U.S. FOREIGN POLICY
AND THE LAW
OF THE SEA

U.S. FOREIGN POLICY
AND THE LAW
OF THE SEA

ANN L. HOLLICK

PRINCETON UNIVERSITY PRESS
PRINCETON, NEW JERSEY

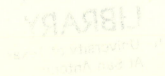

Library of Congress Cataloging in Publication Data will be
found on the last printed page of this book

Publication of this book has been aided by the
Whitney Darrow Publication Reserve Fund of
Princeton University Press

This book has been composed in linotype Electra

Clothbound editions of Princeton University Press books
are printed on acid-free paper, and binding materials are
chosen for strength and durability

Printed in the United States of America by Princeton
University Press, Princeton, New Jersey

TO MY FAMILY

CONTENTS

CONTENTS

LIST OF TABLES AND CHARTS

LIST OF APPENDICES

ACKNOWLEDGMENTS

THIS IS A BOOK about the political and legal aspects of the United States' relationship to the oceans. Although it began as a study of current ocean policy and events, it gradually expanded into a broader history to lend some depth and perspective to the subject. As a history of the past forty years of U.S. oceans policy, the book falls untidily into several fields— international and domestic politics, international law, and occasionally economics.

My interest in the subject of oceans policy began in 1967 when I first learned of the prospect of mining manganese nodules from the deep seabed and envisioned the political difficulties that were bound to arise over any plan to recover this resource. This interest in ocean mining quickly broadened into the full range of marine issues as it became evident that oceans interests and activities were closely linked —technologically, environmentally, legally, and politically. I was fortunate to discover a dynamic and fascinating oceans community of fishermen, naval officers, marine scientists, oil men, lobbyists, government officials, foreign diplomats, and scholars. To the members of this community, I am indebted for their patience and generosity in providing information and for their stimulating and valuable criticism of my work.

So many people contributed to this book in so many ways that a complete rendition of their input would fill a volume. However, I must single out two colleagues who took the time and trouble to provide extensive editorial comment on the entire manuscript. Professor William T. Burke of the University of Washington encouraged my work on the early fisheries problems, reduced the factual errors in the manuscript, and did his best to see that I did justice to the legal aspects of my subject. Professor Joseph S. Nye, Harvard University, was a source of stimulation and insight through his own work on oceans policy, and his helpful comments on this and other oceans manuscripts contributed to the final shape of the book. As to errors of fact and interpretation in this book, the standard disclaimer applies to these and other colleagues who are hereby absolved of all responsibility.

A fundamental debt must be acknowledged to my academic mentors: Robert E. Osgood, Robert W. Tucker, and George Liska of Johns Hopkins University. They not only nurtured my understanding of international law, politics, and American foreign policy but they also had the flexibility to let me apply my knowledge to the oceans—a subject area that was little explored and certainly outside the traditional realm of political science in 1970. Each contributed in his own way to this volume, no doubt more than any of them would care to admit.

During the four years spent working on this book, a number of institutions have contributed to my intellectual improvement and financial welfare. Two centers, the Woodrow Wilson International Center for Scholars, Washington, D.C., and the Harvard Center for International Affairs, Cambridge, Massachusetts, provided the time and resources to enable me to complete the historical research and writing. Work on the more recent periods was undertaken while I was a member of the faculty of the Johns Hopkins School of Advanced International Studies and directing the Ocean Policy Project. The contributors to the Ocean Policy Project not only financed the time I devoted to research but also the invaluable services of my assistant, Barbara Bowersox, who helped research, edit, and prepare the manuscript. Her critical contributions to this effort went well beyond support services to include the gentle pressure and moral support indispensable to the completion of a project of this scope.

Excerpts from some of the author's previously published works appear herein by permission of the publishers:

An abbreviated version of Chapter 2 appeared as "U.S. Oceans Policy: The Truman Proclamations," 17 VA. J. INT'L L. 23-55 (Fall 1976). Excerpts from that article are included herein on pages 19-21, 37-43, 45, 49-50, 52, and 56-57. Reprinted by permission of the editor-in-chief. Copyright © 1977, Virginia Journal of International Law Association.

Portions of Chapters 6 and 7 are drawn from material published in Ann L. Hollick and Robert E. Osgood, *New Era of Ocean Politics*, copyright © 1974 by The Johns Hopkins University Press.

U.S. FOREIGN POLICY
AND THE LAW
OF THE SEA

THE LAW OF THE SEA
IN TRANSITION: AN OVERVIEW

THE DISTINCTIVE FEATURE of the planet earth is its abundant water. Water covers 70 percent of the earth's surface and has been of major importance in all aspects of the development of civilization. In addition to its crucial role in moderating global climate, the world ocean has served as a source of food, a medium for transport and commerce, a protective barrier, a laboratory for understanding the earth's physical and biological history, and a receptacle for waste disposal.

Man's earliest uses of the oceans and the corresponding legal regime to govern these activities remained relatively constant for hundreds of years. Radical changes, however, began in the 20th century. After the Second World War, nations turned their attention increasingly to the oceans to seek more resources for their burgeoning populations. Rapid scientific and technological advances went hand in hand with expanding demand and revolutionized the scale and variety of ocean uses. Increased and diversified use of the oceans combined with fundamental strategic changes and new environmental concerns to transform the oceans into a politically volatile arena. Under these pressures, the law of the sea underwent rapid transformation. In this book we will discover how changing oceans technology and activities have affected the international law and politics of the sea, as seen through the lens of an evolving U.S. policy toward the oceans.

Perhaps the most significant change in the oceans area has been the crowding and interaction of ocean users that has resulted from intensified marine activities. In the 1930s and 1940s, the level of ocean use was such that activities of different ocean users were not linked to one another. This situation had changed by the 1950s, and the United States and the international community negotiated four law of the sea treaties in 1958 that provided distinct legal regimes for ocean fishing, offshore oil recovery, and navigation. Yet the conventions on fisheries, the continental shelf, the territorial sea, and the high seas produced by the First United Nations Conference on the Law of the Sea (UNCLOS I, 1958) were backward looking in that they focused on jurisdictional

3

claims and neglected management concepts. Where technology permitted substantial resource exploitation, nations sought to extend national jurisdiction while permitting unrestricted navigation elsewhere.

In the 1960s and 1970s, and throughout the Third United Nations Conference on the Law of the Sea (UNCLOS III, 1973-1981), the new political force represented by the developing world resisted strategies to provide separate regimes for distinct ocean activities. Political rather than management considerations led them to link jurisdictional issues to one another and to the issue of deep seabed mining. Despite visible evidence of crowding and conflict among ocean activities in near-shore areas, cooperative management and regulatory schemes were eschewed. Instead, coastal nations expanded their jurisdiction over vast new areas without adopting concrete and binding guidelines for managing activities that affected other nations or international areas.

In the remainder of this chapter, we will sketch out some of the general themes of this book, including the legal background of the UNCLOS III negotiations and the economic, technological, and political forces at work. Alternative approaches to U.S. policy are discussed and some forecasts hazarded regarding the future international oceans regime.

Law of the Sea: Background

Civilization's early reliance on the oceans for food and transport led to the development of several general precepts to govern the interaction of political groups such as city states, the Roman empire, and nation states. In the era of small populations and limited technologies, problems of congestion or overexploitation rarely occurred. The principal ocean activities of fishing and navigation could be pursued with little concern for the impact on other interests. The legal regime that periodically prevailed under these conditions came to be known as "freedom of the seas." According to this principle, activities on the oceans could be freely pursued with due regard for other users.

A contrasting legal principle that has alternated with freedom of the seas is that of enclosure or division of the oceans. This concept has been most often applied in nearshore areas. Various Greek and later Italian city states, as well as the Romans, attempted to exercise control over areas off their shores insofar as their technological capabilities permitted. By the 15th century, the invention of gunpowder and the development of the cannon allowed nations to exert their sovereignty more effectively over offshore areas. Increasing interest in ocean resources simultaneously spurred state efforts to control the coastal waters.

The tension between the concept of free use of the seas and the enclosure principle took an interesting turn in the 16th century. At this time Spain and Portugal carried the practice of enclosure to new extremes and claimed, under the Treaty of Tordesillas,[1] to divide the new world and Atlantic waters into spheres of influence along a longitude running 1,000 miles west of the Cape Verde Islands. While they excluded third parties, they acknowledged limited rights of navigation for each other in their respective areas.

This extreme version of enclosure generated a major legal debate in the early 17th century. As the Dutch and British developed commercial interests throughout the world, they came into direct confrontation with the Spanish and Portuguese claims to a *mare clausum* and to a monopoly on trade. Political, economic, and military clashes ensued. The legal case of the rising maritime nations was eloquently championed in 1609 in the famous chapter on "Mare Liberum" (of *De Jure Praedae Commentaries*) by Hugo de Groat or Grotius.[2] Grotius's argument on the right of neutral vessels to use the sea freely became the basis of subsequent doctrine on the freedom of the seas, and was embodied in the Treaty of Paris of 1856.

The interest of coastal states in reserving offshore areas for limited or general purposes persisted, and provided the impetus to claims over a territorial sea as well as to special-purpose contiguous zones. John Selden's argument for a *mare clausum* sought to restrict foreign fishing off British shores.[3] Cornelius van Bynkershoek later expounded the principle that coastal state dominion over offshore areas extended to the point at which the coastal state's power effectively ended.[4] In the early 18th century this was viewed as the distance within cannon shot range, or three nautical miles as practiced in the Mediterranean. Scandinavian territorial claims, on the other hand, extended to a continuous belt of water four nautical miles wide (the Scandinavian "league"), as described by Samuel von Puffendorf.[5]

In the 20th century, the tension between pressures for enclosure and for maritime freedom has continued. Early in the century expanding use of the oceans generated growing interest in reaching some sort of general agreement on the width of the territorial sea and of a special-purpose contiguous zone. Under the auspices of the League of Nations, a Conference for the Codification of International Law met in The Hague in 1930. The Second Committee discussed the territorial sea and contiguous zone. While it was agreed that the territorial sea formed

5

part of the territory of the coastal states and that other waters were "free," there was no agreement on the width of the territorial sea or on the nature and breadth of the contiguous zone. Prevailing political forces supported the concept of the freedom of the seas beyond a narrow territorial sea. The ground was laid, however, for subsequent United Nations conferences to deal with coastal-state offshore jurisdiction and the status of the areas beyond. In the second half of the 20th century the tide has turned substantially in favor of the forces for enclosure.

Expanding Ocean Uses

Intensified use of the oceans in the 20th century has stemmed from two causes: (1) increased technological capabilities creating new and facilitating old uses; and (2) rising demand for ocean resources due to steadily growing population pressures and rising incomes. With the development of new and expanded uses have come problems of resource depletion and crowding in the heavily used nearshore areas.

Developments in ocean shipping are illustrative of some of the radical changes that have taken place in the oceans since World War II. In the short span of the two decades after 1950, the world's merchant fleet virtually doubled in numbers, and quadrupled in tonnage. By the end of the 1970s, the age of the supership had arrived, with tankers of 500,000 tons in production and vessels of a million tons on the drawing boards. Unprecedented speeds—up to 33 knot averages in some ships— had also been achieved. The more than 65,000 ships that comprise the world merchant fleet[6] testify to the fact that ocean transport remains the cheapest way—and often the only way—to move bulk goods. Some 55 percent of the world's petroleum products, for example, is moved by ship.

Most international shipping lanes lie in the calmer waters close to shore, a pattern that poses obvious problems since the maneuverability and safety of ships have not kept pace with increases in size and speed. Similarly, the training of crews and provision of navigational aids have not matched the management needs arising in congested areas. As a result of these deficiencies, collisions and groundings are common occurrences[7] and, given prevailing traffic patterns, such accidents usually occur within a few miles of some coastline.

Another time-honored ocean use—fishing—has also undergone dramatic changes in this century. No longer the random, lonely hunting operation it once was, fishing is now conducted from large, modern vessels equipped with sonar to locate the catch, and capable of spend-

6

ing long periods at sea. The development of block and tackle and multiple processing lines has made it possible for a single vessel to harvest and process hundreds of tons of fish daily.

The world fish catch, after more than tripling from 1950 to 1969, began to level off at roughly 70 million metric tons a year in the 1970s.[8] No one knows whether this level can be maintained or increased. Experts suggest that 100 million metric tons may be the upper limit on world catch. Overfishing and climatic change periodically have caused fishery levels to drop dramatically in some areas of the world. In the face of climatic and biological uncertainty, fishing efforts will need to be regulated if overall catch is to be maintained or increased. As with shipping routes, the most valuable fishing grounds lie within 200 miles of shore. Approximately 90 percent of world fisheries are found in this broad belt, with as much as 20 percent off North America alone.

Among the more recent uses of the ocean is its increasingly vital role as a source of energy, principally in the form of offshore oil and gas. By the year 2000, however, it is anticipated that the stored solar energy of the oceans can be recovered through ocean thermal energy conversion (OTEC) devices which will utilize the temperature differences between surface and bottom layers of the ocean. Wave motions and extreme tidal fluctuations in certain areas of the world can also be used to generate energy. And much farther down the road, ocean currents themselves may be harnessed to generate energy.

Offshore oil and gas are recovered from the continental margin (that part of the continent that extends underwater) at depths of up to 200 meters. The continental margin includes several geological areas—the continental shelf, the continental slope, and the continental rise—and varies widely from one coastal area to another. While the margin along the west coast of South America drops away very steeply, the continental margins of other nations such as Canada and Australia slope

CHART 1-A
Ocean Space Definitions

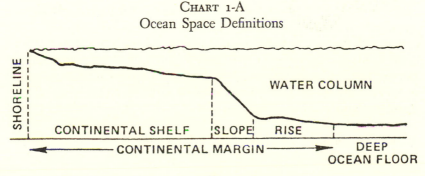

7

gradually outward to distances of over 500 miles before meeting the deep ocean floor. Not all of these wide margins, however, necessarily offer petroleum deposits. Indeed, offshore deposits are generally correlated with onshore reserves such as in the Middle East, Venezuela, and Indonesia. In the 1970s, 20 percent of all oil and gas production came from offshore areas, a figure that has risen to 30 percent in the 1980s. As in the case of fisheries, coastal states have been quick to lay claim to offshore minerals. This was accomplished as early as 1958 in the Geneva Convention on the Continental Shelf which granted coastal states sovereign rights over the seabed resources off their shores.

Other minerals of great interest but still undetermined value lie scattered about the ocean floor in the form of manganese nodules. While these nodules were discovered as long ago as the 1870s, it was only with the development of a recovery capability nearly 100 years later that they began to assume commercial importance. Ranging in size from small pebbles to large rocks, manganese nodules contain significant quantities of nickel, copper, cobalt, and manganese, and are found at depths of 12,000 to 20,000 feet, well removed from continental margins. The greatest concentrations are in the North and South Pacific oceans. Once the technological means to mine the ocean floor had been developed, it became apparent that the existing law of the sea was inadequate to deal with the jurisdictional problems posed by a midocean resource. Under the 1958 Convention on the Continental Shelf, each nation could conceivably extend its boundaries to the middle of the ocean as it developed the capability to harvest manganese nodules. Such an approach would clearly benefit those nations fronting on vast oceans while offering little for other countries.

One use of the oceans that often competes with recreational and fishing interests is that of waste disposal. Urban societies have clustered along coastlines, often with severe consequences for adjacent waters. It is only recently that we have come to appreciate the value—and the danger—of dumping sewage into the oceans. The oceans are the ultimate sink for world pollutants whether they arrive there via the atmosphere, rivers, or through direct disposal. Little is known of the capacity of the oceans to absorb our wastes. Knowledge is being gained —often the hard way—of the tolerance levels of closed areas such as the Mediterranean and of specific coastal environments. As information is being gathered on the time it takes to disperse pollution in specific locales, attention must also be given to the overall condition of oceans over time.

Another important use which we make of the oceans is as a laboratory for scientific research. The assimilative capacity of the oceans is only one of many questions to which the oceans hold the answers and which are vital to the future of civilization. The oceans are the source of our weather, of winds and storms. Ultimately our ability to prepare for ocean storms requires improved capabilities for prediction and perhaps control of the weather. Marine scientific research can advance this capability. The ocean floor holds the story of the history of our planet, the movement of the continents and the record of volcanic activity. To learn more of this history, a number of research institutions are conducting marine scientific research into the tectonic plates that comprise the outer crust of the earth. Other research on natural upwellings and tides and currents should teach us more about the living resources of the oceans.

Mention must also be made of our use of the oceans for military purposes. All major naval powers have used the oceans as a medium for projecting influence over smaller countries, while smaller countries have benefited from the protective barrier that the oceans have sometimes offered. The seas have been used to convoy military supplies, to show the flag, to launch attacks, and to evacuate nationals from the shores of other countries. More recently, the oceans have provided the world with the means for a stable deterrent from nuclear attack. As long as the oceans remain opaque—that is, as long as submarine concealment outpaces detection capabilities—this underwater deterrent should remain invulnerable.

TECHNOLOGY, ECONOMICS, POLITICS, AND THE LAW

In the second half of the 20th century, the development of new and the intensification of old uses of the oceans accelerated the pace of change in the law of the sea. At the beginning of the century, the oceans could be characterized economically as a common property resource and politically and socially as a global commons. This situation, in which ocean resources exceeded man's capabilities to utilize them, has changed dramatically, and the scarcity problem has arisen with regard to a number of marine resources. As early as the middle of this century, some fisheries and whale species were already being overfished. The growth of shipping traffic posed the problem of crowding and the danger of collision in certain restricted sea areas. And in the nearshore waters of Europe and Japan, the ocean's absorptive capacity for land and ship-source pollutants had been exceeded.

As ocean resources gained a scarcity value, the governments of the world tried in various ways to lay claim to these resources, that is, to appropriate portions of the global commons. The predominant means of subjecting ocean resources to national control has been through the extension of coastal state jurisdiction to ever larger offshore areas. This process may be traced through the major international conferences convened to consider the law of the sea. At the Hague Conference of 1930, the discussion revolved around a territorial sea of three or four miles with a small contiguous zone beyond.

In 1958 and 1960, UNCLOS I and II failed by a narrow margin to agree on a six-mile territorial sea and an additional six-mile contiguous zone for fiscal, sanitation, and customs enforcement (as detailed in Chapter 5). Even more significant was the codification of new means of expanding coastal-state jurisdiction through the use of straight base-lines from which offshore zones would be measured. A further national appropriation of coastal resources was recognized in the 1958 Convention on the Continental Shelf, which granted the coastal state "sovereign rights" to seabed resources out to depths of 200 meters or beyond that point to water depths at which exploitation is possible. The underlying cause of these extensions of coastal-state jurisdiction, namely the demand for marine resources, was captured in the "exploitability clause" of the Convention on the Continental Shelf.

UNCLOS III carried the process even further. The settlement emerging from that conference includes 12-mile territorial seas, 200-mile economic zones, coastal-state rights to areas of the continental margin which extend beyond 200 miles, and a new archipelago concept which allows island groups to enclose the waters between their islands with straight baselines. What is clear from the history of these efforts to develop a law to regulate ocean use is that man has borrowed the concepts of free use and enclosure from his experiences on land and sought to apply them to the oceans, an approach which has persisted from UNCLOS I through UNCLOS III. Due, however, to new technologies and to man's capability to exploit intensively and even to occupy the ocean, the contending concepts of sovereignty and freedom are inadequate to cope with present and prospective resource and environmental problems. Coordinated management offers a more hopeful approach for the long term.

The relationship of national extensions or claims to actual technological capabilities is complex. The acquisitive impulse set in motion by technological improvements has never been precise. That is, there has been little correlation between the claims made and the actual technology available for development. In most cases, the claims process has moved well ahead of technological capability, commercial viability, or even concrete evidence of significant resources. The most extreme example of this was Chile's claim to a 200-mile zone in 1947 (see Chapter 3). Another example in the 1940s was U.S. industry and government interest in claiming areas up to 100 or 150 miles from shore and to depths of around 600 feet even though the deepest offshore well was operating at only 60 feet (Chapters 2 and 4). The same instincts were apparent in UNCLOS III where states with broad continental margins demanded the most extensive definitions of the legal continental shelf although the capability to operate in remote offshore areas did not exist, and there was no compelling evidence of petroleum resources (Chapter 9).

Although the law of the sea has evolved with a momentum based indirectly upon technological innovation, it has been periodically affected by the overriding political conflicts of the age. The early naval clashes of the Second World War sparked claims to protective zones by neutral states (Chapters 2 and 3). The ensuing cold war similarly heightened concern over the nature and extent of the territorial sea and transit rights through straits. As a result, the U.S.-Soviet contest dominated the 1958 and 1960 UN Conferences on the Law of the Sea (Chapter 5). While East-West differences continued to affect law of the sea policies and perceptions, economic and political differences between developed and less developed nations began to play a greater role in the late 1960s. Even when it became apparent by 1975 that the jurisdictional issues before UNCLOS III pitted coastal against non-coastal states, a high level of North-South rhetoric was maintained on the issue of deep seabed mining (Chapters 9 and 10). Despite the changing political context, the law of the sea has evoked unusual alliances and evidenced a unique momentum stemming from technological and territorial imperatives. In the 20th century, these imperatives have led to the enclosure of vast ocean areas under national jurisdiction.

U.S. Ocean Policy

The United States has played a key role in the development of the law of the sea in this century. The U.S. impact on ocean law has been felt in several ways. In the first place, the United States has developed and disseminated much of the technology that has facilitated intensified ocean uses. Secondly, as a major power, the United States has exercised its influence bilaterally and within the UNCLOS conferences and other multilateral fora to affect the policies of other nations. And finally, U.S. national claims and actions have laid the basis for the claims of other states and hence the formation of customary international law. Indeed, the major innovations in the law of the sea—the concepts of the 200-mile zone and the continental shelf—can both be traced to the actions of the U.S. (Chapters 2 and 3).

Like other areas of U.S. foreign policy, U.S. ocean policy may be examined and explained at various analytical levels or levels of generality. At the broadest or macro perspective, U.S. ocean policy might be viewed in terms of technological imperatives or in terms of the nation's geographic situation or its resource needs. Through a focus on the "American character," the analyst can come to terms with American traditions of isolationism and anti-Europeanism and the countervailing traditions of unilateral action, the "open door" policy, and expansionism. In this manner the analyst can trace American maritime policy from its isolationist origins where the oceans served as a protective barrier to its interventionist phase where the oceans served as a medium to project American power globally.

An alternative but complementary macro-approach to U.S. foreign policy would analyze U.S. ocean policy in terms of the U.S. role in the prevailing international system. In this instance, U.S. policies in the 1930s could be explained as those of a middle-range power seeking to protect narrow resource interests, and the 1940s would mark the transition to the status of a global or superpower (Chapters 2-4). By the 1950s and 1960s, the U.S., as the preeminent world power, became cognizant of the impact of its claims and the denial of its claims by other states and sought to maximize its naval mobility in order to extend its influence throughout the world (Chapters 5-7). In the 1970s and 1980s, the U.S. returned to a more limited view of its capabilities in the wake of the Vietnam War, growing Soviet power, and the dispersion of economic power to Japan and Western Europe (Chapters 8-10).

While it is important to be attentive to these broad levels of explanation, they do not offer, in and of themselves, a sufficient understanding of national ocean policy. To explain ocean policy, the analyst must supplement the macro-approaches with micro-level analysis focusing on the decision-making or policy process. In this context, the actions of key individuals, interest groups, bureaucratic actors, and the legislature occupy center stage while the larger forces serve as the background. In U.S. oceans policy as in other foreign policy areas, decision-making analysis is complemented and reinforced by an appreciation of the macro-forces that drive national policy.

The Truman Proclamations extending U.S. claims to offshore areas offer one example of how micro- and macro-forces provide complementary explanations (Chapter 2). In this policy process, key individuals such as Secretary of the Interior Harold Ickes and President Franklin Roosevelt embodied and translated the perceptions of an isolationist, middle-range power into concrete policies at a time when the U.S. position in the world was changing radically. Technological developments were reflected in the pressure of interest groups (U.S. fishermen and oil men) operating outside of government agencies. At the same time, the relevant government agencies were operating according to bureaucratic imperatives to try to expand their scope of competence (e.g., the Department of Interior's effort to expand the federal claim to the continental shelf vis-à-vis the states and foreign governments). The success of these agencies and groups varied according both to the skills of key individuals and to the reinforcing or countervailing national and international trends.

The importance of individual personalities, capabilities, and contacts to ocean policy decision making at various points in time should be underscored. Given the absence of sustained high-level or presidential attention, skillful bureaucratic actors have made a major impact on U.S. ocean policy, particularly when their policy preferences have been reinforced by external factors. An example would be the increased importance ascribed to a Defense Department position where there was concern about the Soviet threat, or the weight given oil industry views when an energy shortage developed.

When a president has given ocean issues his attention, his attitudes have had a major effect on policy, at least temporarily. The two principal instances of presidential impact were under Franklin Roosevelt and Richard Nixon. While Roosevelt's orientation favored the extension of U.S. claims to offshore areas (Chapter 2), that of Nixon favored restricting national claims in order to maximize U.S. naval mobility (Chapter 7). But Roosevelt's death in office and Nixon's retreat from office under the Watergate cloud meant that their respective impacts on ocean policy were brief.

UNCLOS I, II, AND III

The United States policy on the oceans has evolved in the context of, and been reflected in, the three principal international efforts to reach agreement on a law of the sea, UNCLOS I, II, and III. These conferences were interspersed in a series of ongoing multi- and bilateral negotiations and were accompanied by a steadily evolving customary law. As ocean uses have expanded with improved technology, the pursuit of agreement on a widely accepted convention on the law of the sea has become ever more difficult. By 1973, UNCLOS III was clearly the most complex, ambitious multilateral treaty negotiation ever attempted.

UNCLOS I and II dealt primarily with the nature and extent of coastal-state jurisdiction in offshore areas (Chapters 4 and 5). UNCLOS III dealt not only with coastal-state jurisdiction but also with the specifics of a regime for the seabed beyond national jurisdiction (Chapters 8-10). In all ocean negotiations, resources of significant and near-term value are at issue, unlike those of outer space. The importance of the ocean resources accounts in part for the length and difficulty of the negotiations.

Technological and political factors also account for the problems in coming to agreement on a law of the sea. Behind the political difficulties of the conferences lie the diverse perspectives of the participants. When the UN was founded in 1945, there were fifty member nations. By the time of the 1958 and 1960 conferences, just under ninety nations were represented. UNCLOS III saw the number of participants increase to 158. With each expansion of conference membership, the negotiating difficulties increased.

An additional problem plagued UNCLOS III. While UNCLOS I and II had limited agendas and began after extensive preparatory work had been completed by the International Law Commission, UNCLOS III was saddled with a long agenda and inadequate preparation. The combination of an agenda of some 25 items (and over 100 subitems) and the large number of participating nations resulted in a constant fluctuation of political groups coalescing around different issues. The preparatory work that had been completed by the Seabed Committee was uneven and generally in need of substantial additional work, thereby further handicapping the work of the conference.

However, if one assesses UNCLOS III by what was possible, rather than desirable, a number of positive statements can be made. The conference did manage to overcome the handicaps of poor preparation, too many participants, and too long an agenda. It did provide an opportunity for small nations to learn about the law of the sea and to express their own views. Because the conference could not definitively resolve strongly contested issues such as boundary delimitation or the status of the economic zone, UNCLOS III necessarily resorted to ambiguous language. The merit of ambiguity is that it leaves it to state practice to determine the evolution of customary law and the interpretation of the treaty.

It was inevitable, however, that the UNCLOS text would reflect past, rather than future, technological developments and ocean uses. The retrospective nature of the treaty process raises grave questions as to the utility of such an effort, and suggests the possible value of an ongoing semipermanent negotiating body. In a universal and highly politicized forum it is virtually impossible to negotiate a definitive document providing for sound management of fisheries, marine pollution, and navigation. And given the prospect of new technical developments and ocean resource discoveries, an ongoing forum is better suited to develop the legal regime as the need arises.

FUTURE DIRECTIONS AND PROSPECTS

With or without a widely accepted law of the sea treaty, general trends in the use of marine resources and national claims to offshore jurisdiction can be anticipated. Whether a conference text is ultimately ratified by a sufficient number of states, UNCLOS III produced texts and a legislative history that delineate certain general rules. With a widely accepted treaty, the evolution of the law of the sea will be somewhat more tidy than in its absence, at least during the rest of the 20th century. Disputes will nonetheless continue to arise within a broadly legitimized framework.

In a brief overview, one can anticipate a troubled common where the prevailing order will be periodically strained by disputes. The coming decades will witness a continued increase in ocean resource exploitation with the concomitant problems of crowding, ocean pollution, and overfishing. A law of the sea treaty will have to be supplemented by bilateral and multilateral agreements since it neither (1) addresses the principal sources of pollution (land-based activities), nor (2) imposes effective constraints on coastal-state fishing rights. The bulk of ocean resource activities will be carried on within 200-mile zones under the regulation and control of national governments.

Conflicts will continue over the delineation of national boundaries as well as over the interaction of national and international uses of the zone and their impact on neighboring states. National regulations over activities in the zone will be expanded gradually before states press for further seaward extensions of jurisdiction. In the near term it will be difficult to restrict national activities in the zone in the face of strong coastal-state proprietary instincts.

Marine scientific research will have to develop new bilateral and multilateral mechanisms under the consent regime that emerged at UNCLOS III. Marine scientists will be required to seek consent for research throughout the continental margin as well as within the 200-mile zones. Coastal state efforts to limit publication of research results concerning areas of national jurisdiction will reduce the interest of acadmic researchers in research off foreign shores.

Mining of maganese nodules in the Pacific Ocean will not begin until the late 1980s, whether under an internationally agreed regime or in accordance with national legislation. Given present and projected supply and demand for nodule minerals, there is no pressing need to undertake deep-sea mining before then.

Whether a treaty is widely accepted or not, certain aspects of the present approach to ocean management are intrinsically unstable. Nations are attempting to regulate ocean space as if it were land by drawing arbitrary boundaries through waters that constitute an ecological whole. In the 1980s it will become increasingly evident to coastal states that they cannot successfully manage the resources of their coastal zones without reference to adjacent ocean areas.

The activities of other coastal states, whether in adjacent zones or on the high seas, will undercut even the best of management schemes for conservation, environmental protection, or resource exploitation. When this fact becomes unavoidable, two trends will emerge: regional management and coastal-state expansion. Where the economic zones of two or more states are adjacent, coastal states will be forced to adopt cooperative approaches for the management of fisheries, offshore industry, and the like. Particularly in enclosed and semienclosed seas, the need for regional management of ocean resources will be unavoidable. Even as diverse and incompatible a group as the Mediterranean littoral states has come to the reluctant conclusion that offshore pollution problems can only be resolved cooperatively.

The second and inconsistent trend will be toward expanded coastal-state claims where offshore areas front on open (i.e., unclaimed) ocean. The high seas activities of flag states—whether for navigation, fishing, use of ocean thermal energy, or deep-sea mining—will have a potential impact on the coastal state's management of resources within its 200-mile zone. And even if there is no significant impact, the resources just beyond 200 miles will become tempting to coastal states as they consolidate their control over those within 200 miles. In the absence of agreement on the proposed deep seabed regime, there will be little to weigh against coastal-state expansionism. If, for instance, a technologically advanced nation were to begin mining manganese nodules 250 miles off the Pacific coast of Latin America, the nearest coastal state might well extend its jurisdiction to include the prospective site. A case in point is the insistence of broad margin states at UNCLOS III on controlling the mineral resources of the continental margin where it extends beyond 200 miles.

In the absence of forceful and concerted disapprobation, a logical endpoint of national moves would be the total carving up of ocean space into national areas with international cooperative efforts dictated by the circumstances of particular areas and uses. Countervailing pressures would develop for international regulatory approaches to a number of issues. The oceans' critical role in facilitating world transportation might generate a truly global international approach to shipping and the attendant problems of pollution. A similarly global approach to all marine pollution might be useful because of the intermingling of ocean waters, but it would probably rest primarily on regional arrangements. Fishing could ultimately dictate cooperation on the basis of ecologically interdependent stocks with special management regimes required for anadromous and highly migratory species. Offshore oil recovery would not inspire an international management approach except where the common pool problem arises or where drilling activities pose environmental hazards for other states. None of thesse international or regional approaches to ocean management are likely to be undertaken through foresighted national planning. Coastal states will only be driven to cooperation after strictly national approaches are clearly proven to be inadequate. Thus, as in the case of Mediterranean pollution, we must expect to see near-crisis situations of pollution, overfishing, or maritime accidents before states gradually move to cooperative measures.

THE TRUMAN PROCLAMATIONS:

1935-1945

IN SEPTEMBER 1945 the United States government issued two proclamations and two companion executive orders concerning U.S. jurisdiction over natural resources in coastal areas. Although the policy itself was formulated during the administration of President Roosevelt, it fell to his successor to implement what have come to be known as the "Truman Proclamations." The better remembered proclamation asserted U.S. jurisdiction and control over the natural resources of the continental shelf contiguous to the United States.[1] The continental shelf proclamation called for the determination of boundaries with adjacent states on the basis of equitable principles and for the retention of the high seas character of the waters above the continental shelf. The second proclamation, dealing with fisheries,[2] has been largely forgotten in the United States. It declared a U.S. right to establish conservation zones for the protection of fisheries in certain areas of the high seas contiguous to the United States where fishing activities had or would be maintained on a substantial scale. Areas which had been traditionally fished by U.S. nationals alone were to be subject to the regulation and control of the United States and might, when conditions warranted, be limited to U.S. nationals. In areas which had been fished by nationals of other states, provision could be made for joint management by the United States and the other nations traditionally fishing the areas and, if necessary, for the exclusion of new entrants to the fisheries in question. The fisheries proclamation, like that on the continental shelf, specified that the conservation zones were to retain their character as high seas and would in no way affect the right of free and unimpeded navigation in the areas.

The Truman Proclamations mark a period of transition in the relationship of the United States to the oceans. From a regional power with a primarily coastal orientation, the United States had evolved during the Second World War into a major maritime power with global concerns. The proclamations embody both the coastal and the global perspectives. The origins of the two claims are to be found in the 1930s when an expansive United States government sought to control resources off U.S. shores by excluding foreign access. The acquisitive forces behind these proclamations were ultimately tempered by a global perspective that emerged within the government toward the end of World War II. U.S. interests were newly perceived to include facilitating liberal trade policies by limiting offshore claims and setting a precedent for other states to emulate. Although qualified in their final formulation by international factors, the thrust of the Truman Proclamations was expansionist. Moreover, they were adopted unilaterally rather than through multilateral negotiations with other states. The response to the claims of the world's foremost power was the prompt adoption by other states of a variety of claims emulating the unilateral mode, if not the substance, of the U.S. action. The United States was to spend the next thirty years trying to roll back and limit the expansive moves of other states.

OFFSHORE ISSUES IN THE 1930S

The Truman Proclamations fall into a long history of coastal-state claims to offshore jurisdiction beyond the traditional maritime limits of three miles, or one marine league. In the Western hemisphere, a number of resource-oriented claims had been advanced prior to the U.S. proclamations. In 1907, for instance, Argentina declared a ten-mile fishing zone,[3] while in 1923 Colombia claimed a twelve-mile territorial sea for hydrocarbons and fishing.[4] In 1935 Mexico revised its earlier claim to waters up to 20 kilometers from shore to a claim of sovereignty to a distance of nine miles. In Europe, the new power represented by the Soviet Union laid claim to a twelve-mile territorial sea in an act reflecting its middle-power perceptions as well as its ability to defy the rules of the international system.

The United States' own claims to offshore jurisdiction were ambivalent from the beginning of its history. As a new republic, the United States was too weak to defy the regime established by the maritime powers, but at the same time its remoteness from Britain gave it a certain freedom of action. On the whole, the United States has maintained territorial waters of one marine league, or three miles, from shore.[5] However, Thomas Jefferson spoke in favor of reserving the country's rights to "as broad a margin of protected navigation as any nation whatever."[6] And in 1806, James Madison noted that U.S. immunity from belligerent warfare could be extended to a zone as wide as the Gulf Stream current.[7]

19

President Franklin D. Roosevelt's willingness to extend coastal jurisdiction for a variety of purposes was particularly striking. In the decade
prior to the Truman Proclamations, his proclivities resulted in a number of claims characteristic of a regional or middle power strong enough
to defy the prevailing legal system, yet too weak to impose a new legal
regime. In 1935, the United States enacted antismuggling legislation
that authorized the president to proclaim a customs control area extending 100 miles north and south from where a suspected ship was
hovering and including all seas extending fifty miles from the twelve-
mile customs zone.[8] Then in September of 1939, the United States proposed to an Inter-American meeting of Ministers of Foreign Affairs
that a zone of neutrality be created around the hemisphere to be
patrolled individually or collectively by the American republics.[9] The
U.S. concept of a neutrality zone was subsequently adopted by the
meeting and developed into a regional approach for the Western
hemisphere, excluding Canada, by means of the Declaration of Panama. The declaration specified that: "the American Republics, so long
as they maintain their neutrality, are as of inherent right entitled to
have those waters adjacent to the American continent, which they regard as of primary concern and direct utility in their relations, free
from the commission of any hostile act by any non-American belligerent nation."[10] The defense zone which was proposed by the U.S. and
agreed to in this declaration extended 300 miles and more from shore.
President Roosevelt personally delimited the connecting straight lines
of the zone which extended the defense area well beyond 300 miles in
some places.[11] The belligerents, whose activities were to be regulated
by the declaration, never acquiesced in its infringement upon their
belligerent rights. Indeed, the only notable consequence of the neutrality zone was its subsequent use by Chile and Peru as a legal precedent upon which to base their claims to 200-mile zones.[12]

The president's interest in extending U.S. coastal jurisdiction was not
limited to customs or wartime considerations. He was equally eager to
expand U.S. control over offshore resources. In the context of a dispute between the U.S. and Japan over Japanese salmon fishing off
Alaska, the president freely contemplated extending jurisdiction to any
distance that would protect the salmon resource. One presidential suggestion was "a Presidential Proclamation closing the sea area along
the Alaska coast to all fishing—Japanese, Canadian and American—a
kind of marine refuge."[13] Stimulated by a subsequent memorandum in
which the secretary of state described the continental shelf as a "bridge
between the deep sea and the inland rivers and lakes where salmon

spawn,"[14] the president modified his proposal for a U.S. extension of jurisdiction to one that would "forbid fishing on this 'shelf' and to a distance of perhaps twelve miles beyond it into real deep water."[15] In a conversation with Under Secretary of State Sumner Welles, the president further indicated that he was considering an executive proclamation that would declare the waters of the Pacific Ocean between the three-mile limit and a depth of 100 fathoms as being territorial waters. Fishing within this area would only be allowed under a license granted by the U.S. government.[16]

In advancing these proposals, President Roosevelt acknowledged that he was uncertain as to which depth contour would afford "complete protection"[17] for the salmon and asked for further technical information to this end. His interest in depth as a means of delimitation can be traced to a remark by Secretary Hull indicating that the Japanese were capturing salmon where the runs came near the surface because of the shallowness of the waters. Were this indeed the only area in which salmon could be caught, a depth criterion might have prevented continued open ocean salmon catches. The State Department's response, however, was not encouraging to the president. The counselor of the department pointed out that even a limit of fifty miles or more could not effectively protect the industry if the Japanese were fishing with long gill nets at distances of seventy-five or one hundred miles offshore. The only way to protect the U.S. industry was to get Japanese assurances that they would forgo fishing activities for a "very considerable distance" beyond the U.S. coastline.[18] Hence a diplomatic solution was indicated. Moreover, it fell to the State Department to call to the president's attention the fact that such a claim to control fishing beyond three miles would set a troublesome precedent in U.S. relations with other countries.

What was significant about this episode was the president's enthusiasm for ad hoc extensions of jurisdiction. Also notable was the president's lack of familiarity with the issue coupled with the limited amount of time he spent on the question. Apart from some intense activity on the subject during Sunday and Monday, November 20 and 21, 1937, there is no record of any further presidential attention to the problem until two months later. Then, in a Cabinet meeting on January 18, 1938, the president again raised the issue of the Alaska coastline, this time with regard to crabs as well as salmon. Having forgotten the State Department's admonition on the difficulties of setting a limit that would protect salmon, the president was once again proposing a limit of twenty miles or more. When the issue of a presidential proclamation was raised, the Cabinet indicated a preference for seeking legislation first.[19] The president's clearly expressed concerns were with conservation of a natural resource and security of the American food supply. Missing from the president's treatment of the subject was any perception of the impact of such a unilateral action on U.S. interests elsewhere and any sense that U.S. interests might transcend those of a middle-range, regional power.

U.S.-Japanese Salmon Controversy

The 1945 fisheries proclamation can be traced to the dispute between the United States and Japan over salmon in the 1930s. Many of the State Department officials involved in the 1930s negotiations with Japan were subsequently active in the departmental process leading up to the Truman Proclamations. Their attitudes, as well as those of the president, were clearly affected by the 1930s dispute.[20]

Intimations of the salmon controversy may be found as early as 1930. In that year the Department of Commerce, then the lead agency in fisheries, warned the State Department of the adverse industry reaction if the Japanese were to fish for or pack salmon in international waters off the coast of Alaska. At the instigation of the Commerce Department, the State Department suggested to the Japanese government that it withhold licenses from Japanese fishing vessels for fishing in Bristol Bay. While the Japanese were unwilling to give assurances to this effect, they did indicate that no license would be issued to Japanese fishing vessels to catch salmon in the area without prior notification to the United States.[21]

In the years after 1930, this understanding was generally observed by the Japanese government. Occasionally, Japanese vessels fished off the Alaska coast for cod, halibut, hake, and crabs, and from time to time floating crab canneries operated in the international waters of Bristol Bay. Every year the Japanese government sent one or two research vessels to study the fishing resources off the Alaska coast. Despite this low level of effort and the absence of any evidence that the Japanese were fishing for salmon in Bristol Bay, the Alaskan salmon industry became increasingly alarmed at "manifestations of increasing interest of the Japanese in the fishing resources of the Bering Sea."[22] As a result, the State Department approached the Japanese government about the possibility of negotiating a convention that would prohibit Japanese nationals from fishing for salmon in certain international areas of Bristol Bay.[23] The Japanese responded that they could not decide whether to enter such negotiations until they had concluded their investigations of the fishing resources of Bristol Bay. These would run from 1936 for a period of three years. Moreover, the Japanese government gave assurances that it would issue no licenses to fish for salmon for the time being.

This arrangement proved insufficient to allay the fears of the Northeast Pacific fishermen. Pressures were apparently building in Japan for an expansion of Japanese fishing into the Northeast Pacific salmon industry, and these were reported in the U.S.[24] As American public concern mounted, so did congressional activity. In mid-1937, Senator Homer T. Bone of Washington introduced a bill (S.2679) that would declare salmon hatched in Alaska to be the property of the United States and subject to regulation by the secretary of commerce. Bill S.2679 would also have given the president the authority to extend U.S. jurisdiction of salmon fishing law enforcement areas up to four leagues (twelve miles) from shore or beyond that to waters less than 100 fathoms deep.[25] In response to a request for comments on the proposed legislation, Secretary of State Hull pointed out that under the provisions of the bill, U.S. jurisdiction could be asserted to waters as far as 200 miles from the coast. Such action, he noted, was without legal precedent, and "the dangers of international controversies and dissensions inherent in such a proposal" were evident. Moreover, if the United States were to adopt such measures "it would find it difficult to object to the application of the principle against our own nationals and vessels." As a result of these considerations, the Department of State came to "the conclusion that the solution should be sought through the medium of diplomatic negotiations with the governments chiefly concerned.[26]

As time went on, however, the State Department found itself caught in an increasingly difficult position between the influential salmon lobby and its allies[27] on the one hand, and the Japanese government on the other. With the exception of one vessel that was sighted fishing for salmon in the Bering Sea in 1936, there was no evidence that the Japanese were fishing for salmon. Nonetheless, Alaskan fishing interests as well as the president and the secretary of the interior, were firmly convinced that they were harvesting salmon in Bristol Bay.[28] In this inconclusive situation, the State Department sent Leo D. Sturgeon (Division of Far Eastern Affairs) to investigate the allegations together with represesntatives of the Commerce Department's Bureau of Fisheries and the fishing industry. The survey was conducted from July 30 to August 11, 1937, and did not turn up conclusive evidence of Japanese salmon fishing. The report resulting from the investigation recommended further studies to determine the state of the salmon fishery and suggested continued representations to the Japanese government to arrive at a negotiated solution to the problem.[29] These recommendations reaffirmed the State Department's predilection for a negotiated outcome.

Yet diplomatic negotiations were becoming more and more difficult for the two countries as relations became increasingly strained in the late 1930s. By November of 1937 the Alaska fishermen's association and the Pacific Coast union of seamen and longshoremen were supporting a boycott of Japanese goods even though the United States had uncovered no evidence of Japanese salmon fishing. The U.S. was asking the Japanese government to voluntarily forgo the right to fish for a single species of fish in waters the Japanese regarded as international on the grounds of a special U.S. economic interest in the fishery and in the absence of any evidence as to the rate of harvest that the fishery could sustain. A final factor contributing to the difficulties for the State Department was the president's enthusiasm for extending jurisdiction discussed above.

Under these various pressures the State Department pressed the Japanese government very hard beginning in mid-November of 1937. U.S. Ambassador to Japan Joseph C. Grew was asked to inform the Japanese government that the U.S. was no longer willing to await the outcome of its three-year study. The U.S. wanted immediate assurances that the operation of all Japanese fishing vessels in the offshore salmon fishing areas of Alaska would be prohibited pending agreement on a "comprehensive arrangement for the general protection of the fisheries of the North Pacific Ocean." Moreover, "the Japanese Government should be discouraged from any thought that we anticipate sharing with Japan the salmon resources of Alaska."[30] After preliminary discussions with the Japanese government, the United States limited its demands to four points: "(a) assurance that Japanese nationals will not be granted licenses to fish for salmon in Alaskan waters, (b) discontinuance of the Japanese Government's fishing survey, (c) consent to visit and inspection of fishing vessels, and (d) consent of the Japanese Government to a suitable public statement by the American Government regarding the agreement."[31]

The Japanese position in the negotiation was predictable. The Japanese government was unwilling to make any statement which might prejudice its rights under international law to fish on the high seas. It was, however, willing to discontinue its fishing survey. With regard to the inspection of Japanese vessels, the Japanese were unwilling to agree to the right of friendly search of their vessels on the high seas. If, however, indisputable evidence were presented that a Japanese crab or fish meal vessel were in fact fishing for salmon, the government was prepared to consider cancellation of the vessel's license. On the issue of publicizing the agreement, the Japanese insisted that any public statement by the American government be referred to the Japanese government prior to publication.[32]

The negotiations were lengthy and difficult. Significant differences existed over the press communiqué that the United States wished to issue. Finally, on March 25, 1938, an agreement was reached and the following statement was released to the press:

As a result of discussions between the American Government and the Government of Japan in regard to the salmon fishing activities of Japanese nationals in the off-shore waters of Alaska . . . the Japanese Government has given, without prejudice to the question of rights under international law, assurances as follows: (1) that the Japanese Government is suspending the three-year salmon fishing survey which has been in progress since 1936 in the waters in question; (2) that inasmuch as salmon fishing by Japanese vessels is not permitted without licenses from the Japanese Government and as the Government has been refraining from issuing such licenses to those vessels which desired to proceed to the Bristol Bay area to fish for salmon, it will, on its own initiative, continue to suspend the issuance of such licenses; that in order to make effective this assurance the Japanese Government is prepared to take, if and when conclusive evidence is presented that any Japanese vessels engage in salmon fishing on a commercial scale in the waters in question, necessary and proper measures to prevent any such further operations.

The American Government appreciates these assurances which the Japanese Government has given in the spirit of collaboration in the efforts of the American Government to conserve and protect the Alaskan salmon fishery resources . . .

In view of the above assurances it is evident that if ever Japanese vessels, which were present in the waters in question to engage in crab fishing or in production of fish meal, caught salmon in commercial quantities in the past, such fishing was conducted without the knowledge of the Japanese Government.

Furthermore, these assurances of the Japanese Government are regarded as regulating the situation until such time as the problems involved may call for, and circumstances may render practicable, the taking of other measures.[33]

Upon the conclusion of negotiations, Ambassador Grew provided Washington with his assessment of the outcome. Grew pointed out that "had it not been for the hostilities with China and the otherwise delicate state of Japan's international relations, the arrangement just concluded would not have been possible." Moreover, he predicted, the agreement did not represent a permanent solution to the problem and the question of Japanese fishing in Alaskan waters would be raised again.[34]

Grew's predictions were soon to be realized—sooner, no doubt, than even he expected. For in October of the same year, Secretary Hull asked him to once again raise the issue with the Japanese government with an eye to "a permanent arrangement which will give unmistakeable recognition and protection to the established American interest and claim in the salmon fishing of Alaska."[35] Although the March agreement had calmed "the immediate apprehensions of interested Pacific Coast communities," the general view was that it was a temporary expedient, and agitation for a definitive exclusion of the Japanese continued within interested segments of the public and the Congress. The United States government was urged to assert control over offshore areas as far as was necessary to protect the salmon.[36] In response to these pressures, an outline of a salmon fishing agreement was drafted within the State Department and forwarded to Ambassador Grew.[37] In it the point was made that wherever nationals of a particular country have developed a fishery in waters adjacent to their country, that country enjoyed "a prior interest and claim" to the fishery in question. Here we find an early expression of the policy that was elaborated in the Truman fishery proclamation seven years later.

Ambassador Grew's response to these new pressures was to the point. Given Japanese fishing interests elsewhere, Grew could see "no prospect whatever of the Japanese Government modifying its initial position and giving its assent at this time or in the near future to the agreement envisaged by the Department." The timing of such an initiative was, in Grew's view, particularly inopportune. To raise the issue then would confirm Japanese suspicions that the fishing question was being kept alive for political purposes relating to its controversy with the United States over China. To do so would simply exacerbate growing U.S. difficulties with Japan.[38]

The weight of coastal-oriented private and public pressures rested heavily on the State Department in 1938 and 1939. The Department was repeatedly accused of negligence in protecting the nation's economic interests.[39] Therefore, despite Ambassador Grew's assessment, the department continued to favor a further approach to the Japanese government on the issue. It was willing, however, to reduce the initiative from that of a formal proposal for fresh negotiations to that of an informal information memorandum to the foreign office detailing the situation within the United States and the possibility of legislative action. This memorandum should leave it to the Japanese government to decide whether it wished to renegotiate the salmon arrangement.[40]

At the same time that the State Department was applying pressure on the Japanese government it was also trying to stave off congressional action. At a meeting with Delegate Anthony J. Dimond in January 1939, the State Department's counselor presented Commerce Department data on the extent of American interests in the waters off other countries' shores. The economic values involved were substantial, he noted, and might be jeopardized if the U.S. afforded other countries a precedent for unilateral extensions of coastal jurisdiction.[41] While Dimond was impressed with the magnitude of U.S. fishing off foreign shores, he continued to regard salmon as a special case. If the bill extending U.S. jurisdiction were to pass, Dimond went on, it could only do so if not opposed by the State Department. On behalf of the State Department, the counselor indicated official concern that other countries might not accept the U.S. distinction between salmon and other fisheries and stressed his anticipation of "serious repercussions from unilateral action."[42] State Department officials indicated that they would, however, continue to keep in touch with Dimond and would initiate general discussions with the Canadian legation on the salmon problem.

Meanwhile, as Grew had anticipated, the response of Japanese foreign ministry officials to the U.S. suggestion regarding further discussions was unequivocally negative. In fact, the foreign office officials did not transmit word of the U.S. proposal to other agencies or high-level officials in Japan because of the strong negative feelings that would have been aroused. In the absence of any new developments since the March 1938 agreement, the Japanese foreign ministry indicated that it would continue to consider the matter closed.[43]

With the rapid deterioration of U.S.-Japanese relations, the salmon dispute was engulfed by other more pressing issues. This piece of unfinished business was, however, the original impetus for the 1945 fisheries proclamation. The outbreak of the war offered only a brief respite from this troublesome dispute and the issue was to come once again before the State Department in 1943.

Offshore Oil Jurisdiction

The petroleum issues that were addressed in the Truman Proclamation on the Continental Shelf find their origins in the period of the 1930s. By the mid-1930s technological capabilities had reached the stage where the prospects for substantial offshore oil were generating widespread interest. The development of recovery capabilities had been gradual after the first well beneath the sea was drilled in 1898. At the turn of the century, the first offshore oil was recovered off the California coast. Early wells were often located on land with slanted pipes to recover oil beneath the waters. Prior to 1921 oil was removed from offshore areas without any authority from either the state or federal governments.[44] Then in 1921 the state of California passed a leasing act under which it subsequently issued leases and received royalties. Extensive development began off California around 1928, and by the 1940s wells had been drilled at depths ranging up to sixty feet.[45] Interest in offshore oil in the Gulf of Mexico developed in the late 1930s.

The rapid advance of technological capabilities began to raise problems of conflicting jurisdictional claims when it became apparent that deposits of offshore oil were substantial. The jurisdictional problems were of two distinct types: (1) the question of ownership as between the federal government and individual states and (2) the limit of U.S. jurisdiction as opposed to that of other nations. Drilling off California occurred well within three miles of shore due to the steep incline of the continental shelf. It posed, therefore, only the issue of state versus federal ownership. Exploration in the shallow Gulf of Mexico, however, was quite another matter. Among the areas of interest in the Caribbean were portions of the Bahamas Bank beyond three miles of the U.S. coast.[46]

Prior to 1938, the two jurisdictional issues remained distinct. The position of the federal government was summed up in a widely reported letter from Secretary of the Interior Harold L. Ickes to Olin S. Proctor dated December 22, 1933.[47] In it, Secretary Ickes declined to issue a lease under the leasing act of February 25, 1920 (41 Stat. 437) on the grounds that "title to the soil under the ocean within the three-mile limit is in the State of California." On August 21, 1935, the 1920 Mineral Leasing Act was amended (49 Stat. 674) and a number of leases were filed with the General Land Office of the Interior Department.

Until the summer of 1937, these leases were denied[48] and the government accepted the principle of state ownership of submerged lands.

Then in the summer of 1937, Secretary Ickes persuaded Senator Gerald Nye to introduce a bill (S.2164) to the 75th Congress asserting a federal government claim to petroleum deposits in submerged lands off the entire coast of the United States. In the course of the debate, the bill was transformed into a resolution (S.J. Res. 208) that directed Attorney General Francis Biddle to assert federal title over the offshore lands. The resolution passed the Senate on August 16, 1937. The House Judiciary Committee held hearings on the resolution and amended it to restrict the claim to the coast of California. It was not acted on by the House of Representatives. These and additional versions of the bill were reintroduced in the 76th Congress (H.J. Res. 176, 181, and S.J. Res. 24, 83, and 92). In response to a request by the Navy, it was proposed in one set of bills (H.J. Res. 176, S.J. Res. 92) that the entire continental shelf be set aside as a naval petroleum reserve.[49] The Navy maintained strong support for these and similar legislative proposals.

Navy's interest in offshore petroleum resources was shared by the president and several agencies of the federal government. The Interior Department supported Navy's bid for turning the offshore lands into naval oil reserves, but continued to express doubts regarding the federal title to these lands.[50] Nonetheless, with the advent of legislation in the Congress, the Interior Department began to suspend decisions on applications for licenses and ceased to deny federal jurisdiction. The states' response was predictable. In 1938, Louisiana claimed a limit of twenty-four marine miles seaward from a three-mile belt and in 1939 California resumed offshore leasing after a hiatus of several years. These developments left an eager oil industry in a state of uncertainty as to the status of areas in which it might operate.

In the summer of 1938, the president, with his characteristic exuberance for extensive claims, requested that Assistant Secretary of the Interior E. K. Burlew explore the possibility of issuing an executive order that would set up "naval oil reserves on the coast beginning with the shore line and extending halfway across the oceans."[51] In one fell swoop, the president would merge the federal-state issue in an extensive bid for offshore jurisdiction. The Interior Department response was not encouraging. Within the three-mile limit, the president was told, an executive order would represent an exercise of his inherent and statutory powers to withdraw and reserve public lands for public purposes. This would have the advantage of promoting the passage of suitable legislation in the Congress. But beyond the three-mile limit, the president was told, he was "without the authority to promulgate the suggested order prior to the actual occupation of the lands by drilling or mining for oil."[52]

The president was not easily daunted. On July 1, 1939, he addressed a memorandum to the attorney general and the secretaries of state, navy and interior in which he said:

> I am still convinced that: (a) Federal as opposed to State jurisdiction exists below low-water mark . . . and that (b) Federal jurisdiction can well be exercised as far out into the ocean as it is mechanically possible to drill wells.
>
> I recognize that new principles of international law might have to be asserted but such principles would not in effect be wholly new, because they would be based on the consideration that inventive genius has moved jurisdiction out to sea to the limit of inventive genius.
>
> I suggest, therefore, that this matter be studied by a joint interdepartmental committee of Justice, State, Navy and Interior, with the Attorney General as Chairman.
>
> I am, therefore, asking the Attorney General to undertake this task with your cooperation, with a view to the introduction of the necessary legislation at the next session.[53]

This memo is notable for the president's persistence in seeking to extend jurisdiction and his willingness to shift means, from an executive order to a legislative approach. His introduction of a limit set by "inventive genius" also displays the president's own ingenuity.

Under the president's mandate, the Interdepartmental Committee to Study Title to Submerged Oil Lands set to work, and on March 13, 1940, had completed its efforts with a report to the president. In examining the possible legal bases on which to predicate a claim, the committee came to the conclusion that the rights of the government "should be defined through appropriate court proceedings. While legislation would be helpful as an exercise of those rights, it is not deemed indispensable to the assertion of them." The Navy, however, the report noted, was "very strongly of the opinion that every effort should be made to pass . . . legislation, setting aside submerged oil lands as a naval reserve." While this memorandum addressed itself to the national jurisdictional dispute, it made no proposals regarding the outer limits of national jurisdiction. The study concluded that the matter should be referred "to the Attorney General with instructions to take all steps by way of judicial proceedings, or legislation, or both.[54]

This result was congenial to the secretary of the interior. As early as 1938 he noted in his diary his concern to pursue both judicial and legislative routes to determine the title of offshore lands. Now with the conclusions of the interdepartmental study in hand, he intensified his pressure on the attorney general. Ickes wrote to Acting Attorney General Francis Biddle in May and November of 1940 and in January, March, June, and July of 1941, asking him to file suit to assert U.S. rights to offshore lands. In response to his last letter of July 2, 1941, the attorney general told the secretary that there had been a significant change in the plan worked out by the Interdepartmental Committee. The attorney general advised the secretary that enabling legislation would be necessary to advance the federal government's case and that a draft statute had been sent to the president in the fall of 1940. The president had had the bill under consideration since then but had not found it advisable to proceed at that juncture.

Apparently the administration's plan to press the government's case in the courts and in the Congress had run afoul of the national presidential election. Leaks to the press had revealed government plans, and the opposition candidate, Wendell Wilkie, adopted the politically popular role of preserving states' rights.[55] The president was quick to back off from plans for instituting legal proceedings. As of March 31, 1942, Ickes was notified that, at the president's suggestion, the matter was dormant.[56] The bills to effect federal jurisdiction had died with the 76th Congress and the only bills pending by 1942 were those seeking to confirm the title of the several states (H.J. Res. 5 and H.J. Res. 34).

DECISION-MAKING PROCESS
IN THE ROOSEVELT ADMINISTRATION

The period of the Second World War provided only a brief interruption in the evolution of fisheries and offshore oil problems from the 1930s. And despite the war, bureaucratic politics continued as usual. Agency actors maintained efforts to increase their authority vis-à-vis one another, other branches of the government, and the states. Because of the exigencies of mobilizing the nation to wage a major war, some agencies were in a better position to enhance their positions than others. Thus while the war led to an increase in the powers of the federal government and of the executive branch in particular, it especially fortified those agencies and administrators that were in charge of meeting wartime needs.

Among those departments most successful in enhancing their bureaucratic authority during the war was the Department of the Interior under Harold Ickes. Ickes's efforts to enlarge his authority date from his earliest days in office. In 1934, for instance, he noted his desire to transfer the Bureau of Commercial Fisheries from the Department of Commerce to the Department of the Interior[57] as well as to extract the Forestry Division from the Department of Agriculture. Ickes's express goal was to convert the Interior Department into a Department of Conservation.

Hence Ickes was particularly active in the 1938 congressional battle over a reorganization bill that would enhance the president's authority to shift certain bureaus from agency to agency.[58] With the passage of the bill, Ickes turned his attention to the president. In response to Ickes's numerous requests, Roosevelt transferred to Interior the Fisheries Bureau, the Biological Survey, and the Insular Affairs Bureau from the Departments of Commerce, Agriculture, and War respectively. To the secretary's extreme annoyance, however, the president did not give him the Forestry Division or the Coast and Geodetic Survey. Moreover, the president removed several bureaus from Interior's control.[59]

Despite Ickes's pique, it is evident that the Interior Department fared well in the bureaucratic reorganization of 1939. With the transfer of the Bureau of Fisheries and the Biological Survey (53 Stat. 1431), Interior became the lead agency in offshore living resources. This was acknowledged in 1940 by the consolidation of the two bureaus into the Fish and Wildlife Service (54 Stat. 230). On this organizational base, the Interior Department, through Ickes, lost no time in interjecting itself into the Alaska salmon dispute. In 1941, Interior created a departmental committee to consider legislation regarding the Alaska fisheries.[60] At the same time, Interior began to build a base of support with the fishing industry. By these means, Interior began to challenge the pivotal role that the State Department had occupied in the fisheries controversy of the 1930s.[61]

During the early 1940s Ickes seldom let up in his persistent pressure on the president for new authority. In March of 1942, Ickes proposed that Roosevelt make him "fishery coordinator" in order to assure the contribution of the fishing industry to the national food supply.[62] After several reminders from Ickes,[63] the president finally granted his request in July 1942 to last for the duration of the war.[64] Ickes used this new title to further enhance his base of authority with industry and other agencies.[65] Ickes was after the president less than a month later with a request that his title be changed from that of fishery coordinator to coordinator of fisheries.[66]

While intent upon consolidating his power in the area of living resources, Ickes never neglected to expand his authority in regard to petroleum resources. During the war, Ickes regularly agitated within the executive branch for new powers over energy. Throughout 1941, he was continually at odds with the State Department over which agency should be in charge of decisions regarding the shipment of oil overseas. As petroleum coordinator for national defense, he periodically interjected himself into matters affecting foreign policy, and the State Department was thrust into the position of having to go directly to the president to keep Ickes in hand.[67] While State, backed by the War Department, prevailed in 1941, Ickes continued to wring new powers from the president. In November 1941 he was made the coordinator of hard fuels. And in 1942, the president signed an executive order giving Ickes, as petroleum administrator for the war, the power to promulgate conservation measures relating to offshore deposits.[68]

Interior Seizes the Initiative

While Ickes actively jockeyed for position with other federal agencies throughout the war, he left the question of federal versus state authority over offshore lands temporarily in abeyance. Wartime needs required maximum production efforts from the petroleum companies, efforts which would not be forthcoming if there were a dispute over title. The war also presented an opportunity for Ickes since the authority of the federal government was expanding rapidly. Two jurisdictional problems needed to be resolved: the respective powers of the federal versus state governments and the extent of national jurisdiction. With this in mind, Ickes began in 1943 to stir the federal government into action.

The timing of the Ickes moves to expand U.S. jurisdiction is particularly noteworthy, coming as it did toward the end of the war. The United States was to emerge from the war as the preeminent world power, forced against its traditions to adopt a global or international perspective. Ickes's plan, however, reflected the goals of a middle-range power limited to coastal preoccupations.

The move to extend U.S. jurisdiction originated within the Interior Department's General Land Office (GLO). In a May 28, 1943, memorandum to the secretary, GLO officials pointed out that the wartime situation offered the ideal opportunity to strike "from our own thinking and international law the shackles of the three-mile limit for territorial waters."[69] "In the interest of national and domestic security" the U.S. should adopt a "line of 100 or 150 miles from our shores" thereby taking the U.S. "beyond the continental shelf and reserving this valuable asset for the United States." A draft letter to the president was enclosed for Ickes's signature. On behalf of the Interior Department, Secretary Ickes forwarded the proposed letter to President Roosevelt on June 5, 1943. It called for a study of the legal and policy problems involved in "availing ourselves fully of the riches in this submerged land (the continental shelf) and in the waters over them." In language proposed to him by GLO officials, Ickes argued that:

> The War has impressed us with the necessity for an augmented supply of natural resources. In this connection I draw your attention to the importance of the Continental Shelf . . . The Continental Shelf extending some 100 or 150 miles from our shores forms a fine breeding place for fish of all kinds; it is an excellent hiding place for submarines, and since it is a continuation of our continent, it probably contains ore and other resources similar to those found in our States.
>
> I suggest the advisability of laying the groundwork now for availing ourselves fully of the riches in this submerged land and in the waters over them.

The letter went on to propose that the Interior Department undertake a study of the legal and policy problems involved, in collaboration with the Departments of State and Justice and the National Resources Planning Board.[70]

In addition to serving the purposes of the General Land Office, the Ickes letter to Roosevelt represented a continuation of the secretary's efforts to ensure his department's primacy in fisheries policy. To be sure, the Japanese were not fishing off Alaska for salmon—or for any other species for that matter—in 1943. Nonetheless, the Pacific coast fishing industry continued to agitate for control of offshore fisheries and several pieces of legislation to this effect had been reintroduced in the Congress. Ickes's calculation that the war presented the optimum time to make a unilateral move was evidently shared by some on Capitol Hill.[71] The Ickes memo of June 1943 also represented an effort to secure Interior's participation in the fisheries' decision-making process and to enlarge its role vis-à-vis the State Department. In May of 1943, the Department of State had established a "Departmental Committee to study the problems of protection and utilization of, and jurisdiction over, coastal fisheries and other marine resources."[72] This organizational move was made to prepare for a North Atlantic fisheries meeting in London in October 1943,[73] and Interior wanted to be included in the planning.

The president's response to Ickes's initiative was immediate and favorable. It reflected the same expansionist sentiments the president had expressed in 1937 with no evidence that he had been persuaded of the detrimental consequences of unilateral claims to jurisdiction. On June

9, Roosevelt sent a memo to the secretary of state, Cordell Hull, expressing the view that:

> I think Harold Ickes has the right slant on this. For many years, I have felt that the old three-mile limit or twenty-mile limit should be superseded by a rule of common sense. For instance, the Gulf of Mexico is bounded on the south by Mexico and on the north by the United States. In parts of the Gulf, shallow water extends very many miles off shore. It seems to me that the Mexican Government should be entitled to drill for oil in the southern half of the Gulf and we in the northern half of the Gulf. That would be far more sensible than allowing some European nation, for example, to come in there and drill.
>
> Another case which we have all talked about relates to the shelf in the bend of Alaska. Japanese fishing vessels netted habitually for salmon and crabs, twenty-five, thirty or forty miles offshore, catching them on their way to the shores and rivers of Alaska for the purpose of spawning.
>
> Would you agree to setting up a Board as he suggests, with representatives of the State Department, Interior Department, National Resources Planning Board, and the Department of Justice?[74]

Roosevelt's two principal concerns are strikingly those of the leader of a regional or middle-range power. There is no intimation that he recognized the fact of American preeminence in the world or that he understood the regime-creating effect of the actions taken by global powers. Roosevelt's first concern, that a European nation would exploit oil in the Gulf of Mexico, echoes the posture of the historic Monroe Doctrine. It was desirable in Roosevelt's view to divide the Gulf of Mexico between the U.S. and Mexico in order to exclude "some European nation," presumably the British. The threat of unauthorized petroleum exploitation near U.S. shores seems implausible at best, especially in 1943. The second aspect of the Roosevelt rationale—namely the desire to restrict Japanese fishing off Alaska—represents the legacy of the 1937 to 1938 dispute with Japan. Despite Japanese assurances and the lack of any evidence as to Japanese fishing for salmon, the president had accepted the popular view that such fishing had indeed taken place. What is striking about the 1943 Roosevelt memo is the persistence of the president's earlier views in a period when they were even less suitable, as well as his hostile attitude toward other developed nations—allies as well as enemies—in the absence of any compelling foreign threat in 1943 to U.S. offshore resources.

Given the president's enthusiasm for the Ickes proposal, the secretary of state's response was prompt and affirmative. Upon replying to the president's memo, Cordell Hull did take the occasion to point out that the State Department had already formed a committee to study the problem. Moreover, Hull suggested that it might be "appropriate and advantageous" to include the Department of the Navy in the proposed interdepartmental study group.[75] Hull's effort to broaden the participation of the study group was reasonable in terms of the Navy's earlier interest in establishing offshore naval petroleum reserves. Moreover, the Navy's participation would have had the advantage of diluting the domestic resource thrust of the study group. Hull's efforts, however, were to no avail, and the Navy never became a member of the interagency body.[76]

Roosevelt formally approved Ickes's proposal in May 1944 and told Interior to "go ahead with State and Justice" in the absence of the National Resources Planning Board which had "met an untimely death."[77] Neither in Ickes's initial proposal, nor in his April 18, 1944, reminder to the president, did he recommend Navy's participation. As a result, the president approved creation of an interdepartmental study group consisting only of Interior, State, and Justice.

With the president's instructions in hand, Ickes set out on a two-pronged program that would not only extend U.S. continental shelf jurisdiction vis-à-vis other countries, but would also secure federal vs. state ownership of the shelf. Roosevelt had not foreseen the domestic side of the strategy although he had included the Justice Department in the study group at Ickes's suggestion. Moreover, the president had envisioned the formation of a single study group. Upon the advice of his associates, however, Ickes preferred to handle "the international phases of the problem" with the State Department and the "domestic phases" with the Justice Department.[78] Such a separation, of course, maintained a pivotal role for the Interior Department.

According to the plan, Ickes sent letters to Cordell Hull and to Attorney General Biddle on May 23 asking each to meet with him to designate the appropriate officials in their agencies to carry out the president's memorandum. In his letter to the attorney general Ickes detailed his concern with winning ownership of offshore lands by asserting that "the study which the president has approved necessarily involves the question of the respective sovereign and proprietary roles of the Federal Government and of the several coastal States with respect to the submerged lands off our shores."[79] On these grounds Ickes went on to remind the attorney general of the recommendation of the interdepartmental group in 1940 that the matter of state-federal jurisdiction be referred "to the Attorney General with instructions to take all steps by way of judicial proceedings or legislation, or both." Ickes pointed out that neither step had been taken. In fact, he acknowledged, efforts to obtain legislation in 1938 on the part of Navy, Justice, and Interior had been to no avail. It was, therefore, necessary to proceed with litigation. He concluded, "I would like to discuss these matters with you at your earliest convenience with the object of having the suit brought as soon as possible and arranging for the participation by your Department in the domestic aspects of the study which the President has directed us to make."

The Ickes memo indicates a gradual evolution of his views from his 1933 acceptance of state jurisdiction through a willingness to wait for a legal and legislative determination of the issue to a resolve to gain federal control of the continental shelf by any means whatsoever. As late as April 14, 1943, Ickes had argued to Senator Truman that, given the pressing wartime need for oil, then was not the time to disrupt production by initiating legislation against the states.[80] However, Ickes noted at the time that all operators on the continental shelf were subject to conservation measures he might invoke as petroleum administrator for the war. By 1944, Ickes's public stance against litigation was no longer visible. Citing the fact that the states were draining the strategically valuable reserves of the shelf, Ickes importuned the president to "suggest to the Attorney General that he immediately either commence the suit or request Congress to pass the legislation he considers desirable."[81] Simultaneously, alternative approaches were being considered in the Interior Department. Ickes was advised by his staff that under the War Powers Act he could, with the authorization of the president, institute condemnation litigation to establish military petroleum reserves as a device to determine ownership of the offshore lands.[82] The secretary's increased zeal in pursuing federal ownership may have resulted from a combination of factors: his appointment as petroleum administrator for the war; the expanded use by states of the continental shelf; the growing knowledge of substantial petroleum resources in the area.

Despite Ickes's determination, the attorney general was not willing to be pressed into litigation before the Justice Department felt it had a case. Biddle sent Ickes a memo responding to his May 23 request for a meeting and drawing a clear distinction between the plan to bring judicial proceedings and the president's approval for a study of extending control over offshore resources. Biddle indicated his department's readiness to participate in the study which the president had proposed. On the question of litigation, however, Biddle went over Ickes's head directly to the president[83] and informed the president of specific plans that Ickes had to initiate a test case based on an application for license by the Regent Oil Company. Biddle reminded the president that Justice saw little chance of a successful suit unless a statute was first passed supporting the government's policy. Moreover, he argued that this was not the "time to inflame California, Louisiana, Texas and the other oil states." Opposed to both the timing and means contemplated by Ickes, Biddle concluded, "I feel it so important that I hope you will say a word to Harold about it." Biddle then forwarded a copy of his advice to the president directly to Ickes.

Recognizing that he had been thwarted by the attorney general, Ickes agreed to withhold action to provoke a test case. He did ask that conversations be continued between his department and the Justice Department as to how "the Government's claims to these lands may be most advantageously brought before the courts."[84] The upshot of these discussions, as reported by Fowler Harper, solicitor for Interior, was that Justice was annoyed with the "recurring suggestion of this Department that the question be litigated to conclusion."[85] The prime difference was over the timing of litigation, and, given Biddle's ready access to the president, Justice maintained the upper hand in this regard.

While Ickes did not fare well in his plan to press the domestic side of offshore jurisdiction, he was in a stronger position in dealing with the State Department. In response to Ickes's request that Hull designate an official to study the question of extending jurisdiction, the secretary nominated Assistant Secretary of State Breckinridge Long.[86] On behalf of the Interior Department, Michael Straus, an assistant secretary, contacted Long and arranged the first meeting of the interdepartmental group for July 13.[87]

This meeting was chaired jointly by Long and Straus. The offices represented within the Department of the Interior included those of the Solicitor, the General Land Office, the Geological Survey, and the Fish and Wildlife Service. The offices represented from the Department of State were the Office of the Petroleum Advisor, the Division of Geography and Cartography, and the Office of Economic Affairs.[88] The assistant secretaries from both departments were in agreement on the need to free the U.S. from the "handicaps of the rule of the three-mile limit." They also agreed that "the extent of the continental shelf appeared to offer a reasonable basis on which to assert a wider jurisdiction." Dr. Ira Gabrielson, the director of the Fish and Wildlife Service, stressed the immediacy of the fisheries problem and the need to take action to prevent "encroachment by foreign nationals" in the postwar period. Other officials raised the question of the possible adverse impact on U.S. fishing activities near other countries of unilateral action to limit foreign fishing near U.S. shores.

As there seemed to be a large measure of agreement between officials of both agencies, a subcommittee of four was named to "develop a formula which might be recommended" to the secretaries of state and interior.[89] According to published and unpublished memoranda, this group, consisting of two representatives from each agency, met twice in the following week. Under review were two drafts, one on fisheries and the other on the shelf. The paper on fisheries was prepared by the State Department's Committee on Offshore Resources on the basis of the latest draft of an agreement that was being negotiated between the United States, Canada, and Newfoundland. The paper on the continental shelf was drafted in the Interior Department.[90]

Six State Department officials met on July 25 to consider the two drafts. The bulk of that meeting was devoted to fisheries policy and the procedure by which the draft statement should be made public. The draft statements were regarded as satisfactory by most of those present, and the main item of discussion was that of procedure. The sentiment of the meeting appeared to favor keeping the two policies separate although they might be announced simultaneously. And those that had been most actively involved in negotiation of the fisheries question with Canada and Newfoundland weighed in strongly in favor of prior agreement with these two countries.[91] The general view was that a joint announcement by two or more countries would be most effective.[92]

Bureaucratic Differences

The contrasting accounts of this State Department meeting reveal the first intimations of differences of opinion among government officials. Those differences were over whether a joint announcement, involving at the least Canada and Newfoundland, was absolutely necessary, and they stemmed from the fact that during the fourteen months of its existence the State Department Committee on Offshore Resources had developed a preferred method of proceeding. As articulated by Mr. Sturgeon of the Office of Economic Affairs (ECA), this was that "the declaration of policy regarding fisheries would be embodied in an exchange of notes between the United States, Canada, and Newfoundland." In the course of discussions with the other North Americans over problems with Japan and in the Northwest Atlantic, the State Department's Committee on Offshore Resources and its ECA representative had developed a firm commitment to a joint regional approach to fisheries policy.

The outcome of the meeting was somewhat confused. On the one hand it seemed to be resolved that in deference to Sturgeon's position, "no announcement of the new policy should be made until agreement is reached with the Canadians and that before the agreement with Canada is announced, the USSR should be informed." Yet elsewhere there seemed to be agreement that both policy statements should be made public simultaneously, without any indication of whether Canadian concurrence in the continental shelf policy would also be sought. The one course of action clearly rejected was that of a Senate resolution or congressional legislation. Several members of the group did point out that "federal legislation would be necessary to give effect to the new policy regarding fisheries"[93] in order to enable enforcement by the Interior Department.

On August 3, Assistant Secretary Long forwarded the draft texts to a meeting of the State Department's Policy Committee before issuing a departmental approval. By this time bureaucratic differences within the State Department could no longer be papered over with vague language. The depth of these differences is reflected in the suggestion made by the Office of Economic Affairs that the issue be referred to it for further study—in other words, buried. Several memoranda indicated the importance ECA attached to proceeding on a regional or "limited international basis."[94] A number of long intradepartmental meetings between ECA and other officials ensued, but to no avail.

Assistant Secretary Long was finally compelled to refer the deadlock to the secretary of state for resolution. In a memorandum dated September 23, Long set the matter before the secretary with an explanation of the difficulties in reaching agreement and with a reference to the pressure being exerted by the Department of the Interior to come to a decision. The overriding "purpose" at that point in time, as Long perceived it, was to reach "an agreement with the Department of the Interior on a question of policy." Long felt that ECA concern to determine the manner of proceeding was "irrelevant to the present purpose," and he asked the secretary to approve the policy.

The objections of the Office of Economic Affairs were spelled out in a lengthy memorandum accompanying Assistant Secretary Long's letter to the secretary.[95] The ECA statement stressed the importance of procedures by which the new policy toward offshore jurisdiction would be implemented. The memorandum noted that "so significant a departure from past practices under the law of nations cannot be wholly separated from the method by which it might be put into effect." The adoption of the fisheries policy contemplated could, it was argued, "lead to misunderstanding, suspicion, and opposition on the part of many other countries." The U.S., therefore, "should not announce this policy without some form of international consultation with at least the countries that would feel themselves interested in and affected thereby." ECA listed "Canada, Newfoundland, the United Kingdom, the Soviet Union, Mexico, Ecuador, et cetera" as countries whose concurrence was "essential" before the U.S. proceeded to any announcement or action. The same case was made for consultation with other governments concerning the extension of U.S. jurisdiction over the continental shelf, but foreign concurrence in this policy was not described as essential. This memorandum reveals a significant evolution in ECA thinking in the direction of an international rather than a regional approach to the expansion of offshore jurisdiction.[96] The number of countries whose concurrence ECA felt must be sought in the extension of fisheries jurisdiction had significantly increased.[97] Moreover, a unilateral announcement on continental shelf resources as opposed to that on fisheries was no longer acceptable to ECA by the end of 1944.

The ECA policy statements on fisheries and continental shelf jurisdiction[98] reveal that, contrary to Long's statement that the difference between ECA and other segments of State was simply over procedure, there was indeed a fundamental and widening divergence over substance. In addition to providing a longer and more elaborated statement of proposed policy (which was said to be consistent with Canadian preferences), the ECA specified that in the exercise of its jurisdiction, the U.S. government should pursue a policy of "equality of treatment as between its own nationals and those of any other state" with regard to access to the resources of the continental shelf and to coastal fisheries. "In any international agreements into which the United States may enter on this subject, the Government . . . will endeavor to secure recognition of the principle of equality of treatment by all states parties to such agreements." Such an approach was inconsistent with the exclusionary policy contemplated by the other offices of State and Interior, and was a sign of the growing recognition within segments of U.S. officialdom of the country's interest in a liberal, universal economic system. With such an outlook, regional, much less unilateral, approaches were to be eschewed.

The forces for moving ahead to an agreement with Interior and ultimately to a policy pronouncement were, however, more powerful than this new perception. Long had, from the outset, been an avowed proponent of extending U.S. jurisdiction beyond three miles.[99] He seemingly prevailed when Acting Secretary of State Edward Stettinius, Jr. decided on behalf of the State Department to officially forward the draft statements to the Department of the Interior on November 28.[100] The drafts did not include ECA's substantive views on equality of treatment for nationals of all countries. Stettinius's decision to forward the policy drafts to Interior was taken two months after the Long memorandum. Several factors account for his delay in acting. The transition from Hull to Stettinius meant that time was lost in familiarizing the new secretary with the issue. Moreover, Stettinius, unlike his predecessor, was drawn into the absorbing issue of wartime diplomacy and the postwar order, leaving him little time for a sustained consideration of offshore resource policy.

While State with its many concerns was consistently slow in its procedures, the same cannot be said of Interior. Secretary Stettinius sent the two approved drafts to Interior on December 5, 1944.[101] Two days later, Secretary Ickes responded with complete approval of both policies.[102] Striking while the iron was hot, Ickes went on to propose that a memorandum be sent to the president calling for the simultaneous announcement of both proclamations. Other governments, Ickes pointed out, might be notified informally of the impending policy pronouncement.

Stettinius, on behalf of the State Department, responded negatively to Ickes's preferred method of proceeding. While he had been willing to approve and forward the two drafts to Interior and to ignore the issue of equality of treatment for foreign nationals, Stettinius had evidently been persuaded by ECA's argument in favor of an international approach. The international route commended itself to Stettinius for personal as well as bureaucratic reasons. He was personally committed to the evolution of the United Nations organization and other cooperative postwar relationships. In addition, Stettinius had agency reasons for preferring a consultative approach. To move unilaterally at this point in time would preclude the successful completion of two years of State Department discussions with the governments of Newfoundland, Canada, and more recently Mexico over fisheries jurisdiction. Stettinius felt that "from the standpoint of our foreign relations with Canada, especially, it would be desirable to avoid public unilateral action by our Government until the Canadian Government has been informed of the action proposed."[103] Indeed, Stettinius pointed out, the governments of Canada and Newfoundland had "contributed materially in the formulation of the statement on fisheries; and it is believed that both these countries will be in substantial agreement with the policy and may welcome an opportunity to take joint action with us, or to take unilateral action concurrently with ours, in making known their adherence to the proposed principles."[104]

As a result of these considerations, Stettinius proposed an alternative course of action to Ickes. In essence, it was first to ask the president for a general approval of the overall policy. Then the views of other governments would be sought through consultations. And finally, "when the reactions of the foreign governments concerned have been learned, a decision can be made regarding the steps which might be taken to make the policy public, such as the issuance of proclamations."[105] "This procedure," Stettinius felt, "would more likely keep the other governments in a favorable frame of mind."[106] The Stettinius proposal was summed up in a draft memorandum to be sent to the president for his approval. The memorandum included a description of the policy, a long middle section detailing the need for consultation with other governments, and a concluding paragraph recommending a presidential decision after these consultations.

Ickes was plainly alarmed by the prospect that, following consultations with other governments, there might be further delays in proceeding to a policy announcement due either to foreign opposition or to State Department indecision. He therefore altered his strategy. Ickes proposed a course which provided that a two-month period would elapse between presidential approval of the policy and the official announcement, thereby giving the appearance of consultation while in fact avoiding a procedure which might alter U.S. policy on the basis of the foreign response. Ickes set this out in a January 4, 1945 memo to Stettinius: "In the interest of expediting this project, might it not be desirable to obtain a decision from the President on all questions of substance prior to the proposed consultation with other governments? This is particularly important in connection with the timing of the public declarations of policy which, I think, should come at the earliest practicable moment."[107] Ickes proposed the following formulation to replace the last paragraph of the Stettinius memo: "Within a period of two months from the date of your approval and after consultation with the foreign governments concerned, the necessary documents will be submitted for signature and promulgation by you."[108] As subsequent events were to show, the word "consultation" in the Ickes scenario meant "notification" and such a procedure would not have satisfied the concerns expressed in Stettinius's earlier response to Ickes.

CHAPTER 2

Discontinuity in Decision Making

We do not know what the new secretary's reaction would have been since, just at this time, his attention became absorbed in preparations for the Yalta meeting of the Allies. The proposal to extend offshore jurisdiction, with other less weighty matters, devolved upon Acting Secretary of State Joseph C. Grew. It was Grew who gave his approval to the Ickes plan for proceeding and who signed off on the January memo to the president. As ambassador to Japan, Under Secretary Grew had represented the U.S. in the Alaska salmon controversy and doubtless had vivid recollections of the difficulties of negotiating fisheries issues. Apart from that single episode, Grew had little background on the issue of offshore resources and, like most of the State Department officials, the little experience he had was limited to fisheries.[109]

In 1944 and 1945, the upper levels of the State Department as well as the presidency underwent changes disruptive of sustained consideration of policy.[110] Moreover, the conduct of the war had generated a number of incongruities in the process of foreign policy decision making. Several centers of foreign policy power had developed over which the State Department had little or no control. The War Department conducted its foreign affairs, sometimes in coordination with the president and the State Department and sometimes not. The president, for his part, undertook his own foreign policies without consulting Secretary Hull. With Hull's departure in late 1944 and the illness and death of Roosevelt in 1945, subsequent secretaries of state were engulfed in the difficult problems of wartime diplomacy and the postwar settlement. The situation of the State Department, therefore, went from one in which it was relegated responsibility for only the most routine aspects of foreign affairs to one in which it was absorbed in assisting a new president with the pressing problems of the postwar order. Superimposed on this transition was a succession of three secretaries of state and two presidents within a six-month period including the critical first months of 1945.[111] In this context, less urgent problems, such as that of the status of offshore resources, were necessarily disposed of by the lower levels of government. Officials at these levels were rarely able to engage the focused attention of their harried superiors.

The absence of high-level policy guidance accounts in part for the announcement in 1945 of an offshore resources policy that was inconsistent with other trends in U.S. foreign policy. While the government was becoming more deeply concerned with consolidating its relations with its allies and with the viability of the new international organization in the face of an intransigent Soviet Union, the Truman Proclamations represented a blow to multilateral cooperative approaches. That this policy went forward may be traced to Grew's acquiescence in Ickes's proposal for altering the last paragraph of the Stettinius memorandum. In light of his earlier objections, it is doubtful that Stettinius would have agreed to this procedure.

The result of grafting Interior's timetable for proceeding onto the original State Department memorandum was a highly ambivalent policy directive. The central sections of the memorandum laid strong emphasis on the need to proceed jointly with other governments but the concluding paragraph merely recommended that the U.S. in effect notify other governments over a two-month period of its intention to extend jurisdiction. The contradictory nature of this memo as it went to President Roosevelt was subsequently to plague those U.S. officials who were charged with notifying foreign governments. The ambivalence provided an opportunity for delay of the policy pronouncements by those U.S. officials who continued to oppose it. The opening, however, was not sufficient to reverse the policy process once the Ickes procedure had been adopted and the president had signed off on the memorandum.

President Roosevelt approved the Grew-Ickes memorandum two months later, on March 31, 1945. The approval was issued from Warm Springs where the president had gone on March 30 to recuperate. It is unlikely that Roosevelt, engrossed as he had been in the February Yalta meeting and increasingly weakened by illness, gave the policy much thought before signing it. Less than two weeks after approving the memo, the president died, leaving his successor virtually committed to a policy of expanding offshore jurisdiction—a policy which was ironically to be termed the "Truman Proclamations."

RATIONALE FOR THE TRUMAN PROCLAMATIONS

Before turning to consider the events leading from President Roosevelt's approval of the policy to its public announcement, it is useful to examine in some detail the case that was being made within the government for extending offshore jurisdiction. This sheds some light on the premises behind the Truman Proclamations and provides a basis for evaluating them. The most comprehensive collection of official U.S. reasoning is set forth in a memo drafted by William Bishop of the State Department's Legal Advisor's Office. This lengthy explanatory statement was drafted for use in consultations with other governments. It constitutes a virtual "grab bag" of arguments—some legal, some social, some geological, and some economic. The Bishop document was transmitted to

45

selected foreign governments and its ideas were drawn upon in direct conversations with representatives of other countries.

The legal advisor's memorandum justifying U.S. policy was divided into two sections, one dealing with fisheries and the other with the continental shelf. The explanation of U.S. fisheries proposals began on a high-minded note. The avowed purpose of U.S. policy was to improve "the jurisdictional basis of conservation measures and international cooperation in this field." This was followed by an elaborate principled justification of U.S. policy:

1. The fisheries are essential both to the coastal communities which are dependent upon them for a livelihood and to allied and related industries. . . .
2. Progressive development of new methods in fishing . . . contribute to intensified exploitation over wide areas. In important instances coastal fisheries are seriously exposed to unregulated exploitation and depletion, thus creating general anxiety for their future among the people whose economic welfare and security depend upon them. In consequence a clear need has arisen for an improved basis for the regulation and protection of fisheries in the high seas contiguous to the coasts.
3. Equity and justice require that natural resources which have been built up by systematic conservation and self-denying restricted utilization . . . be protected and reserved from destructive exploitation by interests which have not contributed to their growth and development.
4. The fisheries differ in species, abundance, and other characteristics, from sea to sea and area to area; regulatory measures . . . must be diversified and adapted to conditions peculiar to each region, with due regard to the special rights and equities of the coastal state and of any other state which has participated in the fishery of the region. Regulation and control of coastal fishery resources should therefore be treated on a regional basis.
5. Regulatory arrangements for a particular fishing area or region should be made among the states whose continued use of or relative proximity to the affected resources gives them the interest and intimate knowledge necessary for wise and effective control, and cannot achieve full success unless made applicable to all persons and vessels of whatsoever nationality engaged in fishing therein.[112]

The task of the legal advisor in finding a legal rationale to protect U.S. fishing interests was complicated by the diversity of those interests.

46

On the one hand, a status quo doctrine had to be elaborated to protect declining U.S. coastal fishing industries while, on the other hand, legal protection was needed for growing U.S. distant-water fishing interests. The skills of State Department lawyers were equal to the task. To preserve U.S. distant-water fishing interests, the Bishop memo specified that "the right of all states which have taken any substantial part in the fishery are preserved. It is not intended to disturb in any way well-established or historic fishing activities." Instead, what the U.S. proposed was "the establishment of clearly defined conservation zones in areas of the high seas contiguous to the coasts." In these zones freedom of navigation and purposes other than fishing would be preserved. Coastal-state control of fisheries activities was to be viewed as a special and limited case. The legal memorandum spelled out a carefully constructed rationale for the exercise of this control: "(a) proximity to the coasts of the state; (b) the development and maintenance of well-established fishing activities on a substantial scale by a state's nationals; (c) the absence in that area of any well-established fishing activities on the part of nationals of states other than those seeking to exercise such authority; and (d) the existence of established conservation practices, or the need for such practices, in relation to the fisheries of the area in question."[113]

In virtually all respects, the policy and its rationale were designed to protect U.S. salmon resources from the Japanese. Indeed, this was made explicit by the inclusion in the memorandum of a statement made by Secretary Hull in 1938, in the context of the U.S.-Japanese dispute. "An industry . . . which has been built up by the nationals of one country cannot in fairness be left to be destroyed by the nationals of other countries." The message was clear. New entrants were not to be allowed into a developed fishery.

In addition to attempting a rationale of the substance of U.S. policies, the Bishop memorandum tackled the difficult problem of justifying the unilateral method adopted by the U.S. in asserting offshore claims. This was done by raising the preferred U.S. policy from the realm of national interest to the level of principles of universal applicability. The memo invited other governments to join with the United States in the "practical application of the principles set forth above." These governments were urged to adopt "a similar policy as a substantial step . . . toward the improvement of the basis of international cooperation in the fisheries field."

The second portion of the legal advisor's memorandum dealt equally skillfully with the U.S. claim to continental shelf resources with arguments tailored to the matter at hand. The universalist reasons for the

47

U.S. policy included concern for "the long-range worldwide need for new sources of petroleum and other minerals."[114] Claims to living resources of the shelf were based on universally recognized historic claims to offshore sedentary fisheries. Occupation and contiguity were the legal basis for these claims.

To supplement the customary law arguments, the memorandum went on to elaborate geological, economic, national security, and conservation arguments indicating why it was "reasonable and just" to lay claim to the U.S. continental shelf:

> (a) the continental shelf may be regarded on geographic and physiological grounds as an extension of the land mass of the coastal state and thus naturally appurtenant to it; (b) these resources often form part of a pool or deposit extending seaward from within the state and their utilization may affect resources therein; (c) the effectiveness of measures which may be adopted to utilize or conserve these resources would be contingent upon cooperation and protection from the coastal state; (d) self-protection compels the coastal state to keep close watch over activities off its shores which are of the nature and relative permanence necessary for utilization of resources of the subsoil and sea bed of the continental shelf; (e) prudent conservation and practical utilization of these resources are dependent upon a clear governmental policy defining their jurisdictional status; and (f) the government of the country to whose shores the resources are contiguous is clearly the logical government to exercise jurisdiction and control over these resources.[115]

The legal memorandum threw in a few additional points for good measure and regardless of the inconsistencies they posed. It asserted that "no foreign state would have reason to object to utilization and conservation by the United States of undersea mineral resources within a reasonable distance of its coasts."[116] As a result, it was possible to distinguish between a coastal fisheries policy in which other states might share a legitimate interest with the U.S. and a continental shelf resources policy in which they would not. However, just in case a foreign power entertained any designs over U.S. continental shelf resources, the memorandum pointed out that as "an exercise of its rights of self-protection and as a matter of national defense," the U.S. would view such a foreign activity with "serious concern." As if all of this were not sufficient, the memorandum also threw in the industry argument calling for "reasonable assurance of title." In the absence of the assurance which would result from extending U.S. jurisdiction over the continental shelf, it was argued, industry could not proceed to make the investments that were needed to promote the production of petroleum. Why other governments would, in the absence of such recognized title, consider drilling off U.S. shores without permission is never explained. The case is simply asserted that recognized jurisdiction over resources is "required in the interest of their conservation and prudent utilization."[117]

The legal advisor's definition of what composed the continental shelf differed from the distance criterion of 100 or 150 miles from shore cited in the original Ickes memorandum to the president. The legal advisor's formula stated: "The continental shelf extends seaward for varying distances off the shores, and in most places terminates in a fairly definite 'drop off.' The continental shelf is usually defined as that part of the undersea land mass adjacent to the coast, over which the sea is not more than 100 fathoms (600 feet) in depth." The term "shelf" was here taken to include "the shallow waters around this nation's islands as well as off the continental United States."[118] As in the case of the explicitly bounded fishery conservation zones, the U.S. claim to continental shelf resources was not to affect the high seas status of the superjacent waters.

This lengthy document sets forth most comprehensively the premises behind the Truman Proclamations. The various reasons for extending U.S. resources jurisdiction bear a striking resemblance to arguments heard in the United States in the 1970s. They include the need to secure control of vital natural resources, national security, dependence of local communities, conservation, economic necessity, geological reality, and technological pressures.

Although the legal memorandum was distributed in its entirety to several foreign governments, in discussions with foreign officials the arguments in it were stressed selectively depending upon the concerns of the particular audience. It is difficult in this circumstance to assign a weight to the several lines of argumentation as being greater or lesser factors in the decision to pursue a policy of extending offshore jurisdiction. It is equally difficult to distinguish between those arguments which were merely expedient as opposed to those which were genuinely felt. This is particularly true where reasons cited were partially contradictory.

TRUMAN PERIOD

The memorandum signed by President Roosevelt on March 31, 1945, specified that the U.S. would publicly announce its claim to offshore resources within two months. The Truman Proclamations, however, were not issued until September 28. In the intervening six-month period a succession of domestic and foreign events prompted a delay, but none was sufficient to either modify or prevent the policy announcement.

The forces of opposition within the U.S. and foreign governments struggled futilely to alter the course of a resolute Interior Department marching under the standard of the dead president's imprimatur. President Truman himself was notified of the proposed policy only after discussions were already underway with foreign governments. In the face of this momentum (and Interior Department persistence), he would have had the greatest difficulty reversing the policy had he wished to.[119] To be sure, Roosevelt's death, less than two weeks after signing off on the coastal resources policy, proved inconvenient to the Interior Department schedule as did the turnover of the secretaryship of state during this period. The inconvenience and the opposition, however, came too late to avert the policy pronouncements.

On April 24, about two weeks after Roosevelt's death, Acting Secretary Grew charged Eugene Dooman, special assistant to the assistant secretary of state for commonwealth affairs, with the conduct of discussions with foreign governments.[120] The selection of a representative from the Office of Commonwealth Affairs reflected the lingering sentiment that the concurrence of the other North American governments was desirable. Within the next three days, Dooman had officially notified the Canadian and then the Mexican governments of U.S. policy regarding jurisdiction over offshore resources.[121] Only then did the State Department apprise the new president of the proposed policy. The notification, when it came, was drafted in such a manner as to ensure Truman's approval. In an April 30 memo drafted by Assistant Secretary of State Dean Acheson and signed by Grew and Ickes, Truman was told of the policy which President Roosevelt had approved before his death. President Truman was advised:

> The effect of the adoption of these formulae will be to assert jurisdiction and control over the mineral and other resources under the sea bed of the continental shelf, and to assert the policy of establishing conservation zones for the protection of coastal fishery resources. These zones are to be controlled and regulated exclusively by the United States in areas where only our nationals have developed and maintained fishing activities on a substantial scale. In areas where legitimate fishery activities have been developed and maintained by nationals of other countries, their rights are safeguarded and such countries are permitted to join in the regulation

and control. The right of other countries to establish similar conservation zones off their shores in accordance with the same principles is conceded.[122]

The last sentence of that portion of the memorandum signed by Grew[123] asked: "May we have your instructions as to whether you approve the course outlined and wish the two departments to proceed?" Secretary Ickes was not so reticent. Playing on the desires of the non-elected president to maintain the continuity of policy of a popular predecessor, Ickes added the statement, "I recommend the reaffirmation by you of the policy approved by President Roosevelt in the attached memorandum and I urge that the Secretary of State be instructed to proceed promptly to consult the remaining foreign governments concerned in order that the original two months' schedule be met and appropriate documents submitted to you on May 31, 1945."

As this memorandum reveals, the title "Truman Proclamation" is a misnomer as applied to the policy of extending U.S. control to offshore resources. In fact, the question was raised after Roosevelt's death as to whether even *he* had taken any direct interest in the extension of U.S. control over offshore resources.[124] The background to the proclamations reveals that Roosevelt did, indeed, have a strong interest in extending the offshore jurisdiction of the United States to distances as far as the middle of the ocean. The record shows, however, that this consistent intent was not matched by any consistent view as to suitable means. Roosevelt considered executive proclamations, legislation, and litigation in turn. There is no evidence, moreover, that he had ever recognized the problems of legal precedent or international reaction to such actions on the part of a major world power. Certainly at the time that he signed the instructions to proceed with the proclamations, only two weeks before his death, it is unlikely that he gave any sustained attention to the question of procedure.

On the basis of a scanty historical record, the extent of Truman's recognition of the international consequences of the proclamations is even more difficult to determine. In signing the proclamations, Truman describes his intention as that of establishing fishing conservation zones. Elsewhere, he discusses at greater length the continental shelf proclamation.[125] The weight of these remarks, however, reflects a preoccupation with the federal-state conflict over offshore petroleum to which he had fallen heir. Given the pressing considerations of winding down the war in Europe and ending the war in the Pacific, the new president could scarcely devote significant time to the issue of offshore resources.

If presidential interest in the proclamations was indeed minimal or if the actions taken were uninformed, this would not be the first time that more knowledgeable lesser officials formulated and implemented a policy in the name of an unsuspecting president.

The Truman reply to the Grew-Ickes memo was forthcoming within the first week of May. As far as the records indicate, the presidential response was twofold. Truman returned the documents to Joseph Grew and "expressed verbally his approval of the policy papers."[126] Then in a written response dated May 4, President Truman raised questions concerning the impact of the policy on federal-state jurisdictional claims.[127] The president's ten years in the Senate had educated him on this aspect of the problem. He inquired as to the effect of this policy on state control of resources to the low-tide mark and in the area beyond that extending to three miles. His own view was that "federal control should exist, beyond low tide." Apart from the state versus federal government issues, there is no published record of the president's views on the international ramifications of the policy.[128]

Also scanty is the record, published and unpublished, of the opposition that developed within the U.S. government to unilateral action. What does emerge from these limited documents is that the center of the opposition to the proposed policy continued to be in the State Department offices charged with responsibility for the creation of a new liberal economic order in the postwar period.

By 1945, the International Trade Policy Division had replaced the Office of Economic Affairs as the leading opponent of extending U.S. offshore jurisdiction. The thrust of its differences with the policy continued to be twofold: (1) it preferred a genuinely international approach to a unilateral announcement and, (2) it sought to assure equal treatment to foreign nationals in the exploitation of U.S. coastal resources. Perhaps the clearest statement of the international economic perspective on procedure and substance is found in a memorandum by Deputy Assistant Secretary of State W. C. Thorp to the secretary of state.[129] Written in mid-August, Thorp's memo points out, with regard to procedure, that although twelve foreign governments had been consulted, there had been only one positive indication of attitude (Cuba). The others had not replied, with the exception of an informal negative comment from the Canadian deputy minister of fisheries to the assistant chief of the State Department's Commodities Division.[130] The international response to U.S. policy, or lack thereof, prompted Thorp to recommend an alternate procedure to unilateral announcement. "In the light of the present effort to use international cooperation whenever possible, it would seem more appropriate either to follow up the matter directly with the various governments, or to use the appropriate interested agency, the FAO, as a means to develop an international policy."

With regard to substance, Thorp made some equally telling remarks:

> There is one point at which the policy is not clear—the extent to which it is a form of protectionism, keeping American fishery areas for Americans. Our fundamental principle in this area is that of equal access to resources. The program as outlined does not assure equal treatment to foreign nationals, although it is avowedly established as a conservation of resources program and not one of protection of American business interests. . . . This seems inconsistent with the international economic program of reducing protective devices and eliminating trade restrictions. The principle of equal access can be incorporated in the program without disturbing the concept of jurisdiction over the continental shelf.

Thorp explicitly acknowledges that U.S. business interests would be greatly disturbed by the principle of equal access to resources. He is also explicit about the "substantial pressure from the fisheries industry and the Department of the Interior for prompt unilateral action."

The August memorandum may be viewed as a last futile effort to stave off a policy which in style and substance was inconsistent with a newly developing policy of U.S. economic leadership through international cooperative mechanisms. As the war was drawing to a close, economic planners within the State Department were eager to pursue the goal of eliminating discrimination in international commerce through the reduction of tariffs and other trade barriers. The motives behind the U.S. desire to create a new postwar economic order have been the subject of considerable debate. While some argue that U.S. imperialist instincts prompted what was an effort to keep markets open to U.S. goods and to maintain sources of raw materials,[131] others argue that the U.S. pursued a liberal economic order as a means of increasing interdependence and thereby averting future wars.[132] The true motivation of U.S. economic policy during this period doubtless lies somewhere in a blend of these two concerns. This same blend of motives was probably present in the opposition of economic officials to the Truman Proclamations. While it may be the case that their preference for equal treatment of U.S. and foreign nationals in access to offshore resources was intended to secure U.S. access to resources off other countries, there was no doubt also a measure of genuine commitment to the view that a liberalized world economic order was conducive to the general welfare.

The Congress

The relative absence of direct congressional participation in the events immediately leading up to the Truman Proclamations is a striking example of executive domination of foreign policy during wartime. Prior to U.S. involvement in the war, the Congress had played a major role, first in stimulating executive concern with offshore policy by the threat of legislation, and then through direct involvement in the negotiations with Japan. The war disrupted this pattern of consultation between the executive and Capitol Hill. It did not alter, however, the views that had developed in both branches of government in the course of the 1930s negotiations. Early in 1944, Senator Waldgren submitted the Alaskan Fisheries Bill (S.930) for the explicit purpose of once again applying pressure on the executive branch. When the secretary of state indicated that congressional action might impede negotiated settlement of the problem, Waldgren amended the bill to apply only to waters to which U.S. jurisdiction might be extended by valid treaty or subsequent congressional action.[133] Such an amendment was not satisfactory to fishery interests who continued to press for the immediate extension of jurisdiction to fifty or sixty miles from shore. Others favored a negotiated agreement between the U.S. and Canada which might be forced on Japan after the war was over. In effect, the range of opinions that existed within the executive was also to be found within the Congress.

The coincidence of executive and congressional views on U.S. fisheries policy did not extend to policy regarding the continental shelf. Once it was decided to announce the two policies simultaneously, therefore, it became evident to those anxious to proceed rapidly that consultation with the full Congress would delay, if not halt, the public announcement. Ickes had seen to it, in his revision of the Stettinius memorandum to the president, that the proposed seeking of congressional concurrence was watered down to optional "communication" with the Congress. The original Stettinius memo to the president of December 1944 had included the following: ". . . the Departments would welcome an expression of your opinion whether you would wish to inform the Congress and obtain its concurrence in connection with the issuance of any proclamations."[134]

The Ickes revision, however, that went to the president read otherwise: ". . . you may wish to consider the advisability of formal or informal communication with the Congress or with some of its leaders prior to the issuance of any proclamations."[135]

Just as genuine consultation with foreign governments would have altered or delayed the proposed policy, so too would the need for congressional concurrence.

An additional reason for the lack of consultation with the Congress was the absence of high-level direction on the question. The final Grew-Ickes memo presented "formal or informal communication" with the Congress as something the president might wish to consider. When Roosevelt signed the memorandum, however, he did not specify how the Congress was to be informed. In the April 30 memo to President Truman, therefore, it was pointed out that among the procedures Roosevelt had approved was "a discussion between the President or, if he should prefer, the Secretaries of State and Interior, or both, and appropriate members of the House and Senate before releasing the documents." When Truman responded orally to the Grew-Ickes request he did not specify how the executive was to proceed in its dealings with Congress although he had himself raised the question of state-federal relations.

Thus on May 15, 1945, Eugene Dooman found himself in a quandary. He had been authorized by Joseph Grew to continue discussions with foreign governments as per the presidential memo. "The President did not, however, give any directive with regard to discussions with appropriate members of the House and Senate."[136] Dooman consequently turned to Assistant Secretary of State Dean Acheson for instructions, "in light of the circumstances above set forth, in the manner of discussions with members of the House and Senate." Although Acheson's response to Dooman is unavailable in the published and unpublished records, it appears from available documents that Acheson and an Interior Department representative did approach Senator Joseph O'Mahoney of Wyoming (chairman of a special committee investigating petroleum resources) sometime between mid-May and early July.[137]

The next reference to notifying the Congress came on July 5. In response to a testy missive from Ickes urging immediate action on the policy, the new secretary of state, James F. Byrnes, recommended that he and Ickes meet with Senator O'Mahoney and Senator Tom Conally (Texas—chairman of the Senate Foreign Relations Committee) and perhaps other Senators from the Foreign Relations and Public Lands Committees.[138] Not until September 14, however, three days before the policy was publicly announced, did Acheson, as acting secretary of state, meet with Senator Conally.[139] What remains uncertain is whether Ickes met with congressional representatives. Given his intentions with regard to asserting federal jurisdiction over offshore lands and his haste to see the policy implemented, Ickes's communications with the Congress were probably minimal. A disposition to engage the Congress in this policy was not evident in the State Department in any event. Indeed, Byrnes's memorandum may have stemmed from a greater interest in deferring the policy pronouncement than in involving the Congress. The fact that Congress never moved to implement the Truman Proclamations through legislation is at least partly due to this executive branch inattention.

The lack of contact with the Congress during 1945 was less a result of calculation than of confusion. Indeed, the communications of the period show the disarray prevailing within the Department of State as James F. Byrnes succeeded Stettinius (and Acting Secretary Grew) as secretary of state.[140] In the proposed proclamations, Secretary Byrnes was confronted with a policy about which he knew very little. While it was strongly supported by the Interior Department, it was equally strongly opposed by economic affairs officials within his own agency. An additional confusion was lent to the issue by the delayed foreign responses to informal U.S. notification and the mounting British and Canadian opposition.

FOREIGN REACTION

The Byrnes-Ickes interchange in the summer of 1945 is notable in a number of respects. In addition to illuminating the disarray within the foreign policy establishment and the lack of attention to Congress, it reveals a measure of discontinuity and confusion in U.S. exchanges with foreign governments. Ickes, by June of 1945, had grown increasingly testy over the delays in implementing the policy and procedures which he had so deliberately set up. Without the support of his friend, President Roosevelt, he was reduced to writing badgering letters to a procession of secretaries of state. To make matters worse, he learned that the State Department was sitting on the proposed proclamations rather than signing them and forwarding them to the president. On June 28, Ickes addressed a memorandum to Acting Secretary Joseph Grew reminding him of their initial joint memorandum to Roosevelt and pointing out that the two-month period provided for therein had expired May 31.

> On June 13, I signed a joint memorandum to the President prepared for the signatures of the Secretaries of State and Interior and approved proposed proclamations and Executive orders. These papers were delivered to Assistant Secretary Acheson that day. It was our understanding in this Department that the signing and ap-

proval of these documents by Acting Secretary Grew was at this point a formality which, along with the submission of the papers to the President for his signature, would be speedily accomplished.

Despite all this, the papers have not as yet been signed by Acting Secretary Grew or submitted to the President. I should have supposed that the time for obstruction was over when two Presidents, to say nothing of the Secretary of State, have made a decision. I am sure that you will not think it unreasonable of me to ask that the proposed proclamations and Executive orders be submitted to the President for signature as soon as possible.[141]

Byrnes's July 5 response to the Ickes memorandum was noncommittal. Byrnes pointed out that the issue was new to him and suggested that before they act on the policy, both secretaries should meet with congressional leaders. Over six weeks elapsed before Byrnes again contacted Ickes in writing. During that period there was apparently at least one conversation between the two secretaries.[142] While the content of that discussion is not known, Byrnes evidently did not take the opportunity to agree to proceed with the policy announcement. Indeed, in his letter to Ickes dated August 27, Byrnes's attitude toward the proposed proclamations seems to have gone from uninformed to opposed. The Byrnes letter attributed this opposition to an offer that had recently come in from the British government.[143] In that offer, the British suggested an international arrangement between the two countries in which each country would reciprocally recognize the "jurisdiction over oil exploration and exploitation" of the other beyond the territorial waters of the U.S. on the one hand, and of the Bahamas, the Turks, and the Caicos islands on the other. This British offer, however, did not refer to general U.S. plans to extend offshore resources jurisdiction. Nonetheless, Byrnes argued that despite the omission, "a careful study of the note would seem to warrant the conclusion that the British Government is now prepared to take a position wholly in line with the principles set forth in our draft statement of policy with regard to the resources of the Continental Shelf." Therefore, in light of the British offer, Byrnes told Ickes that "the Department has considered whether it would be desirable to abandon the procedure previously envisaged, that is, that of proclaiming the United States position along the lines of the draft statement of policy, and entering into bilateral arrangements with interested countries such as that now proposed by the British Embassy. Another procedure, which the Department is inclined to favor, would be for the United States to proclaim its position and subsequently support such position by bilateral arrangements."

The distinction between these two modes of proceeding is a fine one at best. The preferred State Department procedure did nonetheless seem to presuppose a higher degree of international cooperation. No doubt this course of action would have been a source of some distress to Secretary Ickes. Under the circumstances, however, he had little occasion for concern. Byrnes's attempts to mitigate the appearance of a unilateral pronouncement apparently came too late. Moreover, Byrnes's efforts were based on a British offer which in fact did not accept the general principles behind U.S. proposals to extend jurisdiction but which was directed instead to a specific bilateral issue between the two countries.[144] The British attitude toward the proclamations became unmistakably clear when on August 31 (only four days after Byrnes's note suggesting that the British would adopt a policy similar to that of the U.S.) the British government forwarded a strong note disassociating itself from the U.S. decision on the continental shelf or any explanatory statement thereof.[145] Thus the efforts of the secretary of state to link a broad statement of U.S. policy to bilateral arrangements with Britain and other nations was clearly not viable. The original alternative—to proclaim the U.S. position and support it if and when possible by bilateral agreements—seemed to be the only course left open to the State Department.

Of the several diplomatic efforts underway at this point, the exchange with the British is particularly illuminating of the foreign reaction to the proposed U.S. policies. The process of notifying other governments was handled in a manner that initially misled the British into thinking they were being consulted, not notified. With regard to the fisheries proclamation, the British government requested (July 4) that the proposed U.S. fisheries policy be tailored to suit the specific situation confronting the U.S. in offshore fisheries.[146] The American response (July 6) was that it was too late to make changes in the proposed policy pronouncements.[147] Eugene Dooman argued that the U.S. fisheries principles were not applicable "anywhere other than the waters in the Western Hemisphere."[148] He promised, moreover, that the press release accompanying the proclamation would use such phrases as "in the Western Hemisphere" or in "North American waters" to indicate that the policy could not be stretched to apply to European waters.[149] The U.S. government strongly preferred to cloak its perceived national policy interests in protecting salmon within the broader rhetoric of universal principle.

The British responses to the proposed U.S. policies came from several sources within the government, but were not inconsistent. The first British reaction, which was limited to fisheries policy, came in mid-

June. Then in early August the United Kingdom offered to deal with the issue of the continental shelf in the Carribean on a bilateral basis. Although willing to negotiate at a specific level, the British offered no comment on the overall U.S. approach to extending national resources jurisdiction. The British would not support a broad statement of principle on the continental shelf. In a communication dated August 31, the United Kingdom announced that "His Majesty's Government do not wish to be associated with this Decision and would prefer that, when it is announced, no reference should be made to prior consultation with His Majesty's Government."[150] The British did not disassociate themselves from the fisheries proclamation apparently due to the assurances they had received that the explanatory press release would indicate that the proclamation was not intended to have universal application.

The application of the fisheries proclamation to North American or Western Hemisphere waters, however, posed problems for a number of British colonies and commonwealth states. It is particularly noteworthy that the governments of Canada and Newfoundland, whose concurrence had been so strongly advocated, never did offer the U.S. their official support. Indeed, the Canadian response ultimately fell somewhere between negative and noncommittal. An informal comment of the Canadian (deputy) minister of fisheries was negative.[151] In other conversations, Canadian officials were evasive, citing general elections in Canada and other domestic factors as the reasons for Canada's inability to act with the United States. To explain the Canadian unwillingness to support the U.S. in the Truman Proclamations, Dooman, as the State Department liaison, cited the effects of the June 11 elections in Canada. A more compelling reason, however, was that set out by the Canadian minister of fisheries himself. Dr. Finn is quoted by Francis Linville of the State Department's Commodities Division as saying that

> he agreed that the present day world needs a greater control over fishing than formerly existed, but did not think that the United States was proceeding in the best manner. He then raised most of the objections which have disturbed ITP [International Trade Policy]. He said he thought it would be better if the control over waters beyond a three-mile limit should be worked out in agreements with the other countries concerned and should not be used in an exclusive fashion. He mentioned that adopting the New Policy would possibly cause some trouble for us when other countries began applying somewhat similar policies. He said that he did not

59

believe that the matter was particularly urgent or serious at the moment because the Japanese are not fishing in our waters and we should be able to control their fishing after the war. He added that the fact that the United States has not received any serious complaints from other countries concerning the New Policy certainly did not mean that other countries approve of the policy which we have told them we are going to announce.[152]

This Canadian view as conveyed by Finn was basically the same as that of the State Department's International Trade Policy Division. It faulted the Truman Proclamations on the grounds of substance as well as procedure. Moreover, it made the telling point that such a policy was simply unnecessary at the time. Perhaps Finn's most perspicacious comment was the reference to the precedent that would be set for other countries to pursue similar policies.

By the time of the announcement of the proclamations, the Canadian government had come to no internal decision and therefore offered no official reply to the United States notification.[153] Whatever the domestic differences, it was clear that the Canadian government saw no reason to join with the United States in a unilateral policy that was unnecessary and that moreover would have a negative impact on relations with other countries. Similarly, the government of Newfoundland had not completed its internal deliberations before the U.S. policy was announced. Its contemplated response, however, was indifferent to the shelf proclamation and concerned about the fisheries proclamation. Like Canada, Newfoundland preferred a policy that would be agreed upon by the three North American states. Without such an agreement, unilateral action by one would simply lead to the concentration of foreign fishing in the waters of the other two states. Moreover, Newfoundland questioned the acceptability of the policy to other states.[154] Newfoundland's reaction never reached the United States because the proclamations were announced on September 28. Once the proclamations were made public, Newfoundland officials fully realized that the U.S. had intended to proceed unilaterally, not in consultation with other governments, and that the U.S. expected no reply. Nonetheless, representations were considered concerning any administrative actions the United States might take under the proclamation.[155] It soon became apparent to Newfoundland, however, that U.S. administrative action was unlikely in the Atlantic and that representations would be unnecessary.[156]

The only support ever received during the period of informal "consultations" with other governments was from Cuba and was contingent upon Cuba's being included in the management of areas traditionally fished by its fishermen.[157] With the exception of the United Kingdom, all other governments were officially noncommittal,[158] or, in the case of Canada and Newfoundland, privately negative.

An assessment of the merits of the September 28, 1945, Truman Proclamations is bleak. The proclamations provoked short-term ill feeling on the part of Britain and Canada over the U.S. manner of proceeding. And the longer term consequences were equally unfortunate. The proclamations unleashed a series of claims throughout Latin America, claims which often went well beyond the original U.S. proclamations. The U.S. protested national claims that exceeded the U.S. proclamations in scope, but to no avail. The unilateral approach taken in adopting the Truman Proclamations had undermined the credibility of U.S. opposition to the unilateral pronouncements of other countries. Indeed, the proclamations had set the stage for subsequent coastal-state claims.

The fact that neither proclamation was officially protested by other nations underscores the fact that U.S. offshore resources were not in danger of foreign exploitation in 1945. The exhaustion of U.S. allies and enemies emerging from the Second World War provided the opportunity for securing an acceptable legal regime for offshore resources on a multilateral basis. The United States was the strongest nation in the world and, not coincidentally, a prime supporter of international institutions. As the preeminent world power, the U.S. could have secured wide agreement to the substance of its proclamations and thereby strengthened its hand in dealing with nations that sought to advance excessive claims. In a period when the United States was creating a United Nations, a liberalized international trade system, and a global monetary order, the Truman Proclamations struck a discordant note.

U.S. FISHERIES PROBLEMS:

1946-1956

THE SECOND WORLD WAR both stimulated and retarded developments in fisheries. The war resulted in severe food shortages in many countries since the belligerents had to curtail their fishing efforts due to fear of attack and the need to allocate commercial vessels to military uses. The result was that some fisheries which had been overfished had an opportunity to bounce back. The war also promoted great advances in ocean-related technologies ranging from improved radar and navigational systems to the replacement of cotton with nylon fishing nets. Fishermen could travel greater distances from their home ports, and catch and store more fish. These economic and technological developments increased pressures for access to offshore living resources. The war, however, had retarded the evolution of management schemes. The preoccupation with winning the war and the dictates of alliance policy constrained most nations from moving to implement or negotiate fisheries policies suited to the changing technological circumstances. The Truman Proclamations rang the starting bell in the postwar race for resources.

The Second World War also accelerated the change in the international political system. The Euro-centered prewar system was replaced with one in which the United States was politically and economically preeminent in a world of small states and exhausted former powers. The Department of State quickly recognized that the Truman Proclamation on fisheries was not a suitable policy for a nation with global interests. It was soon abandoned but not before the damage had been done and it had been widely emulated—in spirit if not substance— throughout Latin America. In any event, U.S. economic and political preeminence was not easily translatable into effective power to influence international fisheries policy.[1] Since fisheries policy is scarcely a prominent concern in the hierarchy of national policies, the full weight of governmental influence would never be brought to bear in this area. Moreover, U.S. fishing interests were mutually inconsistent—including distant-water and coastal fisheries as well as the special case of salmon fishermen—and a single national policy was difficult to formulate. Thus U.S. fisheries policy in the postwar period was characterized by efforts to protect status-quo special interests. The United States was unable to prevail in fisheries negotiations within the Organization of American States (OAS). When the United States succeeded in moving the locus of fisheries discussions from the OAS to other UN bodies such as the Technical Conference on the Conservation of Living Resources and to the International Law Commission, it was more successful in advancing its fisheries policies.

A further product of the Second World War was the significant increase in the size and the powers of the federal government over the several state and local interests. In the case of fisheries, however, local interests acting through the Congress maintained a high profile. In response to nagging fisheries problems, the State Department created an office in 1948 in an attempt to manage the vocal and diverse fishing groups and to negotiate international arrangements that would be acceptable to them. The creation of this office gave State a new role vis-à-vis the domestic interests. Once the industry had direct access to full-time fisheries negotiators in the State Department, the Interior Department did not have to mediate or intervene in international fisheries questions.

U.S. fishing groups and the concomitant postwar problem areas for the U.S. government can be divided into three geographical areas: the Northwest Atlantic Ocean, the Northeast Pacific Ocean, and Latin America (the west coast and the Gulf of Mexico). The offshore areas of North America have been among the richest in the world. The New England fishing grounds were rich in haddock, cod, rosefish (red fish), white hake, red hake pollock, and cusk. Off the coasts of the northwest states and Alaska, fish stocks of principal concern to the coastal fishermen were salmon, halibut, herring, and later crab and shrimp. U.S. distant-water fishing had moved down the coast of Latin American during and after the war. The shrimp industry operated out of the Gulf states, covered the Gulf of Mexico, and ultimately reached the shores of Brazil. The tuna industry operated out of San Diego and fished off the west coast of Latin America. By the end of the war, the United States did very little whaling but maintained an active interest in conserving the resource. Each segment of the fishing industry posed different problems for the United States government in developing an overall fisheries policy.

Northwest Atlantic Fisheries

The fishing grounds off the shores of Eastern Canada and the United States are among the most abundant in the world and have been fished for centuries by the nations of Western Europe. Scientific research on the living resources of the area was coordinated from 1920-1938 by a North American Council on Fishing Investigations, established as a counterpart to the International Council for the Exploration of the Sea (ICES). Its members included Canada, France, Newfoundland, and the United States. When, in the 1930s, the problem of overfishing in the Atlantic became apparent, the British government convened a conference to address the issue. It met in London in 1937 and adopted a "Convention on the Regulation of Meshes of Fishing Nets and Size Limits of Fish." The convention was intended to apply to the Atlantic Ocean north of the equator and to portions of the Arctic Ocean. The convention was signed by ten Western European countries but failed to come into effect.[2]

The British tried again in 1943 and 1946. While the United States did not participate in the 1937 conference, it sent observers to the 1943 and 1946 meetings.[3] Agreement at the 1943 meeting was blocked by differences over the size of the area to which the convention would apply. Canada supported the application of the convention to the western as well as the eastern Atlantic, covering waters as far west as 60° west longitude or even 75° west longitude. The United States, however, preferred "separate regulatory treatment of the fisheries of the Eastern and Western Atlantic" dividing the ocean along 40° west longitude into two roughly equal areas.[4] The United States argued (much as Chile, Ecuador, and Peru were to do a few years later) that "regulatory arrangements for a particular fishing area or region can best be made among the nations whose proximity to the affected resource gives them the intimate knowledge and interest necessary to wise and effective control." The Canadian approach reflected the fact that European nations were already fishing the Newfoundland Banks. Canada also recognized that the U.S. approach would leave Canada isolated in a regional arrangement with her more powerful southern neighbor and she opted instead for a larger regulatory area in which she would have British influence to counter that of the United States.

This dispute placed Britain in a difficult position between her dominion and her major wartime ally. On behalf of the U.S., however, the United Kingdom proposed that the area of the convention be shifted further east than the Canadian proposal had specified. In the period between the 1943 and 1946 conferences, the United States met informally with the governments of Newfoundland and Canada to discuss the scope of regional arrangements. The United Kingdom encouraged these discussions and gently urged the Canadians to consider separate arrangements for the East and West Atlantic.[5] Under these pressures, Canada acquiesced and in April 1946, a Convention for the Regulation of the Meshes of Fishing Nets and the Size Limits of Fish[6] was adopted in London. The area to which the convention applied was the Atlantic and Arctic Oceans north of 48° north latitude and between 42° west longitude and 32° east longitude.

Agreement on regulations limited to the Northeast Atlantic left the Northwest Atlantic exposed to fishing by nations reluctant to submit to mesh size regulations. The legal regime for the area was already clouded by the abortive 1937 convention and the Truman fisheries proclamation of 1945 (see Chapter 2). For their part, the governments of Canada and Newfoundland recognized that any efforts by the United States to implement the proclamation, that is to negotiate or unilaterally establish fishing conservation zones off U.S. shores, would simply shift foreign fishing from U.S. grounds to more northern waters. Thus both Canada and Newfoundland considered issuing proclamations along similar lines when the U.S. notified them informally of its intended actions. Once the proclamations had been announced in September 1945, the prime consideration for Canada and Newfoundland was how or whether the U.S. would implement the proclamation. Canada found herself under substantial domestic pressures to join with the United States in "controlling her offshore fishing waters."[7] In 1947, the Canadian government briefly (June-July) considered introducing a joint resolution in the Parliament "similar in terms to the Proclamation issued by the President of the United States."[8]

Apprised of this situation, the British government was prompt to discourage the issuance of fisheries proclamations by its two former colonies. The British held to the view that "at the time the Proclamation was made . . . it had a particular bearing on the quest for oil,"[9] and was assumed to be principally the concern of the United States and Mexico. By 1947 the United States itself was no longer keen on the issuance of fisheries proclamations "lest . . . [they] . . . should be misinterpreted."[10] State Department officials were already alarmed by Latin American fisheries claims that had misinterpreted and gone well beyond the U.S. proclamation. The precipitate U.S. action of 1945 had been taken to deal with the single problem of conserving Alaska salmon, the

British recalled. But as of 1947, British officials surmised that the United States had no practical program in mind.[11]

The British assessment of the U.S. situation was on the mark. Faced with growing conflicts off Latin America and having no regulatory arrangements for U.S. coastal waters, the State Department was increasingly preoccupied with fishing matters. In 1948, State established an Office of the Special Assistant to the Under Secretary for Fisheries and Wildlife. The first incumbent was Wilbert McLeod Chapman. Among his initial concerns was to establish a conservation regime for the New England coast. In 1948, his office issued invitations to an International Northwest Atlantic Fisheries Conference to meet in Washington on January 17, 1949. The U.S. extended invitations to Canada, Denmark, France, Great Britain, Iceland, Newfoundland, Norway, Portugal, and Spain. Shortly before the conference, the United States issued a draft convention prepared by the United States and discussed by Canada, Newfoundland, and U.S. officials at a preliminary meeting in June 1948.

A month before the conference was to take place, Canada had second thoughts about the proposed convention. She notified Washington that she favored postponing the conference for a year. Among Canada's concerns was the need to concert policy with Newfoundland, which was soon to become a Canadian province. The draft convention had adopted Newfoundland's traditional narrow territorial waters and Ottawa feared that including these limits in an international convention would make it difficult to revise Newfoundland's offshore limits outward at a future time. Canada also was concerned with the size of the proposed commission, enforcement aspects of the treaty, and the limited regulatory powers specified. Her preference was to further limit the powers of the commission to those of investigation and recommendation. During a hasty trip to Ottawa, Mr. Chapman persuaded the Canadian government to participate in the conference in return for limiting the powers of the new international commission to investigation.

The conference went ahead in Washington in January 1949 as scheduled and concluded the Northwest Atlantic Fisheries Convention.[12] The convention area, north of 39° north latitude and west of 42° west longitude, was divided into five subareas. Panels were established for each subarea with membership determined by substantial exploitation in, or adjacency to, the subarea. An overall international commission (ICNAF) was established for the convention area with each contracting government having one vote. An advisory committee was provided to represent private fishing interests. Recommendations for regulations were to be made by subarea with the unanimous consent of each gov-

66

ernment represented on the appropriate panel. Provision was made for liaison with FAO and ICES.

The convention entered into force on July 3, 1950, and the first meeting of ICNAF was held in Washington in 1951. By 1953, all ten signatories had become parties. The Federal Republic of Germany adhered to the convention on June 27, 1957. Halifax was chosen as the headquarters of the organization, but the convention was amended in 1956 to permit the holding of annual meetings outside of North America for the benefit of European members.

Fisheries Relations with Latin America

Upon the announcement of the Truman Proclamations, claims to offshore areas proliferated throughout Latin America and elsewhere. While technological advances and food shortages had generated the perceived need for such national extensions, the U.S. announcement in September of 1945 established a legal situation in which the less powerful countries hoped that their national claims might be internationally accepted.

The role of the Truman Proclamation on fisheries in setting a precedent for the evolution of the law of the sea merits careful evaluation. The fisheries proclamation reflected the diverse interests that had participated in its formulation and it contained a critical distinction. It proposed, at one and the same time, a unilateral approach *and* a negotiated or multilateral approach to the conservation of offshore fisheries. The former method might apply to those fisheries which were historically reserved exclusively to U.S. nationals while the latter approach was to be employed where foreign fishermen had developed a long-standing interest in the fishery. This finely tuned distinction had been carefully devised within the State Department to suit diverse U.S. fishing needs and not just the interests of the salmon industry. It was, however, subject to genuine misunderstanding or deliberate misinterpretation where it did not meet the needs and interests of other governments. The unilateral aspect of the fisheries policy was enhanced by its having been issued as a national proclamation together with a declaration of national jurisdiction over the resources of the shelf.

The requisites of the fishing industries in other countries of the Western Hemisphere did not coincide with those of the United States. While U.S. tuna fishermen had operated off South American shores since the 1930s and U.S. shrimp fisheries had expanded their operations

67

to the shores of other nations during the war, most Latin American nations fished only off their own coasts. Thus they were not attracted to a declaration of national jurisdiction that provided for reciprocity in recognizing the rights of established foreign fishermen off their shores. The style of the Truman Proclamations, however, if not their precise content, provided the occasion for other nations of the hemisphere to consider policies and advance claims tailored to their respective situations.

Broadly speaking, the Latin American claims of the 1940s and 1950s took two directions. The first established varying degrees of national jurisdiction or sovereignty over the continental shelf and the superjacent waters without reference to a particular distance criterion. The second set of claims incorporated under national sovereignty the continental shelf and offshore waters to a distance of 200 miles.[13]

The Early Claims

MEXICO.   In regard to the first category of claims—those claiming the shelf and overlying waters but specifying no distance criterion—Mexico was the first country to announce its claims after the September 1945 proclamations. On October 29, the president of Mexico incorporated as national territory the continental shelf adjacent to Mexico to a depth of 200 meters and all of its resources. With regard to the superjacent waters the presidential declaration provided for "the supervision, use and control" of zones needed to conserve fisheries.[14] An amendment to the Mexican Constitution (December 6, 1945) took the claim further, declaring that the waters covering the continental shelf were the property of the nation. Although the amendment was approved by the Mexican Congress and the requisite number of states, it was never promulgated by the executive.[15]

Mexico's prompt action following the U.S. proclamations occurred within the context of a decade-old controversy between the two countries. In 1935, President Cárdenas had issued a decree claiming sovereignty over territorial waters of nine nautical miles.[16] The United States promptly reserved its rights under the new decree. A heated correspondence then ensued wherein the Mexican government based its claim to a nine-mile territorial sea on the Treaty of Guadalupe Hidalgo establishing the boundary between the U.S. and Mexico in 1848.[17] Mexico reiterated its nine-mile claim in the National Property Law of 1941 but no protest was lodged by the U.S. until 1948.[18] Instead, boundary issues lay dormant during the war. When the United States government planned to extend its own offshore jurisdiction, Mexico was among those countries given advance notice in the summer of 1945. Thus Mexico was ready to move quickly to make her own offshore claims once the U.S. acted publicly. This she did one month later.

The U.S. announcement of the Truman Proclamations interrupted bilateral fishing discussions then underway between the two countries. These talks, initiated in the early 1940s, dealt with Japanese fishing off the coasts of the U.S. and Mexico, and they continued to serve as a vehicle for surmounting different national interpretations of offshore jurisdiction.[19] These differences were to become more acute as the California-based tuna industry increased the level of its effort in Mexican waters during the war. The Informal Joint Mexican-American Committee on International Fisheries had met in Washington in September 1944 and developed recommendations on a treaty between the two countries.[20] Both governments had agreed informally that pending a fisheries treaty, no changes would be made in existing arrangements for licensing U.S. tuna vessels.[21] A year later (August 1945) the United States presented a revised draft fisheries treaty for the Pacific coast for consideration by the Mexican government.[22] Before the Mexican reply could be received, the Truman Proclamations were announced, leaving the Mexicans uncertain as to the status of the fishery negotiations then in train. The U.S. tuna industry, eager to protect its fishing grounds off Mexico's Pacific coast, was as bewildered as the Mexican government.[23] The official U.S. acknowledgement of Mexico's corresponding claim did little to clarify the U.S. government's intentions as to the continued relevance of the 1945 draft U.S. fisheries treaty.[24] Instead, the State Department, under pressure from the tuna industry, concentrated on cautioning Mexico that the United States would recognize the Mexican claim only if it were consistent with the U.S. fisheries proclamation, i.e., only "on the condition that adequate recognition is given to United States fishing interests in . . . the establishment of such zones."[25]

In this confused legal context, the jurisdictional dispute heated up in the fall of 1946. In September, the Mexican Coast Guard apprehended two groups of U.S. vessels fishing for shrimp off the Campeche coast, brought them to port, and fined the first group. The distances from shore at which these vessels were apprehended were disputed, but were probably 17 and 30 miles respectively. The initial Mexican reaction to U.S. protests was to claim that the fishing boats were fishing illegally under the newly defined limits of continental shelf waters.[26] U.S. officials remonstrated to the Foreign Affairs Ministry, insisting that the new claim would not become law until it had been ratified by the requisite number of Mexican states and promulgated in the *Diario Oficial*. By

February 1947, therefore, the Mexican government had shifted ground and was asserting that the seizures had taken place four miles from land and were based on the Mexican claim to a nine-mile territorial sea.[27]

U.S. officials recognized that regardless of the facts of the seizure, the conflict between the two countries was based on divergent legal principles as to the acceptable breadth of the territorial sea and the establishment of restricted fishing zones. The three-pronged course adopted by the State Department and conveyed to its ambassador in Mexico was to maintain the official position in support of a three-mile territorial limit, to reiterate the conditions under which fishing conservation zones would be recognized by the United States,[28] and to press forward with efforts to negotiate a fisheries treaty.[29]

The U.S. decision to proceed toward a bilateral treaty was ultimately successful, at least with regard to the Pacific coast. In December 1946, the ambassador conveyed the message that the U.S. maintained the right for its nationals to fish freely off the coast of Mexico beyond three miles "pending the conclusion of a fisheries treaty between the United States and Mexico."[30] And the United States continued to await the Mexican response to the draft treaty it had proposed in August 1945. Once the Mexican government realized that the United States intended to proceed with the negotiation of a treaty for Pacific coast fisheries, a response to the U.S. draft was forthcoming.[31] The Mexicans objected to a number of features of the draft, including its provisions on territorial waters and continental shelf waters and the absence of reciprocal fishing rights. Among the Mexican suggestions offered in January 1947 was that the treaty be made applicable to the Gulf as well as to the Pacific coasts. The U.S. shrimp fishery was expanding rapidly in the Gulf and the 1946 seziures there were repeated again in January and April of 1947.

The United States government considered the Mexican response to its 1945 draft and in September of 1947 indicated its willingess to commence direct and informal negotiations.[32] These negotiations took place in Mexico City in October and November of 1948. The resulting Convention for the Establishment of an International Commission for the Scientific Investigation of Tuna provided for a commission to investigate the condition of the tuna and bait fisheries in the "waters of the Pacific Ocean off the coasts of both countries."[33] This agreement represented the first of many U.S. efforts to assist the rapidly growing tuna industry in the Pacific. It entered into force in 1950 but the commission was never activated.

The problem of fishing along the Gulf coasts remained unsettled. In essence, an unstable equilibrium developed wherein the United States officially maintained its right to fish beyond three miles of the shores of other nations,[34] and the Mexican government continued to support its claim to a nine-mile territorial sea on the basis of the 1848 treaty. In 1947, Mexico buttressed its case by pointing to the fact that the U.S. had agreed at the Inter-American Conference for the Maintenance of Continental Peace and Security (1947) to the establishment of a hemispheric security region whose boundaries extended hundreds of miles to sea.[35] After further seizures in 1950, the U.S. shrimp industry instructed masters of its vessels not to fish within nine miles of Mexican shores,[36] and the immediate problem subsided with the issue of jurisdiction remaining unsettled.

PANAMA.   The second country to react to the U.S. proclamations by claiming sovereignty over the shelf and the superjacent waters to an unspecified distance was Panama. In March 1946, Panama claimed the territorial sea and the continental shelf as national territory.[37] In December of the same year, Panama declared that national jurisdiction for purposes of fishing extended throughout ocean space covering the continental shelf.[38] The differences between the Panamanian and the U.S. claims may have been based on misunderstanding of the fine distinctions in the U.S. proclamations. Panama's claims did not result in seizures of foreign vessels or in U.S. protests. In part, this was due to Panama's willingess to license U.S. bait fishing vessels at a reasonable rate. The absence of overt conflict may also be attributed to the active efforts of the American Tunaboat Association and local U.S. embassy officials to resolve fishing differences informally and to persuade the Panamanians to back off from their claims.

ARGENTINA.   In the case of Argentina, the third state to respond to U.S. actions, the Truman Proclamations provided an occasion for justifying or amplifying preexisting claims to offshore jurisdiction beyond a three-mile territorial sea. In January of 1944, Argentina had decreed that the zones of the epicontinental sea were to be temporary zones of mineral reserves.[39] This presidential decree did not proclaim sovereignty over the submarine areas and superjacent waters; rather it addressed itself to the mineral resources of the shelf. Following the announcement of the Truman Proclamations, however, President Peron issued another decree purportedly amplifying article 2 of the 1944 decree.[40] Citing the U.S. actions in its preamble, the October 1946 decree claimed sovereignty, property rights, and the incorporation as national territory of the Argentine continental shelf and its epicontinental sea. No specific mention was made of fisheries although by implication they were embraced within the claim to the epicontinental sea. Navigation in these waters was declared unaffected.

The Argentine action could scarcely be termed a precise use of the U.S. proclamations as precedent. Argentina merely took the opportunity of U.S. unilateral action to advance its own claims, either misunderstanding or misinterpreting the U.S. claim.

The official U.S. protest was slow in coming. Faced with a rash of unilateral claims in 1946 and 1947, the State Department did not reply to Argentina until July 2, 1948 when it noted that the U.S. "reserves the rights and interests of the United States" so far as the 1946 declaration was concerned. In this letter, identical copies of which went to Peru and Chile, the U.S. argued that the principles of Argentina's claim "differ in large measure from those of the United States Proclamations and appear to be at variance with the generally accepted principles of international law." The U.S. note pointed in particular to the fact that sovereignty was claimed beyond "the generally accepted limits of territorial waters" and that U.S. rights and interests off the coasts of Argentina were not accorded recognition.[41] Argentina's response was to reject U.S. reservations and to maintain its claim.[42] Thus the two countries in the 1950s were in a standoff between divergent interpretations of the international law of the sea.

COSTA RICA.   The case of Costa Rica in the period under consideration falls between the first and the second categories of policies. That is, it was influenced first by U.S. claims to the continental shelf and fishery conservation zones and subsequently by the claims of Chile and Peru to 200 miles. Between 1947 and 1949, Costa Rica issued and reissued varying offshore claims. This confused and complex situation resulted from two principal factors: (1) differences among Costa Rican government agencies, and (2) direct involvement by U.S. nationals in the fishing industry of the country.

During the war, U.S. tuna fishermen had increased the level of their fishing efforts along the Pacific coast of Latin America. By the close of the war, the industry was beginning to relocate to other countries. Most of Costa Rica's fishing interests were U.S. owned, and centered in the Gulf of Nicoya.[43] In order to regulate and profit from this growing industry, the Costa Rican government began to consider fisheries legislation in 1947. Among the measures under consideration were some contemplating an extension of territorial jurisdiction to 50 miles.[44] Domestic sentiment in favor of extending jurisdiction centered in the Ministry of Agriculture and Industries and received support from those fishing organizations already headquartered in Costa Rica. Indeed, the threat of relocating or withholding planned onshore investment in Costa Rica was used by the major U.S. fishing companies to seek legislation that would favor vessels with shore bases in Costa Rica.[45]

The ministries of foreign affairs and finance did not support proposals for an extension of jurisdiction in the face of the international (read U.S.) reaction and given the absence of a single patrol boat to enforce an extended jurisdiction.[46] The Department of State made its views on extension unequivocally clear in an aide-mémoire delivered to the Foreign Affairs Ministry on June 18.[47] In this document, the U.S. reserved its rights in advance of any extension of jurisdiction and reiterated the principles upon which its own proclamation had been based. Caught between local U.S. firms on the one hand and the U.S. government on the other, the Costa Rican Foreign Affairs Ministry requested the State Department to send a fisheries expert to advise on pending fisheries legislation.[48] In response to this request, John Kask, a nongovernmental fisheries expert, was sent to Costa Rica from July 14 to August 8, 1947 to advise and hopefully influence the Costa Rican government.[49] With the under secretary of agriculture, Kask assisted in the revision of draft fisheries legislation that had been drawn up by the minister of agriculture and industries. While the proposed legislation favored shore-based fishing in terms of tax treatment, it did not establish an extended area of exclusive fishing jurisdiction.

Political disturbances in the country delayed the issuance of these new fisheries regulations until September 27, 1947.[50] Then immediately upon promulgation, those groups favoring greater protection for shore-based tuna fishing instituted a press campaign against the new regulations. The debate was couched in terms of differences over fishing gear, with the shore-based fishing industry (which relied on bait fishing) opposed to the purse-seining techniques of vessels operating out of San Pedro, California. In the face of this vocal opposition both within and outside his government, the president suspended the fisheries decree on October 18.[51]

Nine months elapsed before new regulations were declared, this time extending national sovereignty to 200 miles. During this period, the ministries of finance and foreign affairs sought to have the U.S. embassy bring direct pressure to bear within the Ministry of Agriculture and Industries.[52] U.S. policy, however, was to "avoid any further involvement in these policy questions so long as there is not actual undue interference with American commercial operations."[53]

The Costa Rican decree of July 27, 1948[54] represented a victory for the Ministry of Agriculture within the government and for locally-based, albeit U.S.-owned, fishing interests. It also reflected the influence of previous claims to 200 miles that had been made by Chile and Peru. And, of course, it cited the U.S. proclamations as well. Costa Rica's decree proclaimed and confirmed national sovereignty over the continental shelf and over the seas adjacent to the coast to a distance of 200 miles. The decree was not self-executing, however, and would require the promulgation of regulations for implementation. The U.S. government immediately authorized its embassy to "make friendly representations to appropriate Costa Rican officials now before the regulations are issued and incidents occur."[55] The U.S. position was that long-standing U.S. fishing interests in high seas tuna off Costa Rica precluded U.S. recognition of unilaterally declared conservation zones. At this point, therefore, the U.S. urged the "negotiation of a fisheries agreement with Costa Rica whereby a high seas conservation zone off Costa Rica might be established and fishing regulations issued."[56]

With these instructions, embassy officials went to work immediately, first trying to ascertain what U.S. official policy was, then trying to promote negotiations on a treaty. The Costa Rican reaction to the proposal was predictably divided. The acting foreign minister was favorably disposed to negotiations,[57] while the director of the Fishery Department in the Ministry of Agriculture was not.[58] The latter pointed out that Costa Rica had little to gain from a treaty since a treaty would not compensate Costa Rica for the resources removed from her waters.

Despite the Ministry of Agriculture, U.S. governmental views were reflected in initial regulations issued September 29 on the "Law of Maritime Fishing and Hunting."[59] These regulations deliberately left vague the extent of the area to which they applied, assuming that that issue could be resolved in the course of negotiations. Furthermore, the acting foreign minister indicated privately that, pending agreement on a treaty, the Costa Rican government did not intend to enforce the regulations beyond three miles.[60]

In the light of these assurances, the State Department decided to postpone announcing its reservations to the initial decree pending the negotiation of a treaty. Such an action might have fueled domestic sentiment and strengthened the position of those groups in Costa Rica that were opposed to a treaty. With these groups in mind, the government of Costa Rica issued regulations in January 1949 providing for fisheries enforcement to a distance of six miles from shore.[61] One month later the State Department was prepared to commence negotiations with Costa Rica; indeed State hoped to use the convention just signed in Mexico as a model on which to base an agreement with Costa Rica. Given the favorable disposition of the Foreign Affairs Ministry, negotiations were successful and on May 31, 1949, a Convention for the Establishment of an Inter-American Tropical Tuna Commission (IATTC)[62] was signed in Washington by representatives of the two countries.

The U.S.-Costa Rican agreement differed in several respects from that between the U.S. and Mexico. While the latter agreement applied to the waters off the Pacific coasts of the two countries, the former convention was made broadly applicable to the "waters of the Eastern Pacific Ocean." Moreover, the treaty with Costa Rica was opened to adherence by all nations having an interest in the fishery.[63] Both tuna fisheries treaties provided for the establishment of a strictly investigatory body, but the mandate of the IATTC was more detailed and included the authority (1) to make recommendations directed toward maintaining the maximum sustainable catch and (2) to publish and disseminate its findings. And, most important, neither convention specified a limit to national jurisdiction. In this fashion all parties were able to maintain their official positions, yet U.S. fishing interests were safeguarded by participation in the investigatory process upon which a decision to establish a conservation zone would presumably be based.

The Costa Rican 200-mile decree was further qualified in late 1949. In Decree No. 803,[64] the government introduced a distinction between its "sovereignty" over the continental shelf and its "rights and interests" in the waters adjacent to its coasts.

The 200-Mile Claims

The second category of national claims to offshore jurisdiction in Latin America is characterized by common acceptance of the outer limit of 200 nautical miles. The motivations behind the 200-mile claims differed from country to country as did the precise nature of the jurisdiction claimed. The causes for and origins of the 200-mile claims have been obscured by the development of sophisticated legal rationales to buttress a claim which, at the outset, served a very limited range of economic interests and found little support in the then prevailing international law of the sea.[65]

CHILE. An understanding of the origins of the 200-mile zone claims must begin with the first assertion of such jurisdiction—that of Chile in June 1947. The considerations motivating Chile's action were several. Chilean business interests sought this means to protect their new offshore whaling operations. The return of European whalers after the war posed a threat to Chile's infant industry. And a zone of 200 miles was selected as a protective measure on the mistaken assumption that such a claim was consistent with the security zone adopted in the 1939 Declaration of Panama.[66]

Wartime business measures and a threatening postwar development provided the context in which Chile's 200-mile claim seemed both necessary and reasonable. During the Second World War, European pelagic whaling operations in Antarctic waters had been suspended. Cut off from European sources of fats and oils and protected from competition with foreign whalers, a Chilean firm, Compañía Industrial, went into the whaling business to supply its production of soap and cooking oils. The attractiveness of this whaling venture was enhanced by the development of a new technology for dehydrogenizing the meat of the sperm whale (cachalote).[67]

While Compañía Industrial was developing a substantial interest in its protected whaling operations, the war in Europe was drawing to a close and plans were being laid for a return to Antarctic whaling. The European interest in a prompt renewal of whaling operations reflected serious food shortages in Europe and dwindling supplies of fats and oils.[68]

European interest in an early all-out whaling effort was potentially circumscribed by a number of international conservation agreements which had been reached in the 1930s to regulate pelagic whaling.[69] Britain took the lead in pressing for a temporary relaxation of these agreements. In early 1944 Britain convened a meeting in London and, with the support of the Norwegian government in exile, proposed that the open season on whaling should extend from November 24 to March 24 in the first whaling season after the termination of hostilities in Europe. The years of the first whaling season were not specified in the interests of security but were privately agreed to refer to 1944-1945.[70] Other proposals for easing the restrictions of the 1937 agreement were resisted by the United States, among others, which was concerned to preserve the whale resources. It was agreed, therefore, to continue to restrict the operation of factory ships to Antarctic waters. The United States and Norway were successful, moreover, in pressing for a maximum limit on catch in Antarctic waters of 16,000 blue whale units.[71] This represented the first total limit that had ever been set.

Given the absence of Irish accession to the 1944 protocol, a supplementary protocol[72] was concluded in London in October 1945 to bring the 1944 protocol into effect for those nations that had adopted it. The delay in effecting the 1944 protocol shifted the period of temporary relaxation of treaty provisions to a first season occurring in 1945-1946. The shortage of fats and oils and the rationale for relaxing regulations continued to apply in 1946. A protocol of March 15, 1946,[73] was, therefore, agreed to permit certain factory ships to continue whaling operations after March 24. Then on December 2, 1946, a further protocol[74] was signed in Washington extending the relaxation of whaling regulations into a second season, 1946-1947.

Due to physical constraints, the full intent of whaling nations to resume whaling could not be realized. The whaling vessels that it was hoped would be released upon the termination of the war simply did not exist. Moreover, it seems clear in retrospect that the whale stocks had not recovered from extensive prewar whaling.[75] Thus, during the stipulated 1946-1947 season, the total allowable blue whale units could not be caught in the allotted time. In these circumstances it was agreed to again extend the whaling season. Moreover, because of dire food shortages in Japan and the undercapacity of other whaling nations, two Japanese factory ships were allowed to operate in the Antarctic under the supervision of the Supreme Allied Command in the Pacific (SCAP).[76] By the 1947-1948 whaling season, however, problems of undercapacity no longer existed in Europe. Indeed, with U.S. plans to allow a further "emergency" Japanese whaling expedition in 1947-1948 (despite the strenuous objections of its allies in the Far Eastern Commission),[77] the situation of overcapacity in Antarctic whaling would once again obtain.

Thus, by 1947 Chile's infant whaling industry found itself threatened by ever increasing levels of competition with efficient distant-water whaling fleets. Further unwelcome possibilities were held out by the prospect that the Chilean government might participate in international agreements which would limit the access of Chilean companies to the offshore whaling resource. Although the international protocols of the 1930s and mid-1940s were instruments of the pelagic whaling powers, the Chilean government participated in the Whaling Conference that met in Washington in December 1946. In addition to extending the protocol that had been agreed upon in March to relax the 1937 whaling regulations, the Washington conference reached agreement on an International Convention for the Regulation of Whaling to completely replace the 1937 agreement. The convention established an International Whaling Commission which was empowered to amend the code of regulations attached to the convention "by adopting regulations designating protected species, fixing closed seasons and waters, limiting total catches and the sizes of whales taken."[78] The commission was authorized to make recommendations to contracting governments to effectuate its regulations. Chile (and Peru) signed but never ratified the provisions of this convention.

Before the Chilean government could proceed further down the path of international regulation of offshore whaling, the officials of Compañía Industrial contacted the Chilean president regarding their special problem and recommended a plan to resolve that problem.[79] In developing a proposal to exclude foreign whaling from nearshore areas, Helmuth Heinzen, the general manager of Compañía Industrial, had sought the assistance of Fernando Guarello, the firm's lawyer. Sr. Guarello was unable to find a suitable measure within existing Chilean laws and regulations. He therefore turned to an international legal expert, Jermán Fischer, to seek possible international precedents for a claim to offshore jurisdiction.

The task was not an easy one, by Sr. Fischer's account. After substantial research, the most promising precedent seemed to be that of the October 1939 Declaration of Panama. Sr. Fischer found an account of this declaration together with a rough sketch of the zones in a Chilean periodical in his library.[80]

The extent as well as the terms of the 1939 declaration were ill-suited to serve the needs of the Chilean whaling company. As to its purpose, the zone had been established at U.S. initiative upon the outbreak of war in Europe to serve as a "neutral" or "safety zone." Within the limits of this zone, belligerents were to be prohibited from engaging in hostilities.[81] The security zone never applied to Canadian waters and ceased to be relevant when the U.S. became a belligerent. Even before then, it was apparent that the zone served as a hiding place for belligerent vessels and that its neutrality was not observed. As to its extent, the Declaration of Panama security zone varied in width from 300 to 500 miles.[82] The zone off Chile had been closer to 300 miles wide, although the map that was part of the journal article available to Sr. Fischer made it seem somewhat less.

When notified of a possible legal precedent for a claim to 200 or 300 miles from shore, the company officials were initially reluctant. Given the limited scope of their whaling operations, they were looking for protection only to roughly 50 miles. Sr. Fischer was persuasive. He argued that in order to withstand the foreign reactions that would be generated by a claim to exclude distant-water whaling, it was necessary to base the action on some international precedent, in this case on the Declaration of Panama.

Once convinced of the need to claim a 200-mile zone, company officials began consultations at home and in neighboring countries to garner support. Fernando Guarello secured the support of Chile's president, Gabriel González Videla.[83] Helmuth Heinzen sought out businessmen in Peru and Ecuador who might want the protection afforded by extended national offshore zones. At the same time, Guarello together with Tobias Barros Ortíz, a former chancellor and Chilean ambassador, visited government officials in the same countries.

PERU. Although the offshore resource interests of Chile's neighbors differed from those of Chile, both Ecuador and Peru were favorably disposed toward offshore claims, albeit for different reasons. Neither Peru nor Ecuador had coastal waters within the Antarctic region that would be subjected to international regulations. Occasional foreign whaling expeditions took place off their shores but their own local fishermen rarely operated beyond twenty-five miles from shore.[84] Nonetheless, they wanted to protect their fishing fleets and the prospect of American tuna fishing in waters off their shores was growing. Peru was particularly interested in developing a fishmeal industry based on its vast anchoveta resources and to this end had imported equipment from the dying California sardine industry.[85] Thus Peru adopted a 200-mile policy[86] shortly after Chile and Ecuador formally took this step in 1951.

Chile's 200-mile zone was proclaimed on June 23 and Peru's was promulgated on August 1, 1947. The differences between the two pronouncements reflect the different national goals that each was seeking to fulfill. The Peruvian claim, for instance, omits any reference to the protection of whaling so prominently featured in the Chilean claim. Instead, Peruvian concerns centered on protecting the abundant fisheries off its shore from close neighbors as well as distant-water fishing states. Thus, Peru did not include the stipulation found in the Chilean decree that reciprocal fishing rights would be observed with other states. Peru's fisheries are richer than those of Chile and the Peruvian interest in fishing off Chile or, for that matter, off any other country was and remains remote at best.

The similarities between the Chilean and Peruvian 200-mile proclamations are equally noteworthy. Both claims are justified in terms of the precedents afforded by other states' claims. Not only are the Truman Proclamations cited as precedent, they are also reflected in the texts of the Chilean and Peruvian claims. Although the west coast of Latin America has only a very narrow continental shelf, an effort was made to model the Chilean and Peruvian claims along the lines of the Truman Proclamations on the continental shelf and on fisheries. Thus both the Chilean and Peruvian 200-mile claims make separate mention of the shelf and the superjacent waters. The incorporation of elements of the Truman Proclamation on the continental shelf was an afterthought at most, since the contents of the Chilean and Peruvian claims clearly reveal a preoccupation with offshore living resources, not with the resources of the continental shelf.

79

Thus, in this case the Truman Proclamations constituted an indirect influence on the 200-mile claims and a legal opportunity to assert the claims rather than a direct stimulus as in the case of Mexico, Panama, and Argentina. However, in all six of the claims occurring between October 1945 and October 1947, the fact of a U.S. unilateral claim was viewed as giving sanction to other states to make unilateral claims. Indeed, every single one of the Latin claims cited the Truman Proclamations as precedent. That the claims did not correctly emulate those of the United States reflects the different interests of the coastal states. It is not clear that the misunderstanding and misinterpretations of the U.S. claims were deliberate, at least at the outset.

The opportunity for misunderstanding U.S. policy was increased by U.S. efforts in 1947 to revive the Declaration of Panama in a new form. As the cold war was developing, U.S. military advisers supported the delineation of a zone of security covering the same area as the 1939 declaration but extended to embrace Canada as well. This zone was embodied in the Inter-American Treaty of Reciprocal Assistance. Signed September 2, 1947 in Rio de Janeiro,[87] the treaty was described as one of collective self-defense. The preference of the United States military for reviving the security zone of the 1939 declaration simply fueled proprietary sentiments of Latin states toward areas off their shores while giving the appearance of U.S. concurrence with the substance if not the method of security claims. It is noteworthy that most of the Latin American 200-mile claims included security as well as resource aspects.

Governmental Coordination of Policy

The confusion in Latin American governments over the exact nature of U.S. fisheries policy was shared by a number of American officials in foreign capitals and in Washington.[88] This was compounded where U.S.-owned fishery interests based in Latin America were pursuing policies contrary to those of the U.S. government. These transnational actors worked at cross-purposes with distant-water fishing interests operating out of the United States. Domestically based fishing groups included Alaskan and Northwest Pacific salmon interests, California-based tuna operators, the New England ground fish industry, and an expanding Gulf of Mexico shrimp industry. The policy preferences of those different groups vis-à-vis other countries ran in contrary directions. The salmon industry wanted to exclude foreign, namely Japanese, fishing. The New England fishermen feared an influx of European fishing off their region. The tuna industry had pushed its operations down the west coast of Latin America and did not want to be shut out from these or future fishing grounds. The shrimp industry was developing new fishing grounds throughout the Gulf of Mexico but lacked political support because Gulf coast state governments were preoccupied with wresting control of offshore lands from the federal government rather than with advancing U.S. distant-water interests. As if these diverse and contentious pressure groups were not enough, the State Department was beset with a U.S. military establishment that was pressing for extensive "security zones" for hemispheric defense at a time when strategic security interests called for maintaining high seas freedoms.

The Office of the Special Assistant to the Secretary for Fisheries and Wildlife was established within the State Department in 1947-1948 in response to industry pressure and growing international fisheries problems.[89] The impact of this new office and of the experience of its particular incumbents was visible in the evolution of U.S. policy after 1948. The first incumbent, Wilbert McLeod Chapman, had served as the director of the School of Fisheries, University of Washington prior to joining the government.[90] He was succeeded in 1951 (to 1966) by William Herrington, whose previous fisheries experience included supervision of Japanese fishing during the Occupation. The State Department fisheries office quickly became the central point within the government for coordination and formulation of U.S. fisheries policy vis-à-vis other governments.

In 1956, the Congress sought to increase the role of the Interior Department through the enactment of the Fish and Wildlife Act of 1956.[91] This act provided for the creation of two new bureaus within the Interior Department—the Bureau of Commercial Fisheries and the Bureau of Sport Fisheries and Wildlife. It also stipulated that the secretary of state should include an official designated by the Interior Department in all international meetings concerning fisheries. This effort to ensure the participation of the Interior Department in international negotiations was negated when President Eisenhower signed the bill into law. The president noted that such a directive would be unconstitutional, hence he construed the provision to be merely an indication of congressional desires.[92] In any event, the State Department's fisheries office was firmly in control of U.S. international fisheries policy by the mid-1950s.

Prior to the creation of the Office of the Special Assistant in 1948, the international fisheries policy of the United States was sporadic and ad hoc. Responses to and ways of dealing with the claims of Latin American countries depended upon general U.S. relations with the country in question, upon the activities of local U.S.-owned fishery businesses and of U.S. embassy officials in the country. The U.S. was uniformly more successful in pressing its case in Central American countries close to and dependent upon the United States than in South America. And informal bilateral negotiations were generally more fruitful than official remonstrances and challenges. Mexico's claim (October 1945), for instance, was met with a prompt, mildly worded elaboration of U.S. views on the proper interpretation of such offshore claims and on the reservation of U.S. rights and interests in waters beyond three miles. The U.S. then took the initiative in resuming bilateral negotiations and confrontations were avoided. In the case of Costa Rica, U.S. views were conveyed in an informal aide-mémoire (June 1946), and influenced subsequent Costa Rican fisheries regulations (September 1946). In 1947, the United States did not protest Costa Rica's claim to a 200-mile zone (June), pursuing instead bilateral negotiations toward a fisheries treaty. Similarly, the U.S. issued no formal protest or reservations to Panama's claim (December 1946). Instead, officials of the American Tunaboat Association and the U.S. embassy worked quietly with Panamanian officials to achieve a *modus vivendi*, and in 1953 Panama became a member of the Inter-American Tropical Tuna Commission.

After the Office of the Special Assistant was established, an effort was made to define U.S. policy for the benefit of U.S. and foreign officials,[93] and to tidy up the U.S. position on foreign claims to offshore areas. The State Department issued protests on July 2, 1948, to the claims made by Argentina (in October 1946), Chile (in June 1947), and Peru (in August 1947).[94] This policy of issuing public protests was not conducive to reaching an eventual accommodation because the protests were viewed as challenges to national sovereignty and they led the claimants to dig in rather than lose face. With only four professional staff members, the new office did not have the resources to negotiate with all countries issuing claims. Mr. Chapman found it necessary to reserve the U.S. position on some claims while dealing with other disputes that were more pressing. The negotiations on Northwest Atlantic fisheries, and with Costa Rica, Mexico, and Japan were most pressing in terms of the existing levels of U.S. fisheries activities. Since the 1930s, the U.S. had had only limited whaling operations and relatively few tuna boats fishing off Ecuador.[95] Only after the discovery in 1947 of a rich tuna fishing ground sixty miles off the Peruvian coast[96] did the level of U.S. fishing efforts there increase significantly.

The U.S. interest in retaining access to these prospective tuna grounds was reflected in her July 1948 protests of the Chilean and Peruvian claims. The Office of the Special Assistant was delayed in undertaking informal negotiations with the 200-mile claimants due to other negotiations. In the meantime, U.S. tuna fleets based in Peru and California fished within 100 miles of the Peruvian coast up to the early 1950s with relatively few difficulties.[97]

Then in the early 1950s, the California sardine fishing disappeared with a radical change in water temperatures. The idled sardine vessels were subsequently used to fish off Latin America and some were sold to Peru which was developing its fishmeal industry.[98] With the influx of new foreign fishing, Latin American governments moved to protect their local fishing industries, many of which were foreign-owned, by extending jurisdiction over offshore areas.

The Response in Latin America:
Individual Claims, 1950-1951

After the United States had delivered its strong protests to Argentina, Chile, and Peru in mid-1948, no new claims were forthcoming for over a year. In fact the only activity in the fisheries area in 1949 was Costa Rica's decision to revise its 200-mile policy back to one claiming sovereignty over the continental shelf and rights and interests in offshore waters. In the early 1950s, however, a flood of claims swept through Latin America. The timing of these claims may have been linked to the heating up of the cold war via the outbreak of war in Korea, as well as to the influx of new U.S. fishing vessels. Indeed, some of the claims of the period made specific reference to security zones. In addition to the impetus given by wartime uncertainty and fears of resource shortages, the Korean War diverted the attention of the United States, by then the main opponent of expansionist offshore claims. In 1950, six countries—Mexico, Honduras, El Salvador, Nicaragua, Ecuador, and Brazil—issued new claims or regulations. Among these, El Salvador was the only one to join the 200-mile club. Mexico's Law of Fisheries (January 16) was followed in April by seizures of five U.S. fishing vessels in the Gulf. Nicaragua,[99] Ecuador,[100] and Brazil[101] laid claim to the continental shelf (to a depth of 200 meters in Ecuador's case) and in some cases included the waters over the shelf.

More problematic from the United States' legal perspective were the claims made by Honduras and El Salvador. Honduras laid claim to its continental shelves and the waters above them and in the same decree claimed a territorial sea twelve kilometers wide. The United Kingdom issued a note of protest, but none by the United States has been found.[102] The claim made by El Salvador to a 200-mile territorial sea[103] was undoubtedly of greater concern to the United States. It declared the seas, airspace, and continental shelf to a distance of 200 miles to be "irreducible." On the other hand, it provided for freedom of navigation which would not have obtained in a proper territorial sea. U.S. alarm at the Salvadorian claim was apparent in the prompt protest that was delivered.[104] In this note, the U.S. government reiterated its adherence to the concept of a three-mile territorial sea and stated categorically that it did not consider its nationals, vessels, or aircraft to be subject to the provisions of the Salvadorian claim. It appears in retrospect that the phrasing of the Salvadorian claim in regard to the 200-mile territorial sea was a mistake on the part of the drafters, and five years later a decree was issued defining the coastal sea and exclusive fishing zone as twelve miles.[105]

The year 1951 was equally ominous for U.S. policy in terms of the proliferation of confused and expansive Latin American offshore claims. In January, Honduras extended its "protection and supervision" to a distance of 200 miles.[106] It also claimed the continental shelf and decreed zones of fishing protection to be specified subsequently. With respect to these three elements, the decree stipulated that it did "not deny similar lawful rights of other States, nor affect the freedom of navigation." The announcement cited as precedents the claims of the U.S., Mexico, Argentina, Chile, Peru, and Costa Rica. It was unique, however, in explicitly distinguishing between the continental shelf, potential zones of fishery protection, and a vague 200-mile security zone. (While the 200-mile concepts of Chile and Peru had combined and confused functional claims to security and resources, other nations had limited themselves to offshore resource claims.) The influence of the United States was apparent in the fact that no further reference was made in the 1951 Honduran claim to the twelve-kilometer territorial sea claimed a year earlier.

The Ecuadorian claim, made a month later, specified a territorial sea of twelve miles in which the coastal state would control fishing.[107] The territorial sea was to be measured "from the low-water mark of the outermost islands of the Galapagos Islands" as well as "from the low-water mark at the most salient points of the Ecuadorian coast and of the adjacent islands." Within a line joining these points, gulfs, bays, straits, and channels became internal waters. The Ecuadorian decree also referred to areas of "maritime policing or protection" such as that established by the 1947 Treaty of Mutual Assistance specifying security zones of 300 and more miles, and stipulated that such areas were to be enforced as part of the present decree. And finally, the decree provided for control and protection of the fisheries "appertaining" to the continental shelf to a depth of 200 meters. Since the money collected from the sale of licenses was turned over directly to the navy, enforcement officials were diligent in their duties where unlicensed vessels were concerned.[108] In May 1951, Ecuador made her first seizures of U.S. fishing vessels under her new claim.

In the same month, the U.S. delivered its protest to the Ecuadorian claim.[109] The United States took issue with four aspects of the claim: (1) the twelve-mile territorial sea; (2) the single belt of territorial waters that was to be created around the entire Colon Archipelago; (3) the use of straight baselines; and (4) the concept of exclusive fishing areas corresponding to the continental shelf. The U.S. adhered to a three-mile territorial sea, separate belts of territorial sea for each island, baselines following the sinuosities of the coast,[110] and the right to limit exclusive fisheries jurisdiction to territorial waters.

Chile, Ecuador, and Peru
Coordinate Claims: 1952-1955

The individual claims to offshore jurisdiction of various Latin American countries were rewarded with official protests where they exceeded the resource claims embodied in the Truman Proclamations or the three-mile territorial sea. The states issuing protests included the maritime nations of Europe as well as the United States.[111] After the State Department had established an office for fisheries matters in 1948, the United States responded to each unacceptable claim either with informal efforts to influence the implementation of the claim or with a prompt and specific official protest and statement of U.S. policy. In some cases both policies were pursued.

Confronted with this powerful opposition, Chile and Peru resolved to concert their actions to defend their policies. They were soon joined by Ecuador. Throughout their subsequent efforts, Peru played the most active role. Actions to gain support for the 200-mile policy took two principal directions. One was to band tightly together in enforcing the policy vis-à-vis other states. The second was to work through regional organizations to secure wider support and acceptance of a 200-mile zone. In the process, the nature of the rights claimed by the individual coastal states in the zone became even more confused.

The first tripartite conference of the "CEP" countries, as they came to be known, was held in Santiago, Chile from August 11 to 18, 1952. This "First Conference on the Exploitation and Conservation of the Maritime Resources of the South Pacific" marks Ecuador's entry into the 200-mile club. The meeting was kept secret[112] until agreement had been worked out among the participants. The four agreements announced at the conference represented a successful effort to compromise and satisfy the diverse interests of the three participants. The agreements included (1) a Declaration on the Maritime Zone, (2) the organization of the Standing Committee of the Conference on the Use and Conservation of the Marine Resources of the South Pacific, (3) a Joint Declaration on Fishery Problems in the South Pacific, and (4) Regulations Governing Whaling in the Waters of the South Pacific.[113] In these agreements, the three countries asserted "sole sovereignty and jurisdiction" over a zone (including the sea floor) to a distance of 200 miles from the coasts or from islands. "Innocent and inoffensive passage" of vessels of other nations was permitted in the zone.[114]

A Permanent South Pacific Fisheries Commission was established by these agreements to standardize regulations and coordinate policies in the claimed areas. To promote fisheries conservation, the agreements recommended the establishment of marine biological stations and the coordination of national and international research. The fourth agreement represents the CEP answer to the International Whaling regulations promulgated three years earlier at the Washington conference. Chile and Peru had signed but not ratified the 1949 convention. In their 1952 pronouncement, the three South American states banned all foreign fishing for baleen whales within the newly declared zone and allowed it under strict regulations only for toothed whales. Land stations were deemed more efficient for the conduct of whaling than factory ships, thereby rationalizing the exclusion of foreign whaling to a distance of 200 miles from shore.

The 1952 Santiago declarations specified that the three governments intended to effect the principles embodied in the declarations through appropriate national regulations. The Santiago Declaration was not ratified and incorporated into law in Ecuador until February 1955[115] and in Peru until May of 1955.[116] Nonetheless, Ecuador and Peru started to enforce their fisheries jurisdiction more rigorously after the Santiago conference. In doing so, Peru relied on her presidential decree of 1947 and Ecuador on her 1950 and 1951 claims to a twelve-mile territorial sea beyond straight baselines, and to the waters above the shelf. Ecuador withdrew the previous system of granting licenses for fishing in her territorial waters.[117] Then in July of 1952, these waters were reopened to foreign vessels which were contracted by one of the two national fishing companies.[118] Chile, on the other hand, made no seizures of foreign fishing vessels during this period. This absence of Chilean seizures was due either to the fact that the government was not enforcing its claims, or to the fact that fewer foreign fishing vessels operate in Chilean waters, which are more remote and less fertile than those off Ecuador and Peru.

Renewed enforcement efforts by Ecuador and Peru resulted in an escalating number of seizures. Ecuadorian seizures of U.S. vessels in March 1953 were followed by bilateral negotiations between the two countries. At this conference (March 25-April 14, 1953), Ecuador agreed on an interim basis to issue licenses by radio to U.S. fishermen to fish in the territorial waters of her continental coast. She did not, however, revise her claims. The final statement of the conference elaborated the outstanding differences between the two countries. It recommended the early convening of a second bilateral negotiation, preferably by the end of May, to consider these differences as well as the possibilities of constructing a fueling station in Ecuador and the prospect of Ecuador's becoming a member of the IATTC. It was agreed that U.S.-Ecuadorian differences over offshore claims were "matters for determination only by the general agreement of maritime states."[119] That is, the test of the validity of their respective legal approaches would be found in the extent of support that could be garnered among other states. The second negotiation between the two countries never took place and Ecuador resumed seizures of foreign fishing vessels found within waters it claimed. Problems with Ecuador subsided after the May 9, 1955, law opening Ecuadorian territorial waters once again to foreign fishing.

Of the various seizures, perhaps the most serious incident occurred when Ecuador captured two U.S. fishing boats 14 to 25 miles off a coastal island, and, in the process, wounded a U.S. seaman.[120] The most spectacular seizure by a CEP nation took place in November 1954 when Peru seized five whaling vessels of the Onassis whaling fleet at distances of 160 to 364 miles from shore. The five vessels, including a factory vessel, were fined $3 million dollars and were detained until the fines were paid.[121]

By 1954, a total of around twenty U.S. tuna vessels had been seized by Peru, Ecuador, Colombia, El Salvador, or Panama.[122] The seizures were accompanied by various fines. As these difficulties mounted, the U.S. government responded with a range of policies—unilateral, bilateral, and multilateral. Under pressure from the fishing industry, Congress enacted a law that would reimburse a fisherman for fines and payments incurred if a U.S. vessel was seized in an area which the U.S. government regarded as high seas. Further, the act specified that the secretary of state "shall take such action as he may deem appropriate to make and collect on claims against a foreign country for amounts expended by the United States under provisions of this Act."[123]

The United States also sought multilateral support for its policy from European maritime nations. The United Kingdom took a major part in arousing European concern. In 1954, the CEP countries received protest notes from the United States,[124] Sweden, the United Kingdom, and the Netherlands.[125] In addition, the United States had promoted consideration by the International Law Commission (ILC) of legal regimes for offshore areas. By 1953 and 1954 ILC drafting was well along the way toward an ultimate codification conference. In encouraging the consideration of the issue within United Nations bodies such as the ILC and the Rome Technical Conference, the United States was seeking to outflank the CEP nations by drawing the issue to a global forum where U.S. policy would receive broader support.[126] The CEP for its part preferred to deliberate the offshore jurisdictional issue in the OAS.

In the face of international opposition and U.S. pressures for bilateral negotiations, the CEP held a second tripartite conference to bind themselves closer together. Meeting in Lima, December 1 to 4, 1954, the three participants signed agreements supplementary to the Declaration of Sovereignty over the Maritime Zone of 200 miles and relating to: (1) penalties; (2) measures of supervision and control in the maritime zones; (3) permits for the exploitation of the maritime resources of the South Pacific; (4) regular annual meetings of the standing committee and; (5) a special maritime frontier zone.[127] The agreements reiterated previous claims and bound the three nations not to agree to anything that would diminish sovereignty over the zone. With regard to licensing foreign whaling fleets, no nation could act without the unanimous agreement of others through the CEP standing committee established in 1952. A problem between the adjacent member nations was addressed in the creation of a ten-mile zone (beginning at twelve miles from shore) extending to 200 miles from shore on each side of the boundary between neighboring states. In this zone the accidental presence of fishing vessels of the neighboring state would not be considered a violation of the coastal state's zone. Peru was unwilling to concede more than this to Chile, which had proposed free fishing in a fifty-mile zone on each side of its boundary. On the whole, the spirit of the 1954 supplementary agreement resembled a pact which tried to prevent the adherents from seeking their individual advantage at the expense of the others.

The pledge of solidarity inherent in the 1954 agreements was soon tested. When in March 1955 the Ecuadorian seizure of U.S. vessels resulted in the wounding of a seaman, the U.S. issued an immediate note of protest[128] and proposed bilateral negotiations between the two governments. Because of the 1954 pledge, Ecuador did not agree.[129] As a result, the United States made a dual proposal to the three CEP countries in May 1955.[130] It proposed that the dispute over their claims to a 200-mile maritime zone be submitted to the International Court of Justice (ICJ) and that the U.S. and CEP countries negotiate toward an agreement for the conservation of fishing resources in which they had a common concern. In the meantime, the U.S. called for an informal understanding that would allow both sides to resolve their legal positions "and avoid further incidents."

The response of the CEP was predictable. None of them had accepted the compulsory jurisdiction of the ICJ and they were not prepared to submit the dispute to the court at that time. There was little doubt that the ICJ would rule against the 200-mile claims. On the other hand, the CEP responded that they were prepared to begin negotiations with the U.S. toward a conservation agreement, and that they wished "as far as possible" to avoid further incidents with the U.S. Despite its preference for submitting the controversy to the ICJ, the United States agreed to begin negotiations with the three countries. In the U.S. view, the agreement would have to avoid reference to the claims of the different governments.

The agreement toward which the United States hoped to work would, the U.S. specified, conform to the conclusions on the technical aspects of fishery conservation approved by the UN International Technical Conference on the Living Resources of the Sea.[131] This conference among forty-five states had taken place in Rome from April 18 to May 10, 1955, and the "guiding principles" which it espoused for the formulation of fishery conventions reflected U.S. preferences. That is, "all States fishing the resource and adjacent coastal States should have opportunity of joining the convention and of participating in the consideration and discussion of regulatory measures." Another aspect of the Rome conclusions that was increasingly playing a role in U.S. fisheries policy was the approach to regulation on the basis of the fishery stocks in question. Stocks of each species were to be managed individually, where separable, and according to area, where required by intermingling of stocks. The delegations of Chile, Ecuador, and Peru had abstained from voting on the conclusions of the final report on the grounds that they exceeded the competence of the conference and that they reflected the thinking of a group that did not have a decisive majority.[132]

The negotiations between the U.S. and the CEP opened in Santiago on September 14, and closed October 5, 1955.[133] During the proceedings, Chile, Ecuador, and Peru acted as a single unit in advancing proposals. Although the subject of the conference was ostensibly the conservation of fishery resources of the Southeast Pacific, the unstated agenda was the legal rights of coastal states. The United States, for its part, wished to see established a commission along the lines of the Inter-American Tropical Tuna Commission. Under such a commission, states that would be deemed to have an "interest" in the conservation of a stock included those who fished it as well as coastal states adjacent to it.[134]

The CEP adopted a quite different view of which countries had an interest in a fishery—a view which was based on a 200-mile zone but which finessed its status as a territorial sea. Within a twelve-mile zone the coastal state would have exclusive control of fisheries. Beyond that, a coastal state could designate a 50- or 60-mile zone which constituted areas "traditionally" exploited by it. Fishing here would also be controlled by licenses issued by the coastal state. By adopting a timeframe of thirty years, the concept of "traditional fishing" was used to exclude virtually all distant-water fleets (apart from whaling) since they had not arrived off the CEP coasts until the 1930s and then only in small numbers. In the remainder of the area covered by the agreement, i.e., to 200 miles, existing conservation regulations already adopted by the CEP would apply. In this area the coastal state would have enforcement powers as well as preferential rights with respect to any quotas that might be established.

The area out to 62 or 72 miles from shore seems to have been of particular interest to the fishing industries of the CEP countries. A great deal of attention had been given in the local press to the 200-mile claim over the previous years, however, and it would have been difficult for any government to have compromised this national claim in negotiations with the United States. In effect, matters had gone too far for a public resolution of the differences between the U.S. and the 200-milers. The instructions to the delegations allowed of no mutually agreeable position. Domestic opinion in the respective countries was too aroused[135] to permit a governmentally negotiated sleight of hand that would have prevented future conflicts.

There was a strong desire on the part of interested parties on both sides, however, to avoid further incidents. Thus after the four-power conference concluded in Santiago, an informal agreement was worked out directly between the American Tunaboat Association, on behalf of the tuna industry, and the government of Peru.[136] In essence, the agreement continued the practice (adopted after World War II) of U.S.

boats buying licenses to fish for bait fish which were found close to shore. The arrangement provided for the licensing of U.S. vessels fishing in coastal waters but did not specify the exact extent of those waters. In this fashion, purchase of licenses need not imply recognition of the 200-mile claim. These understandings led to a decline in the rate of seizures until the 1960s when purse seining displaced bait fishing as the preferred method for harvesting tuna. When nylon nets replaced cotton nets, purse seining became the optimal fishing mode in distant waters. Because costly trips to nearshore waters to obtain bait fish were no longer necessary, U.S. vessels stopped buying licenses.

Due to the strength of public opinion and the strictures of the agreement between Chile, Ecuador, and Peru, secret efforts to reach a bilateral accommodation with Washington were politically damaging to the government of any CEP country. One such agreement in 1956 between Secretary of State John Foster Dulles and the new president of Peru, Dr. Manuel Prado, failed due to public exposure. In this understanding, Peru's president agreed in principle to drop the claim to 200-mile territorial waters in the context of a South Pacific fisheries agreement among interested nations. Signatory nations would be allowed to fish specified areas off South America.[137]

Dulles then stopped in Ecuador to discuss the same possibilities. Upon his return to Washington, the *New York Times* revealed the nature of the U.S. understanding with Peru and Peru's willingness to reconsider its 200-mile claim. Chile and Ecuador were incensed at Peru's breaking ranks and the Peruvian president responded by recourse to ambiguity. On the one hand he indicated his intention to observe Peru's agreements with her neighbors. On the other hand, Peruvian officials indicated that the president's agreement with Dulles still remained in principle.[138]

Ten years later, the Ecuadorian junta found itself in the same predicament. In 1963, a military junta assumed power and negotiated a secret agreement with the U.S. whereby the U.S. recognized Ecuador's twelve-mile limit to tax foreign fishing and Ecuador agreed to refrain from seizures beyond the twelve-mile limit.[139] The public revelation of this agreement in 1965 contributed to undermining the government and in 1966 the new government abrogated the agreement.[140]

Regional Support for 200 Miles

The CEP countries consistently sought support among the states of the region for a policy of each state's right to determine the extent of its offshore resource jurisdiction. This approach won ready support from those states that had found their claims contested by the United States. Thus the CEP countries not only aroused domestic sentiment for 200 miles, but they also gained support among other Latin American countries. A retreat from their claims in the mid to late 1950s would have meant a loss of face both at home and among their neighbors.

At the Ninth International Conference of American states in Bogota, April 1948, the charter of the Organization of American States was drafted.[141] A principal supporter of the body, the United States soon experienced difficulty in asserting its leadership in some of the sub-organs of the OAS. In April 1950, the Inter-American Council of Jurists (the full 21 members of the OAS) assigned the task of studying "the system of Territorial Waters and Related Questions" to its nine-member permanent committee.[142] This Inter-American Juridical Committee met in July 1952 and quickly fell under the influence of the more extreme proponents of 200-mile claims. These members pushed through, by a narrow margin, a draft convention that would recognize the "exclusive sovereignty" of the coastal state over the continental shelf and superjacent waters and airspace. It also recognized the coastal state's right to establish "an area of protection, control, and economic exploitation to a distance of 200 miles."[143] The U.S., Colombia, and Brazil dissented on the grounds that the text went beyond the committee's mandate and was not founded in international law.

The draft convention pushed through the Inter-American Juridical Committee by the CEP was returned to the committee by the Council of Jurists for further study. The council admonished the committee to stay within its procedural guidelines this time, that is, it was to refer draft reports to member governments of the Council of Jurists to allow them to make comments before a final report was prepared.[144] The council had in mind that the general study it was recommending would be preparatory to a special Inter-American Conference which would try to reach agreement on the subject of territorial waters and related questions.

The following spring (1954) the Tenth Inter-American Conference authorized the council of the OAS to convene such a conference under the title "Conservation of Natural Resources: The Continental Shelf and Marine Waters."[145] The OAS-sponsored conference was delayed until 1956 due to U.S. efforts to schedule a UN fisheries conference in advance. Assisted by Garcia Amador, chairman of the International Law Commission, and Hans Andersen of Iceland, William Herrington succeeded at the 1954 General Assembly in getting a resolution to convene in 1955 the UN Technical Conference on the Conservation of the Living Resources of the Seas. This pushed back the date of the

OAS Conference at Ciudad Trujillo to 1956.[146] To maintain his alliance in pursuit of an early UN Technical Conference, the special assistant for fisheries and wildlife had to support Iceland's resolution to refer all aspects of the law of the sea to the International Law Commission. This was contrary to the efforts of the State Department legal advisor to get a separate General Assembly resolution on the continental shelf. In the interests, however, of moving fisheries matters into a more congenial forum, the special assistant was prepared to sacrifice the legal advisor's goal. The debate on international fisheries problems was successfully shifted to a global technical forum. The results of the Rome Technical Conference affected the subsequent OAS meeting and became the basis of ILC deliberations and ultimately of the UN Geneva Conference on the Law of the Sea in 1958 and 1960.

In preparation for the OAS Conference on the "Conservation of Natural Resources," the Council of Jurists had been asked to prepare a background study on the legal aspects of the matter. The council once again had turned to its Juridical Committee requesting a study. In light of its previous difficulties, the Juridical Committee declined the task.[147] Thus when the Council of Jurists met in Mexico City in January 1956, two months before the conference was to begin in Ciudad Trujillo, it had no preparatory documents before it. In this situation, the CEP were in a position to dominate the preparatory meeting. Together with Argentina, El Salvador, Guatemala, Mexico, and Uruguay they introduced a draft resolution embodying their particular claims. The resolution rejected a three-mile territorial sea and declared that each state was competent to establish its territorial waters "taking into account geographical, geological and biological factors, as well as the economic needs of its population, and its security and defense." The resolution further provided for the coastal state's "right of exclusive exploitation of species" related to the coast as well as for straight baselines to measure the inner boundary of territorial waters.[148]

The proponents of this resolution effectively prevented debate within the Council of Jurists. At the single session held to discuss the resolution, they would not respond to objections, and the committee allowed no further time for consideration of the proposal.[149] The resolution was then pressed to a vote in committee and in plenary where it was adopted by a vote of 15 to 1 (the United States) with 5 abstentions (Bolivia, Colombia, Cuba, Dominican Republic, Nicaragua). The "Principles of Mexico," as they came to be known, reflected a tenuous solidarity. Among the reservations offered to the principles, five states voting for the resolution (Panama, Brazil, Honduras, Guatemala, Venezuela) indicated that their support was partial.[150] Thus the Cuban motion reducing the resolution from the status of a declaration to that of a preparatory study was passed by a vote of 11 to 9. In this category, the "Principles of Mexico" were transmitted to the Specialized Conference.

The Specialized Conference on the Conservation of Natural Resources: Continental Shelf and Marine Waters met in Ciudad Trujillo from March 15 to 28, 1956, only a few weeks before the ILC's final meeting on its law of the sea draft. Unlike the meeting of the Juridical Committee in Mexico, the Specialized Conference dealt with a single issue and had before it around forty technical papers drafted by national and international scientific groups. The "Principles of Mexico" was simply one of several preparatory documents. Participants included technical experts as well as lawyers.

The conference began by accepting a U.S. proposal that no final decisions be made except by unanimous vote. The U.S. had made it clear that it would not tolerate a repetition of the Mexico meeting. The U.S. negotiator, William Herrington, took the lead in submitting proposals for the consideration of the delegates.[151] In fact, the final resolution was based on a draft originally submitted by the United States.[152] The brief document carefully laid out the areas of agreement and disagreement among the OAS members. Indeed, it represents the best single statement of the state of claims in the mid-1950s.[153] The only area of substantive agreement was on the definition of the continental shelf. In a formula subsequently adopted by the 1958 Geneva Conference on the Law of the Sea, the Ciudad Trujillo resolution stated that "the sea-bed and subsoil of the continental shelf . . . adjacent to the coastal state, outside the area of the territorial sea, and to a depth of 200 meters or, beyond that limit, to where the depth of the superjacent waters admits of the exploitation of the natural resources . . . appertain exclusively to that state and are subject to its jurisdiction and control."[154] The resolution noted the absence of agreement as to the juridical regime applicable to waters above the shelf as well as to what living resources might be said to pertain to the shelf.

With regard to fisheries the resolution noted that international cooperation was desirable, in the form of agreements among states directly interested in the resources, in order to achieve optimum sustainable yield. There was agreement on the fact that the coastal state had a special interest in the productivity of the resources of the high seas adjacent to its territorial sea, but no agreement was possible on the nature or scope of that interest. Finally, the resolution noted the "diversity of positions" among the participants on the breadth of the territorial sea. In conclusion, the resolution did not take a stance with regard to the positions of the participants, but recommended instead that the American states continue efforts to reach a solution of their differences. However, the OAS did not resume consideration of these issues until 1971.

The moderate tone of the Ciudad Trujillo resolution reflected the inability of the CEP countries to carry the day against the well-prepared U.S. and Cuban negotiators. It also reflected the very strong U.S. stand against the more extreme Latin American positions. The U.S. went so far as to threaten withdrawal from the Organization of American States if these positions were not modified.[155] The U.S. strategy, under the guidance of William Herrington, was to diffuse the issue in the OAS and move law of the sea issues from the OAS context into other United Nations forums where the U.S. could expect greater support.

NORTHEAST PACIFIC FISHERIES:
RELATIONS WITH JAPAN

Before turning to consider the U.S. pursuit of its fisheries goals through the International Law Commission and the UN Conferences on the Law of the Sea, one more area of postwar U.S. fisheries policy merits consideration—that pertaining to fisheries resources of the North Pacific. The threat of Japanese fishing of salmon spawned in North American rivers had troubled relations between the countries before the war and had led ultimately to the Truman Proclamation on fisheries. During the war the Northeast Pacific fishing interests, supported by the Congress, had been eager to move quickly to preclude the resumption of Japanese fishing. As we have noted, however, not all U.S. fishing interests favored the implementation of the Truman Proclamation "conservation zones" through executive decree or legislation. The interests of the powerful Northeast Pacific fishing groups, which included halibut and herring as well as salmon fishermen, had to be pursued in a manner that would not preclude the entry of U.S. tuna and shrimp fishing vessels into new grounds. That means was developed through what was to be known as the "abstention principle," a concept that was a variation of U.S. policy in the 1930s. The "abstention principle" was elevated to a principle of international law and based on conservation goals and scientific means. The United States signed the peace treaty with Japan in 1951 and negotiated the abstention principle into its fishing relations with Japan in the same year. Prior to the treaty, U.S.-Japanese relations were those between a victorious and a vanquished power.

95

Japan as a Defeated Power: 1946-1951

From Japan's surrender in August 1945, the United States took an active role in controlling the direction of the country's postwar policies. This was true in the area of fisheries as in all others. The United States, in the person of its Supreme Commander of the Allies in the Pacific (SCAP), General Douglas MacArthur, ran Japan's fisheries policy from the outset of the occupation to the signing of the peace treaty. In theory, of course, the Far Eastern Commission (FEC), through its Subcommittee on Fishing,[156] was to have a major role in guiding that policy. In practice, however, SCAP headquarters acted unilaterally and according to its own best judgment.

Nowhere is this clearer than in the controversy over the Japanese Antarctic whaling expedition authorized by SCAP for the 1947 whaling season.[157] In 1946, SCAP issued "interim directives" for a SCAP-administered Japanese-manned Antarctic whaling project (two factory ships) as an "emergency measure" for one season only. The grounds given by the U.S. government were the food shortages then prevailing in Japan and the U.S. concern to alleviate that shortage. The Congress, it was argued, would not support a major U.S. effort to supply the food needs of Japan, nor were the allies offering any assistance in the way of food products.[158] Humanitarian needs, therefore, dictated this course.

The United States was isolated in its support of the Japanese whaling expedition. The other members of the FEC, led most vocally by Australia and the United Kingdom, protested the absence of consultation between the FEC and SCAP. They favored restricting Japanese fishing to a limited area.[159] As to Japan's food needs, they insisted that Japanese whaling vessels be turned over to them as reparations and they would use the ships to provide the whale products needed in Japan. The issue was argued at various levels of technical detail between the U.S. on one side and other FEC members on the other. Problems were addressed such as the possibility that Antarctic whaling capacity had been reached, the fact that western crews could not use boats built for smaller Japanese crew members, the difficulties in defining the administrative prerogatives of SCAP, and so on.

Behind the technical issues, however, was a basic difference of opinion on the direction that Japan's postwar fishing efforts would take. Australia was adamantly opposed to any resumption of Japanese fishing south of the equator. She was supported by other members of the FEC in her goal of seeing to it that future Japanese fishing should be severely limited in extent. The United States government adopted a very different approach. It was of the view that fishing was of fundamental importance to the Japanese economy "(a) as a source of food, (b) as a means of employment, and (c) as a source of exports to provide foreign exchange for essential imports."[160] Consequently, a revival of the Japanese fishing industry should be encouraged. Given its own coastal fishing industries, it is understandable that the United States was opposed to restricting such resumed Japanese fishing to the Northern hemisphere, i.e., to U.S. offshore fishing grounds.

To distribute the burden of a renewed Japanese fishing effort while accommodating the Pacific Northwest and Alaskan fishing interests, the U.S. proposed to the FEC that Japanese fishing not be permitted within fifty miles of land. Additionally, Japanese fishing operations would have to conform to "(a) The provisions of the international whaling agreements; (b) The provisions of other international agreements relating to conservation of fisheries; (c) Recognized conservation practices, including abstinence from pelagic sealing or interference with conservation measures instituted by littoral states."[161] Through these conservation provisions, the U.S. government, as early as 1946 and 1947, was laying the groundwork for subsequently excluding Japan from its North Pacific fishing grounds. The U.S. and Canada had long-standing agreements to conserve halibut and salmon stocks in the area, and according to the conservation principles advanced by the U.S. within the FEC, Japan could be excluded from these fisheries. The trick was to sell this approach to the Japanese government.

This task did not prove difficult. Ultimately, the Japanese government had little choice but to go along with U.S. policy. The Australian-proposed alternative was far more detrimental to the future of Japanese fishing. Under SCAP auspices, Japan was authorized to undertake two Antarctic whaling expeditions and to resume fishing from Japan eastward to the 165th meridian.[162] Under careful U.S. tutelage, Japan adopted "a conservation program for the Japanese fishing industry, developed by General MacArthur's headquarters." This was designed to eliminate "the basis of objections on the part of some nations to the return of Japanese fishing fleets to some portions of their prewar fishing areas." The conservation program was proudly announced by the Departments of State, Interior, and the Army on June 10, 1949. Under it Japanese were being trained in "proper fishery conservation methods" so that they could ultimately "participate in world affairs in a responsible manner."

Japan's willingness to adopt self-denying practices was clearly linked to its desire for the conclusion of a peace treaty. Assurances of this willingness were set out in a letter from the prime minister to the U.S. ambassador to Japan on February 7, 1951. The letter specified that,

97

pending negotiations with other countries, the Japanese would "as a voluntary act, implying no waiver of their international rights, prohibit their resident nationals and vessels from carrying on fishing operations in presently conserved fisheries in all waters where arrangements have already been made, either by international or domestic act, to protect the fisheries from overharvesting, and in which fisheries Japanese nationals or vessels were not in the year 1940 conducting operations."[163] The U.S. indicated satisfaction with this assurance but left nothing to chance. Article 9 of the peace treaty stipulated that "Japan will enter promptly into negotiations with the Allied Powers so desiring for the conclusion of bilateral and multilateral agreements providing for the regulation or limitation of fishing and the conservation and development of fisheries on the high seas."[164] With the signing of the treaty of peace on September 8, 1951, full sovereignty was restored to Japan and a new phase of fishing relations with the United States commenced.

Negotiations with Japan and the Abstention Principle

In accordance with the terms of the peace treaty, Japan issued invitations to the United States and Canada to initiate negotiations that would pave the way for a North Pacific fisheries convention. These negotiations were held in Tokyo from November 4 to December 14, 1951, and produced a "proposed International Convention for the High Seas Fisheries of the North Pacific Ocean."[165] After the peace treaty came into effect, the fisheries convention was signed by representatives of the three governments on May 9, 1952. The convention went into force in 1953 and the North Pacific Fisheries Act of 1954 implemented the convention for the United States.

William Herrington, who was by 1951 the State Department's special assistant for fisheries, led the U.S. delegation at the Tokyo negotiations. His account of the negotiations is particularly illuminating. In it he explicitly describes the convention as "the culmination of efforts to obtain recognition of U.S. conservation programs and principles formulated by the fisheries interests of the Northwest and Alaska thirty years ago."[166] These interests had pressed very hard at the closing stages of the war, he noted, for imposing geographic fishing limitations on Japan as a condition of the treaty of peace.[167] "The Government of the United States, however, being concerned with all the varied interests of the fishing industry, promotion of international goodwill, rehabilitation of the Japanese economy, and maintenance of freedom of access to unutilized raw materials of the high seas, has found it impossible to fit such proposals into our overall international policies."[168] In order to satisfy the varied U.S. objectives, the "new and promising approach" embodied in Japan's voluntary abstention from certain fisheries was adopted.[169] (That the approach was not entirely "new" is suggested by U.S. pressures for a similar Japanese abstention from fishing Bristol Bay salmon in the 1930s.) Under this agreement, according to Herrington, "each signatory agrees to abstain from exploitation of specified fish stocks which are already exploited to the maximum by one or both of the other parties provided the latter are carrying out programs for the conservation of the stocks." In practice, what this approach meant was that Japan would abstain from fishing for salmon, halibut, or herring off the North American coast east of 175 degrees west longitude. The convention specified that these stocks were already covered by agreements between the United States and Canada. To allay Canadian concern that its fishermen would be excluded from U.S. coastal waters, the convention provided that "no such abstention should be requested of any parties in waters in which there has been a history of joint conservation activity by such parties, an intermingling of their fleets, and an intermingling of the stocks of fish exploited by their fleets."[170]

The convention created a North Pacific Fisheries Commission which was charged with the responsibility for conserving those fisheries that were not explicitly relegated to bilateral arrangements by the convention. The commission was also charged with promoting and coordinating scientific studies undertaken by national research agencies and with recommending measures based on these findings that would secure the maximum sustained productivity of the stocks. The commission was expected to conduct an annual review of herring, halibut, and salmon stocks to determine if they continued to qualify for abstention. The three contracting parties to the convention were represented on the commission.

Japan's willingness to agree to the North Pacific Fisheries Convention reflected its situation in the early 1950s. Japan was obliged to carry out the terms of article 9 of the peace treaty. Until a convention could be negotiated, Japanese fishermen were committed to voluntarily abstain from certain stocks by the prime minister's letter of February 1951. Then, too, the proposed convention did not deny the general principle that Japanese fishermen might operate anywhere on the high seas. The embodiment of this right in a convention with the United States and Canada would be important to subsequent negotiations between Japan and other coastal states.

The 1952 convention provided for the possibility of alteration. It specified that it would remain in effect for ten years and after that for

99

one year from the date on which any contracting party gave notice of its intent to terminate. The conditions reinforcing Japanese acceptance of the convention disappeared quickly, and within a decade Japan was proposing a major revision of the North Pacific Fisheries Convention.[171] Perhaps the major factor contributing to the pressures for change in this treaty was the abstention line that had been set at 175° west longitude. This line was unfortunate in most respects. From the domestic political perspective, the notion of an exclusionary boundary was anathema to U.S. distant-water fishing interests. (The line encouraged the Korean government to claim a 60-mile conservation zone and a 200-mile fish zone in August 1952.) From the foreign relations perspective, the line soon became a vestige of Japanese humiliation and a source of continuing rancor for that country, despite the fact that it had been included in the agreement at Japanese insistence.[172] And from the practical standpoint of protecting the highly mobile salmon stocks, the line was not effective. The abstention line was drawn about 600 miles west of Bristol Bay and was hoped in 1952 to be sufficiently distant from U.S. spawning grounds to prevent Japanese catches.[173]

The abstention line was to be provisional and subject to change according to new information that would establish the point dividing Asian from North American stocks. It soon became evident, however, that the migratory patterns of the Bristol Bay salmon carried them west of the line and that the range of Asian and North American stocks overlapped.[174] Thus Japanese fishing Asian-spawned salmon west of the line also caught North American salmon. By 1957 reduced salmon stocks in Bristol Bay were once again being blamed on Japanese fishing. In 1958 the State Department notified Japan that the Interior Department was contemplating the closure of Bristol Bay to U.S. nationals fishing for salmon unless the Japanese would further limit their salmon fishing. This step was implemented by the Interior Department in 1959 until the Japanese agreed to a reduction in their salmon quota throughout the North Pacific from 11 million to 8 million fish.[175]

The principle of voluntary abstention, like the drawing of an abstention line, did not provide a durable basis for general international fisheries policy. Not only did it encounter opposition from domestic groups, but it failed to win widespread international support in subsequent U.S. efforts to promote it as a principle of international law. The principle of abstention, borrowing from the policy preferences of the U.S. salmon industry, was advanced as U.S. policy from the outset of the U.S. occupation of Japan. When William Herrington moved from service as the SCAP chief of Fisheries Division to head the Fisheries

Office in the State Department, he brought the policy with him.[176] The negotiation of the principle into the North Pacific Fisheries Convention, however, destroyed a tenuous truce that had been reached between the West Coast salmon and tuna industries. The tuna fishing interests insisted that tuna and California sardine be left out of the protocol to the convention. And they vigorously protested the incorporation into a U.S.-negotiated international convention of a principle they deemed to be exclusionary of distant-water fishing fleets.

Since Herrington's constituents included all segments of the U.S. fishing industry, he faced a difficult task in reconciling their mutually inconsistent interests in an overall U.S. fisheries policy. According to an account by Wilbert Chapman, director of research for the American Tunaboat Association in the 1950s, Herrington built a tenuous coalition on the basis of the needs of the several groups. The tuna industry was beset by increasing Latin American moves to shut it out of its newly discovered fishing grounds. And within the Inter-American meetings of the early 1950s, the 200-mile proponents were winning acceptance of their views. The tuna industry consequently recognized the need to shift fisheries matters out of the OAS context into the broader UN forum of the International Law Commission. Mr. Herrington argued that he needed a united fishing industry supporting him if he were to succeed in this effort. The North Pacific fishing groups, for their part, wanted to see the abstention principle dignified as a principle of international law. To carry the fight for this principle through years of international negotiation, Mr. Herrington argued the need for the support of the entire U.S. fishing community. On this basis, he built a fragile coalition between the coastal and distant-water segments of his industry constituents. This uneasy truce lasted until the final defeat of the abstention principle in the 1958 Geneva Conference on the Law of the Sea.[177]

While the U.S. succeeded in shifting the focal point of international fisheries discussions from the OAS to other United Nations bodies, its policy on abstention suffered repeated defeats. In the 1955 Technical Conference in Rome the United States and Canadian delegations were unable to get the support of their European allies for abstention. The Soviet bloc was also opposed since the Soviet Praesidium had just adopted a policy of rapidly expanding their worldwide fishing efforts. Thus while the Europeans and the Soviets supported the North Americans against the Latin American 200-mile policies, they did not offer similar support for abstention. Consequently, the U.S. and Canada withdrew their jointly sponsored abstention principle before it was defeated in a vote.[178] The next year at the ILC meeting the abstention principle again had to be withdrawn at the last minute. Latin American support for abstention both in the ILC and at the Geneva Conference of 1958 was sufficient to deter European and Soviet support. Thus the abstention principle was defeated at the 1958 conference and was not reintroduced by the United States in 1960.

THE CONTINENTAL SHELF DEBATE:

1945-1956

FROM THE PERSPECTIVE of United States policy, gaining control of the resources of the continental shelf had two principal facets—domestic and international. At issue on the domestic side was whether the federal government or the state governments would own the seabed and its resources under the territorial sea (or related areas claimed by the states). The resolution of this question was pursued first through litigation and then through legislation. During the Truman administration, legislation confirming state rights in offshore lands was vetoed by the president. With Eisenhower's accession to the presidency, the Congress passed the Submerged Lands Act and gave the states title to the seabed within their territorial sea boundaries. The Outer Continental Shelf Lands Act subjected the continental shelf beyond to the jurisdiction of the United States and authorized federal leasing of offshore lands beyond the territorial sea.

At issue internationally was how to extend control to offshore resources without unleashing a host of coastal-state claims that would threaten U.S. high seas interests just as the U.S. was beginning to adopt a global perspective. Although a number of claims, specifically by Latin American countries, went well beyond that of the U.S., the pattern of claim and response through the early 1950s indicated that national rights to the continental shelf, in some form and to some distance, were generally accepted. As a result, the issue was taken up in a succession of regional and international meetings, culminating in the 1958 Convention on the Continental Shelf.

As noted in the preceding chapters, the principal engine for expansion of United States government continental shelf claims during the 1930s and early 1940s was the Interior Department, and in particular its secretary, Harold Ickes. Secretary Ickes worked persistently to gain control of offshore lands for the federal government and to extend the boundary of the continental shelf for the nation. He was willing to pursue any available means including legislation, litigation, and executive proclamation. Less eager to press ahead were the Departments of

Justice and State. Justice officials were unwilling to bring a suit against the states until a strong case could be made for federal title to offshore lands. The State Department was concerned that any offshore claims beyond the three-mile territorial sea might be misinterpreted or misused by other nations to advance claims that would threaten high seas rights. The Interior Department's efforts to assert federal and national rights over offshore areas were sidetracked first by the presidential elections of 1940 and then by U.S. entrance into the Second World War. As the end of the war drew near, Ickes renewed his agency's efforts on both the domestic and the international fronts.

The Truman Proclamation on the "Policy of the United States with Respect to the Natural Resources of the Subsoil and Sea Bed of the Continental Shelf" was the result of the Interior Department's efforts. As finally promulgated, the proclamation was neutral as to the issue of state versus federal government ownership of the submerged lands beyond the coastline. The proclamation claimed "the natural resources of the subsoil and seabed of the continental shelf beneath the high seas but contiguous to the coasts of the United States as appertaining to the United States, subject to its jurisdiction and control." The accompanying executive order "Reserving and Placing Certain Resources of the Continental Shelf under the Control and Jurisdiction of the Secretary of the Interior" specified that "neither this Order nor the aforesaid proclamation shall be deemed to affect the determination by legislation or judicial decree of any issues between the United States and the several states, relating to the ownership or control of the subsoil and seabed of the continental shelf within or outside of the three-mile limit."[1] Despite President Truman's express preference for federal jurisdiction over the offshore lands and Secretary Ickes's active efforts in this direction, this sentence was included upon the suggestion of the Interior Department.[2] Only congressional action or judicial decision, it was recognized, could ultimately resolve this domestic dispute.

For administrative purposes, however, and "pending the enactment of legislation," the natural resources of the subsoil and seabed of the continental shelf were placed under the jurisdiction and control of the secretary of the interior. Secretary Ickes was quick to provide his own interpretation of the Continental Shelf Proclamation. In his annual report for 1945, he stated that the proclamation asserted U.S. "sovereignty over the mineral resources of this ground."[3] He was optimistic about the valuable minerals that could be expected in the newly claimed area out to a depth of 600 feet.[4] He was even more excited about Interior's prospective role in developing the continental shelf.

This Department has been assigned to explore the shelf, and we have developed our plans so far as we can develop them without knowing how much money the Congress will appropriate for the work. We have acquired some of the extraordinary instruments that will be used; we are building or redesigning others. We are formulating a program for cooperative work by geophysicists, geologists, and engineers. Their work will be carried on partly aboard vessels and partly in submarines, and diving bells, and in airplanes. The cost of the survey may run to several millions of dollars if we include the cost of ships and equipment still in the Navy's possession.

Clearly, Secretary Ickes was going to lose no time establishing an active role for his agency and the federal government in the development of the resources of the shelf. Such activity could only improve the federal government's claim to the area. A definitive resolution of the domestic issue of jurisdiction, however, was to be eight years in coming. Only with the passage of the Submerged Lands Act and the Outer Continental Shelf Act in 1953 was the domestic status of the continental shelf finally settled.

Federal-State Contention: 1945-1953

The Truman Period

The opening gun in the eight-year struggle for control of the offshore lands was sounded shortly after Truman's accession to the presidency. A firm proponent of federal jurisdiction over offshore resources, President Truman pressed for judicial action to resolve the issue. In May 1945 he instructed Attorney General Biddle to bring suit in the U.S. district court for the southern district of California against the Pacific Western Oil Corporation as a test case.[5] Thus Ickes's plan to move ahead with litigation against the states had finally been realized.[6] On October 19, 1945, the new attorney general, Tom Clark, was authorized by the president to dismiss the suit against the Pacific Western Oil Corporation and file in the Supreme Court a motion for leave to file an original suit against the state of California. The Justice Department preferred to try this major constitutional issue directly in the Supreme Court. The attorney general's position in the suit was that the United States was "the owner in fee simple of, or possessed of paramount rights in and powers over, the lands, minerals and other things of value underlying the Pacific Ocean, lying seaward of the ordinary low-water mark on the coast of California and outside of the inland waters of the State, extending seaward three nautical miles." The state of California contended that the three-mile belt was within its boundaries, that title to submerged lands within the boundaries of the thirteen original states had been acquired by them from the crown of England, and that since California was admitted on an equal footing with those states, she also enjoyed such offshore boundaries.

On June 23, 1947, the Supreme Court sustained the position of the United States.[7] In an opinion delivered by Justice Black, the Court concluded that the concept of territorial sovereignty over an offshore belt had not developed until after the American Revolution and therefore offshore areas were not part of the domain acquired by the original states from the British crown. Rather, offshore lands had been added to the national domain by action of the federal government. Moreover, the coastal belt was linked to matters of national defense and foreign relations which were concerns of the nation rather than of the several states. Neither earlier congressional acquiescence in state assertions of ownership of the continental shelf nor the failure of previous attempts to pass legislation authorizing this suit (S.J. Res. 92, S. Rept. 1612, 76th Cong., 3rd sess.) were deemed to refute the United States' claim. California protested that six basic propositions of the law were overlooked by the Court, but a request for a new hearing was denied. A decree to effectuate the Court's opinion was entered on October 27, 1947 (332 U.S. 804). It declared the United States to be possessed of "paramount rights in and full dominion and power over, the lands, minerals and other things underlying the Pacific Ocean lying seaward of the ordinary low-water mark on the coast of California."

The federal government's victory was short-lived. Shortly after the Supreme Court ruling, the government received applications for offshore leases under the Mineral Leasing Act of February 25, 1920. In August of 1947, however, the solicitor general of the Interior Department and the attorney general concluded that the 1920 act could not apply to mining of the continental shelf. Thus in September the pending applications for leases had to be denied by the Interior Department. In effect, the federal government had secured paramount rights to lease lands off the California coast, but had no statutory authority to do so. To gain that authority, the secretaries of defense and interior and the attorney general submitted legislation to the Congress on February 6, 1948 "to promote the development and conservation of certain resources in the submerged coastal lands adjacent to the shores of the United States."[8]

The need for congressional action to establish the statutory authority for federal leasing of offshore lands placed the issue of offshore jurisdiction into the arena least hospitable to federal efforts to assert control. By the time of the Supreme Court's decision on California, over fifty bills had been introduced in the Congress that would preclude federal government control of the lands under the marginal sea. No legislation had been introduced during the war, but when President Truman first moved the issue into the courts in 1945, the Congress responded by introducing legislation that would quitclaim to the states the submerged coastal lands within state boundaries at the same time they entered the Union. Hearings on these bills[9] were held in June of 1945, and H.J. Res. 225 passed the House of Representatives the same year. Then in 1946 the Senate also adopted H.J. Res. 225. The measure was vetoed by President Truman on August 1, however, and the House was unable to override the veto. The grounds upon which the president based his veto were that the question of ownership was a legal one and should be determined by the Supreme Court in the California case which was then pending. If the Court determined that "the United States owns these areas, they should not be given away."[10]

Pending the outcome of the California case, no new measures were introduced in 1947. But once the Supreme Court decided in favor of the federal government's claim, the Congress again began to press for legislation promoting state claims to offshore lands. Quitclaim bills[11] were introduced and seventeen days of joint hearings were held by subcommittees of the House and Senate Committees on the Judiciary in February and March 1948 (supplemented by further Senate hearings on May 4 and 5, 1948). In this environment, proposals for federal management legislation[12] to implement the California decision did not fare well.

Despite its inability to gain statutory authority from the Congress to manage offshore lands, the administration began original actions against Louisiana and Texas on December 21, 1948, similar to that against California. These cases differed from the California case, however, in the seaward extent of the areas that were being claimed by the plaintiffs. Louisiana had declared its offshore boundary to be twenty-seven marine miles from the coast[13] and Texas claimed its boundary as the edge of the continental shelf.[14] On June 5, 1950, the Supreme Court ruled against the claims of both Louisiana and Texas.[15] Decrees were entered in both cases on December 11, 1950, declaring the "paramount rights" of the United States in the submerged lands and minerals within twenty-seven marine miles of the Louisiana coast (340 U.S. 899) and to the edge of the continental shelf off the Texas coast (340 U.S. 900).

CONGRESSIONAL-EXECUTIVE STANDOFF. Further rulings of the Supreme Court reiterating its decision in the California case could not resolve the impasse between the Congress and the executive. The Congress could not muster enough support for quitclaim legislation to override a presidential veto and the executive could not win congressional support for legislation that would provide it with statutory authority to manage the offshore lands. The position of the petroleum industry on this controversy is unclear. Both sides charged the other with being in league with special oil interests. State jurisdiction proponents charged that "a few persons and their lawyers . . . are attempting to obtain from the Federal Government, for a nominal consideration, oil and gas leases on parts of the submerged lands."[16] President Truman, on the other hand, viewed it as a question of "the private oil interests, seeking to exploit these oil-rich areas without federal control and supervision."[17] Wherever particular industry representatives stood, it is likely that the overwhelming sentiments of the oil companies lay with a prompt resolution of the issue of jurisdiction. Indeed all parties to the dispute seemed to agree on one thing—the importance of recovering offshore oil and of reaching a definitive settlement to facilitate new development.

Thus in 1949 new efforts were mounted to reach an understanding between the states and the federal government. On February 1, 1949, the secretary of defense (James Forrestal), the attorney general (Tom Clark), and the secretary of the interior (J. A. Krug) submitted a proposed bill "to promote the development and conservation of certain resources in the submerged coastal lands adjacent to the shores of the United States."[18] This bill was similar to the one introduced by the three secretaries during the previous year with regard to federal ownership and management of the offshore lands. It offered a new inducement to compromise, however, in the form of possible sharing of the income that would be derived from oil and gas operations. The federal government's proffered compromise did not go far enough to meet the states' demands. Thus in May, June, and July, the Speaker of the House, the attorney general, the secretary of the interior, and officials of various states met in an effort to try to define possible areas of agreement in the controversy.[19] Accord on fundamental issues proved elusive and the negotiations were terminated in July. Each side then introduced bills which it hoped would be the basis for an overall agreement.[20]

Hearings on these bills were held from August to October 1949. The stalemate between the states and the federal government persisted, however, and negotiations between the opposing parties were once again resumed. As before, neither side could prevail without the support of the other.

Efforts to circumvent the impasse failed. For instance, the federal government considered the feasibility of converting the offshore lands into a naval petroleum reserve. The solicitor general of the Interior Department, however, argued that continuing uncertainty of title would make it difficult to manage these areas, even as a naval petroleum reserve. Consideration was also given to the possibility of federal administration of the marginal sea under the surplus property provision of the General Services Act, but this idea was eventually abandoned.

The Eighty-first Congress spawned a number of creative efforts at compromise based on the distinction between (1) ownership of the submerged lands and resources and (2) the right to develop and use them. The reason that some proponents of states' rights were willing to accept this distinction was their fear that the Supreme Court decisions had tied the ownership of the shelf under the territorial sea so closely to the national government that the ownership of it would be constitutionally inalienable.[21]

Comparable legislation reappeared in the Eighty-second Congress.[22] Hearings on the Senate versions were held in February, March, April, and June of 1952, and by the spring of 1952, fourteen resolutions were also pending in the House. S.J. Res. 20 passed the Senate on April 2 (50 yes, 35 no, 11 abstentions); its amendments channeling revenues to national security and educational purposes did not. It then went to the House where it was passed on May 15 (247 yes, 89 no, and 90 abstentions).[23] In its final form, S.J. Res. 20 quitclaimed to the states the jurisdiction over offshore lands within their historic boundaries.

The presidential veto came as no surprise. President Truman's earlier veto plus subsequent public statements and the position of his agency heads were unequivocally opposed to making "an outright gift of the offshore resources of the country to three states at the expense of the other forty-five."[24] Truman's veto message of May 29, 1952, reiterated his position on the matter.[25] The controversy had, in his view, been "resolved in the only way such legal questions can be resolved under our Constitution—that is, by the courts, and in this case, by the Supreme Court."[26] The president proposed that a reasonable solution of the question would provide for the rapid development of offshore resource for the needs of national defense. This should be done by "federal leases to private parties for exploration and development of the oil and gas deposits in the undersea lands."[27] The president, more-over, should be empowered to set aside any unleased lands of the shelf and reserve them for the purpose of national security. The absence of any provision to this effect in the bill that had reached Truman's desk accounted for the strong Defense Department opposition to his approval of such legislation. The president went on to note his support for the revenue-sharing proposals sponsored in the Senate by Senator O'Mahoney and Senator Hill which would direct oil revenues to aid education. "When you consider . . . how much good such a provision would do for school children throughout the nation, it gives particular emphasis to the necessity for preserving these great assets for the benefit of all the people of the country rather than giving them to a few of the states."[28]

ELECTION POLITICS. President Truman's veto of legislation granting states' rights over offshore lands quickly became an issue in the presidential campaign of 1952. The Republican platform promised "restoration to the States of their rights to all lands and resources beneath navigable inland and offshore waters within their historic boundaries." General Eisenhower was unequivocal in his support of state ownership of offshore lands within historic boundaries. In a speech on October 13 he said: "I favor the recognition of clear legal title to these lands in each of the forty-eight states. . . . The Supreme Court has declared in very recent years that there are certain paramount federal rights in these areas, but the Court expressly recognized the right of Congress to deal with those matters of ownership and title. Twice, by substantial majorities, both houses of Congress have voted to recognize the traditional concept of state ownership of these submerged areas. Twice, these acts of Congress have been vetoed by the President. I would approve such acts of Congress."[29] On the other hand, Adlai Stevenson, the Democratic candidate, was decidedly opposed to turning over offshore lands to the states.

Upon Eisenhower's election to the presidency, Truman made one last effort to secure federal title to the offshore lands through the use of his powers as chief executive. On December 20, 1952, the Interior Department sent President Truman a proposed executive order "creating Naval Petroleum Reserve No. 5" out of the continental shelf lands. The special counsel to the president negotiated the draft through the relevant government agencies.[30] He convened a meeting on January 8 of representatives of the Bureau of the Budget and the Departments of the Interior and Justice to consider the proposed executive order. Justice Department officials expressed strong reservations to the proposal as drafted by Interior. They argued that (a) the proposed reserve could not be created under the Naval Petroleum Reserve Act of June 17, 1944, and (b) the draft should include provisions continuing in effect the 1947 agreement between the attorneys general of the United States and California which permitted continued production by the state of California from the oil wells off its coast. Mr. Murphy asked the solicitor of the Interior Department to revise the proposed order accordingly. This was done and at a meeting two days later (this time including representation from the Department of the Navy), the draft order was approved. On January 12, the Bureau of the Budget formally transmitted it to the attorney general, and on January 16, four days before leaving office, President Truman issued Executive Order 10426 setting aside the United States continental shelf as a naval petroleum reserve.[31]

The Eisenhower Period

President Truman's efforts to preserve federal ownership of offshore lands were quickly reversed under the Eisenhower administration. Immediately following the new president's inauguration, a number of bills were introduced. Like those in the previous Congress, the proposed quitclaim legislation fell into two principal categories. S.J. Res. 13 and S. 294 (H.R. 4198) would confer on the states both the ownership of offshore lands within their historic boundaries and the right to administer the development of the natural resources therein. On the other hand, S. 107 and the Hill amendment provided that the federal government owned the offshore lands but that the respective coastal states had the right to administer and develop the lands and the right to specified portions of the revenue therefrom. The new administration did not submit a federal management bill.

AGENCY VIEWS. Congressional hearings on these bills were conducted in February and March of 1953. During the hearings it became apparent that not all members of the new administration supported President Eisenhower's preference for granting title to offshore lands to the coastal states. On March 2, for instance, Attorney General Brownell testified before the Senate Committee on Interior and Insular Affairs in favor of the federal government retaining title but conferring on the states the right to administer the development of resources within their boundaries.[32] The attorney general also urged the Congress in its legislation to draw the line setting the limits to the area in which the states would have such administrative rights in order to prevent any long litigation. Moreover, Brownell shared the views of his predecessor that

111

President Truman's Executive Order 10426 was legally sufficient to transfer the administrative rights over offshore lands from the Department of the Interior to the Navy, but that did not affect the issue of title.[33]

The Department of State's concerns and policies remained essentially unchanged from those of the previous administration. Correspondence from State Department officials from 1949 through 1953 illustrates State's firmly held conviction that legislative measures extending the national limits would be seized upon by other nations as a justification for their own claims. State Department officials expressed concern with three aspects of the proposed legislation: (1) the manner in which the baseline was drawn, (2) the extent of the area claimed beyond the baseline, and (3) the nature of the claim (i.e., to sovereignty or jurisdiction). The clearest statement of State Department concerns is found in a letter from Assistant Secretary Thruston B. Morton (on behalf of the secretary) to Senator Henry Jackson on March 6, 1953. Morton points out that:

> Extension of the boundary of a State beyond the 3-mile limit would directly conflict with international law, as the United States conceives it, and may, moreover, precipitate developments in international practice to which this Government, in the national interest, is clearly opposed. A number of foreign states are at present showing a clear propensity to extend their sovereignty over considerable areas of their adjacent seas. This restricts the freedom of the sea, and the freedom of the sea has been and is a cornerstone of the United States policy because it is a maritime and naval power. Any change of position regarding the 3-mile limit on the part of the United States is likely to be seized upon by other states as justification or excuse for broader and even extravagant claims over their adjacent seas. Indeed, this is just what happened when this Government made its proclamation of 1945 regarding the resources of the Continental Shelf. It precipitated a chain reaction of claims generally going beyond the terms of the United States proclamation, including claims of sovereignty extending to 200 miles from shore. Extension now of the jurisdictional powers of the States in the high seas beyond those heretofore claimed by the Nation would, of course, be an abandonment of the traditional policy of the United States and negate the determined efforts now being made by this Government to oppose and restrain such actions on the part of others.[34]

The view expressed by Morton in 1953 had been consistently espoused by the State Department throughout the litigation of the Texas and Louisiana cases. The then attorney general, J. Howard McGrath, had called on State for its opinion on international law as it applied to the claims of both states to areas beyond three miles. After the decision had gone against Texas and Louisiana, the states redirected their efforts to extending outward the outer limits of their internal waters from which the federal continental shelf would be measured. Here again, the State Department had an interest in ensuring that the practice of the individual states did not set an adverse international precedent and the attorney general turned to State for an expert opinion. In November 1951, the State Department indicated that it had "traditionally taken the position that territorial waters should be measured from the low-water mark along the coast."[35] The communication went on to note that this same position was taken with regard to small indentations in the coastline and to offshore islands.

In 1952, the State Department continued to adhere to its initial position despite the December 18, 1951, ruling by the International Court of Justice in the fisheries case between the United Kingdom and Norway. This case concerned the method of determining the seaward limit of internal waters from which Norway measured its fisheries zones. The court accepted Norway's position that the baseline should be a series of straight lines drawn between the headlands of indentations on the mainland and running around the outer edge of the farthest offshore islands, rocks, and reefs. In response to an inquiry by the attorney general, Dean Acheson stated the State Department's position that

> the decision of the International Court of Justice in the Fisheries Case does not require the United States to change its previous position with respect to the delimitation of its territorial waters. It is true that some of the principles on which this United States position has been traditionally predicated have been deemed by the Court not to have acquired the authority of a general rule of international law. Among these are the principle that the base line follows the sinuosities of the coast and the principle that in the case of bays no more than 10 miles wide, the base line is a straight line across their opening. These principles, however, are not in conflict with the criteria set forth in the decision of the International Court of Justice. The decision, moreover, leaves the choice of the method of delimitation applicable under such criteria to the national state. The Department accordingly adheres to its statement of the position of the United States with respect to the delimitation of its territorial waters on date of November 13, 1951.[36]

113

In hearings on the Submerged Lands Act and the subsequent outer continental shelf legislation, the deputy legal advisor of State argued the case for asserting jurisdiction, as had been done in the Truman Proclamation, over the natural resources of the seabed rather than laying claim to the seabed itself. The case was twofold. The earlier claim had not been protested and any change now in the U.S. position would simply stir up and confuse other nations.[37] Secondly, there was no reason to claim more than was absolutely necessary.[38]

While the positions of the State and Justice Departments remained consistent from the Truman to the Eisenhower administrations, those of the Navy and the Interior Department did not. The new secretary of defense, C. E. Wilson, was asked in February whether he differed "from the views expressed by the Secretaries of Defense Forrestal, Marshall, Johnson, Lovett, and other officials of the Defense Department as to the necessity for the control and management of the mineral resources of submerged lands of the marginal sea by the Federal Government." Defense Secretary Wilson evaded the question in his answer by pleading ignorance of the views of his predecessors and stressing the "necessity of development of oil reserves wherever they may be located and under whatever administration."[39] Similarly, the new secretary of the navy backed off from earlier department support for a naval petroleum reserve. He simply referred the question to the attorney general.[40]

Douglas McKay, the new secretary of the interior, departed even more clearly from the policy of his predecessor. In hearings before the Interior and Insular Affairs Committee, McKay expressed his willingness to see restored "to the various states the coastal offshore lands to the limits of the line marked by the historical boundaries of each of the respective States."[41] Moreover, McKay seemed to have no misgivings as to whether these lands should extend beyond a national limit of three miles. Clearly McKay's view and that of Defense Secretary Wilson reflected the approach of their president.

THE PRESIDENT AND THE CONGRESS. Eisenhower, while noting his respect for the right of the Departments of State and Justice to distinguish between outright ownership of land and mineral rights, nonetheless pursued a clear policy of (a) restoring ownership to the states, and (b) allowing Congress or the courts to determine the limits of ownership.[42] With such clear-cut presidential support, congressional proponents of state ownership were bound to prevail.

THE SUBMERGED LANDS ACT. Hearings on quitclaim legislation were pressed to a conclusion in March. On April 1, the House of Representatives voted on and passed H.R. 4198 (285 yes, 108 no, 38 not voting). The Senate moved S.J. Res. 13 to the floor where it became bogged down in extensive floor debate and filibusters. On April 24, President Eisenhower wrote Senator Anderson urging "prompt passage" of the submerged lands bill. S.J. Res 13 was finally passed by voice vote in the Senate and was signed into law by the president on May 22.[43]

In brief, the Submerged Lands Act recognized state ownership of the lands beneath inland navigable waters and gave the states title to the bed of the territorial sea within their boundaries. By a floor amendment,[44] the definition of boundaries was subjected to a maximum limit of three miles from the coast in the Atlantic or Pacific or three leagues (nine geographical miles) in the Gulf of Mexico. In this manner, the Congress disregarded the State Department's concern with the foreign policy consequences of claims beyond three miles and the attorney general's request that Congress set a definitive boundary to avoid future lengthy litigation. The State Department's views were taken into account, however, in the formula for determining the baseline from which state ownership would be measured. The coastline was defined as the ordinary low-water line on the open coast, and it marked the seaward limit of inland waters.[45] The Submerged Lands Act adopted a dual approach to (1) the ownership of the offshore lands and (2) the right to develop and use them. Both these rights were assigned to the states. Thus, if the law were subsequently found to be unconstitutional on the grounds that federal ownership was inalienable, the states would still enjoy the right to develop and use these areas. A number of elaborate separability provisions were specified in the act to protect the grant of management rights in the event that the grant of title should be held unconstitutional.

Due to poor draftsmanship as well as to the opposition of a number of inland states, the Submerged Lands Act proved the object of subsequent contention and litigation.[46] Its drafting shortcomings are attributable in part to poor coordination of amendments in committee and on the floor as well as to an unwillingness on the part of its proponents to depart significantly from the measure vetoed by President Truman for fear that the new president might use any such departure as an excuse for reneging on his campaign promise to sign such a bill.[47] As we have seen, such fears were unfounded as President Eisenhower was positively enthusiastic about the measure.

THE OUTER CONTINENTAL SHELF LANDS ACT. As initially proposed in the House of Representatives, H.R. 4198 had a second part which dealt with the management of the continental shelf beyond the submerged lands awarded to the states. The Senate, however, preferred to deal with the two areas separately and thus the outer continental shelf, as it came to be known, was deferred to separate legislation (H.R. 5134 and S. 1901, 83rd Cong., 1st sess.). Hearings on the Outer Continental Shelf Lands Act took place first in the House and then in the Senate and continued from April to the beginning of June. The international aspects of the proposed legislation related to the extent of the claim as well as to its substance. The deputy legal advisor testified on behalf of the State Department. The Department opposed the use of the term "sovereignty," preferring instead the designation "jurisdiction and control." Moreover, the State Department preferred to limit governmental jurisdiction and control to the resources of the continental shelf rather than laying claim to the seabed itself. The Senate Interior and Insular Affairs Committee reported the bill out in June.

On August 7, the Outer Continental Shelf Lands Act was signed into law by the President.[48] It was the first federal act authorized the leasing of offshore lands. As finally enacted, the bill provided "that the subsoil and seabed of the outer continental shelf appertain to the United States and are subject to its jurisdiction, control, and power of disposition," and it authorized the secretary of the interior to lease such lands. Thus while the State Department had succeeded in striking the term "sovereignty" from the claim, it did not succeed in restricting its scope to the resources of the seabed alone. In this regard the Outer Continental Shelf Lands Act went beyond the Truman Proclamation on the continental shelf which it purported to implement. The State Department had obviously impressed upon the drafters the importance of the nation's maritime interests, since the bill stressed the point that the claim "does not in anywise affect the character as high seas of the waters above that seabed and subsoil nor their use with respect to navigation and fishing."[49] The geographic extent of the outer continental shelf claim was also consistent with the Truman Proclamation on the shelf. The inner boundary was defined as the subsoil and seabed appertaining to the United States seaward of the "lands beneath navigable waters" disposed of by the Submerged Lands Act (Sec. 2, 43 U.S.C. 1331). The outer boundary was defined as "the point where the continental slope leading to the true ocean bottom begins. This point is generally regarded as a depth of approximately 100 fathoms, or 600 feet, more or less."[50]

With the promulgation of the Submerged Lands Act and the Outer Continental Shelf Lands Act in 1953, the Truman Proclamation on the continental shelf was at last implemented legislatively.[51] The visions of great wealth in these offshore areas had stimulated this policy and for the time being the government of the United States (if not all the states) was satisfied with its new acquisition. The report of the Senate Committee on Interior and Insular Affairs estimated that the outer continental shelf covered an area of 261,000 square statute miles, or about one tenth of the land area of the U.S.[52] The president gloated that even with the recognition of state claims, the federal government had acquired vastly more in the way of petroleum wealth. "Whereas Louisiana . . . had 250 million barrels of oil within its boundary, the federal government, on its section of the continental shelf off the Louisiana coast, retained 3.75 billion barrels of oil. Whereas Texas, within its three-league limit, has 1.2 billion barrels, the United States government, in its section of the shelf off the Texas coast, retained 7.8 billion."[53] Satisfaction with the newly acquired riches of the continental shelf to a depth of 100 fathoms was short-lived, as we shall see. Within the space of five years, the United States joined with other nations in agreement on an open-ended definition of the outer limit of the national continental shelf.

INTERNATIONAL ASPECTS

The Pattern of Claim and Response

The reaction of other nations to the Truman Proclamation on fisheries has been reviewed in Chapter 3.[54] Several conclusions emerge from that pattern of claim and response. In the first place, there is an obvious relationship between the type of claim made and the offshore resource situation of a nation. Secondly, even where countries did not possess broad continental margins or abundant petroleum resources (such as those on the west coast of Latin America), they nonetheless laid claim to the continental shelf in order to strengthen their claims to offshore fisheries or waters of primary interest. And, finally, the ensuing protests from the maritime countries were directed at those claims affecting high seas rights beyond a narrow territorial sea, not at the claims to the continental shelves. Indeed, the United States and the United Kingdom set the pattern for continental shelf claims by their own examples. The result was that the customary law on the doctrine of national jurisdiction over the continental shelf evolved rapidly until it was widely accepted by the early 1950s. Fisheries and territorial sea claims, however, remained the object of sharp dispute.

A summary review of the continental shelf claims following the Truman Proclamations indicates the broad measure of agreement as well as the areas of divergence in continental shelf claims. In the first year after the Truman Proclamations, Mexico,[55] Panama,[56] and Argentina[57] claimed their continental shelves as national territory. Of the three, Argentina went the furthest in claiming "sovereignty, property rights and incorporation of the shelf and sea as national territory." The Mexican and Panamanian interest was clearly in control over offshore fisheries and the establishment of territorial claims vis-à-vis other nations. Argentina, on the other hand, had a long-standing interest in its extensive continental margin as well as its offshore fisheries. In 1947 and 1948, Chile, Peru, and Costa Rica declared national sovereignty over the continental shelf and seas to a distance of 200 miles from shore. The primary concern of each of these states was in controlling fishery resources off its shores. The inclusion of a reference to the continental shelf claim was, at least at the outset, designed to strengthen the general claim by appearing to emulate the Truman Proclamations. The United States and the United Kingdom protested these claims vigorously insofar as they purported to established coastal-state rights in the high seas. In 1949, Costa Rica modified its claim to one of sovereignty over the continental shelf and rights and interests in the waters off its shores.

During this period, the British played a significant role in limiting the forms of coastal-state claims by means of precedents set through its own policies and those of its dependencies.[58] From 1948 to 1950, Britain laid claim to the continental shelves off a number of its dependencies. In the Caribbean, Britain claimed the seabed and subsoil of the continental shelf off the Bahamas,[59] Jamaica,[60] and British Honduras.[61] The boundaries of the Falkland Islands were also extended to include the continental shelf contiguous to their coasts.[62] On January 10, 1949, the king of Saudi Arabia issued a "Royal Pronouncement concerning the subsoil and sea-bed of the high seas of the Persian Gulf." A number of Arab states under British protection followed suit and issued "Proclamations with respect to the sea-bed and subsoil of the high seas of the Persian Gulf." They were Bahrein (June 5), Qatar (June 8), Abu Dhabi (June 10), Kuwait (June 12), Dubai (June 14), Sharja (June 10), Ras el Khaimad (June 17), Umm al Taiwan (June 20), and Ajman (June 20). Each of the Middle Eastern states had a clear and direct concern with establishing control over the petroleum resources of the shallow Persian Gulf. The Caribbean states were concerned with protecting living resources as well as potential offshore mineral resources. In all of these actions, a principal interest was to delimit boundaries that might be at issue between two or more states so that exploitation of offshore resources might proceed unclouded by jurisdictional uncertainties. The choice of the continental shelf concept as a vehicle for resolving boundary delimitation questions reflected Britain's prevailing concern to preserve the high seas status of waters beyond three miles from shore.

The United States had pursued a less consistent policy than the British throughout the 1930s and 1940s. By the end of the 1940s, however, a fairly clear maritime orientation began to emerge in the foreign policy actions of the U.S. government. With the creation of the Office of the Special Assistant to the Under Secretary of Fisheries and Wildlife, two offices within the State Department managed law of the sea matters. The special assistant's office had responsibility for international fisheries negotiations and the Office of the Legal Advisor handled all other law of the sea issues. Given the direct relationship of fisheries questions to other ocean issues, this division of responsibility inevitably led to different emphases and occasionally to policy conflicts.[63] The overall thrust of U.S. policy by the 1950s, however, was clearly maritime and global in orientation. Domestically, continental shelf issues commanded greater congressional and executive branch attention than did fisheries matters.[64] Whereas the Submerged Lands Act and the Outer Continental Shelf Lands Act implemented the Truman Proclamation on the continental shelf, no similar action was taken on behalf of the fisheries proclamation. The growing prominence of a distant-water orientation in fisheries reflected the fact that newly developed U.S. tuna and shrimp interests had counterbalanced traditional coastal fishing interests. It also reflected an evolving preoccupation with national security based on a global view of U.S. interests.

By 1950 the Department of State had begun systematically communicating its views on acceptable law of the sea policies to other nations. In some instances the diplomatic pressures brought to bear by the United States and Britain, as well as the careful precedents set by the British, were successful in diverting the process of claims from the paths taken by Argentina, Chile, and Peru. In 1949 and 1950, for instance, a number of countries revised or adopted new offshore claims that were acceptable to the maritime countries. Mexico revised its earlier continental shelf claim, while Pakistan,[65] Nicaragua,[66] and Brazil[67] claimed their continental shelves to the depth of 200 meters or 100 fathoms.

Less to British and American liking were claims made by Honduras and El Salvador. In March of 1950, Honduras claimed as part of its national territory "the submarine platform or continental and insular shelf, and the waters which cover it, in both the Atlantic and Pacific Oceans, whatever be its depth and however far it extends." To make matters worse, Honduras went on to claim a twelve-mile territorial sea,[68] which it subsequently eliminated in 1951.[69] The pronouncements of El Salvador were even more sweeping. Going beyond even the Chilean and Peruvian claims, El Salvador claimed that the territory of the Republic "includes the adjacent seas to a distance of two hundred marine miles from the low-water mark and comprises the corresponding aerial space, subsoil and continental shelf."[70] Inconsistencies inherent in the Salvadoran claim have led to the conclusion that what was being claimed was not a 200-mile territorial sea. This view has been reinforced by subsequent Salvadoran practice.[71]

In February 1951, Ecuador promulgated a more sophisticated set of offshore claims designed to assert national jurisdiction to the furthest extent possible while stretching the bounds of evolving customary law to the utmost. Ecuador claimed the continental shelf to a depth of 200 meters, "control and protection of the fisheries appertaining thereto," and a territorial sea of twelve miles measured from straight baselines linking outlying islands and points on the coast. By reference to the treaty of Mutual Assistance, the possibility of claims to even larger areas for maritime policing or protection was held open.[72] The ensuing U.S. protest was directed against Ecuador's claim to straight baselines, a twelve-mile territorial sea, and the fishery resources of the waters over the continental shelf. It did not take issue with the claim to the continental shelf per se or with the claim to an area of maritime protection.

The pattern of claim and response up to and through the early 1950s indicates the areas of agreement and disagreement developing in the law of the sea. National rights to the continental shelf, in some form and to some distance, were generally accepted. On the other hand, there was disagreement on claims affecting the high seas beyond a narrow territorial sea, such as claims to a broader territorial sea, to straight baselines, or to control of high seas fisheries.

Multilateral Approaches

Unilateral efforts to determine the evolution of customary law of the sea were supplemented in the early 1950s by multilateral efforts. The purpose of these international gatherings, from the point of view of national delegates, was to develop a record in favor of each group's preferred point of view. The alternative forums for discussion were the subsidiary bodies of the Organization of American States (OAS) and the universal United Nations bodies such as the Food and Agriculture Organization, the International Law Commission, and the General Assembly.

The Inter-American Juridical Council of the OAS took up law of the sea deliberations in the early 1950s. It quickly became apparent that this and other inter-American bodies would be dominated by those states making extensive offshore claims. In 1952, for instance, the extreme position on offshore claims dominated the nine-member Inter-American Juridical Committee. It passed a draft convention that would recognize the "exclusive sovereignty" of a coastal state over the continental shelf, superjacent waters and airspace, and recognized the right of a state to establish "an area of protection, control, and economic exploitation to a distance of 200 miles."[73]

The United States was similarly outvoted in 1956 at the Mexico meeting of the Inter-American Council of Jurists preparatory to the Ciudad Trujillo Conference on the "Conservation of Natural Resources: The Continental Shelf and Marine Waters." On this occasion the final draft resolution was somewhat milder, reflecting an effort to garner the support of a larger number of Latin American states. Nonetheless, it rejected the concept of a uniform three-mile territorial sea and declared the right of each state to establish its territorial waters according to its national needs and situation. The draft resolution also provided for the use of straight baselines from which to measure territorial waters and for the coastal state's right to exclusively exploit the fisheries off its coasts. The resolution was pressed to a vote and passed over United States objections by a vote of 15 to 1 with 5 abstentions. Only concerted last-minute efforts succeeded in demoting the resolution from the status of a resolution to that of a preparatory study.

At the ensuing Ciudad Trujillo Conference, the United States was more successful in getting its views on the record. By dint of vigorous diplomatic efforts and threats to withdraw from the OAS altogether, U.S. representatives succeeded in moving the conference to a resolution that merely recorded the existing areas of agreement and disagreement as to national claims over offshore areas. The Ciudad Trujillo resolution is of particular interest as an accurate statement of the state of customary law of the sea in 1956. The only area in which there was substantial agreement was on the breadth of the continental shelf. The definition accepted at Ciudad Trujillo and subsequently incorporated in the Geneva Convention on the Continental Shelf was that the continental shelf extended to the depth of 200 meters or beyond that to depths admitting of exploitation. With regard to the juridical regime applicable to the waters over the shelf or to the living resources that might appertain to the shelf, the resolution noted the absence of agreement. Similarly, the resolution noted the "diversity of positions" among participating states on the issue of the breadth of the territorial sea as well as differences over coastal-state rights to control offshore fishery resources.

Apart from its single success at Ciudad Trujillo, the United States found itself increasingly isolated within the OAS deliberations on law of the sea. As this became apparent, U.S. officials worked to move law of the sea discussions to universal United Nations bodies where the U.S. exercised a greater measure of influence. In 1955, the U.S. succeeded in moving fisheries discussions into a conference of the Food and Agriculture Organization (FAO) at Rome which elaborated guidelines for a moderate fisheries policy. And in the early 1950s, the U.S. was among those supporting the efforts of the General Assembly and the International Law Commission to resolve the territorial sea and continental shelf questions. A measure of U.S. success in internationalizing the law of the sea is evident in the fact that although the Ciudad Trujillo resolution recommended that the American states continue efforts to resolve their differences, the OAS did not resume consideration of law of the sea matters until 1971.

The International Law Commission

The activities of the International Law Commission (ILC) laid the groundwork for the first two United Nations conferences on the law of the sea (UNCLOS I and II). Indeed, its deliberations represented the first systematic multilateral effort to deal with law of the sea matters under United Nations auspices.[74] The ILC was established in 1947[75] to fulfill the mandate of Article 13 of the UN charter, "To initiate studies and make recommendations for the purpose of . . . encouraging the progressive development of international law and its codification." Composed initially of fifteen eminent international lawyers elected by the General Assembly,[76] the ILC held its first meeting in 1949. At this session, a provisional list of fourteen topics was selected for codification and sent out for government comments.[77] Two law of the sea items were among the fourteen: the regime of the high seas and the regime of territorial waters. On the basis of General Assembly recommendations and direct governmental responses, the ILC adopted both of these areas for consideration: the high seas (including the contiguous zone and the continental shelf) and the territorial sea. The ILC accorded priority to its work on the high seas regime and on two other items not related to law of the sea. The territorial sea was ranked fourth in priority. Work on the high seas item began in 1950 and was completed in 1956. In the intervening period the commission published two draft resolutions on the high seas based on six reports by a special rapporteur and comments by governments.[78] In 1951 the commission adopted a set of draft articles on high seas matters, including the continental shelf and resources. This was circulated to national governments for comments on the basis of which the ILC prepared a second draft in 1953. That draft resolution dealt with the continental shelf, resources of the high seas, sedentary fisheries and the contiguous zone.[79] ILC work on the regime of the territorial sea began in 1952 on the basis of a report by the special rapporteur dealing with baselines and bays. Issues pertaining to the territorial sea included the issue of an appropriate breadth, the manner of drawing baselines, methods of delimiting boundaries between adjacent or opposite states, the treatment of islands and internal waters, innocent passage, and passage through international straits. In 1954, the ILC completed work on provisional articles on territorial sea issues and forwarded them to national governments for comment. On the basis of their replies, the ILC drew up its final report on the regime of the territorial sea and the regime of the high seas in 1956.

The 1953 draft ILC articles on the high seas had been accompanied by a recommendation that the United Nations convene a general conference on the law of the sea. However, the General Assembly was not prepared at the time to hold a single conference on law of the sea questions. In 1954, it voted instead to convene an FAO fisheries conference in Rome the following year. Moreover, the efforts of the State Department legal advisor's office to prod the General Assembly to vote separately on the continental shelf question were to no avail. The General Assembly resolved to refer all law of the sea issues back to the ILC for further consideration. Thus, while the FAO conference dealt with fisheries matters, the ILC once again reviewed the issues of the high seas, territorial seas, continental shelf, and the whole range of boundary and delimitation problems.

The 1956 ILC report consisted of seventy-three articles divided into two parts.[80] The first part included a general section, a section on the limits of the territorial sea, and a section on innocent passage. The second part included sections on the general regime of the high seas, the contiguous zone, and the continental shelf. On the difficult question of the breadth of the territorial sea, the commission members were unable to agree upon a limit between three and twelve miles. The commission noted that although national practice was not uniform, "international law does not permit an extension of the territorial sea beyond twelve miles" (Art. 3). The commission defined the term high seas as "all parts of the sea that are not included in the territorial sea . . .

or in the internal waters of a State" (Art. 26). "The high seas being open to all nations, no State may validly purport to subject any part of them to its sovereignty. Freedom of the high seas comprises, *inter alia*: (1) freedom of navigation; (2) freedom of fishing; (3) freedom to lay submarine cables and pipelines; (4) freedom to fly over the high seas" (Art. 27).

Similarly, the commission offered a definition of the legal continental shelf. "The term 'continental shelf' is used as referring to the seabed and subsoil of the submarine areas adjacent to the coast but outside the area of the territorial sea, to a depth of 200 meters (approximately 100 fathoms),[81] or, beyond that limit, to where the depth of the superjacent waters admits of the exploitation of the natural resources of the said areas" (Art. 67). With regard to these areas the coastal state has "sovereign rights for the purpose of exploring and exploiting its natural resources" (Art. 68), but those rights "do not affect the legal status of the superjacent waters as high seas, or that of the airspace above those waters" (Art. 69).

The ILC had been considering the regime of the continental shelf since 1950. By 1956, there was agreement among the commission members on the need for a new legal regime to accommodate the fact of increasing coastal-state activities in offshore seabed areas. Differences of opinion existed, however, on three questions: (1) the extent of the legal continental shelf; (2) the nature of coastal-state rights in that area; (3) the resources comprised within the concept of "continental shelf resources." In its final draft, the commission either sought a compromise of these differences or deferred the problem to an international conference.

EXTENT OF THE CONTINENTAL SHELF. Records of the ILC indicate that three principal alternatives were under consideration as to the breadth of the national continental shelf.[82] The first would limit the shelf to the area reaching a depth of 200 meters. The second would allow the national shelf to extend to that point "where the depth of the superjacent waters admits of the exploitation of the natural resources of the seabed and subsoil." The third would establish a continental shelf extending some minimum distance from the shore (such as twenty miles) for the benefit of those countries whose continental shelves sloped steeply away from the coastline. Each of these several definitions was considered but found defective in one respect or other.

In the 1951 draft resolution of the ILC, the definition used was that relating to the depth of exploitability. The advantage of this was seen to be its flexibility and the fact that it would be more acceptable to

countries with narrow margins.[83] There was severe criticism of this definition, nonetheless, and in the 1953 ILC draft resolution the commission reverted to a geological definition restricting the outer edge of the
national continental shelf to a depth of 200 meters.[84] This definition
had its difficulties as well for it would afford vastly different offshore
areas to coastal states according to the vagaries of geography. Those
countries without extensive shallow continental shelves, particularly
those claiming 200-mile areas, would feel unjustly circumscribed.[85] The
final formulation adopted by the ILC in 1956 was based on the results
of the Ciudad Trujillo Conference. In an effort to reach an acceptable
compromise of divergent views, the ILC adopted both the fixed outer
limit formula (200 meters depth) and the flexible or moving outer limit
formula (depth-of-exploitability).[86] This definition was forwarded to
the United Nations conference and became the basis for the definition
finally adopted in the Convention on the Continental Shelf in 1958.

COASTAL STATE RIGHTS ON THE SHELF.   The second area of disagreement
within the ILC concerning the continental shelf doctrine was the nature of the rights that the coastal state would enjoy over the shelf. The
United States position in the debate coincided with the more restrictive
concept of national rights. The Truman Proclamation had called for
jurisdiction and control over the resources of the continental shelf, and
the Outer Continental Shelf Lands Act provided for national jurisdiction and control of the subsoil and seabed of the outer continental shelf.
Latin American nations, for their part, wanted to apply the concept of
sovereignty to the continental shelf and had so specified in their various
national claims. The ILC position on this question shifted slightly over
time. In 1951, the draft resolution on the continental shelf referred to
national control and jurisdiction. By 1953, however, the ILC had modified that to "sovereign rights for purposes of exploring and exploiting"
the resources of the shelf. This formulation was acceptable to the U.S.
and others and was retained in the final 1956 draft and forwarded to
the 1958 conference. It represented an effort at compromise between
the two extremes represented among coastal nations and was ultimately
incorporated in Article 2 of the 1958 Convention on the Continental
Shelf.

CONTINENTAL SHELF RESOURCES.   The third area of uncertainty in the
formulation of the new doctrine of the continental shelf was the issue
of exactly which resources pertained to the continental shelf and which
did not. The 1951 ILC draft resolution on the continental shelf limited
shelf resources to the mineral resources of the seabed and subsoil. In

1953, however, the ILC report extended shelf resources to include the sedentary fisheries of the continental shelf. (Although the executive branch of the U.S. government had not favored such a definition of shelf resources, the Submerged Lands Act passed in the same year had incorporated sedentary fisheries within the continental shelf rights of the various states of the country.) In its final report, the ILC referred to the natural resources of the continental shelf without defining the term. It preferred that the task of "examination of the scientific aspects of that question should be left to the experts" (Art. 68, Commentary). The commentary to the commission's 1956 report did, however, describe sedentary fisheries as those permanently attached to the bed of the sea, although it failed to define "attached." Ultimately, Article 2 of the Convention on the Continental Shelf encompassed within its view of continental shelf resources "the mineral and other non-living resources of the seabed and subsoil together with living organisms belonging to sedentary species, that is to say, organisms which, at the harvestable stage, either are immobile on or under the seabed or are unable to move except in constant physical contact with the seabed or the subsoil."

With the submission of its second comprehensive report in 1956, the International Law Commission proposed for a second time that an international conference be convened to consider law of the sea questions, and, where agreement was possible, to draw up the appropriate international conventions. Unlike in 1954, the General Assembly was now prepared to authorize such a conference. Following debate in the sixth committee, the General Assembly in February 1957 voted to convene the first United Nations Conference on the Law of the Sea.[87]

THE FIRST AND SECOND UN CONFERENCES ON THE LAW OF THE SEA: 1958 AND 1960

THE FIRST UNITED NATIONS CONFERENCE on the Law of the Sea met in Geneva from February 24 to April 28, 1958. Preparations for the conference had been underway for several years. The International Law Commission had begun its work on law of the sea questions in 1950 and in 1956 had produced a text of seventy-three draft articles which served as the basic working document for the conference. A series of regional meetings in 1955 and 1956 also produced resolutions or recommendations that were considered at the 1958 conference. A further preparatory input were the debates held in the Sixth (Legal) Committee of the General Assembly. The General Assembly authorized the secretary general to select experts to assist the Secretariat in the preparation of documents for the conference. And finally, a meeting of the landlocked states immediately prior to the conference resulted in the creation of an additional main committee of the conference.

Evidence of the prevailing East-West conflict was discernible throughout the conference as the principal blocs vied for broad support of their respective positions. Among the contentious issues were the territorial sea and fisheries zone question; the proper means of drawing baselines; and the outer limits of the continental shelf. In some cases contention resulted from cold war issues that were only indirectly related to the work of the conference. The overriding goal of the U.S. government was an international agreement on offshore limits for the territorial sea and a fishing zone. Within this framework, the U.S. delegation had some flexibility, but was constrained from making major concessions by its defense and fishing groups. The United States was able to consider a territorial sea of up to six miles and a twelve-mile contiguous fishing zone.

Due largely to the careful preparatory work of the ILC and the Secretariat, the 1958 conference produced four conventions: (1) a Convention on the Territorial Sea and the Contiguous Zone; (2) a Convention on the High Seas; (3) a Convention on Fishing and Conservation of the Living Resources of the High Seas; and (4) a Convention on the Continental Shelf. Because the conference failed to reach agreement on the breadth of the territorial sea, one of its resolutions was the convening of a second conference. The second conference met in Geneva from March 17 to April 26, 1960, but was also unsuccessful in reaching agreement on the difficult issue of the breadth of the territorial sea and the related fishing zone.

Conference Preparation

International Law Commission

The articles drafted by the International Law Commission served as the basic document for the work of the 1958 Geneva conference. The ILC's interest in the law of the sea can be traced to its first meeting in 1949 where it selected both the regime of the high seas and the regime of the territorial seas as topics whose codification seemed desirable and feasible. The regime of the high seas was included among those subjects given priority and Professor J.P.A. François of the Netherlands was chosen to be special rapporteur. Then, upon the recommendation of the General Assembly,[1] the ILC at its third session (1951) began work on the regime of the territorial sea and appointed Professor François as special rapporteur for that topic as well.

The work of the ILC on the law of the sea proceeded over a period of six years. During that time, a number of drafts were presented to national governments for comment.[2] In addition to government inputs, the ILC was aided in its drafting efforts by the work of several international conferences. The results of the Food and Agriculture Organization (FAO) International Technical Conference on the Living Resources of the Sea held in Rome in 1955 are visible in the ILC's draft articles on fisheries.[3] So, too, are the conclusions of the OAS-sponsored Conference on the Conservation of Marine Resources: Continental Shelf and Marine Waters held in Ciudad Trujillo in 1956. Where the issues had proven politically intractable, as in the cases of the regime of the territorial sea and the management of fishery resources, the ILC had to resort to texts which had been negotiated in broader international forums.[4]

FISHERIES. The FAO International Technical Conference on the Living Resources of the Sea adopted an approach to fisheries management based on international conventions covering the geographical and biological distribution of fisheries populations. While the conference recognized the special interests of the coastal state in maintaining the productivity of the resources of the high seas near to its coast, it did not acknowledge a coastal-state right to establish exclusive offshore fishing zones to claim these resources. The conference report stressed the need for conservation in any rational exploitation of the living resources of the sea and stated that "the principal objective of conservation of the living resources of the seas is to obtain the optimum sustainable yield so as to secure a maximum supply of food and other marine products."[5]

The ILC included twelve articles (49-60) on fishing in Part II of its final draft dealing with the high seas. These articles followed the approach laid out at the Rome conference. Article 49 provided that "all States have the right for their nationals to engage in fishing on the high seas, subject to their treaty obligations and to the provisions contained" in the ILC draft. "Optimum sustainable yield" was adopted from the Rome conference as the criterion for conservation measures (Art. 50). Article 51 imposed an obligation upon the state to adopt conservation measures when necessary where its nationals were fishing alone on the high seas. Where nationals of two or more states were fishing the same stock in the same area of the high seas, the governments were obligated, at the request of any one state, to enter into a conservation agreement (Art. 52). If the states involved did not reach agreement within a reasonable period of time, any of the states could invoke the compulsory arbitration procedure contained in Article 57. If newcomers began fishing the same stocks of fish, the conservation measures adopted should apply to them. If the newcomers did not accept the measures, then the compulsory arbitration procedure could be invoked (Art. 53), and the conservation regulations would remain in force pending a decision.[6]

Article 54 specified that the "coastal State has a special interest in maintaining the productivity of the living resources in the high seas adjacent to its territorial sea." It was, moreover, "entitled to take part on an equal footing in any system of research and regulation in that area," even though its nationals did not fish there. In the event of lack of agreement among the states concerned, appeal could be made to the arbitral procedure. If negotiations did not lead to agreement within a reasonable period of time, a coastal state could unilaterally adopt regulations for offshore conservation provided that three criteria were met: (a) scientific evidence indicating an urgent need for conservation measures was provided, (b) the measures adopted were based on appropriate scientific findings, and (c) the measures did not discriminate against foreign fishermen.

Article 56 established the right of a state to request nations fishing an area in which it had an interest but did not fish itself to adopt conservation measures. Articles 57 to 59 dealt with the resort to an arbitral commission of seven members where a fisheries dispute should arise under Articles 52 through 56. The arbitral commission would have the power to prevent the application of unilateral measures pending its award and its decisions would be binding on the states concerned.

In the preparation of these articles, as in the International Technical Conference in Rome, there was a strong difference of opinion among those states that wished to claim the resources within broad offshore zones of a fixed distance and the major distant-water fishing nations that wanted to prevent an expansion of any coastal-state rights beyond a narrow territorial sea.[7] Although the Rome conference and the ILC had not adopted the U.S. proposal for abstention, the final product of these efforts was acceptable to the United States[8] and other maritime powers. The ILC draft did not recognize claims to fishery or special resource zones. Instead it emphasized the goal of optimum sustainable yield through conservation and the means of internationally negotiated agreements with a resort to compulsory arbitration where negotiations failed.

TERRITORIAL SEA. The preparation of draft articles on the territorial sea raised issues similar to those raised in ILC discussions on fisheries. The major maritime states—the United States and European nations—found themselves defending a narrow territorial limit of three miles. Other nations claimed sovereignty in offshore areas of up to twelve miles and a few Latin American nations claimed as much as 200 miles. The reasons cited for extensive territorial claims were economic need and security considerations. As noted in Chapter 3, the expansionist coastal states had prevailed in all of the OAS meetings up to the Conference on the Conservation of Marine Resources at Ciudad Trujillo in 1956.[9] There, however, the United States succeeded in pushing through a statement that merely recorded the "diversity of positions among the states represented at this Conference with respect to the breadth of the territorial sea."[10] As a result of this diversity, the conference did "not express an opinion concerning the positions of the various participating states on the matters on which agreement has not been reached." The resolution of the Ciudad Trujillo conference coincided in part with the direction that the ILC was then taking in its drafts on the breadth of the territorial sea. The ILC went further than Ciudad Trujillo, however, in rejecting altogether the very extensive claims of the Latin American states.

Within the ILC, the difference of opinion over the width of the territorial sea was limited to a range of three to twelve miles.[11] From the outset of ILC deliberations, various attempts were made to deal with this difference of opinion. In his first report to the commission in 1952, the rapporteur, Professor François, proposed a compromise article in which "the breadth of the belt of sea defined in Article 1 shall be fixed by the coastal State but may not exceed six marine miles."[12] The major maritime powers, in particular the British, were strongly opposed to any proposal that would extend the territorial sea beyond a three-mile limit.[13] Taking account of the strong British reaction, the ILC then adopted a different approach. In its seventh report (1955) on the breadth of the territorial sea, Article 3 stipulated that:

1. The Commission recognizes that international practice is not uniform as regards the traditional limitation of the territorial sea to three miles.
2. The Commission considers that international law does not justify an extension of the territorial sea beyond twelve miles.
3. The Commission, without taking any decision as to the breadth of the territorial sea within that limit, considers that international law does not require States to recognize a breadth beyond three miles.[14]

The 1955 ILC draft is notable for its categorical rejection of territorial sea claims beyond twelve miles, for its references to a "traditional" territorial sea of three miles, and for its strong statement that states claiming three-mile seas need not recognize any greater claims.

This draft went a long way toward satisfying the major maritime countries.[15] The replies of other governments, however, were less favorable. As a result, the 1956 draft of the ILC was more neutral in its formulation. It replaced the earlier statement that countries need not recognize claims greater than three miles with a factual statement to the effect that some countries do not recognize such claims. It also ceased to use three miles as the reference point for traditional international practice. Like the Ciudad Trujillo resolution, it merely noted the diversity of claims. But the 1956 ILC draft did maintain its strong position against territorial sea claims greater than twelve miles.

1. The Commission recognizes that international practice is not uniform as regards the delimitation of the territorial sea.
2. The Commission considers that international law does not permit an extension of the territorial sea beyond twelve miles.
3. The Commission, without taking any decision as to the breadth

of the territorial sea up to that limit, notes on the one hand, that many States have fixed a breadth greater than three miles and, on the other hand, that many States do not recognize such a breadth when that of their own territorial sea is less.

The commission concluded the article by stating "that the breadth of the territorial sea should be fixed by an international conference."[16]

By the end of its eighth session in 1956, the ILC had produced seventy-three draft articles dealing with the territorial sea and contiguous zone, the high seas, the continental shelf, fisheries, and the conservation of living resources. A detailed commentary accompanied the articles and explained the evolution of the ideas behind each article.

The General Assembly

The report of the International Law Commission, including its draft articles, was referred to the Sixth Committee of the United Nations General Assembly. From November 28 to December 20, 1956, the Sixth Committee held a general debate on the commission's report and considered a resolution recommending the holding of an international conference to examine the law of the sea.[17] The draft resolution[18] took up the ILC's recommendation that an international conference should be convened to examine the law of the sea and that the results of its work should be embodied in one or more international conventions or other appropriate instruments. The resolution asked the secretary-general to convene the conference and to "arrange for the necessary staff and facilities which would be required," including the technical services of experts. The resolution further specified that the ILC's report should be referred to the conference "as the basis for its consideration of the various problems involved in the development and codification of the law of the sea," and that the secretary-general should transmit the record of the debates of the General Assembly on this question to the conference. The cosponsors of the draft resolution included among their members those states which were generally satisfied with the ILC report, and which wished to move to an international conference without further substantive preparatory work. This position was espoused most forcefully by the representatives of the United States and the United Kingdom.[19] The opponents of this view wanted to ensure that the ILC report was not the only basic document before the conference. Mexico, for example, objected to "the hasty and premature submission of the draft resolution before us."[20] The particular goal of the latter group was to establish a record of the significant opposition to the three-mile territorial limit. Because the ILC draft did not do this, they urged that more preparatory work be undertaken. Those countries that wished to limit further preparatory efforts to purely administrative and technical considerations were extremely hostile to such proposals.[21]

On February 21, 1957, the General Assembly authorized the convening of a conference on the law of the sea to take place early in March 1958.[22] The resolution as finally drafted attempted a compromise between those wishing further preliminary work and those favoring only administrative and technical preparations. The resolution asked the secretary-general

> to invite appropriate experts to advise and assist the Secretariat in preparing the conference, with the following terms of reference:
> (a) To obtain, in the manner which they think most appropriate, from the governments invited to the conference any further provisional comments that the governments may wish to make on the Commission's report and related matters, and to present to the conference in systematic form any comments made by the governments, as well as the relevant statements made in the Sixth Committee at the eleventh and previous sessions of the General Assembly;
> (b) To present to the Conference recommendations concerning its method of work and procedures, and other questions of an administrative nature;
> (c) To prepare, or arrange for the preparation of, working documents of a legal, technical, scientific or economic nature in order to facilitate the work of the conference.

This approach allowed those governments that were opposed to some of the ILC draft articles to ensure that their views were on the record. Thus, although the resolution stipulated that the ILC report would be referred to the conference as "the basis for its consideration of the various problems in the development and codification of the law of the sea," direct governmental comments plus the verbatim records of the relevant General Assembly debates would also be considered "by the conference in conjunction with the Commission's report."[23]

The Secretariat

As authorized by the General Assembly, the secretary-general selected "appropriate experts" to assist the Secretariat in preparation for the conference. They included representatives from Australia, Chile, Cuba, Czechoslovakia, Egypt, India, Mexico, the Netherlands, the United

Kingdom, and the United States. The first responsibility of the Secretariat and its experts was to solicit further comments on the ILC report or related matters and to present these comments to the conference with the verbatim records of the General Assembly debates. Only twenty governments expressed their views[24] and they were largely those that had already submitted comments on the ILC drafts at earlier stages.

The second task of the Secretariat and its team of experts was to draft the provisional agenda, determine the rules of procedure, set up the committee structure of the conference, and propose methods of work. In fulfillment of this mandate, the secretary-general submitted (1) Provisional Agenda of the Conference (A/CONF.13/9); (2) Provisional Rules of Procedure of the Conference (A/CONF.13/10); (3) Memorandum concerning the Method of Work and Procedures of the Conference (A/CONF.13/11); and (4) Report of the Secretary-General on the Preparation of the Conference (A/CONF.13/20). In brief, these provided that (1) the conference should have four main committees dealing with appropriate portions of the ILC draft while the issue of free access to the sea for landlocked countries would be referred to a special committee; (2) the committees of the conference should arrive at decisions on all issues by a simple majority of representatives present and voting; (3) the conference would take decisions on questions of procedure by a simple majority of those present and voting, but on questions of substance a two-thirds majority of those present and voting would be required; (4) a drafting committee would be established at an early stage.

The third responsibility of the Secretariat and the experts was to prepare or arrange for working documents of a legal, technical, scientific, or economic nature to facilitate the work of the conference. Twenty-four documents were produced under secretariat auspices and distributed to the conference as an Initial List of Documents (A/CONF.13/33.)[25] Included among these were studies on historic bays, the slave trade, pollution of the sea by oil, the rights of landlocked countries, the territorial waters of archipelagoes, decisions of international tribunals on the law of the sea, the principle of abstention, fishing methods, the economic importance of fisheries to various states, and bibliographies of the literature on the law of the sea.

A final input into preparations for the law of the sea conference was made by the landlocked countries that wanted the question of access to the sea included in the agenda. As a result of an amendment submitted by several landlocked states,[26] the Sixth Committee had recommended to the General Assembly that the conference study the question of free access to the sea for landlocked countries. The General Assembly accepted the recommendation but did not provide for a preparatory study on the subject. The Secretariat, in its preparations, specified that the free access question should be referred to a special committee of the conference, and prepared a memorandum on the matter.[27] Unsatisfied, the landlocked countries met from February 10 to 14 and recommended that the committee on the question of free access to the sea be given the status of a main committee. This proposal was accepted by the plenary conference as were the provisional rules of procedure recommended by the Secretariat, and on February 24, 1958, the first UN Conference on the Law of the Sea convened.

THE 1958 CONFERENCE

The first UN Conference on the Law of the Sea brought to Geneva approximately 700 delegates from 86 countries (87 if Egypt and Syria are counted separately) and, as observers, seven specialized agencies[28] and nine intergovernmental organizations. The task of reconciling in a single body of international law the views of these disparate nations and organizations was formidable. In addition to sharp differences over the territorial sea and fisheries issues, the conference participants were at odds on questions only indirectly related to the law of the sea. Due largely to the careful preparatory work of the ILC and the Secretariat, the conference reached agreement on four conventions, one optional protocol, and nine resolutions. The conventions embodied the work of the ILC with relatively few changes. Agreement eluded the conference, however, on the breadth of the territorial sea and the related fishing zone. The political maneuvering surrounding these and other contentious issues before the conference provides an illuminating glimpse of the state of ocean law and politics in the late 1950s.

Conference Politics

POLITICAL DIVISIONS. The predominant political cleavage of the first and second conferences on the law of the sea was that between the East and the West. In addition to the cold war clash, the beginnings of a North-South fissure can be discerned in the anticolonial sentiment evident among the new nations who wished to revise the traditional maritime law to serve their needs. Supplementing these major groupings[29] were numerous smaller constellations based on regional or other considerations.

From the U.S. perspective, the principal antagonist to a satisfactory law of the sea outcome was the Soviet Union.[30] The Soviet Union commanded an Eastern European bloc of ten votes in favor of a twelve-mile territorial sea. In this territorial sea, warships would require prior authorization for innocent passage. A strong Soviet stand on sovereign immunity was joined to an equally firm opposition to compulsory arbitration of disputes.[31] In this and a number of its other policies, the Soviet position coincided with that of the newer nations. In its desire to identify with the developing world, the Soviet bloc expressed appreciation for the position of archipelagic states.[32] Similarly, the Soviet group joined forces with the fourteen landlocked states in support of free access to the sea, a position consistent with the interests of its landlocked satellites in Eastern Europe. Easy ideological points were scored by Soviet opposition to high seas testing of atomic weapons by the United States.[33] Where the Soviet group position did not coincide with that of the newer nations, as in the case of fisheries, it attempted to finesse the issue through conservation schemes not unlike those of the United States.[34]

The newer nations had as a common theme their opposition to a maritime law that had been developed by their former colonial masters. Linked to this was a vigorous commitment to national sovereignty plus an opposition to compulsory dispute settlement. While these attitudes were generalized among the Afro-Asian delegates at the conference,[35] they took concrete form in the specific concerns of the Arab and Latin American States. The ten Arab states were united behind a twelve-mile territorial sea. Under such a regime, the Gulf of Aqaba would be largely comprised of territorial seas and the Straits of Tiran would cease to be an international strait, thereby closing off shipping to the Israeli port of Eilat. Latin American nations encompassed a variety of views, but those with long coastlines shared a concern to protect their coastal fisheries from foreign distant-water fishing and to see their offshore claims recognized in international law.

A number of specific economic or geographic problems were reflected in the policies of individual states. Iceland's substantial dependence on offshore fisheries led to her support for a twelve-mile territorial sea and divided the NATO coalition.[36] Canadian policy combined several elements. While concerned to protect her fisheries from U.S. fishermen to a distance of twelve miles beyond liberally drawn straight baselines,[37] Canada also reflected in her policy "a thirst for recognition as a young, growing and virile leader of world opinion and independence in foreign affairs from the United States."[38] The Philippines and Indonesia opposed virtually all territorial sea proposals in an effort to preserve their claim that waters between the islands of an archipelago should be treated as internal waters and that territorial waters should extend outward from straight baselines drawn between the islands.[39] Burma was concerned to protect herself from Japanese fishing while Morocco and Tunisia were threatened by French fishing.[40]

The United States and the nations of Western Europe and NATO constituted the final major grouping at the conference.[41] This group included major shipping, naval, and fishing nations. As such, they shared a concern to protect maritime mobility and traditional high seas rights. The Western nations differed among themselves, however, on just how to go about protecting maritime freedoms. While the continental Europeans, particularly the French and the Swedes, were conservative in outlook, the United States and the United Kingdom were relatively flexible as to a territorial sea of three to six miles and a contiguous zone of up to twelve miles.[42]

U.S. GOALS. Although somewhat flexible in its means, the U.S. position was quite consistent in its goals and priorities. As articulated repeatedly by Arthur Dean, the head of the U.S. delegation, the U.S. was concerned with military security, commercial navigation, and fishing interests. To increase the breadth of the territorial sea from three to twelve miles would, in the U.S. view, seriously inhibit the operational flexibility of the U.S. fleet and air force because it would close off vital straits in the Aegean and the Eastern Mediterranean, and in Indonesia, the Philippines, and Japan. While surface warships could continue to operate in straits linking international bodies of water, submarines would be required to transit on the surface and airplanes would be denied the right to overfly. This limitation on maritime mobility would be particularly unfortunate just as the U.S. was developing the Polaris submarine which, in the absence of territorial sea extensions, could offer the U.S. a deterrent capability not requiring "complicated base agreements with other countries."[43] U.S. commercial considerations included a fear that the Soviets, as a continental power, were seeking to disrupt free world commerce through their support for a twelve-mile territorial sea. A further U.S. economic concern was to protect both its coastal and its distant-water fishing activities.

The United States sought international agreement on uniform offshore limits for the territorial sea and a fishing zone. Within this framework, the government was willing to be somewhat flexible, but was constrained by defense[44] and fishing interests. The first U.S. effort to reach an acceptable compromise preserved U.S. security interests at the expense of distant-water fishing. It combined a three-mile territorial sea with an additional nine-mile contiguous zone in which the coastal state would enjoy exclusive fishing rights.[45] When it became apparent that a three-mile territorial sea was not internationally saleable, the U.S. then pressed its security concerns by proposing a six-mile territorial sea. Despite the reservations of defense representatives, the delegation was authorized to move beyond its initial support for a three-mile territorial sea. In this second compromise, U.S. and European distant-water fishing interests would be protected by an additional six-mile contiguous zone in which historic fishing rights would be recognized.[46] The second U.S. compromise offered less to coastal fishing nations than its first proposal and was more satisfactory to U.S. and European distant-water fishing interests. Defense interests, on the other hand, were unhappy.

U.S. efforts to reach agreement on an internationally acceptable territorial sea breadth reflected the difficulty of protecting the diverse interests of both allies and domestic interests groups. Given the size and composition of the U.S. delegation, negotiations within the U.S. government to effect these compromises were particularly difficult. The forty-five member delegation reflected a range of public agencies and private interests, and included seven representatives, one alternate representative, one congressional adviser, three senior advisers, twenty-nine other advisers, and four secretarial officers.[47] Government agencies included State, Defense, Interior, Commerce, Treasury, the Federal Communications Commission, and the Atomic Energy Commission. Private interests included U.S. representatives on fisheries commissions, distant-water and coastal fishermen, and communications interests. Of the various U.S. interests, defense and fisheries were the most amply represented.[48] The changing U.S. compromises on territorial seas and fisheries indicate that these two interests were the primary competitors for influence within the U.S. delegation.

CONTENTIOUS ISSUES. The territorial sea and fisheries zone question was the single most intractable law of the sea issue before the conference, requiring a delicate balancing of various domestic and international considerations. The conference was beset with other difficult issues as well. Differences existed over the proper means of drawing baselines to delimit internal waters. The continental shelf issue raised questions of which resources pertained to the shelf and how its outer limits were to be defined. Fisheries discussions revolved around conservation schemes, dispute settlement provisions, and the abstention principle.

Finally, a host of troublesome issues that were only indirectly related to the central work of the conference surfaced. They included membership, piracy, nuclear testing, the Middle East, and landlocked states. For the most part, these were linked to the prevailing cold war struggle.

The first of these obstacles to beset the conference plenary was the argument over membership. Conference participation was limited to members of the UN or of one of its specialized agencies. The absence of mainland China, the German Democratic Republic, North Korea, and North Vietnam was vociferously protested by the Soviet bloc with support from the nonaligned states.[49]

Two cold war issues that troubled the deliberations on the high seas were piracy and nuclear testing. The piracy issue arose with a Soviet bloc effort to have the definition of piracy expanded from the actions of private ships to include acts of public vessels undertaken for political reasons.[50] Their proposal to curtail Chinese nationalist seizures of merchant vessels bound for China was not adopted.[51] The Soviet bloc also led a movement to prohibit nuclear testing on the high seas,[52] a position that had the sympathy of many opponents of nuclear testing. The United States was successful in having the matter referred to the General Assembly.[53]

Another issue arising at the conference was the Arab-Israeli dispute over the straits of Tiran. The Arab stance on a twelve-mile territorial sea must be viewed in the context of the complex Middle Eastern situation. Israeli occupation of the Gaza strip and Sharm el Sheikh was being cited by Arab nations as a reason for opposing innocent passage through the straits of Tiran and for their support of a twelve-mile territorial sea. While the Israelis were being obdurate, the U.S. was attempting to promote both Israeli withdrawal from occupied territories and Israeli navigation rights in the Gulf of Aqaba.[54] The solid Arab support for a twelve-mile territorial sea, added to that of the Soviet bloc, brought to twenty the number of states that were firmly committed to oppose any compromise proposals for lesser distances.

An additional contentious issue with both cold war overtones and geographic aspects was the landlocked states' desire for access to the sea. This problem was compounded when the Soviet bloc came out in support of landlocked access. Neighboring states of Western Europe as well as Yugoslavia were fearful that unfettered transit rights for Soviet satellites would provide the occasion for espionage activities.

Organization and Work of the Conference

Despite the extensive preparatory work of the ILC and the Secretariat, deliberations within the main committees proceeded slowly. Ignoring the secretary-general's recommendation that the main committees limit themselves to short general debate on the issues before them, the four original committees spent a total of fifty-one meetings on general de-

139

bate. In addition, the committees were confronted with 502 amendments or proposals for changing or adding articles. Despite these difficulties, the conference concluded just three days behind schedule, having agreed upon four conventions, one protocol, and nine resolutions. Although extensively debated, the conclusions of the 1956 ILC report were adopted with relatively few changes.

The work of the conference was apportioned among four main committees. The first committee dealt with issues related to the territorial sea and contiguous zone. The second committee was assigned the regime of the high seas. The third committee handled fisheries questions, and the fourth committee was responsible for questions concerning the continental shelf. The work of each committee was directly related to, and in some cases overlapped, that of the other committees. Fisheries problems, for instance, arose in connection with the contiguous zone under consideration in Committee One and the continental shelf in Committee Four, as well as in the Committee Three deliberations. Given coastal-state desires to control offshore marine resources, the fisheries question was troublesome wherever it surfaced. Noneconomic considerations—either political or defense-related—were equally contentious throughout the work of the conference.

COMMITTEE ONE: TERRITORIAL SEA AND CONTIGUOUS ZONE.   The concepts of the territorial sea and the contiguous zone were closely linked in the deliberations of Committee One. The territorial sea provided for a zone of full coastal-state sovereignty (including the airspace and seabed) subject only to the right of innocent passage by other states. The contiguous zone, on the other hand, was intended to allow the coastal state to control specific functions or activities beyond the territorial sea. Given their military and economic implications, these two issues proved to be the most difficult of the conference. The breadth of the territorial sea was perceived to have consequences for the flow of world military and commercial traffic, particularly through international straits that would be overlapped by a twelve-mile territorial sea. The contiguous zone, on the other hand, became a major focus for those states that wanted to extend their control over offshore fishery resources.

The juridical status of the territorial sea as an area of sovereignty was spelled out in Articles 1 and 2 of the ILC proposals on the territorial sea. The commission was unable to reach agreement on the breadth of the territorial sea. Thus, in Article 3, it simply observed that international practice regarding the delimitation of the territorial sea was not uniform, but that "international law does not permit an extension of the territorial sea beyond twelve miles." Within that maximum limit, the commission suggested "that the breadth of the territorial sea should be fixed by an international conference."[55]

The ILC also spelled out the special rights that the coastal state might exercise in the contiguous zone, including "the control necessary to (a) prevent infringement of its customs, fiscal or sanitary regulations within the territory or territorial sea; (b) punish infringement of the above regulations committed within its territory or territorial sea" (Art. 66). The ILC set an outer limit on the contiguous zone of twelve miles. If the breadth of the territorial sea were to be resolved at twelve miles, a contiguous zone would become unnecessary under the ILC formulation.

The issue of the territorial sea boundary proved no more soluble for the conference than it had been for the ILC. A number of coastal states sought to protect offshore fisheries and to create security zones either by revising the status of the contiguous zone or by pushing the territorial sea out as far as possible or by some combination of these two methods. The maritime states and those with distant-water fishing interests resisted such efforts to reduce the extent of the high seas.

Thirteen basic proposals were presented to Committee One on the limit of the territorial sea,[56] and all were closely linked to a contiguous fisheries zone. None succeeded, in committee or in plenary, in commanding the necessary conference majority. Of the many proposals before the committee, four main proposals reflect the range of views represented at the conference. The United States introduced a revised proposal[57] that stipulated a six-mile territorial sea and a six-mile fishery zone, with the proviso that states that had fished for a period of at least five years in the outer six-mile area would continue to have the right to do so.[58] The Canadians, fearful of the access that such a proposal would grant to Canadian fisheries, proposed a six-mile territorial sea with an additional six-mile exclusive fishery zone.[59] The third proposal was initially advanced by Mexico and India and subsequently adapted to one advanced by Mexico, Burma, Colombia, Indonesia, Morocco, Saudi Arabia, the United Arab Republic, and Venezuela. It provided that states determine the breadth of their territorial sea up to twelve miles. Where a state claimed less than a twelve-mile territorial sea, it could claim an exclusive contiguous fishing zone of up to twelve miles.[60] The fourth major proposal, advanced by the Soviet Union, provided that each state could determine the width of its territorial sea up to twelve miles.[61]

None of the four full proposals received the necessary simple majority in first committee voting.[62] The Canadian proposal, however, was voted on paragraph by paragraph. While its section on a territorial sea was defeated, the twelve-mile contiguous zone was adopted (37 to 25 with 9 abstentions). Thus the first committee could only report to plenary a twelve-mile fishing zone under Article 3. Adoption of articles in plenary required a two-thirds majority, so a resolution of the territorial sea limit was even more difficult there than in Committee One. The U.S. proposal received the largest number of votes but fell seven votes short of the required two-thirds majority. The Canadian proposal on a twelve-mile contiguous fishing zone was defeated in plenary. The coalition proposal authorizing a territorial sea of up to twelve miles received only a one vote majority. And the Soviet proposal was defeated again.

Other delimitation questions, such as the drawing of baselines and the status of bays, proved more manageable than the outer limit of the territorial sea. The baseline serves as the point from which the territorial sea or contiguous zone is measured. Coastal states seek to increase their offshore jurisdiction by various formulae designed to move the baseline further from shore. The ILC submitted two articles concerning baselines; Article 4 on "normal baselines" and Article 5 on "straight baselines." The baseline for normal situations was generally regarded as the low-water line along the coast and the substance of the ILC article to this effect was adopted and became Article 3 of the convention. The use of straight baselines for irregular coasts, however, was more contentious. The ILC had adopted, in Article 5, the approach of the International Court of Justice (ICJ) in the "Anglo-Norwegian Fisheries Case."[63] This specified that, when a coastline was deeply indented or cut into and there were islands in the vicinity, a straight baseline might be used to link appropriate points as long as it did not depart appreciably from the general direction of the coast. Where the straight baseline enclosed as internal waters areas that had formerly been part of the high seas or territorial sea, a right of innocent passage would apply.

Eighteen states submitted amendments to the ILC's article on straight baselines. Most of these were states opposed to extending the territorial sea beyond a narrow limit. After informal negotiations, the opponents of the ILC formulation united behind an amended version of a British proposal[64] which was designed to reduce the number of situations in which straight baselines might be used and to retain preexisting rights in areas newly brought under a straight baseline regime. Although the British proposal survived voting in the committee,[65] it did not obtain the required two-thirds majority in plenary.

Proponents of narrow offshore claims were equally unsuccessful in their effort to restrict the length of straight baselines, or closing lines, used to delimit bays. The ILC had proposed a formula for limiting bays to "well-marked indentations" and the use of a closing line of fifteen miles (Art. 7). If the mouth of a bay exceeded fifteen miles, a fifteen-mile line could be drawn within the bay to enclose the maximum area of internal waters. Narrow territorial sea advocates, including the United Kingdom, Greece, the Federal Republic of Germany and the United States proposed that the maximum limit of the closing line be ten miles.[66] Instead, the conference, both in the first committee and plenary, adopted twenty-four-mile closing lines for bays as advocated by the Soviet Union, Poland, Bulgaria, and Guatemala.[67] These closing lines were to apply within as well as across the mouths of bays.[68]

Consideration of the substantive aspects of the territorial sea evoked roughly the same maritime and coastal-state coalitions as did the boundary and delimitation issues. The ILC articles (1 and 2) on the juridical status of the territorial sea, the superjacent airspace, and the seabed were adopted without significant changes. Differences arose, however, over the meaning of innocent passage and the attendant questions of coastal-state and third-party rights and duties. The ILC draft article (15) on the "meaning of the right of innocent passage" defined it as passage that "does not use the territorial sea for committing any acts prejudicial to the security of the coastal states." This single criterion of innocent passage was attacked by coastal states as providing insufficient protection for coastal interests. In the final outcome, the reference to specific acts was dropped and additional criteria were added to the effect that passage itself could not be prejudicial to the "peace and good order" of the coastal state.[69] The ILC provision that submarines were required to navigate on the surface was retained with the additional provision that they must show the flag when transiting a territorial sea.

Maritime states were more successful in their efforts to protect their navigation rights in straits used for international navigation. The original ILC article (17) provided that "there must be no suspension of the innocent passage of foreign ships through straits normally used for international navigation between two parts of the high seas." The maritime nations strongly resisted the limitation of international straits to (a) those linking two parts of the high seas and (b) those "normally" used for international navigation. A principal concern of the U.S. was that, under the ILC formulation, the straits of Tiran leading to the Gulf of Aqaba might be closed to shipping to the Israeli port of Eilat.[70] A proposal by the Netherlands, Portugal, and the United Kingdom[71] altering these provisions narrowly made it through Committee One (31 in favor, 30 opposed, 10 abstaining) and into the final convention.[72] The convention provides that "there shall be no suspension of the innocent passage of foreign ships through straits which are used for international navigation between one part of the high seas and another part of the high seas or the territorial sea of a foreign state."[73]

The NATO nations and other maritime and naval powers were also successful on the troublesome issue of whether warships were required to get coastal state authorization in order to traverse a territorial sea. The ILC had proposed in its Article 24 that "the coastal state may make the passage of warships through the territorial sea subject to previous authorization or notification." This provision was defended by the Soviet bloc nations as well as by many of the developing nations and nations bordering straits.[74] The major maritime nations fought unsuccessfully in Committee One to remove the requirement for authorization. In plenary, however, the naval powers succeeded by a vote of 50 to 24 with 5 abstentions in having the word "authorization" removed from the text. In response, the proponents of prior authorization succeeded in mustering a two-thirds majority against an article requiring only notification for the transit of a warship.[75] The final convention, therefore, made no mention of either prior notification or authorization for the passage of warships through the territorial sea.

The Convention on the Territorial Sea and Contiguous Zone reflected the extensive preparatory work of the ILC and a great deal of hard bargaining over troublesome issues. It provided for a twelve-mile contiguous zone for limited (i.e., nonfishery) purposes and a territorial sea of undetermined distance but not to exceed twelve miles. It authorized the use of straight baselines to enclose internal waters, including areas within bays less than 24 miles wide. It prescribed extensive rules for innocent passage and forbad the suspension of passage for foreign ships passing through international straits linking two parts of the high seas or linking the territorial waters of another state to the high seas.

The failure to reach agreement on the breadth of the territorial sea was regarded by many as the major weakness of the 1958 conventions. To rectify this defect, the conference recommended that the Thirteenth General Assembly (1958) consider convening a second conference to deal with the breadth of the territorial sea and the contiguous zone. The resolution was adopted 48 to 2 with 26 abstentions.

COMMITTEE TWO: THE HIGH SEAS. The work of Committee Two on the regime of the high seas was less controversial than the work of Committee One. The second committee was charged with the definition of the high seas and high seas freedoms, the nationality and status of ships, safety and rights of navigation, visit and hot pursuit, illegal acts such as piracy and slavery, and the prevention of pollution. The definition of the high seas related directly to the work of Committee One since, as provided by the ILC and adopted by the conference, the high seas were defined as all parts of the sea that are not included in the territorial sea or internal waters of a state. Equally acceptable was the ILC language (Art. 27) specifying that "the high seas being open to all nations, no State may validly purport to subject any part of them to its sovereignty."

It was more difficult to agree upon which high seas freedoms, if any, should be listed in the convention and what types of activities might be proscribed. The ILC specified four high seas freedoms: (1) freedom of navigation; (2) freedom of fishing; (3) freedom to lay submarine cables and pipelines; and (4) freedom to fly over the high seas. This list was embodied without change in the Convention on the High Seas,[76] but not without substantial controversy. Some states were opposed to the freedoms that were listed. The Peruvians, for instance, contested the specific mention of fishing as a high seas freedom.[77] Other states, such as Portugal, wanted to add other freedoms to the list, such as scientifiic research.[78] Still others claimed that by enumerating any list of freedoms, all those activities not specified might be inferred to enjoy less than a high seas status. And it was conversely argued that the ILC comments and the use of "inter alia" when listing high seas freedoms indicated that the list was not exhaustive and other freedoms were protected.[79] The French proposed eliminating the list entirely.[80] None of these proposals, however, received the necessary majority and the list remained unchanged.

In addition to efforts to alter the ILC list of freedoms, there were proposals to add to the ILC text a reference to those activities that should be proscribed on the high seas. This movement was spearheaded by the Soviet Union and its allies and opposed by the U.S. and its NATO allies. Albania, Bulgaria, and the Soviet Union proposed a clause prohibiting designation of naval training areas on the high seas near other countries or international shipping routes. The proposal failed of adoption in committee in the face of concerted NATO resistance.[81] Another Soviet bloc proposal to prohibit the testing of nuclear weapons on the high seas generated prolonged debate in the committee.[82] Yugoslavia and Romania argued that nuclear testing on the high seas interfered with other states' high seas freedoms, such as fishing, and, moreover, was illegal because it generated pollution. The Western nuclear powers refused to address the substance of these charges. Instead, they took the approach that this issue was not within the competence of the Law of the Sea Conference and therefore should be handled by the U.N. Disarmament Commission. Because a number of states felt strongly about high seas nuclear testing, yet did not want to allow what was essentially a bipolar issue to damage the conference, they were unwilling merely to refer the question to the General Assembly as proposed by the United Kingdom.[83] A compromise was found in an Indian proposal that would (a) refer the issue to the General Assembly (b) in conjunction with a resolution recognizing the "serious and genuine apprehension on the part of many States that nuclear explosions constitute an infringement of the freedom of the high seas."[84] Although the United States was scarcely enthusiastic about the resolution, it facilitated the voting on it in order to forestall the Soviet bloc proposal. The Indian proposal passed (51 to 1, with 14 abstentions) and the Soviet bloc proposal was dropped from consideration.[85]

A number of other skirmishes were fought over Soviet bloc efforts to include a phrase proscribing activities that might adversely affect the use of the high seas by other states.[86] The language finally adopted in Article 2 of the Convention on the High Seas was proposed by the United Kingdom and was less restrictive of high seas military activities. It specified that the enumerated high seas freedoms "and others which are recognized by the general principles of international law, shall be exercised by all States with reasonable regard to the interests of other States in their exercise of the freedom of the high seas."[87]

The issue of nuclear testing surfaced in Committee Two discussions on pollution of the high seas as well as on high seas freedoms. Article 48 of the ILC draft referred to "regulations to prevent pollution of the seas from the dumping of radioactive wastes" (paragraph 2) and "regulations with a view to prevention of pollution of the seas or airspace above, resulting from experiments or activities with radioactive materials or other harmful agents" (paragraph 3). The United States and the United Kingdom sought to have these paragraphs deleted in conjunction with a resolution on the subject. Their joint proposal was adopted by a majority of one vote.[88] A number of developing nations, in addition to the Soviet bloc, were unhappy with such an outcome and four states (Argentina, Ceylon, India, Mexico) reintroduced the deleted paragraphs as a new article.[89] The U.S. and the United Kingdom did not oppose reintroduction of the paragraphs.[90] Instead, they worked with the four sponsors to improve the language and agreed to delete the reference to "experiments." The revised proposal was then adopted without dissent.[91]

While nuclear testing on the high seas was the most disputed issue before the second committee, bipolar confrontations developed on a number of other questions. One clash, which mirrored a similar disagreement in Committee One, was over whether immunity should extend to all government-owned ships or just to warships and other noncommercial vessels. The Soviet Union defended the ILC draft which afforded warships (Art. 32) and other government ships (Art. 33) "complete immunity from the jurisdiction of any State other than the flag State."[92] The Western bloc nations carried the day in their efforts to restrict immunity to warships and other noncommercial government ships when the U.S. proposal to this effect passed with a comfortable majority.[93]

COMMITTEE THREE: FISHERIES. The ILC provisions on fisheries were based on the principles worked out at the UN Technical Conference on Living Resources of the Sea held in Rome in 1955.[94] They had been reiterated in the resolution emanating from the Specialized Conference on the Conservation of Natural Resources: Continental Shelf and Marine Waters held in Ciudad Trujillo the following year.[95] Given the repeated international deliberations that had preceded the ILC articles, it was a foregone conclusion that few of the basic ideas or the balance of the articles would be changed.

The third committee was further fortunate in having the contentious issue of the contiguous fishing zone relegated to Committee One. Similarly, the troublesome question of jurisdiction over the living resources of the continental shelf was handled in Committee Four. This allowed the third committee to concentrate on fisheries conservation and management in zones of unspecified dimensions. Management and conservation, however, were destined to serve as yet another battleground between coastal and maritime forces.

The ILC articles before the conference covered (1) definitions, (2) areas fished by a single state, (3) areas fished by two or more states, (4) new entrants into a regulated fishery, (5) the special interest of a coastal state in offshore waters, (6) the coastal state's rights to adopt unilateral but nondiscriminatory measures, (7) the special interest of third parties in conservation measures, and (8) the establishment of an arbitral commission.[96]

To the ILC definitions of the right to fish and the meaning of the term conservation, coastal states proposed the addition of references to the special interest of the coastal state.[97] The special interest of the coastal state was ultimately incorporated in the definition of the right to fish,[98] but was not approved by the committee in drawing up conservation programs. Article 51 of the ILC text provided that a single state could issue conservation regulations to govern fishing by its nationals on the high seas. Article 52 provided for negotiations where two or more parties fished a single area and wished to establish fishery conservation measures. When, after a period of time, the states were unable to reach agreement, either party could request a settlement by an arbitral commission as set out in Article 57. Coastal states seeking stronger rights were opposed to a compulsory review procedure, preferring instead a more general reference to UN dispute settlement.[99] The distant-water fishing nations, excluding the Soviet Union,[100] were insistent upon such a requirement. Thus the committee turned to consider Articles 57 and 58 on dispute settlement before proceeding further with the discussion of conservation measures.

ILC Article 57 providing for an arbitral body was completely replaced by a U.S.-Greek proposal for a special commission.[101] The membership of the body was increased from three to five and the selection procedures altered. The time allowed for reaching a decision was lengthened from three to five months with the possibility of extension. Article 58 of the ILC provided that the arbitral commission could determine that controversial measures would not be applied pending the outcome of the dispute settlement. This article was replaced by a proposal sponsored by Greece, Pakistan, and the United States which provided that the commission could suspend unilaterally declared conservation measures where there was evidence that the urgent application of such measures was not necessary.[102] The adoption of this measure represented a victory for those countries who feared that coastal states would unilaterally impose regulations using conservation as a justification.

Once the issue of the arbitral commission was decided, Committee Three returned to consider the operational articles on regulation. Article 53 provided that a conservation regime already in force would be applicable to newcomers fishing the area. If the new entrant objected, the issue would be subject to the dispute settlement procedures provided in Articles 57 and 58. The United States and several Western European states proposed a procedure whereby the FAO would be notified of new conservation measures and the measures would not become applicable to new entrants until seven months after notification.[103] This proposal was adopted over the opposition of the coastal states who resisted any delay in the application of new conservation measures to new entrants.

The ILC articles 54 and 55 dealt with the coastal state's special interest in and rights to take measures to conserve fishing resources off its shores. A number of amendments and additions were proposed for Article 54 on the coastal state's interest in offshore fisheries.[104] Ultimately, coastal and maritime forces coalesced around two proposals. Proponents of coastal-state rights supported a proposal which would prohibit enforcement of conservation measures "which are opposed to those which have been adopted by the coastal state."[105] The proposal favored by distant-water fishing nations would authorize a coastal state to request a state fishing off its shores to enter into negotiations toward a conservation regime.[106] Both proposals were ultimately adopted and incorporated into what was to become Article 6 of the Convention on Fishing.

Article 55 on the coastal state's right to adopt conservation measures was the subject of sharp disagreement. Distant-water fishing interests, represented by a group of Western European states, advanced a proposal that would lay out specific prerequisites for a coastal state's unilateral conservation measures.[107] The proponents of coastal-state rights, at the other extreme, proposed that unilateral control over offshore fisheries could be imposed without the need for negotiations and that in any scheme entailing restrictions on fishing effort, the coastal state would receive special consideration. The original coastal-state proposal generated such opposition that a revised version was submitted providing for a six-month negotiating period and for the continued application of the disputed unilateral measures pending settlement by the arbitral commission.[108] Although disliked by the most adamant distant-water fishing nations, the moderated version of the coastal-state proposal was accepted and the Western European proposal was shunted aside.[109]

Article 56 dealt with the special interest a state might have in seeing conservation regimes established for areas which it does not fish and which are not off its own coast. Such a state could request fishing states to impose conservation measures in these areas. The substance of the ILC proposal was unchanged by the proposals subsequently incorporated.[110]

In addition to the broad division of Committee Three members into distant-water and coastal fishing nations, there were a number of coastal nations that sought the adoption of articles tailored to their special needs. Peru urged special protection for its anchoveta fishery, India for its trap and chank fisheries, and Iceland for its continental shelf fisheries.[111] The United States and Canada continued to seek international recognition of the abstention principle which had been embodied in the 1952 North Pacific Fisheries Convention negotiated with Japan. The abstention approach called for a new entrant to a regulated fishing area to abstain from exploiting those fish stocks which were already exploited to the maximum, provided that the regulating states were carrying out programs to conserve the stocks in question. As noted elsewhere,[112] the U.S. and Canada were unsuccessful in advancing this proposal both within the 1955 FAO Technical Conference and at the subsequent ILC meeting to draft fisheries articles. The principal support for the North American position at the Geneva Conference came from the Latin American delegations. This was sufficient to alarm the distant-water fishing nations, and the abstention principle was opposed by the Soviets, the Europeans, and the Japanese. Rather than allow the abstention principle to be defeated in a committee vote, the U.S. and Canadian delegations decided to withdraw the proposal in favor of a resolution that merely recommended that nations consider the abstention approach when such a problem arose.[113] Even this pallid resolution lost in the plenary vote.

The articles ultimately comprising the Convention on Fishing and Conservation of the Living Resources of the High Seas[114] were carefully balanced between coastal and distant-water fishing interests. To avoid a situation in which states could alter the balance of the convention by submitting reservations to those articles which they disliked, it was agreed to add an article (Art. 19) proscribing the filing of reservations to the key articles of the text. As a consequence, the Soviet Union and its allies did not sign the convention. The Soviets indicated their support for the substantive part of the document but would not become party to a convention that called for compulsory arbitration of disputes.[115]

COMMITTEE FOUR: THE CONTINENTAL SHELF. The fourth committee dealt with the drafting of a legal regime for the continental shelf. As in the case of other jurisdictional issues, the debate was between states with primarily coastal interests and states with maritime interests.[116] The continental shelf, however, unlike the territorial sea, was a relatively new and untested legal concept. Like the definition of the territorial sea, the definition of the continental shelf involved problems of delimiting its extent or width as well as determining the substance or functional content of the shelf regime.

The basis of Committee Four's deliberations were seven articles (Articles 67-73)[117] drafted by the ILC defining the continental shelf, describing and setting limits on coastal-state rights, elaborating coastal-state rights and obligations with regard to installations on the shelf, delimiting the shelf between two or more neighboring states, and settling disputes by referral to the International Court of Justice. Article 67 defined the continental shelf as the "seabed and subsoil of the submarine areas adjacent to the coast but outside the area of the territorial sea, to a depth of 200 meters [approximately 100 fathoms] or, beyond that limit, to where the depth of the superjacent waters admits of the exploitation of the natural resources of the said areas." While some nations preferred a single criterion according to a depth of 500 meters, others, such as Argentina, favored no criteria at all for setting an outer limit.[118] The ILC formulation of an expandable boundary was sufficiently flexible for resource-hungry coastal states and was incorporated unchanged in the convention. The only successful amendment to this article was a Philippine proposal stipulating that the continental shelf definition would apply to islands as well.[119]

Article 68 addressed the substance or functional content of the continental shelf regime and was the subject of substantial dispute. The ILC provided that the "coastal state exercises over the shelf sovereign rights for the purpose of exploring and exploiting its natural resources." Dispute centered on the meaning of "sovereign rights" and the meaning of "natural resources." Several Latin American nations contended that "sovereign rights" must be replaced with full "sovereignty" since the latter was indivisible.[120] The Federal Republic of Germany, at the other extreme, preferred merely to accord the coastal state "rights" to explore and exploit the mineral resources of the shelf.[121] The United States proposed that "sovereign rights" be replaced with "exclusive rights."[122] This formulation was adopted by the committee but in plenary the U.S. backed away from its proposal leaving the Europeans as the sole supporters. The plenary then moved to restore the term "sovereign rights."[123] New provisions were added to the definition of coastal-state rights in committee stipulating that the rights do not depend on actual occupation and that in the absence of the coastal state's action to exploit its own shelf, no other state could undertake such activities.

The ILC articles did not specify what was meant by the natural resources over which the coastal state exercised sovereign rights. This task was left to a divided fourth committee. The nations seeking restrictions on coastal-state extensions proposed that natural resources should be limited to mineral resources.[124] At the other extreme, newer nations sought coastal-state sovereignty over all living resources even if these resources only occasionally inhabited the seabed.[125] The majority of nations fell somewhere within these two extremes but were confronted with a serious technical difficulty in deciding how to define living seabed resources in a fashion that would not lend itself to continuing dispute. The definition finally agreed upon defined natural resources to encompass "mineral and other non-living resources of the seabed and subsoil together with living organisms belonging to sedentary species, that is to say, organisms which, at the harvestable stage, either are immobile on or under the seabed or are unable to move except in constant physical contact with the seabed."[126]

Articles 69 and 70 of the ILC draft provided that the coastal state's rights on the continental shelf would not affect the high seas status of the superjacent waters and the right of other states to lay or maintain submarine cables on the shelf. The only change in these articles was the addition of submarine pipelines to those third-party activities protected from the coastal state.[127] Article 71 provided that the coastal state's exploration and exploitation of its shelf was not to result in any unjustifiable interference with navigation, fishing, or conservation of living resources. It further provided for the construction of installations for resource purposes by the coastal state on its continental shelf. A number of additions were made to the ILC draft. Denmark[128] and France[129] proposed respectively that the exploration and exploitation of the continental shelf must not interfere with scientific research but that research concerning the continental shelf required the consent of the coastal state. Yugoslavia proposed that safety zones around installations be set at 500 meters and that the coastal state be required to undertake measures to protect living resources in the safety zones.[130] A final United Kingdom proposal incorporated in the convention was that the coastal state was required to remove installations when they were no longer in use.[131]

Article 72 providing for delimitation of the continental shelf between opposite and adjacent states remained essentially unchanged from the ILC draft. Boundaries were to be arrived at by agreement and, failing that, by median or equidistance principles if special circumstances did not apply.

The final ILC Article (73) provided that disputes concerning the interpretation of the continental shelf articles would be referred to the International Court of Justice at the request of any of the parties unless they agreed on another form of dispute settlement. This article was unacceptable to the Soviet bloc for the same reasons they opposed compulsory dispute settlement in Committee Three. Other states that hoped to press exaggerated shelf claims were equally opposed to such a dispute settlement provision. Thus, although the article passed the committee by the necessary majority, it failed to receive a two-thirds vote in plenary and was dropped from the convention.

The first UN Conference on the Law of the Sea concluded on April 28, 1958. Two months of effort had produced four conventions: (1) Convention on the Territorial Sea and Contiguous Zone[132]; (2) Convention on the High Seas[133]; (3) Convention on Fishing and Conservation of the Living Resources of the High Seas[134]; and (4) Convention on the Continental Shelf.[135] The conference also adopted nine resolutions[136] covering nuclear tests on the high seas, pollution of the high seas by radioactive materials, international fishing conservation conventions, cooperation in conservation measures, humane killing of marine life, special situations relating to coastal fisheries, the regime of historic waters, convening a second UN Conference on the Law of the Sea, and a tribute to the International Law Commission. And finally, the conference produced an Optional Protocol of Signature concerning the Compulsory Settlement of Disputes.[137]

The last substantive proposal voted on by the conference was the recommendation to the General Assembly that it convene a new conference on law of the sea which would deal with the unresolved question of the territorial sea breadth and the related issue of the contiguous fishing zone. This request was acted on by the General Assembly at its thirteenth session. Resolution 1307, adopted by an almost unanimous vote,[138] asked the secretary-general to convoke a second law of the sea conference in March or April 1960 "for the purpose of considering further the questions of the breadth of the territorial sea and fishery limits."

INTERREGNUM: 1958-1960

In the period between the first and second UN conferences, two conflicting trends were discernible in law of the sea. On the one hand, a number of small states increased their claims to territorial seas or contiguous fishing zones of twelve miles. On the other hand, maritime powers such as the United States, Britain, and Japan attempted to hold the line on new claims and reaffirmed their traditional policies on offshore limits.

States expanding their offshore claims were widely dispersed around the globe and relatively few in number. None of them claimed ocean areas beyond twelve miles, that is beyond the maximum limit that had been under consideration at the 1958 conference. In Asia, China extended her territorial sea to twelve miles.[139] In Latin America, Panama moved from a three- to a twelve-mile territorial sea.[140] On June 30, 1958, Iceland adopted a twelve-mile contiguous fishing zone to take effect in September of the same year.[141] In the Middle East, a series of states moved to adopt territorial seas of twelve miles: the Sudan,[142] Iraq (from three to twelve),[143] Libya (from six to twelve),[144] and Iran (from six to twelve).[145]

The trend reflected in these claims did not augur well for the 1960 conference. The six-mile territorial sea plus six-mile contiguous zone formula had commanded the largest majority in 1958. It was likely, therefore, that some variant of the six-plus-six formula would have to be the basis for compromise in 1960.[146] Coastal-state extensions to a full twelve-mile territorial sea strengthened the Soviet-Mexican camp and made ultimate compromise more difficult.

In the face of these new claims, the maritime nations issued protests and reaffirmed their stand that three miles was the maximum breadth of the territorial sea.[147] In its protest of the Panamanian twelve-mile claim, the U.S. affirmed that "no basis exists in international law for claims to a territorial sea in excess of three nautical miles. . . . Furthermore there is no obligation on the part of states adhering to the three-mile rule to recognize claims on the part of other states to a greater breadth of territorial sea." The note went on to point out that Panama's action was particularly "regrettable in view of the recent action of the United Nations General Assembly in voting overwhelmingly to call an international conference to consider the breadth of the territorial sea and fishery matters." The British issued a similar protest.[148]

In the case of the Icelandic claim to a twelve-mile fishing zone, matters went far beyond an exchange of notes. The Icelandic move was met with a concerted response by fishing vessel owners from Britain, Denmark, Holland, Belgium, France, and Spain. The owners met in Holland and agreed to continue fishing waters beyond four miles from the Icelandic coast and they called upon their respective governments for assistance in this policy. The British government announced its intention to provide armed escorts for its trawlers if necessary.[149] NATO efforts to resolve the dispute were unsuccessful and the new law went into effect in September. British escorts therefore accompanied British trawlers and a number of encounters ensued with the Icelandic coast guard.[150] The British distant-water fishing industry began an aggressive campaign—restrained in part by the United Kingdom's delegation to the UN—of providing information within the UN General Assembly and subsequently of making extensive contacts with leaders of the fishing industries of Western European and North America.[151]

While the British were carrying out their more visible resistance to unacceptable claims, the United States conducted a diplomatic campaign to gain support for a compromise formula on the territorial sea and contiguous fishing zone. In the period between the two conferences, the U.S. government consulted with more than forty countries from Latin America, Asia, and Western Europe.[152] On the basis of these discussions, the U.S. concluded that the basic preferences of most countries were not changed from those expressed at the 1958 conference. There was, however, the perception of the need for compromise if agreement were to be possible in 1960. Moreover, in the U.S. view, it was apparent that the area of possible compromise was quite narrow, falling somewhere between the final U.S. and Canadian proposals of 1958.[153]

The United States therefore devised two variants on the six-plus-six formula. The first proposal, favored by the U.S., would allow states that had fished the six- to twelve-mile area to continue to do so but with restrictions as to level of effort, areas fished, and classes of fish. The second proposal provided for states that had fished the outer six miles to continue fishing for a limited number of years.[154] It was acceptable to distant-water fishing interests only as a last resort if the first proposal were clearly unacceptable.[155] The effort to retain some historic fishing rights in the outer six-mile zone reflected the desire of the Northwest fishermen to continue fishing off of British Columbia.[156] The U.S. received indications from Argentina, Uruguay, Costa Rica, and El Salvador that her new proposals might provide a basis for their support. Brazilian assistance was expected to persuade Argentina, Uruguay, and others.[157] The eight Latin American states that had supported the earlier U.S. proposal seemed willing to support U.S. compromise efforts. Indeed, even Chile indicated a willingness to support a narrow territorial sea and to recast the justification of its 200-mile claim from that of a territorial sea to that of a high seas conservation zone.[158] In its lobbying efforts with Latin American nations, the U.S. repeatedly stressed the importance of a narrow territorial sea to hemispheric defense and the difficulty of carrying out U.S. obligations under the Rio Treaty without a narrow territorial sea.

Consultations with Asian countries showed few changes in basic attitudes. The Indian government declared itself uncommitted to any proposals. The Commonwealth nations had a generally favorable reaction to U.S. compromise efforts but they did point to the administrative difficulties that would be involved in trying to determine and control the level of fishing effort by nations based upon their historic rights.

The 1960 Conference

The protests, admonitions, and intersessional consultations seem to have had little or no impact on the national positions adopted at the 1960 Conference on the Law of the Sea.[159] The positions of the 88 participating nations showed only slight movement from the 1958 conference. The second conference was relatively brief, lasting from March 17 to April 26, 1960. The agenda was limited to the interrelated questions of the breadth of the territorial sea and the contiguous fishing zone and the discussions were conducted in a Committee of the Whole.

155

The second conference was as polarized as the first around support for a twelve-mile territorial sea on the one hand and support for a six-mile territorial sea plus fishing zone on the other.

A number of proposals were initially advanced in the Committee of the Whole. The Soviets proposed that states could opt for a twelve-mile territorial sea or a twelve-mile contiguous fishing zone if its territorial sea were narrower.[160] Mexico submitted an ingenious proposal according to which a state would be accorded a wider fishing zone if it claimed a narrow territorial sea. A state claiming a twelve-mile territorial sea, for instance, would have no additional fishing zone while one claiming three to six miles as territorial sea could have a fishing zone extending up to eighteen miles from the baseline.[161] The other proposals were less novel. The U.S. introduced its initial proposal for a six-mile territorial sea combined with a twelve-mile fishing zone in which historic fishing rights would be honored. The only difference in this proposal from that which the U.S. introduced in 1958 was that it specified that fishing had to have occurred within the five years preceding 1958 and that the average level of fishing by a state in the outer six miles during this five-year period would serve as an upper limit on the catch it could take in the future.[162] Canada reintroduced her six-plus-six proposal according to which the coastal state enjoyed exclusive fishing rights in the outer contiguous fishing zone.[163] And finally a group of sixteen developing nations offered a proposal similar to that of the Soviet Union allowing each state to fix its territorial sea breadth up to a limit of twelve miles.[164] One other major proposal—also from the 1958 conference—was introduced in the main committee. Iceland proposed that where the people of a state are "overwhelmingly dependent upon [the state's] coastal fisheries for [their] livelihood or economic development and it becomes necessary to limit the total catch of a stock or stocks of fish in areas adjacent to the coastal fisheries zone, the coastal State shall have preferential rights under such limitations."[165]

Following initial debate, a number of these proposals were withdrawn or revised. The United States and Canada withdrew their respective proposals and introduced a compromise scheme based on the fallback position that the U.S. had developed in its preconference consultations. Not only did the scheme require fishing to have taken place for five years in order to establish historic rights in the outer six-mile contiguous zone, it also provided that those rights would be phased out over a ten-year period to begin in late 1960.[166] The joint proposal served thenceforth as the pole around which the maritime or distant-water fishing states and their supporters coalesced.

Those nations favoring twelve-mile territorial seas dropped their earlier proposals in favor of an eighteen-nation[167] proposal that states could fix their territorial seas or fishing zones at twelve miles.[168] The Soviet Union withdrew its proposal in favor of the eighteen-nation scheme.

The two new proposals, two amendments to the joint proposal,[169] and the Icelandic proposal were put to a vote in the Committee of the Whole on April 13. The eighteen-power proposal was defeated (39 to 36, with 13 abstentions), as were the amendments to the U.S.-Canadian proposal. The joint proposal was adopted (43 to 33, with 12 abstentions), as was the Icelandic proposal (31 to 11, with 46 abstentions).[170]

In addition to the two proposals adopted by the Committee of the Whole, other proposals were advanced in plenary. One proposal, vigorously opposed by the developed nations, was advanced by ten members[171] of the eighteen-nation group that sponsored a twelve-mile territorial sea in the Committee of the Whole. It would postpone until 1965 the fixing of the territorial sea breadth by another UN conference. In the meantime, all those nations that were independent before 1945 could not alter their territorial sea or fishing zone claims while all others might do so up to a limit of twelve miles.[172] The proposal was rejected by the conferees (38 votes to 32, with 18 abstentions).

Another proposal was advanced as an amendment to the U.S.-Canadian proposal. Sponsored by Brazil, Cuba, and Uruguay, it was accepted by the U.S. and Canada in order to promote acceptance of their proposal by the 200-mile states. In fact, its adoption would have constituted a reversal of the purpose of the joint proposal. The tristate amendment would have allowed the coastal state to claim preferential fishing rights in areas of the high seas adjacent to the contiguous fishing zone. It also would have provided that a "special situation" would be considered to exist when fisheries and the economic development of the coastal state were intimately linked.[173] Canadian willingness to accept such an amendment was understandable in light of Canada's interest in extending its control over offshore fisheries. The U.S. situation was less clear-cut. Such a "giveaway" had been anticipated and vigorously opposed by U.S. distant-water fishermen.[174] The Navy remained unenthusiastic about a six-mile territorial sea, but did want to see a definitive limit established.[175] U.S. willingness to support the Latin amendment therefore reflected the intense pressure to reach agreement that had developed by the end of the conference. The head of the U.S. delegation, Arthur Dean, had launched a massive campaign in the closing weeks to secure the needed affirmative votes or abstentions. Hand-delivered letters from President Eisenhower were directed to a few critical rulers. In other capitals, U.S. ambassadors contacted the appropriate local officials. In such a crisis atmosphere, the Brazil-Cuba-Uruguay proposal appeared to be necessary to secure the needed votes for the U.S.-Canadian six-plus-six formula.[176]

Voting began in plenary on April 26. Both the Icelandic and U.S.-Canadian proposals were rejected. The joint proposal failed by only one vote to obtain the required two-thirds majority (54 votes to 28, with 5 abstentions) in spite of the fact that the Brazil-Cuba-Uruguay amendment on fisheries had been adopted (58 votes to 19, with 10 abstentions). At the last minute, Ecuador voted no instead of abstaining because Mr. Dean could not agree to revoke the fines that the U.S. had levied against Ecuador under the Fisherman's Protective Act. (Mr. Dean had, however, privately agreed to an executive agreement with Ecuador in which the U.S. would renounce its rights to fish within twelve miles of Ecuador.) A U.S. proposal for a reconsideration of the joint proposal failed.

Only two resolutions were affirmatively voted by the 1960 conference. One, suggested by Ethiopia, Ghana, and Liberia, was in the form of a resolution urging technical assistance to help developing countries improve their fishing capabilities.[177] The second proposal, sponsored by Mexico, requested that the General Assembly vote sufficient funds to publish the records of the 1960 conference.[178]

The failure of the conference to adopt the U.S.-Canadian proposal with the Brazil-Cuba-Uruguay amendment was, according to one participant, the source of jubilation for both distant-water fishing and naval interests in the U.S. delegation.[179] The Navy had only reluctantly agreed to support a six-mile territorial sea while U.S. distant-water fishing interests were positively horrified by the prospect of coastal-state preferential rights beyond twelve miles. Thus the absence of agreement came as a relief to both U.S. interest groups. It is probably fair to say that the joint proposal as amended by Brazil, Cuba, and Uruguay was a compromise that satisfied no single group's interest at the conference. If it had received the additional vote needed for adoption, it is uncertain what type of international support such a treaty would have received. On the other hand, it was the only proposal in the treaty that went to the heart of the critical issue of allocation of fishery resources. Without a provision allocating fisheries within and beyond twelve miles, the fisheries treaty was doomed from the outset to be irrelevant.[180]

The salient weakness of the UNCLOS I and II efforts was the failure to reach agreement on the breadth of the territorial sea. While a contiguous zone for customs, fiscal, and sanitary purposes was set at twelve miles, no territorial waters limit was specified. A further weakness, which was to become more apparent as ocean mining moved further offshore, was the failure to limit the scope of the national continental shelf. Under the 1958 convention, coastal-state jurisdiction could expand as exploitation at greater depths was possible. Moreover, it was not at all clear which fisheries would qualify as resources of the shelf and thereby be subject to coastal-state control. And a final defect of the 1958 agreements was the complexity of the provisions of the Convention on Fishing and Conservation of the Living Resources of the High Seas. This convention did not meet the concerns of the coastal states for greater control over offshore areas nor did it provide widely acceptable procedures for joint conservation of living resources.

Even though only twenty-two ratifications were required, it took a number of years before all of the 1958 Geneva conventions came into effect.[181] The Convention on the High Seas was the first to receive the necessary ratifications, in September 1962. Then in June and September of 1964, the Convention on the Continental Shelf and the Convention on the Territorial Sea and the Contiguous Zone were respectively adopted. The Convention on Fishing and Conservation of the Living Resources of the High Seas did not receive the requisite twenty-two ratifications until 1966. By that time the number of independent states had grown to the point where twenty-two states represented a small fraction of the international community. Those states, largely African, that had not participated at the first and second UN conferences on the law of the sea were not inclined to endorse the outcomes. Moreover, those developing states that were denied twelve-mile territorial seas and fishing zones at the 1958 and 1960 conferences were unenthusiastic about the conference results. Maritime nations were equally unhappy about the lack of international agreement on the breadth of the territorial sea. In this climate of dissatisfaction, it is scant surprise that efforts to settle the territorial sea and fisheries problems continued in the 1960s. By the end of the decade, the UN was moving toward yet another conference on the law of the sea.

OCEAN POLICY INTERREGNUM:

THE 1960s

THE DECADE of the 1960s marked an interlude between two protracted treaty-making efforts. The failure of the first two UN Conferences on the Law of the Sea to reach agreement on the breadth of the territorial sea created substantial uncertainty as to the legitimacy of various off-shore claims to jurisdiction. Customary law evolved in the 1960s through the process of claim and response, a process that was marked by numerous clashes and ad hoc settlements. The determination of functional and jurisdictional rights was made all the more urgent by the rapid pace of marine technological developments in this period. Not only were the petroleum and offshore mining industries operating at ever greater depths, but developments in fishing techniques were mak-ing distant-water fishing more attractive at the same time that coastal nations were developing their own offshore capabilities.

Ocean politics were inevitably affected by the pervasive political con-flict of the 1960s between the U.S. and the Soviet Union. From overt technological competition to repeated efforts to improve decision-mak-ing capabilities, the East-West conflict proved a catalyst to intensified civilian and military ocean efforts. Where competition proved too costly for both sides of the political divide or when common interests were compelling, the superpowers reached specific or limited agreements. While détente in the oceans was progressing, however, problems be-tween the developed and the developing nations were intensifying— most conspicuously in the form of repeated seizures of foreign fishing vessels by coastal states of South America. As the 1960s progressed, con-tinuing legal uncertainty, technological advances, and persistent politi-cal problems brought ocean questions back to the UN forum.

AN UNCERTAIN LAW OF THE SEA

The four conventions produced by the 1958 UN Conference on the Law of the Sea[1] set the international legal framework for the ocean regime of the 1960s. The Convention on the High Seas came into effect in September 1962, the Continental Shelf Convention in June 1964, the Convention on the Territorial Sea and Contiguous Zone in September 1964, and the Fishing Convention in March 1966. The Conventions on the High Seas and the Continental Shelf received the most signatures—forty-nine each by February 1972. The weaknesses or deficiencies of these conventions reflected the inability of the international community to agree on critical jurisdictional issues in 1958.

The failure of the 1960 conference to reach agreement on the breadth of the territorial sea and a contiguous fishing zone marked the end of efforts to seek universal agreement on a territorial sea for a decade. Multilateral efforts, however, persisted. One such effort was mounted because fifty-four nations (one short of the requisite two-thirds majority) had voted at Geneva for a six-mile territorial sea plus an additional six-mile fishing zone.[2] After the 1960 conference, the British and Canadian governments canvassed other nations around the world seeking support for such a formula.[3] Although the U.S. government officially returned to its stance on a three-mile territorial sea at the close of UNCLOS II, it indicated that it would be willing to consider a multilateral approach depending on the outcome of the British-Canadian survey. After a worldwide campaign, the British, Canadian, and Australian governments gained the support of forty-four nations for the six-plus-six formula, contingent upon the agreement of the United States and other major powers.[4] By 1962, however, United States support for a limited multilateral territorial sea agreement had waned[5] and the multilateral effort therefore collapsed. While the British then turned to a regional law of the sea effort, Canada opted for a unilateral approach to offshore claims. In July 1964, Canada passed legislation creating a nine-mile fishing zone beyond the three-mile territorial sea and empowering the government to draw straight baselines from which these zones would be measured.[6] As other nations followed suit, the salient characteristic of the 1960s law of the sea soon became a wide variety of claims to territorial sea, fishing zones, and continental shelves. The diverse claims provoked numerous fishing incidents as well as efforts at formal and informal accommodation along bilateral and regional lines.

Claims

Prior to UNCLOS I and II, national claims to offshore jurisdiction ranged from a three-mile territorial sea claimed by maritime states to the 200-mile territorial seas claimed by Chile and Peru. The Soviet Union, China, and several Middle Eastern countries were among thirteen nations claiming a twelve-mile territorial sea. After the law of the sea conferences, a growing number of states began to adopt twelve-mile limits either as territorial seas or as fishing zones.

Territorial sea claims of twelve miles were advanced in Africa, Asia, and Latin America throughout the 1960s.[7] In 1963, Algeria and Syria adopted such a claim, followed in 1964 by Cyprus, Togo, and North Vietnam. In 1965 Honduras followed suit; then in 1966, Pakistan and Thailand. This desultory pattern of twelve-mile territorial sea claims continued and by 1968, six more states had joined the list—Burma, Dahomey, India, Kuwait, Liberia, and Senegal.

Claims to twelve-mile fishing zones also proliferated after the multi-lateral effort failed to gain the necessary U.S. support. Norway, Tunisia, and South Africa moved between 1961 and 1963. And the United Kingdom agreed in 1961 to a twelve-mile fishing zone around Iceland to become effective in 1964. All of these claims represented fully exclusive fishing zones. Then in 1964, as a result of the British-sponsored European Fisheries Conference, fourteen European nations[8] adopted a variant on the twelve-mile fishing zone. Within an inner belt of six miles the coastal state would enjoy exclusive fishing rights while in the outer six-mile belt, fishermen who had habitually fished the area would be allowed to continue fishing under coastal-state controls.[9] By 1966, a growing Russian and European fishery off North America prompted the U.S. to adopt a twelve-mile fishing zone.[10] Mexico added a three-mile fishing zone to its nine-mile territorial sea two months later.[11]

Less modest offshore claims in the second half of the 1960s followed the example of Chile and Peru. In 1965 Nicaragua laid claim to a fishing zone of 200 miles.[12] In 1966, Ecuador officially claimed a 200-mile territorial sea,[13] as did Argentina.[14] The following year, Panama extended its territorial waters to 200 miles.[15] Two-hundred-mile claims resumed again two years later when Uruguay[16] (1969) and Brazil[17] (1970) claimed territorial seas of this breadth.

Fishing Incidents

The failure of the Geneva conferences to agree upon the extent of coastal-state offshore jurisdiction opened the door to a series of vessel seizures and other incidents that lasted throughout the 1960s. The driving forces behind the confrontations were new marine technologies that made possible an intensified use of the ocean's limited resources. The introduction of the purse seine into tuna fishing yielded substantial increases in catch per unit time fished. As distant-water fishing operations were becoming more profitable, coastal states were stimulating the development of indigenous fishing industries to increase domestic production of protein. The concerted Soviet program to develop a major high seas fishery came to fruition in the 1960s at the same time that the Japanese were expanding into new fishing grounds. The Soviet fishing fleet first appeared on the Georges Bank in 1961.[18]

Among the best documented and reported confrontations are those between the American tuna fleet and the nations along the west coast of Latin America.[19] Because the U.S. government did not recognize claims to offshore waters beyond a three-mile territorial sea, U.S. fishermen were advised not to purchase licenses to fish in zones greater than three miles (subsequently twelve miles when the U.S. adopted a contiguous fishing zone of this breadth). Intent upon enforcing their claims, South American nations repeatedly seized and fined U.S. vessels operating within claimed waters. Ecuador and Colombia seized and fined ten vessels in 1962 and eleven in 1963. After a year's respite, seizures resumed and rose from ten in 1965 to sixteen in 1967. The State Department estimated that from 1959 to 1967, there had been 102 seizures of U.S. fishing vessels by Mexico, Colombia, Ecuador, El Salvador, Honduras, Panama, and Peru.[20]

The U.S. response to vessel seizures centered in the Congress and built upon the retaliatory measures adopted in the 1950s. Ecuador had been the first country to seize a U.S. tuna vessel in 1951. From then to 1960, a total of forty-two U.S. tuna boats were seized. In 1954, the Congress had responded by passing the Fishermen's Protective Act under which U.S. fishermen were reimbursed for fines paid to foreign governments that had seized U.S. vessels fishing in what the U.S. regarded as international waters.[21] The secretary of state was authorized to take appropriate action to collect the claims reimbursed by the U.S. government from the seizing government.

With the return of systematic seizures after the first and second UN conferences on the law of the sea, Congress resumed consideration of retaliatory legislative measures. One such bill was the Kuchel amendment to the foreign aid bill of 1965. It required the president to consider ending foreign aid to nations that seized or harassed American fishing vessels on the high seas.[22] Another measure designed to encourage U.S. distant-water fishing was a bill to broaden the Fishermen's Protective Act of 1954. Public Law 90-482 (August 12, 1968) stipulated that the U.S. government would not only reimburse the fine levied by the seizing government, but all the costs incurred by the owner of a detained fishing vessel. The state seizing the vessel would be called upon to repay the U.S. government or the amount of the fine could be deducted from its foreign aid allocation.[23] A third measure was the Naval

Vessels Loan Extension Act of 1967, which provided that any vessels loaned to a foreign government might be recalled if that government conducted illegal seizures of U.S. vessels.[24] A fourth measure was appended by the Congress to the Foreign Military Sales Act in 1968.[25] Sponsored by Thomas M. Pelly, it provided that no defense article or service should be sold by the U.S. to any country that seized or fined a U.S. vessel fishing more than twelve miles from shore. The president was empowered to waive this provision on national security grounds. This act was applied to Peru the following year after Peru seized two U.S. tuna vessels.[26]

Ad Hoc Settlements

The persistent conflicts stemming from differing interpretations of national jurisdiction spurred equally persistent efforts to reach bilateral and regional resolutions and understandings. The U.S. pursued regional arrangements with the CEP countries (Chile, Ecuador, and Peru), but settled for bilateral agreements where possible. Similarly, the U.S. negotiated bilateral or tripartite understandings as appropriate with Japan and Canada. While Japan pursued a number of bilaterals, the Europeans settled on a regional approach. Such arrangements were imperative where fishing pressures were greatest. The bilateral efforts were pragmatic attempts to allocate a finite resource between contending states and, in addition, to coordinate research among participating nations. The successful agreements allowed welcome respites from conflict unwanted by the contracting parties.[27]

CHILE, ECUADOR, AND PERU AND THE UNITED STATES. Throughout the 1960s the United States sought to reach various understandings—some formal, others informal—with Latin American nations. Upon conclusion of the Geneva conferences, Ecuadorian seizures became a major problem for the U.S. The rapid conversion of distant-water tuna fleets to purse seining meant that bait boats no longer needed to seek licenses to fish within three miles of the coast. At the same time, unseasonable weather caused a drop in catch for the nascent tuna industry operating out of Ecuador. In response to domestic pressures, the Ecuadorian government passed a decree banning purse-seining operations out to forty miles in one area of the coast. In the face of U.S. protests and offers of technical assistance to the affected coastal fishermen, Ecuador's president ordered the navy not to enforce the decree.[28] When the Ecuadorian government was overthrown in 1963, the Kennedy administration extended recognition and negotiated a secret *modus vivendi* under

which the United States recognized Ecuadorian exclusive fishing jurisdiction to twelve miles and in certain areas. The Ecuadorians agreed to
license U.S. fishermen within twelve miles and to desist from seizing
U.S. vessels beyond.[29] For over two years, this understanding prevented
significant conflicts between the two countries. A similar agreement may
also have been in force between the U.S. and Peru since it too retreated
from fining U.S. vessels during the same period.[30] Like Ecuador, Peru
was adversely affected by the shift to purse seining. Peru had counted
on revenues from licensing bait fishing to meet its portion of payments
for a special fund fishing project begun in 1960.[31] In 1965, the understanding between the U.S. and Ecuador was revealed and became one
of the major factors leading to the overthrow of the junta. Also in 1965,
Peru laid claim to the airspace above its 200 mile zone[32] and Ecuador
moved in 1966 to establish an unequivocal 200-mile territorial sea.

As Ecuadorian and Peruvian seizures resumed in 1965, the U.S. tried
again to reach an understanding—this time a formal one with the CEP
group. In February 1967, the State Department proposed that the question of territorial waters be submitted either to the International Court
of Justice or to arbitration or to a multilateral conference that would
include Canada and Japan, nations that also maintained a tuna fishery.
The CEP response was initially negative.[33] Subsequently, however, the
CEP indicated that they would be willing to meet with the U.S. to
discuss technical and scientific aspects of fisheries conservation. Informal talks between the four nations began in April 1968 revolving
around a U.S. proposal to create an organization that would facilitate
cooperation regarding problems of conservation, development, exploitation, and seizures. There was no immediate response, and by early 1969
it was evident that the CEP countries were divided over how to react to
the U.S. proposal. While Chile was willing to go to a conference, Peru
was negative, fearing that the U.S. would use a conference to open the
issue of CEP 200-mile claims. Ecuador was undecided.[34]

CEP differences over whether to meet with the U.S. were overtaken
by crisis when Peru seized and fired on more U.S. fishing vessels in
early 1969. Confronted with this hostile act, yet unable to get the Latins
to the negotiating table, the United States cancelled deliveries of military equipment to Peru in accordance with the Foreign Military Sales
Act of 1968.[35] Peru responded by kicking the U.S. military mission out
of the country. The CEP then argued that they could not negotiate
with the U.S. as long as the U.S. arms sale sanction was in effect. When
the U.S. suspended the ban in June 1969, it was announced that a
four-power conference would be held. With the lifting of the arms sale
ban, the CEP were spurred into formal discussions by the congressional

threat to prohibit imports of fish from any country seizing U.S. vessels in international waters (H.R. 10607).

The quadripartite conference met in Buenos Aires in August 1969 and again in September 1970. The agenda reflected the concerns of both sides. The CEP demanded that the U.S. eliminate its tariff on canned fish products and its labeling restrictions on bonito.[36] They were also concerned about the operation of factory ships in the South Pacific. The U.S. was interested in promoting a Regional Fishing Institute to regulate the concession of fishing licenses and conservation within the zone. In a far-reaching proposal, the U.S. in effect conceded CEP jurisdiction by agreeing to collect the fees set by the CEP from its own vessels fishing in the area. It would then turn these monies over to the coastal-state governments.[37] Fearful that such an arrangement would reflect some diminution of their sovereignty in the 200-mile zones, the CEP turned the proposal down and the talks recessed without agreement.

CANADA, JAPAN, AND THE UNITED STATES. In addition to problems with the west coast South American states, the United States faced problems in multilateral negotiations on fisheries off its own shores. The U.S., Canada, and Japan found themselves unable to agree on a new regime for the fisheries of the North East Pacific. Since 1953, fishing relations among the three had been governed by the International Convention for the High Seas Fisheries of the North Pacific Ocean (see Chapter 3). During that time Japanese trawlers had moved into areas of concern to U.S. halibut and king crab fishermen. While the regime had been successful in regulating Japanese entry into some fisheries,[38] the Japanese were dissatisfied with a system based on the principle of abstention —a principle which had not received wide support at the 1958 UN Conference on the Law of the Sea. In June and September of 1963, the three parties, at Japanese initiative, sought alternative means of regulating salmon and salmon-trout fishing. Japan supported joint use of fishing resources based on scientific stock surveys. Canada and the U.S., however, sought a framework that would preserve their historic rights in the North Pacific fishery. Meeting again in 1964, the three parties agreed on the possibility of forgoing the abstention principle as the basis for the management regime, but were unable to agree on an alternative management approach.[39]

JAPAN AND SOUTH KOREA. One of the more successful bilateral fishing agreements of the 1960s was between Japan and South Korea, despite centuries of troubled fishing relations. A new chapter in their ongoing controversy began with Korea's Presidential Proclamation of Sovereignty over the Adjacent Sea on January 18, 1952. Anticipating the removal of the fishing boundary established during the U.S. occupation,[40] the Koreans emulated Peru and claimed sovereignty over an area extending from 20 to 100 miles from shore. The Korean claim was protested by the United States, Britain, China, and, of course, Japan. Undeterred, the Korean government continued to seize foreign fishing vessels as they had under the MacArthur line. Between 1947 and 1964, Korea seized more than 200 Japanese vessels in proscribed areas.[41]

The 1958 Geneva Fisheries Convention contributed little to the resolution of the Japanese-Korean dispute. Neither did the 1960 failure to reach agreement on offshore fishing limits. Desirous, however, of improving economic relations, both countries met in 1963-1964 to seek a mutually acceptable settlement of their fishery dispute.[42] Despite long-standing differences, the negotiators agreed on a settlement in which both parties made substantial concessions. The final agreement authorized each party to establish a twelve-mile fishery zone and created a joint control zone adjacent to Korea's exclusive fishing zone. Within the joint zone, resources were to be shared on an equal basis. Each party was responsible for policing its own vessels and could notify the other government where infractions of the regulations were suspected.[43] This settlement represented a substantial retreat for the Koreans from their former expansive claim. For Japan, the settlement marked the first time that she formally recognized a coastal-state claim greater than three miles. With the resolution of this acrimonious issue, the way was paved for the two nations to establish normal relations. The treaty remained in force beyond its initial five-year period with both parties seemingly satisfied with the results.

JAPAN, THE USSR, AND THE UNITED STATES. Another set of U.S. bilateral negotiations was stimulated by the evolving regime of the continental shelf. The Bartlett Act,[44] passed by the Congress in 1964, anticipated the coming into effect of the Geneva Convention on the Continental Shelf. It prohibited foreign vessels from fishing in U.S. territorial waters and from taking living resources of the continental shelf. The secretary of the interior, in consultation with the secretary of state, was authorized to determine which living resources were to be classified as pertaining to the continental shelf, that is, which species were immobile or unable to move except in constant physical contact with the seabed. It was important to U.S. distant-water shrimp fishermen that any classification of continental shelf resources should be based on careful scientific evaluation and in accordance with the definition set out in the

Geneva Convention on the Continental Shelf. This concern for the reciprocal effects on U.S. distant-water fishing explains why king crab was not defined as a continental shelf resource until 1968.

The delay in classifying the king crab resource did not retard U.S. efforts to reduce the level of Japanese and Soviet pressure on the stocks. Negotiations with Japan and the USSR began in late 1964 and early 1965 respectively. The Japanese government argued that king crab constituted a high seas resource and was not subject to the exclusive use and control of the U.S. Moreover, Japan could not be bound by the Geneva Convention on the Continental Shelf to which it was not a party.[45] Negotiations ensued producing an agreement which came into force on November 25, 1964. This two-year arrangement allowed both parties to reserve their differing positions on whether crab was a continental shelf resource, and subject to the coastal state's "exclusive jurisdiction, control and rights of exploration." Japan agreed to limit its catch of king crab in the eastern Bering Sea, to provide scientific data, and to use crab pots only in certain restricted areas. While this agreement did not eliminate friction altogether, its utility was evident to both parties. It was renegotiated periodically, with Japan agreeing each time to a further reduction in its allotment and to a wider use of crab pots.[46] The agreement was eventually superceded by the U.S. declaration of a 200-mile fishing zone in 1977.

Negotiations with the Soviet government were even smoother than those with Japan. The Soviets agreed with the U.S. desire to classify king crab as a continental shelf resource, but pointed out that an abrupt end to their fishing on the U.S. continental shelf would cause economic dislocation. Moreover, U.S. fishermen could not fully exploit the Alaska fishery.[47] The two countries agreed in February 1965 to provisions for a reduced Soviet catch, exchange of scientific data, use of only crab pots in certain areas, and no Soviet king crab fishing south of the Aleutian Islands.[48] Like the agreement with Japan, this arrangement has been renegotiated periodically and the Soviet allowable catch reduced while areas restricted to crab pots have been increased.[49]

EUROPE. The situation of European fisheries after the 1958 and 1960 Geneva conferences was one of differing claims to offshore jurisdiction and bilateral and multilateral efforts to reach agreement. The range of differences among nations was relatively narrow, and the Europeans were able to come to short-term agreements on fisheries matters. Britain took a leading role, after the second law of the sea conference, in resolving outstanding jurisdictional disputes. In February 1961 the English reached an agreement with Iceland in which Iceland, after a three-year period, might claim a twelve-mile exclusive fishery limit off its shores. Shortly thereafter, the English also came to an understanding with Norway under which the Norwegians would extend their fishery limits from four to six miles. Moreover, the English agreed not to fish during certain periods in four areas from six to twelve miles off Norway. In return, Norway recognized Britain's right to keep fishing an outer six-mile zone until 1970.[50]

In 1962 the English found themselves challenged by the attempts of other countries to close them out of their traditional fishing grounds. In March, the Soviets terminated a fisheries agreement under which the English had fished in certain areas of the Barents Sea up to three miles from shore within the Soviet twelve-mile territorial sea. Similarly, the Danish government notified the United Kingdom of its intention to terminate their agreement allowing the British to fish within six to twelve miles of the Faroe Islands.[51]

In light of this evolving situation and of Britain's preference for multilateral agreement on a six-mile territorial sea plus six-mile fishing zone policy, the United Kingdom notified a number of countries of her intention to withdraw from existing fishing agreements.[52] Freed from prior obligations, the British then invited the nations of the northeastern Atlantic to meet on fishing problems. The conference met in London three times between December 1963 and March 1964. The Commission of the European Economic Community and sixteen countries were represented: Austria, Belgium, Denmark, France, Federal Republic of Germany, Iceland, Ireland, Italy, Luxembourg, Netherlands, Norway, Portugal, Spain, Sweden, Switzerland, and the United Kingdom. The conference adopted a Fisheries Convention, Protocol of Provisional Application, and related agreements. The convention specified that coastal states would have exclusive fishery rights within six miles of shore after a brief phaseout period for foreign vessels. In an outer six-mile belt, fishing could be reserved to the coastal state and to those states that had traditionally fished the area during the preceding ten years. Straight baselines and closing lines for bays were to be applied in accordance with the Geneva Convention on the Territorial Sea.[53] The convention was signed by fourteen participants, excluding Denmark and Norway which had already reached agreement with Britain on twelve-mile fishing zones. The British moved quickly to implement the Fisheries Convention[54] and others followed more slowly.

The Fisheries Convention transposed the Permanent Commission (established in 1954 due to delays in ratifying the 1946 Northeast Atlantic Fisheries Convention) into a new Northeast Atlantic Fisheries Commission (NEAFC) to promote conservation measures in the area beyond national jurisdiction. While the new commission continued to rely heavily on ICES for scientific advice, its scope was expanded beyond conservation measures limited to mesh size and size limits of fish. NEAFC was allowed to consider fishing gear, closed seasons and areas, fluctuations in the stocks, and control of catches and level of effort.[55] The convention and the new commission provided the basis for stable fishing relations throughout the 1960s and up to the Third UN Conference on the Law of the Sea.

THE CHANGING INTERNATIONAL POLITICAL SCENE

The uncertainty evident in the law of the sea of the 1960s was fostered by and in turn influenced the larger political context. The process of offshore claims, response, and ad hoc agreement was carried on within an era of international economic, military, and political ferment. At the beginning of the decade the conflict between the ideologies of the East and the West structured the international political system. In the first and second law of the sea conferences, this division was evident in the two broad groupings of states that could be found on most issues. By the end of the decade, however, the rhetoric of the cold war was muted and episodic. The structure of alignments once provided by the bipolar conflict between alternative social systems was in disarray. Instead, the end of the 1960s witnessed the emergence of a new political structure based on a perceived global conflict between the developed and the developing nations.

North-South Differences

The conflict between developed and developing nations emerged from the first meeting of the United Nations Conference on Trade and Development (UNCTAD) in 1964. UNCTAD and its subsidiary organs focused on the needs of developing countries and the measures required to close the gap between the rich and poor nations. UNCTAD subsequently became institutionalized as a permanent part of the UN General Assembly and a forum for airing the concerns of the Third World. The concerns on which the North-South division was based evolved gradually into a program for a New International Economic Order (NIEO). According to the rationale for this program, the disparity in wealth between the developed and developing nations constituted evidence of centuries of colonial exploitation by the countries of the North of the peoples of the South. Under the NIEO, past inequities would be rectified through massive transfers of income and technology to the poorer nations of the world. These transfers would be effected through major changes in the structure of the international system which had heretofore been designed to benefit the developed nations.

The application of the premises of the NIEO to the law of the sea required a certain finesse, especially when it came to the central issue of coastal-state jurisdiction. Geographical circumstance has favored a small number of developed nations and some nations of South America with long coastlines.[56] Thus it was not self-evident that expansion of coastal-state jurisdiction would be an issue susceptible of North-South politics. Nonetheless, by combining the problems of offshore jurisdiction with the question of an international regime for the deep seabed, a few South American nations succeeded in maintaining the appearance of a North-South division until 1975. Thereafter geographic and resource interests seriously undermined the fragile solidarity of the Third World coalition known as the Group of 77 on jurisdictional issues.

The rationale that was used to maintain a developing nation coalition behind broad coastal-state jurisdiction was that a regime of narrow offshore jurisdiction benefitted only the developed maritime nations. The naval powers, it was argued, had always opposed expansive claims that might prevent them from extending their influence as far as possible throughout the oceans. The necessary response to such a policy on the part of the developing countries was to extend coastal-state jurisdiction over vast offshore areas. While the prospect of new wealth excited those developing nations with coastlines fronting on open oceans, little attention was devoted to the fact that the 200-mile zone (a) reduced the "common heritage of mankind"[57] and (b) primarily benefitted the developed nations and the richest of the developing nations.

The ability of a few Latin American states to maintain the cohesion of the Group of 77 behind 200-mile zone policies in law of the sea negotiations for a number of years is a tribute to their diplomatic skills. It also testifies to the development within those countries of strong nationalist sentiments as fishing conflicts with the distant-water fishing nations increased and the cold war waned. Offshore jurisdiction was merely one of many points of friction between the United States and the countries to the south, but it synthesized Latin concern for control over their own resources in areas of perceived national sovereignty. U.S. involvement in Vietnam brought home the irrelevance of the cold war to Latin America while it distracted U.S. attention from its own hemisphere. At the same time, Fidel Castro's complete break with the United States provided an alternate model for relations between the two parts of the hemisphere. Apart from targeting missiles at the heart of the United States, it seemed that small nations could pursue independent, even disruptive policies with impunity right in the traditional U.S. "backyard."

Relations with Canada and Allies

These lsssons were not lost on the northernmost neighbor of the U.S. Indeed, U.S. relations with Canada on law of the sea matters demonstrate the radical political changes of the period.[58] After the collaborative policies of the 1958 and 1960 Geneva conferences, the Canadian government was extremely disappointed when in 1962 the U.S. rejected the multilateral approach based on the six-plus-six formula. Turning then to an independent program of self-help, Canada in 1964 proceeded to legislate a nine-mile contiguous fishing zone beyond its three-mile territorial sea and to establish extensive straight baselines along the sinuosities of the coast.[59]

The U.S. government quickly protested the Canadian claims, but only two years later the Congress passed legislation for a nine-mile fishing zone of its own.[60] U.S. legislation, however, did not provide for straight baselines, and this became a source of friction between the two countries. In 1966, the Canadians indicated their intention to use straight baselines that would make the Gulf of St. Lawrence and the Hecate Strait (of Queen Charlotte Sound) into internal waters. The State Department's legal advisor protested that some of the proposed baselines exceeded those permissible under international law and did not follow the general direction of the coast. Concern was registered at the highest levels. While President Johnson intervened directly with Prime Minister Pearson, Under Secretary of State Rostow bluntly notified the Canadian minister of external affairs that the U.S. would challenge and test any baseline claims that would close the Hecate Strait.[61]

Determined to press ahead with expanding jurisdiction, the Canadian government was fortified in this resolve by the U.S. adoption of a fishing zone. In 1967, therefore, Canada began to move ahead with its new baselines. It announced the first series of straight baselines along the coast of Labrador and the southern and eastern coasts of Newfoundland.[62] Although these baselines were more moderate than those originally envisioned by the Canadians, the U.S. protested them as inconsistent with international law. Then in April 1969, Canada announced its intention to claim straight baselines along the east coast of Nova Scotia and the west coasts of Vancouver Island and the Queen Charlotte Islands.[63] To close Hecate Strait and other areas to U.S. fishing, the Canadians devised a new concept of "fisheries closing lines." Presumably these would be more acceptable to U.S. naval interests than would the expansion of Canada's internal waters via straight baselines. Fisheries closing lines were used in 1970 across the Gulf of St. Lawrence, the Bay of Fundy, Queen Charlotte Sound, and Dixon Entrance.[64]

By 1970, fisheries closing lines represented only a small part of the law of the sea difficulties between the two nations. In the same year, Canada asserted its statutory authority to govern all aspects of exploration and exploitation throughout the entire continental margin. Canada also established a twelve-mile territorial sea[65] and a 100-mile pollution prevention zone above the 60° parallel of north latitude and throughout closed fishery areas.[66] United States protests went unheeded as Canada turned to the United Nations negotiating forum to find support for its expansionist policies.

The Canadian example clearly demonstrates the impact of détente on the Western alliance in the 1960s. The same impact can be seen in relations between Iceland and other NATO allies during the 1960s. Iceland's special fisheries concerns had led her to pursue a policy of expanded coastal-state jurisdiction throughout the first and second law of the sea conferences. The cod war between England and Iceland was contributing to NATO instability at the same time that General de Gaulle was raising questions about the utility of a North Atlantic alliance. Sparked by the British Trawler Federation operating out of the villages of Hull and Grimsby, incidents were occurring with increasing frequency. Because of the importance of the NATO base at Keflavik to monitoring and interdiction of Soviet naval movements, there were strong incentives for the British to settle this dispute amicably.[67] The agreement to Iceland's twelve-mile fishing zone (effective 1964) reflected overriding cold war concerns of the early 1960s. Iceland's interest in controlling its offshore fisheries again took precedence over intra-alliance harmony when in 1972 Iceland claimed a fifty-mile fishing zone.

East-West Relations

The waning of the cold war was a principal factor accounting for the new flexibility of American allies. The success of the policy of détente was visible in their reduced concern with a Soviet or communist threat. The evolution of new attitudes, however, was not a progressive or smooth transition. The 1960s were marked with periodic flashes of East-West conflict in a larger context of emerging superpower accommodation. The Soviet capability to compete with the United States in the skies had been demonstrated by the launching of Sputnik in 1957 and reaffirmed in the shooting down of the U-2 spy plane in 1960. The expansion of Soviet naval capabilities, begun in the mid-1950s, was somewhat slower. The U.S. ability to blockade Soviet delivery of missiles to Cuba in 1962 was based on clear naval superiority in the area as well as on an obvious determination to prevent the emplacement of intercontinental ballistic missiles in the Western hemisphere. The lesson of the Cuban missile crisis was not lost on the Soviets, however. The Soviet drive to enhance its maritime role spurred simultaneous expansion of the fishing and merchant marine fleets as well as of Soviet naval and oceanographic capabilities.[68] By 1965 the Soviets were vying with the U.S. navy in the Mediterranean. Indeed, the U.S. charged the Soviets with interfering with U.S. naval operations on the high seas. The Soviets in turn protested the visit of two U.S. destroyers to the Black Sea in 1968.

Where the Soviets were able to compete successfully with the United States, both countries found that mutual interest dictated some form of accommodation. After the 1961 Berlin crisis, the two nations resumed atomic tests in the atmosphere which had been suspended due to the public outcry over nuclear fallout. By July 1963, however, they were able to agree on the Limited Nuclear Test Ban Treaty and to set up a teletype "hot line" between the two capitals. When China tested its first nuclear device in 1964 and hydrogen bomb in 1967, the U.S. and USSR were able to reach agreement in July 1968 on a Non-Proliferation Treaty. Intense competition in space led both sides to arrive at a Treaty Prohibiting Use of Outer Space for Military Purposes in January 1967.

The same process of U.S. superiority, followed by Soviet advances, ultimate parity, and mutual accommodation occurred in the oceans. One instance of this dynamic was superpower agreement in 1969 to a Treaty Banning Offensive Weapons from the Seabed after two years of negotiation. Even more revealing was an informal U.S.-Soviet understanding on the need for a new law of the sea treaty to protect maritime and distant-water freedoms. In 1967, Soviet officials expressed their concern to U.S. counterparts over the direction of coastal-state claims. The Soviets were encountering increased problems in fishing off the coast of Argentina.[69] Prolonged discussions brought the Soviets and Americans to an understanding on a three-part program for a new law of the sea. The U.S. indicated its willingness to accept a twelve-mile territorial sea if freedom of transit, not innocent passage, could be provided through and over all international straits that would be overlapped by such territorial seas. The third aspect of the desired regime was a provision for coastal-state preferential fishing rights beyond the territorial sea.[70]

By the late 1960s, the Soviets had clearly come to share U.S. maritime concerns. Having adopted a twelve-mile territorial sea as early as 1927, they were unable to renounce their traditional policy. Therefore a straits regime providing for free transit was ideally suited to a Soviet state with limited means of ice-free access to the sea. Knowing that the U.S. would be adamant on such a transit regime, they put greater stress on their concern to limit coastal states' offshore fishing rights. The vital interest of their distant-water fishing fleets could not, they insisted, be jeopardized by restrictive provisions favoring coastal fishing nations.[71] The United States, with extensive coastal as well as distant-water fishing interests, argued in turn that the third article would have to be generous to coastal fishing interests in order to induce a majority of nations to accede to a treaty providing for a twelve-mile territorial sea and for freedom of transit through international straits. Draft articles were drawn up providing for agreement on a twelve-mile territorial sea, free transit through international straits, and for coastal-state fisheries rights. These articles were discussed with a number of governments around the world. Accommodation between the superpowers on these points proved easier to achieve than the acquiescence of their respective allies. In discussions with her NATO allies, it was evident that the U.S. interest in narrow zones of offshore jurisdiction was not widely shared. Italy, Greece, and Denmark were particularly resistant to the proposed provisions on freedom of transit through international straits. The Soviets encountered similar opposition in their discussions with Warsaw Pact nations.

IMPACT OF TECHNOLOGICAL CHANGE
ON U.S. MARINE INTERESTS

A principal factor behind the rapid changes in law of the sea and related international politics during the 1960s was the pace of marine technological developments. These changes were reflected in new fishing techniques, the expansion of marine science research, the progressive movement of offshore oil recovery to greater depths, and advances in naval and antisubmarine warfare capabilities. The impact of these developments was multiple and complex. On the international side, new marine capabilities offered prospects to all coastal countries, large and small, of enhancing the national resource base. The result was evident as nations undertook piecemeal efforts to bring offshore areas under some form of national control. Ocean resources were newly perceived to be finite, and extending national jurisdiction was the obvious and simplest means of allocation, at least for those countries that had long coastlines.

At the domestic level, marine technological advances set in train a form of competition similar to that practiced among nations. The traditional ocean activities of fishing and shipping were now affected by oil rigs dotting the nearshore areas and new naval uses necessitating restricted or security zones. Given the finite coastal areas available to any nation, competition for limited space was inevitable. For U.S. coastal interests, crowding first became a problem in the 1960s. To compound the difficulties, the U.S. had acquired interests that cut in opposite directions—interests that were both global and coastal. Thus whatever action the U.S. government took with regard to coastal resources set a precedent that other nations might apply to the detriment of U.S. distant-water interests. For the first time, the U.S. was confronted with the need to make a sustained effort to coordinate its coastal policies with its distant-water concerns.

Fishing

In the 1960s, fishing represented the most valuable economic use of ocean resources.[72] Although the fishing industry was the oldest and once the most prosperous of United States industries, its importance in the United States had declined both absolutely and relatively since the Second World War. In 1967, the catch of the U.S. fishing industry was a little less than its catches in 1934 and 1947. In 1948, U.S. fishermen had caught around 4.5 billion pounds of fish for 80 percent of the nation's domestic use. While domestic use doubled by 1967, U.S. fishermen caught less than 40 percent of it, and the United States had gone on to become the world's biggest importer of fish and fish products.[73] The U.S. commercial fishing fleet, moreover, had deteriorated badly. During the mid-1950s, the United States had slipped from second to fifth place among fishing nations—behind the Soviet Union, China, Japan, and Peru. In the 1960s, as the Soviets and Japanese increased their harvest off U.S. coasts, the United States slipped to sixth place behind Norway.[74] The declining economic importance of the fishing interest was reflected in the small sums expended by the government on fishery development and seafood technology. Spending on fisheries from the mid-1960s averaged under 10 percent of the total Federal Marine Science Program (see Table 6-1).

Table 6-1

Total Federal Marine Science Program and Percent of Total by Major Purpose: FYs 1966-1970

Major Purpose	1966 $	1966 %	1967 $	1967 %	1968 $	1968 %	Estimated 1969 $	1969 %	Estimated 1970 $	1970 %
National Security	125.4	37.6	161.8	36.9	119.9	27.8	127.2	27.4	127.0	24.7
Oceanographic Research	71.6	21.5	61.5	14.0	78.1	18.1	78.4	16.9	78.4	15.2
Ocean Exploration, Mapping, Charting and Geodesy	32.3	9.7	77.4	17.7	75.7	17.5	79.7	17.2	89.9	17.5
Fishery Development and Seafood Technology	38.7	11.6	38.1	8.7	40.1	9.3	45.3	9.8	49.8	9.7
Development of Coastal Zone	19.9	6.0	21.4	4.9	27.6	6.4	32.1	6.9	43.5	8.5
Environmental Observation and Prediction	13.7	4.1	24.4	5.6	28.8	6.7	33.7	7.3	39.8	7.7
Transportation	10.4	3.1	11.9	2.7	11.1	2.6	16.7	3.6	23.5	4.5
General Purpose Ocean Engineering	3.5	1.0	14.8	3.4	19.2	4.4	19.1	4.1	24.8	4.8
International Cooperation and Collaboration	5.1	1.5	7.1	1.5	9.6	2.2	8.4	1.8	10.0	1.9
Health	5.1	1.5	6.6	1.5	5.3	1.2	6.0	1.4	5.4	1.0
Non-living Resources	3.8	1.1	7.2	1.6	7.3	1.7	8.0	1.7	10.5	2.4
Education	2.2	0.7	4.0	0.9	7.0	1.6	6.7	1.4	8.2	1.6
National Data Centers	1.7	0.5	1.8	0.4	2.1	0.5	2.2	0.4	2.6	0.5
Total	333.4	100.0	438.0	100.0	431.8	100.0	463.4	100.0	513.3	100.0

Note: All dollars are in millions, all percentages are of yearly totals.
Sources: For FY data 1966-1970 see the following publications by the U.S. National Council on Marine Resources and Engineering Development, Government Printing Office, Washington, D.C.

1966: *Marine Science Affairs—A Year of Transition,* February, 1967, p. 105.
1967: *Marine Science Affairs—A Year of Plans and Progress,* March, 1968, p. 171.
1968: *Marine Science Affairs—A Year of Broadened Participation,* January, 1969, p. 205.
1969: *Marine Science Affairs—Selecting Priority Programs,* April, 1970, p. 202.
1970: *Marine Science Affairs,* April, 1971, p. 13.

Within the government, there were two major spokesmen for domestic fishing interests: the Office of the Special Assistant for Fisheries and Wildlife in the State Department, and the Bureau of Commercial Fisheries (BCF) in the Interior Department. The more influential of the two by the end of the decade was the special assistant for fisheries and wildlife. The Bureau of Commercial Fisheries lost stature with the industry when its dynamic director, Donald McKernan, left the bureau to take over the fisheries post in the State Department. The BCF was also receiving diminished support within the Interior Department as the agency's marine interests became increasingly oriented toward the more lucrative offshore oil operations.

At the same time that the fishing industry had to compete with new ocean users, the interests of the coastal and distant-water segments of the industry moved further and further apart.[75] Intense foreign fishing off U.S. coasts brought severe hardships for groups such as the New England ground fishermen. It was these fishing groups that convinced Congress to establish a nine-mile contiguous fishing zone beyond the U.S. territorial sea in 1966.[76] New foreign fishing capabilities were making it difficult for the aging U.S. coastal fleets to compete. And in some species, overfishing was becoming a problem. The typical response, in the U.S. as elsewhere, was protectionist measures designed to reduce competition in coastal areas through a variety of claims.[77] On the other hand, the shrimp fishermen in the Gulf of Mexico and the tuna fleets based in San Diego and Puerto Rico wanted to avoid such extensions of jurisdiction by other nations, and opposed any U.S. actions that might set an adverse precedent. The distant-water fishing groups pushed a stream of legislation through the Congress designed to protect their interest in narrow national fishing zones.[78]

Marine Science

The early 1960s marked the high point of national confidence in the benefits of science and technology, and science was heralded as the basis of U.S. political and economic power. U.S. marine science shared in the general euphoria and financial largesse of the period, and marine scientists were assured by the highest government officials of their special importance to the conduct of U.S. foreign policy.[79] The position of the marine scientist in ocean policy matters was initially facilitated by the inherent difficulty of distinguishing between the pure and applied uses of marine scientific research. The close connection between improved scientific knowledge and enhanced applied ocean capabilities, however, came to haunt the ocean science community in the 1970s.

In the 1960s, marine science vacillated between depicting itself as a profession serving all mankind and pointing out its important contribution to furthering specific national uses of the oceans.[80] When the marine scientist sought a privileged status among ocean users he stressed the fact that his activities provided benefits to mankind as a whole.[81] Since science could benefit the international community while furthering national marine goals, the scientist argued that it was in the interest of all, "the United States, specifically, and the international community of nations, in general, to allow for and advocate the greatest degree of freedom of research in the high seas."[82] When, on the other hand, the marine scientist sought increased funding for research, the scientific spokesmen stressed the link between science and military or commercial uses of the ocean.[83] "Goals for a national ocean program must, of course, be based on marine interests of the United States. These interests are threefold: social, economic, and strategic. Science and technology support these three concerns."[84] In one ingenious formulation it was estimated that an annual investment of $165 million in oceanography (excluding expenditures on national defense) would result in savings to the nation of around $3 billion annually as well as an annual production of an equal amount.[85]

Whether arguing the national or the international benefits of his work, the marine scientist defined his distinctive goal as that of observing and describing marine phenomena for the purpose of improving knowledge of the ocean environment.[86] And, freedom to conduct research on the ocean floor and in the superjacent waters beyond the limits of the territorial sea was the cardinal principle of marine science.[87]

Toward the end of the 1960s, disillusionment began to set in as to the benefits of science and technology. For the marine scientist this trend was evident in assertions of coastal-state jurisdiction over the conduct of marine research.[88] The implications of this trend for the future of marine science were ominous indeed and were not lost on the scientific community. "It is already quite plain that considerations of national security, fears of foreign 'invasion' of nearby ocean regions, pure xenophobia, and general national aggrandizement have had undesirable and hampering effects on marine science. Ocean regions formerly open to undisturbed inquiry are now completely closed to all scientific research and vast submarine regions are accessible for inquiry only upon the discretionary consent of the adjacent state."[89]

This threat to the status of science stemmed from changes in attitude attending the war in Vietnam and the waning of the cold war. Domestically as well as internationally, the relationship of science to military and commercial applications was being seriously questioned. In the case of developing nations, this was related to the growing conviction that scientific research did not uniformly benefit each member of the international community. In their view, developed nations could expect to benefit far more than the poor nations from the conduct of marine research.[90] The consequences of these diverse concerns were evident by the end of the 1960s. The 200-mile claimants in South America had placed such stringent requirements on research that a number of operators cancelled cruises to the area. Even before Brazil adopted a 200-mile territorial sea in 1970, it used its Research Decree of 1968 to discourage research in waters over its continental shelf.[91] The trend was clear. As technology sparked new concerns to control offshore resources, distant-water scientific research would find itself subject to national restrictions in those areas most vital to marine research.

Offshore Oil

Of the several economic or commercial interest groups concerned with ocean policy, the petroleum industry has wielded the greatest influence. The power of this interest derived in the 1960s, as today, from the fact that oil and gas are the principal sources of energy and, as such, vital to the economic well-being of the nation. In the early 1960s, oil supplied the United States with 45 percent of its total fuel energy requirements while natural gas provided another 25 percent.[92] In part, the sheer size of the petroleum companies and of the industry as a whole accounted for the power of this interest. In 1959 the ten largest petroleum corporations had assets of more than a billion dollars each,[93] and the next ten ranged from assets of $856 to $408 million each.

Looking exclusively at offshore oil, statistics indicate an extensive industry commitment to offshore operations by the 1960s. From 1949, when the first mobile rig (capable of operating in twenty feet of water) was built, to 1969, the petroleum industry invested nearly $13 billion off U.S. shores alone to supply about 15 percent of total U.S. production (1.25 million barrels per day).[94] On a global basis, offshore oil production accounted for 16 percent of total production by 1969. From an $800 million business in 1965, the offshore oil business (drilling, production platforms, gathering facilities, and pipelines) had grown to an estimated $1 billion business in 1967, and was projected at $25 billion for the following decade.[95]

The petroleum interest group encompassed a wide range of private organizations, individuals, public agencies, and officials. At the core of the interest group were the major petroleum companies. The majors —Standard Oil (New Jersey), Mobil, Texaco, Standard of California, and Gulf Oil—had the greatest interest in offshore oil since smaller independent producers lacked the capital to bid for offshore leases, much less to carry out costly offshore operations.[96] In fact, in the 1960s, when excess capacity was troubling the industry, the independents openly opposed continued offshore leasing. Congressman Jim Wright (Texas) spoke on behalf of the independents when he urged the Interior Department to delay a lease sale for the Gulf of Mexico scheduled in April 1962. He argued that the first priority should be "to get the domestic on-shore oil business in a stronger, healthier condition before encouraging the development of the outer continental shelf."[97]

The major firms acted through industry trade associations to influence the direction of national policy. Among the most important of these associations was the American Petroleum Institute (API) with an annual budget of around $10 million. Although it purported to represent all segments of the industry, the API was dominated by the large oil companies.[98] In late 1969, the API board of directors adopted a policy favoring expansive national claims to the continental shelf, a position contrary to the view of the independents but consistent with the desire of the major companies to extend drilling operations as far offshore as possible. A policy of extensive coastal-state jurisdiction over the continental shelf was also advanced by the National Petroleum Council (NPC), the industry group most active in the 1960s law of the sea deliberations. The NPC was set up in 1946 to serve as an industry advisory and study body to the Interior Department and had developed a close working relationship with the agency. Many members of the API executive committee served on the NPC.

It has been claimed that at times the secretary of the interior acted "as the chief administrative lobbyist within the federal system for the de facto government of oil."[99] It should be noted, however, that as concerns offshore oil, the Interior Department's interests were complementary but not identical to those of the majors. The Interior Department was responsible for issuing leases, prescribing regulations, supervising operations, and administering the substantial revenues from offshore leasing. As a result, the agency had a natural interest in expanding offshore operations. Interior Department officials were frank in acknowledging that, of all seabed resources, they viewed petroleum resources as of paramount importance.[100] The petroleum majors and their trade associations, on the other hand, were concerned with assuring maximum profitable access to offshore resources, providing security for their investments in this uncertain environment, and guaranteeing suitable returns on investment with a minimum of government control.[101] Given the close working relationship between the Interior Department and the National Petroleum Council and given their complementary interests, it is not surprising that they should have adopted compatible policy positions on the continental shelf boundary.

From the beginning, the majors sought the retention of special incentives and privileges in both offshore and land-based operations.[102] These goals did not initially imply a uniform policy on what the U.S. might claim as the outer boundary of the legal continental shelf or on the nature of the seabed regime beyond. Indeed, it was not until the late 1960s that the National Petroleum Council and other interested groups settled on a policy claiming the entire continental margin, including the geological continental shelf, slope, and rise. New information and developments had persuaded the industry that this was the preferred position.

The principal factor in this policy decision was the movement of offshore operations to greater distances from shore. Although by the mid-1960s offshore operations had been underway for three decades, they were confined to the shallow areas of the continental shelf. Beyond these depths knowledge of petroleum resources was sketchy. On January 1, 1966, only four rigs were operating off the United States in water depths of over 300 feet. Costs and difficulties of operating at depths greater than 150 feet were great. While drilling itself posed no particular problem, distance from shore hampered well completion and production. Consequently, industry interest in areas as deep as 200 meters (656 feet) was remote. Resource estimates varied, but were quite low compared to estimates made less than two years later. In 1966 the ultimate petroleum potential of the U.S. continental shelves was considered to be between 15 to 35 billion barrels of petroleum liquids and 90 to 170 trillion cubic feet of natural gas.[103]

In 1967 and early 1968 new discoveries and developments led the petroleum industry to reevaluate its interest in the deepest offshore areas. The Malta proposal at the United Nations for an international seabed organization raised hopes of boundless seabed treasures while simultaneously threatening to jeopardize national access to them. In the same period, estimates of the magnitude of offshore petroleum resources were skyrocketing while technological advances were lowering the cost of deep-water operations. Then in early 1968 U.S. geologists resolved that petroleum resources in significant commercial quantities were limited to the continental block (which includes the entire continental margin).[104] This information, combined with the threat of an international seabed regime, spurred the petroleum industry to unite behind a policy that called for national jurisdiction over the resources of the continental shelf to extend to the outer edge of the continental margin (including the geologic continental shelf, slope, and rise). Such a position was consistent with the Interior Department's interest in extending its bureaucratic reach over expanded operations. Moreover, given the exploitability clause of the Geneva Convention on the Continental Shelf, there were no international legal barriers to such a position apart from the flexible concept of "adjacency." Indeed, such a policy was consistent with the prevailing political trend toward moving coastal-state jurisdiction further from shore.

Defense Interests

The most influential group concerned with law of the sea and offshore jurisdiction in the 1960s was the Defense Department, led by the Navy. The size of defense interests in the oceans is reflected in the department budget of the period. The Navy alone accounted for $19.8 billion of a Defense Department budget of about $78 billion.[105] In federal expenditures on the national marine science program, the Defense Department regularly accounted for over 50 percent of the annual budget (see Table 6-2). Within the department, the Navy was normally allocated over 95 percent of this sum. If budget allocations and expenditures serve as any index of political power within the government, it is evident that the Defense Department, and the Navy in particular, constituted the single most powerful federal agency involved in marine affairs.

The problems and possibilities posed by rapidly changing marine technologies were significant factors in the defense policy of the 1960s. From the beginning, naval technology had determined the military significance of the oceans for the United States. In the first days of the republic, the oceans had offered for the inward-directed young nation a protective barrier between it and the quarrels of Europe. With the closing of the frontier in the late 19th century, the oceans offered another prospect—that of expanding U.S. influence to the shores of other nations. These time-honored defensive and offensive aspects of the oceans were present in the naval policies of the 1960s, albeit with new technological variations. In the early 1960s, the Defense Department developed an antisubmarine warfare system for emplacement on the continental shelf of the Atlantic. The Caesar system, as it was called, consisted of bottom-mounted hydrophone arrays linked to onshore power sources and monitoring facilities.[106] The seabed was also considered a promising site for offensive weapon systems. It was thought that fixed offensive weapons might be difficult to find if emplaced on our

TABLE 6-2

Total Federal Marine Science Program by Department and Independent Agency: FYs 1966-1970

Agency	1966		1967		1968		Estimated 1969		Estimated 1970	
	$	%	$	%	$	%	$	%	$	%
Department of Defense	174.9	52.8	277.7	63.4	240.6	55.7	259.7	56.0	263.7	51.2
Department of Interior	56.5	15.2	64.1	14.6	70.5	16.3	80.8	17.4	29.2	5.6
National Science Foundation	47.7	14.4	24.8	5.7	38.1	8.6	34.9	7.5	30.3	6.4
Department of Commerce	25.0	7.5	35.3	8.0	33.6	7.8	38.1	8.2	118.3	23.1
Department of Transportation	8.1	2.4	8.3	1.9	15.4	3.6	19.8	4.3	23.4	4.5
Atomic Energy Commission	8.3	2.5	11.3	2.6	13.8	3.2	10.6	2.3	9.5	1.9
Department of Health, Education and Welfare	5.4	1.6	7.7	1.8	6.5	1.5	7.3	1.6	6.5	1.3
State Department	5.0	1.5	5.1	1.2	6.6	1.5	6.9	1.5	7.7	1.5
Smithsonian Institution	1.5	0.4	1.6	0.4	1.9	0.4	1.9	0.4	1.9	0.3
Agency for Internat'l Development	0.1	b	2.0	0.5	3.0	0.7	1.5	0.3	2.3	0.4
National Aeronautics and Space Administration	0.9	b*	0.1	b*	1.8	0.4	1.9	0.4	2.3	0.4
Environmental Protection Agency									18.2	3.4
Total	333.4	100.0	438.0	100.0	431.8	100.0	463.4	100.0	513.3	100.0

Note: All dollars are in millions, all percentages are of yearly totals.

Sources: For FY data 1966-1970 see the following publications by the U.S. National Council on Marine Resources and Engineering Development, Government Printing Office, Washington, D.C.

1966: *Marine Science Affairs—A Year of Transition,* February, 1967, p. 109.
1967: *Marine Science Affairs—A Year of Plans and Progress,* March, 1968, p. 176.
1968: *Marine Science Affairs—A Year of Broadened Participation,* January, 1969, p. 211.
1969: *Marine Science Affairs—Selecting Priority Programs,* April, 1970, p. 201.
1970: *Marine Science Affairs,* April, 1971, p. 13.
* Less than 0.05 percent.

own continental shelves or those of other nations.[107] Mobile systems that crept along the ocean floor might be even less vulnerable to detection.

At the same time that the Defense Department was considering alternative military uses that might be made of the ocean floor, Navy law of the sea specialists supported the extension of national jurisdiction over the seabed by means of the Geneva Convention on the Continental Shelf. Indeed in the early 1960s, the military was complacent both about the pace with which deep seabed exploitation would come and about the impact of such resource activity on the superjacent waters.[108] As one naval spokesman pointed out, "the Continental Shelf Convention did not sacrifice the hard-won freedom of the seas. . . . The legal status of superjacent waters as high seas is not affected by the extension of coastal state control over the shelf."[109] Because the Navy assumed that the freedom of the seas could be maintained under an expanding shelf regime, it evinced no hostility in this early period toward the "historic proclamation" issued by President Truman in 1945.[110] Moreover, the Geneva Convention on the Continental Shelf, which was seen as evolving naturally from the Truman proclamation, was described as having provided "a sound foundation for the orderly development of the ocean's shelf resources."[111] The Continental Shelf Convention, it was pointed out, "by and large applies the customary test of reasonable accommodation."[112] The "real genius" of the convention lay in the way that "it solved most of the problems at hand and, by adopting the exploitability test, assured that no major revision would be needed for quite some time."[113]

The central problem then, arising from the exploitation of seabed resources, was not that of creeping jurisdiction. Rather it was the need to provide for the accommodation of multiple uses of the ocean environment. "The principal legal problem that we face in the regime of the deep seas is basically one of conflict and competition: conflict of users or potential users and competition within and between industries."[114] The military was understandably concerned that the new uses of the seabed would "interfere with or restrict the free movement of naval vessels on and under the high seas."[115] The Navy, however, was "a firm believer in the concept of the accommodation of many different users." Therefore, "while this 'crowding' of the oceans is of concern to the military, it does not pose an insurmountable problem."[116] The Navy was generally indifferent to the location of the continental shelf boundary as long as "sovereignty over the continental shelves (whatever their seaward boundary) should be closely limited." Of greater concern to

185

the military was the extension of territorial sea boundaries, which they wished to see held to a minimum.[117]

This attitude of accommodation with commercial users was put to the test early in the 1960s. In 1962, Navy plans for the use of the continental shelf off California were threatened by a proposed Interior Department lease for phosphate mining.[118] The Navy was unable to prevail upon the Interior Department to insert stipulations in the lease to prevent interference with defense operations in the same area. The uncooperative attitude of the Interior Department was a harbinger of future problems for defense interests in the seabed as the pace of offshore leasing accelerated in the 1960s.

In addition to raising problems of conflicting ocean uses, evolving marine technology dictated a reevaluation of prospects for military uses of the seabed and continental shelf. In the course of the decade it became evident that fixed seabed weapons would not only be costly, but detectable, and therefore vulnerable. Acknowledging this technological blind alley, the U.S. and USSR agreed to prohibit the emplacement of weapons of mass destruction on the seabed beyond twelve miles from shore.[119]

The Navy's concern with the projection of military force took on increased importance in the context of the Vietnam War. The Navy developed the capability to furnish troops and supplies for a sustained period of time to this distant Southeast Asian nation. This mission reinforced the global orientation or "blue water" policy of the United States. Events in the furthest part of the world were viewed as of direct concern to a newly imperial America. Once such a capability was established, organizational compulsion dictated that it be maintained.[120] Thus, U.S. naval predominance achieved by the late 1960s represented a capability that the Defense Department naturally sought to protect. And freedom of the seas was clearly the base upon which that global maritime presence rested.

"Freedom of the seas" is a term often used to indicate the desire of certain ocean users to freely use the ocean environment for a variety of purposes. For the military, these purposes were predicated in the 1960s on the view that "the United States is a maritime nation. Its allies, enemies, and vital foreign interests lie beyond the seas."[121] The time-honored military use of the seas had been for the deployment of surface naval vessels. This use had broadened by 1960 to include the movement of forces on the "surface, subsurface, and in the air above the seas."[122] The newest use of the oceans, of course, was for purposes of concealment. A large portion of U.S. strategic forces had become sea-based, and "the viability of the submarine-based missile force to a very large degree depends upon concealment and dispersion, as well as mobility."[123]

Just as the Navy was articulating its interest in the freedom of the seas, law of the sea developments throughout the world were throwing that interest into jeopardy. Coastal nations were increasing their claims to offshore areas. And the UN, at the instigation of Malta, was considering a regime for seabed mining that would eschew military uses of the ocean floor. In the late 1960s, a number of groups and individuals systematically evaluated the impact of these developments on U.S. security concerns. These studies were instrumental in prompting the defense establishment to reconsider its earlier complacency in relation to expanding national jurisdiction over the continental shelf.

THE HENKIN REPORT AND THE STRATTON COMMISSION REPORT. In 1967 and 1968, the newly established National Council on Marine Resources and Engineering Development commissioned several studies on problems resulting from new and traditional uses of the oceans.[124] One study that was to have a major impact on subsequent military thinking on offshore limits was prepared by Professor Louis Henkin and dealt with international legal problems involved in the exploiting of mineral resources.[125] Professor Henkin made explicit the inherent contradiction between an appropriate legal regime for the recovery of seabed minerals and a regime suited to the military interest in freedom of the seas. While mineral interests suggested a system that would keep seabed minerals in American control, other national interests dictated a substantially different system. "The principal interest of the United States," in Henkin's view, was "national security." With this as the nation's first priority, the United States should not adopt any proposal that would threaten "the existing, substantial freedom of American and allied naval operations." Because "national 'sovereign rights' over mineral resources tend to expand, and threaten the rights of other states to use the area for other purposes," Professor Henkin believed that the adoption of a position favoring a broad or expanding continental shelf would be dangerous. He leaned instead "to the view that American military interests point to a narrow continental shelf, as they do to a narrow territorial sea." "Beyond the shelf," Henkin speculated, "United States military interests would tend to profit from law that avoided national 'sovereignty' and exclusive rights in the seabed." Moreover, "a measure of loose international authority in regard to mining is less likely to be troublesome than most autonomous national regimes." It was therefore "desirable—and probably inevitable—. . . to establish a 'mixed national-international' regime for mining in the deep sea." Such a regime could be either a registry or a licensing system. With regard to petroleum interests, Professor Henkin recommended a compromise in the form of a buffer zone within which only the coastal state could authorize the exploitation of seabed minerals.

✳ Adopting many of the same assumptions and elaborating in greater detail the concept of a deep seabed regime, the National Commission on Marine Science, Engineering and Resources (the Stratton Commission after its chairman, Dr. Julius Stratton) presented a report entitled *Our Nation and the Sea* in January 1969 that also influenced military thinking on the seabed question.[126] In its report the commission unequivocally rejected the National Petroleum Council's proposal for locating the outer limit of the nation's continental shelf at the point where the submerged continental land mass reached the abyssal ocean floor. The commission considered such a proposal "contrary to the best interests of the United States" for several reasons. First "it would benefit other coastal nations of the world proportionately more than the United States and give them exclusive authority over the natural resources of immense subsea areas." Secondly, it was "unfair to the inland nations of the world" and to those coastal nations lacking important mineral deposits on their continental margins.

The final and most important objection to the NPC proposal was that it "would create the danger that some coastal nations without important mineral deposits on or under their continental slopes and rises will feel justified in claiming exclusive access to the superjacent waters, the living resources in them, and the air above them." This phenomenon of expanding national jurisdiction had, for instance, "materialized as an unforeseen and undesirable consequence of the Truman Proclamation." "Such developments," the report went on, "are obviously contrary to the traditional U.S. policy to limit national claims to the sea in the interest of the maximum freedom essential to the multiple uses, including military uses, which the United States makes of the oceans. National security and world peace are best served by the narrowest possible definition of the continental shelf for purposes of mineral resources development."

For these reasons the commission recommended "that the United States take the initiative to secure international agreement on a redefinition of the 'continental shelf.' . . . The seaward limit of each coastal nation's 'continental shelf' should be fixed at the 200-meter isobath, or fifty nautical miles from the baseline . . . whichever alternative gives it the greater area." The commission pointed out that this "redefined 'continental shelf' would be a 'narrow shelf' with precise outer limits thus serving the interests of the United States."

The commission made a point that subsequently became an integral part of military thinking. It insisted that in any future negotiations with other coastal nations "the question of fixing the outer limits of the continental shelf is inseparable from that of the [legal-political] framework applicable beyond these limits." The importance of the seabed regime to United States interests should not be underestimated. "Unless a new international framework is devised which removes legal uncertainty from mineral resource exploration and exploitation in every area of the seabed . . . some venturesome governments and private entrepreneurs will act to create *faits accomplis* that will be difficult to undo, even though they adversely affect the interests of the United States and the international community."

By elaborating the problem of "creeping jurisdiction" and by pointing out its long-term consequences for the freedom of the seas, the Henkin and Stratton Commission studies aroused Defense Department apprehensions over trends in seabed resource development and their implications for military uses of the oceans. Both reports, however, offered a partial solution to the problem by (1) adopting, through international agreement, narrow offshore zones of jurisdiction and (2) by vesting limited rights to regulate seabed mining in an international authority. By indicating that an international organization for seabed exploitation would be more susceptible to U.S. influence than would coastal nations in control of seabed areas, these studies pointed the way toward consideration by the military of international control over seabed minerals exploitation. The premise of both reports was that force could not or would not be used in pursuing the nation's interest in the oceans.

A review of the Defense Department policy adopted in the late 1960s reveals the contribution of the Henkin and Stratton Commission reports. The basic shift in military thinking was the discovery of a crisis stemming from "the growing chaos in the law of the sea."[127] Not only was the pace of exploitation of seabed resources far more rapid than the military had expected, but it was now equally apparent that military interests would be difficult to reconcile with a regime suitable to mineral interests. Even more of a problem than accommodating the activities of offshore mining operations was the impact of seabed exploitation on developing coastal nations. The process the military perceived was one whereby the limited claim of a developed nation "eventually . . . tends to expand. Either its own claim expands or subsequent claims by other countries which purport to copy the original claim expand."[128] The Department of Defense was "very concerned about the tendency

189

to allow these rights to expand, the rights to the continental shelf, the right to the superjacent waters and then to the air space above it."[129] The central problem for the military, superceding that of accommodating multiple uses of the oceans, had become the need to halt the process of creeping jurisdiction.

U.S. GOVERNMENT ORGANIZATION

As rapid technological change stimulated new ocean uses, crowding and conflict among disparate U.S. ocean interests became more serious. At the outset of the 1960s the organization of marine affairs within the U.S. government reflected conditions of the 1950s when separate agencies were able to pursue different ocean goals with little need for cooperation, much less for overall coordination. Of the federal agencies with maritime interests the Navy was the most active in coordinating federal oceanographic programs. As early as 1956 the Office of Naval Research established a Coordinating Committee on Oceanography to oversee marine research activities of other agencies as well as of the Navy. The Department of State was one of eleven federal agencies represented on this committee.[130] Again at the request of the Navy, a new committee was established in 1959 in line with the recommendations of the report of the National Academy of Sciences Committee on Oceanography.[131] This Interagency Committee on Oceanography (ICO) operated within the framework of the Federal Council for Science and Technology. Its executive secretary was charged with improving the organization and operation of the U.S. government in marine affairs.[132] On January 22, 1960, the ICO became a permanent committee of the Federal Council.[133]

On January 11, 1962, the ICO formally established a Panel on International Programs and International Cooperative Organizations (PIPICO)[134] in response to the formation of the Intergovernmental Oceanographic Commission (IOC) in UNESCO in 1961.[135] The IOC had been established to promote scientific cooperation in oceanography, and President Kennedy anticipated full United States participation in its activities.[136] PIPICO was charged with coordinating and supporting this involvement and it became the U.S. coordinating forum for international oceanographic programs. PIPICO also advised the State Department on programs and policies in oceanography that related to national objectives in the international arena and assisted the department in the preparation of position papers to be presented at meetings of the Intergovernmental Oceanographic Commission.

Congress and the Marine Resources Act

The momentum needed to develop a national ocean program came from the Congress. Many in the Congress recognized the need for a national policy regarding the oceans and felt that the Interagency Committee on Oceanography was not sufficient to the task.[137] The pressure of ocean interest groups, concerned marine bureaucrats, and congressional staffs, combined with Soviet advances in the ocean, further stimulated congressional concern. On June 17, 1966, Congress enacted the Marine Resources and Engineering Development Act (P.L. 89-454).[138] The purpose of the act was to provide for a comprehensive, long-range national program in marine science by coordinating the ocean-related activities of twenty-nine bureaus in eleven federal agencies and of thirty-three subcommittees of the Congress.

The act established two bodies to promote the coordination of United States ocean activities where the ICO had failed. To assist and advise the president, a National Council on Marine Resources and Engineering Development (the Marine Sciences Council) was created at the cabinet level chaired by Vice-President Hubert Humphrey. Members of the Marine Sciences Council included the secretaries of state, navy, interior, commerce, health, education and welfare, and transportation and the heads of the Atomic Energy Commission and the National Science Foundation. Appointed as observers were the heads of NASA, AID, the Smithsonian, the Bureau of the Budget, the Council of Economic Advisers, and the Office of Science and Technology. Dr. Edward Wenk, Jr. was appointed executive secretary of the council. On July 13, 1966, the ICO was formally reconstituted as a subcommittee of the Marine Sciences Council and was renamed the Committee on Marine Research, Education and Facilities.

The second body created by the legislation was the Commission on Marine Science, Engineering and Resources, or the Stratton Commission, after its chairman. Appointed January 9, 1967, this presidential advisory commission was composed of fifteen eminent citizens from industry, universities, the state and federal governments, with four congressional advisors. The Stratton Commission was charged with the responsibility for a comprehensive study of all aspects of marine science in order to recommend an overall plan for an adequate national program to meet present and future national needs. The commission would disband and the council's authority would terminate 120 days after the commission completed its report.[139]

From the foreign policy viewpoint, the Marine Resources and Engineering Development Act stipulated that U.S. marine activities should be conducted so as to contribute to "the cooperation by the United States with other nations and groups of nations and international organizations in marine science activity when such cooperation is in the national interest." The act further stated that "the Council, under the foreign policy guidance of the President and as he may request, shall coordinate a program of international cooperation in work done pursuant to this act." (sec. 6, p. 270).

This foreign policy mandate foreshadowed a conflict of jurisdiction between the Marine Sciences Council and the Department of State, charged with overall foreign policy responsibility. Indeed, the potential threat to State Department jurisdiction accelerated the department's efforts to coordinate U.S. ocean policy. Subsequent to the first council meetings, which were held in August 1966, the jurisdictional problem was dealt with, if not solved, by the establishment in early May 1967 of an Ad Hoc Interagency Committee on International Policy in the Marine Sciences.[140] The Ad Hoc Interagency Committee operated as a State Department committee and was only nominally responsible to the Marine Sciences Council. It was chaired by Foy Kohler, deputy under secretary of state. Herman Pollack, the director of the Office of Science and Technology, served as vice-chairman and took over the day-to-day operation of the committee.[141]

The Ad Hoc Interagency Committee assumed from PIPICO overall responsibility for formulating and coordinating U.S. policy on the international aspects of marine affairs. PIPICO, however, continued to operate with a new double identity. Chaired by William Sullivan of the Department of State, it became part of the Ad Hoc Interagency Committee and reported directly to Pollack.[142] In this capacity, PIPICO was responsible for recommending policy arrived at through interagency consultation to the parent committee. At the same time PIPICO continued as a subcommittee of the Committee on Marine Research, Education and Facilities, the successor to the Interagency Committee on Oceanography, PIPICO's original parent committee.

The State Department and the UN

The level of State Department activity in ocean matters increased gradually in the 1960s. Its initial inattention to ocean matters was due largely to the diplomatic mission of the department. Country or regional concerns of the foreign service typically predominant over functionally specific operations. Far from playing an important role in the Interagency Committee on Oceanography, for instance, the State Department did not even become a member until May 18, 1961, when it

CHART 6-A
Marine Science Affairs in the Federal Government, 1967

The Congress

The President

President's Commission on Marine Science, Engineering and Resources

International Aspects of Marine Affairs

Basic Science & Research

Marine Engineering and Technology

Marine Resources

Environmental Problems

Industrial and Private Development

Education and Training

National Council on Marine Resources and Engineering Development (Chn., Vice President)

Comm. on Food from the Sea

Comm. on Multiple Uses of Coastal Zone

Comm. on Marine Research, Education & Facilities

Panel on Research

Panel on Int'l Programs & Int'l Cooperative Orgs.

Panel on Ocean Engineering

Panel on Education

Sub-Panel on Facilities

Joint Panel CMREF/ICAS on Air-Sea Interaction

Panel on Domestic Law

Comm. on Ocean Exploration & Environmental Services

Panel on International Law

Comm. on International Policy in Marine Sciences

Panel on Living Resources

Panel on Pollution in Ocean Environment

Panel on Cooperation in Use of Submersibles and other Advanced Underwater Technology

Sub-Panel on Exploration/Exploitation

Panel on National Security

Panel on U.S. Regional Policies and Programs

Panel on Internat'l Scientific Research & Exploitation/ Exploitation of Mineral Resources

Sub-Panel on Scientific Research

joined as an observer. As the number of international programs in oceanography grew during the decade, the State Department increased its activities in the field, though still in a supportive role.

The earliest State Department interest in the oceans had centered on the management of international fisheries problems. The Office of Special Assistant for Fisheries and Wildlife, created in 1947-1948, was headed successively by three able fisheries negotiators—Wilbert McLeod Chapman, William C. Herrington, and Donald C. McKernan (see Chapter 3). The number of bilateral disputes involving U.S. fishermen and the number of ad hoc agreements negotiated in the 1960s attest to the volume of work performed by this office. From its inception to the mid-1960s, however, the size of the office had grown from four to only five professional staff members. By 1965, members of the office staff, the fisheries community, and congressional staffs were consulting on proposals for upgrading the level of the operation within the State Department and increasing the size of the professional staff.[143] Through congressional pressure, ocean groups hoped to raise marine affairs to a more prominent role within the State Department and throughout the government.

State Department reluctance to be drawn into general ocean matters is illustrated by the departmental response to a congressional initiative calling for a study of the international legal implications of developing ocean resources. In a letter of May 3, 1965, to the chairman of the House Committee on Merchant Marine and Fisheries, State's Assistant Secretary for Congressional Relations Douglas MacArthur II wrote that the State Department was unaware of any need for a study of international law or foreign policy relating to the development of the natural resources of the oceans. In what must be ranked as one of the State Department's most short-lived pronouncements, MacArthur stated that if such a study were deemed necessary from a domestic point of view, then the Department of the Interior would be the appropriate agency to carry it out.[144]

State Department complacency was overtaken by pressures developing at the United Nations, pressures that were fueled in part by those offices in State having functional responsibilities in the oceans. Less than a year after MacArthur's response to the Merchant Marine and Fisheries Committee, James Roosevelt, U.S. delegate to the United Nations, proposed that the secretary-general undertake a study of the state of knowledge concerning undersea resources and exploitation technology.[145] On March 7, 1966, the UN Economic and Social Council (ECOSOC) adopted Resolution 1112 (XL), which requested the secretary-general to survey the existing knowledge of marine resources (excluding fish) beyond the continental shelf and the techniques for exploiting them. As part of the survey, the secretary-general was asked to identify those resources now considered to be capable of economic exploitation, especially for the benefit of developing countries, and to identify gaps in knowledge concerning them.

Later that year the United States delegation, at the instigation of the special assistant for fisheries and wildlife, took the lead in sponsoring a resolution that was adopted by the United Nations General Assembly on December 6, 1966. Resolution 2172 on the resources of the sea endorsed the ECOSOC request for a survey of the state of knowledge of marine resources and asked also that the secretary-general prepare a comprehensive survey of activities in marine science and technology, specifically of mineral resources development, undertaken by members of the United Nations. The findings were to be submitted to the Twenty-third General Assembly two years thence. The thrust of the U.S. proposal was to establish a small group of experts that would be responsible for handling ocean affairs within the UN. The intent of the special assistant for fisheries and wildlife, who was the originator of the proposal, was even more far-reaching. It was to have the UN secretary-general appoint a body of experts who would in turn recommend a world oceanic organization.[146] Within the Office of the Special Assistant for Fisheries and Wildlife, a first draft of such a world oceanic organization had been drawn up as early as 1965. The plans of officials within the State Department were soon overtaken, however, by events within the United Nations.

A NEW BEGINNING: THE U.S.
ADOPTS AN OCEANS POLICY

THE TWENTY-FIFTH GENERAL ASSEMBLY voted in December 1970 to convene the Third UN Conference on the Law of the Sea (UNCLOS III) in 1973. Three initiatives were instrumental in prompting this decision. The first was a proposal by Ambassador Arvid Pardo of Malta to create an international regime for the deep seabed. This proposal sparked the creation of the UN Seabed Committee to negotiate principles to govern an international seabed regime. The second action that laid the groundwork for UNCLOS III was the formulation by the U.S. government of a detailed draft treaty on a seabed mining regime for the area beyond the 200-meter isobath. The U.S. presented its draft to the UN Seabed Committee in August of 1970. The proposal signalled U.S. willingness to negotiate seriously on a deep seabed mining regime. The third major impetus to a conference evolved from bilateral discussions between the United States and the Soviet Union. Sharing similar navigational concerns, both powers proposed an international negotiation that would address the related issues of the territorial sea, transit through international straits, and fisheries. The U.S. officially announced its position on these three issues in the spring of 1970 and called for an international negotiation. The sentiment prevailing among developing nations in the UN Seabed Committee augured ill for separating negotiations on seabed issues from those on territorial sea-related questions. Instead, developing countries pressed for a single conference to handle all law of the sea questions. They hoped in this manner to secure greater concessions from the developed world. Despite U.S. and Soviet concern over the feasibility of such a comprehensive undertaking, the UN General Assembly voted in favor of a comprehensive UN conference on the law of the sea.

The international politics of law of the sea influenced, and were in turn affected by, domestic U.S. ocean policy. International pressure was channeled into the U.S. decision-making process through the UN negotiations. The U.S. government felt compelled to be responsive in the negotiations and sought in vain to formulate policies that would cast the U.S. in a leadership role. The development of a national policy acceptable to the various agencies of government and interest groups proved a formidable task. Prior to the establishment of the UN Seabed Committee, agencies such as Interior, Defense, and the National Science Foundation had pursued their individual ocean policies with little coordination and occasional conflict (see Chapter 6). As the use of the oceans intensified, defense considerations seemed to suggest a very different policy from that suited to seabed resource concerns. This emerging divergence in policy developed into a direct confrontation in 1969 and 1970. In spite of the need to formulate a national policy for the UN Seabed Committee, the Defense and Interior Departments could not agree on the optimal outer limit for the national continental shelf or the nature of the seabed regime beyond.

Under the new Nixon administration, the dispute was processed through the National Security Council system presided over by Henry Kissinger. The policy ultimately selected by President Nixon in May 1970 was transposed into treaty language and presented to the UN Seabed Committee in August 1970 as a draft treaty on the seabed. It reflected a temporary victory for security concerns in that it limited national jurisdiction over the continental shelf to areas within the 200-meter isobath. Although this policy was subsequently eroded by the combined forces of domestic coastal resource interests and foreign coastal states, it set the direction for U.S. policy for two to three years. The process of arriving at the 1970 policy had an even more lasting impact. The policy dispute brought new actors into the debate. It also impelled the principal protagonists to consolidate the law of the sea offices within their respective agencies. And finally, it led to the establishment of an interagency coordinating mechanism which managed law of the sea questions for the duration of the UN negotiations.

THE U.S. AND THE UN SEABED COMMITTEE: 1967-1968

The Malta Initiative

On August 17, 1967, the Mission of Malta to the United Nations proposed including in the agenda of the General Assembly an item entitled "Declaration and Treaty Concerning the Reservation Exclusively for Peaceful Purposes of the Sea-Bed and of the Ocean Floor, Underlying the Seas Beyond the Limits of Present National Jurisdiction, and the Use of their Resources in the Interests of Mankind."[1] The memorandum attached to the proposal expressed concern that the rapid development of marine technology by developed countries would promote national claims to the seabed, the appropriation of seabed resources for the benefit of the few, and the use of the ocean floor for military purposes. To prevent such a course of events, the memorandum went on, the seabed should be declared the "common heritage of mankind" and a treaty should be drafted which would provide that the seabed would not be subject to national appropriation, would be reserved exclusively for peaceful purposes, would be explored by means consistent with the principles and purposes of the UN charter, and would be used and exploited in the "interests of mankind." It further provided that the net financial benefits from such activities would be used primarily to assist the development of poor countries, and it suggested that an international agency be established to assure international jurisdiction over the seabed. No reference was made to aspects of the law of the sea unrelated to the seabed.

On September 21, 1967, when Ambassador Pardo presented his reasons for proposing this item to the General Assembly's General Committee, the response of the United States ambassador, Arthur J. Goldberg, was highly favorable. Ambassador Goldberg declared that the Maltese item was of great importance and wholeheartedly supported its inscription on the General Assembly agenda. He agreed with Ambassador Pardo that efforts in ocean research must "be put on a more effective international footing." Goldberg then strongly endorsed "the expanding interest of the General Assembly in this field." He pointed out that "this organization is in a position to assume leadership in enlisting the peaceful cooperation of all nations in developing the world's oceans and ocean floor." He concluded that the item should be given "early consideration" in the first committee.[2]

THE CONGRESS. Ambassador Goldberg's enthusiasm for the Maltese proposal was not shared on Capitol Hill. Upon its appearance, resolutions pro and con were introduced in the Congress with the cons largely outnumbering the pros. Nearly two dozen resolutions were introduced in the House opposing any move to vest control over seabed resources in an international organization.[3] A similar resolution was introduced in the United States Senate.[4]

The House resolutions relating to the Malta proposal were referred to the Committee on Foreign Affairs and assigned to the Subcommittee on International Organizations and Actions. The House hearings began on September 22 and continued intermittently through October. In the course of the hearings, a number of congressmen expressed a deep hostility toward the United Nations. This hostility was combined with the

conviction that the Maltese proposal for internationalizing seabed resources was highly detrimental to the national economic interest. In
some cases the economic interest was perceived as requiring access for
American industry to seabed resources extending as far as the middle
of the oceans.[5]

THE STATE DEPARTMENT. The State Department position on the Malta
proposal was ambivalent, reflecting a division of opinion within the
department as well as among the interested agencies. On the day after
the enthusiastic Goldberg statement, David H. Popper, deputy assistant
secretary of state for international organization affairs, displayed a notable lack of enthusiasm for the Malta proposal in testimony before the
foreign affairs subcommittee. Mr. Popper assured the congressmen present that "we have no intention of taking substantive action on this
proposal at this time," and that "we do not intend, in the course of
consideration of the question in this General Assembly, to dispose of
title to the deep-sea bottom, either to the United Nations or to any
other recipient."[6] The tenor of Mr. Popper's remarks may be partially
explained by State's desire to prevent Congress from adopting restrictive
measures. To this end, he assured the foreign affairs subcommittee that
Congress would be fully consulted regarding any proposals that the
United States might contemplate.

The attitude of the Congress was not uniform, however, and could
not have been the sole cause of the State Department's vacillation on
the Maltese item. Several resolutions were introduced in the House
supporting the Maltese approach,[7] and two of the three resolutions
introduced in the Senate also favored it.[8] The Senate resolutions were
referred to the Committee on Foreign Relations and a hearing was
scheduled for November 29. At the hearing, before a committee not
unfavorably disposed to the Malta proposal, State Department officials
clung to the view that a U.S. government position on the Malta proposal was premature at that time. Questioned about the merits of resolutions as far-reaching and detailed as those of Senator Pell (S. Res. 172,
S. Res. 186), Joseph Sisco, assistant secretary of state for international
organization affairs responded that the executive branch was "in favor
of moving as rapidly as the accumulation of knowledge will permit . . .
and we would hope that we can begin to move ahead with reasonable
speed."[9]

The inconsistency and hesitancy plaguing State Department efforts to
develop a position on the Malta proposal were in large measure the result of simple unpreparedness. At the October 19 hearing before the
House Foreign Affairs Committee, Herman Pollack, the director of the

State Department's Bureau of International Scientific and Technological Affairs, confessed that the progress of the Ad Hoc Interagency Committee in reaching a government position had been very slow. In existence since early May and apprised of the Malta item since August, the Ad Hoc Interagency Committee was "still developing preliminary governmental attitudes toward the question." When the committee had been established, Pollack said, we had simply not "quite anticipated the speed at which the problem would be put before us."[10] Over a month later, Mr. Pollack again testified on the progress of the ad hoc committee, this time before the Senate Foreign Relations Committee. Mr. Pollack indicated "that a number of working groups and task forces have been established to consider the variety of problems that are posed by the future of the ocean floor, and that the principal consequence at this point in time has been to scope the problem, to examine some of the possible alternatives."[11] This was the extent of progress in the interagency committee during the three and one-half months following the Malta resolution.

The official position of the U.S. government as it emerged at the end of 1967 indicated a backing off from the approbation for the Malta proposal expressed in Goldberg's September 21 statement.[12] Ambassador Goldberg's intervention in Committee One on November 8 accurately expressed this changed attitude and was notably reserved in its evaluation of the Malta proposal. Goldberg presented three suggestions that were intended as conservative alternatives to the Pardo proposal. He proposed that the General Assembly establish a committee on the oceans to plan a comprehensive program of international cooperation, and that the General Assembly, through the committee on the oceans, begin to develop "general standards and principles to guide states and their nationals in the exploration and use of the deep ocean floor."[13]

The manner in which the three proposals had been developed within the government indicates the extent of interagency disagreement on a U.S. position and illustrates the relatively free hand that the State Department had to formulate ocean policy in 1967. The Ad Hoc Interagency Committee had been unable to secure the concurrence of all its members to the proposals and, in the absence of agency-wide agreement, the committee could not formally recommend or endorse them. Herman Pollack nonetheless presented the proposals to the Congress and Ambassador Goldberg took them to the UN. Although obviously free to formulate ocean policy without the unanimous support of the Ad Hoc Interagency Committee, the State Department did not use this freedom to devise far-reaching proposals. Instead, the Department tacitly acknowledged the strength of the opposition to the Malta proposal in Congress and the executive branch by limiting itself to three very cautious offerings. The proposals for an ocean committee, a program of international cooperation, and the formulation of principles to guide ocean use merely skirted the Malta proposal while trying to lead UN deliberations in less dangerous directions.

UN SEABED COMMITTEE. The most important outcome of the Malta proposal in the Twenty-second General Assembly was the establishment of a committee to give sustained consideration to the seabed resources question. The General Assembly rejected both the Soviet position in favor of leaving ocean issues to the Intergovernmental Oceanographic Commission and the U.S. proposal for a committee dealing with all ocean issues. It voted instead to establish a thirty-five nation "Ad Hoc Committee to Study the Peaceful Uses of the Sea-Beds and Ocean Floor Beyond the Limits of National Jurisdiction."[14] The Ad Hoc Seabed Committee was charged with preparing a study of "practical means to promote international cooperation in the exploration, conservation and use of the seabed and the ocean floor, and the subsoil thereof . . . and of their resources."

The U.S. Response

ORGANIZATIONAL CHANGES. Within the U.S. government and the State Department in particular, the Malta proposal and the creation of the Ad Hoc Seabed Committee engendered new interest in a national marine resources policy and new efforts to organize the decision-making process. In the wake of the Ad Hoc Interagency Committee's failure to secure a department-wide position, efforts were undertaken to streamline its operations and consolidate its chaotic structure. In December 1967 the Ad Hoc Interagency Committee was converted into the permanent Committee on International Policy in the Marine Environment (CIPME). CIPME's new chairman was Charles Bohlen, deputy under secretary of state for political affairs. Herman Pollack continued in the position of vice-chairman and conducted most of the meetings.

The membership of CIPME was smaller than that of its predecessor. Organized at the assistant secretary level, the agencies represented were the Departments of the Interior, Defense, Commerce, Transportation, the National Science Foundation, and the Marine Sciences Council. To enhance its effectiveness, CIPME's panel structure was greatly consolidated. The three CIPME subcommittees were the Committee on Legal Aspects of Scientific Research, the resilient Panel on International Programs and International Cooperative Organizations

(PIPICO), and a legal working group on the Seabed and the Deep Ocean Floor (SADOF). Despite its new attachment to CIPME, PIPICO continued to operate reasonably independently. Herman Pollack took charge of SADOF, the official center for decision making regarding the seabed in the Department of State. Members of SADOF included the Departments of Defense, Commerce, Interior, and Transportation, as well as State.[15] In practice, SADOF and CIPME were official forums for bilateral discussions among member agencies.[16] These discussions became more and more difficult as the seabed issue rose to prominence in the UN.

U.S. PROPOSALS. With its streamlined ocean policy machinery, the Department of State was eager to dispel the negative impression left at the UN by U.S. unwillingness to support the Pardo seabed proposal. In the course of 1968, the State Department formulated and advanced four ocean proposals in the Ad Hoc Seabed Committee, the General Assembly, and other forums. The first proposal called for a ban on weapons of mass destruction from the seabed and was put before the Eighteen-Nation Disarmament Committee (ENDC). The other three initiatives were developed within the CIPME framework and presented to the Ad Hoc Seabed Committee. They included establishing international marine preserves, launching an International Decade of Ocean Development, and preparing a declaration of principles to govern the use of the seabed.

The United States proposal for banning weapons of mass destruction from the seabed was in reality a response to a Soviet initiative. At the first meeting of the Ad Hoc Seabed Committee, the Soviet Union announced support for the principle of prohibiting all military uses of the seabed beyond the limits of national jurisdiction.[17] The scope of the Soviet-proposed ban was taken as a sign that the Soviets were lagging behind the Americans in the development of underwater detection devices. A comprehensive ban on military uses of the seabed would limit the use of such devices against Soviet missile-carrying submarines.[18] Regardless of Soviet motives, the move was popular in the United Nations and placed the U.S. government in the uncomfortable position of having to urge caution. The United States argued that the use of the seabed for peaceful purposes did not preclude all military activities and that the U.S. was willing to discuss a ban on weapons of mass destruction. In a draft resolution the United States proposed that the Eighteen-Nation Disarmament Committee in Geneva "take up the question of arms limitation on the seabed and the ocean floor with a view to defining those factors vital to a workable, verifiable and effective international agreement which would prevent the utilization of this new environment for the emplacement of weapons of mass destruction."[19] All arms limitation discussions were eventually referred to ENDC.

The U.S. proposal on international marine preserves was made at the second session of the Ad Hoc Seabed Committee held in June and July. It called for international agreements to set aside certain virgin marine areas for scientific research and the preservation of marine life. The United States offered Rose Island, an uninhabited coral atoll in the South Pacific, as a marine preserve. This proposal attracted little interest at the UN.[20]

The other two U.S. initiatives were foreshadowed in the November 1967 Goldberg statement to the General Assembly. The proposal to stimulate the investigation of ocean resources within an international cooperative framework was jointly formulated by SADOF and the Marine Sciences Council. It surfaced on January 17, 1968 in President Johnson's State of the Union message. The president suggested that the United States "launch, with other nations, an exploration of the ocean depth to tap its wealth and its energy and its abundance."[21] Then on March 8, in a conservation message to the Congress, the president added that he had "instructed the Secretary of State to consult with other nations on the steps that could be taken to launch an historic and unprecedented adventure—an International Decade of Ocean Exploration for the 1970's."[22] The Marine Sciences Council elaborated on the presidential announcements in a May 9 "white paper." The council described the decade as a "period of intensified collaborative planning, development of national capabilities, and execution of national and international programs of oceanic research and resource exploration."[23] As envisioned, the decade would be oriented toward both marine resource exploration and marine science research. Although the endorsement of the United Nations was desired, it was not intended that the Ad Hoc Seabed Committee coordinate the decade program.[24]

At the second session of the Ad Hoc Seabed Committee, the U.S. representative reiterated and elaborated on the plans for an oceanographic decade. In this and other forums, the United States entered into discussions with more than fifty nations. By the time of the twenty-third General Assembly, the United States had received a favorable reaction from a majority of member nations as well as from the ad hoc committee. The decade proposal was adopted by the plenary session of the General Assembly on December 21.

The United States proposal for a draft declaration of principles was the only U.S. initiative in 1968 directly related to the establishment of a seabed regime. The principles were intended to serve several purposes.

One was to stall for time. Another was to ensure that the United States would "be as much as possible in charge of the direction of events in the U.N. and not . . . be in the position of lacking firm proposals." The principles were further intended to allay the fears of developing nations that technologically advanced countries would appropriate the resources of the ocean floor for themselves.

Officially developed within CIPME, the U.S. draft declaration of principles was formulated by David Popper, the assistant secretary for international organization affairs, and an advisory group. With the establishment at the United Nations of the Ad Hoc Seabed Committee, the Bureau of International Organization Affairs had come to play an expanding role in the formulation and coordination of seabed policy. While members of this bureau took the initiative in developing the principles and in handling procedural and administrative aspects of their presentation to the Ad Hoc Seabed Committee, Herman Pollack's office provided the technical background and expertise. The principles were reviewed by a special group within CIPME which included representatives of the Departments of State, Interior, Defense, Commerce, Transportation, and the National Science Foundation.[25]

The draft declaration of principles was introduced in June at the second session of the Ad Hoc Seabed Committee. When submitting the principles to that committee's legal group, Leonard Meeker, the legal advisor of the State Department, reiterated the United States position that it was desirable "to consider the adoption of certain principles which would then serve as a guide to states in the conduct of their activities and also as general lines of direction to be observed in the working out of more detailed and internationally agreed arrangements that might be required later."[26] In developing such principles, the U.S. was taking its lead from the statement of President Johnson at the commissioning of the oceanographic vessel, "The Oceanographer," in 1966: "Under no circumstances, we believe, must we ever allow the prospects of rich harvest and mineral wealth to create a new form of colonial competition among the maritime nations. We must be careful to avoid a race to grab and hold the lands under the high seas. We must ensure that the deep seas and the ocean bottoms are, and remain, the legacy of all human beings."[27]

The principles were: (1) that no state might claim or exercise sovereignty or sovereign rights over any part of the deep ocean floor; (2) that internationally agreed arrangements to govern exploitation of deep-sea resources should be established as soon as practicable, with provisions for the orderly development of resources and for the dedication of a part of the value of the resources to "international community purposes";

(3) that an internationally agreed precise boundary for the deep ocean floor be established as soon as practicable, with the understanding that exploitation of the natural resources of the ocean floor prior to such delimitation would not prejudice its eventual location; (4) that states and their nationals would conduct themselves in accordance with international law in the use of the seabeds; (5) that states encourage cooperation in scientific investigation and dissemination of information; (6) that states show reasonable regard for the interests of other states by avoiding unjustifiable interference with the freedom of the sea and scientific research and by adopting safeguards to minimize pollution; (7) that states assist one another in the event of accidents or emergencies resulting from seabed activities.

Neither the seven principles advanced by the United States nor those proposed by other nations generated unanimous support within the Ad Hoc Seabed Committee. Much of the opposition to attempts to formulate principles on the seabed came from the Soviet bloc. Other countries did not agree to the draft principles for different reasons. While some believed that the Geneva Convention on the Continental Shelf needed to be revised in order to arrive at a more precise definition of the limits of national jurisdiction, others felt that discussions on a seabed regime could begin without a precise definition. Still others were reluctant to discuss the issue at all, fearing a loss of rights that had been recognized by the 1958 Geneva Convention.[28]

At the third meeting of the Ad Hoc Seabed Committee in August, the United States resumed its efforts to get agreement on a set of principles. The U.S. representative introduced a greatly abbreviated version of principles on which agreement was said to be most desirable. This condensed set of principles specified that there was an area of the seabed beyond national jurisdiction for which there should be a boundary and an internationally accepted regime for the exploitation of resources. This regime should be based on principles such as prohibiting national appropriation of seabed areas beyond national jurisdiction, nondiscrimination in exploitation rights, the conduct of resource exploitation for the benefit of mankind, and the reservation of the area for peaceful purposes. These suggested areas of agreement, stipulated Meeker, were "not a substitute for the more comprehensive draft resolution on principles which was advanced by the United States two months ago."[29]

Despite U.S. efforts, the Ad Hoc Seabed Committee failed to arrive at a consensus on principles by the end of the August meeting. It therefore incorporated in its report to the General Assembly two very different formulations of principles. The one, a "draft declaration of general principles" or set "A," reflected the views of delegations from six Latin

American and nine Afro-Asian countries. The other, a "draft resolution of agreed principles" or set "B," was based in large measure on the principles advanced by the United States and was supported by many members of the "Western European and others" group.[30]

The seven principles formulated in the State Department and re-formulated for the August meeting of the Ad Hoc Seabed Committee marked a substantial advance in the development of a U.S. position on the seabeds. In fact, the draft principles were to constitute the only U.S. policy on the seabed issue, apart from the question of military uses, until 1970. In light of the subsequent difficulties, the U.S. encountered in trying to move beyond this set of principles, it is noteworthy that in 1968 the principles had the endorsement of all agencies represented on CIPME, that is of the Departments of Defense, State, Interior, Commerce, Transportation, and the National Science Foundation. Agreement on the exact location of the continental shelf boundary or on the details of a seabed regime was not possible. Meeker alluded to the interagency differences when he said that the United States had two kinds of interests which were at times "not wholly working in the same direction." Not only was the United States a coastal nation, it was also a "considerable maritime power with the ability to do things far from our shores."[31] The conflict between these two orientations was just beginning to be realized in 1968.

The closing months of 1968 marked the end of the initial period of development of seabed policy both within the government and within the United Nations. From the Malta proposal to the end of the Johnson administration, the United States had moved gradually to develop broadly defined goals in the seabed. After reviewing the work of the executive and of the UN Ad Hoc Seabed Committee, the House Foreign Affairs Committee issued its report in October in which it generally supported the State Department's initiatives at the UN, while conveying the need for caution in further commitments. The committee also specified that "during the coming months, serious effort should be exerted by the concerned agencies of the U.S. government to work out their differences and to arrive at unified interagency positions on issues relating to the seabeds." In particular, the committee urged prompt action "to establish suitable arrangements for clarifying the limits of the territorial waters and to define the area of the ocean floor which lies beyond the limits of present national jurisdictions."[32]

At the United Nations a period of initial enquiry and study drew to a close in December.[33] The report of the secretary-general pursuant to Resolution 2172 (xxi) was in the hands of the General Assembly; the report of the Ad Hoc Seabed Committee was adopted on August 30 and also went to the General Assembly. After debate on these reports in Committees I and II, the plenary adopted three resolutions. Resolution 2413 (XXIII) on the "Exploitation and Conservation of Living Marine Resources," invited member nations to increase their cooperation in international development and exploitation organizations. Resolution 2412 (XXIII) on "International Co-operation in Problems Related to the Oceans" endorsed the concept of a long-term program of oceanographic research.

On the last day of the twenty-third session, the General Assembly adopted Resolution 2467 dealing with issues raised by the Ad Hoc Seabed Committee's report.[34] Separate votes were taken on this four-part resolution. By a vote of 112 to none with seven abstentions, part A of Resolution 2467 established a forty-two-member Committee on the Peaceful Uses of the Seabed and the Ocean Floor Beyond the Limits of National Jurisdiction. The committee was instructed (1) to study the elaboration of legal principles that would promote international cooperation in the use of the seabed and ensure the exploitation of seabed resources for the benefit of mankind; (2) to study ways to promote seabed resource exploitation; (3) to review other studies; (4) to examine antipollution measures; (5) to study the question of the reservation of the seabed for peaceful purposes; and (6) to report on its work at subsequent sessions of the General Assembly. Part B of this resolution was adopted by a vote of 119 to none. It requested the secretary-general, in cooperation with appropriate organizations, to undertake a study on the control of marine pollution.

Part C of Resolution 2467 encountered opposition from the United States, the Soviet Union, and several other nations. It was adopted in the plenary session by a vote of 85 to 9 with 25 abstentions. In it the General Assembly requested the secretary-general to study the means of establishing "appropriate international machinery for the promotion of the exploration and exploitation of the resources of this area [seabed], and the use of these resources in the interests of mankind." The resolution was unacceptable to nations that opposed a supranational seabed authority. Other countries considered it inappropriate to refer this question to the Secretariat when the new Seabed Committee had just been assigned the task of recommending an acceptable seabed regime. The United States abstained "because it had made no decision as to the desirability of such international machinery, and felt the resolution, which called for a study on the question by the Secretary-General, in effect prejudged this issue."[35]

The ocean resolutions adopted by the twenty-third session of the General Assembly were significant in several respects.[36] The establishment of a permanent Seabed Committee to succeed the Ad Hoc Seabed Committee ensured that the issue of seabed resources, their exploitation and allocation, would thenceforth be accorded prominence within the United Nations. The resolutions calling for expanded research and exploration on the subjects of fisheries, marine pollution, and other aspects of the marine environment signified an awareness of the need for increased knowledge of the oceans. At the same time, the reports requested of the secretary-general and the new Seabed Committee indicated that, while studies of the marine environment were in progress, a majority of nations wished to move toward concrete administrative arrangements for seabed resource exploitation.

The U.S. Draft Seabed Treaty

The years 1968 and 1969 were ones of stalemate and frustration within the U.S. government as well as in the UN Seabed Committee. Within the U.S., efforts to move beyond the 1968 draft declaration of principles were frustrated by the conflict between strategic and coastal resource interests. At the United Nations, efforts to reach agreement on seabed principles were blocked by nations who feared a threat to their coastal interests as well as by nations who feared any moves in the direction of a supranational seabed authority. With regard to seabed arms control, the United States and the Soviet Union did reach agreement on a draft treaty banning weapons of mass destruction from the ocean floor, only to have it rejected by the General Assembly.

Seabed and Continental Shelf Debate

By the time the Nixon administration took office, several powerful groups had developed new conceptions of their interests in the seabed and the policies needed to protect those interests. The Department of the Interior became the principal government representative of the view that the U.S. economic interest required direct control over the petroleum resources of a broadly defined continental margin (although Interior was divided over broad versus narrow jurisdiction for fishery resources). Interior was also sympathetic to the concerns of the hard mineral industry that sought a laissez-faire regime for deep seabed mining. The Defense Department, on the other hand, represented the naval interest in maintaining a global U.S. presence, unimpaired by extensive and comprehensive coastal-state claims to offshore areas. Fearing that limited claims to seabed areas would evolve into more expansive claims, Defense favored a narrow continental shelf boundary as well as an international seabed regime beyond to deter further national extensions.

The direct conflict between the preferred policies of these powerful protagonists placed the State Department in an uncomfortable position. Its Committee for International Policy in the Marine Environment (CIPME) was unable to find a suitable position that would command interagency agreement and therefore could not develop new policies for the UN Seabed Committee. Moreover, under the new administration, the State Department lacked the power to unilaterally impose a policy on the other agencies. Through the National Security Council system under Henry Kissinger, only the White House had the authority to resolve such a dispute.

The lack of agreement between Defense and Interior over the continental shelf boundary and the seabed regime was a product of the rapid development of ocean mineral recovery capabilities. While in 1963 and 1964 the Department of the Interior had issued oil leases in depths of over 200 meters, none resulted in production.[37] Primary interest therefore continued to focus on the shallow areas of the continental shelf. The leasing of seventy-one tracts in 1968 in the Santa Barbara channel signalled a significant change in this situation. More than half of the acreage leased at this auction was beyond depths of 600 feet (182 meters). Of the seventy-one tracts, eight were at depths of more than 1,200 feet (364 meters).[38] Returns to the U.S. Treasury from all outer continental shelf operations in 1968 were substantial, totaling almost $2 billion.[39] Royalty payments alone came to $201 million and increased to $214 million in 1969.[40] By the end of 1969, the government had issued oil leases out to 1,320 feet (400 meters) and exploration was underway.[41] The U.S. Geological Survey was reporting recoverable reserves on the U.S. continental margin of 180 to 220 billion barrels of petroleum liquids and from 820 to 1,100 trillion cubic feet of gas.[42]

With the Department of the Interior's determination to continue this lucrative leasing policy, the Department of Defense became increasingly concerned over the threat implied to its global interest in narrow national zones of offshore jurisdiction. Although the deepest producing well was only in 340 feet (103 meters) of water, the fact that the U.S. government, through its Interior Department, was issuing leases at depths well beyond that constituted a de facto claim to seabed jurisdiction based on the legal concept of exploitability. With exploratory wells already at depths of 1,300 feet (396 meters), the National Petroleum Council (NPC) was predicting a technical capability to drill and produce at depths of up to 1,500 feet (457 meters) by 1974.[43] It would not

209

be long, the Defense Department feared, before other nations would follow the U.S. example and make equal or even greater seabed claims.

OFFSHORE OIL AND THE INTERIOR DEPARTMENT. If the advance of technology toward increasing depths of exploitability had not encouraged the petroleum industry to pursue its continental shelf policy forcefully, the advent of the Nixon administration would doubtless have done so. It was clear during the Nixon presidential campaign and the early days of the new administration that the petroleum industry could expect sympathetic treatment at the highest levels of government. The new president announced that oil policy would be made in the White House and not in the Department of the Interior as had been the case during the Johnson administration.[44] Since Walter J. Hickel, the new secretary of the interior, was favorably regarded by the petroleum industry anyway, the industry looked forward to a double insurance that its interests would be protected.

By mid-1969 the Department of the Interior had arrived at a position of active support for a continental shelf policy substantially in line with the position of the National Petroleum Council. In its July 1968 Interim Report, the NPC first announced its support for a unilateral interpretation of the Geneva Convention on the Continental Shelf as providing a national continental shelf embracing the entire continental margin. Its position in favor of "parallel uniform declarations" of jurisdiction over the "submerged portion of the continent" was reaffirmed in its March 1969 final report.[45] In this report, the NPC stressed the point that it was neither necessary nor desirable to reach a new international agreement on the boundary of the national continental shelf, since the existing Geneva Convention sufficed. The NPC took issue, therefore, with the U.S. government position in the United Nations that exploitation prior to the establishment of the boundary should not prejudice its ultimate location.[46]

As financial returns from leasing at greater and greater depths increased, the Department of the Interior's support for a broad continental shelf grew accordingly. A careful reading of the congressional testimony of Interior Department officials over a period of several years indicates that the department had not always advocated such a boundary. Not long after the Malta initiative, the department's assistant secretary for fish and wildlife and parks testified that the question of the continental shelf boundary was "a little fuzzy" due to the exploitability clause of the Geneva Convention on the Continental Shelf.[47] In June 1968 department officials had little to add to their earlier uncertainty except to stress the desirability of agreeing upon a precise boundary.

At this hearing the Department of the Interior's solicitor, Edward Weinberg, testified that the department had participated in "the development and review of" the principles formulated within CIPME and presented later that month to the UN Seabed Committee. It was in the interests of the concerns for which the Interior Department was responsible, Mr. Weinberg said, to arrive "at a determination of this line of demarcation, so that" they could proceed with the issuance of licenses secure in "the knowledge that there is a line which is ascertainable, and within which there can be no question as to . . . the right of the United States to develop the resources."[48]

By 1969 the Department of the Interior was no longer speaking in terms of the ambiguous continental shelf boundary nor was its support for the June 1968 principles any longer unequivocal. On September 24, 1969, Russell E. Train, the new under secretary of the interior, presented a defense of the position favoring the extension of the national continental shelf to the foot of the continental margin. The Interior Department's position, as he expressed it, diverged from that of the NPC over the question of whether the nation's continental shelf already extended to the seaward portion of the rise or would do so with the advance of technology. The Interior Department favored the concept of the moving boundary. It therefore considered its "issuance of mineral leases beyond the 200-meter isobath as clearly a legitimate exercise of the rights afforded to the United States by virtue of the 1958 Geneva Convention."[49]

Under Secretary Train acknowledged that the Interior Department had participated in the formulation of the original June 1968 principles and in their reformulation for the just concluded August 1969 meeting of the UN Seabed Committee. In his restatement of the U.S. government's principles, however, Mr. Train was understandably selective.[50] For the most part he referred to the revised principles of 1969, since they were more congenial to the department's changed position than were the principles to which Interior had agreed in 1968. The 1969 principles omitted any reference to the provision calling for "an internationally agreed precise boundary between the deep ocean floor and the 'continental shelf.' " The Interior Department agreed with the NPC that no new international agreement need be negotiated since the provisions of the Geneva Convention on the Continental Shelf sufficed to establish the boundary.

The under secretary, in his interpretation of the government's principles, stressed the need to accommodate multiple ocean uses. It was the position of the Interior Department, Mr. Train explained, that the right to exploit the resources of the juridical continental shelf was expressly limited by the Geneva Convention on the Continental Shelf and did not include rights to the seabed itself or to the superjacent waters.[51] Therefore, as there was no legal basis for "creeping jurisdiction," a broad continental shelf should not be viewed as a potential threat to the freedom of the seas. The best way to deal with the problem of expanding national claims, in his view, did "not lie in limiting the access of this Nation to the resources of its own continental shelf but rather in reaching international agreements on the limits of the territorial sea." Mr. Train referred to the separate discussions being conducted on the limits of the territorial sea and pointed out that, if this important boundary question could be resolved, the danger of creeping jurisdiction would be eliminated.

DEFENSE DEPARTMENT. As the Interior Department moved toward a position favoring a broad continental shelf in 1969, the Defense Department position moved perceptibly in the opposite direction. This shift reflected the impact on Defense Department thinking of recent technological advances in offshore mining, the Interior Department's leasing policy, developments in the UN Seabed Committee, and the Henkin and Stratton Commission studies analyzing the effect of these developments on future military uses of the oceans (see Chapter 6).

The change in Defense Department attitudes can be traced through public pronouncements from 1967 to 1969. Several months after the Malta proposal, Assistant Secretary of the Navy Robert Frosch and Rear Admiral Wilfred A. Hearn had argued that proposals to internationalize the deep ocean floor were premature. Since ocean floor exploitation at great depths would not occur "for quite some time," there was no need to make a decision for a while. The admiral was satisfied that the general rule prohibiting "unjustifiable interference" with navigation, fishing, or conservation would adequately protect the defense interest. Moreover, Mr. Frosch argued, "any attempt to deal in a radical legal way with the sea bottom would interfere with some national security enterprise."[52]

By September 1969 the outlines of a less confident Defense Department attitude had begun to emerge. Although not yet prepared to recommend a specific location for the continental shelf boundary, the Defense Department did argue in favor of one that would be "narrower rather than broader." The boundary, moreover, "should be precise and should be defined by international agreement."[53] Department spokesmen stressed the fact that their support for a narrow national continental shelf was based on the national security interest in the freedom of the seas. They viewed this interest as being increasingly threatened by the tendency of rights in the ocean environment to expand from single to multipurpose rights. Starting from the premise that claims to the resources of the continental shelf would inevitably extend to the shelf and to the superjacent waters, Defense Department spokesmen argued that the continental shelf boundary would necessarily affect the territorial sea boundary and they could not therefore be resolved independently of one another as the Interior Department had suggested. In contrast to Interior's efforts to distinguish between the determination of a territorial sea boundary and legal rights to the continental shelf and the superjacent waters, the Department of Defense came in 1969 to link the territorial sea, straits, and fisheries issues to policy on the continental shelf and seabed regime.

The Department of Defense was as selective as the Interior Department in its interpretation of the principles supported by the U.S. government at the United Nations. It neglected the principle stressing the need to accommodate conflicting uses of the ocean environment. Instead Defense Department spokesmen stressed the importance of the principle calling for international agreement on a precise continental shelf boundary, since the expansion of offshore claims· occurred by means of unilateral national declarations. Moreover, the Defense Department interpreted "international agreement" to mean an international convention or protocol, and it unequivocally ruled out unilateral declarations of jurisdiction as recommended by the NPC.[54]

MILITARY USES OF THE SEABED.   While advocating a narrow continental shelf, the Department of Defense was less than precise on exactly where the boundary should be located. Warren Nutter, the assistant secretary of defense for international affairs, testified that the Defense Department favored "200 meters as defined in the existing Geneva Convention, but . . . would not preclude consideration of other depths, isobaths, or distance."[55] Where the apparent restriction of fossil fuels to the continental land mass provided the National Petroleum Council and the Interior Department with a clear interest in a continental shelf boundary at the base of the continental block, the several considerations determining the defense interest did not work in a single direction. The Defense Department was concerned to maximize both the area of the high seas and the area of the seabed that would be free from coastal-state jurisdiction over military uses.[56] Therefore, the Defense Department had a double interest in maintaining a narrow continental shelf, providing of course that the military was at liberty to emplace detection devices on the seabed beyond national jurisdiction.[57] That freedom, however, was being brought into question at the meetings of the Eighteen-Nation Disarmament Committee (ENDC) in Geneva where the Soviet Union was urging a ban on all military uses of the seabed.

In brief, the situation within the Eighteen-Nation Disarmament Committee (or the Conference of the Committee on Disarmament as it was later called) was one of superpower disagreement on two central issues.[58] The United States was at odds with the Soviet Union over the types of military activities that should be banned from the seabed and over the extent of the seabed to which the ban should apply. The U.S. position, consonant with its vested interest in using bottom-mounted detection devices, was that some military activities were defensive by nature and were desirable; it was therefore necessary to distinguish "between peaceful uses of the seabed and complete demilitarization of the seabed."[59] The U.S. supported a ban only on nuclear weapons and other weapons of mass destruction fixed on the ocean floor beyond an off-shore zone of three miles.[60] The Soviet Union, less advanced than the United States in the development of underwater surveillance devices, proposed a complete demilitarization of the ocean floor beyond a twelve-mile zone.[61]

The Defense Department's uncertainty then as to the most desirable continental shelf boundary was due to the unresolved issue of military uses of the seabed. If the U.S. position were to prevail at Geneva, the military would be free to use the seabed for surveillance devices and would therefore want as large a non-national seabed area as possible, beginning at the 200-meter isobath. If the Soviet proposal for complete demilitarization of the non-national seabed area should prevail, bottom-mounted detection devices could only be placed on national continental shelves subject to the agreement of the coastal nation. In this event, the military would favor a continental shelf boundary at a depth greater than 200 meters, despite the anticipated difficulty of securing coastal-state agreement to the use of the shelf for detection devices.[62]

By October 1969 the United States and the Soviet Union reached an accommodation on a draft treaty that would forbid only the emplacement of weapons of mass destruction on the seabed beyond an offshore zone of twelve miles.[63] After its initial rejection by other nations and the revision of several provisions,[64] the draft treaty was adopted by the twenty-fifth General Assembly on November 17, 1970 with its restriction to weapons of mass destruction unchanged.[65] The Seabed Arms Control Treaty was signed by the U.S. and the Soviet Union in February 1971.[66] Once U.S.-Soviet agreement had been reached and it was clear that surveillance devices would not be banned from the seabed, the Department of Defense moved to support the narrowest definition of the continental shelf possible—the 200-meter isobath. The central

Defense Department concern became the impact on navigational freedoms of proliferating national claims to offshore areas.

HARD MINERALS INDUSTRY. As the debate between defense and petroleum interests developed, the newly formed seabed hard minerals industry became concerned with the impact of the continental shelf boundary on the deep seabed regime. The industry interest in the boundary question was indirect. Of principal concern to seabed miners were the manganese nodules of the deep seabed, well beyond the continental margins. While all manganese nodules contain varying amounts of a large number of minerals such as manganese, cobalt, copper, nickel, iron, silicon, and aluminum, those nodules of greatest commercial interest were expected to lie in the deepest parts of the Pacific Ocean (at depths of up to 18,000 feet).[67] Because nodules with a high concentration of copper, nickel, and cobalt were rarely found on the continental margin, locating the national continental shelf boundary at any point up to the outer edge of the margin would not directly affect the nodule miner.

The industry concern with the continental shelf boundary, therefore, was largely tactical. That is, it wished to see a boundary settlement that would have positive side effects on the regime for the deep seabed. As a result of changes in industry perceptions, mining industry policy underwent several transitions—from early support for a broad continental shelf, to a policy favoring a moving shelf boundary, to a total disregard of the boundary issue combined with a firm position on the regime beyond national jurisdiction. In August 1968, for example, the petroleum and hard minerals industries were in substantial agreement that the rights of coastal states already extended to the minerals on the entire continental margin. They also agreed that it was premature to consider establishing a regime for the seabed beyond that boundary.[68]

By 1969 the hard minerals interest group broke with the oil industry and began to move away from the wide margin position. The new view was that the Geneva Convention on the Continental Shelf "extends sovereign rights over the seabed beyond the 200-meter line only as technological progress makes exploitation in that area possible in fact."[69] This newly independent position on the continental shelf boundary coincided with greater knowledge about the location of commercially attractive deposits and a growing tactical sophistication. Although the mining industry shared the petroleum industry's aversion to international administrative organizations, it had come to believe that mining companies would be operating in areas beyond the limits of national jurisdiction no matter where the continental shelf boundary was drawn.

215

Ocean miners had to be concerned, therefore, with the nature of the seabed regime which would govern deep-sea exploitation, a concern which was not shared by the petroleum interest given its policy on the extent of national seabed jurisdiction.

Despite the absence of a direct interest in the boundary issue, the hard minerals industry maintained its tactical concern with the boundary dispute through 1969 and 1970. Mining representatives were willing to support a narrow but outward moving boundary if such a boundary could be used to buy a satisfactory seabed regime.[70] By a "satisfactory regime," the hard minerals industry meant a system of freedom to explore the seabed, to stake claims, and to receive exclusive licenses to exploit the claimed areas. An international authority, in this view, should be no more than a registry agency, and its financial exactions should be minimal.

Although the mining industry was willing to trade the petroleum industry's broad continental shelf for a favorable seabed regime, it was soon apparent that the Defense Department was an unreliable ally. To induce other nations to agree to a narrow continental shelf in 1970, Defense promoted the establishment of a powerful and generous seabed authority to administer the exploration and exploitation of seabed resources and to allocate substantial revenues from these activities to an international development fund. The hard minerals industry strongly opposed the Defense Department position, but was not successful in blocking it. Due to its position on the boundary, the hard minerals interest had lost the support of the petroleum industry. And within the Interior Department, hard minerals had to compete with petroleum for the time and energy of government bureaucrats responsible for seabed policy.

U.S. Government Organization

The conflict over the continental shelf boundary posed special problems for the Department of State. Unable to develop a unified U.S. seabed policy, State was powerless to influence developments within the UN Seabed Committee. Moreover, delay in presenting a U.S. position was interpreted by other UN members as a deliberate obstructionism. State officials were particularly concerned about the proliferation of national ocean claims and the threat that this posed to peace and order in the oceans. Only if the U.S. could formulate and implement a policy on national offshore boundaries, they believed, could she successfully influence other countries to moderate their claims accordingly. In the meantime, all the State Department could do was protest claims that it deemed unreasonable.

Within the State Department the CIPME coordinating and policy-formulating role was jeopardized by the interagency dispute. As CIPME failed, the Bureau of International Organization Affairs and the Legal Advisor's Office took the lead in ad hoc efforts to seek interagency compromise. The former was responsible for U.S. positions in the UN Seabed Committee and the latter handled the bilateral negotiations on territorial seas, straits, and fisheries. Both were anxious to see a prompt resolution of the boundary issue and to avoid having the dispute decided by the White House.

In February 1970, the ad hoc link between the Legal Advisor's Office and the Bureau of International Affairs was formalized with the creation of an Interagency Task Force on the Law of the Sea. The mandate of the task force was to coordinate the government's negotiating position on seabed and law of the sea issues. Because of his extensive involvement in the straits and territorial sea negotiations, John Stevenson, the legal advisor, was designated task force chairman,[71] and Joseph Greene, deputy assistant secretary for international organization affairs, was appointed vice-chairman. Herman Pollack, who had been acting as CIPME's chairman, was accorded membership on the task force along with representatives of several other State Department bureaus. Other agencies represented on the task force included the Departments of Defense, Interior, Justice, Commerce, and Transportation, as well as representatives of the National Security Council, the National Science Foundation, and the National Council on Marine Resources and Engineering Development. Ad hoc members included the Bureau of the Budget, the Permanent Mission of the United States to the United Nations, and the CIA.

The Interagency Task Force was divided into four subcommittees, the most powerful of which was the Executive Operations Group, responsible for identifying and assigning tasks to and considering the recommendations of all other working groups. The group had only four members, the chairman and vice-chairman of the task force and the representatives of the Departments of Defense and Interior. The executive group met once or twice a week while the full membership of the task force met once a month for briefing and questions. It was the Executive Operations Group that was effectively in control of U.S. decisions on law of the sea.

The consolidation of law of the sea and continental shelf/seabed issues in the Department of State initiated similar processes in the Departments of Defense and Interior. Until the spring of 1970, separate staffs had serviced each issue area in the Defense Department. In September of 1968, the judge advocate general of the navy served as the Defense Department representative on matters relating to the law of the sea, while the assistant secretary of navy for research and development followed UN seabed issues as the department representative to CIPME. A Defense Advisory Group on Law of the Sea (DAGLOS) had been established to facilitate coordination between these two areas. It was chaired by Leigh Ratiner of the General Counsel's Office and staffed on seabed questions by a representative of the Office of International Security Affairs (ISA). Then a month after the establishment of the Interagency Task Force in State, DAGLOS assumed control over all matters having legal implications for jurisdiction in the seas and on the seabeds, including the territorial sea, the continental shelf, and the regime for the seabed beyond. The DAGLOS membership continued to include representatives of the Office of the Assistant Secretary of Defense for International Security Affairs, the Office of the Chief of Naval Operations, the Office of the Navy Judge Advocate General, the Air Force, the Army, and the Joint Chiefs of Staff.[72] Ratiner continued to serve as the Defense Department's representative to the law of the sea task force.

The Department of the Interior had long-standing responsibilities in both seabed mining and fisheries matters. These issues were handled in separate bureaus. While offshore leasing was managed by the Bureau of Land Management, fisheries questions were the responsibility of the Bureau of Commercial Fisheries. The assistant director for international affairs in the Bureau of Commercial Fisheries had represented Interior in early negotiations on its U.S. fisheries proposals. In 1966, the Department of the Interior had also formed a task force of experts to formulate a marine resources development program, with the assistant secretary for fish and wildlife and parks as program administrator.[73] Concurrently, the solicitor of the department served as its official representative to CIPME.[74]

In 1969, the department appointed an informal law of the sea advisory committee to coordinate its several areas of interest in international developments in this field. In April 1970, the Office of Marine Resources in the Interior Department was transferred to the Office of the Secretary and was renamed the Office of Marine Affairs.[75] In September, David Stang, assistant to the under secretary, took charge of coordinating departmental activities relating to questions of the continental shelf, seabeds, the Arctic, territorial sea, and international fisheries. Stang also served as the Interior Department's representative to the Interagency Task Force.

The Decision Process

In March 1969, Secretary of Defense Melvin Laird requested a National Security Study Memorandum (NSSM) on the continental shelf question. The NSSM[76] proposed that the NSC Under Secretaries Committee meet to consider the position the United States should take at the United Nations regarding the location of the continental shelf boundary. It further suggested that the committee seek to reconcile the U.S. position on the continental shelf boundary with its position on the territorial sea and related issues.

The April NSSM marked the first step in a policy process that was to carry the question of the continental shelf boundary to the president. The process, known as the "NSC options system," was used by the president and his national security adviser, Henry Kissinger, to consolidate control over foreign policy.[77] A NSSM triggered the decision process by eliciting different agency views and recommending policy options. This would then be followed by an Under Secretaries Committee review. If disagreement persisted, the chairman of the Under Secretaries Committee was to forward his report together with the agency options to the National Security Council for staff assessment. The options were ultimately presented to the president with Kissinger's recommendation.[78]

State Department as Mediator

No date was set for the Under Secretaries Committee meeting, and State Department officials continued to hope that a compromise formula might be worked out that would satisfy both sides. To avoid an open impasse, State convened the full membership of CIPME less and less frequently. Instead, department officials promoted bilateral discussions between the principal protagonists. At the same time, State tried to buttress the stature of the rapidly failing CIPME.[79] The office of CIPME chairman was upgraded by replacing Charles Bohlen, deputy under secretary of state, with U. Alexis Johnson, the new under secretary for political affairs.[80] Johnson devoted a substantial portion of his time to CIPME affairs.

The uncomfortable State Department role as a mediator with no power was exacerbated by pressures from the U.S. Congress and the United Nations for an executive position on the continental shelf boundary and seabed regime. As the interagency dispute became known throughout the government, a number of Senate subcommittees sprang up with an interest in influencing the U.S. position. In addition to Senator Claiborne Pell's (D-R.I.) Subcommittee on Ocean Space of the Foreign Relations Committee,[81] two other committees held hearings in 1969. In July the Committee on Commerce established a special study group chaired by Senator Ernest F. Hollings (D-S.C) to consider "the policy which the United States should advocate within the United Nations."[82] This became a Subcommittee on Oceanography charged with the Special Study on United Nations Suboceanic Land Policy. In August the Committee on Interior and Insular Affairs established a Special Subcommittee on the Outer Continental Shelf chaired by Senator Lee Metcalf (D-Montana) "to assist the executive branch . . . in arriving at a policy position that is in our country's best interests."[83]

During the Senate hearings, State Department officials characterized their agency's foreign policy role on the continental shelf question as one of helping to "get a consensus of the interests of the United States and project them into an international setting."[84] In light of the April NSSM, this description represented a not unrealistic assessment of the State Department's relative power and the extent of its influence with the Nixon White House.[85] In congressional testimony, department officials carefully avoided taking a position on the points at issue between the Departments of Interior and Defense. When Senator Pell complained that the State Department was forgoing the exercise of its leadership role and that of the United States by not reaching a decision on these and other seabed questions, U. Alexis Johnson deftly explained that the United States was exercising "a leadership role in keeping options open until we decide where our national interests lie best."[86] In fact, he concluded, the main purpose of the June 1968 principles presented to the Ad Hoc Seabed Committee was to keep U.S. options open until a decision could be made.

Events within the United Nations Seabed Committee belied this optimistic view of the U.S. leadership role. Eager to move ahead with its mandate to elaborate legal principles to promote international cooperation in the use of the seabed, the Seabed Committee had held an organizational meeting in February 1969 and its first substantive session in March. In the summer, an Informal Drafting Group consulted on legal issues, and the secretary-general's report on administrative and organizational arrangements was issued. In the course of these meetings, little progress was made toward agreement on legal principles and the need for a seabed regime. The resulting frustration and antagonism was ultimately directed at the developed nations—the United States and the Soviet Union in particular—for what was viewed as their dilatory tactics.

CHART 7-A
UNCLOS III Preparations: 1968-1970

Ad Hoc Committee to Study the Peaceful Uses of the Sea-bed and the
   Ocean Floor Beyond the Limits of National Jurisdiction. (Created
   by UNGA Res. 2340 [XXII], December 18, 1967, with 35 member
   states.)

1968   March 18-27, New York
       June 17-July 9, New York
       August 19-30, Rio de Janeiro

Committee on the Peaceful Uses of the Sea-Bed and the Ocean Floor
   Beyond the Limits of National Jurisdiction. (Replaces Ad Hoc Committee, UNGA Res. 2467 A [XXIII], December 21, 1968; 42 member
   states.)

1969   February 6 and 7, New York
       March 10-28, New York
       August 11-29, New York
1970   March 2-26, New York
       August 3-28, Geneva

In the face of the Defense-Interior dispute and in light of differences
of opinion within the State Department itself,[87] U.S. delegates to the
United Nations were able to do little more than stall for time. Meanwhile the utility of the U.S. government's June 1968 principles was fast
diminishing. In the face of determined Defense Department and Interior Department efforts to reinterpret the principles according to their
respective interests, even this limited progress toward developing a
United States position was rapidly being eroded.

To counter this trend and to prepare for the August 1969 meeting of
the UN Seabed Committee, the State Department mounted a valiant
effort to redefine the U.S. government position in a manner acceptable
to both Interior and Defense. With the question of the continental
shelf boundary hopelessly deadlocked, other areas of potential agreement were sought. The several U.S. agencies had come to accept the
view of some Latin American delegates that boundary issues could only
be discussed in relation to the seabed question. And the seabed regime
proved to be a subject upon which some accommodation was possible.
Both the Defense and the Interior Departments were willing to accept
a limited international registry scheme for seabed resource exploitation.

This measure of agreement became the core of the U.S. position by the time the UN Seabed Committee reconvened on August 11, 1969.

The revised U.S. position was formulated by the Department of State in three parts.[88] The first part was a bare-bones set of legal principles providing for the use of the seabeds. The second and only new part concerned machinery for seabed resource exploration and exploitation. And the third part dealt with U.S. policy on the continental shelf boundary. This tripartite division was designed to separate areas of agreement from those of disagreement and to enable the U.S. to move ahead on the former. The set of legal principles proposed by the United States in the first part of its August 1969 position was a reworked version of the set "B" principles supported by the U.S. in late 1968. The most controversial provisions were omitted not only to satisfy contending domestic interests but also to improve the chances of reaching a consensus on principles in the Seabed Committee.

The United States omitted the seabed regime issue from its revised legal principles largely to secure their acceptance by the Soviet Union. The issue was too important to developing nations, however, to be omitted from the U.S. position altogether, and it became the second and central facet of the U.S. position in August 1969. The secretary-general's June 18 report on administrative and organizational machinery for seabed resource exploitation was the prime subject under consideration in the August meeting of the Economic and Technical Subcommittee of the UN Seabed Committee. It was in that body that the United States adopted a "preliminary view" favoring "an international registry of claims governed by agreed criteria and supplemented by appropriate procedures." Under this regime, "governments would be responsible for adherence by their nationals to the criteria."[89] The U.S. further proposed "dedication as feasible and practicable of a portion of the value of the resources recovered from the deep seabeds to international community purposes."[90] Although it did not go far enough to satisfy most developing nations, a registry scheme creating a central authority lacking the power to deny claims, enforce standards, or control military uses of the seabed was acceptable to both the Departments of Interior and Defense.[91]

While the State Department had managed to obtain a measure of agreement within the government on a skeletal list of legal principles and on a restricted type of seabed machinery, the third part of its August 1969 position, namely the continental shelf boundary issue, remained unresolved. Although it continued to advocate an internationally agreed precise boundary, the State Department still took no stand on the desirable location of the boundary or on the exact means of agreeing upon it. Department officials did point out that there was "ample precedent for having different boundaries, different areas of jurisdiction for different purposes."[92] This statement on the viability of distinguishing between an ocean floor boundary and boundaries in the water column reflected a trend in State Department thinking toward acceptance of some aspects of the Interior Department's position. As if to confirm that trend, the State Department also adopted a position favoring continued seabed exploration and exploitation pending the establishment of a definitive continental shelf boundary.

The trend in State Department thinking toward accepting portions of the Interior Department policy became even clearer in late 1969 when the department renewed its efforts to find a compromise continental shelf policy. With the CIPME mechanism hopelessly stalled, the Bureau of International Organization Affairs and the Legal Advisor's Office took the lead in seeking a compromise. They produced a proposal on the continental shelf which was circulated in the late fall of 1969. It attempted to accommodate the interests of both the Department of Defense and the Department of the Interior by adopting an intermediate zone for the area between the 200-meter isobath and the outer edge of the continental margin.[93] In this zone the coastal nation would control the exploration and exploitation of seabed resources. Traditional quotas and tariff protection would not apply to the petroleum resources recovered from the intermediate zone. While responsible for enforcing standards to protect against pollution and navigation hazards, the coastal nation would not have the right to exclude other nations from conducting scientific research or military activities on the continental margin beyond the 200-meter isobath. Legitimate scientific research was explicitly guaranteed. A further aspect of the proposal was that the coastal state would guarantee that it would submit any plans to expropriate foreign concessions in its intermediate zone to compulsory arbitration. To induce the developing nations to accept such a proposal, the State Department compromise stipulated that a small royalty of two percent based on the value of mineral resources exploited in the zone be paid to an existing international development fund.[94] The proposal sought to ensure exclusive jurisdiction for the United States and other coastal nations over offshore petroleum resources while guaranteeing continued freedom of navigation and military and scientific access to continental margins below the depth of 200 meters.

State Department hopes to bring the Departments of Defense and Interior into agreement were quickly disappointed. The Department of Defense flatly rejected the new proposal as a cosmetic version of the Department of the Interior position. It argued that by giving the coastal state exclusive jurisdiction over resource exploitation on the continental margin, the proposal jeopardized the freedom of other nations to use that area for other purposes. Guarantees of access for military or scientific purposes, Defense argued, would simply not be acceptable to coastal nations. Moreover, an intermediate zone would be temporary at best, ultimately evolving into a zone of sovereign rights applicable to the superjacent waters as well as to the seabed. What was needed instead was international administration of seabed resource exploitation beyond the 200-meter or the 550-meter isobath. To gain the agreement of developing nations to such a narrow continental shelf, the international regime established beyond the continental shelf boundary would have to provide substantial benefits to the international community and to developing nations in particular. Only by combining a narrow continental shelf with a satisfactory international regime, the Defense Department insisted, would there be any chance of halting the proliferation of unilateral national claims.

Officials in the Department of the Interior objected less strenuously to the State Department proposal, since it satisfied their primary concern to maintain national jurisdiction over petroleum resources of the U.S. continental margin. They were willing to accept the concept of an intermediate zone as long as it did not call into question the ownership of seabed resources of the zone. The Department of the Interior was even willing to go along with a small payoff to the international community if that was required to ensure national jurisdiction over these resources. The National Science Foundation also found that it could support the State Department proposal provided that it maintained absolute protection for scientific research in the intermediate zone.

GENERAL ASSEMBLY RESOLUTION.   While the State Department was seeking consensus among government agencies, events at the UN reached a critical stage. Operating according to the consensus principle, the Seabed Committee had made little progress by the end of the year toward reaching agreement on a seabed regime. In December, the frustration of developing countries over what they viewed as the recalcitrance of the developed nations was expressed in a series of General Assembly resolutions, passed in some cases over the opposition of the United States and the Soviet Union.[95] On December 12, for instance, a two-thirds majority of the General Assembly sent back to the Geneva Conference the Soviet-American draft treaty banning weapons of mass destruction from the ocean floor.[96]

On December 15 the General Assembly adopted Resolution 2574 dealing with the oceans.[97] Part A of that resolution called on the secretary-general to poll the membership on whether to call a conference to discuss all law of the sea issues in order to arrive at an internationally accepted definition of the seabed area beyond national jurisdiction. This resolution was directly contrary to U.S. and Soviet support for a division of law of the sea issues into "manageable packages" that could be separately considered.[98] It carried, nonetheless, by a vote of 65 in favor, 12 opposed, with 30 abstentions. Part B of Resolution 2574 called on the Seabed Committee to expedite its work on developing legal principles and to submit a draft declaration of principles to the twenty-fifth session of the General Assembly. Part C requested the secretary-general to prepare a study on types of international seabed machinery with particular attention given to its status, structure, functions, and powers. Resolution 2574D, or the "moratorium resolution," declared a halt to all exploitation of seabed resources beyond national jurisdiction pending the establishment of an international regime for the seabed. The declaration added that no claim to any part of the seabed area or its resources would be recognized. The developing nations passed the resolution over U.S. and Soviet opposition by a vote of 62 in favor, 28 opposed, and 28 abstentions.[99]

The official U.S. position regarding the moratorium resolution was that it was merely a recommendation and was not, therefore, legally binding.[100] The reasoning behind U.S. opposition was that it was not in the international interest to retard the advance of seabed resource exploitation and technology.[101] The State Department supported the continued exploitation of the seabed with the stipulation that it should not prejudice the eventual settlement of the continental shelf boundary. Although the United States did support a moratorium on further seabed claims, it could not support a resolution that would have the undesirable effect of encouraging governments to claim large offshore areas in order to remove them from the scope of the prohibition contained in the resolution.[102]

While the growing hostility over the perceived dilatory tactics of developed nations furnished an incentive for the U.S. to formulate a position on the seabed regime and the continental shelf boundary, the moratorium resolution introduced an additional source of friction into the Defense-Interior feud. The Defense Department seized the opportunity of the moratorium resolution to challenge Interior's right to continue issuing leases beyond the 200-meter depth contour. Defense had been urging the State Department to adopt an international moratorium on boundary claims as part of the U.S. position on legal principles. In a note to the secretary of the interior, Melvin Laird reportedly asked for a halt on leasing in greater depths of water. Secretary Hickel's response was unequivocally negative. The Department of the Interior had no intention of discontinuing leasing beyond the 200-meter isobath. Nor did it agree with the State Department that continued seabed resource exploitation should not prejudice the eventual location of an internationally accepted continental shelf boundary.[103]

UNDER SECRETARIES COMMITTEE MEETS.   Faced by an intransigent Interior Department, a weak State Department, and a clear policy trend toward increasing assertions of U.S. foreign offshore jurisdiction, the Defense Department resolved to take the dispute to the highest levels of government. Accordingly it pressed for an early meeting of the Under Secretaries Committee. The meeting was scheduled for January 29, 1970, thereby setting in motion a period of intense intragovernmental activity. Law of the sea officials within the Departments of Defense and Interior refined positions and prepared papers. They briefed secretaries, under secretaries, and assistant secretaries on the positions of their agencies, and recruited allies among other agencies and in the White House. The Department of the Interior consolidated the backing of the Department of Commerce and won the support of the Bureau of the Budget and of the White House domestic affairs staff headed by John Ehrlichman. The Department of Defense found support within the Department of Justice and the National Security Council and continued to lobby in the State Department for a revision of the compromise proposal. The State Department lined up the Transportation Department and the National Science Foundation to back up its proposal.

After months of anticipation, the Under Secretaries Committee meeting was brief.[104] The committee was called to order at 4:00 p.m. on January 29, 1970 by Under Secretary of State Elliot L. Richardson. Crowded around the table were representatives of a dozen agencies.[105] The paper officially before the committee was the compromise proposal drawn up in the Department of State. In fact, there were three positions on the continental shelf boundary before the group. The first would establish a narrow boundary at a depth no greater than 550 meters. The second would establish a wide continental shelf with the boundary at the junction of the continental margin and the abyssal ocean floor. The third position would create an intermediate zone in the area between the 200-meter isobath and the ocean floor in which national jurisdiction would be strictly limited to seabed resources. As chairman of the meeting, Under Secretary Richardson saw to it that each of these positions was spelled out.

The outcome of the Under Secretaries Committee meeting was predictably inconclusive. Although the pros and cons of the State, Defense, and Interior positions were heatedly discussed, there was no agreement. The conflict was not to be traced to a fundamental disagreement over national goals, rather it stemmed from different sets of priorities that each agency had regarding the nation's interests in the oceans. These differing priorities reflected the divergent functions, interests, and constituencies of the agencies involved. No agency called for a sacrifice of any of the goals considered paramount by another interest. Instead each of the contenders offered a complete design for guaranteeing the achievement of all the nation's ocean goals. The agency controversy, therefore, took the form of a conflict over means. However, the controversy over means was linked closely to a fundamental difference in outlook as to the nature of international relations and of United States foreign policy. The Departments of State and Defense avowed the need for sustained multilateral dealings with other nations in pursuit of U.S. goals, while the agencies with a domestic orientation adopted a more isolationist posture.

Given the power of the contending interests, an Under Secretary's Committee review could not dictate a settlement.[106] Under the circumstances, the role of the Under Secretaries Committee was to help define the options open to the president, who would make the final decision. With the policy dispute elevated to the White House for presidential resolution, the contending agencies began to lobby more vigorously than ever for the support of other groups in behalf of their positions. The Defense Department and its allies, including Senator Pell and the U.S. mission to the United Nations, made representations to Under Secretary of State Richardson to the effect that the State Department position would not be saleable to many developing nations. In response to these arguments, and in his individual capacity, Richardson proposed a fourth policy position on the continental shelf boundary and the seabed regime for consideration by the president.[107]

Richardson's proposal, formulated in March, represented a compromise between the State Department's position on an intermediate zone and the Defense Department's position on a continental shelf ending at the 200-meter isobath.[108] The under secretary proposed that the concept of the intermediate zone be retained but that the zone be expressly recognized as international in character. The proposal went on to stipulate, however, that within the intermediate zone the coastal state would have the exclusive right to administer natural resource exploitation as a trustee for the international community and to receive certain benefits from this activity. The Richardson proposal further provided for the collection of internationally agreed royalties of a specified amount from exploitation within the seabed area. These royalties were to be used for international community purposes, especially for aid to developing countries. The significant differences between the Richardson proposal and the initial State Department position lay in the form of sovereignty to be established within the intermediate zone—in effect, the location of the legal continental shelf boundary—and the portion of royalties to be allocated to the international community. Given Mr. Richardson's influence and his personal support for a revised position, his proposal soon became the leading position within the State Department.

The reactions of the Departments of Defense and Interior to this new proposal were swift and predictable. While the Defense Department reiterated its opposition to this or any other variation on the concept of the intermediate zone, it acknowledged that the Richardson proposal might prove acceptable as a "fall-back" position. The Department of the Interior vigorously opposed the new proposal. Its main drawback, as Interior saw it, was that it would give the international community the discretionary authority to allow the coastal state to act as a "trustee" in its own intermediate zone. Such authority would mean that the international community, of which underdeveloped nations constituted a majority, would have the power to decide upon and to impose production controls, to fix high royalty payments, to impose other onerous restrictions upon the coastal state, or to exclude the coastal state altogether from its trusteeship zone. Finally the Interior Department expressed concern that the Richardson proposal, unlike the original State Department position, called for the payment of a large amount in royalties to an international fund. For these reasons, the Department of the Interior strongly urged a return to the original State Department position.

THE PRESIDENT DECIDES. With the formulation of the Richardson proposal and the retention of the original State Department proposal at Interior's insistence, there were four policy options to be considered by the White House. These policy positions were drawn up and sent to the president in March, but no decision on the options was forthcoming until the end of May.[109] One reason for the delay was the fact that the continental shelf/seabed regime issue had to compete with more pressing problems such as the war in Vietnam and the U.S. invasion of Cambodia for the time and attention of busy presidential advisors. Related to this source of delay was the absence of technical, legal, and political expertise on ocean matters among the White House staff. In the course of intensive agency lobbying, however, key staff members in the National Security Council and the domestic affairs side of the

White House gradually became familiar with the political issues behind the agency dispute.

With this growing mastery of the continental shelf/seabed regime issue came a new source of delay—a firm difference of opinion among the president's own advisors.[110] John Ehrlichman, presidential assistant for domestic affairs, and his assistant John Whittaker held conversations in March with Secretary of the Interior Walter Hickel and other Interior officials. As a result of these discussions, Ehrlichman came down firmly on the side of the Interior Department. Ehrlichman did not want the president to be accused of giving away the nation's mineral estate. Such politically damaging attacks could be avoided only by adopting either the original State Department position or the Interior Department's proposal. Concerned with the adverse foreign policy implications of these two options, Henry Kissinger and his staff were more receptive to the forceful representations of Secretary of Defense Melvin Laird and other Defense Department officials. The National Security Council, therefore, threw its support behind the Defense Department and the Richardson positions. Only these options, it was believed, would enable the United States to persuade the rest of the international community to accept narrow continental shelf boundaries and a narrow territorial sea. This disagreement between the president's advisors on foreign and domestic affairs prolonged the period of decision.[111]

From March through May, State and Defense Department representatives pressed for a prompt White House decision. They pointed out that a presidential announcement of an attractive seabed proposal during the March meeting of the Seabed Committee would have salutary effects in the committee as well as in U.S. efforts in the territorial sea, straits, and fisheries discussions. When that failed, State and Defense directed White House attention to the deteriorating international situation. A number of nations were making extreme claims to offshore jurisdiction, claims that might be headed off by an attractive U.S. proposal on the continental shelf and the seabed regime. A case in point was the recent action of the Brazilian government, which on March 25 had followed up its claim to prohibit all military activity in the area of its continental margin with an extension of its territorial sea from twelve to 200 miles.[112] Of even greater concern to American officials was impending Canadian legislation that would establish a twelve-mile territorial sea and a 100-mile shipping safety control zone.[113] At the request of the president, the Canadian government had agreed to delay the introduction of this legislation until after the Easter recess.[114] Officials favoring an early presidential decision on the continental shelf question were quick to point out that the United States would be in a better position to restrain the Canadians from taking this course if the president were to promptly announce an internationally appealing position on the continental shelf and the seabed regime.

In the final analysis, the greatest motivation for a presidential decision was the increasing public awareness of the dispute within the government. In the ongoing effort to win acceptance of their respective positions, the contending agencies sought outside sources of support.[115] Leaks to the press proliferated,[116] and the backing of concerned congressmen was solicited.[117] The resulting increase in public and congressional interest in the dispute threatened to circumscribe the president's decision-making freedom.

Particularly important in prompting a White House decision was pressure emanating from Congress to resolve the question. Established to "assist the executive branch . . . in arriving at a policy position," the Subcommittee on the Outer Continental Shelf of the Senate Interior and Insular Affairs Committee had scheduled hearings beginning on April 8 to hear witnesses from the contending agencies.[118] Unwilling to have the agency dispute aired publicly, the White House sent John Whittaker to ask Senator Metcalf for more time to reach a unified government position. Senator Metcalf agreed to a postponement, and April 22 was set as the new date of the hearing.[119] The difference, however, between the domestic and foreign affairs staffs at the White House was not resolved, and on April 17 Senator Metcalf was once again asked to delay the hearings. The Senator agreed but made it clear that although his subcommittee preferred to work with the administration once it had arrived at a position, it would, in the absence of a presidential decision, issue a report on its own.[120] In a letter dated April 28, Kenneth BeLieu, deputy assistant to the president, pledged that the administration would present a unified position to the subcommittee on May 27.[121]

Having made this commitment to the Congress, the White House staff began intense negotiations on the continental shelf/seabed regime issue. With the lines firmly drawn between the domestic affairs and the foreign affairs advisors, the problem came down to one of preparing an option memorandum for the president that was acceptable to both sides. Officially responsible for the drafting, the National Security Council staff prepared a series of memoranda which were reviewed and commented on by the domestic affairs staff. Of paramount concern to Ehrlichman was the National Security Council's initial omission of the original State Department position as one of the options to be sent to the president. It was this position, in Ehrlichman's view, that offered the best compromise between domestic and foreign policy considerations. In a contest between the Richardson and the original State Department proposals, Ehrlichman preferred the latter since it recognized the inherent legal right of states to the resources of their continental margins. It had the further advantage of designating only a small percentage of royalties from exploitation in the intermediate zone to an international fund.

The final version of the option paper took Ehrlichman's views into account, but generally reflected the foreign affairs bias of the National Security Council. It was sent to the president under Kissinger's signature at the end of April. On the basis of this options paper as well as private conversations with his advisors, President Nixon decided in favor of the Richardson position. The president, it may be safely assumed, devoted little time to reaching this decision. Other demands on his attention were far more pressing. The U.S. invasion of Cambodia—to mention just one—was announced on April 30 and in the weeks to follow was to consume a major portion of the president's time.

On May 22, members of the Congress were fully briefed on the White House decision, and on the following morning, Ronald Ziegler, the White House press secretary, and John Stevenson held a press conference to announce the president's seabed policy.[122] The policy, as outlined in the press release and in Stevenson's remarks to the press, was clearly the Richardson proposal. The president called for the renunciation of national claims to seabed resources beyond the depth of 200 meters and for the establishment, beyond this point, of an international regime to govern the exploitation of seabed resources. Two types of machinery would be created to authorize resource exploitation in this international seabed area. To the edge of the continental margin, referred to in the proposal as the "trusteeship zone," the coastal state would act as trustee for the international community in the exploitation of marine resources. In return, the "coastal state would receive a share of the international revenues from the zone in which it acts as trustee." Beyond the continental margin, international machinery would authorize and regulate exploitation and would collect "substantial mineral royalties" to be used for economic assistance to developing countries. In addition, the international regime would formulate "rules to prevent unreasonable interference with other uses of the ocean, to protect the ocean from pollution, to assure the integrity of the investment necessary for such exploitation, and to provide for peaceful and compulsory settlement of disputes."

On the morning of May 27 the twice-delayed hearing on the administration's continental shelf and seabed regime policy was at last convened. Testifying before the Special Subcommittee on the Outer Continental Shelf were Under Secretary Richardson and John Stevenson. Richardson led off with a detailed description of the president's proposal and then went on to explain some of the reasoning behind it. He pointed out that a central concern was to balance a "broad and international interest" on the one hand with the "very legitimate interests on the part of coastal states in the waters off their shores." He also indicated that "for the United States to propose a concept of broad extension of national jurisdiction would have indirect, but serious, national security implications and would impede the freedom of scientific research and other uses of the high seas."[123]

Stevenson addressed his remarks to another important issue—the relationship in the minds of policymakers between the administration's territorial sea and straits proposal of February and the president's seabed proposal. The United States, he acknowledged, was very anxious to get a twelve-mile territorial sea generally accepted and believed "that in order to make progress in the law of the sea area, it is necessary to also make a parallel progress in the seabed area, because a great many countries are going to be looking at progress in the two areas as being interrelated."[124] On a number of subjects the witnesses were unable to go into detail. This was due to the fact, Richardson reminded the Congress, that the May 23 statement represented only an initial "approach to dealing with the exploitation of the continental margin."[125] As the president had promised, the government would introduce more specific proposals at the next meeting of the UN Seabed Committee.

The Treaty is Prepared for the UN

The task of preparing the more specific proposals was to be undertaken by the Department of State in coordination with the Departments of Defense and Interior. Within the State Department the initiative was taken by the Legal Advisor's Office. John Stevenson's Interagency Task Force on the Law of the Sea established an ad hoc drafting committee[126] chaired by Bernard H. Oxman.

The five-man committee went to work immediately in an atmosphere of growing dissension over the president's proposal.[127] Within the space of a month, the group, working around the clock, had prepared an initial version of a draft treaty and began to circulate it for comments. In mid-July, representatives of various industry and marine science groups met with the drafting committee to review early versions of the draft.[128] Most vocal in their opposition to its provisions were representatives of the petroleum industry. At the same time, the draft text was circulated to concerned federal agencies which were given until July 22 to submit their approval or disapproval.[129] On the last day of the deadline, less than two weeks before the Seabed Committee was scheduled to meet in Geneva, the Departments of Commerce and the Interior responded that they could not approve the draft treaty in its present form and that they opposed its presentation to the UN Seabed Committee. On the other side, the Navy and the Joint Chiefs of Staff insisted that the draft treaty be presented.

The Congress meanwhile was studying the draft treaty with care.[130] On June 29 Senator Metcalf had requested that a copy of the draft be sent to his subcommittee.[131] The "subcommittee was unanimous in expressing serious doubts about many of its provisions" and, in a letter to Secretary of State William Rogers, urged that the draft treaty "not be presented at the Geneva conference and instead that it be substantially revised."[132]

With the mushrooming of industry, agency, and congressional opposition, the drafters and proponents of the treaty were undecided as to whether they should attempt to circumvent or accommodate the opposition. Within the White House the decision was taken in favor of limited accommodation of the petroleum interest group's opposition. On July 27 officials from the Departments of State, Defense, and Interior met in executive session with members of the Subcommittee on the Outer Continental Shelf.[133] At the meeting, accommodations were made in the text of the draft. The designated percentage of fees to be paid to the authority from exploitation in the trusteeship area was changed from two-thirds to an unspecified figure between one-half and two-thirds. In addition the status of the draft treaty was reduced to that of a "working paper for discussion purposes," and a disclaimer was added to the effect that "the draft Convention and its Appendices . . . do not necessarily represent the definitive views of the United States Government. The Appendices in particular are included solely by way of example." The senators were satisfied with these modifications in the draft convention and withdrew their opposition to its presentation at Geneva in this altered form. They did indicate, however, that they would hold further hearings on the terms of the draft working paper.[134] After a similar meeting with the supporters of the draft treaty, representatives of the dissenting agencies were reluctantly persuaded that no further modifications could be secured at the time.

With this qualified Senate approval and the grudging acquiescence of the Interior Department, the U.S. delegation rushed the draft working paper to Geneva where it was presented on August 3, the opening day of the United Nations Seabed Committee meeting.[135] The response to the U.S. draft at the August meeting was generally one of stunned surprise. U.S. allies had received barely three days notice of the new U.S. position on the seabed regime. Given the length and detail of the draft convention and given the brief duration of the session (August 3 to 28), the delegates assembled at Geneva could do little more than register their approbation of the U.S. government's serious intent to deal with the problem of a regime for the deep seabed. Beyond that there was little support for the substance of the proposal. The principal short-term result of the U.S. draft treaty was to infuse new life into the moribund deliberations of the UN Seabed Committee which had become bogged down in wrangling over legal principles to govern a seabed regime. The new evidence of U.S. government willingness to move ahead with a seabed regime sparked a UN General Assembly decision a few months later to convene a Third UN Conference on the Law of the Sea.

Territorial Sea, Straits, and Fisheries: 1967-1970

The decision to convene a Third UN Law of the Sea Conference found its antecedents in the negotiations on territorial sea, straits, and fisheries matters. These negotiations began in 1967 at the initiative of the United States and the Soviet Union. The two maritime powers were eager to see international agreement on a twelve-mile territorial sea if freedom of navigation through straits covered by a twelve-mile territorial sea were guaranteed. To satisfy the resource concerns of coastal states, they were prepared to consider some form of preferential fishing rights for coastal states beyond the territorial sea. In discussions with their respective allies, both powers indicated a preference to group the territorial sea and straits question with fisheries as a "manageable package" of trade-offs for a single international negotiation.

After two and a half years of discussions, the U.S. and Soviet governments agreed to begin actively promoting an early international conference to deal only with territorial sea issues. To ensure maximum news coverage, the U.S. announced its new negotiating position to coincide with a statement on the subject included in the president's first Annual Message on Foreign Policy. On February 18, 1970, in his State of the World message, President Nixon said, "The most pressing issue regarding the law of the sea is the need to achieve agreement on the breadth of the territorial sea, to head off the threat of escalating national claims over the ocean. We also believe it important to make parallel progress toward establishing an internationally agreed boundary between the continental shelf and the deep seabeds, and on a regime for exploitation of deep seabed resources."[136] In a speech made in Philadelphia the same day, John Stevenson announced that the United States was prepared to revise its traditional posture on a three-mile territorial sea. The U.S. government was willing to conclude a "new international treaty fixing the limitation of the territorial sea at 12 miles and providing for freedom of transit through and over international straits and carefully defined preferential fishing rights for coastal states on the high seas."[137]

Neither the president's statements nor the Stevenson speech stressed the fact that the U.S. position was conceived in terms of a quid pro quo; that is, the move to a twelve-mile territorial sea was to be predicated on widespread international agreement to unrestricted freedom of passage through and over international straits.[138] Preferential fishing rights were to serve as an added inducement to coastal nations to accept the other provisions. The Defense Department insisted that these points be clarified. On February 25 the State Department issued a statement to the effect that "the United States supports the 12-mile limit . . . only if a treaty can be negotiated which . . . will provide for freedom of navigation through and over international straits. At the same time, the United States will attempt to accommodate the interests of coastal states in the fishery resources off their coasts."[139] In an announcement made on the same day, the Defense Department stressed the point that, until widespread international agreement on the U.S. position was reached, the United States had "no obligation to recognize claims in excess of three miles" and did "not recognize the 12-mile limit." "Any unilateral departure . . . from our historic claims," the statement concluded, would adversely affect "the security and commercial interests of the United States."[140]

The 1970 U.S. territorial sea, straits, and fisheries policy reflected an effort to balance U.S. naval concerns with international considerations that had surfaced in the course of the discussions with the Soviets and other countries. A principal goal of the U.S. Navy was to protect transit through and over international straits. If the breadth of the territorial sea were universally extended to twelve miles, 116 international straits would be covered by territorial waters.[141] The Navy feared that high seas corridors would cease to exist in such straits, and transit would be subject to the regime of innocent passage.[142] To avoid the application of coastal-state discretion to surface vessels, allow submerged transit for submarines, and assure overflight rights for military as well as civilian

235

aircraft, the U.S. would have to insist on a new legal right of freedom of transit in straits less than twenty-four miles wide.

The Soviets, who had adopted a twelve-mile territorial sea in 1927,[143] had become a major maritime power by the mid-1960s. They therefore promoted the same policy as the U.S. on freedom of transit through and over international straits. The British were equally supportive of any regime that would maintain maritime mobility. The interests of the Japanese and Soviets, however, diverged from those of the United States over fisheries. The second and third largest fishing nations of the world respectively, Japan and Russia were not in accord with the preferential fishing rights that the United States was prepared to grant to coastal nations dependent on their coastal fisheries.

The 1970 U.S. proposal on fishing was designed to balance coastal with distant-water fishing interests, but it did not satisfy either group. By the late 1960s, nine Latin American nations had claimed zones of 200 miles to protect fishery resources off their shores. To halt the trend toward such claims and to induce these nations to roll back established claims, the United States was proposing that special or preferential rights over offshore living resources be granted to coastal nations. According to the U.S. concept of preferential rights, a coastal fishing nation would be able to reserve a portion of the catch off its shores for its own fishermen.[144] The amount would be determined by the coastal state's economic dependence on or extent of investment in offshore fisheries. At the insistence of the Department of Defense, this proposal deliberately avoided the concept of a fishing zone that might subsequently evolve into a fixed area of expanded coastal-state jurisdiction.[145]

The preferred U.S.-Soviet scenario for separating seabed negotiations from the territorial-sea-related negotiations did not prove feasible. A number of factors conspired against the plan. In the first place, there was a natural physical relationship between solutions for seabed resources and regimes for the resources of the overlying waters. In the second place, there was significant international opposition to separate negotiations. While U.S. and Soviet allies were, at best, lukewarm about the territorial sea proposals, the developing nations, spearheaded by the Latin Americans, were strongly opposed. To protect their extensive claims, the 200-milers sought to prevent a separate conference on the territorial sea questions. To this end they met in Montevideo in May 1970 and agreed that any law of the sea conference to be convened must deal with the full range of law of the sea issues.[146] They met again the next month in Lima with all the states of Latin America and secured support for their policy of expanding the conference agenda. The principal selling point for this policy was that developing countries could secure concessions from the developed nations on seabed issues in exchange for some accommodation of the developed nations' navigational concerns.

The third and final factor militating against a "manageable packages" scenario was the ongoing difference of opinion within the U.S. government. Interior Department officials were alone in insisting that the regime for the seabed could be separated from that for the superjacent waters. The proponents of a narrow continental shelf regime disagreed and hoped that the generous seabed regime outlined in the U.S. draft seabed treaty would have a favorable impact on U.S. navigational interests in straits transit. The consolidation of State and Defense Department staffs in 1969 reflected the linkage between seabed and territorial sea issues and anticipated a comprehensive conference.

UNITED NATIONS RESOLUTION

By the time the 1970 UN General Assembly was convened, a number of significant developments had occurred in U.S. policy on the law of the sea. At the beginning of the year (February), the U.S. officially announced a new policy accepting twelve-mile territorial seas in conjunction with freedom of transit through and over international straits and with preferential fishing rights for the coastal states. Then on May 23, the president announced a new policy setting the continental shelf boundary at the 200-meter isobath with an intermediate zone and international seabed regime beyond. In August the U.S. delegation presented a draft treaty on the international seabed that filled out the May decision with a financially generous international licensing system. A final important U.S. policy shift came on November 20 when the U.S. presented a draft resolution to Committee I of the UN General Assembly in favor of a single international negotiation on the full range of law of the sea questions. This move represented a backing off from a position favoring separate negotiating packages and was consistent with the preferences of those that wished to use the generous U.S. position on the seabed as a trade-off for free transit through international straits. The combining of issues also reflected the fact that in the course of 1970, the concerned agencies of government had unified their law of the sea staffs into single operations.

The impact of the new U.S. policies was twofold. On the domestic front, they unleashed a wave of opposition and resistance from those groups that had been excluded from the 1970 decision-making process. In the international arena, the 1970 policies evoked surprise and opposit:on, but most importantly they infused new life into the Seabed Committee and sparked the decision to move toward a Third UNCLOS.

The Seabed Committee had been struggling to reach agreement upon legal principles to govern a seabed regime when the U.S. draft treaty simply cut through the process by focusing attention on a concrete proposal. Under pressure to move toward a negotiation of specific technical details, the General Assembly adopted by a vote of 108 to 0 with 14 abstentions, a Declaration of Principles Governing the Sea-bed and Ocean Floor Beyond the Limits of National Jurisdiction.[147] This declaration stated that the resources of the seabed area beyond national limits were the common heritage of mankind. The area should not be subject to appropriation by any means by states or persons and no state should claim or exercise sovereign rights over any parts of it. The declaration called for an international regime to watch over the safe and orderly development and rational management of the area and its resources. This regime was to ensure the equitable sharing by states in the benefits from these resources, taking into account the needs and interests of developing countries. The United States voted for the resolution but indicated its view that the declaration of principles did not preclude U.S. companies from mining manganese nodules on the deep seabed.[148]

Three other oceans resolutions were passed by the twenty-fifth General Assembly.[149] The first called on the UN secretary-general to study the impact that deep seabed mining would have on the prices of minerals on the world market and on the economic well-being of developing countries. This resolution was instigated by the mineral-exporting developing nations who feared that seabed mining would reduce markets and prices for their exports. The next resolution was promoted by the landlocked nations who were becoming increasingly concerned over the prospect of coastal-state division of the oceans. It called on the secretary-general to study the special problems of the landlocked in exploring and exploiting deep seabed resources.

The third General Assembly resolution called for a new conference on the law of the sea to be held in 1973. The conference would deal with the establishment of an international regime for the seabed beyond national jurisdiction as well as a broad range of issues including "the regime of the high seas, the continental shelf, the territorial sea (including the question of its breadth and the question of international straits) and contiguous zone, fishing and conservation of the living resources of the high seas (including the question of preferential rights of coastal states), the preservation of the marine environment (including *inter alia* the prevention of pollution), and scientific research." To handle this range of topics, the Seabed Committee was scheduled to hold pre-paratory conferences in 1971 and 1972. At these preparatory meetings a draft convention for a seabed regime was to be developed in addition to draft articles on all other agenda items. The General Assembly would review the progress of the Seabed Committee on an annual basis and retain the right to postpone the 1973 conference if the progress were deemed insufficient.

PREPARATIONS FOR

A THIRD UN CONFERENCE ON THE LAW

OF THE SEA: 1971-1973

In accordance with the UN resolution calling for a Third UN Conference on the Law of the Sea (UNCLOS III), the UN Seabed Committee became the official preparatory committee for the conference. From 1971 through 1973 it met twice a year for a total of twenty-nine weeks. It produced draft treaty articles that were uneven in quality and completeness. Those dealing with seabed mining suffered least from inadequate drafting, although the use of bracketed and alternative texts reflected strong differences of opinion between developed and developing countries. Subcommittee II, dealing with problems of offshore jurisdiction, was delayed in its drafting efforts because it had the preliminary task of drawing up a list of subjects and issues to serve as the agenda for UNCLOS III. Moreover, its work was plagued by significant differences of view among groups of states with varying geographic situations. It was in Subcommittee II that negotiating blocs such as coastal states, archipelago states, landlocked states, and geographically disadvantaged states first began to emerge.

During the three years of preparatory deliberations, U.S. policies on offshore jurisdiction changed notably from those announced in 1970. These shifts were influenced by the transition in general U.S. foreign policy as well as by pressures from domestic ocean groups and the UN Seabed Committee. Within the U.S., the opposition to the 1970 policies on the seabed and offshore jurisdiction gathered force by 1971. Most private interest groups had been caught by surprise by the 1970 decisions and they insisted that thenceforth they be included in the policy process that affected their interests. By 1973 they had achieved significant changes in the 1970 policies.

The most pronounced U.S. policy shift was from support for a narrow national continental shelf extending to a depth of 200 meters to acceptance of national jurisdiction over the seabed to a distance of 200 miles. There was no discernible change in U.S. policy on a regime for deep-sea mining. Similarly, the United States government continued to espouse positions on fisheries that balanced both coastal and distant-water concerns. The difference was that after 1971 fisheries policy was being directly formulated by U.S. fisheries groups. During difficult deliberations on the agenda in 1972, U.S. policy on freedom of transit through international straits underwent several refinements. The U.S. agreed to a formulation on "right of transit" and gave greater attention to the need for international regulations to provide for traffic lanes and protection of the environment. U.S. policies on the marine environment and scientific research were not elaborated until 1973. In Subcommittee III, the U.S. sought to balance environmental and navigational considerations through a policy that disaggregated standard-setting from enforcement and coastal-state from port-state and flag-state responsibilities. The U.S. also sought to assure access for marine science research to areas under coastal-state control in exchange for the observance of specified obligations by the researcher.

The preparatory work of the Seabed Committee continued into the period designated for the conference. The first session of UNCLOS III was held for two weeks in December 1973 to deal with organizational matters. This session wrangled first over the election of officers and then became bogged down on the rules of procedure. The second session of the conference met for ten weeks in Caracas in the summer of 1974 ostensibly to address substantive issues. The first week of this session was devoted to a resolution of differences over conference procedure. And much of the rest of the Caracas meeting was spent completing the formulation of alternative texts in those committees that had fallen behind in their preparatory work.

Conference Preparations
by the UN Seabed Committee

1971

The Seabed Committee—expanded from forty-two to eighty-six members—held its first sessions in Geneva for two weeks in March and for six weeks in the summer of 1971.[1] The first task of the preparatory committee was to organize its work procedures. The committee first reelected Hamilton S. Amerasinghe of Sri Lanka as chairman. Then a twenty-five-member bureau was established with membership allocated on a regional basis. Using the issues agreed upon in General Assembly Resolution 2750C (xxv), the committee divided its work into three

CHAPTER 8

CHART 8-A
UNCLOS III Preparations: 1971-1973

Committee on the Peaceful Uses of the Sea-Bed and the Ocean Floor Beyond the Limits of National Jurisdiction. (Designated official preparatory committee for Third UN Conference on Law of the Sea to be held in 1973. UNGA Res. 2750 C [xxv], December 17, 1970.)

		Weeks	(Cumulative)
1971	March 12-26, Geneva	2	2
	July 19 - August 27, Geneva	6	8
	October 14, 15, and 22, New York	1	9
1972*	February 28 - March 30, New York	4	13
	July 17 - August 18, Geneva	5	18
1973	March 5 - April 6, New York	4	22
	July 2 - August 24, Geneva	7	29

* Membership increased from 86 to 91 by UNGA Res. 2881, December 21, 1971.

subcommittees.[2] Subcommittee I, chaired by an African, E. E. Seaton of the United Republic of Tanzania, was charged with preparing draft articles on the international regime, including machinery, for the seabed area beyond the limits of national jurisdiction. Subcommittee II was chaired by a Latin American, Reynaldo Galindo Pohl of El Salvador, and had the task of preparing "a comprehensive list of subjects and issues" to serve as an agenda for the upcoming law of the sea conference. The list was to include the regimes of the territorial sea, international straits, the contiguous zone, the continental shelf, fishing, and the high seas. Subcommittee III, chaired by a Western European, A. Van der Essen of Belgium, was allocated the residual issues of marine environment and marine scientific research. It, too, was asked to prepare draft articles for the law of the sea conference.

In August of 1971, it was further decided that (1) the question of the international regime should receive priority by allocating more time to Subcommittee I; (2) the recommendations of Subcommittee II on the precise definition of the boundary between the national and international areas would constitute the basic proposals for the main committee deliberations on the issue; and (3) the question of peaceful uses was allocated to the main committee although each subcommittee could raise the question when it related to its mandate.

The pattern of work followed by each of the three subcommittees was similar.[3] A general debate on the main issues was held during which national delegations submitted working papers, draft conventions, and draft treaty articles for consideration. Then informal working groups prepared draft articles based on the proposals and working papers before each of the subcommittees. While little substantive progress was made in the meetings, they were educational for new members in defining the issues under consideration. In 1971, Subcommittee I held thirty-one meetings during which the member countries set out their preferred positions on an international regime for deep-sea mining. Subcommittee II met twenty-three times and conducted a general debate of the issues before it. Late in the summer session, the subcommittee appointed an eleven-member working group of the whole to conduct negotiations on a list of subjects for the conference agenda. This group met only twice and was not revived in 1972. Subcommittee III met only fourteen times during 1971 because its deliberations on the marine environment were viewed as dependent on the outcome of the UN Conference on the Human Environment to be held in Stockholm in 1972. The committee completed its report to the General Assembly in October. At its twenty-sixth session, the General Assembly noted with satisfaction the preparatory work of the Seabed Committee and added five new members, including the People's Republic of China.[4] It also requested the Seabed Committee to hold two further sessions in 1972.

1972

The committee met for nine weeks in the spring and summer of 1972.[5] Subcommittee I, under a new African chairman, Paul Engo of Cameroon, held thirty meetings during the two sessions. It began its program of work with a debate on the "status, scope and basic provisions of the regime based on the Declaration of Principles, Resolution 2749 (xxv)." It then appointed a thirty-three-nation working group to draw up the principles section of a draft seabed treaty. The membership of the working group would be designated by the respective regional groups for the most part, with the understanding that any member of the subcommittee could participate in the group's discussions. The working group met twenty times during the fall session under the direction of Christopher Pinto of Sri Lanka. The subcommittee then turned to the second item on its program of work, namely the "status, scope, functions and powers of the international machinery" in relation to the organs of an international seabed authority, rules and practices governing exploration and exploitation, sharing of benefits, economic impact of seabed mining, and the needs and interests of land-locked states. By the end of 1972, the working group of Subcommittee I had produced a number of bracketed texts reflecting areas of agreement and disagreement on the provisions of the regime.

Although there was some discussion of fisheries questions, the work of Subcommittee II in 1972 centered on the effort to reach agreement on a list of subjects and issues to serve as the agenda for the law of the sea conference. It met nine times in March and fifteen times at the summer session. Because of the importance of the question to all delegations, the subcommittee was unable to agree upon a procedure for selecting a smaller working group. As a result, it operated as a sub-committee of the whole. Members of the African, Asian, and Latin American regional groups met informally during the March session to resolve the differences between a proposed Latin American list of sub-jects and issues[6] and an African-Asian list.[7] Subcommittee II deferred to the consultations of these coastal developing countries, which took most of the March session. The developing country representatives reached agreement on an agenda of twenty-three main items and sixty-five subitems. It was released on March 24, four working days before the end of the session.[8] Sponsored by fifty-six coastal states, the list provoked a major outcry and spate of amendments[9] from those nations that had been excluded from the deliberations.

The principal U.S. and Soviet objection to the coastal-state list was to the omission of any reference to "free transit through international straits." In connection with straits, the coastal-state text provided for "straits used for international navigation" and "innocent passage." The United States and Soviet delegates were also alarmed with other provisions of the list that would restrict navigational freedoms. The coastal-state list provided only for an exclusive economic zone (Item 6), omit-ting the preferred U.S. alternative of limiting coastal states to preferential rights beyond the territorial sea. In addition, high seas freedoms were restricted to those of navigation and overflight (Item 7). And finally, scientific research was addressed only in terms of regulation and international cooperation (Item 12). The landlocked states were as unhappy as the maritime powers over the absence of special provision for their participation in marine resource exploitation.

The bulk of the summer session was spent on wrangling between the coastal-state drafters of the list of subjects and issues and those coun-tries whose interests had been ignored. Agreement was finally reached on August 16 using two procedures: specific amendments and a general disclaimer. The final list consisted of twenty-five main items and about eighty-five subitems.[10] Following intensive negotiations, the maritime nations and the Group of 77 agreed to a compromise on the straits provision to include, in addition to "straits used for international navigation" and "innocent passage," a section on "other related matters including the question of the right of transit." The maritime states were also succesful in the inclusion of a new Item 7 that provided for types of coastal-state jurisdiction beyond the twelve-mile territorial sea other than the exclusive economic zone. Other concerns were accommodated through an introductory disclaimer which specified that the list of subjects and issues was "not necessarily complete" nor did it "prejudice the position of any State or commit any State with respect to the items on it." The list would serve merely as "a framework for discussion and drafting of necessary articles." While agreement on the list of issues for UNCLOS III represented the major accomplishment of the 1972 preparatory sessions, it also signalled the difficulties that lay ahead in the negotiations. And the size of the list did not augur well for the conference.

The third subcommittee met five times during the spring session and thirteen times in the summer of 1972 to develop a work program and conduct a general debate. The subcommittee developed a five-point work program in March: "A. Preservation of the marine environment (including the sea-bed); B. Elimination and prevention of pollution of the marine environment (including the sea-bed); C. Scientific research concerning the marine environment (including the sea-bed); D. Development and transfer of technology; and E. Other matters." General debate in the subcommittee covered questions of marine environment, scientific research, and technology transfer. Documents relating to environmental activities underway in other forums were brought to the attention of the subcommittee.[11] The work of the subcommittee picked up after the UN Conference on the Human Environment concluded in June of 1972. At the summer session, the general discussion on marine pollution was concluded and a thirty-three-nation working group was formed to draft articles on the preservation of the marine environment. Under its chairman, José-Luis Vallarta of Mexico, the working group held two meetings and invited members of the subcommittee to submit proposals.

One aspect of the 1972 sessions that threatened to be disruptive was a possible new moratorium resolution prohibiting activities relating to exploitation of the deep seabed until the establishment of an international regime. UNCTAD passed such a resolution in the spring of 1972, and the delegation of Kuwait introduced one at the end of the March session of the Seabed Committee. Due to intense bickering over the list of subjects and issues, however, the moratorium resolution seems to have been forgotten. It was not discussed until late in the summer session and then it was not pressed to a vote.

Upon the Seabed Committee's agreement (however precarious) on a list of subjects and issues, the General Assembly reaffirmed the mandate of the committee and requested it to hold two further sessions in 1973 to complete its preparatory work. The Seabed Committee was asked to submit a report with recommendations to the General Assembly at its twenty-eighth session. Resolution 3029 A (xxvii) also requested the secretary-general to convene the first session of UNCLOS III for a two-week period in November-December 1973 "for the purpose of dealing with organizational matters." It then called for a second session to meet in Santiago, Chile in April-May 1974 to deal with substantive matters. The resolution assumed that UNCLOS III would be concluded no later than 1975 and noted that Austria had offered Vienna as a site for a possible 1975 session.[12]

The two other resolutions of the twenty-seventh General Assembly reflected the efforts of the landlocked states to spur a reappraisal of the trend toward expanding coastal-state jurisdiction. Resolution 3029 B (xxvii) requested the secretary-general to prepare a comparative study of the resources available to the international area under each of the different national limits being considered by the Seabed Committee. Resolution 3029 C (xxvii) was a coastal-state response calling on the secretary-general to prepare a comparative study of the economic significance of the alternative national boundaries for the riparian states.

1973

The Seabed Committee held two final preparatory sessions in 1973—the first from March 7-April 5 in New York, and the second from July 3 to August 17 in Geneva.[13] In Subcommittee I, the Pinto working group was the main center of activity. While the subcommittee met only seven times in the spring and again in the fall, the working group held thirty meetings in March-April and thirty-seven in July-August. The working group labored through two readings of the texts on the international regime, systematically trying to narrow the differences among delegations. It then completed two readings of some of the texts pertaining to international machinery. The product, for the use of the law of the sea conference, was a set of bracketed and alternative texts on some of the major issues before the subcommittee. A number of additional issues were not discussed.

After the exhausting battle over the list of subjects and issues, Subcommittee II set out in 1973 to develop a program and method of work. Early in March, it agreed to deal with all items on the agenda that had not been allocated to the two other subcommittees, namely all questions relating to offshore jurisdiction except the marine environment and scientific research. In the course of thirty-two meetings, Subcommittee II conducted a wide-ranging discussion of national views on the many issues before it. As to work procedure, it was again necessary to include all delegations. Thus agreement was reached on a working group of the whole (under Mr. Moncef Kedadi of Tunisia) with the option of creating other subgroups or drafting groups as appropriate. The working group met eleven times in the spring and thirty-one times in the summer to prepare draft articles. July 16 was set as the last date for the submission of national proposals to the working group. These were then incorporated into a comparative table. Where sufficient discussion of proposals had occurred, consolidated texts were prepared on the territorial sea and related items such as straits, the continental shelf, high seas, and archipelagos. Using the comparative table of national proposals and the consolidated texts as a basis, delegates were encouraged to negotiate the basic variants encompassed in these proposals. Some efforts were made to reduce the number of variants before the summer session ended.

In 1973, Subcommittee III held seventeen meetings. In the spring session it conducted general debate on the subject of scientific research after which a working group was established to prepare draft treaty articles on scientific research and the transfer of technology. Transfer of technology was the subject of a brief general debate at the summer session.

The working group on marine pollution met twenty-eight times in 1973 and produced a number of working papers on the basis of proposals and comments of national delegations. The discussion covered proposals that had been submitted on general and particular obligations of states, global and regional cooperation, technical assistance, monitoring, standards, and enforcement. The working group did not have the time to consider all the proposals submitted or the bracketed and alternative texts prepared in informal consultation. It did, however, prepare alternative texts on global and regional cooperation and on the standards for controlling land-based, seabed, and vessel-source pollution. Agreed texts were adopted on monitoring and technical assistance.

The working group on marine scientific research set to work at the summer session and held ten meetings. It discussed the definition and objectives of marine scientific research, the prerequisites for undertaking it, and regulations for its conduct and promotion. Informal consultations produced a number of bracketed and alternative texts reflecting comments and suggestions by the delegations. There was insufficient time, however, to review these texts in the working group.

By the end of its three years of preparatory work, the UN Seabed Committee had produced texts of uneven quality. The most refined texts were those on the deep seabed and marine environment. While the fifty draft articles produced by Subcommittee I were not complete and reflected wide disagreement among delegates by the use of brackets, alternative language, and footnotes, they had at least been reviewed by the working group of the subcommittee. At the other extreme, Subcommittee II had lost so much time in the fight over the agenda that it was able to prepare only a few bracketed and alternative texts, leaving the remaining national proposals in the form of comparative tables. And Subcommittee III had been hampered by the belated interest in its work, particularly while other UN forums were active in the marine environment. Although it produced bracketed and alternative texts on the marine environment by 1973, there had not been time to review these texts.[14]

On November 16, 1973, the General Assembly passed Resolution 3067 (xxviii) officially convening the Third United Nations Conference on the Law of the Sea. It called for an organizational session to be held in New York from December 3-14, 1973 to elect the officers, adopt the agenda and rules of procedure, to establish subsidiary organs of the conference, and to allocate work among them. A second session of the conference was to be convened in the summer of 1974 in Santiago (subsequently changed to Caracas)[15] to deal with substantive work. The possibility of an additional session, not later than 1975, was mentioned. Resolution 3067 (xxviii) invited all states that were members of the UN or its specialized agencies to participate, as well as the Republic of Guinea-Bissau and the Democratic Republic of Vietnam.

The Politics of the Preparatory Period

The progress of the UN Seabed Committee in laying the basis for fruitful negotiation at UNCLOS III was slowed by a number of obstacles including the structure and substance of the negotiations as well as an increasingly unfavorable international political climate. These difficulties persisted into the period of the conference negotiations. The conference began its work with the uneven and inadequate texts prepard by the Seabed Committee. At the First UN Conference on the Law of the Sea, negotiations had been facilitated by the unified texts prepared by the International Law Commission and extensive governmental input over a period of six years. UNCLOS III did not have a comparable basis for its deliberations; indeed, the first two years of the conference were spent on efforts to draft unified texts.

The positive aspects of the Seabed Committee's work in some cases generated potential obstacles to future negotiation. A case in point was the agreement reached in 1972 on a twenty-five-item conference agenda. While that was regarded at the time as a breakthrough and an important step forward, it is apparent, with the benefit of hindsight, that the size of the agenda was a major stumbling block to negotiating an international agreement. To ensure an internationally acceptable law of the sea, the conference membership was based on universal participation. This meant that roughly 150 nations with disparate interests would be required to arrive at a single agreement on a large number of important economic and jurisdictional issues.

CHART 8-B

Comparative Makeup of National Delegations,
1958 (UNCLOS I) and 1974 (UNCLOS III)

	1958	1974
Africa	6	41
Asia	24	41
Latin America	20	24
Communist	10	12
Other	26	29
Total	86	147

In addition to jeopardizing the chance for eventual agreement, the multi-issue approach to the development of a law of the sea regime had other undesirable consequences. In the first place, it meant that each issue would not be negotiated on its merits, that is, according to what might be the preferable regime for each discrete question in terms of global welfare. By linking each issue to everything else, the dominant technique became that of trade-offs and the resulting product was usually the lowest common denominator.

A further difficulty evolved from the trade-off procedure. In such a negotiating situation it was necessary to build coalitions in support of clusters of policies. While the task of coalition building was educational for many delegations, it was extremely time-consuming. When the coalitions papered over disparate interests, they were often fragile. And the more fragile they were, the more time was required to keep them together and the less time for negotiations between groups. In addition, the more tenuous or delicately balanced a group-agreed policy was, the more inflexible the group became in negotiating it and the more difficult it was to rethink coalition positions. Yet take-it-or-leave-it positions were scarcely conducive to negotiations among contending groups.

This dilemma was clearly demonstrated in the negotiation on the list of subjects and issues. The bulk of March 1972 was consumed by negotiations among the African, Asian, and Latin American regional groups. While this effort helped to consolidate a "Group of 77" coalition, it could do so only by giving each of the coastal-state participants what it wanted and disregarding the concerns of maritime, landlocked and geographically disadvantaged states. The result was an inflexible position. And the time taken arriving at it had precluded negotiations with other groups. The phenomenon of spending precious time in building, maintaining, and repairing coalitions was to recur throughout UNCLOS III.

The preparatory period was useful in allowing many of the newly participating developing nations to give some thought to their interests in the oceans. However, the educational aspects of the exercise were less oriented toward ocean use and management than toward the law of the sea. The vast majority of national representatives were lawyers, without technical expertise in the oceans field. What they learned about law of the sea was combined with their skill in North-South negotiating tactics. Indeed, most of the developing nation delegates were UN representatives who were interacting in other forums on a range of North-South issues.

Political Coalitions

The political coalitions that emerged during the six preparatory sessions reflected the early stages of the law of the sea exercise. The three principal groups were the Group of 77, the maritime states, and the landlocked/geographically disadvantaged states (LL/GDS).[16] The Group of 77 coalition included delegates from Africa, Asia, and Latin America. It had its roots in UNCTAD and other UN negotiations. Similarly, the coalition of maritime states included those developed countries that were increasingly the object of attack by the Group of 77 in other international forums. The third coalition, the LL/GDS,[17] included states without coastlines or with restricted offshore areas. This coalition was unique to the law of the sea negotiations and cut across the developed versus developing nation division. Although the LL/GDS group was in an embryonic stage by 1973, it was a harbinger of what a true law of the sea negotiation would involve—namely, specific geographic and economic interests. While the landlocked sought access to the sea for purposes of commerce, the geographically disadvantaged wanted continued access to the resources off the shores of neighboring states. And both groups anticipated a special position in the operation of a deep seabed mining regime. The relative quiescence of the LL/GDS in this period may be attributed to a couple of factors. In the first place, the LL/GDS consituted only 10 percent of the 91-member preparatory committee. When the conference expanded membership to around 150, the LL/GDS grew to a formidable one-third of the membership. In the second place, the distinct interests of the LL/GDS were not sharply focused in the prenegotiating phase. In such a situation, they tended to be absorbed into the dominant developed versus developing state coalitions. Indeed, the coastal developing countries made conscious efforts to keep the landlocked developing countries in the fold and away from a natural alliance with the maritime powers who were also seeking to limit coastal-state jurisdiction.[18] In the heat of the North-South confrontation, the developing LL/GDS were sensitive to accusations of being in the pockets of the developed countries.

While the rhetoric of the period and the absence of genuine negotiations promoted tight Group of 77 and maritime nation groupings, the draft articles and language proposed by individual or groups of states in Subcommittee II of the Seabed Committee suggested the real differences of interest that existed and would ultimately emerge. By 1973, there was a growing awareness of the distinctive geographic and resource circumstances of each country.

On questions of offshore jurisdiction, the principal groupings included the "territorialists," the broad-margin states, the "patrimonialists,"[19] the archipelagic states, the maritime states, and the LL/GDS.

TERRITORIALISTS. The territorialists included those Latin American nations that claimed 200-mile territorial seas, such as Peru, Ecuador, Chile, Panama, and Brazil. Of this group, the Peruvians, Chileans, and Ecuadorians were the most outspoken. Peru, Ecuador, and Panama operated jointly in the submission of draft treaty language on jurisdiction.[20] And Brazil pursued a somewhat independent, almost reluctant role.[21]

BROAD-MARGIN STATES. The broad-margin states counted among their number those countries whose continental margins extended beyond 200 miles. They included such states as Argentina, Australia, Brazil, Canada, India, Norway, and New Zealand. The goal of these countries was to secure "sovereign rights to the resources of the continental shelf throughout its natural prolongation where it extends beyond 200 miles."[22] Other 200-mile states with narrow margins, such as Chile, Iceland, and Mexico, were willing to support a broad-margin approach in order to secure the requisite support for 200 miles. All the broad-margin states were interested in defining the margin's outer limits as expansively as possible. And Canada was intent upon using the margin concept to gain preferential rights to fisheries above the margin but beyond 200 miles.[23]

PATRIMONIALISTS. The patrimonialists included those countries that favored establishing 200-mile economic or resource zones or "patrimonial seas." In these zones the coastal state would have sovereign rights over the renewable resources of the seabed and superjacent waters. The leading patrimonialists in Latin America were Colombia, Mexico, Venezuela, and other states of the Caribbean. On June 7, 1972, fifteen Caribbean states met in Santo Domingo at the Specialized Conference of the Caribbean Countries on Problems of the Sea. They included Barbados, Colombia, Costa Rica, the Dominican Republic, El Salvador, Guatemala, Guyana, Haiti, Honduras, Jamaica, Mexico, Nicaragua, Panama, Trinidad and Tobago, and Venezuela. All other Latin American states were invited as observers. The meeting provided the occasion for the participants to coordinate policy on the patrimonial sea.[24] The resulting Declaration of Santo Domingo served as the basis for patrimonial sea articles that were subsequently presented to the UN Seabed Committee.[25]

In Africa, the concept of a 200-mile economic zone had been adopted by the African States Regional Seminar on the Law of the Sea held in Yaounde from June 20-30, 1972.[26] The African position was further refined in May 1973 by the Council of Ministers of the Organization of African Unity at their conference in Addis Ababa. Cameroon, Ghana, Ivory Coast, Kenya, Lesotho, Liberia, Libya, Madagascar, Mali, Mauritania, Morocco, Senegal, Sierra Leone, Sudan, Swaziland, Tanzania, and Tunisia cosponsored a proposal for such a zone.[27]

Significant differences existed, however, in the Latin and African economic zones. Reflecting the existence of broad-margin states in the southern hemisphere, the Latins were tolerant of claims to the margin beyond 200 miles. The Africans were not. The principal African negotiating problem was to accommodate the interests of their thirteen land-locked and their numerous geographically disadvantaged states. To this end, they called for the right of the LL/GDS to exploit the living resources of the zones of neighboring states. They also referred to possible regional or subregional arrangements for resource management and the need for resolving boundary differences on the basis of equity as well as equidistance.[28]

ARCHIPELAGIC STATES. The archipelagic states sought to expand their jurisdiction over vast areas of ocean space by using the concepts of "archipelagic waters" and 200-mile resource zones. Fiji, Indonesia, Mauritius, and the Philippines[29] proposed that archipelagic waters be created within straight baselines that would link the outermost points of their outermost islands and drying reefs. In the enclosed "archipelagic waters," the island state would enjoy sovereignty and rights to the waters, seabed, subsoil, and airspace. Ships would be allowed to navigate through these waters under a right of innocent passage but would have to observe the sea-lanes, traffic separation schemes, and other navigation-related regulations of the archipelagic states. Foreign warships would not enjoy sovereign immunity.[30] The archipelagic states further proposed that the territorial sea and economic zone should extend seaward from the straight baselines surrounding the archipelago to twelve and 200 miles respectively.[31] High seas would begin beyond the economic zone.[32]

MARITIME STATES. The maritime states shared a concern to protect navigational and distant-water freedoms in the oceans. Although the specific circumstances of each maritime state varied greatly, they all sought to limit and avoid the use of zonal approaches to coastal-state jurisdiction beyond the territorial sea. They were also in general accord on the need to facilitate transit through and over international straits that would be covered by territorial seas. States with maritime interests included the United States, the Soviet Union, Japan, and a number of West and East European countries. Within the group of maritime states, a subgroup of states known as the Group of 5 represented the most advanced maritime capabilities. It included the U.S., the USSR, the United Kingdom, Japan, and France.[33]

Although the perceived U.S. and Soviet maritime interests in maximizing high seas freedoms were virtually identical, the two countries never acted jointly to sponsor proposals. Indeed, each tried to use whatever policy changes it made in a competitive fashion as a concession to the Group of 77. The U.S. had such difficulty agreeing on policy within its own delegation that collaboration was difficult even with allies. The Soviets, of course, perceived the gradual shift in U.S. policy toward a coastal-state approach as a deliberate effort to buy Group of 77 goodwill. When, in late 1973, the Soviets abruptly switched their position to one favoring a 200-mile resource zone, it was billed as an indication of Soviet flexibility[34] but in fact was taken in anticipation of a U.S. move in this direction. Once the Soviets had accepted a 200-mile zone approach, the pressure against U.S. disant-water interests was overwhelming and the U.S. followed suit.

One significant discrepancy between the U.S. and Soviet policies on transit through straits reflected the politics of the Middle East. The Soviets sought freedom of navigation only for straits linking two parts of the high seas. In straits leading from the territorial sea to the high seas, as in the case of the Straits of Tiran, the Soviets were willing to accept innocent passage.[35] The U.S., on the other hand, sought a free transit regime for both geographic situations.

The policy of the United Kingdom on scientific research, straits transit, and navigation was consistently closest to that of the United States.[36] The British, Americans, Japanese, and Soviets all shared a concern with protecting their distant-water fishing interests.[37] While some Western European nations such as Germany shared these distant-water concerns, their positions were arrived at jointly and hence reflected a regional or EEC approach to fisheries management. The EEC members adopted a policy whereby a coastal state could reserve that portion of the catch that its fishermen could take in a zone of unspecified distance.[38] The fact that four members of the EEC were members of the LL/GDS group was consistent with the general maritime orientation of the community and its desire to change existing international law of the sea only minimally.

LANDLOCKED/GEOGRAPHICALLY DISADVANTAGED STATES. The LL/GDS states pursued a multifaceted policy on offshore jurisdiction centering on efforts to limit the distance and the scope of national claims to offshore areas. In 1971 they had called for a study of the implications of various limits (200-meter isobath, 500-meter isobath, 40 nautical miles, 200 nautical miles, and the edge of the continental margin)[39] in an effort to highlight the extent of the resources that would be available to an international regime if narrow national limits were adopted. In the face of strong pressure for 200 miles, including a 200-mile zone proposal by Ambassador Pardo of Malta,[40] the LL/GDS devised a new policy in which the coastal state would have the right to exploit living and nonliving resources in a zone of unspecified distance. However, the adjacent and neighboring LL/GDS would also have a right to participate in the exploitation of living resources. And an unspecified percentage of revenues derived from the exploitation of nonliving resources in the zone would be distributed on the same basis as revenues from the international seabed area.[41] The LL/GDS supported the right of each coastal state to establish a territorial sea of twelve miles as long as it was not exercised in a manner that would cut off the territorial sea of another state from the high seas.[42] And finally, the LL/GDS called for the right of landlocked countries to participate in research conducted by third parties in the zone of a neighboring coastal state.[43]

The diverse geographic and resource circumstances affecting negotiations on offshore jurisdiction did not apply to negotiations on a deep seabed regime. In fact, the interest groups in such a negotiation were quite different. They included states with the technology to mine (among which some were more advanced in seabed mining technology than others), states that exported the minerals found in nodules, states that consumed these minerals, states with likely nodule deposits in or near their economic zones, and so on. In fact, some of these interest groups did surface much later in the negotiations. By 1973, however, the principal negotiating groups were the developing countries on the one hand and the developed on the other. Indeed the conflicts arising over offshore jurisdiction issues seemed to add weight to Group of 77 efforts to maintain cohesion wherever possible on deep seabed issues.

GROUP OF 77. As in other areas, the Latin Americans took a lead role in defining a Group of 77 position on seabed mining. Delegates from Peru, Brazil, and Trinidad and Tobago developed the concept of an "Enterprise" that would mine the seabed area on behalf of the international community under the auspices of an international seabed authority. Peru and Chile engendered sympathetic support for their efforts to limit seabed production to avoid damage to the prices of their own copper production.[44] The issue of production controls and commodity arrangements to protect raw materials producers was of increasing concern to all developing nations. However, there was no well thought-out policy at this stage as was evidenced by the absence of comprehensive joint proposals.[45] The lack of concrete proposals combined with increasing polemics suggest that the seabed negotiation was serving primarily as an opportunity to maintain Group of 77 solidarity and to vent general frustrations. The territorialists found a North-South split on deep-sea mining particularly useful to consolidate developing nation sentiment behind their extreme claims. As the North-South division developed elsewhere in United Nations deliberations, it spread into the law of the sea negotiations, particularly after the oil embargo of 1973 by the Organization of Petroleum Exporting Countries (OPEC).

TECHNOLOGICALLY ADVANCED MINING STATES. The developed nations tried repeatedly to bring the discussions down to the specifics of seabed mining. Where such specifics might threaten Group of 77 solidarity, they were unsuccessful. A common feature of the developed country positions was the expectation that states and parties working under state auspices would mine the seabed.[46] The Japanese and West European proposals also reflected a concern to limit the number of sites any one state might mine to keep United States companies from mining a disproportionate number of promising sites. The Russians gave no detailed consideration to the subject of seabed mining except to point out that a seabed regime should not affect the status of the superjacent waters. Countries such as Norway and Canada evidenced a sympathy for the developing nation position favoring direct exploitation of the seabed by an international authority. They intimated their possible support for a regime that would combine mining by states with that of an international authority.

Evolving U.S. Policy

U.S. ocean policy during the preparatory sessions was influenced by overall trends in the international political climate as well as by domestic pressures. The period 1971-1973 was notable as a time of transition in many areas of U.S. foreign policy. Faced with momentous changes and pressing problems, the highest levels of the government were unable to give sustained attention to the broad range of ocean issues under consideration at UNCLOS III. The single ocean problem commanding sporadic high-level concern was the bilateral confrontations provoked by Latin American seizures of U.S. fishing vessels.

Among the priority issues confronting the administration were promoting détente with the Soviet Union and developing new contacts with China. The Nixon visit to Peking in February 1972 had required several years of delicate negotiations to arrange. The year 1972 was also occupied with the politics of a presidential election. And unbeknownst to the country at the time, it marked the year of the Watergate burglary which came to absorb so much White House attention. The persistent dissent over the U.S. involvement in Vietnam flared up with the president's bombing of Hanoi in December 1972. Meanwhile,

Mr. Kissinger was conducting quiet negotiations with the North Viet-
namese and in January 1973 a cease-fire in Vietnam was announced.
Elsewhere, new resource problems were looming on the horizon. The
nations of OPEC began to increase the price of world oil in large in-
crements. The assertiveness and bargaining power of OPEC fueled the
increasing confidence of Southern nations in a growing North-South
confrontation. And it presaged the oil embargo that followed on the
heels of the October 1973 war in the Middle East.

The impact of these general foreign policy developments on ocean
policy was twofold. First, changing international priorities were mirrored in changing priorities within interagency law of the sea deliberations. A clear example is seen in the gradual decline of defense considerations in U.S. oceans policy coinciding with U.S. efforts to extricate
itself from Southeast Asia. Another example is the increasing weight
of oil interests in law of the sea as OPEC actions raised new concern
over petroleum supplies.

The second impact of general U.S. foreign policy on law of the sea
was in determining the way the oceans policy process worked. With
the highest officials of government absorbed elsewhere, law of the sea
was largely the province of middle-level officials. From 1970 to 1973,
the Office of the Legal Adviser took charge of law of the sea for the
State Department. John R. Stevenson, the legal adviser, chaired the
Interagency Task Force on Law of the Sea and was the principal U.S.
representative to all international negotiations on the law of the sea.
Within State, Stevenson drew on the staff of the Legal Adviser's Office,
the Office of the Coordinator for Ocean Affairs, and the Bureau of
Intelligence and Research.[47]

After Ambassador Stevenson resigned as legal adviser at the end of
1972, there was a period of shifting leadership and organization. The
role of the Interagency Task Force[48] was formalized in January 1973.
It continued to be chaired by State with representation at the assistant
secretary level by the Defense Department, the Interior Department,
the National Oceanic and Atmospheric Administration (NOAA), and
the Treasury Department (as of 1973). Within the task force, an
executive group coordinated the work of ad hoc groups and took decision-making responsibility.

In the spring of 1973, John Norton Moore served as head of the
U.S. delegation to the law of the sea conference. Then in the summer
of 1973, Ambassador Stevenson resumed leadership of the delegation
until 1976. Further developments in 1973 coincided with Henry Kissinger's move from the National Security Council to become secretary

257

of state. The Under Secretaries Committee, chaired by the deputy secretary of state, retained responsibility for reviewing law of the sea policy before it was referred to the president. In practice, this did not result in a consequential role for the Under Secretaries Committee. In September 1973, a new Office of Law of the Sea Negotiations (D/LOS) was established under Deputy Secretary of State Kenneth Rush in his capacity as chairman of the NSC Under Secretaries Committee. Under D/LOS, the functions of the chairman of the Interagency Task Force and the special representative of the president for the law of the sea conference were split between John Norton Moore and John Stevenson respectively. D/LOS staff served both men. The new D/LOS further institutionalized the interagency process and consolidated State Department control over the decision-making process.

The fact that the law of the sea process saw only limited and sporadic input by the highest government officials had both advantages and disadvantages. The advantages were that middle-level officials were specialists who were able to give this complex subject the sustained attention needed to develop and negotiate a coherent policy. The disadvantages of limited high-level involvement were apparent when law of the sea officials could not agree among themselves on a policy. Getting a presidential resolution of interagency differences in 1972, for instance, proved a difficult task. The same problem of getting top officials to sign off on delegation instructions occurred before every session of the Seabed Committee. Instructions generally made it through the clogged National Security Council system several weeks after the sessions had begun. This problem gradually improved after the summer of 1973 when Henry Kissinger took over as secretary of state. His move not only enhanced the authority of the State Department position in law of the sea but it also reduced the importance of the National Security Council process as a means of controlling policy from the White House.

The pressures most directly affecting U.S. oceans policy were those emanating from domestic ocean interest groups and from the Seabed Committee negotiations. After the United States announced in 1970 its policies on seabed mining, the territorial sea, straits, and fisheries, a sharp reaction set in. The vocal sentiment in the Seabed Committee for expanding coastal-state jurisdiction was mirrored on the domestic scene. Under the weight of these external and internal forces, U.S. policy gradually developed a more coastal orientation until in 1974 the government moved to support a 200-mile economic zone. This transition occurred in stages over the three years preceding UNCLOS III.

Seabed and Continental Shelf

U.S. policy on the seabed and continental shelf was the first area to respond to coastal pressures. The president's May 23 statement of policy and the August 1970 draft treaty on seabed mining sparked immediate concern in two very powerful industries. The petroleum industry was adamantly opposed to relinquishing national jurisdiction over resources beyond the 200-meter isobath.[49] It found support for this view within the Senate Committee on Interior and Insular Affairs.[50] The hard minerals industry voiced equally strong opposition to the provisions of the U.S. draft treaty and its annexes,[51] and it too received a sympathetic hearing in Congress. Both industries were careful to direct their fire at the lengthy and complex treaty rather than openly attack the president's May 1970 statement of policy.

This strong negative reaction was not offset by significant domestic or international support for the treaty. The response in Congress on balance was negative.[52] Other maritime states were taken by surprise and were uncertain about the effect of the total U.S. package on their own interests. The landlocked and geographically disadvantaged states were as yet few in number and relatively quiescent. Although they would be the natural beneficiaries of a narrow national continental shelf and a generous international regime beyond, the developing LL/GDS were reluctant to applaud a United States proposal that had clear military purposes.

THE CONTINENTAL SHELF BOUNDARY. In the absence of support for the draft treaty, the official U.S. position on the continental shelf shifted first to support for a coastal seabed zone and then to a full coastal-state resource zone. A year after the 1970 draft treaty, the U.S. delegation was authorized to support a mileage limitation on the outer limit of the trusteeship zone, couched either in general terms or in terms of 200 miles. The delegation was to maintain the substance of its 1970 policy in other respects while being responsive to foreign and domestic concerns.[53]

By August of 1972, the U.S. had evolved a five-point policy that it hoped would balance coastal-state offshore concerns with international benefits and maritime freedoms. The concept of a trusteeship zone was no longer evident. Ambassador Stevenson, the head of the U.S. delegation, told the Seabed Committee that the United States was prepared to accept coastal-state regulation of the exploitation of mineral resources in an area to be negotiated (and in passing he noted widespread acceptance of 200-mile economic zones).[54] Coastal-state rights in the area were to be subject to international standards and compulsory settlement of disputes. Other uses of the area would not be restricted and pollution controls would be internationally determined. Revenues from sea-bed resources were to be shared with the international community and foreign investment in the area would be protected from expropriation. The provisions on compulsory dispute settlement and nationalization were a clear effort to respond to a disgruntled oil industry. The reference to widespread support for 200-mile economic zones reflected a tentative effort to elicit some concessions in exchange for a U.S. recognition of 200 miles.

Given the range of U.S. interests, the ability of the United States to extract concessions for changes in its own position was limited at best. While some U.S. groups adamantly opposed a 200-mile seabed area, others argued over how to adopt it. And the petroleum industry asserted that national jurisdiction over seabed resources already existed throughout the continental margin beyond 200 miles. Thus, when the U.S. introduced draft treaty articles in 1973 that would grant the coastal state exclusive rights to seabed resources in an area yet to be determined and subject to the 1972 provisos,[55] it was not part of any compromise with the coastal states. By 1974, the U.S. had moved toward a full-fledged 200-mile economic zone plus coastal-state jurisdiction throughout the continental margin beyond 200 miles. By this time, the U.S. was following the Soviet lead and was not able to extract any concessions from the coastal states.

Changes in U.S. government policy on the continental shelf occurred at the same time that the petroleum industry was revising its own views, bringing the two closer together. After a strong attack on the U.S. draft treaty in March 1971,[56] the petroleum industry refrained from further official comments on the question of offshore jurisdiction until the end of 1972. During this period, industry representatives continued to lobby in favor of a broad shelf and were warmly received by representatives of coastal nations. However, a perceptible shift was occurring in industry interests and this was soon reflected in petroleum policy. Where they had once supported unilateral coastal-state claims to the resources of the continental margin, industry representatives now moved to stress the need for international standards and regulations to limit coastal-state powers. The industry was particularly eager to deter expropriation of investment in offshore operations and to secure some international tribunal or other mechanism for compulsory dispute settlement.

Rapid shifts in the international scene were complicating the world oil picture in general and oceans petroleum policy in particular. Where formerly domestic sectors of the major petroleum companies had decided industry policy through the Interior Department's National Petroleum Council (NPC), international problems had begun to require the cooperation of the State Department. The multinationals were having their first serious difficulties with the producing nations which were operating as a bloc through OPEC. While this did not propel industry spokesmen to support an international organization to control resources beyond a depth of 200 meters, it did undermine industry confidence in the view that it was safer and more profitable to deal bilaterally with foreign governments. OPEC successes in increasing their revenues buttressed by the growing trend to expropriation, account for the evolution of the NPC position after March 1971.

The new concerns of the petroleum industry are reflected in the National Petroleum Council's December 1972 summary report on the *U.S. Energy Outlook*. In that report the NPC suggested that "any proposed international treaty dealing with seabed mineral resources should confirm the jurisdiction of coastal nations over . . . the mineral resources of the entire submerged continental mass off their coasts."[57] Gone was the former exhortation to the government to unilaterally declare exclusive jurisdiction over the resources of the margin. Instead, the NPC recommended that an international treaty "should provide for security of investment made in resource development in areas of the continental margin pursuant to agreement with or license from the coastal state." To assure these investments, the NPC supported transferring disputes in the area "to an international tribunal for compulsory objective decision."

The muted industry shift toward coastal-state control over offshore resources was facilitated by the prevailing trend toward expansive coastal-state jurisdiction. By 1972, the U.S. government was speaking sympathetically of coastal-state resource zones. And in 1974, when the U.S. defined the continental shelf as extending to the outer limit of the continental margin, the NPC Interim Report on *Ocean Petroleum Resources* indicated a willingness to settle for a 200-mile limit if that would yield broad agreement on the many issues before the law of the sea conference. In the course of achieving their victory on offshore jurisdiction, the multinational oil firms had developed a sophisticated perspective on their own needs for an orderly regime governing ocean resources.

Nowhere was this more apparent than in the case of ocean shipping. The industry came belatedly to a concern for the problems of transporting oil. It had been slow to respond to the implications of Canada's

Arctic waters pollution legislation and to take an active interest in safeguarding transit routes. Several factors account for this delayed reaction. In the first place, the problem of access to offshore resources was given priority over problems of transport in 1970-1971. Then, when the majors did become attentive to the problems of shipping, they were persuaded that coastal nations would treat commercial transport vessels differently from naval vessels. The petroleum industry regarded it as self-evident that the shipment of petroleum products at the lowest possible cost was in the interest of all nations. Thus, as long as the industry took reasonable precautions to avoid polluting the oceans, it need not fear that unreasonable restrictions would be imposed on petroleum shipping.

This sanguine view of the international community interest in facilitating the economic production and distribution of petroleum was spelled out in detail in the 1973 and 1974 NPC reports on ocean issues.[58] In those reports, the industry reiterated and elaborated its support for integrity of investment (or prompt compensation in the event of expropriation) and for compulsory dispute settlement procedures. The NPC noted the "international community interest in unimpeded navigation" for merchant ships. Ships could be required to comply with internationally prescribed standards. Enforcement of these standards would be the prerogative of the flag state, except in the territorial sea, and coastal states would be allowed limited enforcement rights in an area beyond the territorial sea. Clearly the industry policy as outlined in these reports was quite close to the prevailing official U.S. policies on the economic zone, marine pollution, and compulsory settlement of disputes.

DEEP-SEA MINING.   The hard minerals industry did not have the experience of seeing its views converge with government policy. Despite its strenuous opposition to the 1970 U.S. Draft Treaty on the Seabed Regime, the thrust of the original policy on deep-sea mining was not modified. While the petroleum industry found its opposition to the draft treaty in harmony with the majority of coastal developing states, the objections of the hard minerals industry ran counter to the sentiments of the majority in the UN. Most developing nation delegations supported the concept of an international authority that would be able to mine the seabed directly as well as regulate the activities of others. The mining companies, on the other hand, supported limited regimes ranging from laissez faire to an international registry of claims. The drafters of the 1970 treaty consequently found themselves occupying the middle ground between opposing national and international factions.

Finding little support in the Interior Department—or elsewhere in the executive branch for that matter—the industry turned to the U.S. Congress. Several mining firms were beginning to develop deep-sea mining technology and by the beginning of 1972, Hughes Tool Company had started construction of what was reported to be a mining barge.[59] At the request of Senator Lee Metcalf (D-Mont.), the American Mining Congress (AMC) drafted legislation for a seabed regime that would be more congenial to mining interests than the 1970 draft treaty. Introduced originally as S.2801 on November 2, 1971 (HR 13904, March 20, 1972), the AMC bill lapsed with the 92nd Congress.[60] Identical legislation, however, was reintroduced in the 93rd Congress (HR 9, January 3, 1973; S.1134, March 8, 1973).[61] This industry-sponsored legislation[62] was designed to allow U.S. firms to mine the deep seabed under a national licensing system pending the establishment of an international regime. It provided for reciprocal recognition of similar practice by other countries and for the establishment of a fund drawn from income taxes with aid directed to less developed reciprocating states. In January 1974, this legislation was revised in the House Merchant Marine and Fisheries Committee and introduced in the Congress as HR 12233 and S.2878.[63] Although the drafters eliminated several of the more controversial provisions, a new feature of the revised bill was the provision that January 1976 would be the trigger date for the national licensing regime if no international regime had been negotiated by that time.

Both domestic and international opposition to these bills was voiced. Much of the executive branch opposition centered on the provisions for a U.S. government guarantee to reimburse the licensee for any loss of investment or for increased costs resulting from requirements or limitations imposed by a subsequent international regime. This investment guarantee was to be in effect for forty years from the issuance of the license. Opponents pointed out the illogic of a policy whereby the government would guarantee an industry against its own future actions. Foreign as well as domestic opponents also argued that enactment of this legislation could prejudice the character of the international regime to be established through negotiations in the Seabed Committee.[64]

In the Seabed Committee, the executive branch tried to turn the AMC legislation into an asset by using it to speed the pace of the international negotiations. U.S. officials also sought to concert policy on some form of interim legislation with the other technologically advanced nations. Threats of seabed legislation, however, did not alter the leisurely pace of the negotiations. Instead, they had the effect of enhancing Group of 77 solidarity, increasing the strident rhetoric, and provoking periodic intimations of a new moratorium resolution on seabed mining. The Group of 77 was not ready to begin serious negotiations on seabed issues until 1975. Meanwhile, internationalists chaffed and national mining companies proceeded with exploration and the development of technology.[65]

Complicating the intragovernmental deliberations on a seabed regime was the appearance of a new participant in the law of the sea process in March 1973—the Treasury Department. Until then, uncontested responsibility for deep-sea mining had rested with the Interior Department. Through 1971, Interior officials had accorded more attention to petroleum problems than to those of the hard minerals industry. This changed in early 1972 when two officials were recruited from the Defense Department to handle law of the sea for Interior. Interior's new emphasis on deep-sea mining was also promoted by the fact that the petroleum interests were increasingly satisfied with U.S. policy while the hard minerals industry was increasingly alarmed about the direction of the negotiations. While Interior officials predictably did not relish the advent of a new agency concerned with seabed policy, other law of the sea departments were equally alarmed.

Together with the Council of Economic Advisors (CEA), the Council on International Economic Policy (CIEP), and the Office of Management and Budget (OMB), Treasury brought a new perspective to bear on the entire range of law of the sea policies dear to the hearts of the several agencies.[66] With regard to seabed mining, the Treasury Department feared that an international regime with discretionary authority might act to discourage production. In a period of resource scarcity, this would further restrict supply and raise mineral prices to the consuming nations. The 1970 draft treaty sought political gains at the expense of needed resources and economic efficiency. To attempt to generate international revenues by creating an overweighted and discretionary bureaucratic structure would, in the Treasury view, simply deter exploitation and limit seabed development, thereby reducing the revenues that might ultimately be available to developing nations. Similarly inefficient would be the encouragement of mining through guarantees against financial loss as envisioned in the AMC legislation. To foster seabed mining before the cost of land-based sources made the attendant risks acceptable to the mining companies would simply subsidize development of high-cost minerals at the expense of the taxpayer. On the other hand, to hinder development of seabed resources when the risks were commercially acceptable would subsidize the development of higher cost land-based minerals at the expense of the consumer.

The economic perspective brought to bear on the issue of seabed mining reflected the strongly held views of Secretary of the Treasury George Shultz and his deputy, William Simon. Similar approaches were applied to the entire range of law of the sea questions: jurisdiction over the continental shelf, transit through international straits, international standards for marine pollution, and living resources. The direct interest of the top officials in the Treasury Department succeeded in generating a series of government studies and policy reviews despite the resistance of the other agencies. A July 1973 National Security Decision Memorandum (NSDM) directed the Interagency Task Force to review U.S. economic interests in the law of the sea negotiations. Agency studies were solicited. This review process introduced new considerations into a policy process that had previously been dominated by tactical and political concerns.

To apply the brakes when international negotiations were well advanced did not sit well with those agencies whose views had already been accommodated in U.S. policy and who had therefore developed a vested interest in seeing the negotiating process move ahead toward an international law of the sea treaty. One response to this state of affairs was the bureaucratic restructuring in the Department of State and the establishment of D/LOS. The personal involvement of Shultz and Simon as well as White House advisors Kenneth Dam and Peter Flannigan called forth a corresponding level of prominence for law of the sea in other agencies. With Henry Kissinger newly established as secretary of state, State Department officials were in a position to maintain control of the policy process and resist the pressures of economic agencies for change.

In a series of agency clashes between the 1973 spring and summer sessions of the UN Seabed Committee, the economic agencies disputed the economic soundness of agency proposals on international pollution regulations, on licensing provisions subjecting leases beyond 200-meters depth to an international regime proviso,[67] and on the 1970 draft seabed treaty. The conflict came to a head in July when delegates to the UN Seabed Committee were assembling in Geneva. As the meeting opened on July 2, 1973, the U.S. delegation was without instructions. In previous years, this situation had been a result of difficulties in getting the summer White House to sign off on agency-sponsored draft instructions. In 1973, however, the agencies had not been able to agree on draft instructions. To break this impasse, Deputy Secretary Rush convened an Under Secretaries Committee meeting on July 9 and State, Defense, and Interior officials returned to Washington.[68] Trying to strike a middle ground, the committee reached an accommodation providing that existing U.S. proposals were not to be considered definitive pending completion of a thorough economic review of all aspects of law of the sea.

Meanwhile, those who were anxious to proceed with international negotiations were able to do so under the auspices of a decision memorandum focusing on tactical considerations such as narrowing divergent positions, drafting treaty articles, and consolidating texts. Apart from details on marine pollution, the delegation was left free to elaborate all the points stressed by Stevenson in August 1972, as long as no commitments were made on revenue sharing. Making up for lost time, the U.S. delegation issued a series of treaty proposals in rapid succession: on the Coastal Seabed Economic Area (July 16), on Protection of the Marine Environment (July 18), on Marine Scientific Research (July 20), and on Settlement of Disputes (August 22). With the exception of the proposed "chapter" on compulsory dispute settlement, the draft articles reflected a transposition into treaty language of earlier policy pronouncements.

Offshore Jurisdiction

The U.S. policy on offshore jurisdiction over straits, territorial seas, and fisheries underwent a number of changes during the 1971-1973 negotiations. Like U.S. seabed policies, these areas were the subject of some domestic and a great deal of international coastal pressures. The year 1971 was a particularly active period for U.S. fisheries deliberations while 1972 was a significant year for U.S. straits policy.

FISHERIES. When the U.S. announced its support for preferential coastal-state fishing rights beyond a twelve-mile territorial sea in 1970, the policy was directly tied to the U.S. position on straits transit and the territorial sea. The U.S. hoped to negotiate the three issues as a package, using fisheries policy as a carrot for coastal-state concessions on free transit through international straits. The possible fishing concessions were limited by Japanese and Soviet opposition to granting coastal-state rights beyond the territorial sea. And a principal U.S. goal, espoused succinctly by Defense Department officials, was to avoid the concept of a fishing zone that might ultimately develop into an area of general coastal-state jurisdiction.[69] Thus U.S. policy trod a delicate line between appeasing coastal fishing nations while providing some protection for distant-water fishing nations and for U.S. maritime concerns.

A noteworthy aspect of the 1970 fisheries policy was the lack of a direct input by the U.S. fishing industry. Although the fishing industry had been meeting regularly with the special assistant to the secretary of state for fisheries and wildlife on law of the sea policy, the final decisions were taken within the executive group that was officially created early in 1970. Once the industry learned of the policies affecting its interests, it began to use its congressional leverage to get a handle on the formulation of fisheries policy. After 1971, fisheries policy evolved away from explicit links to territorial sea considerations and reflected the determination of the U.S. fishing community of its own best interests. What is striking about the result is that it continued to represent a balance between coastal and distant-water considerations, this time for purely domestic fisheries reasons.

A look at the makeup of the U.S. fishing industry suggests why a composite policy would reflect both coastal and distant-water concerns. U.S. fishing activities fell into several categories, which included recreational or sport fishing, scientific research, and commercial fishing. Commercial fishing interests shared a single goal—to produce and market seafood. Apart from this common purpose, the industry in the early 1970s was highly fragmented. It was divided into producing and processing segments, but more importantly from a law of the sea point of view, it was divided according to location of fishing effort and species harvested. In terms of area fished, some segments of U.S. industry fished off the U.S. coast while others fished in distant waters. Coastal fishermen harvested a variety of species which were found, for the most part, within 200 miles of shore. Different international legal regimes applied to sedentary living resources of the continental shelf as compared to pelagic (oceanic) species. U.S. fishing for anadromous species (those spawning in fresh waters) took place relatively close to or in the spawning rivers, although this differed in the case of salmon which could travel far beyond 200 miles from shore. Distant-water U.S. fishing could similarly be divided according to species harvested. Operating out of San Diego, the U.S. tuna fleet was harvesting a highly migratory species that ranged great distances, within and beyond 200 miles from shore. The U.S. shrimp fleet, on the other hand, fished within 200 miles of shore off the United States, Mexico, Brazil, and other Latin American nations.

The February 1970 statement on fisheries, although sketchy, was sufficient to alert the industry to discussions in progress and to act as an inducement to concerted action. Distant-water segments of the U.S. fishing industry had the same negative reaction to a preferential rights approach as the Soviet Union and Japan. The U.S. coastal fishermen, like the fishermen of developing coastal nations, favored expanding coastal-state fishing rights and were happy to see movement in this direction. Neither segment of the industry, however, was happy about being excluded from policy deliberations. Despite their differences, coastal and distant-water fishing interests recognized that they would have to act in concert if they were to have an input into U.S. fisheries policy.[70]

To gain a voice in policy formulation, the fishing industry began to exert pressure on a number of fronts in 1971. With congressional support, two executive branch voices for the industry gradually strengthened their positions vis-à-vis other actors in the law of the sea policy process. In the State Department, the special assistant to the secretary for fisheries and wildlife was appointed the coordinator for marine affairs in January 1971. The creation of the National Oceanic and Atmospheric Administration (NOAA) in the Commerce Department in October 1970 had seen the transfer of Interior's Bureau of Commercial Fisheries to NOAA's National Marine Fisheries Service.[71] No longer having to compete with petroleum interests for the attention of top officials in Interior, fisheries interests were able to play a larger role in law of the sea fisheries policy with the help of NOAA officials. The industry exerted leverage on the Congress not only at the State level but also through its various Washington offices and through the National Fisheries Institute and National Canners Association. When an Advisory Group on Law of the Sea was formed in 1972, the industry mobilized congressional support to obtain two seats on the U.S. delegation for its fisheries subcommittee. While the extra seat reflected continuing differences among coastal, anadromous, and distant-water interests, the desire for a voice in the policy process continued to promote cooperation.

The U.S. adoption of the "species approach" was the most notable product of industry cooperation. It was first elaborated, together with the U.S. position on straits and the territorial sea, on July 30, 1971, before the UN Seabed Committee.[72] The species approach applied the concept of coastal-state preferential rights to coastal and anadromous stocks of fish beyond an exclusive fishing zone of up to twelve miles. Coastal states would not have preferential rights to highly migratory oceanic species such as tuna, thereby protecting the U.S. fleets off the west coast of Latin America. To provide for U.S., Soviet, and Japanese fishing off the shores of other nations—at least temporarily—the United States proposed that the fishing capacity of a coastal state be used to determine the extent of its preferential rights in its offshore fishery. As that capacity expanded, so would the coastal nation's preferential rights, presenting, of course, the problem of how to phase out fishing efforts of other nations in the area. To deal with this and other difficulties, the U.S. proposal included provisions for international cooperation in inspection and dispute settlement as well as joint conservation measures to prevent overfishing. Only if all other measures failed was unilateral state action deemed acceptable. Like the 1970 U.S. seabed proposal, the U.S. species approach of 1971 envisioned a strong role for international and regional organizations in the regulation of high seas resources and sought thereby to counter pressure for unilateral extension of coastal-state control over offshore resources.

As elaborated in 1971 and revised in 1972, the species approach was an effort to accommodate U.S. fisheries policy to the prevailing trend toward resource zones of up to 200 miles. In Latin America, ten nations —Argentina, Brazil, Chile, Costa Rica, Ecuador, El Salvador, Nicaragua, Panama, Peru, and Uruguay—were claiming such areas. Canada's expanded fishery jurisdiction had gone into effect in February 1971. And even Malta's Ambassador Pardo had spoken out in favor of a 200-mile resource zone.[73]

Within the government the fisheries problems with Latin America received the attention of high-level U.S. officials throughout 1971. Studies and recommendations were solicited on how to manage our disputes with Brazil and the west coast South American states. A National Security Study Memorandum sought agency views on the prospects for applying the trusteeship concept to fishery resources or alternatively of accepting functional or resource zones. One objective of this review was to straighten out U.S. policy priorities among the diverse issues under consideration by the UN Seabed Committee. The result was to disentangle fisheries from other considerations.

The background to the NSSM effort may be found in the troubled U.S.-Latin American fishing relations of the period. The second session of the quadripartite conference (between the U.S., Chile, Ecuador, and Peru) was held in September 1970.[74] Scheduled to reconvene before July 31, 1971, these negotiations were cancelled in the wake of new disputes between Ecuador and the U.S. Between January 11 and 17, 1971, Ecuador seized four U.S. tuna boats operating roughly fifty miles offshore. On January 18, the U.S. suspended sales of military material to Ecuador for one year in accordance with the provisions of the Foreign Military Sales Act (as amended in 1970). Ecuador was told that further financial sanctions were being reviewed.[75] The Ecuadorian government retaliated by charging the U.S. with "aggression and coercion" before the OAS. The OAS called on both parties to negotiate their differences and to avoid exacerbating the dispute.[76] The dispute did not subside, however. The Ecuadorian government expelled the U.S. military mission from the country. In 1971 Ecuador made fifty-one seizures of U.S. fishing vessels and extracted a total of $2.4 million in fines and licenses.[77]

Unable because of Ecuadorian opposition to resume the quadripartite negotiations, the U.S. had to be satisfied with limited measures to protect its distant-water fishing concerns. In the case of Ecuador, these included private conversations between officials of the two governments to soothe relations.[78] In negotiations with Brazil, the U.S. effected a Shrimp Fishing Agreement along the lines of the draft treaty it had been seeking with Chile, Ecuador, and Peru (CEP). Under its terms, a temporary settlement of the conflict was reached that allowed both parties to continue to maintain their claims.[79] In the absence of a resolution of U.S. differences with west coast Latin American nations, the Congress extended to July 1977 the insurance program established under the Fishermen's Protective Act which was due to expire in February 1973.[80] A further development in the U.S.-Latin American dispute was a trend toward U.S. tuna boats shifting to registry under the flags of Latin American countries. From 1967-1973, approximately twenty U.S. tuna boats changed their registry.[81] A final area to which the U.S. turned its attention was to the UN law of the sea conference. It was here that the government hoped to see established a regime that would accommodate both coastal and distant-water concerns.

In August 1972, when the United States once again introduced draft articles on fisheries to the UN Seabed Committee,[82] they were no longer linked to territorial sea and straits policy. In the fisheries articles as well as in seabed policy statements, there were further concessions to coastal-state jurisdiction over offshore resources. U.S. distant-water fishing interests played a role in drafting the articles, as evidenced by retention of the species approach,[83] but widespread foreign sentiment for broad fishing zones was also a major factor behind the 1972 revisions. The new articles provided that the coastal state would regulate harvesting of coastal and anadromous species and that international fisheries organizations would regulate highly migratory stocks. The coastal state had the right to reserve to its flag vessels all the stocks it could harvest. Above that level and to the point of scientifically determined maximum sustainable yield, the coastal state would grant access to other fishing states with priority to those historically fishing the area and then to other states in the region. If its own fishing capacity increased, the coastal state would reduce the amount of catch allocated to the other states.

The U.S. reiterated the species approach in meetings of the Seabed Committee in 1973.[84] When the U.S. succumbed to pressures for a

200-mile zone policy in 1974, it adapted its species approach to the new policy on the economic zone and continental shelf.[85]

THE TERRITORIAL SEA AND INTERNATIONAL STRAITS. If 1971 was the year of the fisherman in U.S. government policy deliberations, then 1972 was the year of straits. Unlike the U.S. position on fisheries, that on the territorial sea and straits remained relatively unchanged from its initial statement in Stevenson's 1970 speech to its formulation as draft articles for the Seabed Committee in August 1971.[86] The articles provided for a maximum territorial sea breadth of up to twelve miles with baselines to be determined in accordance with criteria set out in the 1958 Geneva Convention on the Territorial Sea and Contiguous Zone. In straits used for international navigation, all ships and aircraft would enjoy a high seas freedom of navigation. While coastal states would have the right to designate corridors suitable for transit, those corridors customarily employed would have to be included and international traffic safety regulations would have to be agreed upon. In the statement accompanying these articles, Stevenson indicated that the United States was prepared to accept a twelve-mile limit if the right of free transit were provided for all vessels and aircraft through and over international straits. Stevenson stressed that free transit was "a limited but vital right" and added that the right was merely one of "transiting the straits, not of conducting any other activities."[87]

As noted above, the U.S. proposal on the territorial sea and straits was no longer linked to fisheries policy by 1972. Standing alone, the proposal came under attack by other delegations. While there was wide support in the Seabed Committee for a twelve-mile territorial sea, there was little support for the straits proposal. The major maritime states supported the U.S. position on straits transit and the land-locked and geographically disadvantaged were quiet. Opposition to freedom of transit through straits centered initially in the Spanish delegation. In 1972, the debate over the list of subjects and issues was instrumental in spreading the controversy to states that had no direct interest in the straits question. The omission from the Group of 77 agenda of reference to "free transit through and over international straits" engendered forceful U.S. and Soviet remonstrances. Developing country sympathy with the straits states was based largely on a general policy of opposing U.S. and Soviet policies. Thus the developing coastal states dug in when the U.S. and Soviets insisted that the agenda be revised to include provision for "free transit" through straits.

Not all members of the U.S. delegation were equally concerned about the need to insert a free transit provision in the list of subjects and issues. As the Group of 77 was hurling accusations of intransigence at the U.S. at the end of the spring 1972 session, other U.S. interests became increasingly alarmed at the failing prospects for a successful law of the sea conference. Hoping to modify, if not overrule, Defense Department insistence on a free transit right, officials from the Departments of State and Interior pressed for National Security Council studies of alternative straits policies. With the personal involvement of Secretary of Defense Melvin Laird the Defense view prevailed in the White House review of the alternative policies presented to it.

The NSDM containing the instructions for the U.S. delegation in the summer of 1972 did not modify the U.S. position calling for the inclusion of free transit on the draft agenda. It did, however, allow for an interpretation of free transit to include some environmental qualifications on the right of free transit. In his July 28 statement to Subcommittee II, John Stevenson stressed the interpretation of free transit as a simple and limited right to pass from one end of a strait to another. He stopped referring to transit as a high seas right and began to elaborate certain coastal-state rights in international straits. These included the right to enforce violations of its own laws and regulations committed by ships in transit as well as a right to enforce mandatory internationally accepted traffic safety schemes. The traffic schemes would be decided in the Intergovernmental Maritime Consultative Organization (IMCO) which, under the new U.S. view, would be given enhanced responsibilities in the areas of straits transit and the environment.

The newly articulated limitations on the right of free transit did not persuade the Group of 77 of the desirability of including a reference to the right of free transit in the draft agenda. The United States was equally adamant and the fall 1972 session of the Seabed Committee seemed to be locked in an impasse. Then, following several weeks of hard bargaining, the chairman of the Seabed Committee, Hamilton S. Amerasinghe, proposed that the compromise formulation "right of transit" be included in the straits agenda item. While other delegations waited, the head of the U.S. delegation cabled Washington on August 12 for a change in instructions to accept the compromise. The Departments of Interior and Commerce, concerned with seeing their own interests advanced in the international negotiations, supported the State Department's request for the change. Only Defense remained steadfastly opposed.[88] Meeting three days later in Washington, agency officials were still unable to agree and John Irwin, chairman of the Under Secretaries Committee, was forced to take the dispute to the White House. With Kissinger en route to Saigon and the president in San Clemente, it took over seven days to press the change in delegation instructions to a resolution. The decision taken favored the compromise formula, "right of transit," overruling the Defense Department and making possible the final agreement on an agenda for UNCLOS III.

After the tense negotiations of 1972, 1973 did not see any major problem for U.S. straits policy in the UN Seabed Committee. Although the U.S. had agreed to a formulation on the "right of transit" through international straits, the substance of U.S. policy remained the same and no new treaty articles were submitted. Elsewhere, however, events were emphasizing the importance for the U.S. of assured straits transit. The October 1973 war in the Middle East was soon followed by an oil embargo and an "energy crisis." The paramount lesson of the Middle East conflict, in Defense Department eyes, was the unwillingness of NATO allies to provide refueling and overflight rights in a conflict they did not support. The right of transit through and over the straits of Gibraltar was crucial to U.S. support for Israel. Defense concluded that an internationally guaranteed right of access through international straits was indispensable to the projection of U.S. force. The lesson of the subsequent "energy crisis," as Defense saw it, was the need to protect transport of vital commodities by keeping sea-lanes open.

MARINE ENVIRONMENT. In 1973, the United States government presented draft treaty articles on marine scientific research and the marine environment to the UN Seabed Committee. While the U.S. had indicated what its position on these issues would be in earlier sessions of Subcommittee III, the delay in the work of the subcommittee had reduced the urgency of drafting treaty language until 1973. The United States, it will be recalled, was not enthusiastic in 1970 about expanding the law of the sea agenda to include these items, much less about negotiating all law of the sea questions in a single conference. Thus, the U.S. came to the preparatory sessions of the Seabed Committee with positions on all the major issues before it except marine scientific research and the marine environment.

The lack of an agreed law of the sea position on science and research did not mean that the U.S. lacked a policy on these questions. It did mean that they were handled in other international and regional bodies and that the policies in these forums were not easily transposed into a law of the sea context. The Intergovernmental Oceanographic Commission (IOC) had been handling marine science affairs within UNESCO since 1960. Under its auspices a number of regional cooperative scientific studies had been carried out. The Intergovernmental Maritime

Consultative Organization (IMCO) was the international body charged with negotiating conventions to regulate maritime safety and control marine pollution. It had begun its work in 1959. Regional pollution control arrangements had been undertaken in certain enclosed and semienclosed seas. And the 1972 Stockholm Conference on the International Environment had marine pollution on its agenda.

The pollution of the marine environment first became a politically touchy law of the sea issue in 1969. In that year the tanker *Manhattan* transited the Northwest Passage. The prospect of the increased use of the Northwest Passage sparked the enactment of Canada's Arctic Waters Pollution Prevention Act.[89] Under this legislation, the Canadian government claimed authority over a pollution prevention zone extending 100 nautical miles from land above the 60° parallel of north latitude and elsewhere to coincide with fishery closing lines.[90] In these areas the Canadians claimed the right to issue regulations governing vessel construction, navigational aids, qualification of the master, and so on. The U.S. viewed the implications of such action as harmful for commercial and military navigation elsewhere but was unsuccessful in persuading the Canadians to reconsider their actions.[91]

Indeed it was at Canadian insistence that the marine environment was specified as one of the agenda items by the 1970 General Assembly resolution calling for the Third Law of the Sea Conference. While the U.S. would have preferred to negotiate the issue bilaterally or in IMCO, the Canadians expected to find support for their position from other coastal states at the conference. The initial response of coastal states was favorable to Canada's claim as representing yet another means of expanding coastal-state authority in offshore areas. In the course of the conference, however, this enthusiasm was to wane as developing coastal and shipping states realized that coastal-state pollution controls could be used by developed nations as a nontariff barrier to discriminate against their shipping.

In the conference preparatory sessions, however, control of vessel-source pollution constituted yet another battlefield for the maritime and coastal forces. Within the U.S. government, the agency protagonists fell into their customary roles. Defense opposed coastal-state pollution zones and insisted on exemptions from international standards for military vessels ("vessels of sovereign immunity"). State preferred international standards but wanted to make some effort to accommodate coastal-state sentiment. Interior was anxious to facilitate oil transport while assuming coastal-state control over the resources of the continental margin. The Transportation Department had responsibilities in the area of shipping and pollution through the Coast Guard. And Treasury raised questions as to the economic effects of international as opposed to coastal-state standards on the costs of transport and the prices of goods to be shipped.

Given these domestic factions and an equally divided foreign scene, U.S. environmental policy attempted to balance both coastal and maritime concerns. A hint of the direction U.S. environmental policy would take was given in the U.S. statements on straits transit in the summer of 1972. At that time, Ambassador Stevenson had recommended new responsibilities for IMCO in developing international standards for straits transit and vessel-source pollution. In July 1973, the U.S. submitted a complete set of draft articles which developed and elaborated this approach to the marine environment.[92] The 1973 articles dealing with vessel-source pollution advanced a position similar to that of the petroleum industry. The articles distinguished between the right to set and the right to enforce standards for vessel-source pollution. IMCO would be vested with the power to set international standards relating to design and construction of vessels and equipment, pollution liability and prevention, and damage compensation. IMCO could also approve requests for higher standards to apply to special areas. The U.S. articles differed from the petroleum industry position in that they gave the flag state the right to impose higher standards on vessels flying its flag and the port state the right to impose higher standards on vessels entering its ports. It was presumed that the direct interest of port and flag states in facilitating navigation would preclude arbitrary or unduly restrictive standards.

In the area of enforcement, the U.S. articles relied on a combination of flag-state, coastal-state, and port-state enforcement. Flag states were responsible for implementing international standards for vessel design, construction, and equipment. Internationally accepted discharge standards would be enforced beyond the territorial sea by flag and port states. The articles specified occasions where coastal-state action would be appropriate, in addition to the types of arrangements the coastal state could make with other states to carry out an enforcement action. The coastal state would be authorized to take direct action, including arrest, to prevent, mitigate, or eliminate a pollution danger to its coasts from offshore maritime casualties or a violation of international standards. Moreover, the coastal state could take enforcement actions against vessels of a certain flag if a compulsory dispute settlement had found that the flag state in question had persistently failed to carry out its enforcement responsibilities. For ordinary violations of international standards, the coastal state would require information from the offending vessel and call on the flag state or the next port state to take enforcement action. In the case of port-state enforcement, the vessel was to be promptly released after providing evidence of financial liability.

This complex and detailed policy on vessel-source pollution was designed to prevent harassment or unnecessary stopping and boarding of commercial vessels by coastal states. It presumed the creation of a dispute settlement mechanism to resolve differences. The policy also skirted the issue of pollution zones beyond the territorial sea. The only power proposed by the U.S. for the coastal state was the right to establish standards stricter than those agreed upon internationally for resource exploitation on the continental shelf.

The U.S. articles on the marine environment addressed a number of goals, not all of them environmental. The input of public and governmental environmental spokesmen came relatively late in the policy process. The public Advisory Committee on Law of the Sea (ACLOS), created in 1972, had only two members on its marine environment subcommittee until 1973. The Environmental Protection Agency (EPA) and the Council on Environmental Quality (CEQ) were represented for the first time at the UN Seabed Committee in the summer of 1973. The inclusion of the environmental agencies in the policy process reflects domestic as well as international pressures. By 1973, it was no longer possible to avoid taking a position on the marine environment in the Seabed Committee. Domestically, concern for the environment was being registered in the National Environmental Policy Act of 1969, the Federal Water Pollution Control Act of 1972, and the Coastal Zone Management Act of 1972. Within the U.S. delegation, a new leadership hoped to diffuse the power of the old law of the sea players and an obstreperous Treasury Department by bringing in the new environmental actors. The problem of Treasury intervention had become particularly acute in the context of preparation for the October 1973 IMCO Conference on Marine Pollution.

Insofar as the debate between coastal- and distant-water interests is concerned, environmental issues per se did not evoke a clear-cut national interest. Protection of the marine environment could be sought through coastal or international mechanisms, but no coastal-state restrictions in an offshore zone could guarantee protection from actions taking place farther out to sea. Ultimately, preservation of the marine environment would require international measures that would apply throughout the oceans.

SCIENTIFIC RESEARCH. There is only one mention of marine science in the four conventions that were produced by the 1958 UN Conference on the Law of the Sea. The Convention on the Continental Shelf specifies that "the consent of the coastal state shall be obtained in respect of any research concerning the continental shelf and undertaken there. Nevertheless, the coastal state shall not normally withhold its consent" in the case of purely scientific research, and the coastal state can participate or be represented. This provision was subject to varying interpretations after it was formulated, and was used by some coastal states to prevent or impede scientific research. The United States interpreted research on the continental shelf to mean research that came into physical contact with the shelf. This interpretation was not, however, widely accepted. Nor was there agreement on what constituted fundamental as opposed to applied research. There was no mention of marine science research in the 1958 Convention on the Territorial Sea and Contiguous Zone or in the 1958 Convention on the High Seas. The United States and a few other countries indicated that they considered scientific research to be among the high seas freedoms, although it was not specifically listed as such in the 1958 convention. In practice, the consent of the coastal state was required for the conduct of research in the territorial sea as well as in other zones of national jurisdiction.

After the 1958 conference, policies toward marine science research evolved according to the differing perspectives of developing coastal and developed maritime states. Many coastal nations sought to regulate the conduct of scientific research in offshore zones of national jurisdiction. The developing countries argued that even where research was not of a commercial or military nature, it would benefit the developed researching state more than the technologically backward. Because this would further widen the gap between developed and developing nations, such research should be controlled. The view of the scientific community in developed countries was that scientific research benefited the international community as a whole and that it should remain as free and unrestricted as possible.

Marine scientific research was placed on the agenda of UNCLOS III in the original 1970 General Assembly resolution calling for the conference. It remained on the agenda, was elaborated, and indeed was mentioned in conjunction with several other agenda items when the final conference list of subjects and issues was completed in 1972. Albeit related to a number of issues such as the seabed regime, the main responsibility for marine science research was allocated to Subcommittee III of the UN Seabed Committee and then to its successor, Committee III, when the conference began.

The first detailed U.S. statement on scientific research was made on August 11, 1972, but the United States did not submit draft articles on the subject until July 20, 1973.[93] Compared to other ocean issues, the U.S. developed an official position on marine science relatively late. This delay may be attributed to two related factors. In the first place, the Seabed Committee did not begin a general debate on scientific research in Subcommittee III until the spring of 1973. Thus there was no pressure to come forward with a comprehensive U.S. policy. In the second place, the delay was due to the fact that nongovernment marine scientists did not have direct access to the central policy process until 1972 when the Advisory Committee on the Law of the Sea was formed. A science lobbying group, the Freedom of Ocean Science Task Group (FOSTG), had been established in 1970 under the National Academy of Sciences Committee on Oceanography and then moved to the Ocean Affairs Board of the Academy. The group represented researchers from academic institutions who needed guarantees to protect open research and unrestricted mobility for their study of the marine environment. FOSTG operated through the special assistant to the secretary for fisheries and wildlife and met on occasion directly with the legal advisor.

The academic marine science community often found itself in a difficult or isolated position vis-à-vis other U.S. interests—both commercial and military operators—that conducted scientific research. While often receiving financial support from business or the Navy, academic scientists pursued special goals as far as access to coastal waters was concerned. The academic science community shared the intelligence community's preference for freedom of access to nearshore areas but broke with that group in its search for a special right of access for research intended for open publication. Commercial interests were also not publication-oriented. They were, however, willing and able to negotiate arrangements with coastal states that provided access to resources and benefits for both parties—a capability that the marine science community lacked. It was difficult for a single research institution to devote resources to developing such a capability since academic researchers ranged widely over the oceans rather than concentrating, like commercial researchers, on surveys of a few areas. To be sure, the largest U.S. oceanographic institutions, the Scripps Institution of Oceanography and Woods Hole Oceanographic Institution, had over a number of years gained some experience in dealings with other governments and scientific institutions, but for the most part, academic marine scientists were dependent upon the State Department to facilitate arrangements for research off the coasts of other countries.

The representation of the marine science interest within the government varied during the preconference preparations. Initially, science representatives from government agencies were responsible for preparing agency positions.[94] In the 1970 deliberations on the continental shelf boundary and a seabed regime, the National Science Foundation tried in vain to obtain special guarantees for freedom of scientific research. Although the definition of the continental shelf at 200 meters was consistent with scientists' desires to limit offshore claims, scientific research had not been instrumental in deciding the outcome. Following this setback for NSF, the State Department began to play a greater role in marine science policy. In January 1971, Ambassador Donald McKernan, the department's special assistant for fisheries and wildlife, was appointed marine affairs coordinator. Among his assistant coordinators was one designated especially for marine science. Then in 1972 scientists from the academic institutions began playing a more active role in determining science policy for the law of the sea. In 1973, the National Science Foundation responded by creating a position to represent the scientists on the Interagency Task Force and the U.S. delegation. State's marine affairs coordinator continued to represent the science interest in the international negotiations.

From its first statements on scientific research, the attitudes and policy of the United States remained generally consistent with minor modification until the United States moved to accept a broad economic zone policy in 1974. The U.S. stressed the importance of marine science research in the production of knowledge that is beneficial to all mankind. Since ocean phenomena transcend manmade boundaries, international arrangements should, in the U.S. view, facilitate access for scientific investigations. Scientific research should be conducted in accordance with international environmental standards and, in areas of coastal-state resource jurisdiction, should protect the legitimate economic interests of the coastal state.

More specifically, the United States proposed that the coastal state should have the right to authorize and regulate scientific research in the territorial sea. Beyond that, in areas under national jurisdiction, the coastal state should have the right to control commercial exploitation. With regard to scientific research in the zone, the U.S. consistently advocated seven coastal-state rights or obligations on the researcher: (1) advance notification of the proposed research including a detailed description of the research project; (2) the right of coastal-state participation; (3) sharing of all data and samples with the coastal state; (4) assistance to the coastal state in interpreting the results of research and their relevance to coastal-state interests; (5) open publication as soon as possible of significant research results; (6) compliance with all applicable international environmental standards; and (7) flag-state certification that the research would be conducted in accordance

279

with the treaty by a qualified institution with a view to purely scientific research. While the U.S. ceased to refer to "freedom of scientific research" beyond the territorial sea, it stressed that if the specified obligations were fulfilled, the coastal state could not forbid legitimate scientific research (not related to exploration or exploitation of resources) in areas under coastal-state jurisdiction and beyond twelve miles from shore.

In the three years of preparatory sessions of the Seabed Committee, U.S. policy on offshore jurisdiction adapted itself to the prevailing domestic and international coastal pressures. This evolution culminated in 1974 when the U.S. officially accepted the concept of the 200-mile economic zone. U.S. offshore policies continued to respond to coastal forces but the pace of change was incremental after 1974. U.S. policy on seabed mining, on the other hand, had varied little during the preparatory sessions, but after 1974 began to change rapidly. This coincided with concerted international pressure for U.S. seabed concessions in exchange for an international agreement on offshore jurisdiction issues.

Procedural Session of UNCLOS III

The Seabed Committee came to the end of its work in the fall of 1973 without having drafted a full set of alternative treaty articles for the conference. Among those articles that had been drawn up, some were more refined than others. Despite inadequate preparatory documents, the General Assembly voted to keep to the schedule set up in 1970, that is, to officially begin the Third Law of the Sea Conference in 1973. On November 16, 1973 it resolved to convene the first session of the conference in New York from December 3 to 14 to deal with organizational matters such as the election of officers, the adoption of the agenda and rules of procedure of the conference, the establishment of subsidiary organs, and the allocation of work among those organs.[95] To facilitate this task, the secretary-general was asked to prepare draft rules of procedure for consideration by the conference. The General Assembly scheduled the second session of the conference to consider substantive questions for a ten-week period from June 20 to August 29 in Caracas. And it held open the possibility of a third session or subsequent sessions "to convene not later than 1975."

The Third UN Conference on the Law of the Sea began to consider organizational questions on December 3, 1973. Disputes over membership on the conference bodies followed by differences over the rules of procedure prevented the completion of the procedural work during the two-week session. Unresolved organizational issues were then the topic of discussions in two informal negotiations from February 25-March 1 and June 10-12, 1974. Procedural questions went on to occupy the first week of the Caracas session and were finally resolved on June 27.

The difficulty of agreeing on rules of procedure for the conference did not augur well for subsequent discussions. Indeed the protracted dispute over organizational issues suggests the structural difficulties that would come to plague the conference. The first round of contention arose among and within the regional groups that provided the framework for selecting officers of the conference and membership on committees. The composition and powers of the General Committee and the Drafting Committee were the first disputed issues. Most nations expected these committees to play major roles at the conference, and fought vigorously to secure membership. The African group sought more seats on the General Committee than the Latin Americans and the Asians sought equal representation with the Africans. Within the "Western European and Others" group, the British, French, and Americans sought representation on both the Drafting and General Committees leaving few seats for other members. These disputes turned out to be pointless since, in subsequent negotiations, the Group of 77 ensured that the activity of the conference centered in the three main committees where they were amply represented. The committee chairmen from Africa, Latin America, and Eastern Europe became the centers of power in the UNCLOS drafting process.

A conflict over decision-making procedures for the conference dominated the proceedings after December 11. It highlighted the concern of two conference minorities—the developed maritime states and the landlocked and geographically disadvantaged states—that the procedures for voting should afford maximum protection for their interests. The more numerous coastal-state members of the Group of 77 were equally concerned that a few states should not be given the power to exercise a veto over the will of the majority. The outcome of this clash was, predictably, a compromise. The compromise diverged from the rules that traditionally governed General Assembly decision making by requiring larger majorities.[96] Such an outcome was consistent with the realities of a negotiation to create international law to govern the seas. Without the support of minorities such as the maritime states, no legal regime could survive for long. Indeed the lesson of the 1960s had been the need for general acceptance of a workable law of the sea.

There were several key issues in the debate over the rules of procedure.[97] They all pertained to when and how to vote on disputed issues. To protect the concerns of minorities, a "gentlemen's agreement" had been reached in the Seabed Committee. As finally appended to the rules of procedure, it said: "Bearing in mind that the problems of ocean space are closely interrelated and need to be considered as a whole and the desirability of adopting a Convention on the Law of the Sea which will secure the widest possible acceptance. . . . The Conference should make every effort to reach agreement on substantive matters by way of consensus and there should be no voting on such matters until all efforts at consensus have been exhausted."[98] The conference deliberations centered on how best to give effect to this gentlemen's agreement. Which body or individual should determine whether all efforts to reach consensus had been exhausted? When should a vote be taken and what deferrals should be allowed? When a vote was taken, what types of majorities would be required for passage of procedural and substantive questions? And, of course, a procedural issue that took precedence chronologically was the issue of how decisions were to be taken with regard to the rules of procedure themselves.[99]

These difficult and contentious questions were ultimately resolved through a complex formula encompassed in Rule 37 (requirements for voting) and Rule 39 (required majority). In response to the persistent efforts of the president of the conference, Hamilton S. Amerasinghe, they were resolved by a consensus procedure under the threat of a voting deadline. Rule 37 covered the procedure for determining whether all efforts to reach general agreement had been exhausted. It provided for three forms of deferral: (1) if requested by at least fifteen representatives, (2) on the president's initiative, or (3) by vote of the conference (by a majority of those present and voting). During the period of deferral, Rule 37 called for a special negotiating effort under the direction of the president assisted by the General Committee. Rule 37 then provided that the conference could decide that all efforts to reach consensus had been exhausted by the vote of a two-thirds majority of representatives present and voting, provided that such a majority included at least a majority of the states participating in that session of the conference. Rule 39 then specified that "decisions of the Conference on all matters of substance, including the adoption of the text of the Convention on the Law of the Sea as a whole, shall be taken by a two-thirds majority of the representatives present and voting, provided that such majority shall include at least a majority of the States participating in that session of the Conference." On matters of procedure, decisions were to be taken by a majority of the representatives present and voting. The formula calling for a double majority ensured that over half the members of the conference would have to pass any substantive issues.

On June 27, the discussions on rules of procedure concluded. The conference adopted the gentlemen's agreement on consensus and agreed to its incorporation in the rules of procedure as an appendix. The rules of procedure were then adopted as a whole and without objections. The threat of having to move to a potentially divisive vote was an important source of pressure to reach agreement. Had the developed maritime states been outvoted on the rules of procedure, they would doubtless have reconsidered their further participation in a negotiation where their views were accorded little weight. Instead, the conference proceeded to negotiate an outcome that satisfied no one completely but was acceptable to most. The pattern in the procedural discussions of avoiding votes and pressing for consensus established the pattern for the substantive negotiations that were yet to come.

UNCLOS III:

VARIATIONS ON A THEME

THE THIRD UN CONFERENCE on the Law of the Sea consumed a total of 77 weeks over its first seven years. During this lengthy and protracted negotiation, the same themes and issues recurred, albeit with some variations and an overall gradual evolution toward agreement. While the agenda of the meetings remained constant, the salience of particular issues and the tone of the discussions shifted from session to session depending on progress in one or more committees. The method of work also changed as repeated efforts were made to create representative negotiating groups of manageable size. Minor changes in the composition of interest groups occurred over time. And the product of each session evolved from year to year. The 1974 Caracas session completed the procedural and preparatory work for the conference and yielded a set of draft treaty alternatives in the form of informal working papers as well as a definitive set of rules of procedure. In 1975, the conference conducted its first negotiations to produce the first Informal Single Negotiating Text. This was revised and reissued in 1976 as the Revised Single Negotiating Text. In 1977, the RSNT was replaced by an Informal Composite Negotiating Text which went through three revisions in 1979 and 1980 and emerged in August 1980 as the Draft Convention on the Law of the Sea.

In addition to the agenda, the formal structure of the conference and the conference leadership provided the greatest elements of continuity. The subsidiary bodies included (1) a credentials committee, (2) a steering committee, (3) a drafting committee, and (4) three main committees to deal with substantive issues. The main committees were assigned the same agenda items as the three subcommittees of the UN Seabed Committee.[1] Committee I dealt with seabed mining beyond the limits of national jurisdiction and was chaired by Paul Engo of Cameroon, with its working group chaired by Christopher Pinto of Sri Lanka. Tommy Koh of Singapore handled major negotiations on financial arrangements. Committee II had responsibility for issues pertaining to national jurisdiction such as the economic or resource zone,

CHART 9-A
UNCLOS III Official Sessions: 1973-1981

	Weeks	(Cumulative)
First Session—1973		
December 3-15, New York	2	2
Second Session—1974		
June 20 - August 29, Caracas	10	12
Third Session—1975		
March 17 - May 9, Geneva	8	20
Fourth Session—1976		
March 15 - May 7, New York	8	28
Fifth Session—1976		
August 2 - September 17, New York	7	35
Sixth Session—1977		
May 23 - July 15, New York	8	43
Seventh Session—1978		
March 28 - May 19, Geneva	8	51
August 21 - September 15, New York	4	55
Eighth Session—1979		
March 19 - April 27, Geneva	6	61
July 16 - August 24, New York	6	67
Ninth Session—1980		
February 27 - April 3, New York	5	72
July 28 - August 29, Geneva	5	77
Tenth Session—1981		
March 7 - April 17, New York	6	83

the continental shelf, fishing, the territorial sea, and straits. The chairmanship was at first alternated between two Latin Americans, Reynaldo Galindo Pohl of El Salvador and Andres Aguilar of Venezuela, but after 1975 met regularly under Mr. Aguilar. Two of its rapporteurs, Francis Njenga of Kenya and Satya Nandan of Fiji, were in charge of important working groups and other negotiations of the first and second committees. Committee III was entrusted with the residual jurisdictional questions of marine pollution and scientific research. The committee was chaired by Alexander Yankov of Bulgaria and its working groups on pollution and research were headed by José-Luis Vallarta of Mexico and Cornel Metternich of Germany, respectively.

Other conference officials played an important ongoing role through the numerous formal and informal negotiating groups. Hamilton S. Amerasinghe (Sri Lanka) was reelected president and took a strong hand in guiding the conference until his death in 1980. He played a major role in negotiating the treaty provisions on dispute settlement. J. Alan Beesley of Canada was elected chairman of the drafting committee and represented a developed country with strong coastal interests as well as the concerns of a major nickel producer. Similarly, Jens Evensen of Norway was able to play a major role as chairman of a number of informal and expert negotiating groups on jurisdictional questions, seabed mining, and final clauses.[2] Despite Ambassador Evensen's skills as a negotiator and his importance as a spokesman for a developed country with significant coastal appetites, he occupied no formal position in the conference structure. Mexico's representative, Jorge Castañeda, was also effective in informal negotiations on jurisdictional issues before and after becoming his country's foreign minister. Spokesman for the coastal-state group, Castañeda represented the patrimonialist position on behalf of Mexico and other Central American and Caribbean nations.

The protracted deliberations of UNCLOS III can be traced to a number of factors. As noted elsewhere (Chapter 8), the number of participants, the length of the agenda, and the goal of a single comprehensive treaty presented a formidable negotiating task. There was, moreover, no deadline for the completion of the conference. As early as 1973 and 1974, the prevailing assumption was that there would be a 1975 session. By 1975, there was no reason to not anticipate further sessions. When in 1976 a number of developed countries, including the United States, adopted 200-mile economic or fishing zones, they satisfied internal coastal pressures for extending jurisdiction and removed a substantial source of pressure for a treaty. Thereafter, a principal reason for completing the treaty was to establish a deep seabed regime, but national mining legislation moved more quickly than the UNCLOS debates and was instrumental in spurring the negotiations.

Because the conference lasted so long, the national interests of a number of countries changed more rapidly than the various iterations of the draft treaty. When the United States, the United Kingdom, and the Soviet Union accepted the concept of the 200-mile zone in 1974, it was widely viewed as a victory for the nations of the developing world. By 1976 this view had been succeeded by the more sober recognition that these three maritime nations as well as other developed countries such as Canada, Australia, and Norway were the principal beneficiaries of a global 200-mile zone. Apart from a few South American states, the developing coastal countries would receive narrow slices of 200 miles that were relatively resource-poor and prospectively difficult to manage. When this was recognized, the ranks of those considering themselves geographically disadvantaged[3] swelled, bringing the number of land-locked and geographically disadvantaged states (LL/GDS) to over fifty nations. Despite these developments, however, the broad outlines of the conference settlement had been set by 1976. They included a twelve-mile territorial sea, a 200-mile economic zone, and provision for unim-peded transit through international straits and for coastal-state jurisdic-tion over the continental margin beyond 200 miles. This framework was first elaborated in the Informal Single Negotiating Text (ISNT) by the Committee II chairman. Once it was set in the conference text it was impossible to alter, even though a growing number of states began to have second thoughts.

The UNCLOS III negotiations fall broadly into two phases—the period through 1976 and that from 1977 on. Through 1976, the nego-tiations concerned the full range of ocean issues; after 1976, the prob-lem of seabed mining was the only significant unresolved issue. From 1977 on, the negotiations on seabed mining became progressively more technical and complex. For U.S. policy, the period after 1976 marks a change as well. The departure of the Nixon-Ford administration brought a change in the principal U.S. negotiators, in addition to a different congressional-executive relationship. Throughout the Nixon-Ford years, the administration had had a relatively free hand to deter-mine U.S. policy. The passage of the U.S. claim to a 200-mile fisheries zone by the Congress marked the end of unchallenged executive branch ascendancy.

Apart from the discontinuities between 1976 and 1977, a gradual evolution can be discerned throughout the conference. The interna-tional politics of the Carter years spilled over into the law of the sea negotiations. The new administration's emphasis on human rights and nonproliferation initially troubled its relations with traditional U.S. allies as well as exacerbating relations with the Soviet Union. While U.S. policies on the Panama Canal Treaty, human rights, and civil strife in other countries were more congenial to the Group of 77, the U.S. continued to hold to its economic policies in a number of North-South negotiations. The preoccupation of the period, namely OPEC's oil price increases and the attendant economic effects, generated initial developing country support for restrictive seabed mineral commodity policy. This was followed by a disillusionment with the OPEC coun-tries and growing divisions within the Group of 77.

CARACAS SESSION: 1974

The first substantive session of UNCLOS III met in Caracas from June 20-August 29, 1974.[4] The character of the Caracas meetings was typified by its setting in an oil-rich developing country. Eager to create a new law of the sea that represented what were perceived to be the distinctive interests of developing countries, the third world had pressed for a conference site that would provide a suitable title for the prospective convention. When the Santiago site was withdrawn after the overthrow of the Chilean government, the Caracas offer was preferred over the UN headquarters in New York or Geneva.

Billed as the first substantive negotiating session of UNCLOS III, the Caracas meeting was in fact devoted to completing the inadequate preparatory work of the Seabed Committee and of the procedural session. The massive influx of new participants expanded the conference from the 91-member Seabed Committee to 137 members in Caracas. Substantial time was necessarily spent educating the new participants and integrating them into existing interest groups. Because groups were devoting their energies to the coordination of internal positions, little time was available for negotiations among or between groups.

The Caracas session, like those that followed, was haunted by the problem of developing cohesion within groups that could in turn negotiate with other groups. The Group of 77, regional groups, the European states, coastal states, and the developed nations all experienced serious fissures when they had to address specific negotiating points. These difficulties were presaged in meetings of the LL/GDS and of the Group of 77 before the Caracas session. On March 20-22, the landlocked and shelf-locked states met in Kampala to coordinate their positions for a subsequent meeting of the Group of 77. The resulting Declaration of Kampala elaborated a number of goals: access to the sea and to high seas living resources for landlocked states; the right to exploit and benefit from the resources in the coastal area of neighboring states; the right to sail ships under national flags and use the port facilities of neighboring coastal states on an equal basis; exemption from customs duties or charges except as related to traffic services; and the exploration of the seabed for the benefit of mankind.[5] The LL/GDS then took their position to the meeting of the Group of 77 in Nairobi. The 77 met from March 25 to April 5, vainly seeking a common law of the sea position. A number of disagreements surfaced at the Nairobi meeting, the most pervasive being the difference between the LL/GDS and the coastal states. The coastals refused to acknowledge the concept of geographic disadvantage and were only willing to agree to negotiate arrangements that would include benefits for the landlocked. The only area of agreement that could be found among the Group of 77 was on the deep seabed regime, but even here there were differences.

The division between the LL/GDS and the coastal states plagued the Caracas meeting and subsequent sessions. It split the African regional group and slowed the deliberations of Committee II. It also affected the efforts of the European Community to reach a common position. Because of this split, the Group of 77 intensified efforts to arrive at a unified position on Committee I issues. Due to internal differences and lack of technical expertise, the Group of 77 negotiations were time-consuming. Moreover, once a position was agreed upon, the group could not alter its formulations on the conditions for exploiting the seabed, even when these formulations proved to be an obstacle to negotiations.

While much time was spent on behind-the-scenes coalition building, a major portion of the session was also spent on general debate in plenary and then in the main committees. After the rules of procedure were adopted on June 27, the general debate in plenary lasted through July 15. Although the speakers were intended to be only the fifty or so new participants, a number of states took the occasion to reiterate previous positions, partly in the hope of influencing the newcomers. A total of 115 states and nine nongovernmental organizations addressed the plenary.[6] The interventions covered a variety of issues, and, for the most part, reflected no shifts in position from the earlier negotiations.

The salient issue at the session, and one which all delegates addressed, was that of the limits of national jurisdiction. The most important developments of the session were the changed positions on jurisdiction announced by the Soviet Union,[7] the United Kingdom,[8] and the United States.[9] These three maritime powers had been the principal opponents of extending offshore jurisdiction. In the course of the Seabed Committee deliberations, they had been under internal and external pressures to adopt a more coastal orientation. Finally in 1974 they officially announced policies favoring 200-mile economic zones and national jurisdiction over the resources of the continental margin where it extends beyond 200 miles. Each country specified a number of conditions that must be met for their support of a 200-mile zone but because they had not acted in concert, no reciprocal concessions were won from the coastal states.

The initial reaction of many third world nations was to view the shift of major maritime nations as a victory for the new legal regime that would reflect third world principles. The immediate political impact was to isolate the landlocked and shelf-locked states that were opposing extended national jurisdiction. And the corollary was to make it appear that there was a ground swell of support for a 200-mile zone and a twelve-mile territorial sea. Indeed, the coastal states pressed for a conference product stating that the twelve-mile territorial sea and 200-mile zone represented the general consensus of opinion. Although the LL/GDS, with maritime-state support, successfully resisted such a document, the coastal states, including the U.S., persisted in describing this as the emerging trend.

The product of the Caracas discussions was a more complete set of alternative treaty articles. Committee I completed a third reading of draft articles for a seabed regime. Committee II, led by Ambassador Aguilar, consolidated the national proposals that were submitted into alternative formulations and returned them to the committee for review. The product was a reduced number of detailed treaty articles supported by increasingly cohesive blocs of states. Committee III proceeded in its working groups to review and perfect the texts on marine pollution and scientific research.

Committee I

The first committee adopted its program of work, which envisioned a week of general debate followed by a third reading of articles dealing with the system of seabed exploitation.[10] Although Committee I had progressed further than any other committee in drafting alternative articles, it became the most politically volatile forum of discussion in Caracas. Several explanations for this change may be ascertained. Since it was ahead of the other committees in its drafting efforts, it could afford to expend its time on polemics while it waited for the others to catch up. Moreover, the discussion in Committee I was widely viewed as of secondary importance to Committee II deliberations on the limits of jurisdiction. The developing coastal states therefore used the deep seabed negotiations as leverage and delayed the rate of progress until they could secure their position on offshore jurisdiction. And, with the Group of 77 severely divided on jurisdictional issues, Committee I offered the only opportunity to promote rhetorical Group of 77 solidarity even at the expense of negotiations.

The chairman of the committee, Paul Engo, chaired the general debate and Christopher Pinto chaired the informal working sessions. Three related issues were sources of dissension in these meetings: (1) the question of "who may exploit the area";[11] (2) the conditions of exploitation (i.e., rules and regulations to govern mining); and (3) the economic implications of seabed mining for land-based producers. On each of these questions, there was a wide gap between the technologically advanced countries and the developing countries, although differences of opinion were evident within both groups.

On the issue of who may exploit the deep seabed, the developed countries envisioned a seabed authority that would issue licenses to states or companies to explore and exploit seabed resources. Licenses would be issued on a nondiscriminatory basis to qualified applicants that complied with prescribed rules. In return for an application fee, the licensees would receive exclusive rights for a period of time to a designated area.[12] The Group of 77, on behalf of developing nations, proposed that the exploration and exploitation of the resources of the area, as well as other related activities such as scientific research, be conducted directly by the seabed authority. In recognition of the technological realities, the authority would be empowered to "confer certain tasks on juridical or natural persons, through service contracts or association or through any such means it may determine which ensures its direct and effective control at all times over such activities."[13]

A wide difference of views was evident as well in discussions of the rules and regulations that would govern seabed mining. The developed nations pressed for a detailed "mining code" that would be incorporated in the treaty.[14] Prospective miners would know how the system would work and their rights and duties as well as those of the authority. The United States was particularly eager to limit the power of the authority to discriminate among ocean miners or to impose unreasonable terms and conditions.[15] The developing countries preferred to accord the authority maximum flexibility to determine rules and regulations and wished to insert only general guidelines in the treaty. This position was consistent with their effort to maintain the power of the seabed authority and it also reflected the fact that the Group of 77 had difficulty in producing anything more detailed than general principles.[16]

The third area of contention in Committee I was that of the economic implications of seabed mining for producers of copper, cobalt, nickel, and manganese. The land-based producers, principally Chile,[17] Peru, and Zaire, were fearful that seabed mining would lead to price reductions for their mineral exports. While such price reductions might have a limited effect on more diversified economies, they would be deleterious to the economies of land-based producers because of their heavy dependence on mineral exports. Mineral-exporting countries were supported in their concerns by UN Conference on Trade and Development (UNCTAD) studies that suggested serious consequences for such economies if seabed mining were not limited. The United States was opposed to granting the seabed authority the right to impose production or price controls on seabed mining, either directly or indirectly. Instead, the benefits to all consumers of increased supply of seabed minerals was stressed. A number of studies both within the UN and the United States suggested that seabed production would have minor economic impact on land-based production and this would be limited to cobalt producers (i.e., Zaire).[18]

Despite such evidence, the land-based producers received a sympathetic hearing from other raw materials producers among developing nations. Thus the relatively small group of concerned producers was able to link seabed mining to the expanding North-South debate over the "New International Economic Order." The U.S. argument that the vast majority of developing nations were consumers of seabed minerals and would benefit from new sources of minerals made little headway. The interchange was essentially a dialogue of the deaf. In the aftermath of the OPEC oil embargo, the developed world was intent upon securing assured supplies of seabed minerals. The developing countries, while reeling under the impact of OPEC price increases, were vicariously enjoying the success of the OPEC cartel. By pursuing a common policy, they hoped to expand production controls and price increases to all raw materials, not just seabed minerals. The debate on economic implications was a clear case of substituting polemics and coalition building for negotiations between factions.[19]

While the issues before the committee were difficult enough in the prevailing political climate, neither side contributed to improving the tenor of the exchange. The U.S. team was headed by a representative of the Federal Energy Agency (newly transferred from the Interior Department) with no background in international diplomacy. The other delegates were also, with some notable exceptions, junior representatives on their national delegations. Eager to draw attention to their efforts, they succeeded in turning Committee I into an arena for fireworks rather than for considered negotiations.

By the end of the Caracas meeting, very little progress was discernible in the first committee.[20] The third reading of the draft treaty articles produced few changes or reductions in the number of alternative articles.[21]

Committee II

The work of Committee II on offshore jurisdiction was viewed by all participants as the most important of the session. Committee II dealt with fifteen of the twenty-four agenda items, and it had made the least progress in its preparatory work. The Caracas session was spent making up for lost time. Committee II adopted its work program under the direction of Chairman Andres Aguilar,[22] and conducted a general debate on each of the fifteen items before the committee.[23] When debate on each issue was completed, the officers of the committee prepared a working paper setting out the main trends on the subject. When each working paper was ready, the general debate on the next item was interrupted and the working paper was discussed. Some working papers went through two revisions. Over eighty proposals were submitted in the process.[24] The final product was a series of fifteen working papers comprising a consolidated set of treaty articles for subsequent negotiation.[25]

Items before Committee II included the territorial sea, transit through straits, the economic zone, and the related issues of fishing, the high seas regime, and the continental shelf beyond 200 miles. Issues of importance to certain groups of states were the regimes for achipelagos and islands.

TERRITORIAL SEA AND STRAITS TRANSIT.   There was widespread agreement at Caracas on a twelve-mile territorial sea,[26] but subject to certain conditions. Developing coastal states insisted that a twelve-mile territorial sea be combined with coastal-state jurisdiction over offshore resources to 200 miles. And maritime states linked their acceptance of a twelve-mile territorial sea to a regime of unimpeded transit through and over straits that would be covered by territorial seas of twelve miles. The maritime states were willing to accommodate the environmental and safety concerns of the states bordering such straits. The United States supported the right of straits states to designate corridors for transit and to propose traffic separation schemes in crowded straits. Although the U.S. recognized that special standards might be necessary in straits where unusual circumstances pertained, it otherwise preferred to see international regulations and procedures applied to the promotion of safety and the prevention of pollution in international straits.[27] The maritime states stressed the importance they attached to a successful resolution of the straits issue for an acceptable treaty.[28]

States bordering international straits evidenced a variety of concerns, some of which went beyond safety and environmental considerations. Their governing assumption was that the regime of innocent passage should pertain throughout their territorial seas, even when they overlapped straits less than twenty-four miles wide. Under such a regime, straits states proposed to exercise a number of controls over navigation.

These were clearly set out in a set of draft articles submitted in 1973 by Cyprus, Greece, Indonesia, Morocco, Spain, and Yemen.[29] According to this draft, the straits state would have the right to regulate transit and could apply certain provisions to vessels with special characteristics, such as tankers, nuclear-powered ships, and ships carrying nuclear weapons. Submarines would be required to navigate on the surface and to show the flag. And all warships or noncommercial government ships would be required to give prior notice of transit and to be authorized by the coastal state.

The majority of states at the Caracas session fell somewhere between the maritime states and the straits states. A few members of the Group of 77 supported the straits state position for ideological reasons, that is, since it represented a move to increase coastal-state authority, it was taken in opposition to the major maritime states. The Arab states were in a difficult situation. While they wished to close the Straits of Tiran to Israeli shipping, they needed unrestricted passage through the Straits of Hormuz and Gibraltar. Most states shared the Arab concern to facilitate shipping of petroleum and other goods. As a result, a great deal of support was given to a middle-of-the-road proposal by Fiji under which coastal states could regulate transit, but the regulation could be no more restrictive than internationally accepted IMCO rules on matters such as ship design, construction, manning, and equipment.

THE ECONOMIC ZONE, LIVING RESOURCES, AND THE CONTINENTAL SHELF. The configuration of political forces on the question of a 200-mile economic or resource zone broke down according to geographic interests. The maritime states, the United Kingdom, the United States, and the Soviet Union, conditioned their acceptance of 200-mile economic zones upon guarantees for the conduct of nonresource-related activities by other states. This policy accommodated their distant-water naval concerns with their interest in controlling the resources off their own vast coasts. In their view, it was important that the resource rights of the coastal state be carefully elaborated in the treaty and that residual rights (i.e., rights not specifically granted to the coastal state) be retained by the international community. Compulsory dispute settlement was needed to resolve differences that might arise.

The landlocked and geographically disadvantaged states were decidedly unenthusiastic about the concept of an economic zone unless provision could be made to allow them access to the resources of the zone and to the revenues generated therefrom.[30] At the other extreme from the LL/GDS were the territorialists such as Brazil, Panama, Peru, and Ecuador, which sought to convert the 200-mile zone into a full territorial sea.[31] Occupying a position between the territorialists and the maritime states were a number of developing coastal states. The "patrimonialists" of Latin America, such as Mexico, Venezuela, and Argentina, and the African coastal states sought exclusive jurisdiction throughout a 200-mile national zone in which the international community would have carefully defined but restricted rights.[32] Implicit in the issue of whether the coastal state or the international community enjoyed residual rights in the zone was the question of whether the zone beyond the territorial sea was to be regarded as high seas.

The controversy over the economic zone derived from coastal-state concern to control the living resources of the economic zone and the mineral resources of the continental shelf. With regard to fishery resources, developing coastal states sought exclusive jurisdiction over the resources of their zone and the right to permit foreign fishing only at their own discretion. Distant-water fishing states were willing to concede only preferential rights to the coastal state. Where the coastal state did not have the capacity to harvest the total allowable catch, they wanted foreign fishing to be permitted.[33] The LL/GDS sought even more. They proposed that they should have the right to participate in fishing in the zone of neighboring coastal states "on an equal and non-discriminatory basis."[34] The coastal developing states recognized that neighboring states might have an interest, but opposed the concept of preferential rights as derogating from their sovereignty over natural resources in the zone. The European Community, without the British, attempted a regional approach to the fisheries problem.[35]

Special fisheries problems developed among those states having an interest in highly migratory species (primarily tuna) and anadromous species (salmon). Developing coastal states insisted on the right to all fish that entered their economic zone, regardless of their migratory habits, whereas the United States sought an international regime to manage tuna throughout its cycle.[36] In the case of salmon, the host states where salmon spawned sought exclusive jurisdiction over the fishery throughout its migratory cycle.[37] Japan, the major high seas fisher of salmon, proposed international management of anadromous species by all interested parties.[38]

In the case of the continental shelf, there was also a rather clear division among groups according to their geographic interests. States with margins extending beyond 200 miles promoted coastal-state jurisdiction over the resources of the margin to the point where it meets the abyssal plain. While some were willing to consider revenue sharing in the margin beyond 200 miles (e.g., the United States,[39] New Zealand, and Canada), others were not (e.g., Argentina, Australia, and the

United Kingdom). Opposed to the wide-margin position were Japan,[40] the LL/GDS, and a number of African coastal states.

ARCHIPELAGOS AND ISLANDS. Archipelago states sought a regime in which they would draw straight baselines between their outermost islands and enclose "archipelagic waters" within. Other zones of jurisdiction, such as the exclusive economic zone, would extend outward from the baselines. States claiming archipelagic status included Fiji, Mauritius, Indonesia, Malaysia, the Philippines, and the Bahamas.[41] Maritime powers were concerned that these claims to vast areas of ocean space would restrict traditionally used shipping areas and they sought means to guarantee passage through these waters.

In the case of islands, the central question was whether islands should be treated like the land masses in the allocation of offshore areas, that is, should an island receive a full economic zone, and should it be used as a baseline from which to delimit boundaries between opposite and adjacent states, and so on. Here too, national positions coincided with the facts of national geography. The salient controversy over islands was between Greece and Turkey.[42]

Upon the completion of the session, Ambassador Aguilar made a statement summing up the work of Committee II. This was issued as an official document after the territorialists, who were opposed to the statement, were threatened with a vote on the issue. According to Chairman Aguilar,

> The idea of a territorial sea of twelve miles and an exclusive economic zone beyond the territorial sea up to a total maximum distance of 200 miles is, at least at this time, the keystone of the compromise solution favoured by the majority of States participating in the Conference. . . .
>
> Acceptance of this idea is, of course, dependent on the satisfactory solution of other issues, especially the issue of passage through straits used for international navigation, the outermost limit of the continental shelf and the actual retention of this concept, and, last but not least, the aspirations of the land-locked countries and other countries which, for one reason or another, consider themselves geographically disadvantaged.
>
> There are, in addition, other problems to be studied and solved in connection with this idea, for example, those relating to archipelagoes and the regime of islands in general.
>
> It is also necessary to go further into the matter of the nature

and characteristics of the concept of the exclusive economic zone, a subject on which important differences of opinion still persist.[43]

Committee III

The third committee adopted its program of work[44] and broke into two informal groups, the one on marine pollution headed by José-Luis Vallarta and the other on scientific research led by Cornel Metternich.[45]

MARINE ENVIRONMENT. The marine environment working group made little headway beyond a review of the articles that had been drafted in the Seabed Committee in 1973.[46] Leading coastal states, such as Brazil, India, and Kenya, wanted to prevent any resolution of environmental questions before the broad issues on offshore jurisdiction in Committee II were settled.

Environmental questions facing the working group in 1974 had several components: a general obligation to protect the marine environment, minimum standards for resource exploitation activities in the economic zone, and vessel-source pollution. Land-based sources of pollution, which constituted the major threat to the ocean environment, were deemed beyond the competence of UNCLOS III.

Nations adopted a variety of positions on environmental issues, but there were some broad differences of opinion that corresponded with the coastal orientation of many developing states and the maritime concerns of the developed world. On the question of a general obligation to protect the environment, developing nations pressed for language that would allow a double standard to be applied.[47] In their eyes, development took priority over environmental protection as it had done in the industrialization of the developed world. Developing countries, therefore, resisted the argument that minimum international standards should be applied to coastal-state activities in the economic zone. A number of coastal states were opposed to international standards as derogating from their sovereignty in a national zone.

The debate over the management of vessel-source pollution broke down along similar lines. Maritime states preferred to see international standards enforced by flag states in the economic zone with coastal-state enforcement limited to emergency situations.[48] The United States sought a combination of international and port-state standards with flag-state and port-state enforcement. Proponents of coastal-state rights preferred to expand coastal-state powers to adopt and enforce pollution control standards. Developing countries, however, indicated that these powers should not normally extend to construction, design, manning, or equipment standards which they feared might be used to discriminate against their own shipping.[49]

MARINE SCIENCE. The positions adopted on the subject of marine scientific research coincided with the major political divisions of the session between coastal developing states, the technologically developed, and the LL/GDS.[50] The contentious issue was that of the conditions under which scientific research could be conducted in the economic zone. Developed states sought to preserve free access for their vessels to conduct research in the economic zones of other states. Developing coastal states insisted that all research be subject to the prior consent of the coastal state. And the LL/GDS proposed a regime which allowed them to participate in research activities within the zones of neighboring coastal states.[51]

In the course of the discussions in the Working Group on Scientific Research and Transfer of Technology, four main trends emerged: (1) Some coastal members of the Group of 77 proposed that the coastal state have exclusive rights to control research in the economic zone and the seabed authority in the international area[52]; (2) Ireland, Mexico, and Spain suggested a consent regime that required the researchers to fulfill specified obligations. Consent would not normally be withheld if the obligations were met; (3) The Netherlands, the Federal Republic of Germany, and the United States proposed a regime under which coastal-state consent was not required and the researcher had to meet a number of obligations including advance notification, right of the coastal state to participate, sharing of data and samples, assistance in interpreting the research results, open publication of findings, compliance with international environmental standards, and flag-state certification of the researching institution[53]; (4) the United Kingdom, Denmark, the USSR, and Switzerland proposed that marine scientific research in the coastal areas would only be subject to coastal-state consent if it was aimed directly at the exploitation of resources over which the coastal state exercised jurisdiction. It was hoped that these main trends could be reduced to a set of alternative treaty articles at subsequent sessions of the informal working group.

Nigeria and Sri Lanka led a group of twenty developing states in sponsoring a proposal on technology transfer.[54] It called for the transfer of marine technology, including patented and nonpatented technology, through the appropriate international organizations and agreements. The seabed authority was to ensure that nationals of developing states be trained and that patents on seabed mining technology be made available to developing nations on request. Regional scientific and technological research centers were to be established to provide training, data, and technical assistance for the countries of the region.

Dispute Settlement

Toward the end of the session about thirty states with wide geographic representation met regularly on an informal basis to consider ideas for the dispute settlement chapter of the convention. This group was chaired by Ambassador Galindo Pohl (El Salvador) and Ambassador Ralph Harry (Australia) with Louis Sohn (U.S.) as a rapporteur. By the last week of the session the group produced a working paper containing notes and draft alternative texts on eleven basic points.[55] These included a general obligation for peaceful dispute settlement, means chosen by parties, relation of law of the sea treaty obligations to other obligations, settlement procedures entailing binding or nonbinding decisions, relationship of general to functional approaches, parties to a dispute, exhaustion of local remedies, advisory adjudication, applicable law, and exceptions and reservations to the dispute settlement provisions.

The Caracas session concluded on August 29 after ten weeks of formal and informal meetings. The three committees produced over 250 draft texts containing alternative treaty articles or provisions. The delegates recommended to the General Assembly that a further eight-week session be held in Geneva in the spring of 1975 and that a final session should be held at an unspecified date in Caracas to sign the resulting final documents. While some nations viewed the prospect of further sessions after 1975 as likely, the U.S. delegation was opposed to protracted negotiations which would present it with the difficult task of containing legislative initiatives.[56]

GENEVA SESSION: 1975

The third session of UNCLOS III met in Geneva from March 17 to May 10, 1975.[57] The product and the politics of the third session showed an evolution from the Caracas meeting. The documents before the conference were alternative texts with a few consolidated texts on noncontroversial issues. By the end of the session, the chairmen of the three main committees had prepared an Informal Single Negotiating Text (ISNT) covering most of the issues before the conference.[58] The chairman of the dispute settlement group also submitted a text to the president of the conference. The unified text then became the basis for subsequent negotiation. The texts represented the judgment of the committee chairmen rather than negotiated or compromise texts.

The decision to entrust the drafting of the text to the three chairmen was taken out of desperation midway through the session when all efforts to establish representative negotiating groups had failed. Several weeks into the session, it was apparent that the negotiations were running into difficulty. Committee I was returning to the ideological posturing of Caracas and Committee II was splintering into a large number of special negotiating groups. In the fourth week of the session, President Amerasinghe tried to elicit support for the formation of small, representative negotiating groups with members to be selected by regional groups. This proposal received an overwhelmingly negative response from the majority of delegations who would necessarily be excluded from such groups and were unwilling to have other states represent them.[59]

A week later President Amerasinghe tried again. The goal, he stated, was to produce a unified text. He therefore proposed that the chairmen of the committees with their respective bureaus would prepare unified texts for presentation to the conference. These texts would represent the best assessment by the chairmen of what a compromise position looked like and would serve as a basis for future negotiations. Delegates would be free to propose amendments after the texts were submitted. Because responsibility for the texts would be placed in the hands of the three chairmen, most delegates accepted the Amerasinghe proposal.[60] Under such a procedure, they could always disavow whatever the chairman proposed as not representing a negotiated position.

Once this procedure was agreed upon on April 18, the process of drafting texts for submission to the chairmen began in earnest. The important negotiations of the conference continued to be conducted outside of the committees within a large number of small informal groups.[61] Indeed, the proliferation of informal groups marked a clear transition from the Caracas session and reflected the seriousness of purpose with which the session began. But the sheer number of groups also constituted an obstacle to the negotiations. The fragmentation of the conference into smaller groups did not spill over into Committee I where the Group of 77 managed to maintain a united front against the developed nations. To do so, however, the 77 could not develop compromise positions and were therefore unable to negotiate with the developed countries. In Committee II, on the other hand, the Group of 77 was in disarray, although the Latin American coastal states continued to exercise substantial influence. Since Caracas, the LL/GDS group had expanded to 48 members and was increasingly behaving according to its geographic rather than ideological interests. As the LL/ GDS became more threatening, individual coastal states periodically issued dire warnings that the landlocked could lose all rights to access to the sea if they jeopardized the treaty sought by the coastal states. The coastal states also tried to separate the developed from the developing LL/GDS as well as the landlocked from the geographically disadvantaged. These efforts were largely unsuccessful. In the absence of effective institutional mechanisms for structuring the negotiations there was growing frustration over delays in progress.

Committee I

The negotiations in Committee I shifted in tone from the first half of the Geneva session to the second half. During the first four weeks, the tenor of the negotiations was hopeful and characterized by a seeming willingness on the part of the developed countries and the Group of 77 to be flexible. In the fifth week of the session, discussions on seabed mining returned to the ideological posturing that had typified the Caracas meeting. The radical elements within the Group of 77 opposed any efforts to meet the concerns of the developed countries on conditions of exploitation and machinery to govern seabed mining. Moreover, this division within the group made it virtually impossible for the 77 spokesmen to go beyond the original negotiating positions advanced at Caracas.[62]

The chairman of the informal working group, Christopher Pinto, presided over the negotiation of two broad sets of issues—the conditions of exploitation and machinery for seabed mining. These negotiations were attempted in several forums as difficulties persisted in creating representative negotiating groups of manageable size. At the beginning of the session, the fifty-country negotiating group on conditions of exploitation was reestablished. Pressures to expand the size soon converted it into a Working Group of the Whole Committee with over 100 delegations typically represented. The chairman had to resort to several smaller consultative or private negotiating groups to assist him in reaching compromise formulae.

Most of the session was devoted to discussions on the system of exploitation. The working group had five proposals before it from the United States (L.6), the Group of 77 (L.7), the European Community (L.8), Japan (L.9), and the Soviet Union (L.12). The discussion during the first half of the session focused on the issue of joint ventures as the possible system for exploiting the seabed. This represented a concession on both sides, the Group of 77 preferring exploitation by the authority only and the developed countries preferring exploitation by states or state-sponsored private entities. The Group of 77 felt that it had made a significant concession in Caracas by agreeing to include articles on basic conditions of exploitation in the treaty. The United States responded at the Geneva session by withdrawing its proposal for detailed rules and regulations in favor of more general provisions on conditions of exploitation. The U.S. also agreed to consider a system of joint ventures as the single method of exploitation. The system would include profit sharing with the authority and the reservation or banking of sites for the authority. Each applicant would submit two sites of which the authority would select one as a reserved area. In these areas the authority would negotiate with applicants for the best financial arrangements and transfer of technology.[63]

On the basis of the accommodations made by both sides, Chairman Pinto produced a personal draft of a text on basic conditions of exploitation.[64] The Pinto draft was based on the Group of 77 approach and lacked detailed regulations. It sought to accommodate developed countries through a parallel system of contractual joint ventures where sites would be reserved for states as well as for direct exploitation by the authority. In the course of discussions of the Pinto draft, the Group of 77 became increasingly a prisoner of its most radical members. The Pinto text had captured the essence of the emerging compromise through a system which would permit mining by both the authority and states and states parties. By making the compromise explicit, however, the draft became the target of radical delegations (Algeria, Tanzania) who decried any effort to "carve up" the common heritage of mankind.

A number of factors account for the ability of the radical members of the Group of 77 to hold the rest back from making further concessions. An underlying factor was the desire of all members of the group to maintain solidarity in the face of the developed states. Thus a few determined delegates were able to hold the rest in check. Moreover, the radicals were able to argue that if the group simply stood firm, more concessions would be forthcoming from those states anxious to mine the seabed. Unilateral mining was unlikely but if it should happen, it would serve the purpose of those eager to promote the ideological conflict between the North and the South. The few land-based producers with a concrete interest in an international seabed regime were far outnumbered by the states for whom the seabed was of no importance except as a North-South issue. And in the North-South discussions, the radical delegates stressed the relevance of a powerful seabed authority to the concerns evident in commodity negotiations on raw materials and to the deliberations of the Sixth Special Session of the General Assembly.

The compromise centered on a parallel system fell apart toward the end of the session as the Group of 77 returned to its original position on direct and effective control of seabed mining by the authority. The group did indicate a willingness to consider guidelines to set standards for mining. An irate U.S. response polarized the discussion and played into the hands of the radicals. Subsequent drafting efforts were based on informal consultations conducted by the chairman of the working group. After these discussions, Chairman Pinto drafted a new text on the conditions of exploitation and transmitted it to the chairman of Committee I from the working group. This list of twenty-one articles was appended to the body of the ICNT.

Chairman Pinto also conducted negotiations on machinery for seabed mining. There were only three formal sessions held to discuss the powers and responsibilities of the various organs of the authority. The central differences aired in this debate were over the respective powers of the council and the assembly and the related issue of the voting structure in the council (i.e., regional distribution of seats or allocation according to special interests). On the basis of his informal consultations, Chairman Pinto forwarded his draft text to the chairman of Committee I for inclusion in the Informal Single Negotiating Text (ISNT). Chairman Engo, eager to regain some leverage in the Committee I discussions, set about revising the negotiated Pinto draft. In a bid for popularity with the Group of 77, Engo altered the draft in the direction of the Group of 77 position. Among the notable changes in the Engo draft was the reduced protection afforded the special interests of developed countries in the council.[65]

The seventy-five articles on the regime and machinery negotiated by Pinto and revised by Engo became the core of Part I of the Informal Single Negotiating Text,[66] supplemented by the twenty-one articles on the Basic Conditions of General Survey, Exploration and Exploitation negotiated by Mr. Pinto.

Committee II

The negotiations on Committee II items were officially conducted in two phases. From March 18 to April 4, the committee completed a second reading of the "main trends" document[67] produced at Caracas, and tried to reduce the number of alternative formulations of each article. During the rest of the session, informal consultative groups met from one to seven times each to try to negotiate consolidated articles.

They included consultative groups on (1) baselines, (2) historic bays and historic waters, (3) the contiguous zone, (4) innocent passage, (5) high seas, (6) transit for landlocked states, (7) the continental shelf, (8) the exclusive economic zone, (9) straits, (10) enclosed and semi-enclosed seas, (11) islands, and (12) delimitation.[68] The groups were open-ended and consequently too large to conduct negotiations. They did stimulate a number of smaller working groups to deal with specific issues.

Negotiations on Committee II issues were also conducted in a number of official and unofficial regional and special interest groups.[69] One of the most important negotiating groups was the "Juridical Experts" or "Evensen Group" (named after its chairman, Jens Evensen of Norway). This group of some forty delegation heads had been meeting since 1973 to try to prepare agreed texts on issues before Committee II. The articles that it produced in 1975 reflected the predominately coastal orientation of the group, and were rejected by the LL/GDS. The expanded LL/GDS group had become more coherent and vocal in the course of the Geneva negotiations. The outcome of Caracas and the product of groups such as Evensen's Group convinced them that the trends in the conference were decidedly detrimental to their interests. Opposition to the Evensen texts was also voiced by individual countries that had not been included in the consultations.

In the vast array of issues before Committee II, the politics and legal formulations of a few items were particularly significant: (1) territorial seas, (2) straits and archipelagos, (3) the economic zone, and (4) the continental shelf.

TERRITORIAL SEA. Several issues related to the territorial sea were discussed in the informal consultative groups on historic waters, baselines, and innocent passage. Of special interest were the changes in the 1958 Convention on the Territorial Sea that emerged from these discussions. There was general agreement on a territorial sea of twelve miles. There was also support for two changes that would allow a coastal state to extend its baselines further out to sea. Where a coastline was unstable, the coastal state was allowed to use straight baselines to link the farthest points of the low-water line. In addition, straight baselines could be drawn to low-tide elevations (above water only at low tide) even if no structures were built on them (Pt. II, Art. 6 of ISNT).

In the area of innocent passage, there was support for a more precise definition of what constituted passage that was prejudicial to the peace, good order, or security of the coastal state. There was agreement on a number of items relating to the security concerns of the coastal state.

In the final ISNT, however, Galindo Pohl added to the list of non-innocent activities the conduct of scientific research, pollution, and "any other activity not having a bearing on passage" (Pt. II, Art. 16). There was also support for a list prescribing the competence of the coastal state to make laws and regulations in its territorial sea (Pt. II, Art. 18).

STRAITS AND ARCHIPELAGOS. At the Geneva session, the archipelagic negotiations were very closely linked to the straits negotiations. The essence of the regimes for straits and archipelagos that emerged in the 1975 negotiations held firm for the rest of the conference. Transit passage and overflight were provided for straits used for international navigation subject to compliance with international regulations for safety at sea and prevention of pollution (Pt. II, Art. 39). In straits as in archipelagic waters, the coastal state could designate sea-lanes in accordance with certain procedures.

In order to win the support of archipelagic states for its straits policy, the U.S. was prepared to meet many of the demands of Fiji, Indonesia, Malaysia, Mauritius, and the Philippines. The final archipelago articles (Pt. II, Arts. 117-130) were extremely generous to the archipelagic group. Archipelago states were allowed to draw straight baselines linking the outermost points of their outermost islands and drying reefs to enclose archipelagic waters. The ratio of water to land was to be no more than nine to one, but "land" could be loosely defined to include waters within fringing reefs. Although the straight baselines should not exceed eighty miles, one 125-nautical-mile baseline was accepted. Beyond the baseline enclosing archipelagic waters, the state could lay claim to 200-mile economic zones. In return for acquiescence in their claims to vast areas of ocean space, the archipelago states supported archipelagic sea-lanes passage for ships and aircraft under certain prescribed rules.

The bargain struck with the archipelagic states left the coastal straits states[70] isolated. Their isolation was aggravated by the growing perception on the part of most developing countries of their dependence on straits transit for exports and imports, particularly of oil. The issue was increasingly perceived to be less one of maritime state abuse and more one of potential straits state abuse in the hindrance of foreign shipping.

The formulation of the articles on the straits regimes was done principally through an informal consultative group of nineteen members chaired by the United Kingdom and Fiji. The group relied on texts which the two countries had proposed in Caracas.[71] It forwarded a draft text on straits to Galindo Pohl for circulation to Committee II after adopting the text by consensus. Other negotiations were conducted bilaterally as well as in informal consultative groups.

ECONOMIC ZONE. Negotiations on issues pertaining to the economic zone occurred in a number of groups including the Evensen Group, the Group of 77, regional groups, and the LL/GDS. The Evensen Group produced a text dealing with all aspects of the economic zone except highly migratory species, pollution, and marine scientific research. It presented its text to the Committee II chairman and all delegations. Apart from resentment over exclusion from the group, the most serious substantive objections to the text were raised by the LL/GDS. They succeeded in exerting pressure within the Contact Group of the Group of 77 in Committee II. In his capacity as chairman of the Contact Group, Francis Njenga of Kenya attempted a series of drafts designed to provide developing LL/GDS with access to a "fair and equitable" share of the living resources in the economic zones of neighboring states. This effort provoked a strong coastal-state reaction in the Group of 77. Njenga's third draft was forwarded to Galindo Pohl though there was no consensus within the Group of 77.

In addition to submissions from Evensen and the Group of 77 on the economic zone, Galindo Pohl received articles from the European Community (without the United Kingdom), the landlocked states, and the geographically disadvantaged states. The European approach, like the Evensen text, stressed the role of regional and global organizations in fisheries conservation and management. The English were unenthusiastic about being a party to a regional fishing zone. The LL/GDS forwarded a note to Galindo Pohl completely dissociating themselves from the Evensen text. The landlocked were unable to agree with the geographically disadvantaged states on draft articles to be forwarded to the chairman. As a result, they revived an earlier proposal for regional or subregional economic zones[72] and forwarded that. The geographically disadvantaged group submitted a separate proposal under which the rights of the coastal state in its zone would be balanced with the rights of other states.

With the mandate to produce a single text, Galindo Pohl was free to pick and choose among the texts before him. He totally disregarded the landlocked and the geographically disadvantaged drafts as well as the EEC articles and the Group of 77 compromise formulation on LL/GDS access to fisheries. He relied instead on the Evensen Group text but superimposed portions of the Group of 77 text that would enhance the authority of the coastal state. The final text (Pt. II, Arts.

45-61) added coastal-state jurisdiction over marine scientific research and pollution to the Evensen text, even though these were the subject of Committee III deliberations. Article 45 also accorded the coastal state exclusive rights and jurisdiction over all artificial islands and installations, not just those related to coastal-state resource rights. The role of international fisheries organizations in setting guidelines for conservation and rational utilization disappeared in the Galindo Pohl draft. Instead the coastal state was unequivocally given the right to determine the allowable catch of fisheries in its economic zone. The Galindo Pohl text adopted the Group of 77 position requiring coastal-state consent for scientific research in the economic zone.

CONTINENTAL SHELF. Negotiations on the delimitation of the continental shelf had resolved themselves into three approaches by 1975. The LL/GDS and Africans wanted the shelf to coincide with the 200-mile zone. The states with margins extending beyond 200 miles wanted sovereign rights over resources to the outer edge of the margin. States seeking a compromise between these two positions argued for revenue sharing on the margin beyond 200 miles. The U.S. offered a specific proposal for sharing under which the coastal state would contribute one percent of the value of production after five years of operation at a site. That figure would increase by one percent each subsequent year until the tenth year.

There was also the issue of how the edge of the continental margin would be defined if a broad limit were accepted. The U.S. proposed that a state be granted an additional sixty miles beyond the foot of the continental slope (the "Hedberg formula" after Hollis Hedberg). Others sought a formula that would allow them to claim the entire continental rise, that is, all sedimentary materials that had washed off the continental margin. At the time, the United States believed that such a definition would be too imprecise. There was substantial agreement on the need for a Boundary Review Commission to prevent imprecise and unreasonable claims.

Galindo Pohl's text on the continental shelf (Pt. II, Arts. 62-72) provided for coastal-state "sovereign rights for the purpose of exploring and exploiting its natural resources." The shelf was to extend throughout the continental margin or to the distance of 200 miles from shore, whichever was further. The ISNT did not attempt to define the means of measuring the outer edge of the margin. And although it called on the coastal state to share revenues beyond 200 miles, it left the rate of payment blank. Drilling or research on the continental shelf was subject to coastal-state consent. As with the exclusive economic zone, the chairman of Committee II adopted an approach on the continental shelf that was most conducive to expanding coastal-state jurisdiction.

The procedure agreed upon at the 1975 session accorded the committee chairman complete latitude in drawing up his section of the single negotiating text. Galindo Pohl used that discretion to produce a text that enhanced the rights of coastal, archipelagic, and wide-margin states over vast, newly acquired areas. The inputs of maritime states and the LL/GDS regarding the economic zone and the continental shelf were largely ignored except on the issue of straits where the Fiji-UK group was able to submit a negotiated document that commanded consensus. Where Galindo Pohl was able to choose from among the Evensen Group, Group of 77, EEC, and LL/GDS drafts on the economic zone, he unerringly chose the most coastal formulations. The chairman interpreted his mandate so broadly that he even produced articles on marine science and pollution, despite the fact that these issues were not before his committee. Not surprisingly, the Galindo Pohl formulations on science and pollution accorded greater authority to the coastal state than those negotiated in Committee III.

Unwilling to face the response to his product, Galindo Pohl left Geneva before the text was distributed on the last day of the session. Although the document was clearly not a negotiated or compromise formulation, it served as the basis for future negotiations. Thereafter, the conference consisted of efforts by the maritime states and LL/GDS to make the text more balanced.

Committee III

The work of this committee continued to be closely related to that of Committee II both in substance and tactics. As in Committees I and II, the chairman, Alexander Yankov, was free to select those articles for the final text that he found most congenial. The official program of work continued as it had in Caracas to be divided into informal working groups on the marine environment, chaired by José-Luis Vallarta, and on scientific research and transfer of technology, chaired by Cornel Metternich. These groups met on alternate days to consider the least controversial issues before the committee.

MARINE ENVIRONMENT. The informal working group on the marine environment dealt with the relatively uncontentious issues of (1) land-based pollution, (2) monitoring and environmental assessment, and (3) measures to control pollution from activities (including dumping) in the economic zone and on the continental shelf. The Evensen Group and other private negotiating groups considered the difficult problems of vessel-source pollution.

The articles that emerged from the informal working group were generally hortatory and not binding on states. States were enjoined, for instance, to prevent, reduce, and control pollution from land and to endeavor to establish global and regional rules and practices taking into account regional factors and the economic capacity of developing countries (Pt. III, Art. 16). The provisions on monitoring and environmental assessment were equally weak. The text on monitoring said that "states shall, consistent with the rights of other States, endeavor, as much as practicable . . . to observe, measure, evaluate and analyze . . . effects of pollution of the marine environment" (Pt. III, Art. 13). States were asked to assess the potential effects of planned activities in their offshore areas "as far as practicable" where there were "reasonable grounds" for suspecting they would cause "substantial pollution" (Pt. III, Art. 15).

The highly qualified nature of these provisions reflected two currents of thought. The first, espoused by Brazil, was opposed to any provisions that might limit the sovereign rights of the coastal state. The second encompassed developing country views that economic development should be accorded priority over protection of the marine environment in areas of national jurisdiction. Environmental restrictions were viewed as a threat to the rate of development and developing countries, therefore, sought to have separate provisions for themselves as opposed to developing states. Nowhere were these views more forcefully pronounced than in the Committee III discussions of measures to regulate marine pollution from activities (excluding vessel transit) in the economic zone and on the continental shelf. The resulting formulation was that national measures "shall be no less effective than generally accepted international rules" (Pt. III, Art. 17). A similar article was devised for coastal-state measures to control dumping in offshore waters (Pt. III, Art. 18).

The regulation of pollution from ships operating in the territorial sea and economic zone raised even more sharply the issue of accommodating coastal-state rights with international uses of offshore areas. This difficult question was negotiated in the Evensen Group where the final outcome largely reflected flag- and maritime-state concerns. The maritime position was represented in a new proposal submitted to the committee in March.[73] The Group of 77 was unable to agree upon a formal proposal. After Caracas many members of the group had begun to move away from support for the Canadian position on standard-setting authority for the coastal state in the economic zone.[74] The developing nations feared that vesting such rights in the coastal state would result in barriers to the navigation of their own vessels.

With the extreme coastal viewpoint unable to prevail in the Group of 77, the outcome of the Evensen text and the ISNT was weighted to the protection of maritime- and flag-state interests.[75] With regard to standard setting, the flag state should adopt regulations that would be "no less effective than generally accepted international rules." In the territorial sea, the coastal state could establish regulations that were "more effective" for the prevention of pollution but they could not have the "practical effect of hampering innocent passage through the territorial sea." Finally, the coastal state was allowed to adopt special measures for "special areas" if the appropriate international organization approved and where "particularly severe climatic conditions" pertained and marine pollution could cause "irreversible disturbance of the ecological balance" (Pt. III, Art. 20). There was no provision for port-state standard setting.

The ISNT provisions for enforcement similarly accorded a great deal of power to the flag state. The flag state was to enforce compliance of its vessels with international standards wherever those violations occurred (Pt. III, Art. 26). A port state could enforce violations of international discharge standards that occurred within a distance of the coast (to be specified later), but might have its proceedings preempted by the flag state (Pt. III, Art. 27). A coastal state could enforce international discharge and construction standards against vessels in its territorial sea, but its decisions were subject to subsequent flag-state preemption (Pt. III, Art. 28). Finally, the coastal state could take action against a vessel at an unspecified distance from shore at the request of another state off whose shores an illegal discharge took place. This, too, was subject to flag-state preemption. The only penalties that could be imposed by a coastal state were monetary (Pt. III, Art. 28).

Forces within the negotiations on the marine environment were moving in the opposite direction from those in Committee II. Many developing states were able to discern their interest in commercial navigation and joined the maritime and flag states in opposing coastal-state efforts to enhance their authority over pollution control. The Canadians, Australians, Brazilians, and U.S. environmentalists were isolated. And the Bulgarian chairman was willing to follow the prevailing trend. Thus Canada and other extreme coastal states had to turn to Galindo Pohl in Committee II to insert language in the ISNT according coastal-state jurisdiction over preservation of the marine environment throughout the exclusive economic zone (Pt. II, Art. 45).

MARINE SCIENCE. The informal sessions of the committee reviewed the legal status of scientific installations and state liability for damage caused by scientific research. The informal working group under Chairman Metternich pursued negotiations on the conduct of research in the economic zone and the international area, as did a number of private groups. Several new proposals were introduced reflecting the formation of new coalitions.

The major development during the 1975 session was the emergence of three trends that served as the basis for the chairman's decision on the unified text. In the first approach, the Group of 77 continued to insist that all scientific research in areas under coastal-state jurisdiction could be conducted only with the explicit consent of the coastal state.[76] In the international area the authority would conduct all research. The second approach, favored by most western maritime states, and amended by the LL/GDS, specified that research could be conducted in the economic zone if a list of internationally accepted obligations were fulfilled and subject to dispute settlement provisions.[77] Some of the LL/GDS included among the obligations a provision for notifying neighboring LL/GDS of the planned research and allowing their participation on the same terms as the coastal state.[78] The third approach was first proposed by the Soviet Union[79] and then picked up by Mexico and other moderate Latin American states.[80] This proposal would distinguish between research associated with resources and research which was not resource-related. Coastal-state consent was required for the conduct of the former in the zone and on the continental shelf. Fundamental research, on the other hand, would require only compliance with internationally agreed obligations including advance notification of the coastal state.

The Soviet approach was the subject of most discussion during the session. Within the Group of 77 it caused a split between the territorialists, who sought a pure consent regime, and the moderates who were willing to compromise. The position submitted by the patrimonialists toward the end of the session was essentially the same as the Soviet proposal. The Bulgarian chairman therefore adopted this formulation in his unified text. It required the researcher to provide notice and certain information to the coastal state as well as the right to participate in the program and assistance in interpreting the data and samples resulting from the research. If the research was resource-related, the coastal state had to give explicit consent to its conduct as well as to the publication of research results. The issue of whether a project was fundamental or resource-related would be settled by the dispute settlement procedures to be provided in the convention.

Dispute Settlement

The discussions on dispute settlement in Geneva were cochaired by Ambassadors Harry, Galindo Pohl, and A. O. Adede (Kenya). Over sixty countries took part. The group began with the alternative texts on eleven basic issues produced at Caracas. It produced four introductory articles and three annexes for submission to the president of the conference.[81]

There were significant difficulties in trying to reach agreement on an overall system for dispute settlement. Some countries favored the International Court of Justice, others preferred arbitration or conciliation, and still others wanted a special law of the sea tribunal. No single system commanded overwhelming support and an annex was produced (Arts. 5-17) whereby a state would choose one or more of these methods when it ratified the convention. When a case was brought against a contracting party, it had to be in the form selected by that party. Other states preferred a functional approach whereby binding dispute settlement procedures would be specified for only a few specific areas. This approach was reflected in a second annex.

The articles generally agreed upon by the dispute settlement group provided that (1) the contracting parties would settle their disputes by peaceful means, (2) that they might choose the means to settle their disputes, (3) that they might resort to arbitration or judicial settlement in accordance with another agreement to which they were a party, and (4) that they would exchange views whenever a dispute arose or a settlement procedure failed.

The salient fact of the ISNT produced by the three chairmen in 1975 was its uneven quality, both in terms of its quality as a legal document as well as in terms of its success at striking a middle ground between diverse interests. In all cases, the texts reflected the personal biases and political concerns of the individual chairman. Where negotiated texts became part of the ISNT, they were generally consistent with the predilections of the relevant chairman. The interests of some groups were therefore satisfied while others were not. The Committee I text left the developed nations dissatisfied while it met the concerns of the developing nations. The Committee II text pleased the maritime states on straits, coastal states (except the territorialists) on the economic zone, and archipelagic states. It did not satisfy the straits states, the LL/GDS, and the maritime states on the economic zone. Distant-water fishing states were unhappy with provisions on fishing and researching states with provisions on marine science. The Committee III text on marine pollution did not meet the concerns of a few coastal states. The text on scientific research, on the other hand, favored coastal-state interests to the dismay of the researching states.

NEW YORK SESSIONS: 1976

The Law of the Sea Conference met twice in 1976—from March 14 to May 7 and again from August 2 to September 17.[82] Despite fifteen weeks of negotiations, the fourth and fifth sessions made little progress. At the end of the spring session, the committee chairmen produced a Revised Single Negotiating Text (RSNT).[83] The chairmen issued reports on the work of their committees at the end of the summer session.[84]

The goal of the deliberations in 1976 was to revise the texts produced by the chairmen at Geneva into genuinely negotiated texts representing widely supported compromises on the broad range of issues. Each committee adopted a different procedure to achieve that goal and some came closer to achieving it than others. Committee I had the most difficulty in developing a procedure and an atmosphere conducive to negotiations. It continued to be plagued with the problem of constructing a representative negotiating group that could make compromises on behalf of all delegations. At the spring session, the negotiations were ostensibly conducted in informal meetings of the committee. In fact, two small groups met in private to negotiate and review texts on behalf of the chairman. When these private negotiations were discovered, the countries that had been excluded reacted negatively to the procedure as well as to the resulting text. Thus in the summer, Committee I reverted to informal sessions of the committee, this time under the cochairmanship of a developed and a developing country representative. The main result of the summer deliberations was to discredit the RSNT.

Committee II negotiations, on the other hand, worked to strengthen the ISNT and then the RSNT. Following the president's recommendation, the committee conducted an article-by-article review of the ISNT under a rule of silence. Delegates who remained silent were taken as supporting an article while those that spoke out were recognized as seeking change. This procedure served to underline a great deal of support for most of the articles. It also served to single out issues that needed further negotiation. This was undertaken by small groups in the summer session with limited results. In Committee III the working

groups on marine environment and scientific research resumed deliberations under their traditional chairmen assisted by private negotiating
groups. While an accommodation was achieved on marine environment
issues, the Committee III chairman did not seek similar balance in the
text on scientific research.

Several developments in the United States affected the 1976 negotiations directly or indirectly. On April 13, 1976, the U.S. Congress established a 200-mile fishery conservation and management zone to
become effective on March 1, 1977.[85] President Ford approved this
action, over the opposition of the State and Defense Departments, principally because of election-year politics. The bill not only reduced the
support of U.S. coastal fishermen for a treaty but it alerted other nations to the fact that the U.S. would move unilaterally if the conference
failed to move toward agreement. This had the salutary effect of stimulating land-based mineral producers to undertake seabed negotiations
with renewed interest.

The threat of further unilateral legislation, however, had the adverse
effect of putting U.S. negotiators under great pressure to produce a
result in the New York meetings. When the spring session concluded
with only a hotly contested RSNT in hand, the U.S. delegation mounted
a massive campaign to convene another session later in the summer.
Because the U.S. encountered strong resistance to a second session from
other delegations, it took its proposal directly to home governments.
Thus, many delegations voted for a second session upon instructions
from governments and against their better judgment. This left a legacy
of ill will which was to pervade the summer session and to ensure that
it was unproductive.

This unfortunate U.S. policy reflected the fact that the delegation
was under new and inexperienced leadership. With Ambassador Stevenson's return to private law practice, President Ford appointed Vincent T. Learson, former chairman of IBM, to head the U.S. delegation.
With John Norton Moore's abrupt departure as head of the Interagency Task Force, the delegation lost the continuity and experience
of its senior officials.

Any implication that the change in delegation leadership reflected
U.S. disinterest in the negotiations was counteracted by Henry Kissinger's personal involvement in the law of the sea negotiations in 1976.
As a part of his new interest in the developing countries and the growing North-South confrontation, Secretary Kissinger made a major address on the law of the sea in the spring[86] and participated directly in
the development of U.S. policy in the New York negotiations.[87]

Committee I

The deliberations on seabed mining took on a new importance by 1976 as the major issues in the other committees were gradually being settled. While jurisdictional issues were being resolved by negotiations among interested states, Committee I negotiations engaged all nations at the conference. Suitable mechanisms for reducing the discussions to select but representative groups could not be found. An indication of the difficulties in finding acceptable compromise positions is evident in the notable differences between the RSNT at the end of the spring session and the ISNT produced in Geneva. While the developed countries disowned the ISNT, many members of the Group of 77 felt equally negative about the RSNT. In the first case, the chairman had included provisions on his own authority in order to win the support of the Group of 77. In the case of the RSNT, the chairman had relied on the product of two small negotiating groups, the Brazil group and a "friends of Engo" group.

The pattern of negotiation for the spring session was set in the intersessional period. The two small groups of states began meeting in New York on seabed issues a month before the session. One was chaired by Paul Engo and the other by Sergio Thompson-Flores of Brazil. Members of the groups included land-based producers who feared the passage of U.S. legislation to mine the seabed, developing countries that hoped to mine the seabed themselves, moderate developing states, and the U.S. and France. Theses two groups continued their deliberations in private throughout the session while the committee was reviewing the ISNT seabed articles. When the Brazil group was able to agree on negotiated texts on an item, these were forwarded to Chairman Engo who discussed them with his private group. They were then circulated to the committees as PBEs (using the chairman's initials). Toward the end of the session, the Mexican delegation revealed the existence of the Brazil group (of which it was a member) and accused its members of having betrayed the Group of 77. The Algerian and Indian delegates then led the charge against Chairman Engo. In the face of the withering allegation of "selling out" the Group of 77, the developing country members of the private negotiating groups quickly faded into the woodwork. The RSNT drawn up by Engo on the basis of the PBEs found its sole support—and this only partial— from the developed countries that had participated in the negotiations. Once again a few countries with no interest in a treaty were able to discredit a compromise text using solidarity as their slogan.

The fundamental compromise of the RSNT was the provision for a parallel system where both the Enterprise and states and private companies would exploit the seabed on equal terms. The Group of 77 attack on this feature of the RSNT took up the bulk of the summer session. Spokesmen for the Group of 77 argued that the discretionary powers of the authority should not be circumscribed by any provision that would guarantee access for states or states parties. This discussion of the system of exploitation was conducted in a workshop cochaired by S. P. Jagota of India and H.H.M. Sondaal of the Netherlands. The resort to cochairmen and a workshop of the whole was yet another futile effort to come up with some format in which negotiations might be possible. The only outcome of the session was to discredit the compromise reached in the RSNT.

In the course of the 1976 negotiations the United States proffered a number of compromises. They included (1) the right of the Enterprise to mine; (2) a system for banking sites; (3) transfer of mining technology to the authority; (4) financing of the authority; (5) a production control formula; and (6) periodic review conferences. In return, the U.S. sought guaranteed nondiscriminatory access for states and states parties and suitable provisions for the composition of the proposed council and the method of voting. There were some favorable unofficial responses, but time did not permit a discussion of the compromises offered by Kissinger at the summer session.

Committee II

Andres Aguilar resumed the chairmanship of the second committee and under his direction six and a half weeks were spent in an article-by-article review of the text produced by Galindo Pohl at Geneva. This exercise was extremely useful in Committee II since there was widespread discontent among the LL/GDS and the states that had been excluded from the Evensen Group, whose text had served as the basis for the ISNT. Such a review in informal working sessions of the full committee served to clarify the extent of support for or opposition to every part of the text. Under the "rule of silence," delegates who were opposed to an article and sought amendments had to speak out.

This exercise consumed most of the spring session. Compared to Geneva, relatively little time was spent in small group consultations because of the press of work in the committee. At the end of the session, the chairman produced a revised text. In his report he noted that most of the articles of the ISNT were widely accepted and therefore were retained in the RSNT. A few articles were altered to reflect a clear trend for amendment. And a third category of articles required further negotiation, in which cases a suitable compromise was delineated. The two most contentious issues, requiring further work, were the juridical status of the economic zone and LL/GDS access to the resources of the zone.

In the debate on the juridical status of the economic zone, about fifty maritime and LL/GDS nations spoke in favor of retaining the status of the zone as high seas except for the resource rights specifically accorded to coastal states. About fifty states argued in opposition that, apart from rights delegated to third parties for purposes of navigation, overflight, and communication, residual rights in the economic zone should be vested in the coastal state. In his final report, Chairman Aguilar sought to compromise these seemingly irreconcilable positions. He noted that there is no "doubt that the exclusive economic zone is neither the high seas nor the territorial sea. It is a zone *sui generis*."[88]

The LL/GDS were equally outspoken on the subject of access to the resources of regional economic zones. With the addition of Jamaica and Algeria, the LL/GDS numbered fifty-one countries and they emerged in the 1976 sessions as a powerful force. Their disappointment with the ISNT had been a strong inducement to group solidarity and their new cohesiveness provoked a pronounced coastal-state backlash. Jens Evensen convened a group during the session to try to find an acceptable compromise on access to living resources of regional zones.[89] A text was produced for submission to the chairman containing minor improvements for the LL/GDS, although wide differences of opinion remained.

In his report on the spring session, the chairman noted a number of priority issues that required further negotiation. These became the subject of intensive discussions in the summer session. Open-ended negotiating groups were initially established to deal with (1) the juridical status of the economic zone and the rights and duties of states in the zone, (2) the outer boundary of the continental shelf and revenue sharing, and (3) access to the sea by landlocked states. Then two additional open-ended negotiating groups were formed to deal with transit through straits used for international navigation (a small but vocal number of straits states had opposed the ISNT in the spring) and the delimitation of boundaries between opposite and adjacent states. After the negotiations had proceeded as far as they could in these groups, they moved into smaller negotiating groups of thirty states. An informal contact group of coastal states (led by Mexico) and LL/

317

GDS (led by Austria) met outside the conference structure to deal with LL/GDS access to living resources in the zone.

The U.S. was adamantly opposed to the provisions of the RSNT on the juridical status of the economic zone. In his visits to the conference, Secretary Kissinger stressed the U.S. position that the zone must be explicitly recognized as high seas, except for coastal-state resource rights. Little movement was discernible on either side. Problems persisted also in the continental shelf boundary discussions where developing states wanted to be exempt from revenue sharing on the margin beyond 200 miles. The United States had modified its position on delimitation to a willingness to accept either the Hedberg formula (sixty miles beyond the foot of the slope)[90] or a depth-of-sediment formula.

Discussions between the LL/GDS and the coastal states were successful in some areas and not in others. The goals that the LL/GDS pursued most actively at the summer session were (1) landlocked transit rights and access to the sea, (2) limiting the continental shelf to 200 miles unless revenue sharing was provided for the margin beyond, and (3) preferential rights to living resources in the zones of the states of the region. They encountered the greatest difficulty over access to living resources. The straits states, because they were so few in number, experienced similar difficulties in seeking revisions of the RSNT.

A final issue which proved even more intractable than the rest was that of delimitation between opposite and adjacent states. Where the topography of the continental shelf was highly irregular, delimitation could follow bottom contours which would be at variance with an equidistance formula. The two contending principles of delimitation were "equitable principles" or equidistance. The RSNT provided for seabed delimitation according to equitable principles taking into account, where appropriate, the median or equidistance line.[91]

At the end of the summer session, Chairman Aguilar afforded the opportunity for delegates to raise issues of importance to them that had not been the subject of negotiation in the informal groups. A variety of concerns were voiced on issues such as baselines, enclosed and semienclosed seas, the breadth of the territorial, sea and archipelagos. Although this airing of national views indicated that there were discontents on a range of items, these were each limited to too few states to warrant consideration by the full committee.[92] Thus many provisions of the ISNT, now embodied in the RSNT, went unchanged. The issues that were the subject of negotiation in the summer of 1976 remained unresolved. In the face of a stalled Committee I negotiation, no one was prepared to negotiate difficult concessions in Committee II.

Committee III

The Committee III negotiations proceeded in two different directions. While deliberations on marine pollution sought to balance navigation with coastal concerns, negotiations on scientific research went consistently in the direction of increased coastal-state control.

MARINE ENVIRONMENT.   Negotiations on the marine environment were once again situated in the working group of the whole under Chairman Vallarta. In the preparation of a revised text for the chairman of the committee he relied on the intersessional work of the Evensen Group and on private consultations. The working group focused on several issues: regulations on land-based pollution, continental shelf pollution, ocean dumping, and vessel-source pollution.

Salient aspects of the vessel-source pollution discussions were coastal-state rights in the territorial sea and standard setting and enforcement in the economic zone. The United States and the other maritime states were divided on whether the coastal state should be authorized to establish construction, design, equipment, and manning standards in the territorial sea stricter than international regulations. The U.S. view reflected its Ports and Waterways Safety Act of 1972, and was embodied in the Committee III RSNT (Arts. 2, 3). It provided for coastal-state rights to establish stricter standards provided that they did not hamper the right of innocent passage. The position of Japan, the UK, most other Western European nations, and the USSR was embodied in the Committee II text (Arts. 20, 23) and expressly prohibited coastal-state adoption of stricter standards in the territorial sea. The differences in the Committee II and III texts were not ironed out at the summer session.

On standard setting and enforcement of vessel-source pollution in the economic zone, the concern for protecting navigation was evident in the RSNT. On standard setting, the text provided that international regulations would prevail except in two types of areas: "special areas" and "ice-covered areas." In special areas, strict national discharge standards could be applied if IMCO agreed that conditions in the area corresponded to certain requirements (Pt. III, Art. 21). In response to Canadian pressure, the coastal state could establish nondiscriminatory laws and regulations on the basis of scientific criteria to protect vulnerable ice-covered areas (Pt. III, Art. 43).

Enforcement measures within the economic zone continued to rely heavily on a flag-state obligation to take effective action (Pt. III, Sect. 7,

Arts. 23-30). Port states were empowered to prosecute vessels in their ports for violations of international discharge standards wherever they occurred. And coastal states could enforce against "gross or flagrant" violations of international discharge regulations that caused major damage or threat thereof to coastal-state interests. The flag state had the right to preempt prosecution undertaken by port or coastal states for violations beyond the territorial sea unless (a) the flag state was a persistent violator of its enforcement obligations, or (b) the violation had caused major damages. All these provisions were coupled with protections for navigation such as prompt release of a vessel once adequate bond was provided, penalties limited to monetary ones, a three-year statute of limitation on criminal proceedings under the treaty, liability for unreasonable enforcement, and sovereign immunity. The RSNT struck a balance between coastal and navigational interests and was generally supported at the summer session.

MARINE SCIENCE. Unlike the negotiations on marine pollution, those on scientific research did not reconcile coastal and maritime interests. Instead, the discussions and the RSNT moved notably toward full coastal-state powers over marine research in the 200-mile zone. The Geneva ISNT had provided for two categories of research—resource-related and fundamental—and coastal-state consent would be required only for the former. In New York, many developing coastal states argued that it was virtually impossible to distinguish between resource-related and other research and that a consent regime should apply to all research in the economic zone. Other countries defended the distinction as a means of finding a compromise and Secretary Kissinger indicated a U.S. willingness to accept such a distinction if it were coupled with compulsory dispute settlement.

Cornel Metternich, chairman of the working group, reported to Chairman Yankov that a suitable compromise on research would have to be a mixed regime in which some research activities were subject to coastal-state consent and others were not. Chairman Yankov, however, had goals apart from those of finding a middle ground. The Soviets had adopted the Group of 77 position and now supported coastal-state consent for all research in the zone with the proviso that consent would not be withheld if research were not related to resources. It was this position that Yankov incorporated into the RSNT. Marine science research was to be subject not only to a list of obligations but also to the requirement of coastal-state consent.

The United States found itself fighting an uphill battle at the summer session. Secretary Kissinger stressed the importance to the U.S. of marine science. A regime providing for coastal-state consent in the 200-mile economic zone was decried as a functional equivalent of a territorial sea. Most states indicated a willingness to search for some compromise such as a specified and limited list of criteria for denying consent. While Chairman Yankov was officially receptive to small, group efforts to pursue compromise, he repeatedly urged that the RSNT was the basis for compromise and in his report on the session, he ignored the compromise proposals that were put forward.

Dispute Settlement

In the course of the 1976 sessions, the text on dispute settlement was brought up to a status equal to that of the rest of the text. This was accomplished in two stages. At the spring session the president of the conference conducted six days of plenary debate on dispute settlement and heard from seventy-two speakers. On the basis of this debate, he was authorized to produce a single negotiating text.[93] The plenary of the conference met again during the summer session under President Amerasinghe and, in his absence, under Acting President Jens Evensen. The informal plenary conducted a complete review of the ISNT provisions on dispute settlement and the president issued a Revised Single Negotiating Text on these articles.[94] Thus for the first time there was a single text on the full range of law of the sea issues.

Progress in the evolution of the text reflected a growing acceptance by many delegates of the need for binding dispute settlement in the oceans. It did not, however, signify agreement on just how dispute settlement would work. Some states were adamant about excluding any disputes related to coastal-state rights in the economic zone (ISNT, Art. 18). Other states felt that it was in exactly this area that dispute settlement would be necessary. And states continued to differ over the procedures to be applied and whether the defendant should always have the right to choose a preferred forum.

President Amerasinghe produced a compromise in the ISNT (Art. 9) that was to be the heart of the system for dispute settlement. Under it, each contracting party could choose to accept one of four procedures —the International Court of Justice, arbitration, the law of the sea tribunal, or a system of special procedures spelled out in Annex II. This compromise held firm in the RSNT. The major shift was in the case of a dispute where the parties had not accepted the same procedure. Whereas the ISNT (Art. 9, Par. 7) specified that the forum might only be that selected by the defendant, the RSNT (Art. 9, Par. 5) was changed to allow the plaintiff to choose between the forum selected by the defendant or arbitration.

On the extent of applicability of dispute settlement, the 1976 sessions did not make any headway in expanding the scope of dispute settlement. Both the ISNT and the RSNT (Arts. 18 and 17-18, respectively) limited dispute settlement pertaining to the exercise of coastal-state rights in offshore areas to those instances where the coastal state was charged with violating provisions of the convention on international standards for the marine environment or scientific research. On ratifying the convention, states could also choose to except from settlement procedures (1) disputes concerning sea boundaries, (2) military activities, or (3) disputes before the Security Council of the UN.

There was some movement on the question of what parties—states only, or states, the seabed authority, and private contractors—would have access to dispute settlement procedures. The ISNT left the question of access for mining entities up to the Committee I negotiators (Art. 13). The RSNT went further in saying that any "procedure specified in the present Convention shall be open to entities other than Contracting Parties whenever the provisions of the present Convention so permit" (Art. 13). Yet progress on access to dispute settlement procedures, as on other issues, was tied to progress in the work of other committees. The willingness of states to accept dispute settlement relating to the exercise of coastal-state jurisdiction in the zone awaited resolution of questions such as the legal status of the zone. Similarly, the first committee had to move on the matter of a seabed disputes chamber as part of a broader law of the sea tribunal.

By the end of 1976, it was clear that a few key questions were holding up further progress in the rest of the conference. Of particular concern was the impasse in Committee I. On the last day of the session, the conference agreed to reassemble in May 1977 and devote its first few weeks exclusively to negotiations on seabed mining. For the United States, the intervening months were to bring a new administration and a new head of delegation and negotiating team on seabed mining.

New York Session: 1977

The sixth session of UNCLOS III met from May 24 to July 15, 1977 in New York.[95] This eight-week session produced an Informal Composite Negotiating Text (ICNT)[96] which was initially scheduled for release in the fifth or sixth week of the session but did not appear until July 20. The ICNT integrated the four parts of the RSNT into a comprehensive treaty text. It was organized in sixteen parts with the first eight proceeding from areas of nearshore jurisdiction to the international deep seabed.

Problems of structuring the negotiations and decision-making authority continued to plague the conference. The subject of who would exercise final authority in drafting the new text was hotly debated at the beginning of the session. President Amerasinghe sought a mandate to prepare the final text in consultation with the committee chairmen and the chairman of the drafting committee but was vigorously opposed by the Latin Americans and the Eastern Europeans. The latter preferred to retain power in their committee chairmen. Due to this powerful opposition, Amerasinghe had to settle for a system in which he could offer his suggestions but the committee chairmen would continue to have the final word on the precise language to be incorporated into the text.

A new approach was taken to the structure of the negotiations in an effort to advance the work of Committee I. The work of the sixth session was conducted in two stages with the first three weeks of the session devoted exclusively to Committee I negotiations. Jens Evensen presided over these deliberations in a Chairman's Working Group of the Whole with the approval of the committee and Chairman Engo. After discussion in committee, Evensen produced a succession of texts that served as the basis for further discussion and revision. Although neither the developed nor the developing countries were happy with what Evensen produced, the texts had a certain authority because they were the product of an open discussion by the full membership and they clearly sought middle positions between the extremes. When Chairman Engo revised the text according to the preferences of a few members of the Group of 77 at the end of the session, the resulting ICNT ceased to have the authority enjoyed by the Evensen product. The U.S. and other developed countries loudly protested Engo's unexpected intervention in the drafting process.

Committees II, III, and the plenary began their work in the fourth week of the session. Committee II carried out much of its work in small negotiating or consulting groups of about thirty countries. It dealt with (1) the legal status of the economic zone, (2) the outer limit of the continental shelf and revenue sharing, and (3) delimitation between opposite and adjacent states. A twenty-one-nation contact group discussed the issue of LL/GDS access to fisheries in the economic zones of neighboring states. Committee III focused most of its efforts on the marine environment since scientific research was being considered in the context of private discussions on the economic zone. A special group of fifteen states met under the leadership of Jorge Castañeda during the last weeks of the session. It prcduced texts on the status of the economic zone, marine scientific research, and dispute settlement for fisheries. These texts were then transmitted to the Committee II and III chairmen and a number of them found their way into the ICNT.[97]

Committee I

By 1977 it was widely perceived that negotiations on the deep seabed constituted the principal obstacle to a law of the sea treaty. There were, however, a few new factors that provided some occasion for optimism with respect to the possibility of reaching agreement. In the first place, Henry Kissinger had made a number of proposals at the 1976 sessions that could provide the basis for a fruitful discussion—financing and technology for the Enterprise, production limitation, and a twenty-five-year review clause. In the second place, the Group of 77 hoped that the new Carter administration might offer some additional compromises. Thirdly, a growing number of developing countries were ready to begin serious negotiations because they feared that further impasse would thwart a treaty and provoke unilateral mining by developed countries. And finally, the intersessional discussions held in Geneva from February 24 to March 11, 1977 had reflected a growing acceptance of an ill-defined system of parallel access.[98]

In light of these expectations, the sixth session proved disappointing. The deliberations got off to a positive start during the first three weeks reserved for seabed negotiations. The Working Group under Jens Evensen dealt with the system of exploration, resource policy (including production controls for seabed minerals), financing the Enterprise, and a review clause. After the committee discussed each article, Evensen produced draft compromise texts which were first reviewed by a small group of developed and developing countries: the U.S., the Soviet Union, the U.K., Peru, Chile, Mexico, Nigeria, and from time to time, Sri Lanka, India, Indonesia, Canada, and Australia, and then by the whole committee. On the basis of these discussions, the texts were revised and forwarded to Chairman Engo who then consulted with his own small advisory group. When Evensen left New York for a week, the pace of deliberations ground to a halt, and to further complicate matters, Engo began indicating his intention to alter the Evensen texts in an effort to regain some authority over the Committee I negotiations.

Upon Evensen's return, however, he resumed leadership of the Committee I discussions and produced additional articles on institutional issues, the statute of the Enterprise, and dispute settlement. In the meantime, Engo sponsored small negotiating groups on specific issues, such as a group led by Christopher Pinto on technical problems relating to production controls, and another small group on financial arrangements. Engo further began a series of private meetings intended to provide him with a basis for revising the Evensen texts and for regaining his ebbing political power.

The typical Evensen negotiating procedure was to find a compromise position between two extremes. Thus he proposed that two-thirds of the growth in the nickel market should be reserved for seabed mining rather than the 100 percent sought by the U.S. or the 50 percent proposed by the Group of 77. Similarly on the question of voting in the council, Evensen arrived at a middle ground. The U.S. had proposed weighted voting for producers and consumers of seabed minerals, other developed and developing countries, and the LL/GDS. The Europeans proposed a council consisting of chambers for industrial countries, developing countries, producers and consumers, with a majority vote in several of these chambers required for council decisions. The Group of 77 sought a strictly geographic or regional distribution of council membership. Evensen proposed a five-chambered voting system that would have two-thirds of its members from developing countries with chambers based on investment, consumption, production, developing country, and geographic factors. Affirmative votes would be required by four of the five chambers.

The Evensen technique of splitting the difference between opposing views resulted in some texts which the U.S. considered unacceptable and in which it sought revisions. The quick and firm U.S. retorts to the Evensen texts[99] came as a surprise to members of the Group of 77. Under the former Interior Department negotiator, they had grown accustomed to a more accommodating U.S. policy and kept expecting the compromises that the U.S. had proffered at previous sessions. The U.S. negotiators, on the other hand, were trying to change this pattern of negotiations, to present positions directly on their merits, and to reduce the range of further U.S. compromise. Many delegations were slow to recognize the change in approach and kept expecting further compromises throughout the 1977 session.

Evensen's final revisions were prepared the first week of July, and contained points that were acceptable to the United States, and others that were unacceptable. His texts retained the parallel system and limited the authority's discretion in contracting procedures. The Enterprise would receive initial financing from loan guarantees by member states. States would be broadly obliged to transfer technology but the contractor would not. The provisions for a review after twenty years would not result inevitably in a phaseout of the parallel system. And the production control formula allowed seabed mining to fill 100 percent of the growth segment of the nickel market for seven years, and two-thirds thereafter.

The texts were then forwarded to Chairman Engo who closeted himself with several of his closest advisors from the Group of 77. The changes made by this group were kept secret until the ICNT was released after the session concluded, at which point they were categorically rejected by the U.S. Rather than assure access for private or state firms, the Engo draft made technology transfer by contractors and acceptance of mandated joint ventures with the authority into conditions of access. Moreover, the text did not include limits on the financial burdens to be borne by contractors. It set a more stringent limit on seabed production than had the Evensen text and it would allow the seabed authority the power to regulate all mineral production from the seabed. Other problems included new powers for the authority to regulate scientific research, reduced voting protection for the developed countries in the council, allocation of benefits from seabed mining to states and peoples that were not party to the convention, and the provision that the mining regime would become a "unitary" system after twenty-five years if the review conference was unable to reach agreement. The United States protested the Engo revisions as unacceptable in both content and in process. Ambassador Richardson indicated that, as a result, the U.S. would undertake "a most serious and searching review of both the substance and procedures of the conference."[100]

Committee II

During the first three weeks of the 1977 session, some informal consultations were held on Committee II issues. During the last five weeks of the session the work of the committee was carried out in negotiating groups and small consulting groups. The committee held more than thirty informal meetings on issues of importance to various delegations.

ECONOMIC ZONE. The introduction to the RSNT provided that the economic zone was neither high seas nor territorial sea; rather, it was a zone *sui generis*. Further discussions in the thirty-member consulting group revealed a persistent dichotomy between the territorialists on the one hand and maritime states on the other. As the impasse continued, a representative fifteen-state negotiating group was established under the direction of Jorge Castañeda. The principal negotiations during the last three weeks of the session occurred in this group. In addition to the status of the economic zone, the group discussed scientific research and dispute settlement for fisheries. The Castañeda group produced texts on the economic zone that were deliberately ambiguous. Through a system of cross-references between Articles 57, 58, 86, 87, and 89, the Castañeda text allowed each side to claim a victory. The U.S. could argue that it had maintained high seas freedoms in the zone while the patrimonialists and territorialists could claim that the zone was not high seas. The Castañeda text was forwarded to Chairman Aguilar who brought it to the attention of the committee. The text was greeted with apprehension by states that had been excluded from the group. The LL/GDS reserved their position on the proposals. And some states that had been a part of the Castañeda group (e.g., Peru) carried on some nitpicking. However, most of the Castañeda product on Committee II issues was incorporated into the ICNT.

CONTINENTAL SHELF. The continental shelf question centered, as at previous sessions, on delimiting the outer boundary and revenue sharing in the area between 200 miles and that boundary. Among those states that favored a continental shelf limit greater than 200 miles, the preferred alternatives were (1) a limit sixty miles beyond the foot of the continental slope (the "Hedberg formula"), or (2) a limit set at the point where the thickness of the sediment was at least one percent of the distance from the foot of the slope ("Irish formula"). States with extensive continental rises preferred the latter formula. The U.S. delegation supported the broad-margin states in the belief that their support was essential to any treaty. The LL/GDS with African and Arab support continued to oppose a broad-margin policy. Because of the pronounced differences on this question, the ICNT provided only for coastal-state control throughout the continental margin without specifying a means of delimitation.[101]

Greater progress was made on revenue sharing beyond 200 miles. There was partial agreement on a coastal-state obligation to pay one percent of the value of production beginning in the sixth year of commercial production after which it would rise to a maximum of 5 percent by the tenth year (Art. 82 of ICNT). The authority would serve as the distributing mechanism. On the issue of which states would have the obligation to share revenues, differences persisted. Some broad-margin developing coastal states continued to insist on an exemption. The result was the replacement of the RSNT exclusion for developing coastal states (RSNT, Art. 70 [3]) with a provision exempting broad-margin developing states that were net importers of a mineral resource produced from their continental shelves.

OTHER ISSUES. The delimitation of the economic zone and continental shelf between opposite and adjacent states continued to be hotly contested between the proponents of the equidistance method on the one hand and proponents of equitable principles or relevant circumstances on the other. Because support for the two opposing views continued to be relatively equal, the RSNT formula was carried over into the ICNT (Arts. 74 and 83). According to its provisions, delimitation would be "effected by agreement in accordance with equitable principles, employing, where appropriate, the median or equidistance line and taking account of all relevant circumstances."

Transit rights for the landlocked and LL/GDS access to the fisheries resources of neighboring coastal states continued to be subjects of contention. A group of twenty-one (ten LL/GDS and ten coastal states plus the chairman) met unsuccessfully to resolve the issues. In the absence of agreement, Articles 69 and 70 of the ICNT were retained from the RSNT. Read in conjunction with articles 61 and 62, they gave the LL/GDS the right to participate in exploiting the fisheries in the zones of neighboring states subject to (a) the coastal state's right to determine the extent, if any, of the surplus catch that it could not harvest and (b) bilateral, regional, or subregional agreements to be negotiated. The LL/GDS sought the right to fish even if there was no declared surplus.

Informal discussions were held among interested parties on highly migratory species and anadromous species. They produced no changes in the text. Similarly, small numbers of states unhappy with the straits provisions, coastal fisheries articles, and articles on islands and semi-enclosed seas were unable to force changes in the relevant provisions of the ICNT.

Committee III

Committee III began to meet regularly during the fourth week of the session. José-Luis Vallarta again chaired the informal working group on marine pollution while Chairman Yankov chaired the working group on scientific research.

MARINE ENVIRONMENT. The discussions on protection of the environment concentrated on key issues such as vessel-source pollution, coastal-state enforcement rights, port-state enforcement, and standard setting in the territorial sea. There was significant support for the RSNT, except in a few instances where minor technical changes were required. In general the text seemed to strike a balanced compromise.

A noteworthy aspect of the discussions was that the United States was often on the side of Canada and other coastal states in its efforts to increase coastal-state rights in protecting the environment. In discussions on coastal-state enforcement rights in ports, the territorial sea, and the economic zone for vessel-source pollution violations, several maritime states proposed amendments to limit enforcement to violation of discharge regulations. Canada led the opposition to such modifications and in turn sought to strengthen coastal-state enforcement authority. The U.S. expressed support for the existing balance in the RSNT (Art. 30). The only modification in Article 30 occurred on the issue of arrest of vessels (par. 7). The delegates agreed to a text that allowed a vessel to avoid arrest for pollution violations in the economic zone if bonding or another form of financial security were provided.

There was some consideration of whether port-state jurisdiction should extend to discharge violations occurring beyond 200 miles (Art. 28). Maritime-state amendments to require flag-state consent for prosecution of such violations were opposed by the U.S. and Canada. On the other hand, there was significant opposition to proposals to increase port-state authority over discharge violations in the economic zone. In the end, no major changes were made in Article 28.

On coastal-state standard setting in the territorial sea, a few states sought increased coastal-state competence over design, construction, manning, and equipment of foreign vessels. There was, however, strong maritime opposition to such standards. In the wake of a series of disastrous oil spills off U.S. shores, the U.S. delegation found itself under increasing domestic pressure to pursue environmental rather than maritime considerations.[102] The resulting ICNT (Arts. 21, 212[3], and 221[2]) reflected the changed U.S. concerns. It permitted the coastal state to establish and enforce national standards in the territorial sea regarding vessel-source pollution but not to fix design, construction, manning, and equipment standards. It also permitted the coastal state even greater standard-setting powers as a condition for port entry (ICNT 25[2] and 221[1]).

In the area of flag-state preemption rights, amendments were proposed by shipping states to increase the number of cases where flag states could preempt coastal or port-state prosecutions for pollution violations, even in the case of major damage to the coastal state and where the flag state had repeatedly ignored its enforcement obligations.

Opposition to these proposals prevented any major changes in the ICNT.

Some changes were made in the text. The U.S. proposed an amendment (to RSNT Art. 19) that would require flag states to establish laws as stringent as international rules to prevent pollution from deepsea mining including processing at sea. This proposal was incorporated into the ICNT. So, too, was a French amendment to Article 29 requiring the port state to prevent an unseaworthy ship from sailing but requiring immediate release of the ship when the condition in question was rectified. This was adopted in the ICNT in a compromise form.

MARINE SCIENCE. Discussions chaired by Yankov covered the regime for the conduct of marine scientific research (RSNT Art. 60), researching state obligations (RSNT Art. 59), tacit consent (RSNT Art. 64), coastal-state rights to stop ongoing projects (RSNT Art. 65), and settlement of disputes. Scientific research was also considered by the informal Castañeda group dealing with the economic zone. The texts that emerged from the Castañeda group were forwarded to the committee chairmen. While Ambassador Aguilar incorporated most of them into his text, Ambassador Yankov made a number of changes which strengthened the coastal state's powers over scientific research. In doing so, he was reflecting Soviet efforts to curry favor with the Group of 77. The United States found itself isolated and waging a losing battle in trying to limit the circumstances in which consent could be denied.

By 1977 the elements of the regime for scientific research included (1) specified obligations to be fulfilled by the researcher, (2) the requirement to seek coastal-state consent, (3) the obligation of the coastal state to grant consent, and (4) provision that the researcher could proceed if the coastal state did not respond to a request for consent in a given period of time, namely implied consent. The problem was that of striking a balance between the coastal-state right to deny consent and its duty to grant consent where that was not inconsistent with its economic and environmental interests. A formula was finally agreed upon whereby the coastal state would grant consent "in normal circumstances" to projects in the economic zone or on the continental shelf that were consistent with the convention. However, coastal states could withhold their consent if the project in question (a) was directly significant for resource exploitation, (b) involved drilling into the continental shelf, the use of explosives, or the introduction of harmful substances into the environment, (c) involved the use of artificial islands or structures, (d) supplied inaccurate information regarding its nature or objectives, or (e) if the researching state or sponsoring international organization had outstanding obligations to the coastal state from a prior research project (ICNT, Art. 247). The chairman's proposal to replace "in normal circumstances" with "normally" was successfully resisted as being too broad a mandate for coastal-state denials.

An additional issue was that of how much control the coastal state should have over the researcher's future publication. The U.S. succeeded in getting a provision calling for the coastal state to specify its intentions regarding publication at the time it granted consent so that the scientists could make a decision as to whether to proceed with the project.

The ICNT (Article 248) further provided that a coastal state that joined or had a bilateral agreement with a regional or global organization should be deemed to have authorized in advance any project which that organization carried out in its economic zone and on its continental shelf if that state approved the project when it was decided upon in the organization.

Dispute Settlement

The informal plenary dealing with dispute settlement focused on the choice of settlement procedures, provisional measures, optional exceptions to dispute settlement jurisdiction, limitations on jurisdiction, and dispute settlement for the deep seabed. It was resolved by a majority of delegations that there should be a single Law of the Sea Tribunal with a Seabed Disputes Chamber rather than special functional tribunals as proposed by the Soviets. The Seabed Disputes Chamber would have jurisdiction over all disputes arising under the seabed articles of the treaty and its members would be selected from the members of the full tribunal. Apart from the Seabed Disputes Chamber to which all signatories would be parties, states would be able to choose among four dispute settlement procedures upon consenting to the convention: the International Court of Justice, the Law of the Sea Tribunal, arbitration, and a special arbitral tribunal. If the parties to a dispute chose different procedures on acceding to the convention, arbitration would be the common forum (Art. 287, ICNT).

The optional exceptions to compulsory jurisdiction were modified only slightly in 1977. Upon ratifying the convention a state could declare that it would not submit to dispute settlement any controversies pertaining to (a) the delimitation of boundaries between opposite and adjacent states, (b) military and law enforcement activities, and (c) disputes before the Security Council (ICNT, Art. 297). The inclusion of law enforcement activities in the exercise of a state's jurisdiction under the convention was the major change in this article, and it effectively reduced the potential for dispute settlement in the zone.

Other areas where states sought to avoid compulsory dispute settlement pertained to the exercise of coastal-state rights over scientific research and fishing in the economic zone. A rather complex formula was spelled out in Article 296 (ICNT) whereby coastal states sought to protect the authority granted to them elsewhere in the convention. The result was a severely circumscribed ability to submit coastal-state discretionary rights to compulsory dispute settlement. There was, on the other hand, no major effort to exempt the coastal state from dispute settlement when the issue was coastal-state contravention of freedoms of navigation, overflight, or the laying of submarine cables or pipelines.

The relationship between Committee I's work on dispute settlement and that of the informal plenary was resolved by allocating articles relating to the structure and procedure of dispute settlement to the plenary and those pertaining to the jurisdiction of the Seabed Disputes Chamber to Committee I. The debate on jurisdiction was over whether the discretionary acts of the authority should be subject to compulsory adjudication. The Group of 77 was predictably opposed to any limits on the authority's discretion. The Evensen text attempted a compromise whereby the Seabed Disputes Chamber would have compulsory jurisdiction over disputes between states parties or their nationals and the authority relating to activities in the area, including actions taken by organs of the authority in cases of lack of jurisdiction or misuse of power. The chamber was not empowered to adjudicate disputes on whether rules, regulations, or procedures adopted by the authority conformed with the convention or on the authority's exercise of discretionary powers (ICNT Arts. 187 and 191).

GENEVA AND NEW YORK SESSION: 1978

The seventh session of UNCLOS III met in two stages—first in Geneva for an eight-week period from March 28 to May 18, and then in New York for an additional four weeks, August 21 to September 15.[103] The session produced new formulations of a number of ICNT articles, each having varying degrees of support.[104] The revised articles were based, in some cases, on ad referendum compromises and in other cases were closely linked to potential compromises in other articles. The new articles were not incorporated into a revised ICNT. The conference decided to meet again in the spring of 1979 with the option of a second session that year by which time it hoped to revise the ICNT and possibly to "formalize" the revised text.[105]

As at previous sessions the problem of organizing and structuring the negotiations absorbed substantial amounts of time. The core issue, as always, was which groups or individuals should have the authority to revise the text. Since 1975, when the chairmen of the three main committees had been given authority to draft a single negotiating text, they had exercised decisive control over the final version of successive texts. When, in 1977, Chairmen Engo and Yankov refused to incorporate the results of representative negotiating groups into the ICNT, pressures began to build within the conference for a new structure that would limit the role and arbitrary power of the chairmen. This sentiment was generally shared by the Africans and Asians as well as by the U.S. and some members of the Western European group. The Latin Americans, however, were eager to ensure Chairman Aguilar's final authority over the jurisdictional aspects of the text. So while they were willing to agree to arrangements to circumvent Engo in Committee I, they could not accede to any diminution of Aguilar's powers over the Committee II text.

The issue of control over revision of the ICNT produced the greatest confrontation of the conference to date. President Amerasinghe, with U.S. support, came to the session firmly intending to take over responsibility for final revisions of the text from the committee chairmen. Fearing that he was planning to reduce coastal-state rights in the economic zone, the Latins argued that Amerasinghe could no longer serve as president of the conference since, under the new government of Sri Lanka, he was no longer a member of his nation's delegation. The Sri Lanka government, for its part, did not oppose Amerasinghe's continuation as president and the Africans and Asians strongly supported his tenure. Thus the more substantive differences in the issue of control were subsumed under the question of whether a conference president had to be a member of a national delegation. After two weeks of fruitless bickering, a resolution confirming Amerasinghe was adopted by a procedural vote of 75 in favor (including the U.S.), 18 against (the Latin Americans), with 13 abstentions and 21 not participating (largely East and West Europeans).

The third week of the session then turned to the structure of the negotiations and responsibility for changes in the ICNT. To ensure a limited role for Engo, the work of Committee I was apportioned among three negotiating groups with Engo chairing the group devoted to the least urgent issue. Four other negotiating groups (NGs) were assigned other unresolved issues centering on offshore jurisdiction. The groups and their chairmen included:

(a) NG 1—"System of exploration and exploitation and resource policy (Chairman, Frank Njenga, Kenya);

(b) NG 2—"Financial arrangements" (Chairman, Tommy Koh, Singapore);

(c) NG 3—"Organs of the Authority, their composition, powers and function" (Committee I Chairman, Paul Engo, Cameroon);

(4) NG 4—"Right of access of landlocked States and certain developing coastal States in a subregion or region to the living resources of the exclusive economic zone."

"Rights of access of landlocked and geographically disadvantaged States to the living resources of· the economic zone" (Chairman, Satya Nandan, Fiji);

(e) NG 5—"The question of settlement of disputes relating to the exercise of the sovereign rights of coastal States in the exclusive economic zone" (Chairman, Constantine Stavropoulos, Greece);

(f) NG 6—"Definition of the outer limit of the Continental Shelf and the question of Payments and Contributions with respect to the continental shelf beyond 200 miles."

"Definition of the outer limits of the continental shelf and the question of revenue sharing" (Committee II Chairman, Andres Aguilar, Venezuela)[106];

(g) NG 7—"Delimitation of maritime boundaries between adjacent and opposite States and settlement of disputes thereon (Chairman, E. J. Manner, Finland).

Committees II and III and the marine pollution group also continued their work during the session.

The final compromise on revision of the ICNT worked to limit the power of both the committee chairmen and the president in favor of a collegial system. It specified that any revisions were to be the collective responsibility of the president and the chairmen of the main committees "acting together as a team headed by the President" in association with the drafting committee chairman and the rapporteur-general. "Any modification or revisions to be made in the Informal Composite Negotiating Text should emerge from the negotiations themselves and should not be introduced on the initiative of any single person, whether it be the President or a Chairman of a Committee, unless presented to the Plenary and found, from the widespread and substantial support prevailing in Plenary, to offer a substantially improved prospect of a consensus."[107] While protecting the conference from the whims of a few individuals, these new procedural requirements clearly made revision of the ICNT more problematic.

Substantive negotiations began the fourth week of the seventh session and proceeded at an intense pace during the remainder of the Geneva meeting. During the four weeks spent in New York the delegates made little additional headway, despite the fact that the seabed and continental margin issues required substantial further work. The follow-up session in New York had been decided upon by a narrow margin of 51 to 46, with 12 abstentions and this widespread lack of enthusiasm for further negotiations was evident in the desultory pace of the session.

Seabed Negotiating Groups

NG 1 produced revised texts on technology transfer, production control, and the review conference at the Geneva session, and devoted the bulk of the resumed session to discussing the selection of applicants. The new text on transfer of technology, negotiated by the U.S., Tanzania, and Brazil, provided that the contractor would transfer technology to the Enterprise, upon the award of a contract, on reasonable commercial terms that would be subject to compulsory conciliation and arbitration. Loss of the contracted site was a possible penalty for failure to negotiate a satisfactory technology transfer agreement. A requirement for the transfer of technology to developing countries on similar terms was also included to satisfy Brazil. Articles on the review conference were changed to provide that the assembly could impose a moratorium on new contracts if the review conference failed to reach agreement after five years, eliminating the earlier provision for automatic conversion to a unitary system. The authority also lost its mandate to harmonize and coordinate marine science research in the area. And finally, the U.S. and Canada negotiated a production control formula outside the group of technical experts that had been reviewing the issue. It provided that seabed mining should be allocated 60 percent of the growth in nickel consumption for a twenty-five-year period beginning five years before the first commercial production. During that five years the growth segment would be allowed to build up at a rate of 100 percent. The production control formula commanded the support of land-based nickel and copper producers but not of the Western Europeans. At the resumed session, Chairman Njenga produced a text on the selection of applicants.

The chairman of NG 2 produced articles on the financing of the authority and the Enterprise at the Geneva session and revised them in New York to include suggested figures. Assuming that seabed mining would be profitable, the developing countries were concerned to assure adequate financing for the Enterprise. Developed countries, on the other hand, were seeking a fee structure that would not deter investment in this risky new business. The former emphasized front-end fees while the latter concentrated on profit sharing. Chairman Koh's paper on financial arrangements sought to balance these divergent concerns. It provided for an application fee, an annual fee creditable against royalties, a royalty-only system, or a mixed system of royalties plus profit sharing. The Koh paper provided that seabed recovery should be attributed forty percent of net proceeds, that the contractor would not have to move to higher levels of payment until he recovered his development costs and for a fifteen percent rate of return if the assumptions of the MIT model on which it was based were borne out.

NG 3 discussed at Geneva the composition of the council, the rules for voting, and the relationship of the council to the assembly. No texts were produced on these questions. In New York, NG 3 turned to consider the subsidiary organs of the council and their relation to the council. The resulting revised texts made minor changes in the ICNT, such as shifting the functions of the commissions, and they clearly defined the several commissions as advisory bodies of the council.

Committee II and Relevant Negotiating Groups

The work of Committee II was carried out in two forums. Four negotiating groups discussed what were viewed as "hard-core" issues requiring special attention while the committee met in informal session to review articles suggested by delegations. Aguilar resisted all efforts to create special working groups apart from the NGs and he insisted that any changes to the text would have to have overwhelming support in the committee.

Aguilar conducted an article-by-article review of the text. While a number of proposals for change were made by groups of states, none of them commanded sufficient support. Spain, Morocco, Greece, the Republic of Korea, Oman, and Yeman voiced their continued opposition to the straits articles. In Geneva and New York, the Soviets, supported by the East Europeans, proposed the deletion of Article 86 to clarify the high seas status of the economic zone. Having rejected a package deal on the status of the economic zone, access to fisheries, and scientific research offered by the Mexican head of the coastal-state group in 1977, the Soviets had lost what little leverage they had by

1978. Given vigorous coastal-state opposition, they were unsuccessful in getting further changes in the economic zone articles. The Soviets were also unable to muster support for revising the articles on enclosed and semienclosed seas. Developing coastal states periodically raised the issue of the need to restrict military vessels and activities of third parties in the economic zone.

In Geneva a nine-nation proposal revising Article 66 on anadromous species by strengthening the powers of the state of origin did not generate opposition. In New York, a U.S. proposal to clarify the conservation requirements for marine mammals (Art. 65) engendered an informal consulting group that proposed modifications to Article 65 at the eighth session. The Committee II discussion once again underlined the fact that many articles were close to their final formulation.

At Geneva, NG 4 considered the sensitive issue of LL/GDS fishing in the economic zones of coastal states of the region. The chairman produced a text that sought a right for LL/GDS to an appropriate part of the surplus of living resources within the coastal-state economic zone.[108] It sought further to protect LL/GDS interests when the coastal state was able to harvest the entire allowable catch. Preference was specified for developing over developed LL/GDS and GDS were defined as "states with special geographical characteristics" that were dependent on the living resources in the economic zones of neighboring states. From the LL/GDS perspective, these changes were only marginally better than the ICNT, but with the increasing resort to national 200-mile claims, LL/GDS ability to get more protection was waning. The coastal-state group warned in Geneva and again in New York that the LL/GDS could not expect further concessions. They therefore urged the LL/GDS to stop linking the issue of fisheries access to progress on the delimitation of the continental margin.

NG 5 wrestled with the issue of dispute settlement pertaining to the exercise of coastal-state rights in the economic zone (Art. 296). On the one side, the LL/GDS and distant-water fishing states argued that all disputes regarding living resources in the economic zone and particularly the access of other states to fisheries should be subject to compulsory and binding settlement. The coastal states, for their part, opposed any kind of compulsory procedures for fishing disputes in their economic zones. The outcome resembled the provisions of the Castañeda group package which had not been incorporated into the ICNT in 1977 in that, it called for compulsory (but not binding) conciliation. This procedure could be invoked where the coastal state had (a) manifestly failed to ensure proper conservation and management measures thereby endangering fishery resources, (b) arbitrarily refused to determine the allowable catch or its own harvesting capacity for stocks in which other states were interested, or (c) arbitrarily refused to allocate the surplus under the terms of Articles 62, 69, and 70. This compromise did not satisfy the Soviets and the Japanese who wanted binding settlement on the issue of access. When the Soviets tried to reopen the question at the single session of NG 5 in New York, there were immediate coastal-state rejoinders and the chairman deferred further discussion to early in the eighth session. The conditional consensus on this text was widely viewed as being linked to compromises in NGs 4 and 6.

NG 6 was unable to bridge the differences at Geneva or New York on the delimitation of the continental margin. Three positions emerged at Geneva. The Irish or alternatively the Hedberg formula continued to be favored by the broad-margin states and picked up support from other coastal states. The Arab group on behalf of the LL/GDS supported limiting the margin to 200 miles. And the Soviets advanced a new proposal which would limit the continental margin to no more than 100 miles beyond the 200-mile economic zone on the basis of geological criteria. By default, there was a fourth position—namely, that embodied in the ICNT leaving the continental shelf limit defined as the outer edge of the continental margin with no specific formula for delimiting the margin. The LL/GDS linked their acceptance of the Irish formula to a favorable settlement on LL/GDS access to fisheries of the economic zone. NG 6 spent little time discussing revenue sharing from resource exploitation of the shelf beyond 200 miles. On behalf of the Africans, the Seychelles submitted a proposal for sharing 10 percent of the revenue beyond 200 miles as the price for support of the Irish formula. Broad-margin states, however, resisted attempts to increase the level of revenue sharing above the 5 percent (starting in the tenth year of production) specified in the ICNT.

The issue before NG 7 was the criterion to be applied in delimiting maritime boundaries between opposite and adjacent states. There continued to be a major split between states preferring to use median or equidistance lines and those favoring the use of a flexible formula based on "equitable principles." The ICNT formula (Arts. 74 and 83) specified that delimitation was to be reached by agreement "in accordance with equitable principles, employing, where appropriate, the median or equidistance line, and taking account of all relevant circumstances." While this did not command a consensus, agreement could not be reached on another approach. With the talks on delimitation at an impasse, the New York session turned to consider the means of dispute settlement for boundary delimitation. States were divided between those that preferred compulsory dispute settlement and those that did not. As for interim measures pending the resolution of boundary disputes, some states preferred the interim application of the equidistance principle while others accepted only interim arrangements that could be agreed upon between the parties.

Committee III

Most of the discussion in Committee III concerned enforcement of the regulations against vessel-source pollution. At the New York session, the United States submitted a list of minor amendments to the ICNT on scientific research that sought to restore the language of the 1977 Castañeda text. The U.S. had received some support from other developed countries as well as Mexico. The Soviets had privately agreed not to oppose the restoration of the Castañeda language when the U.S. had made it clear that continued obstruction would lead the U.S. to reconsider whether it would renew the World Oceans Agreement. Full discussion of the proposed U.S. amendments was expected at the eighth session.

Marine pollution issues were discussed in informal meetings of Committee III and in the negotiating group directed by José-Luis Vallarta. It had been generally assumed at the end of the sixth session that negotiations on Part XII of the ICNT were concluded. Thus it came as a surprise when the United States and France insisted on reopening the text to strengthen the enforcement powers of the coastal states. The French position had changed in the wake of the Amoco Cadiz grounding off the coast of Brittany and the U.S. delegation was responding to congressional reaction to a series of oil spills off the U.S. coast.[109]

The new proposals would modify the ICNT in several respects. One proposal would authorize the coastal state to arrest a vessel for violating international pollution standards in the territorial sea or economic zone where there was "clear objective evidence" of a violation that resulted in a "discharge causing major damage or threat of major damage" to the coast. The ICNT (Art. 221) only authorized "proceedings" against ships guilty of "flagrant or gross violation" of international standards. Another proposal specified that ships guilty of a "willful and serious act of pollution in the territorial sea" might be subject to penalties exceeding purely monetary ones. The ICNT (Art. 231) provided only for monetary penalties.

Another proposal would reword Article 222 to the effect that nothing in the convention would prejudice the right of states to adopt and enforce measures beyond the territorial sea in cases of ship collision or other maritime casualities that may result in major harm. And yet another controversial proposed change called for cooperative regional arrangements where a ship in the territorial sea of one state could be forced to indicate whether it complied with the port entry requirements of the state to which it was headed.

These French and U.S. proposals received some support from Australia, Bulgaria, Germany, the Netherlands, New Zealand, and Tunisia. The USSR agreed to support them if the U.S. would promise not to make further revisions in the text and the UK on the understanding that the administration would seek to revise section 311 of the Clean Water Act. Reservations to the proposals were expressed by a number of developing and shipping countries including Algeria, Brazil, Chile, Colombia, India, Israel, Liberia, Madagascar, Nigeria, Pakistan, Singapore, Turkey, the UAE, and Tanzania. The chairman therefore placed these proposals in "Category II," which included provisions with substantial support but on which there were still reservations and objections.[110] In Category I, Yankov included consensus revisions such as the adoption of ship-routing systems to prevent accidents, coastal-state rights to regulate against pollution by ships in the territorial sea, and coastal-state responsibilities in the preservation of fragile ecosystems and endangered species. Category III proposals comprised those on which, due to lack of time, no compromise formulae emerged.[111]

Other Issues

The conference held its first preliminary discussion of the preamble and final clauses of the convention and related matters at Geneva. Many delegates felt it was premature to discuss the problems of reservations, provisional application, signature by entities other than states, and the relation of the convention to other treaties until the convention was nearer to its final form. The initial discussion indeed conveyed significant differences on many of these issues. The twenty-three-member drafting committee met informally during the resumed session to consider the Secretariat papers dealing with the problems of harmonizing internal references and recurring expressions in the text.

Geneva and New York Session: 1979

The eighth session of the conference followed the pattern of the previous year, meeting for six weeks in Geneva in the spring and six weeks in New York in the summer.[112] On the basis of earlier negotiations, the first part of the session was able to issue a revision of the Informal Composite Negotiating Text (ICNT/Rev. 1) including new texts on seabed mining, the continental shelf, environment, and other issues. The resumed session continued negotiations on these issues, including scientific research and delimitation of maritime boundaries. Rather than further revise the ICNT/Rev. 1, the committee chairmen issued reports reflecting evolving accommodation in a number of areas. The outstanding issues, including seabed mining, scientific research, marine mammals, and the continental shelf, were deferred to the ninth session.

The eighth session continued to rely on the seven negotiating groups created the previous year. At the urging of the Group of 77, a Working Group of 21 was established to deal with seabed mining issues. Under its auspices, Engo, Koh, Njenga, and Nandan coordinated the work on conditions of exploration and exploitation, financial arrangements, production control, and institutional arrangements. The purpose of this device was to limit the number of delegates to a manageable negotiating forum (10 developed, 10 developing, and China) and to finesse the leadership problem in the first committee. Yet, due to pressure from nonparticipants to expand the forum, alternate delegates were added and the group again became open-ended. As such, it allowed the chairmen of the three seabed negotiating groups to propose and test new ideas. In the absence of a negotiating forum of limited size, negotiations and consultations on seabed mining continued to be carried on in ad hoc informal groups set up by the chairmen. Special groups of "legal experts" were also established to deal with technical issues such as dispute settlement and production limitation.

Negotiating groups 4 and 5 ceased to function during the resumed session because the ICNT/Rev. 1 incorporated new and satisfactory texts on LL/GDS access to living resources in the economic zones of coastal states in a region and on conciliation of fisheries disputes. NG 6 (continental shelf) and NG 7 (delimitation of maritime boundaries between opposite and adjacent states) continued to meet throughout the session without agreement, thus preventing the completion of the work of Committee II. Chairman Aguilar was strategically absent throughout much of the session thereby limiting the opportunity to reopen a number of Committee II issues. And Committee III continued negotiations over U.S. proposals for scientific research.

The Drafting Committee reviewed the work of the language groups (English, French, Spanish, Arabic, Chinese, and Russian). The subject of final clauses was discussed for the first time in an Informal Plenary on Final Clauses and in a group of legal experts under Jens Evensen.

Seabed Mining

The issues before NG 1 on the system of exploration and exploitation continued to be coordinated by Frank Njenga with Satya Nandan chairing a small group of interested states on production limitation. The ICNT/Rev. 1 issued at the end of the spring meeting included new texts on a number of issues discussed by this group: sharing of benefits, scientific research, nondiscrimination, title to minerals, qualification of applicants, transfer of technology, approval of work plans and selection of applicants, joint arrangements, and activities conducted by the authority. The new texts did not represent a consensus; rather, they were described as offering an improved prospect for achieving consensus. Nandan issued a summary of what little progress had been made on production control.

While some of the ICNT/Rev. 1 texts represented an improvement over the ICNT in the U.S. view, others remained unchanged or became less acceptable. The United States registered satisfaction with improvements in the texts on technology transfer (obligation was made contingent upon the nonavailability of a technology on the market) and more objective criteria for selecting applicants for contracts. However, the provision for technology transfer to developing countries to operate in areas reserved for the enterprise remained in the text. And no progress was made on the review conference. A new provision giving the enterprise preference over other applicants in a situation of production limitation made the text less acceptable to the U.S.

At the resumed session, Njenga chaired discussion of the NG 1 issues in the context of the Working Group of 21 and issued revised texts (WG-21/2). The production limitation group chaired by Nandan (and briefly by Okoth of Kenya) developed new ideas on minimum tonnages and the split between seabed and land-based production (namely one that would allow the seabed segment of the market to grow from 60 to 65 percent over time). Despite the last-minute efforts of the Australian delegation, Canadian objections prevented agreement on a satisfactory report on production limitation. Njenga's new text included revisions and clarifications of a number of articles. The highly restrictive French antimonopoly proposal was not debated at length.

The consultations on financial arrangements of NG 2 continued to be conducted by Tommy Koh. In the course of the session he issued a number of drafts and experimented with a variety of formulae on financing the Enterprise and arranging for payments by contractors. In addition to new texts for the ICNT/Rev. 1, he produced a text halfway through the spring meeting (NG2/12) and a new proposal at the end of the summer meeting. While the U.S. was displeased with the financial arrangements text in the ICNT/Rev. 1, it was more hopeful about Koh's summer proposal. With regard to payments by contractors, Koh sought in his last paper to apply a flexible formula for revenue sharing. The provisions of the ICNT/Rev. 1 for financing the Enterprise were little changed, however, in the final Koh draft. The United States continued to oppose the formula whereby states parties would provide half of the Enterprise's financing for its first site in interest-free loans and the other half in loan guarantees.

The question of the organs of the authority was discussed in NG 3 under Chairman Engo in Geneva and in the Working Group of 21 in New York. In Geneva, the group reviewed provisions dealing with the authority and the statute of the Enterprise and held a brief debate on the council. A group of legal experts was formed under Dr. Harry Wuensche (German Democratic Republic) to deal with compulsory dispute settlement. Changes in the ICNT/Rev. 1 were in texts dealing with the privileges and immunities of the Enterprise (Art. 169), council suspension of mining in cases of serious harm to the marine environment (Art. 160), the character of the Secretariat (Art. 168), jurisdiction of the Seabed Disputes Chamber (Art. 187), and limits on jurisdiction with regard to the authority's decisions.

During the second half of the session, the Working Group of 21 addressed the politically volatile question of decision making in the International Seabed Authority at greater length. At issue were the relationship of the council to the assembly, the composition of the council, and voting procedures in the council. On the basis of these discussions, Chairman Engo produced revised texts on a range of issues (WG 21/2). The new texts continued to specify the assembly as the "supreme organ" but did so in the context of the assembly's representation of all members (Art. 158). Moreover, the texts specified that the powers and functions of the assembly were those expressly conferred by the convention (Art. 157) and that the council and the assembly would not impede the functions conferred upon the other (Art. 158).

The issue of the composition of the council was not discussed in depth. The various groups—land-based producers, mining and consuming countries, developing countries, and small industrialized countries —pressed for increased numbers of seats and the United States urged that the council represent at least 50 percent of the world's production and of the world's consumption of minerals that would be produced from the seabed. On decision making by the council, the issue for the U.S. was initially one of how to guarantee that the council could not block the acceptance of mining contracts that would be granted accord-

343

ing to objective criteria, e.g., to assure that plans of work would be approved unless disapproved by a three-fourths majority of the council. In response to a Group of 77 proposal, the issue for the U.S. shifted to one of how it could secure a minimum number of members that could block council decisions adverse to U.S. interests. A plan of work would be automatically approved if the council did not act on it within sixty days. The United States sought a blocking group of five while the Group of 77 was willing to consider a number within a range of seven to nine.

Within the first committee, a group of legal experts was formed to review the provisions on compulsory settlement of disputes for seabed activities (Pt. xi, Sec. 6). Under the chairmanship of Dr. Wuensche, this group produced new texts for the ICNT/Rev. 1, as well as further revisions at the New York meeting. Areas of attention were the selection of members of the Seabed Disputes Chamber of the Tribunal, an ad hoc chamber to deal with disputes between states, disputes between states and natural or juridical persons, limitation of the jurisdiction of the authority, and commercial arbitration.

Committee II

Informal meetings of Committee II continued to germinate proposals for amendments to numerous articles. The eighth session succeeded in putting to rest, however, the work of NG 4 (LL/GDS access to fisheries) and NG 5 (settlement of disputes in the economic zone). After a single meeting of each group, it was decided that the texts developed in 1978 came as close to an acceptable compromise as possible. On this basis, Chairman Aguilar incorporated the texts into the ICNT/Rev. 1.

The primary areas of Committee II attention were the issues before NG 6 and NG 7. NG 6 debate centered on (1) setting the outer limits of the continental shelf, (2) the regime to apply to the shelf beyond 200 miles, and (3) revenue sharing beyond 200 miles.[113] Despite the preference of the Arab group and other LL/GDS for a shelf limit of 200 miles, the text that Aguilar incorporated in the ICNT/Rev. 1 was the expansive Irish formula (sixty miles from foot of slope or sediment thickness test), together with the Soviet amendment limiting the shelf to 350 miles from the baseline or 100 miles from the 2500-meter isobath (Art. 76). Aguilar changed the revenue-sharing formula slightly in the ICNT/Rev. 1 to provide that after five years revenues from the area would rise one percent a year until the twentieth year when they would remain at 7 percent. The broad-margin states were unwilling to allow the construction of artificial islands or installations on the shelf beyond 200 miles but were willing to discuss protection for other uses.

At the resumed session, it was belatedly discovered that the ICNT/Rev. 1 formula would allow states situated on midoceanic ridges to claim much of the deep seabed. Despite Iceland and Portugal's satisfaction with such a situation, attention was given to distinguishing between ridges formed of oceanic crust and ridges of continental origin. The LL/GDS persisted in opposing any extension beyond 200 miles and Japan proposed a formula that would limit claims to midoceanic ridges to 200 miles. Sri Lanka continued to pursue a special exception. And the wide-margin developing countries were steadfast in seeking an exemption from revenue sharing. The United States proposed a formula that would allow wide-margin developing countries that were net importers of hydrocarbons to opt in or out of the revenue-sharing system.

NG 7 was unable to reach agreement on the problems before it: (1) criteria to be applied in delimiting boundaries, (2) interim measures pending agreement, (3) dispute settlement in event of disagreement.[114] On rules or criteria for delimitation, states continued to divide between those favoring equitable principles and those favoring a median line modified by special circumstances. On the provisional regime to apply pending delimitation, the equitable principles states preferred a provisional regime determined by agreement while the other group preferred a median line. On dispute settlement, the equidistance states tended to favor compulsory and binding dispute settlement while the equitable principles states were opposed. By the end of the resumed session, Judge Manner was unable to develop compromise texts for inclusion in the ICNT/Rev. 1.

The question of marine mammals had not been turned over to a negotiating group as a major outstanding issue. Nonetheless, at U.S. instigation, several meetings were held in Geneva and New York of twenty to twenty-five states to consider new language on conservation of cetaceans and marine mammal protection (Art. 68). Although no changes were reflected in the ICNT/Rev. 1, Chairman Aguilar incorporated a redrafted text in his final report as a basis for further discussion.

Committee III

The work of Committee III on the marine environment was concluded during the spring meeting, while that on marine scientific research continued into the resumed session.[115] Those marine environment issues that it was agreed at the seventh session offered the prospect for consensus were incorporated into the ICNT/Rev. 1. Category 3 issues, those on which no compromise formulae had emerged, occupied the bulk of the spring session. On the whole, they continued to be too controversial to be incorporated into the ICNT/Rev. 1.

Progress in accommodating U.S. views on marine scientific research was much slower. U.S.-proposed amendments to clarify or alter the ICNT were opposed by developing coastal states. The only new text added to the ICNT/Rev. 1 was on promoting national marine scientific and technological research centers in developing countries. The United States continued to insist, however, on changes in the ICNT and Chairman Yankov (Bulgaria), with the tactit approval of the Soviets, included new compromise texts in his report to the plenary. While none of the changes significantly altered the consent regime, some offered useful clarification. The provision requiring the coastal state to grant consent "in normal circumstances" was amended to indicate that the absence of diplomatic relations between the researchers' state and the coastal state did not in and of itself signify that relations were abnormal. A compromise on research on the continental shelf beyond 200 miles was also negotiated whereby consent was necessary only in areas that the coastal state had publicly designated as areas of actual or potential exploration. There was only slight improvement in the article restricting the researcher's right to publish research results. The remaining issues were deferred for consideration at the 1980 session.

Other Issues

The six language groups of the Drafting Committee continued to study the Secretariat paper on harmonization (Informal Paper 2/Add. 1) and a concordance text (A/CONF.62/DC/WP. 1) which put each article of the ICNT together in all six languages. The Drafting Committee then sought to produce a set of provisional recommendations on harmonization problems that rested on the Secretariat's identification of problem areas. With the reissuance of a concordance text based on the ICNT/Rev. 1, the group expected to begin an article-by-article review at the 1980 session.

At the resumed session, the conference began extensive work on the final clauses of the convention. Negotiations went on in the informal plenary where each issue was considered before it was turned over to the Group of Legal Experts (of roughly fifty-five members) for further consideration. The more controversial issues included amendment or revision, reservations, relation to other conventions, entry into force, transitional provisions, and denunciation. All political questions were relegated to the plenary for decision.

New York and Geneva Session: 1980

Following the format of previous years, the ninth session of the conference met in a split session—five weeks in New York in the spring, followed by five weeks in Geneva in the summer.[116] The first part of the session negotiated a second revision of the Informal Composite Negotiating Text (ICNT/Rev. 2). The remaining issues included voting in the council of the seabed authority, boundary delimitation, and agreement on the final clauses of the treaty.

Before the ninth session resumed, the United States passed seabed mining legislation. Once the initial protests died down in the summer meeting, the delegates moved quickly to develop a text on the composition of and voting in the council. This was embodied in a third revision of the ICNT that emerged at the end of the session as the Draft Convention on the Law of the Sea (Informal Text).[117]

Committee I

Seabed mining negotiations were the most difficult ones confronting the ninth session. Nonetheless, Committee I was relatively successful in negotiating outstanding issues, despite—or perhaps because of—previous setbacks and the passage of U.S. mining legislation. Among the important changes negotiated in the ICNT/Rev. 2 was the replacement of a moratorium on seabed mining if the Review Conference failed with a provision enabling two-thirds of the states' parties to amend the system of exploitation (Art. 155). The antimonopoly provisions were modified to redefine the area assigned to a state to include only nonreserved sites and to limit the area allowed each state to 2 percent of the total. A minimum floor and a maximum cap (Art. 151) were added to the production control formula in negotiations conducted by Ambassador Nandan.

The critical compromise on the 36-member council of the seabed authority appeared in Article 161 of the Draft Convention. It specified that different voting majorities would be required for different categories of issues. While issues of procedure could be decided by a simple majority, more difficult substantive questions might require a two-thirds or three-fourths majority or a consensus. The compromise in essence moved the question of assured access from the council's decision-making

347

process to that of the Legal and Technical Commission, since a consensus was required to overturn a positive decision of the commission and a three-fourths vote to reverse a negative decision.

Committee II

While a number of states remained dissatisfied with a variety of narrow jurisdictional issues, most of the Committee II texts were not changed. Article 76 delimiting the outer edge of the continental shelf was further revised to limit jurisdiction over submarine ridges to 350 miles when they are not "natural components of the continental margin." This expansive definition implied that coastal states could claim areas at greater distances if they were "natural components" of the continental margin.

NG 7 was finally able to finish its work on delimitation of boundaries between opposite and adjacent states. The final formulation balanced equitable principles with the median line approach and included new references to international law.

ICNT/Rev. 2 also included the U.S. language on marine mammals strengthening the role of the International Whaling Commission and regional organizations (Art. 65). Clarifying language on the temporary suspension of innocent passage during weapons exercises was also added (Art. 25).

Committee III

A number of texts on marine scientific research were reopened during the spring meeting. As a result drafting changes were made in the provisions for scientific research on the shelf beyond 200 miles (Art. 246). Similarly, coastal state rights to suspend or terminate research in progress were strengthened (Art. 253). And Article 247 on promoting research under the auspices of regional or global organizations was weakened from the researching state viewpoint. Taken together, the changes went further down the road to reducing the incentives for the future conduct of distant-water marine science.

Informal Plenary

The informal plenary under President Amerasinghe met throughout the ninth session to discuss the preamble and final clauses of the draft treaty as well as a preparatory commission. The president drafted a preamble that was well received by all parties. The informal plenary reviewed draft texts submitted by Evensen's Group of Legal Experts. A compromise position was reached to the effect that the treaty would enter into force twelve months after 60 states ratified the convention, and the assembly of the seabed authority would convene on that day. Finally, the informal plenary discussed a draft resolution that would create a preparatory commission to function between the signature and the entry into force of the treaty. The commission would be authorized to draft rules and regulations for the seabed authority and its several organs. The U.S. proposed that it also be authorized to bank sites for the Enterprise until the treaty entered into force.

The six language groups met to harmonize and review the texts, but problems emerged periodically when members of a group attempted to insert substantive changes in the text. Because extensive work remained to be done, seven weeks were set aside for the drafting committee to meet before the tenth session.

In the view of the conference leadership, only a few critical issues remained to be settled by the tenth session prior to formalizing the text. The first was the sensitive question of which states and groups could be signatories of the treaty, such as the Palestine Liberation Organization or the European Community. The second task of the tenth session was to establish a preparatory commission that would operate until the treaty entered into force. And thirdly, the 1981 session needed to develop a means of encouraging early exploration in seabed mining and the development of technology by protecting interim investment. This protection would be crucial in linking the activities of companies operating under national legislation to an ultimate international mining regime.

UNITED STATES POLICY AND
LESSONS FOR THE FUTURE

THE THIRD LAW OF THE SEA CONFERENCE and its preparations spanned more than a decade, and during this period each administration appointed different law of the sea negotiators. Significant changes in the domestic and international environment also affected the direction and content of U.S. law of the sea policy. The Watergate scandal and U.S. withdrawal from the Vietnam War contributed to a weakening of U.S. political leadership at the same time that the OPEC oil embargo and subsequent price rises posed grave economic problems of inflation and a declining dollar.

U.S. relations with other states fluctuated correspondingly during the 1970s. As Germany and Japan became major economic powers, United States preeminence decreased accordingly and U.S. allies became more independent and assertive. Relations with the Soviet Union swung from the détente of the Nixon administration, to the troubled years of the Carter White House, and became markedly worse with the Soviet invasion of Afghanistan. Relations with developing countries followed the path of the broader dialogue on North-South affairs. In the aftermath of the OPEC oil embargo, the Group of 77 was exhilarated, cohesive, and uncompromising on a wide range of "New International Economic Order" issues. In the second half of the 1970s, disillusionment with their OPEC brethren and scant returns from the confrontation strategy generated fissures between the poorer and richer developing countries which were evident in a number of North-South forums.

Changes in the broad pattern of relations among states spilled over into the law of the sea negotiations and into the U.S. policy process. From 1970 to 1974, United States policy, under the force of domestic and international pressures, shifted from a heavily maritime orientation to one that attempted to balance coastal with maritime interests. With the assertion of congressional prerogatives in the mid-1970s, the thrust of U.S. policy became progressively more coastal through 1977. This trend was partially reversed during the Carter administration as Elliot Richardson, with the support of Zbigniew Brzezinski, began actively to promote U.S. strategic interests. The government pursued a concerted policy of exercising U.S. legal rights on the seas in order to maintain the American juridical position and to prevent customary law from obviating the need for a new convention.

The number and variety of U.S. law of the sea actors and interest groups continued to complicate the process of decision making in the first years of the conference. At its peak in 1974, membership on the Interagency Task Force was up to twenty agencies. As negotiations proceeded, the pressures on the U.S. delegation to compromise some of its interests in pursuit of a comprehensive treaty text intensified. This exacerbated the already tense relations between distant-water and coastal interests and agencies. The size of the U.S. delegations sent to Caracas in 1974 (116), Geneva in 1975 (78), and New York in 1976 (107) reflected the perception of the several interest groups that direct representation was necessary to protect against any unwanted trade-offs. As a result, the U.S. delegation during the early years of the conference was usually the scene of more intense negotiations than was UNCLOS itself. Large, unwieldy, and contentious, the delegation often spoke with many voices. With the passage of the U.S. 200-mile fishing zone in 1976, a major coastal interest group was satisfied and gradually lost interest in the negotiations. Thereafter, the size of the American delegations decreased from 93 in 1977, to 77 in 1978, to 61 in 1979, and with the end in sight, went back up marginally in 1980 and 1981.

The array of crosscutting U.S. interests contributed to the difficulty U.S. officials found in coordinating policy with other like-minded states in the early years. Even in the Group of 5,[1] a coordinating group of maritime states, the changing U.S. policies were a source of discontent and suspicion. Contributing to the unpredictability of U.S. policy was independent congressional action. As the UNCLOS deliberations wore on, Congress became impatient with the pace of negotiations and began to pass legislation to promote United States oceans interests.

THE NIXON-FORD YEARS: 1974-1976

From 1973 through 1976 UNCLOS III held thirty-five weeks of negotiations. This period marked the first leg of a long journey to a law of the sea treaty. During this time, progress was made in defining the outlines of a treaty settlement on offshore jurisdiction. The U.S. adoption of a 200-mile fisheries zone reflected the growing acceptance of the 200-mile zone concept. Significant differences remained to be negotiated on the status of the zone beyond the twelve mile territorial sea. Also unresolved were access for the landlocked and geographically disadvantaged states (LL/GDS) to the living resources of the zone and the delimitation of the continental margin. An even greater obstacle to final agreement was the wide divergence of opinion over deep seabed mining. By 1976 the conference had produced two very different texts, neither of which commanded full support.

Problems in the larger policy environment contributed to the difficulties the U.S. experienced in the law of the sea from 1974 to 1976. Following President Nixon's resignation under the pressures of Watergate revelations, the humiliating withdrawal from Vietnam heightened the general sense of demoralization. When President Ford succeeded Nixon in 1974, he faced an independent-minded Congress. And 1976, his final year in office, was beset with the politics of a presidential election. The erosion of executive branch leadership at home was mirrored in a reduced ability to command support within international negotiations. From 1974-1976, the Group of 77 was elated by OPEC's ability to unilaterally impose a massive income transfer on the developed world. The full impact of the resulting world recession and economic interdependence had not yet been understood and the goal of the 77 remained the pursuit of OPEC-like successes through group solidarity. The international and domestic environment was not propitious for the negotiation of a balanced, comprehensive law of the sea regime.

During this period an important, albeit unpredictable, force in U.S. policy was the secretary of state himself. Henry Kissinger's interest in law of the sea in 1976 arose out of a broader concern to intervene visibly in the North-South debate. Thus the policy concessions he offered the Group of 77 in 1977 were not evolved within the delegation. Rather, they came out of the secretary's office with the support of a few members of the U.S. delegation. In such a situation, it was not possible to coordinate policy with U.S. allies or to use concessions to maximum effect in return for compromises on the other side.

Congressional Activism

In the 93rd Congress, legislation to extend jurisdiction to 200 miles (the Emergency Marine Fisheries Act of 1974, S. 1988) and to promote mining of the deep seabed (Deep Seabed Hard Minerals Act, H.R. 12233) was debated but not passed. Similarly, the Energy Supply Act of 1974 (S. 3221) that would amend the Outer Continental Shelf Lands Act to increase U.S. energy supplies did not pass the Congress. Another piece of legislation responding in part to the energy shortage was more successful. The Deepwater Port Act of 1974 (P.L. 93-627) provided for a licensing and regulatory program to develop deepwater ports beyond the recognized territorial limits of the U.S.

More typical of the 93rd Congress was the passage of legislation implementing U.S. participation in international programs or conventions, legislation which revealed a willingness to pursue international solutions. The Congress approved an administration bill implementing the IMCO Convention Relating to the Intervention on the High Seas in Cases of Oil Pollution Casualties, 1969 (P.L. 93-248) and passed legislation incorporating parts of the Convention on the Prevention of Marine Pollution by Dumping of Wastes and Other Matter into the Marine Protection Research and Sanctuaries Act (Ocean Dumping Act, P.L. 93-254). The Congress also authorized funds for U.S. participation in the International Ocean Exposition (P.L. 93-304) to be held in Japan in 1975. And the Congress amended the Northwest Fisheries Act of 1950 to permit U.S. participation in international enforcement measures in an expanded area under the International Convention for Northwest Atlantic Fisheries, 1949, as amended (P.L. 93-339).

The 94th Congress, on the other hand, developed a preference for national over international action. In 1975 the Congress passed legislation to implement the 1966 Convention for the Conservation of Atlantic Tunas (Atlantic Tunas Convention Act of 1975, P.L. 94-70) and the 1975 Brazilian Shrimp Agreement (P.L. 94-58). However, IMCO conventions began to run into increasing difficulty on Capitol Hill. The 1969 Convention on Civil Liability for Oil Pollution Damage and the 1971 Convention on the Establishment of an International Fund for Compensation for Oil Pollution Damage were introduced but not passed. Once again the Congress considered seabed mining legislation (S. 713 and H.R. 11879) and the extension of fisheries jurisdiction to 200 miles (S. 961 and H.R. 200).

While seabed legislation failed to pass, the Congress approved the Fishery Conservation and Management Act of 1976 extending the U.S. exclusive fishery zone from twelve to 200 miles to take effect in March 1977.[2] In this zone the U.S. claimed exclusive rights to all fish except highly migratory species (tuna). Beyond 200 miles, the U.S. claimed exclusive rights to anadromous fish. Foreign fishing would be allowed in the 200-mile zone for surplus stocks not claimed by U.S. fishermen. To this end, agreements would be negotiated by the secretary of state and permits issued. The 200-mile zone extension was passed over the strenuous objections of State and Defense Department negotiators.[3] In their view, the unilateral claim undercut U.S. efforts to negotiate international obligations to be observed by the coastal state in managing offshore areas.

U.S. Government Organization

The Department of State was the lead agency for law of the sea within the government and had the task of formulating and coordinating policy in the face of substantial agency differences. During John R. Stevenson's tenure through 1975 the principal means of coordinating the policy process in the State Department was through its task force on law of the sea. It included all of the geographic bureaus and a number of functional bureaus such as the Legal Advisor's Office, the Policy Planning Staff, the Bureau of Intelligence and Research, the Bureau of International Organization Affairs, the Bureau of Economic and Business Affairs, and the Bureau of Oceans, International Environmental and Scientific Affairs. This task force met on major policy issues to coordinate State Department policy before the executive group of the Interagency Task Force met.

The Interagency Task Force grew to roughly twenty agencies by 1974 from its original contingent of State, Defense, Commerce, and Interior. The major new agencies were the National Security Council, Treasury, Transportation (Coast Guard), the National Science Foundation, the Office of Management and Budget, the Federal Energy Administration, the Council on International Economic Policy, the Environmental Protection Agency, the Council on Environmental Quality, and the Justice Department. The Interagency Task Force met several times a year, usually after each conference session. Its executive group of about a dozen agencies carried out most of the work of the task force and met every other week.

In 1974 and 1975 the functions of the chairman of the Interagency Task Force and the special representative of the president for the law of the sea conference remained divided between John Norton Moore and Ambassador Stevenson. The D/LOS staff served both men. In August 1974 the policy-making apparatus was divided at higher levels when responsibility for the law of the sea negotiations was assigned to the under secretary of state for security assistance. The deputy secretary of state, as chairman of the Under Secretaries Committee, continued to oversee law of the sea interagency activities, in fact assuming a reduced role. The Under Secretaries Committee met about once a year but typically convened only when one or more agencies were unhappy with some aspect of U.S. policy.

After Stevenson's retirement from government in December 1975, Moore sought to reunite the interagency and the negotiating functions under his direction. President Ford, however, appointed Vincent T.

Learson, former chairman of the board of IBM to head the law of the sea negotiations. Ambassador Learson then unified the functions of the Interagency Task Force and the president's special representative under himself and Moore left the government. The State Department task force and D/LOS became part of an enlarged staff with more coordinating and fewer substantive functions. A deputy to Ambassador Learson served as director of the D/LOS staff. In September of 1976, interagency coordination and law of the sea policymaking were joined again under the deputy secretary. A high-level policy-planning group was also created under the deputy secretary.[4]

Policy Changes

From 1974 to 1976, U.S. policy on seabed mining shifted significantly. That on offshore jurisdiction continued to evolve in a coastal direction. These changes are evident when comparing official U.S. pronouncements at the first substantive session of UNCLOS III with those made by Secretary Kissinger in 1976.

SEABED MINING. U.S. policy changes after 1974 represented an effort to compromise with the Group of 77 position and be responsive to its concerns. In 1974 the U.S. position on seabed mining was similar to that of 1970, although the area in question no longer included the seabed beyond the 200-meter isobath. Thus in 1974 the United States still insisted that only states or states' parties could mine the seabed under legal arrangements made with the authority. The authority would issue two-year certificates authorizing commercial prospecting by applicants. The authority would also grant, on a first-come, first-served basis, the exclusive right to mine a specified category of minerals in a certain area. In addition to manganese nodules, these categories might include hard minerals below the seabed or "fluids." Revenues would be paid to the seabed authority after the evaluation phase (fifteen years) and during the exploitation phase (twenty years).[5]

By 1976, the United States was still struggling to gain acceptance of the concept that states and private parties had the right to mine the seabed. By then the international authority had taken on a much more complex institutional structure than a mere licensing body and the U.S.'s development approach of 1974 was replaced by a willingness to consider limits on production. The new U.S. policies were articulated by Secretary Kissinger in the spring and summer of 1976.[6] In the spring, Secretary Kissinger outlined the latest U.S. views on seabed machinery.

He noted that the structure of the council (the main decision-making body) should reflect the producer and consumer interests of those states most concerned with seabed mining. The assembly would give general policy guidance and a tribunal would adjudicate questions of interpretation of the treaty and the powers of the authority raised by states or private companies. Kissinger went on to note that the U.S. was willing to make a number of concessions in exchange for assurances of guaranteed access. The first concession was that an international Enterprise would be given the right to mine the seabed under equal conditions. The second was that each prospective miner was to propose two sites to the authority, one of which could be reserved for mining by the Enterprise or by developing countries. In addition, revenues would be generated for the poorest countries based either on royalties or on a system of profit sharing. As a final concession, Kissinger proposed that incentives should be established for private companies to share technology with and train personnel from developing countries that wanted to mine the seabed.

By the summer of 1976, Kissinger went even further in his concessions to gain assured access. He indicated U.S. willingness to agree to a means of financing the Enterprise so that it could begin mining concurrently with states. To this end he reiterated U.S. willingness to transfer mining technology. And, as a further inducement, he proposed periodic review conferences where the mining system might be reexamined. A final area in which Kissinger made new proposals was on limiting production of seabed minerals. To get the land-based producers behind a parallel system, Kissinger indicated that the U.S. was prepared to accept a temporary limitation, for a period fixed in the treaty, on production of seabed minerals tied to the projected growth in the nickel market, then estimated to be about 6 percent a year. The authority would have the right to participate in international agreements on seabed-produced commodities in accordance with the amount of production for which it was directly responsible.

OFFSHORE JURISDICTION. The changes in U.S. policy on questions relating to offshore jurisdiction were less clearly articulated, but nonetheless significant, especially to the distant-water interests that were losing ground. They can be deduced by comparing 1976 official U.S. statements accepting provisions of the ISNT or the RSNT with the more detailed formulation of U.S. policy made in 1974. In such an analysis, it is apparent that the U.S. progressively accepted ever greater extensions of coastal-state rights and restrictions on maritime freedoms. Only the government's policy on the territorial sea and straits transit did not change significantly.[7]

The major shift in U.S. policy after 1970 occurred when the United States officially adopted the concept of a 200-mile economic zone. While preexisting policies on marine environment[8] and scientific research[9] were not explicitly superceded by new policies on these subjects, they were ultimately overtaken by the implications of a zonal approach. In its 1974 formulation, the U.S. 200-mile zone proposal concentrated on coastal-state resource rights in the economic zone and the continental margin and on the balance between these rights and high seas freedoms.[10] In the U.S. proposal, the coastal state would exercise jurisdiction and sovereign and exclusive rights in a zone of up to 200 miles for the purpose of exploiting the resources of the seabed, subsoil, and superjacent waters. While the coastal state had the right to authorize and regulate all drilling and installations used for economic purposes, high seas freedoms were to be preserved, including navigation, overflight, and other non-resource uses. The coastal state would have jurisdiction over the resources of the entire continental margin, even where it extended beyond 200 miles but would share revenues from the area beyond the territorial sea or the 200-meter isobath. The coastal state would be required to respect the legal arrangements it entered into with states or their nationals to exploit the seabed or it would provide just compensation if it took their property.

The coastal state would also be constrained by international duties in regard to its exclusive fishing rights. To ensure conservation and full utilization of fisheries, the coastal state would allow traditional fishing states and other states of the region to harvest the portion of total allowable catch that it was unable to fish. For areas beyond the economic zone, the coastal states would enter into international management arrangements with FAO assistance. International arrangements would apply to the management of highly migratory species throughout their range but anadromous stocks could be fished only with the authorization of the state of origin. The coastal state was also required to respect international environmental standards and to prevent unjustifiable interference with nonresource uses (such as scientific research). Specific U.S. proposals on the marine environment and science protected distant-water interests. Compulsory dispute settlement would be provided for controversies arising out of activities in the economic zone.

By 1976 the United States delegation was forced to surrender language that would impose international obligations on the coastal state in its economic zone. This retreat was due to domestic rather than international pressures. In the heat of election politics, President Ford had promised Massachusetts and New Hampshire supporters that he would accept the pending legislation creating a 200-mile exclusive fisheries zone. Contrary to the advice of the Departments of State, Defense, and Justice, therefore, the president did not veto the Fishery Conservation and Management Act of 1976. The bill had been drafted in the Congress with no executive branch input, and as a result it included few constraints on the rights of coastal states.

Henry Kissinger's April speech[11] offers a definitive statement of U.S. concerns as of 1976. Secretary Kissinger depicted the conference as having made "significant progress" on the issue of twelve-mile territorial seas and "guaranteed unimpeded transit through and over straits used for international navigation." He also expressed satisfaction with the conference provisions for a 200-mile zone, which he depicted as allowing coastal-state control of fisheries, mineral, and other resource activities. He went on to note that "freedom of navigation and other freedoms of the international community must be retained—in this sense the economic zone remains part of the high seas." And, in passing, he said that "the Treaty must protect certain international interests, such as ensuring adequate food supply, conserving highly migratory species, and accommodating the concerns of states . . . that otherwise would derive little benefit from the economic zone."

On the subject of the continental margin, by 1976 the U.S. was notably more reluctant to share revenues from exploitation within 200 miles. The U.S. called for coastal-state jurisdiction over continental margin resources beyond 200 miles to a precisely defined limit. The coastal state would pay a royalty based on value of production at the wellhead for exploitation beyond 200 miles in accordance with a formula to be fixed in the treaty.

Major issues to be resolved, in the U.S. view, were marine scientific research and compulsory settlement of disputes. In the case of research, Kissinger offered what the U.S. then considered to be a major concession. He said that the U.S. would "agree to coastal-state control of scientific research which is directly related to the exploration and exploitation of the resources of the economic zone." But the U.S. would "also insist that other marine and scientific research not be hampered." Where there were differences over whether research was related to resource exploitation, an impartial body would resolve the question. The U.S. was also prepared to endorse a list of obligations (advance notification, participation, provision of data and results, assistance in interpreting results) which would be required of the researcher in any undertaking with the researching state. This shift was made without the agreement of the U.S. scientific community and was intended to be the final U.S. position on the question of research.[12] In addition, Secretary Kissinger stressed the importance of establishing an impartial mechanism to settle disputes over the rights of states in the economic zone. Its findings would be binding on all states.

What emerges from this inventory of Kissinger's concessions in 1976 is that the United States was determined to conclude an international treaty. To this end, the government was unilaterally making, rather than negotiating, compromises—most of them to coastal-state interests. Unfortunately, the practice of bestowing concessions on the opposing side simply increased the appetite for more U.S. concessions without evoking a corresponding response from the coastal states or the Group of 77.

THE CARTER YEARS: 1977-1981

The advent of the Carter administration brought new faces to the U.S. policy process in law of the sea. On January 25, 1977, the new president signalled the importance he attached to this negotiation by appointing Elliot L. Richardson to serve as ambassador at large and special representative of the president for the law of the sea conference. Richardson brought his own team, Richard G. Darman and John T. Smith, to serve as vice-chairmen of the delegation and to head the Committee I negotiations. The Committee II and III negotiators remained unchanged.

In the UN forum, the new negotiating team confronted a politically charged situation complicated by Group of 77 expectations that the new administration would make major concessions on mining. While the broad outlines of a settlement on offshore jurisdiction had been agreed upon, important details remained for resolution. And in the case of seabed mining, the Kissinger concessions needed to be translated into a concrete U.S. policy. Domestically, the new administration found diminished support for and interest in a law of the sea treaty. With the passage of the Fishery Conservation and Management Act, fishery groups ceased to focus on UNCLOS III and the general trend toward expanding jurisdiction satisfied other coastal groups including segments of the petroleum industry and the environmental community. The deepsea mining industry was becoming progressively more alarmed at the direction of the negotiations and retained a strong preference for seabed mining legislation. On the other hand, distant-water interests were playing a reduced role. The Navy's influence had diminished and the marine science interests were clearly bound to suffer further in the negotiations.

A New Approach

In the absence of a strong domestic constituency and in the face of a difficult negotiating situation, Ambassador Richardson evolved a multifaceted strategy to revive domestic support for a treaty, to control other government agencies, and to use domestic legislation to break the stalemate in the negotiations. As a first step, the new administration launched two major law of the sea review processes in 1977. Elliot Richardson requested that the national intelligence agencies examine the United States interest in and need for a law of the sea treaty. He also sought presidential instructions for a government-wide review of U.S. law of the sea policy. The presidential review process (called PRM process for "presidential review memoranda") solicited three sets of decisions. The first decisions under the PRM provided instructions for the delegation at the intersessional meetings in Geneva from February 24 to March 11, 1977. The second part of the PRM called for a review of previous law of the sea positions and examination of U.S. options. The third part was directly related to the second and called for decisions on seabed legislation.

In the request for instructions that went forward to the president, there was agency-wide agreement on (1) production limitation, (2) the quota or antidominant clause, and (3) review of the treaty in twenty to twenty-five years. On production limitation, the administration accepted a 1976 proposal by Kissinger to limit seabed mining to 100 percent of the projected cumulative growth segment of nickel demand. The agencies also agreed with the Kissinger proposal on a review of the treaty after twenty to twenty-five years. And the U.S. continued to oppose the efforts of developed countries to impose quotas on seabed mining. These policies received presidential concurrence.

On the composition of the council and its voting procedures, there was some disagreement on exactly how much protection the U.S. had to seek in the voting structure. The Presidential Review Committee (PRC) decided that the options on voting were too ill-defined and, in any event, the question did not require a presidential decision at that time. A fifth set of issues dealing with the system of exploitation and access for mining firms did go to the president for decision. Agencies disagreed on whether the miners should have to negotiate joint ventures on the sites banked by the Enterprise and, if so, just how often. By the time the president issued instructions to the delegation on this issue, the approved U.S. policy was no longer germane to the 1977 session and Evensen had already drafted this portion of the text. The Group of 77 were pressing for a mixed system based on joint ventures between the authority and private miners in one half of the system and mining directly by the Enterprise in the other.

Going into the 1977 session, the U.S. delegation was limited by the three concessions that had been made by Henry Kissinger. In 1976, the U.S. had agreed—in addition to its acceptance of the parallel system—that an international Enterprise could mine the seabed and that it would be given sites under the "banking system." Secondly, the U.S. had conceded the principle of production control and agreed to a limit on seabed production of 100 percent of the projected growth in the nickel market.[13] And finally, Secretary Kissinger had promised that the U.S. would help to ensure that the Enterprise began mining promptly through financing of commercial development of its first site and the transfer of technology.

Contrary to the expectations of the developing countries, the United States did not offer any new compromise proposals. Instead, the new U.S. Committee I team under Darman and Smith attempted to give effect to the Kissinger compromises of 1976 through detailed proposals on promoting the Enterprise and general financial arrangements. Elliot Richardson outlined a scheme to finance the first operation of the Enterprise through the use of loan guarantees by member states. On financial arrangements, the U.S. proposed that a mining operator could either pay the authority royalties or share profits according to specified rates. The U.S. sought to explain in detail the basis for its proposals and to engage the Group of 77 in serious technical discussions.

The U.S. approach to negotiations had changed notably in two respects. Within the delegation, participation by all interested agencies in the formulation of policies was encouraged. Thus the positions finally arrived at represented agency-wide acceptance and particular attention was paid to the precedent that might be set for other international negotiations.[14] Secondly, and related to the first, the delegation was not prepared to alter policies that it viewed as appropriate and optimally beneficial to all parties. By no longer offering concessions in the hope of evoking a positive response, the delegation significantly changed the style and substance of the U.S. approach to seabed mining.

While the U.S. was trying to negotiate an international treaty, the new administration was under heavy pressure from members of the Congress to indicate whether it supported domestic legislation to mine the seabed. The third part of the PRM elicited agency views on this. Initial government agreement was reached on a policy of cautious attention to the issues in such legislation. Agencies could testify on what they did or did not like about the bills before the Congress, but they could not support any of them. The president concurred in the view that future legislation should not attempt to restrict processing plants to the U.S. and should provide benefits for the international community. In adopting the policy of working with the Congress, the delegation showed that it had benefitted from its experience with fisheries legislation. Through continuing consultation and comment on the bills passing through Congress, the administration was determined to influence the final product.

While the PRM process was producing a series of presidential decisions, the intelligence community reviewed all aspects of the law of the sea in order to make a judgment on the extent of U.S. interest in a law of the sea treaty. The resulting National Intelligence Estimate (NIE) indicated that a widely accepted law of the sea treaty might indeed be useful in restricting the rate at which national claims expanded and in promoting some uniformity among differing regimes. No treaty, however, could restrict all claims and therefore, while useful, a treaty could not be decisive.[15]

Just as the initial PRM and NIE processes were drawing to a close, Richardson launched another review process, this time in response to events at the 1977 New York session. On July 20, Ambassador Richardson issued a press release in which he condemned both the substance of the final text on deep seabed mining and the lack of fair and open processes in its final preparation. Given the "unfortunate, last minute deviation from what had seemed to be an emerging direction of promise in the deep seabed negotiations," Richardson recommended "to the President of the United States that our Government must review not only the balance among our substantive interests, but also whether an agreement acceptable to all governments can best be achieved through the kind of negotiations which have thus far taken place." The last-minute changes in the text by Chairman Engo had been made without wide consultation and had disrupted the delicate balance embodied in the Evensen texts.

In Committee III as well, the United States was disappointed that Chairman Yankov chose to ignore the negotiated language on marine scientific research from the Castañeda group. While U.S. scientists were unhappy with the Castañeda product, they were even less enthusiastic about the Yankov changes. The U.S. had less cause for complaint on the Committee II text on the legal status of the economic zone. The ambiguous formula negotiated by Ambassador Richardson on behalf of the U.S. in the Castañeda negotiating group was incorporated by Chairman Aguilar in his text. However unsatisfactory the language, the U.S. was thenceforth committed to maintaining the formulation even against subsequent Soviet attempts to clarify the high seas status of the economic zone.

At the end of 1977, therefore, the general U.S. reaction to the sixth session was one of dismay at the high-handed procedures of two of the committee chairmen. This spurred an extensive review of U.S. options in the law of the sea. The full range of alternatives—from single-minded pursuit of a treaty to going it alone or with like-minded states—was spelled out to the interested agencies for comment by December. The views of the Advisory Committee were also solicited. The preferred options emerging from these consultations were then to go to the president for final decision.

Events, however, did not lead to a final presidential review. Instead, the preferred options passed from one stage of the review process to another, but ultimately dropped from sight after Darman and Smith left the government early in 1978. The results of the review reflected the Darman and Smith preferences for a two-pronged strategy whereby the U.S. government would continue its efforts to negotiate an international treaty and a minitreaty of like-minded states at the same time that it sought to mold and promote appropriate seabed mining legislation.[16] Indeed, a group of seven "like-minded" states with an interest in seabed mining met in November 1977 to discuss the possibility of a limited treaty to either complement national legislation or to serve as a contingency against a conference failure. On the other hand, some members of the delegation, including Ambassador Richardson, had come to the independent conclusion that a comprehensive treaty was the overriding goal.

Return to Compromise

Within the U.S. delegation, the interest in a minitreaty began to wane in 1978 as the prospects for acceptable procedural arrangements at UNCLOS improved. Richardson and his new Committee I negotiator, Ambassador George Aldrich, sought assurances on new conference procedures. During intersessional negotiations, they solicited agreement that the committee chairmen would not be free to alter the treaty text and to disregard negotiated language. Richardson further hoped to ensure a system where Amerasinghe, as president of the conference, would have a controlling voice, in consultation with interested states, in the formulation of the texts.

When the session opened in 1978, Richardson was confident that the requisite procedural approach was agreed and was once again hopeful about the negotiations.[17] The problem of Engo's unpredictable behavior was to be handled by putting the significant seabed negotiations in the hands of the respected Francis Njenga (Kenya) and Tommy Koh (Singapore). And according to Richardson, future negotiations would be the "overall responsibility of the President of the Conference with the advice of the Committee Chairmen." Ambassador Richardson was also heartened on the substantive aspects of the negotiations, as he found a widespread willingness "to get down to realistic negotiations on a workable system."[18]

The resolution of procedural difficulties was particularly important to the U.S. since it had decided, on the basis of intersessional discussions, that "it was impractical to find a way of introducing a new text which could be broadly accepted as the basis for negotiation."[19] Thus the U.S. backed away from its earlier statement that the ICNT was fundamentally unacceptable as a basis for negotiation. Indeed, Ambassador Richardson, without his former seabed negotiators, came to the view after the spring 1978 negotiations that "the text is still better than the situation that would be likely to exist in the absence of a treaty."[20] Richardson placed weight on the value of the navigational provisions of the treaty, contrary to the findings of the NIE.

While U.S. views on the merits of the ICNT and a minitreaty versus a global treaty shifted from 1977 to 1978, the sixth session of UNCLOS had led to consensus in favor of domestic legislation.[21] Richardson explained that the new administration position stemmed from three considerations: (1) legislation would be needed with or without a treaty given the time that would elapse before a convention came into force; (2) seabed mining should be encouraged; (3) if drafted along the lines recommended by the administration, domestic legislation would not negatively affect the conference negotiations. Thus Ambassador Richardson depicted domestic legislation as consistent with ongoing international negotiations and desirable as a fallback position if those negotiations should fail. And he undoubtedly understood the value of mining legislation in pressing the moderates in the Group of 77 to undertake serious negotiations.

The elements of mining legislation sought by the administration were not always those favored by the mining industry or other groups. As elaborated by Richardson, legislation should be transitional pending agreement on a seabed regime. It should proceed on the legal basis that mining is a high seas freedom and should provide for environmental protection, safety of life and property at sea, and law enforcement. The legislation should also establish an international revenue-sharing fund. Furthermore, it should encourage other nations to pattern their deep seabed legislation on the U.S. model by establishing reciprocating state recognition of rights and by requiring mining states to fly either the U.S. flag or that of reciprocating states on their mining or processing vessels. The administration opposed provisions for investment guarantees against financial loss resulting from future ratification of a treaty, authorization of licenses for specific sites, the requirement that processing plants be located in the U.S., and any flag requirements for ore transport vessels.

By the end of the 1978 session, the U.S. approach combined firm commitment to international negotiation with a willingness to resort to national mining legislation as an interim or a fallback measure.[22] Elliot Richardson orchestrated the delicate strategy of balancing domestic legislation and international negotiations. Under his direction, the several agencies contributed to shaping a mining bill that was acceptable to the administration and was pushed through the House (July 26, 1978) and almost through the Senate.[23] In the last-minute crush of business of the 95th Congress, the mining legislation became snagged in committee by a single senatorial lame-duck opponent. While the authority of the secretary of state would have been sufficient to pry it loose, Secretary Vance's attention was diverted by more pressing problems in South Africa and the Middle East. In any event, his enthusiasm for the legislation had been reduced by the numerous demarches made by foreign ministers at the UN General Assembly opposing U.S. mining legislation. The legislation narrowly missed passage by the 95th Congress.

Nor did the UNCLOS negotiations in 1978 prove as successful as the U.S. had initially hoped. The basic U.S. assumption that Amerasinghe would have a controlling voice in the preparation of the final text was undermined by the bitter fighting over Amerasinghe's continued role as president. However, the creation of negotiating groups and the establishment of a collegial process for revision of the text did serve to reduce the ability of individual chairmen to arbitrarily alter negotiated texts. On this basis, Ambassador Richardson showed a willingness to negotiate new and far-reaching concessions. Since he was still operating under the 1977 PRM instructions, these were discussed on an ad referendum basis. At the spring session, the U.S. negotiated compromises on the mandatory transfer of technology to the Enterprise (NG 1) and on a formula limiting seabed production to 60 percent of the growth rate in nickel. At the summer session, the U.S. submitted figures to NG 2 on financing the Enterprise.

In offering these concessions, the delegation was going well beyond the Kissinger production control formula of 1976 and was reinterpreting the promise he had made then to ensure that the parallel system would in fact be parallel. As Ambassadors Richardson and Aldrich saw it in 1978, there had to be a mandatory transfer of technology from private companies to the Enterprise to ensure that the Enterprise could begin mining the seabed at an early date. Generous financial arrangements, rather than the guarantees offered in 1977, were also proposed to the same end. The production control formula negotiated with Canada represented a U.S. effort to get the assistance of the Peruvian and Chilean delegates in moving the Group of 77 toward negotiations as well as to mollify Canada's nickel concerns.

The strategy of pressing the negotiations as far and as fast as possible evoked a predictable backlash in the mining industry and the economic agencies where the compromises made were deemed to be contrary to U.S. interests and to overall policies in other areas. When U.S. compromises at the first part of the seventh session produced rumblings of agency discontent, Richardson reiterated his view that at least the production control formula was negotiated ad referendum and he promised to remind the continued session that the U.S. had not definitively accepted any of the spring compromises.[24] However, the thrust of his efforts after the spring session was to create the semblance of progress by producing texts upon which there was seemingly some agreement. The lack of progress on many issues at the second session undermined this effort to promote momentum.

From 1978 through 1980, Ambassador Richardson worked hard to keep those Committee II and III portions of the ICNT that had been agreed to from unraveling while trying to make minor amendments where these would build a domestic constituency for the treaty. After the divisive battle over the presidency, the Latin American position on offshore jurisdiction was subject to attack from Afro-Asian members of the Group of 77 as well as from the maritime states. The U.S., however, continued to oppose Soviet efforts to make the economic zone into a clear high seas area as disruptive of the 1977 Castañeda agreement. When NG 5 produced a text giving the international community few dispute settlement protections against coastal-state fishing rights in the economic zone, the U.S. again did not support Soviet attempts to revise the text at the resumed session. Similarly, the U.S. did not support the efforts of the Arabs, Soviets, and the LL/GDS to place 200- or 300-mile limits on the extension of the continental shelf. The delegation was firmly persuaded that it needed the wide-margin states if the treaty was to be viable and that these states would only accept a treaty that recognized their maximum demands. The final compromise on the extent of the continental shelf, therefore, allowed an extension to 350 miles for seabed ridges, and beyond that where the margin was of continental origin.

The only areas where the U.S. sought treaty changes were those that had the prospect of building domestic support for the treaty. Richardson's goal was to add marine scientists and environmentalists to his Defense Department constituents. In response to congressional action to convert the U.S. 200-mile fishing zone into an environmental protection zone as well,[25] Richardson shifted environmental policy from its earlier focus on protecting navigation. He involved U.S. environmentalists in the fight for amendments to enhance coastal-state enforcement rights in the economic zone as well as in efforts to protect marine mammals. In the same fashion, he engaged U.S. marine scientists in the formulation of draft amendments which were presented to the conference at the resumed session in 1978 and negotiated in 1979 and 1980.

While trying to be more responsive to coastal environmental concerns at the seventh session, the U.S. delegation sought changes in the 1977 amendments to Section 311 of the Federal Water Pollution Control Act. As amended, Section 311 provided for civil and criminal penalties for the discharge of oil or hazardous substances in navigable waters of the U.S. and throughout the 200-mile fishing zone and established liability limits. These provisions were unacceptable to other maritime states as well as to U.S. shipping interests who could be subject to reciprocal action by other states. They went well beyond existing customary law and beyond the terms being negotiated in the ICNT.[26] With the agreement of Senator Edmund Muskie in the closing days of the 95th Congress, the administration succeeded in downgrading the penalty for discharge within 200 miles of shore to financial liability and in establishing that the federal government could not enforce against discharges of hazardous substances by foreign vessels beyond twelve miles from shore unless the government otherwise had jurisdiction over them.

Congress and Coastal Pressures

The Richardson effort to mitigate the unilateral antinavigational aspects of the Clean Waters Act represented a small victory in the face of a growing coastal trend in the Congress and elsewhere in the government. The 1977 amendments to the Clean Waters Act reflected a general shift from executive to congressional leadership in setting policy direction for offshore areas. During the Nixon-Ford period, the executive branch played an active role in pressing IMCO for international measures to regulate pollution from vessels, and the Congress gave its general support to that course.[27] With the assertion of congressional powers during the Carter administration, the trend was toward unilateral coastal action and away from support for international measures. An important factor in this trend was the large number of tanker spills that occurred in the winter of 1976-1977.[28]

The 95th Congress, for example, took no action on the International Convention for the Prevention of Pollution from Ships (MARPOL) negotiated in 1973.[29] Although the convention would substantially reduce the amount of oil allowed in discharged ballast and provide that new tankers over 70,000 dwt have a load-on-top capability and segregated ballast, it fell short of the stricter standards sought by environmental groups and the Congress (and that had been implemented in Coast Guard regulations since 1976).[30] Instead the Congress chose to act nationally to implement stricter standards than those provided by MARPOL. It enacted the Port and Tanker Safety Act (P.L. 95-474), amending the Port and Waterways Safety Act of 1972, to regulate foreign vessels in U.S. waters and to ban vessels carrying oil and hazardous materials if they did not comply with U.S. regulations. Because the Port and Tanker Safety Act went beyond the MARPOL provisions, Congress directed the secretaries of state and transportation to seek acceptance of these regulations as international standards.[31]

In a similar vein, the Congress did not act on the 1971 International Convention on the Establishment of an International Fund for Compensation for Oil Pollution Damage and the 1969 International Convention on Civil Liability for Oil Pollution Damage (effective in 1975), which had been introduced by the administration in the 94th Congress together with a domestic scheme. Instead, the 95th Congress preferred a solely national approach with legislation that would establish stricter liability for owners and operators of discharging vessels in the high seas as well as U.S. navigable waters (Oil Pollution Liability and Compensation Act or "Superfund"). The bill would have created a $200 million back-up compensation fund, but it narrowly missed completion by the 95th Congress.[32]

The 94th Congress passed the Fishery Conservation and Management Act (FCMA) of 1976 (P.L. 94-265) which established U.S. authority and enforcement over a 200-nautical-mile fishing conservation zone effective March 1, 1977. The 95th Congress devoted substantial time to the problems that stemmed from this fisheries legislation. Its international efforts, consistent with the FCMA, were limited to amending existing international conventions and extending the Fishermen's Protective Act of 1967. The FCMA authorized the granting of permits for foreign fishing in the U.S. zone under Governing International Fishery Agreements (GIFAs). In 1977, some accommodations were made to facilitate uninterrupted fishing by foreign vessels pending the entry into force of the negotiated GIFAs,[33] and by the end of 1977 ten GIFAs had been approved. In addition to promoting foreign investment in the U.S. fishing industry, the FCMA allowed U.S. fishing vessels to sell their harvest to foreign processing ships operating within the 200-mile zone. An outcry from U.S. processors led to a bill that limited foreign processing vessels to buying only those harvests from U.S. fishermen that could not be utilized by U.S. fish processors (P.L. 95-354). A Reciprocal Fisheries Agreement with Canada was approved (P.L. 95-73).

The new U.S. legislation rendered a number of agreements to which the U.S. was a party ineffective and generated the need for new international arrangements for anadromous and highly migratory species. In 1977 the Congress amended the Atlantic Tunas Convention Act of 1975 by extending it to September 1980 and by redefining the term "fisheries zone" from a zone of twelve to a zone of 200 miles. The International Convention for the High Seas Fisheries of the North Pacific (INPFC) was also renegotiated by the U.S., Canada, and Japan to make it more consistent with the FCMA.[34] The U.S. and Canada succeeded in reducing the area available for Japanese fishing of salmon of North American origin.

The 95th Congress extended the provisions of the Fishermen's Protective Act of 1967 and amended it to provide new benefits for U.S. fishermen operating in the U.S. fisheries zone (P.L. 95-194). The act provided for reimbursement to U.S. fishermen of any direct charges assessed by a foreign government for fishing in areas where coastal-state claims were not recognized by the United States. Because migratory fisheries were excluded from exclusive U.S. authority under the FCMA, the Fishermen's Protective Act continued to provide reimbursement to U.S. tuna vessels seized in foreign waters. An amendment to the act provided a loan program for U.S. vessels if a vessel or its gear were damaged by foreign fishermen operating in the U.S. 200-mile zone.

Although the U.S. did not recognize foreign claims to control U.S. tuna fishing within 200 miles of shore, most Pacific states made such claims. It therefore proved difficult to renegotiate the Inter-American Tropical Tuna Commission after Mexico announced its withdrawal in September 1977. The State Department undertook protracted negotiations to agree on a new multilateral organization to manage tuna. These discussions continued sporadically through 1980.

Other problems confronting the U.S. tuna industry stemmed from the Marine Mammal Protection Act of 1972 (P.L. 92-522) which set limits on the number of porpoises and dolphins that could be caught accidentally in tuna nets. Efforts to aid the tuna industry included a program for development of the tuna resources of the South Pacific (South Pacific Fisheries Development Act Amendment, P.L. 95-295).

The 96th Congress continued to legislate national approaches to ocean issues, the most notable example being the Deep Seabed Hard Mineral Resources Act (P.L. 96-283) passed in June 1980. During the course of 1979, the Congress became increasingly concerned with the direction of the seabed negotiations and with the concessions made by the U.S. delegation. Congressional concern was heightened by executive branch support for a draft treaty on the moon and other celestial bodies negotiated by the UN Committee on the Peaceful Uses of Outer Space.[35] The implications of the law of the sea treaty for future negotiations on outer space resources led many to take a critical look at the emerging seabed regime. After initially delaying the seabed bill in 1979, Ambassador Richardson worked closely with congressional leaders in 1980 to craft legislation that would secure continued investment by the mining companies while not disrupting the Geneva session of the conference. The Deep Seabed Hard Mineral Resources Act that finally emerged was designed to satisfy congressional and executive branch concerns and to be consistent with a future international mining regime.

Slow But Steady Progress

While the Congress concentrated on national approaches to oceans problems, the executive branch continued to seek an internationally accepted law of the sea treaty. In 1979 and 1980, Ambassador Richardson's goal of a comprehensive treaty moved closer to fruition, but the process of negotiating minor improvements in the unacceptable ICNT was a difficult, uphill struggle. The task was made somewhat easier by the fact that important negotiating groups were chaired and controlled by Group of 77 moderates and that the Soviets allowed the Committee III chairman to be more responsive to U.S. concerns. In a number of areas—such as scientific research, seabed mining, and marine pollution —the United States won minor changes. Successive revisions of the ICNT were each described as improvements over the preceding text. From the U.S. perspective, the text was generally moving in the right direction.

To maintain the momentum for a treaty, Ambassador Richardson promoted two important policies in 1979 and 1980. In the first place, he regularized the U.S. policy of opposing national claims greater than those of the U.S. and exercising U.S. juridical rights in the oceans. Secondly, he timed the movement of seabed mining legislation through the Congress to stimulate further progress in the law of the sea negotiations. The policy of protesting excessive national claims and exercising U.S. maritime rights was under deliberation for a number of months before it was leaked to the press in August 1979.[36] In the absence of a comprehensive treaty, the United States recognized only a three-mile territorial sea and a 200-mile fishing zone. The U.S. did not recognize archipelagic claims or claims to territorial seas of twelve or more miles that might restrict either navigation or overflight through straits. Early in 1979, the government decided to clarify this legal position by protesting unacceptable claims and exercising U.S. navigation rights.[37] An additional goal of the delegation to UNCLOS was doubtless to revive the interests of coastal states in securing their offshore claims through an international treaty. The immediate reaction at the eighth session was a predictable protest from several coastal states led by the Latin Americans. Objections to U.S. enforcement policy continued bilaterally and periodically surfaced at the ninth session.

The Richardson policy of delaying seabed mining legislation in the fall of 1979 was equally controversial, but in this case the protests came from the Congress, executive branch agencies, and the mining industry. Richardson, however, had the support of Secretary of State Vance, National Security Advisor Zbigniew Brzezinski, and the leaders of a few key congressional committees when he halted the progress of legislation. He argued that if the bill passed the Congress before substantive negotiations were completed on a second revision of the ICNT, the delicate negotiating balance would be upset and the power of the Group of 77 moderates would be undermined. Once the ICNT/Rev. 2 was drafted, however, the prevailing consideration became the rapid decline in U.S. investment in seabed mining. The concern was to establish an interim legal regime that would satisfy domestic and international concerns pending the entry into force of an acceptable law of the sea treaty. The U.S., therefore, sought to encourage and protect seabed investment and exploration during the years between completion and signature of the treaty and its adoption by the requisite number of states. At the same time, the U.S. supported approaches that would allow the seabed authority and the Enterprise to begin operation immediately when the treaty came into force.

The Deep Seabed Hard Mineral Resources Act was intended to set the framework for such an interim legal regime, and it became the basis for discussions with other states intending to pass similar legislation. It licensed exploration of the seabed after July 1, 1981, but exploitation was not permitted until January 1, 1988. Once the law of the sea treaty came into force for the United States, it would supersede the mining bill. In the meantime the companies were afforded the security they needed to continue investment in seabed mining. To accelerate the entry into force of the treaty, Richardson supported reducing from 70 to 50 the number of ratifications necessary to bring the treaty into effect. A compromise on 60 states was reached in the Draft Convention. One advantage of national legislation with a built-in deadline was that it provided a new impetus for an early completion of the negotiations. After an initial outburst by the Group of 77 at UNCLOS, the negotiations moved ahead in 1980 and 1981 to address unresolved problems.

The remaining issues centered on the relationship of national seabed mining activities to the interim regime and ultimately to the international seabed authority. Also unresolved was the issue of assured access for seabed miners, since the critical problem of decision making was shifted from the council to the Legal and Technical Commission. The shape of a multifaceted seabed regime for the 1980s began to emerge by the tenth session. Negotiations would proceed on several tracks. National mining legislation would be harmonized among reciprocating states while a preparatory commission would continue the work of UNCLOS III and would draft provisional rules and regulations for the seabed authority. The preparatory commission might also bank mining sites for the Enterprise in exchange for which it would recognize early explorers' prior right to mine. With the continuation of UNCLOS III or its transformation into a preparatory commission or an international seabed authority, it is clear that law of the sea is an evolutionary process requiring continued adjustments through international negotiations.

Lessons from the Past

In the development of national and international oceans policy over the past half-century, technological innovation has been a silent but driving force. It has enhanced man's capabilities to recover ocean resources and, in so doing, has raised new problems of crowding and over-exploitation. The typical political and legal response to the expansion of ocean uses has been the expansion of national claims over ocean areas and the exclusion of foreign users. While clear ownership or title should facilitate the adoption of sound management policies, proper management has been an afterthought for most nations. Exclusive national control has been the goal. The claims that have been advanced have generally anticipated the existence of resources as well as the capability to control or exploit them. The Truman Proclamations in 1945, the 200-

mile claims in Latin America in the 1940s and 1950s, and the continental shelf definitions in the First and Third Law of the Sea Conferences were all based on expectation, not prevailing use.

A second and more variable influence on U.S. oceans policy and the law of the sea negotiations has been the spillover from other political issues and problems, whether bilateral or global in scope. The frequent oceans problems that the United States has had with Canada over offshore claims and boundaries as well as in the UN negotiations have been fueled and compounded by Canada's anti-American form of nationalism deriving from a long history of bilateral issues. In the regional and global law of the sea negotiations, broad political forces such as East-West tensions or North-South differences have generated fluctuating patterns of policy and alignments. In the 1950s, fears of Soviet expansionism and the prevailing cold war generated a certain amount of cohesion and support from allies and developing states for U.S. policies and leadership. When U.S. and Soviet oceans interests began to converge in the 1970s, bloc support for U.S. policy was replaced by ad hoc support on discrete issues of mutual interest.

Not only did former allies begin to go their own way in the 1970s, but the developing nations began to operate as a bloc to oppose any and all Soviet and U.S. policies. The North-South division was fed by the protracted U.S. involvement in the Vietnam War and the demoralization of the Watergate period of American history. And many developing countries were bound into a coalition that often pursued policies that were inimical to particular national interests on behalf of the goal of group solidarity. The United States found itself in the position of having a large body of nations react negatively to whatever policies or proposals it adopted. Having led the "free world" coalition of the 1950s, the U.S. itself became the victim of UN bloc politics in the 1970s.

Even at its politically strongest in the 1950s, the United States was not always able to translate its national power into the ability to determine the international law of the sea, either through custom or convention. The multiplicity of U.S. interests made it virtually impossible to adopt coherent policies and to enforce the American view of customary law. The difficulties in adopting a single uniform policy on jurisdiction were exemplified by the U.S. neutrality zone of 1939 and the Truman Proclamations of 1945. Both of these policies came back to haunt U.S. policymakers when South American states began to claim 200-mile zones. Because of its earlier policies, subsequent U.S. insistence on a three-mile territorial sea lacked credibility.

When it came to enforcing its view of customary law, the United States often found that an exercise of its maritime rights against any particular country would adversely affect other aspects of its relations with that country. And the issuance of blanket protests, unmatched by selective action to confirm U.S. claims, further reduced the credibility of the U.S. position. In the absence of an executive branch enforcement policy, the Congress passed preventive legislation which usually exacerbated relations with states as much as or more than a military response. The obvious result was that U.S. protests carried little weight. Only the French and the British used military escorts with effect to support their juridical positions. Indeed, when the Soviets indicated a willingness to act in support of mutually agreed legal positions, the United States was opposed to their intervention in the Western hemisphere.

The belated administration move in 1979 to resist national claims made outside of a treaty context was designed to give other states a stake in signing the UNCLOS treaty rather than to ensure a three-mile territorial sea and a 200-mile fishing zone. At the same time, the exercise of rights policy simply highlighted the fact that the United States had been unable to muster support for its initial policies on offshore jurisdiction. In 1958 and 1960, the U.S. was not able to arrive at an accepted limit for the territorial sea. And in UNCLOS III, the United States was only able to gain support for an international treaty by accepting the most extensive coastal-state claims to continental margins, 200-mile exclusive economic zones, and archipelagic waters. Instead of leading other countries to adopt its preferred policy of limiting offshore jurisdiction, the United States after 1975 resorted to a policy of "buying off" coastal states in exchange for a dubious gain on international straits transit.

U.S. Policy Process

Since the Second World War, the contest among multiple U.S. domestic interests has led to what appears from the outside to be an oceans policy of fits and starts. The U.S. government has often found itself tripping over its own policies when it has moved one way and then another. This has happened when the U.S. has adopted policies to respond to specific needs without thinking through the precedent-setting impact of a given move.

When one looks beneath the label "U.S. government" to discover the agency and interest group actors that determine national policy, the source of the discontinuity in policy becomes intelligible. A host of incompatible and self-interested coastal and distant-water concerns are vying constantly to determine national policy. On any given set of issues one side may prevail; then the other may win the next policy victory. These fluctuations are evident in a cursory scan of postwar history. In the 1940s, President Roosevelt's own coastal inclinations were reinforced by oil and fisheries interests acting through the Interior Department, and were ultimately embodied in the Truman Proclamations. Subsequent military concern to maintain U.S. naval mobility, fortified by the cold war as well as by a growing U.S. interest in distant-water fishing, led in the 1950s to a disintegration in relations with the west coast states of South America and to some limited gains for distant-water interests in the 1958 conventions on law of the sea. However, these interests were frustrated again in 1960 by their inability to promote agreement on a convention limiting the territorial sea.

In the 1960s U.S. coastal forces began to reassert themselves, led by the petroleum industry concern to appropriate all potential offshore oil to national control. While U.S. distant-water interests succeeded in holding their own until 1972, coastal considerations came increasingly to dominate. The Fishery Conservation and Management Act of 1976 extending U.S. fisheries jurisdiction to 200 miles was a victory for coastal interests operating through the Congress. The petroleum industry achieved its continental margin goals through the law of the sea negotiations in the same period of time.

It is interesting to note that particular U.S. interest groups, in addition to being poor judges of the broader national interest, have often misread or been shortsighted in evaluating their own interests. In the late 1960s, for example, the petroleum industry assumed that its existing pattern of relations with developing countries would continue indefinitely. The companies had majority holdings in other countries and were in a controlling position. As a result, the industry asserted the need for extended national jurisdiction and opposed the principle of international control of resources beyond a narrow limit. With the subsequent series of oil company nationalizations and the growing need to transport petroleum products to consumers around the world, the industry belatedly modified its policies to emphasize the need for greater international protection for shipping and offshore oil recovery.

In a similar fashion, the military came to a revised perception of the legal regime needed to protect U.S. security interests. From insistence on a three-mile territorial sea, the Defense Department, in the face of evolving customary law, came to accept a twelve-mile territorial sea with free transit through and over international straits of less than twenty-four-mile width. Security interests also accommodated themselves to expanded economic zones and continental shelves which they had earlier resisted. In each case, these groups have misread their interests by looking to the past for guidance without anticipating future trends and the optimal ways of adapting to them.

The U.S. policy process with regard to oceans makes it difficult to anticipate future contingencies. Particular groups pursue conceptions of interest based on the past, and these are translated into national policy through a process of contention, trade-offs, and compromise. Where compromise has not been possible, as in the case of the 1970 policy on offshore limits, the issue has gone to the president for decision. This happens relatively infrequently because lower level government officials prefer to retain control of policy and will tend to compromise rather than relinquish their power. In those instances where decisions have required presidential attention, the issues have been framed by the contending parties, and, therefore, reflect the retrospective goals of the parties. Thus policymakers at the higher levels have not been in a position to anticipate future needs or to determine a long-term or overarching national interest.

When high-level officials have chosen to intervene in an oceans policy, it has been a mixed blessing at best. Franklin Roosevelt's ingenious efforts to justify expanded U.S. claims lacked any conception that the actions of a great power set important precedents for other states. Indeed, he was personally behind the Neutrality Proclamation of 1939 and the Truman Proclamations in 1945, both of which troubled U.S. policymakers for decades after. In 1976, Secretary of State Kissinger's intervention in law of the sea policy similarly handicapped the efforts of subsequent U.S. negotiators on seabed mining. Because of his desire to play a larger role in the North-South dialogue that had been underway for a number of years, he sought out several negotiations in which to make compromises and UNCLOS III was one of them. Since the compromises were not negotiated through the government agencies, officials spent the subsequent years trying to interpret and negotiate them. Kissinger, of course, was long gone from the scene. A further outcome of the Kissinger compromises was that they misled conference participants into expecting that the U.S. would offer new concessions at each session of the negotiation.

The high rate of turnover of U.S. law of the sea negotiators in UNCLOS III was due to the succession of administrations during the 1970s and to the political nature of the negotiators' position. While bringing in an outside head of the delegation for a brief or one-shot affair such as UNCLOS I or II posed few problems, the turnover of negotiators between 1973 and 1981 had a number of adverse consequences for U.S. policy in UNCLOS III. In the first place, new negotiators are at a disadvantage in a negotiation in relation to more seasoned participants, even when they have an excellent back-up team.

And they are less able to maintain control and policy continuity within their own delegation.

A second disadvantage of short-term negotiators is their desire to get the negotiation concluded quickly during their own tenure. This has led repeatedly in UNCLOS III to a succession of U.S. compromises, each offered in hopes that it would induce the other side to be forth-coming and bring the negotiations to a speedy conclusion. The irony, of course, is that each compromise generates expectations of further U.S. compromises and encourages other states to prolong the negotia-tions to secure additional concessions. Only when it became apparent to other countries in 1977 that further U.S. compromises would have to be achieved through intense negotiations did seabed mining negoti-ations begin in earnest. In the face of a protracted negotiation where foreign negotiators maintain a high degree of continuity, U.S. interests would be better served by appointing a U.S. negotiator for the duration, even one who is not at the highest policy levels.

The diversity of U.S. interests and the discontinuity in U.S. law of the sea leadership led at UNCLOS I, II, and III to a preoccupation with negotiating agreements within the U.S. delegation, particularly from 1973 to 1977. When internal compromises were finally agreed upon, an exhausted delegation often handed them over without extract-ing compromises from the other delegations. In addition, protracted U.S. negotiations often meant late policy decisions and made it diffi-cult to coordinate approaches with U.S. allies and like-minded states. After 1977, U.S. negotiators adopted the opposite approach to negotia-tions on seabed mining. They would negotiate ad referendum compro-mises with the Group of 77 and then try to sell them to the domestic interest groups. In a number of cases, such as production controls and technology transfer, the compromise was deemed unacceptable and the negotiators were enjoined to do better.

United Nations Negotiations

There is a great deal to be learned from the record of U.S. participation in the law of the sea negotiations, particularly in UNCLOS III. The UNCLOS III vehicle was unsatisfactory in many respects, but the alter-native arenas for negotiating an international law of the sea were limited. Indeed, in the 1950s it was the United States that shifted law of the sea discussions out of the OAS context, where the U.S. was badly out-numbered, into the UN General Assembly framework. Once there, after 1958 and 1960, law of the sea could no longer be moved elsewhere, even

377

though the forum ceased to be congenial for the U.S. At best, the U.S. might hope for a return to more fruitful technical and management discussions in UN functional bodies such as the IOC, IMCO, and FAO. These too, however, became increasingly politicized as the membership grew to include a large number of developing states that could field technical delegations.

If the law of the sea negotiations in 1958 and 1960 were barely manageable despite extensive ILC preparations, the Third Law of the Sea Conference suffered even graver problems. The bloc negotiations between East and West were transformed into a curious amalgam of East, West, and South blocs. And the number of participants—over 150—became a major impediment to successful negotiations. When large numbers of states wielding very little power in world events are transformed in the United Nations through the concept of sovereignty into countries with power equal to all others, the discrepancy between political reality within and outside the organization produces incongruous negotiating situations.

The problem of too many participants was compounded in UNCLOS III by the creation of a negotiating agenda covering too many issues. Throughout the decade-long conference, repeated efforts were made to develop viable negotiating mechanisms based on representative groups. Time and again, these mechanisms failed whenever groups of limited size were created or when secret negotiating groups were publicly discredited. On any issue of importance, no state was willing to be excluded from a negotiation or to allow its interests to be represented by others. As a result, the conference turned over final drafting responsibilities to the chairmen of the main negotiating committees. Secret and informal negotiating groups were developed to feed the chairmen compromise language. Given the power of the chairmen to draft the texts, however, the negotiating groups were at the mercy of the chairmen who might or might not accept the results of extensive private negotiations. The dilemmas inherent in this situation were particularly evident in negotiations on seabed mining where many delegations were unhappy with the chairman and yet could not wrest the drafting power from him. A great deal of precious time and talent were expended at UNCLOS III to cope with this problem.

If the pattern of relying on chairmen for major decisions occurs at subsequent negotiations, effective power will reside in the African, Asian, and Latin American regional groups which typically claim important chairmanships. The Western European and other groups get less important positions, and the United States and the Soviet Union never chair major committees, preferring instead to have membership on the general and drafting committees. In UNCLOS III these committees were relatively unimportant and as a result, the major maritime powers had few formal levers to protect their minority interest. The critical chairmanship on offshore issues went to a Latin American who in essence determined the outlines of the law of the sea text with his 1975 draft. In the ensuing years, the LL/GDS and maritime states pursued a fruitless struggle to regain a few of the maritime rights which they had lost in the 1975 draft.

In addition to revealing changes in patterns of institutional power in international organizations, UNCLOS III typified the difficulties of North-South negotiations based on fragile coalitions. Up until 1975 when the draft texts clearly hurt the LL/GDS, the developing countries were able to maintain a precarious coalition based on opposition to maritime powers in matters of seabed mining as well as offshore jurisdiction. When the coastal developing countries sold out the interests of developing LL/GDS in the 1975 text, the coalition fell apart on jurisdictional issues but continued to hold together on seabed mining. Because the Group of 77 encompasses such a large number of states with diverse interests, it has been difficult to maintain and has required substantial efforts to keep itself intact. Unfortunately, these efforts have consumed long periods of time that could have been spent in negotiating with other states. It is also unfortunate that some of the more extreme members of the Group of 77 have been allowed to dominate the group. When the extremists refused to move toward a compromise or even negotiate on an issue, the entire Group of 77 was stymied from fear of losing its cohesiveness and whatever strength it might have through numbers. As a result, sterile rhetorical exchanges dominated much of the history of the conference. Only in 1977 when the threat of unilateral mining by developed states became credible did the moderate members of the Group of 77 begin to participate actively in secret negotiating groups with the developed states.

UNCLOS III was expensive and unnecessarily long on the one hand while on the other it offered a forum for communication and served as an educational vehicle for smaller states. Where the developed countries sent delegations staffed with technical as well as legal experts, the developing countries fielded a few overworked individuals who shared responsibility for several other North-South negotiations. As such, although they were short on technical mastery of ocean issues they were strong on bloc tactics and rhetorical skills and were well grounded in the goals of the New International Economic Order (NIEO). Since they were active in a number of negotiating fora—UNCLOS III, the UN Conference on Trade and Development (UNCTAD), the UN

Committee on the Peaceful Uses of Outer Space, and the UN Conference on Science and Technology for Development (UNCSTD)—they were also better equipped than developed country negotiators to relate developments in one negotiation to those in another.

Perhaps the clearest lesson of UNCLOS III is that the treaty on seabed issues was determined more by the structure and norms of the conference than by the underlying capabilities of the participating states. A treaty negotiation among 150 nations, each commanding an equal vote, puts a premium on the ability to build and maintain coalitions rather than on the power of the negotiating countries. As a result, the Group of 77, when it maintains group solidarity, can determine the outcome through the tactical and strategic skills of its principal negotiators rather than through the influence of their governments. The important role played by Kenya, Peru, Singapore, and Sri Lanka on seabed negotiations is a striking example. Without the United Nations context and the Group of 77 coalition, the role of such countries compared to that of seabed mining states would have been negligible.

In addition to the impact of structure, the underlying norms of UNCLOS III worked against the developed countries. Through the early acceptance of the concept that the seabed beyond national jurisdiction is the "common heritage of mankind," the Group of 77 established an important premise for what was essentially a negotiation over a common property resource. In addition, the developing countries transferred many of the norms of the NIEO from other negotiations, such as mandatory transfer of technology, production controls, and limitations on access for developed states. Applying NIEO concepts to the allocation of a common property resource eliminates the advantage of states technically able to recover a resource. In UNCLOS III, the technical capability to recover manganese nodules was not decisive, particularly because the mining negotiations had been linked to other important issues. U.S. willingness to compromise its mining interests clearly stemmed from U.S. concern to secure consensus on a treaty that protected certain navigation rights. In effect, the outcome of the seabed negotiations was determined in the early 1970s when the jurisdictional issues were grouped with seabed mining in a single conference.

As the law of the sea conference illustrates, there is little advantage from the standpoint of developed states to negotiating regimes for common property resources in the United Nations context. The combination of voting structure and NIEO ideology give the developing nations a position of influence far out of proportion to their capability to contribute to or enforce a regime. Recognition of this fact explains the strong motivation of the Antarctic Treaty powers to ensure the viability of their Consultative Group and to develop regimes for Antarctic resources outside of the United Nations.

Nonetheless, the concurrence of a majority of nations is vital to legitimize certain resource management regimes. This is all the more important when disenchanted nations have the power to disrupt use of a resource even if they do not have the ability to use it themselves. The negotiations in the World Administrative Radio Conference (WARC) over the allocation of the radio spectrum is such a case. A related example is the debate over apportioning geostationary orbits in the outer space meetings.

Given the constraints and operating principles of these UN discussions, developed countries will want to place greater emphasis in the future on the role of customary law in determining regimes. They will want to use multilateral conferences less often, and then only to legitimize the prevailing regime or to address issues that cannot be managed by unilateral and cooperative action. Developing countries, on the other hand, will seek to expand the definition of common property resources and will attempt to negotiate common property issues in the United Nations. In the meetings of UNCSTD and UNCTAD, for instance, the Group of 77 has tried to define science and technology as a common property resource that should be made available to developing countries.

GUIDEPOSTS FOR THE FUTURE

The experiences of the past suggest the likely directions of the future, including potential opportunities and problems. While particular events and the timing of emerging problems cannot be precisely pinpointed, general trends can be identified. Based on historical evidence, we can safely assume that, whatever the outcome of UNCLOS III, the evolution of the law of the sea will be an ongoing process. An UNCLOS III treaty might capture the legal picture at one point in time, but any treaty is doomed to be retrospective. Ocean technologies will continue to evolve, generating new uses and new political and economic processes. The law of the sea will have to follow, either through practice and custom or future codification conferences or some combination of the two.

The product of UNCLOS III and the level of general acceptance will affect the pace and the manner in which ocean law will evolve. Widespread ratification and acceptance of an UNCLOS treaty would slow the rate of change in customary law and would channel future developments in the law back to large multilateral conferences. On the other hand, an UNCLOS treaty that is not widely recognized will result in a more confused political and legal situation, especially with regard to seabed mining. In the absence of a widely accepted regime, unilateral mining by the developed countries can be expected to provoke a strong political reaction by the Group of 77.

The probable oceans regime for the last two decades of the 20th century can be briefly summarized. During this period ocean resource exploitation will continue to increase as will the problems of crowding and "negative externalities," such as ocean pollution and overfishing. The bulk of ocean resource activities will be carried on within 200-mile zones under the regulation and control of national governments. Conflicts will arise over the delineation of national boundaries as well as over the interaction of national and international uses of the zone and their impact on neighboring states. Mining of manganese nodules will begin in the Pacific Ocean, either under the auspices of an international regulatory authority or through private and state organizations operating without reference to an international organization.

Jurisdictional Disputes

Contention over the substance and the scope of coastal-state jurisdiction in the oceans will be a salient feature of the future oceans regime. Substantive conflicts may take a number of forms. Traditional high seas freedoms, such as navigation or the laying of pipelines and cables, will have to be reconciled with the coastal state's new authority over zones of 200 miles or more. Other conflicts may arise among and between neighboring coastal states where activities within a nation's offshore zones, such as the dumping or discharge of wastes, have adverse consequences for nearby states.

The determination of the physical extent of a coastal state's jurisdiction in accordance with the conflicting norms that have been advocated at UNCLOS III will be problematical. States that are situated opposite or adjacent to one another will have to resolve their boundary differences by negotiation or force where the equidistance or median line principle applicable to the waters does not coincide with the depth contours of a shared continental shelf area. The problems of this nature between the United States and Canada are minor compared to those in the South and East China Seas or in the Aegean, where a multiplicity of states and significant historical and political animosities further complicate the difficulties posed by geography. Islands of disputed ownership create particular difficulties and it is possible that these disputes will take a violent direction where valuable offshore resources are

involved. Uninhabited rocks and even submerged coral atolls are accepted in the conference negotiating text as points from which national
jurisdiction might be measured. Scrambles to acquire and control such
pieces of economic real estate will doubtless enliven the ocean scene
of the 1980s.

Where states front on the major oceans, it is likely that, with or without a treaty, justifications will be found for the extension of coastal-
state control beyond 200 miles even where there is no continental margin. Peru has already indicated its interest in the migratory fisheries
beyond 200 miles; Canada and Argentina are intent upon controlling
foreign fishing beyond their 200-mile fishing zones; and Mexico is eye-
ing the prospect of nodule mining in the North Pacific beyond 200
miles. The opposition to the forces behind further national extensions
will be weak in the absence of a widely accepted treaty. The LL/GDS
did not exert significant influence at UNCLOS III. And most of the
maritime states, such as the United States, have substantial coastal interests that preclude wholehearted opposition to extension. In the 1980s,
coastal states will be concentrating on expanding their competence and
jurisdiction within 200 miles and on the continental margin. And in the
1990s, expansionist forces may prevail and further reduce the size of the
"common heritage of mankind."

Problems Within the 200-Mile Zone

Although nationalist sentiments will continue to stimulate claims beyond 200 miles where a coastal state fronts on open ocean, exploration
and exploitation of the resources of the 200-mile economic zone will
absorb most national energies in the 1980s. All of the world's coastal
fisheries, and up to 95 percent of offshore oil, are found in this area.

FISHING. The fishing activities of coastal states in the 1980s will vary
from country to country and region to region. The provisions of the
law of the sea negotiating text point toward the phasing out of most
distant-water fishing activities in favor of coastal-state fishing. Theo-
retically, according to the provisions of the draft treaty, the coastal state
should allow other nations to harvest that portion of the fishery (up to
the level of maximum sustainable yield) that it cannot harvest itself.
In practice, there is no way to contest coastal-state actions under the
proposed treaty if a state decides to prohibit all foreign fishing or, at the
other extreme, to license foreign fishing in excess of what coastal fish
stocks can bear. These decisions will be a matter of domestic politics,
where short-term considerations can be expected to prevail. In the ab-

sence of countervailing forces, a particular government may allow excessive fishing for the sake of its immediate revenue needs. On the other hand, nationalist sentiments spurred by domestic fishing interests may urge a ban on all foreign fishing to reduce the local industry's own costs of operation and regardless of the fishery resource that may go underutilized. In the absence of effective governmental management restricting entry into the coastal fishery, the domestic fishing industries may become overcapitalized and ultimately overfish the national zones. Although the situation will vary from country to country and from government to government, the overall trend will be toward the replacement of long-distance fishing fleets and factory ships with coastal fishermen and shore-based processing operations.

Even where a government chooses to manage a coastal fishery to achieve a maximum sustainable or an optimum yield, its efforts may be undermined by the activities of neighboring states. This problem will be especially acute in enclosed areas such as the Caribbean and the Mediterranean. In these seas, coastal stocks are so intermingled that management must be undertaken on a regional, not a national, basis. The distribution of the fishery resource simply does not coincide with man-made boundaries. It is likely, however, that the 1980s will see serious problems of overfishing before this lesson is learned and regional management practices are adopted. For countries such as the United States and Canada, these problems will only arise where the economic zone directly adjoins that of other states. In these areas, coordinated management will be needed.

Anadromous and highly migratory species, salmon and tuna respectively, pose a special set of problems which cannot be resolved by 200-mile resource zones. Salmon migrate to and from their spawning rivers in patterns that take them well beyond 200 miles from shore. Fishing beyond the 200-mile zone in the 1980s for salmon or coastal stocks could be a major source of contention between distant-water and coastal states. The direction these disputes take will depend upon the overall condition of distant-water fleets and alternative fishing opportunities as well as upon bilateral agreements with coastal fishing states.

The management of tuna stocks will be even more difficult politically since it involves a larger number of states. Tuna travel at high speeds and migrate great distances around and across the Indian, Atlantic, and Pacific Oceans. Management schemes must be applied to the stock as a whole, or the result will be overfishing of the resource. If each country fishes tuna at will as schools pass along the coast within 200 miles of its shores, the fishery will eventually disappear. UNCLOS III was unable to resolve this special management problem, and the prospect for highly migratory species is doubtful.

Whether international management schemes are adopted in the 1980s for migratory species, for anadromous species, or for coastal stocks that move beyond or across national boundaries will depend upon changed perceptions of interdependence and of the need to maintain these sources of protein over the long term. The political will to forgo a degree of national sovereignty in fisheries management may be possible after depletion of stocks and a period of controversy over respective national management schemes.

OCEAN ENERGY. Through the 1970s, most petroleum production from offshore reserves has been in areas close to shore and at depths of less than 200 meters. Over two-thirds of the petroleum reserves of the continental margin are expected to be beyond the territorial sea. Given the fact that petroleum will supply the major portion of world energy needs through the 1980s, the oil and gas of the continental margin remain important elements in the world energy picture. Only 1 to 5 percent of world offshore oil and gas is estimated to lie on the margin beyond 200 miles. The combination of distance from shore and increasing depths as exploitation moves further offshore will restrict commercial activities in the 1980s to areas within the economic zone. As oil exploitation moves to greater depths, surface rigs and platforms will be replaced with underwater mining and storage equipment. This will make them immune to most inclement weather, but, like surface operations, they can pose a hazard to navigation and will have to be well marked.

Assuming the resolution of differences over boundaries, the recovery of petroleum from the continental margin will not pose the same problem as fishing in national 200-mile zones. Unless an oil pool happens to cross an ocean boundary, cooperative management arrangements will not be necessary. Where the common pool problem arises, bilateral or multilateral agreement will be needed to drill the shared pool with least cost. Cooperative arrangements may also prove desirable with regard to the storage of oil or its movement by pipeline or ship. Norwegian oil from the North Sea, for instance, has been brought ashore in Scotland.

With the increased exploitation of offshore reserves in the 1980s will come greater numbers of blowouts and accidental spills. UNCLOS III, however, did not set environmental standards for offshore resource exploitation. Each nation is free to specify its own pollution prevention regulations and may in some instances prefer to set minimal or no standards as an inducement to investment. The development of such "pollution havens" could create negative effects for neighboring zones where environmental goals may be valued for aquaculture, tourism, or esthetic reasons. Given the transnational impact of offshore pollution, states of the region will have to band together in setting standards and liability provisions to preserve environmental goals. Coercive measures may prove to be the only means to ensure that recalcitrant states observe similar pollution prevention measures in their respective zones.

Negative externalities may arise from a number of energy-related activities. In its quest for energy, the coastal state may be expected to turn to its offshore areas for siting of nuclear power plants, for capturing tidal energy, for building vast kelp farms (for bio-conversion), or for harnessing solar energy (ocean thermal energy conversion). Fears of a core meltdown in nuclear power plants is widespread, and offshore siting has become increasingly attractive where public opposition to on-shore locations exists.[38] Indeed, coastal states may respond to domestic pressures by locating plants as far from shore as possible, that is, at the edges or outermost limits of the 200-mile zone. (This might be especially the case where the energy generated supports offshore industrial activities that are not wanted near population centers.) Even in the absence of a power plant failure, the normal operation of a nuclear plant entails environmental change through the discharge of heated water. The attendant impact on the local fisheries population may be positive or negative. That is, raising the water temperature a few degrees may make the environment more or less congenial to fish stocks, depending on normal temperatures and on the types of stocks that might flourish in the warmed waters. In any case, neighboring states will object to action over which they have no control and which poses potential environmental damage. Other nonconventional forms of energy from the oceans will be in the experimental stages in the 1980s and hence will not cause significant friction.

POLLUTION. Pollution of the ocean by dumping waste materials off-shore or by direct emissions of sewage into ocean or river waters has wide-ranging as well as local effects. The use of the ocean as a disposal medium will increase in the 1980s and 1990s with the growth of coastal populations and greater agricultural (pesticides) and industrial activities. The negative impact of dumping and land-source pollution will depend upon a) where the dumping takes place, b) the proximity of other zones, c) the depth of the ocean areas, and d) the direction of winds and ocean currents. International incidents may arise over the dumping of wastes that may be remote from a coastal state's local population but that affects the population or marine resources of other coastal states.

COMMERCIAL NAVIGATION. The world merchant fleet has grown dramatically over the past 25 years, with accompanying increases in both the size and speed of ships. The trend toward more ships for bulk cargo will continue throughout the rest of the century despite a leveling off of demand for imported petroleum. As the volume of merchant shipping has grown, the number of collisions and groundings has increased. Accidents have reached the point where, on the average, a 60,000-ton ship sinks every day.[39] A greater number of ships means that ever more costly accidents will occur in the coming decades. Because the major shipping lanes around the world are within 200 miles of shore, shipping will be competing for space with the increased resource exploitation in the 200-mile zones.

Tanker collisions with unmarked installations can be averted by adopting prominent markings and by requiring the coastal state to issue detailed and updated charts designating obstacles to navigation. Some states may object to the requirement that they facilitate international navigation in their economic zone and may not cooperate. Others may not have the technical capability or financial resources to implement these measures regularly, and will need assistance.

On the subject of navigation, the law of the sea draft text did little more than provide for the right of coastal states to establish traffic lanes in straits overlapped by twelve-mile territorial seas and to protect themselves from ship-source pollution. After several serious collisions, coastal states will be tempted to assert national control over congested areas. This could result in friction between the shippers and the coastal state. Alternatively, the recognition of a mutual interest in regulating traffic in congested areas could lead to international forms of regulation, and states might turn to the Intergovernmental Maritime Consultative Organization (IMCO) with problems of navgiation in congested areas.

Deep Seabed Mining

The commercial recovery of deep seabed manganese nodules will not be underway until the 1990s. It will be an expensive undertaking, and this expense plus the technological uncertainties and political controversies that may attend deep-sea mining will pose problems for the first generation of mining operations. Even if technical and political difficulties are ironed out, the availability of low-cost, land-based supplies of cobalt, manganese, nickel, and copper will slow the rate of growth of deep-sea mining during the rest of the century.

The legal arrangements that will govern deep-sea mining are difficult to predict at this time. Seabed exploration will proceed under the auspices of national legislation harmonized among the developed states. This multilateral regime may be linked to the work of the preparatory commission established to prepare rules and regulations for the international seabed authority. If a treaty does not come into force by the late 1980s, the multilateral regime will proceed from exploration to commercial exploitation. If the law of the sea treaty does come into effect, all seabed miners may become parties to a single international mining regime, or some may choose to stay out and create a dual mining system.

Military Uses

From a military perspective, the oceans are important to maintain the strategic deterrent which makes a first-strike nuclear attack too costly. The opaque ocean environment offers a safe place for United States and Soviet ballistic submarines and thereby contributes to maintaining a fragile peace. Technological change has a major impact on the viability of the strategic balance as both superpowers are continually seeking means to detect enemy submarines while making their own ever more invulnerable. Competitive technological change in antisubmarine warfare (ASW) and in submarine construction will doubtless continue throughout the 1980s. While improvements in ASW technology may render the submarine more vulnerable, a countervailing factor making it more difficult to detect may be the increased background noise resulting from greater commercial use of the oceans. Commercial activities will provide new hiding places and help to mask the characteristic signature of submarines.

No explicit restrictions on military activity per se are evolving out of UNCLOS III. This will create an interesting situation in the 1980s when the coastal state will be consolidating its control over the resources of its 200-mile zone at the same time the area is being used by other nations for strategic or tactical military purposes. The wealthier coastal states will develop naval forces to protect offshore operations from sabotage or harassment. Some coastal states may acquiesce in the use of their zones as hiding places or sanctuaries for submarines and warships of friendly nations. Others may try to monitor or prohibit all ingress by foreign military vessels and installation of ASW equipment. Even small coastal states determined to prevent unwanted activities in their zones may develop the means for raising the costs of foreign military operations. Relatively inexpensive heat-seeking or guided missiles may be installed on patrol boats charged with guarding national economic zones. These can inflict substantial damage to expensive ships or equipment at minimal cost to the coastal state.

As noted above, the oceans regime of the future will be characterized by numerous disagreements and disputes. Coastal patrol fleets may find themselves involved in the controversies that will arise from conflicting or incompatible uses of neighboring or nearby coastal zones or from disputes over the determination of boundaries. Military forces may also be deployed to protect commercial activities beyond national zones, such as deep-sea mining or navigation. The territorial approach adopted by the law of the sea negotiations and the inability to agree on strong provisions for the settlement of disputes will result in a high level of friction in the oceans and the sporadic resort to military force.

For the remainder of the century, two different trends in ocean policy will be visible. In situations where coastal-state zones adjoin open ocean, there will be continuing efforts to extend jurisdiction beyond the 200-mile zone and the continental margin. This trend will be resisted by coastal states lacking such an option, by maritime states, and by whatever seabed authority exists. The other trend will be toward a more cooperative approach to management among those coastal states whose adjoining waters dictate a degree of interdependence. Where transzonal impacts of coastal-state activities are most obvious—as in the case of fisheries or marine pollution—cooperation in managing ocean resources will be necessary. Similarly, a management approach to navigation will be unavoidable where crowding precludes the unrestricted use of the ocean highways. Thus in narrow and congested straits and in crowded nearshore areas, traffic will have to be regulated to assure safe navigation.

These and other management approaches will be adopted reluctantly and only after the adverse consequences of unilateral action in nationally claimed areas become apparent to all.

APPENDIX 1

THE "TRUMAN PROCLAMATIONS"

Proclamation 2667. "Policy of the United States With Respect to the Natural Resources of the Subsoil and Sea Bed of the Continental Shelf," September 28, 1945, 10 *Fed. Reg.* 12303.

"By the President of the United States of America
"A PROCLAMATION

"Whereas the Government of the United States of America, aware of the long range world-wide need for new sources of petroleum and other minerals, holds the view that efforts to discover and make available new supplies of these resources should be encouraged; and

"Whereas its competent experts are of the opinion that such resources underlie many parts of the continental shelf off the coasts of the United States of America, and that with modern technological progress their utilization is already practicable or will become so at an early date; and

"Whereas recognized jurisdiction over these resources is required in the interest of their conservation and prudent utilization when and as development is undertaken; and

"Whereas it is the view of the Government of the United States that the exercise of jurisdiction over the natural resources of the subsoil and sea bed of the continental shelf by the contiguous nation is reasonable and just, since the effectiveness of measures to utilize or conserve these resources would be contingent upon cooperation and protection from the shore, since the continental shelf may be regarded as an extension of the land-mass of the coastal nation and thus naturally appurtenant to it, since these resources frequently form a seaward extension of a pool or deposit lying within the territory, and since self-protection compels the coastal nation to keep close watch over activities off its shores which are of the nature necessary for utilization of these resources;

"Now, therefore, I, Harry S. Truman, President of the United States of America, do hereby proclaim the following policy of the United States of America with respect to the natural resources of the subsoil and sea bed of the continental shelf.

"Having concern for the urgency of conserving and prudently utilizing its natural resources, the Government of the United States regards the natural resources of the subsoil and sea bed of the continental shelf beneath the high seas but contiguous to the coasts of the United States as appertaining to the United States, subject to its jurisdiction and control. In cases where the continental shelf extends to the shores of another State, or is shared with an adjacent State, the boundary shall be determined by the United States and the State concerned in accordance with equitable principles. The character as high seas of the waters above the continental shelf and the right to their free and unimpeded navigation are in no way thus affected.

"IN WITNESS WHEREOF, I have hereunto set my hand and caused the seal of the United States of America to be affixed.

"DONE at the City of Washington this twenty-eighth day of September, in the year of our Lord nineteen hundred and forty-five, [SEAL] and of the Independence of the United States of America the one hundred and seventieth.

HARRY S. TRUMAN

By the President:
DEAN ACHESON
Acting Secretary of State"

Proclamation 2668. "Policy of the United States With Respect to Coastal Fisheries in Certain Areas of the High Seas," September 28, 1945, 10 *Fed. Reg.* 12304.

"BY THE PRESIDENT OF THE UNITED STATES OF AMERICA
"A PROCLAMATION

"WHEREAS for some years the Government of the United States of America has viewed with concern the inadequacy of present arrangements for the protection and perpetuation of the fishery resources contiguous to its coasts, and in view of the potentially disturbing effect of this situation, has carefully studied the possibility of improving the jurisdictional basis for conservation measures and international cooperation in this field; and

"WHEREAS such fishery resources have a special importance to coastal communities as a source of livelihood and to the nation as a food and industrial resource; and

"WHEREAS the progressive development of new methods and techniques contributes to intensified fishing over wide sea areas and in certain cases seriously threatens fisheries with depletion; and

"WHEREAS there is an urgent need to protect coastal fishery resources from destructive exploitation, having due regard to conditions peculiar to each region and situation and to the special rights and equities of the coastal State and of any other State which may have established a legitimate interest therein;

"Now, THEREFORE, I, HARRY S. TRUMAN, President of the United States of America, do hereby proclaim the following policy of the United States of America with respect to coastal fisheries in certain areas of the high seas:

"In view of the pressing need for conservation and protection of fishery resources, the Government of the United States regards it as proper to establish conservation zones in those areas of the high seas contiguous to the coasts of the United States wherein fishing activities have been or in the future may be developed and maintained on a substantial scale. Where such activities have been or shall hereafter be developed and maintained by its nationals alone, the United States regards it as proper to establish explicitly bounded conservation zones in which fishing activities shall be subject to the regulation and control of the United States. Where such activities have been or shall here-after be legitimately developed and maintained jointly by nationals of the United States and nationals of other States, explicitly bounded con-servation zones may be established under agreements between the United States and such other States; and all fishing activities in such zones shall be subject to regulation and control as provided in such agreements. The right of any State to establish conservation zones off its shores in accordance with the above principles is conceded, provided that corresponding recognition is given to any fishing interests of na-tionals of the United States which may exist in such areas. The char-acter as high seas of the areas in which such conservation zones are established and the right to their free and unimpeded navigation are in no way thus affected.

"IN WITNESS WHEREOF, I have hereunto set my hand and caused the seal of the United States of America to be affixed.

"DONE at the City of Washington this twenty-eighth day of Septem-ber, in the year of our Lord nineteen hundred and forty-five, [SEAL] and of the Independence of the United States of America the one hundred and seventieth.

HARRY S. TRUMAN

By the President:
    DEAN ACHESON
        Acting Secretary of State."

APPENDIX 2

*List of Subjects and Issues Relating to the Law of the Sea
—Approved by the Seabed Committee, August 18, 1972*

1. International régime for the sea-bed and the ocean floor beyond national jurisdiction
   1.1 Nature and characteristics
   1.2 International machinery: structure, functions, powers
   1.3 Economic implications
   1.4 Equitable sharing of benefits bearing in mind the special interests and needs of the developing countries, whether coastal or landlocked
   1.5 Definition and limits of the area
   1.6 Use exclusively for peaceful purposes

2. Territorial sea
   2.1 Nature and characteristics, including the question of the unity or plurality of régimes in the territorial sea
   2.2 Historic waters
   2.3 Limits
   2.3.1 Question of the delimitation of the territorial sea; various aspects involved
   2.3.2 Breadth of the territorial sea. Global or regional criteria. Open seas and oceans, semi-closed seas and enclosed seas
   2.4 Innocent passage in the territorial sea
   2.5 Freedom of navigation and overflight resulting from the question of plurality of régimes in the territorial sea

3. Contiguous zone
   3.1 Nature and characteristics
   3.2 Limits
   3.3 Rights of coastal States with regard to national security, customs and fiscal control, sanitation and immigration regulations

4. Straits used for international navigation
   4.1 Innocent passage
   4.2 Other related matters including the question of the right of transit

5. Continental shelf
   5.1 Nature and scope of the sovereign rights of coastal States over the continental shelf. Duties of States
   5.2 Outer limit of the continental shelf: applicable criteria
   5.3 Question of the delimitation between States; various aspects involved
   5.4 Natural resources of the continental shelf
   5.5 Régime for waters superjacent to the continental shelf
   5.6 Scientific research

6. Exclusive economic zone beyond the territorial sea

6.1   Nature and characteristics, including rights and jurisdiction of coastal States in relation to resources, pollution control, and scientific research in the zone. Duties of States

6.2   Resources of the zone

6.3   Freedom of navigation and overflight

6.4   Regional arrangements

6.5   Limits: applicable criteria

6.6   Fisheries

6.6.1   Exclusive fishery zone

6.6.2   Preferential rights of coastal States

6.6.3   Management and conservation

6.6.4   Protection of coastal States' fisheries in enclosed and semi-enclosed seas

6.6.5   Régime of islands under foreign domination and control in relation to zones of exclusive fishing jurisdiction

6.7   Sea-bed within national jurisdiction

6.7.1   Nature and characteristics

6.7.2   Delineation between adjacent and opposite States

6.7.3   Sovereign rights over natural resources

6.7.4   Limits: applicable criteria

6.8   Prevention and control of pollution and other hazards to the marine environment

6.8.1   Rights and responsibilities of coastal States

6.9   Scientific research

7. Coastal State preferential rights or other non-exclusive jurisdiction over resources beyond the territorial sea

7.1   Nature, scope and characteristics

7.2   Sea-bed resources

7.3   Fisheries

7.4   Prevention and control of pollution and other hazards to the marine environment

7.5   International co-operation in the study and rational exploitation of marine resources

7.6   Settlement of disputes

7.7   Other rights and obligations

8. High seas

8.1   Nature and characteristics

8.2   Rights and duties of States

8.3   Question of the freedoms of the high seas and their regulation

8.4   Management and conservation of living resources

8.5   Slavery, piracy, drugs

8.6   Hot pursuit

9. Land-locked countries
    9.1   General Principles of the Law of the Sea concerning the land-locked countries
    9.2   Rights and interests of land-locked countries
    9.2.1 Free access to and from the sea: freedom of transit, means and facilities for transport and communications
    9.2.2 Equality of treatment in the ports of transit States
    9.2.3 Free access to the international sea-bed area beyond national jurisdiction
    9.2.4 Participation in the international régime, including the machinery and the equitable sharing in the benefits of the area
    9.3   Particular interests and needs of developing land-locked countries in the international régime
    9.4   Rights and interests of land-locked countries in regard to living resources of the sea

10. Rights and interests of shelf-locked States and States with narrow shelves or short coastlines
    10.1   International régime
    10.2   Fisheries
    10.3   Special interests and needs of developing shelf-locked States and States with narrow shelves or short coastlines
    10.4   Free access to and from the high seas

11. Rights and interests of States with broad shelves

12. Preservation of the marine environment
    12.1   Sources of pollution and other hazards and measures to combat them
    12.2   Measures to preserve the ecological balance of the marine environment
    12.3   Responsibility and liability for damage to the marine environment and to the coastal State
    12.4   Rights and duties of coastal States
    12.5   International co-operation

13. Scientific research
    13.1   Nature, characteristics and objectives of scientific research of the oceans
    13.2   Access to scientific information
    13.3   International co-operation

14. Development and transfer of technology
    14.1   Development of technological capabilities of developing countries
    14.1.1 Sharing of knowledge and technology between developed and developing countries
    14.1.2 Training of personnel from developing countries
    14.1.3 Transfer of technology to developing countries

15. Regional arrangements
16. Archipelagos
17. Enclosed and semi-enclosed seas
18. Artificial islands and installations

19. Régime of islands:
    (a) Islands under colonial dependence or foreign domination or control;
    (b) Other related matters
20. Responsibility and liability for damage resulting from the use of the marine environment
21. Settlement of disputes
22. Peaceful uses of the ocean space; zones of peace and security
23. Archaeological and historical treasures on the sea-bed and ocean floor beyond the limits of national jurisdiction
24. Transmission from the high seas
25. Enhancing the universal participation of States in multilateral conventions relating to the law of the sea.

APPENDIX 3

LANDLOCKED AND GEOGRAPHICALLY DISADVANTAGED* STATES

Afghanistan**
Austria**
Bahrain
Belgium
Bhutan**
Bolivia**
Botswana**
Burundi**
Byelorussian SSR**
Central African Republic**
Chad**
Czechoslovakia**
Ethiopia
Finland
Gambia
German Democratic Republic
Germany, Federal Republic of
Holy See**
Hungary**
Iraq
Jamaica
Jordan
Kuwait
Laos**

Lesotho**
Liechtenstein**
Luxembourg**
Malawi**
Mali**
Mongolia**
Nepal**
Netherlands
Niger**
Paraguay**
Poland
Qatar
Rwanda**
San Marino**
Singapore
Sudan
Swaziland**
Sweden
Switzerland**
Uganda**
United Arab Emirates
Upper Volta**
Zaire
Zambia**

* Lists of "geographically disadvantaged" states vary considerably, depending on the preparer and the criteria used. The above is the official U.S. Department of State listing.

** 100% landlocked.

APPENDIX 4

NATIONAL SECURITY COUNCIL INTERAGENCY TASK FORCE ON THE LAW OF THE SEA

DEPARTMENTS

Department of State
Department of Defense
Department of Commerce/
  NOAA
Department of Interior
Department of the Treasury
Department of Transportation
Department of Agriculture
Department of Justice

AGENCIES

National Security Council
Office of Management and
  Budget

Environmental Protection
  Agency
Council on Environmental
  Quality
Council on International
  Economic Policy
National Science Foundation
Central Intelligence Agency
Council of Economic Advisors
Agency for International
  Development
Marine Mammal Commission
Federal Energy Administration
  (DOE)

APPENDIX 5

PRODUCT OF THE GENEVA SESSION, UNCLOS III, 1975

I. Committee I Product
   A. Informal Single Negotiating Text: Part 1
      (A/CONF.62/WP.8/Part 1)
      1. Convention on the Seabed and the Ocean Floor and the Subsoil Thereof Beyond the Limits of National Jurisdiction. 75 articles: drafted by Pinto, revised by Engo.
      a. Annex I. Basic Conditions of General Survey Exploration and Exploitation. 21 articles drafted by Pinto and transmitted to Engo from Working Group.

II. Committee II Product
   A. Informal Single Negotiating Text: Part II
      (A/CONF.62/WP.8/Part II)
      Contents: 137 articles drafted by Galindo Pohl and Bureau based on texts from Evensen and other groups.
      1. Territorial Sea and Contiguous Zone
      2. Straits used for International Navigation
      3. Exclusive Economic Zone
      4. Continental Shelf
      5. High Seas
      6. Landlocked States
      7. Archipelagos
      8. Regime of Islands
      9. Enclosed and Semi-Enclosed Seas
      10. Territories under Foreign Occupation or Colonial Domination
      11. Settlement of Disputes
      Annex: Highly Migratory Species

III. Committee III Product
   A. Protection and Preservation of Marine Environment
      1. Four Draft Articles, heavily footnoted
         (A/CONF.62/C.3/L.15, Add. 1)
         a. Monitoring
         b. Environmental Assessment

      c. Standards for Land-based Sources (alternative articles providing double standard for developing countries)

      d. Pollution from Dumping of Wastes at Sea

    2. Proposals introduced as conference room papers (CRPs): (A/CONF.62/C.3/L.30)

B. Science and Transfer of Technology

    1. Possible Consolidated Texts with alternatives (A/CONF.62/C.3/L.31)

      a. Legal Status of Installations for Marine Scientific Research

      b. Responsibility and Liability

      c. Development and Transfer of Technology

    2. Texts Submitted as CRPs

C. Informal Single Negotiating Text (A/CONF.62/WP.8/Part III)

    1. Protection and preservation of Marine Environment: 44 articles drafted by Yankov and Vallarta using L.15 (above) and Evensen text

    2. Marine Scientific Research: 37 articles drafted by Yankov and Metternich using L.31 (above) and Mexican-Irish compromise proposal

    3. Development and Transfer of Technology: 11 articles drafted by Yankov and Metternich using L.31

APPENDIX 6

OFFICIAL AND UNOFFICIAL CONFERENCE GROUPS:
UNCLOS III

OFFICIAL CONFERENCE GROUPS

Conference (Bureau) General Committee

Committee I (Bureau) Working Group—chairman's private consultative groups

Committee II (Bureau) Informal consultative groups (all members—with working groups of smaller sizes for some issues:
1. Baselines Working Group
2. Historic Bays and Historic Waters Working Group
3. Contiguous Zone Working Group
4. Innocent Passage Working Group
5. High Seas Working Group
6. Landlocked and Geographically Disadvantaged Working Group on Access to the Sea
7. Continental Shelf Working Group
8. Exclusive Economic Zone Working Group
9. Straits Working Group
10. Enclosed and Semi-enclosed Seas Working Group
11. Islands Working Group
12. Delimitation Working Group

Committee III (Bureau) two working groups—chairman's private drafting and negotiating groups

Credentials Committee

Drafting Committee

SEMI-OFFICIAL NEGOTIATING GROUPS

Dispute Settlement Group

Juridical Experts (Evensen Group consisting of heads of delegations)

AD HOC OR MISCELLANEOUS ISSUE-ORIENTED GROUPS

Group of 17—Pollution

Group of 13—Science

Amorphous Group—Science

Honduras Group on Continental Shelf

UK/Fiji Group on Straits

REGIONAL GROUPS

African Group—Ivory Coast chairman
Latin American Group—Contacts to Committee I (Rattray) and II
  (Ajala)
  1. Caribbean States
  2. Central American States
Asian group of Group of 77
Arab Group—Separate meetings on each committee
Western European and Others (WEO) Group
European Economic Community
East European Group

INTEREST GROUPS

Group of 77 (Bureau) Kedadi chairman
  Committee I—Working Group (Bureau) Contact Group (deSoto)
    expands from 13 at Caracas to 50 at Geneva
  Committee II—Contact Group (Njenga chairman)
  Committee III—Working Group—Contact Group (Iraq chairman)
Archipelagic States
Oceanic States (Australia, New Zealand, Fiji, Tonga, Western Samoa,
  Micronesia): re coastal-state regulation of highly migratory species in
  economic zone
Landlocked and Geographically Disadvantaged: 48 members (Turkey
  chairman)
  Committee I—Working Group (Czechoslovakia chairman)
  Committee II—Contact Group Questions of Transit
  Working Group on Marine Scientific Research (Netherlands
    chairman)
  Landlocked states of Group of 77
Straits States
Territorialist Group
Coastal States (transformed into Evensen Group)

NOTES

Chapter 1
THE LAW OF THE SEA IN TRANSITION:
AN OVERVIEW

1. Made on June 7, 1494; confirmed by Papal Bull Ea Quae issued by Pope Julius II on January 24, 1506.

2. *The Freedom of the Seas, or the Right Which Belongs to the Dutch to Take Part in the East Indian Trade*, Magoffin translation (New York: Oxford University Press, 1916).

3. John Selden, *Of the Dominion or Ownership of the Sea*, Nedham translation (London, 1652); originally entitled *Mare Clausum sev De Dominio Maris* (1635).

4. Cornelius van Bynkershoek, *De Dominio Maris Dissertatio* (1702) (Oxford: Clarendon Press, 1923).

5. *The Law of Nature and Nations*, 1672.

6. Vessels of 100 gross tons and over. *Lloyd's Register of Shipping Statistical Tables*, 1978 (London, 1979).

7. See Thomas O'Toole, "Merchant Ships Sink at Rate of One a Day," *Washington Post*, August 7, 1972.

8. U.S. Department of Commerce, National Marine Fisheries Service, *Fisheries of the United States*, 1977 (Washington, D.C.: Government Printing Office, 1978).

Chapter 2
THE TRUMAN PROCLAMATIONS: 1935-1945

1. Presidential Proclamation No. 2667, Concerning the Policy of the United States with Respect to the Natural Resources of the Subsoil and Sea-Bed of the Continental Shelf of 28 September 1945. 59 United States Statutes at Large 884. For text, see Appendix 1.

2. Presidential Proclamation No. 2668, Concerning the Policy of the United States with Respect to Coastal Fisheries in Certain Areas of the High Seas of 28 September 1945. 59 United States Statutes at Large 885. For text, see Appendix 2.

3. Presidential Decree Concerning Fishing and Hunting of 18 September 1907, UN Doc. ST/LEG/SER.B/1 at 13.

4. Law No. 14 Amending the Law Concerning Deposits of Hydrocarbons of 31 January 1923. Leyes 498 (1923) UN Doc. ST/LEG/SER.B/15 at 59.

5. Act of Congress, June 5, 1794, c.50. For a discussion of early U.S. claims to special competence in offshore waters see Myres S. McDougal and William T. Burke, *The Public Order of the Oceans*, pp. 587-597.

6. Mr. Jefferson, secretary of state, to M. Genet, French minister, November 8, 1793, quoted in James Kent, *American Law: Commentaries,* 1, 11th ed., p. 31.

7. Ibid., p. 30.

8. Anti-Smuggling Act, 49 *Stat.* 517; 19 U.S.C. 1701-1711, August 3, 1935. Legislation in 1922 (40 *Stat.* 989) built on 1790 legislation extending U.S. authority over smuggling to four leagues from the coast (McDougal and Burke, *Public Order of the Oceans,* p. 587).

9. "Projects of the United States of America Presented to the Congress of Panama," in U.S. Delegation to the Meeting of the Foreign Ministers of the American Republics, September 23-October 3, 1939, *Report* (Washington, D.C.: U.S. Government Printing Office, 1940), pp. 67-73.

10. *Department of State Bulletin,* 1, No. 15 (October 7, 1939), 331-334; U.S. Department of State, *Foreign Relations of the United States 1939,* v, 36-37. (Hereinafter cited as *Foreign Relations,* year and volume number.)

11. "Explanatory Note Regarding Declaration of Panama Map," *Foreign Relations,* ibid; p. 765.

12. Tobias Barrios, "Las Doscientas Millas," *Mercurio,* 19 July 1974; Letter from Jermán L. Fischer to author, 15 March 1976.

13. Memo by president to counselor of the Department of State. *Foreign Relations 1937,* iv, 769.

14. Secretary of State Hull to the ambassador in Japan (Grew), November 10, 1937, *Foreign Relations,* ibid., p. 765.

15. Memo by president to secretary of state, November 22, 1937, *Foreign Relations,* ibid., p. 771.

16. Under secretary to the counselor of the Department of State (Moore), November 22, 1937, *Foreign Relations,* ibid., p. 770.

17. Ibid., p. 771.

18. Ibid., p. 773.

19. *The Secret Diary of Harold L. Ickes,* ii, 296-297.

20. Joseph C. Grew was U.S. ambassador to Japan in 1937 and became acting secretary of state in 1944. Eugene H. Dooman served as counselor of the U.S. embassy in Japan in 1937 and 1938. By 1944, Dooman was special assistant to the assistant secretary of state and in 1945 he was given the task of notifying foreign governments of U.S. plans to extend offshore jurisdiction. Leo D. Sturgeon was with the Division of Far Eastern Affairs in 1937, in which capacity he conducted an investigation of Japanese fishing off Alaska. By 1944 he had moved to the Office of Economic Affairs.

For detailed discussions of the 1930s dispute, see L. Larry Leonard, *International Regulation of Fisheries,* Carnegie Endowment for International Peace, Washington, D.C., Monograph No. 7, 1944, Chapter iii; H. E. Gregory and K. Barnes, *North Pacific Fisheries: With Special Reference to Alaska Salmon* (New York: American Council, Institute of Pacific Relations, 1939), pp. 281-307; Jozo Tomasevich, *International Agreements on Conservation of Marine Resources, With Special Reference to the North*

Pacific (Palo Alto: Stanford University, Food Research Institute, 1943), pp. 219-265.

21. Background enclosure in telegram from the secretary of state to the ambassador in Japan (Grew), June 5, 1937, in *Foreign Relations 1937*, IV, 743.

22. Ibid., p. 744.

23. Department of State Telegram, No. 119, August 3, 1935, *Foreign Relations 1935*, III, 1076.

24. See exchanges between Secretary of State Hull and Ambassador Grew, *Foreign Relations 1937*, IV, 734-737.

25. *Congressional Record*, June 18, 1937, Vol. 81, pt. 6, p. 5953.

26. Secretary of state to chairman of Senate Committee on Commerce (Copeland), August 4, 1937 in *Foreign Relations 1937*, IV, 754-757.

27. For more on the influence of this lobby see James A. Crutchfield and Giulio Pontecorvo, *The Pacific Salmon Fisheries*, pp. 87 ff.; Leonard, *International Regulation of Fisheries*; Gregory and Barnes, *North Pacific Fisheries*.

28. Ickes, *Secret Diary*, II, 296-297.

29. Memorandum by Leo D. Sturgeon, Division of Far Eastern Affairs, *Foreign Relations 1937*, IV, 759-760.

30. Secretary of state to the ambassador in Japan (Grew), November 19, 1937, *Foreign Relations*, ibid., pp. 761-763.

31. Secretary of state to the ambassador in Japan (Grew), January 22, 1938, *Foreign Relations 1939*, II, 164.

32. Ambassador in Japan (Grew) to the secretary of state, January 26, 1938 and February 6, 1938, *Foreign Relations*, ibid., pp. 167-169 and 173.

33. Department of State, *Press Releases*, March 26, 1938, p. 412.

34. Ambassador in Japan (Grew) to the secretary of state, March 31, 1938, *Foreign Relations 1939*, II, 190.

35. Secretary of state to ambassador in Japan (Grew), October 17, 1938, *Foreign Relations*, ibid., p. 191.

36. Joseph Walter Bingham, *Report on the International Law of Pacific Coast Fisheries*.

37. Enclosure, October 17, 1938, *Foreign Relations 1939*, II, 195.

38. Ambassador in Japan (Grew) to the secretary of state, November 15, 1938, *Foreign Relations*, ibid., pp. 197-198. The timing of U.S. fishing claims against Japan was in fact related to Japan's vulnerability before the war. Representative Dimond of Alaska, who introduced legislation both in November 1938 (H.R. 8344) and January 1939 (H.R. 883, "To protect and preserve the salmon fishing of Alaska") was cognizant of the state of Japanese international problems at the time. He explicitly argued that "the preoccupation of Japan in China causes [him] to believe that now would be an admirable time to enact legislation." (Memorandum of conversation by Mr. Leo Sturgeon of the Division of Far Eastern Affairs, January 19, 1939, *Foreign Relations*, ibid., p. 209.)

39. Bingham, *Report*.

40. Acting secretary of state (Welles) to ambassador in Japan (Grew), December 16, 1938, *Foreign Relations 1939*, II, 199-201.

41. The rate of growth of the tuna fleet from the late twenties through the forties was substantial. The fleet operated largely off the west coast of South America. See Henry Reiff, *The United States and the Treaty Law of the Sea*.

42. Memorandum of conversation by Leo D. Sturgeon, Division of Far Eastern Affairs, January 19, 1939, *Foreign Relations 1939*, II, 209.

43. The ambassador in Japan (Grew) to the secretary of state, January 26, 1939, *Foreign Relations*, ibid., pp. 210-211.

44. A concise history of U.S. offshore oil operations is found in unpublished memorandum to the president from the Interdepartmental Committee on Submerged Lands, *Re: Submerged Oil Lands*, March 13, 1940.

45. Drilling in the enclosed waters of Lake Maracaibo, however, had taken place in waters of over 100 feet by 1945. U.S. Congress, Senate, Special Committee Investigating Petroleum Resources, *Hearings, Investigation of Petroleum Resources*, 79th Cong., 1st sess., June 1945, p. 198.

46. See unpublished letter from L. F. McCollum, Standard Oil Company, to the secretary of state, August 5, 1943. National Archives Record Group 48.

47. Unpublished, National Archives Record Group 48.

48. Unpublished memorandum from Office of Solicitor, Department of the Interior, to Interdepartmental Committee to Study Title to Submerged Oil Lands, October 17, 1939. National Archives Record Group 48.

49. For summary information on all these hearings, see U.S. House, Senate, House Judiciary Committee and Special Subcommittee of the Senate Judiciary Committee, *Title to Lands Beneath Tidal and Navigable Waters*; and U.S. Senate, Committee on Interior and Insular Affairs, *Submerged Lands*. See also unpublished memorandum of Interdepartmental Committee on Submerged Lands, March 13, 1940.

50. Ickes, *Secret Diary*, II, entries for May 2, 1937, 217, and March 4, 1938, 330-331.

51. Unpublished memorandum for the first assistant secretary from solicitor, Department of the Interior, Nathan R. Margold, September 16, 1938. National Archives Record Group 48.

52. Unpublished memorandum to the president from first assistant secretary, Department of the Interior, E. K. Burlew, January 16, 1939. National Archives Record Group 48.

53. Unpublished, National Archives Record Group 48.

54. Unpublished memorandum to the secretary of the interior from the assistant solicitor, March 16, 1940. National Archives Record Group 48.

55. See Lorena K. Francis, "End of Tideland Oil Litigation Expected if Wilkie Elected," *Los Angeles Times*, November 1, 1940.

56. Unpublished memorandum from solicitor to secretary of the interior, March 31, 1942. National Archives Record Group 48.

57. Ickes, *Secret Diary*, I, 161.

58. Ickes, *Secret Diary*, II, 338-339; 344-347.

59. Ibid., pp. 630-631; 664-669.

60. Unpublished letter from Ickes to secretary of war, January 22, 1941. Unpublished letter from acting secretary of interior to Representative Dimond, January 27, 1941. National Archives Record Group 48.

61. Interior officials made it clear to State that they intended to be included in any deliberations regarding Alaska salmon. See, for instance, unpublished letter from acting secretary of interior to secretary of state, January 27, 1941. National Archives Record Group 48.

62. Unpublished letter from Secretary Ickes to President Roosevelt, March 18, 1942. National Archives Record Group 48.

63. Unpublished letter from Secretary Ickes to President Roosevelt, July 14, 1942. National Archives Record Group 48.

64. Executive Order 9204, July 21, 1942, F.R. Doc. 42-6998.

65. See, for instance, unpublished letters from Ickes to the secretary of commerce, July 31, 1942; from Ickes to the editor of the *Fishing Gazette* (August 11, 1942); from Ickes to the president of the National Wildlife Federation (August 14, 1942). National Archives Record Group 48.

66. Unpublished letter from Secretary Ickes to President Roosevelt, August 13, 1942. National Archives Record Group 48.

67. Ickes, *Secret Diary*, III, 272-275; 542-569; 590-613.

68. Executive Order No. 9276, December 2, 1942.

69. Unpublished memorandum for the secretary from C. E. Jackson, F. W. Lee, I. D. Wolfsohn of General Land Office, May 28, 1943. National Archives Record Group 48.

70. *Foreign Relations 1945*, II, 1481.

71. See unpublished memorandum, Summary of Material of Interest to Department from hearings on S. 930 held in January 1944, before a subcommittee of the Senate Committee on Commerce, March 2, 1944. National Archives Record Group 48.

72. Under the general supervision of Assistant Secretary of State Breckinridge Long, the committee was composed of representatives of the War Production Board, Committee on Political Planning, Division of Far Eastern Affairs, Division of European Affairs, Division of the American Republics, and the assistant to the legal adviser. *Foreign Relations 1945*, II, 1482.

73. In 1943, the State Department was unequivocally in favor of "regional approaches" to regulation, namely dividing the Atlantic into two distinct regulatory arrangements. Unpublished memorandum, telegram to American embassy, London, by Breckinridge Long, acting for Stettinius, October 19, 1943 (FW 811 0145/8-1944). Among the issues on North Atlantic fisheries that were due to be addressed at the meeting were Canadian efforts to expand the scope of a proposed Northeast Atlantic fisheries convention to the shores of Canada and the preference of others to extend its scope even further to the shores of the United States.

74. *Foreign Relations 1945*, II, 1482.

75. Memorandum from the secretary of state to President Roosevelt, June 10, 1943, *Foreign Relations*, ibid.

76. While documents pertaining to the exclusion of the Navy are not available in the unpublished records or in *Foreign Relations of the United States*, it may be surmised that there was some debate over the composition of the study group. Certainly a lengthy period of time elapsed between Hull's memo of June 10, 1943 recommending Navy's participation and a presidential memo of May 11, 1944 approving the (June 5, 1943) Ickes request for a study.

77. The president's memorandum to the secretary of the interior is described in Ickes's memo to Hull of May 23, 1944, *Foreign Relations 1945*, v, 1483.

78. Unpublished memorandum for the secretary of the interior from the assistant secretary, Michael Straus, May 22, 1944. National Archives Record Group 48.

79. This statement was disingenuous at best since elsewhere he pointed out that there is no "necessary connection between our plan to extend American sovereignty in the soil beneath the sea" and the federal-state issue. Memorandum from Ickes to Solicitor Fowler Harper, August 14, 1944.

80. Unpublished letter from Harold Ickes, petroleum administrator for war, to Senator Harry S. Truman, chairman, Special Committee Investigating the National Defense Program, April 14, 1943. National Archives Record Group 48.

81. Unpublished memorandum to the president, February 28, 1944. National Archives Record Group 48.

82. Unpublished memorandum for the secretary from the solicitor, Fowler Harper, February 28, 1944. National Archives Record Group 48.

83. Unpublished letter from the attorney general to the president, June 9, 1944. National Archives Record Group 48.

84. Unpublished letter from the secretary of the interior to the attorney general, June 15, 1944. National Archives Record Group 48.

85. Unpublished memorandum from the solicitor to the secretary of the interior, July 6, 1944. National Archives Record Group 48.

86. Unpublished letter from Hull to Ickes, June 28, 1944. National Archives Record Group 48.

87. Memoranda between Long and Straus, July 7 and July 10, 1944. National Archives Record Group 48.

88. This sequence of events is described in *Foreign Relations 1945*, II, 1483-1485.

89. Memorandum by L. D. Sturgeon, Office of Economic Affairs, on "Interdepartmental Conference in re Policy for the Protection of Marine Resources," July 15, 1944.

90. Unpublished memorandum from Frederick D. G. Ribble, executive assistant to Assistant Secretary Long, dated July 19, 1944; also memorandum by L. D. Sturgeon, Office of Economic Affairs, July 19, 1944 in Whiteman, *Digest*, 4, 950.

91. The Interior Department's efforts to guide the direction of U.S. policy into a unilateral channel met with early success in the area of fisheries. When Interior first came on the scene, the State Department's committee was beginning to pursue international approaches to the fisheries problem. On June 14, 1943, for instance, the Canadian government had proposed to the Department of State that new principles for the protection of coastal fisheries be worked out between the U.S. and Canada. Eager to stave off congressional legislation (S. 930 on Alaska fisheries was pending), the State Department committee began informal discussions in January and February 1944 with the governments of Newfoundland and Canada. Under consideration were specific proposals dealing with coastal fisheries jurisdiction in the East Pacific and the Northwest Atlantic. Another meeting was scheduled for the summer of 1944. But further discussions with Canada and Newfoundland to negotiate a joint approach to fisheries jurisdiction never occurred. Instead, the State Department committee was successfully coopted into the interdepartmental study group proposed by the Department of the Interior and approved by the president on May 11, 1944.

The history of the State Department's committee is found in memorandum by William V. Bishop, Office of Legal Adviser, "Summary Report on Department Fisheries Committee and Informal Discussions with Canada and Newfoundland," September 4, 1944, in Whiteman, *Digest*, 4, 951-952.

92. Unpublished memorandum to Mr. Long from Mr. Ribble, July 28, 1944; unpublished memo from Mr. Bevans to Barron and Spaulding, July 26, 1944, Department of State MS File 811.0145/7-2644.

93. Memorandum, Bevans to Barron and Spaulding, ibid.

94. L. D. Sturgeon to Mr. Hawkins (director, Office of Economic Affairs), no title, August 7, 1944 and August 8, 1944. Of the interested State Department offices, ECA through Mr. Sturgeon had been most continuously involved with the ongoing negotiations with Canada and Newfoundland. Unpublished Office of Economic Affairs memo to BC, ECA, A-L, A-S, Le, FE, A-M, BF, no title, August 14, 1944. A meeting in Canada in late August may have provided ECA with a further interest in slowing the pace of the decision-making process in Washington. Mr. Sturgeon had been involved on behalf of State in the salmon controversy of 1937.

95. Memorandum by the Office of Economic Affairs, September 23, 1944, *Foreign Relations 1945*, II, 1485-1487.

96. Unpublished documents available in the National Archives (Record Group 48) provide a glimpse of earlier ECA attitudes: Office of Economic Affairs, Memorandum on Interdepartmental Conference in re Policy for the Protection of Marine Resources, July 15, 1944; Division of Research and Publication, Memorandum on Meeting in Mr. Long's office, July 25, to consider statements of policy respecting offshore resources, July 26, 1944; Memo from Sturgeon to Hawkins, Office of Economic Affairs on August 7, 1944 and August 8, 1944.

97. ECA's original plan was to declare U.S. coastal fisheries policy by

means of an exchange of notes between the U.S., Canada, and Newfoundland; Division of Research and Publication, Report of Meeting, July 26, 1944.

98. Proposed Decision with Respect to Fisheries in Certain Areas of the High Seas; Proposed Decision with Respect to Natural Resources of the Subsoil and Sea Bed of the Continental Shelf, September 23, 1944. Department of State MS Files.

99. See untitled, unpublished memorandum from B. L. (Breckinridge Long) to Mr. Hackworth (the Legal Adviser's Office) dated March 8, 1944. Department of State MS Files.

100. Memorandum by the acting secretary of state to the assistant secretary of state (Long), November 28, 1944. *Foreign Relations 1945*, II, 1487.

101. Letter from the secretary of state to the secretary of the interior, *Foreign Relations 1945*, II, 1488.

102. According to a footnote in *Foreign Relations 1945*, II, 1488. The memorandum itself was not included.

103. Letter from the secretary of state to the secretary of the interior, December 19, 1944. *Foreign Relations 1945*, II, 1488-1489.

104. Ibid.

105. *Foreign Relations 1945*, II, 1491, n. 29. The proposed draft memorandum of December 19, 1944 was not included in its entirety.

106. Letter from the secretary of state to the secretary of the interior, December 19, 1944. Department of State MS Files.

107. *Foreign Relations 1945*, II, 1491, n. 29.

108. Memorandum by the acting secretary of state and the secretary of the interior to President Roosevelt, January 22, 1945, *Foreign Relations 1945*, II, 1491.

109. Eugene H. Dooman, a member of the original department committee and special assistant to Assistant Secretary of State Dunn, was given overall responsibility from April-August 1945 for conducting the informal conversations with foreign governments on the extension of offshore jurisdiction (*Foreign Relations 1945*, II, 1493). Leo D. Sturgeon of the Office of Economic Affairs played an active role through 1944. Subsequently, W. C. Thorp of the International Trade Policy Division took up the task of pressing for genuinely international approaches and for equality of treatment on matters of natural resources.

110. The continuity of personnel at the lower levels of the State Department was only somewhat better. Breckinridge Long, the assistant secretary of state to Hull, headed the departmental committee appointed in May 1943 and was actively concerned with marine resources through 1944. The office of the Legal Advisor, under Green H. Hackworth, played a continuous if limited role from May 1943 through the promulgation of the proclamation (*Foreign Relations 1945*, II, 1482).

111. Edward Stettinius replaced Cordell Hull on November 27, 1944;

James Byrnes succeeded Stettinius in June 1945. Harry Truman assumed the presidency upon the death of Roosevelt, April 12, 1945.

112. Explanatory Statement on the Protection and Conservation of Coastal Fisheries, *Foreign Relations 1945*, II, 1496-1497.

113. Ibid., p. 1489.

114. Explanatory Statement on the Proper Utilization and Development of Natural Resources of the Subsoil and Sea Bed of the Continental Shelf, *Foreign Relations 1945*, II, 1499.

115. Ibid., pp. 1500-1501.

116. Ibid., p. 1501.

117. Ibid., p. 1500.

118. Ibid., pp. 1502-1503.

119. The new president was explicit both publicly and privately re his intention "to continue both the foreign and domestic policies of the Roosevelt administration." Harry S. Truman, *Memoirs*, I.

120. *Foreign Relations 1945*, II, 1493, n. 30.

121. Ibid., pp. 1493-1496.

122. Memorandum by the acting secretary of state and the secretary of the interior to President Truman, April 30, 1945, *Foreign Relations 1945*, II, 1503-1504.

123. Signed as the acting secretary of state.

124. Memorandum by Mr. Eugene H. Dooman, special assistant to the assistant secretary of state (Dunn), to Mr. William Phillips, special assistant to the secretary of state, June 15, 1945. *Foreign Relations 1945*, II, 1511.

125. Harry S. Truman, *Memoirs*, II, 480-487. The president sketches out his difficulties with a Congress pressed by "private oil interests seeking to exploit these oil rich areas without federal control and supervision." Despite a federal court ruling in 1947, twice upheld by the U.S. Supreme Court, that the federal government had dominant rights, the Congress passed legislation in 1952 confirming the states' rights. Truman vetoed it on May 29, 1952. While the incoming Republican administration promised support for the states, Truman maintained his stance and four days before leaving office issued an executive order setting aside the continental shelf as a naval petroleum reserve to be administered by the secretary of the navy.

126. *Foreign Relations 1945*, II, 1511.

127. Memorandum by the acting secretary of state and the secretary of the interior (Ickes) to President Truman, with handwritten answer from President Truman thereon, April 30, 1945. *Foreign Relations 1945*, II, 1504. Also unpublished memorandum for Joseph C. Grew, acting secretary, Department of State from Harry S. Truman, president, Subject: Resources of the Continental Shelf and Coastal Fisheries. National Archives Record Group 48.

128. The U.S. Archives seem to be missing a number of documents which are cited but not published in *Foreign Relations 1945*, II. See p. 1525, n. 69.

129. August 17, 1945. *Foreign Relations 1945*, II, 1525.

130. Information on the strong negative British response to the policy seems not to have been shared with Thorp's office.

131. William Appleton Williams, *The Tragedy of American Diplomacy* (New York: Dell, 1972).

132. John Spanier, *American Foreign Policy Since World War II*, chap. 1; Norman A. Graebner, *Cold War Diplomacy, 1945-60*.

133. Unpublished memorandum, summary of material of interest to Department from hearings on S. 930 held in January 1944 before a subcommittee of the Senate Committee on Commerce, March 2, 1944. National Archives Record Group 48.

134. Unpublished memorandum. National Archives Record Group 48.

135. Memorandum by the acting secretary of state and the secretary of the interior to President Roosevelt, January 22, 1945, *Foreign Relations 1945*, II, 1491.

136. Memorandum by Mr. Eugene H. Dooman, special assistant to the assistant secretary of state (Dunn), to the assistant secretary of state (Acheson), May 15, 1945, *Foreign Relations 1945*, II, 1509.

137. Letter from the secretary of state to the secretary of the interior, July 5, 1945, *Foreign Relations 1945*, II, 1519.

138. Ibid., p. 1520.

139. *Foreign Relations 1945*, II, 1527, n. 72.

140. The Byrnes appointment was prompted by the new president's concern over succession to the office of the president. Since the secretary of state was next in line at that time, Truman was concerned to find a secretary of state who had held elective office. Moreover, Byrnes had narrowly missed the nomination as Roosevelt's running mate. (Truman, *Memoirs*, I, 22-23.)

141. *Foreign Relations 1945*, II, 1516.

142. *Foreign Relations 1945*, II, 1526. Letter from the secretary of state to the secretary of the interior, August 27, 1945.

143. Made on August 3. *Foreign Relations 1945*, II, 1523-1524.

144. What Byrnes did not seem to recognize was that the British offer to divide the shelf area between the two countries was established British policy. In 1942, Britain and Venezuela divided the shelf area in the Gulf of Paria.

145. Letter from the second secretary of the British embassy (Cecil) to Mr. William Bishop, assistant to the legal adviser (Hackworth), *Foreign Relations 1945*, II, 1527. (The British responded to the Truman Proclamations by claiming the continental shelves on behalf of the colonies of Jamaica and the Bahamas.)

146. Letter from the counselor of the British embassy (Wright) to Mr. Eugene H. Dooman, special assistant to the assistant secretary of state (Dunn), July 4, 1945, *Foreign Relations 1945*, II, 1516-1517.

147. Letter from Mr. Eugene H. Dooman, special assistant to the as-

sistant secretary of state (Dunn), to the counselor of the British embassy (Wright), July 6, 1945, *Foreign Relations 1945*, II, 1522-1523. See also pp. 1518-1519.

148. Ibid., p. 1518.

149. Unpublished letter from M. R. Wright to R. Dunbar, Treaty Department, Foreign Office, London, dated July 10, 1945. Department of State MS Files.

150. Letter from the second secretary of the British embassy (Cecil) to Mr. William Bishop, assistant to the legal adviser (Hackworth), August 31, 1945, *Foreign Relations 1945*, II, 1527.

151. Unpublished memorandum from Francis A. Linville (Commodities Division) to Mr. Kennedy (CD) and Mr. Wilcox (International Trade Policy), July 27, 1945, describing conversation with Dr. Finn. Department of State MS Files.

152. Ibid.

153. Letter from J. S. Macdonald, high commissioner for Canada, St. Johns, Newfoundland to W. H. Flinn, commissioner for natural resources, Newfoundland, dated January 25, 1946. (Courtesy, Government of Newfoundland.)

154. Telegram No. 43 to secretary of state for dominion affairs from the governor of Newfoundland, dated July 20, 1945. (Courtesy, Government of Newfoundland.)

155. Memorandum from commissioner for natural resources (Newfoundland) to chairman Newfoundland Fisheries Board, 8 December 1945. (Courtesy, Government of Newfoundland.)

156. Letter from commissioner for natural resources (Newfoundland) to Mr. J. S. Macdonald, high commissioner for Canada, St. Johns, dated December 27, 1945; Memorandum for Commission of Government, Subject: North Atlantic Fisheries Control, from W. H. Flinn, commissioner for natural resources (Nfld.), December 27, 1945. (Courtesy, Government of Newfoundland.)

157. Letter from Cuban chargé (Baron) to Mr. Eugene H. Dooman, special assistant to the assistant secretary of state (Dunn), June 19, 1945, *Foreign Relations 1945*, II, 1513-1514.

158. Four governments were notified of U.S. policy regarding both the shelf and fisheries: Canada, Mexico, United Kingdom, Soviet Union. The other seven were notified only of U.S. fisheries policy: Netherlands, Norway, France, Iceland, Denmark, Cuba, Portugal.

Chapter 3
U.S. FISHERIES PROBLEMS: 1946-1956

1. A notable exception is in U.S. dominance of Japanese postwar fishing policy during the occupation.

2. U.S. Naval War College, *International Law: Situation and Documents,*

1956, pp. 317-324; see also Marjorie Whiteman, *Digest of International Law*, 4, 977-978; Henry Reiff, *The United States and the Treaty Law of the Sea*, p. 274.

3. William C. Herrington, in a letter to the author of February 5, 1977, offers the following explanation for U.S. nonparticipation:

The U.S. did not join in for several reasons. (1) Europeans then were not fishing or fishing to a very minor extent on New England fishing grounds and extensive fishing did not appear imminent. Such Western Atlantic fishing as they did carry on was mostly on the Newfoundland Banks . . . and some off eastern Nova Scotia. (2) the European record on conservation management of fisheries was not very good and their procedures in keeping research (ICES) separate from the management body did not appeal to us as providing the most timely and flexible procedure. We were much more favorably inclined toward the Halibut and Salmon Commission type of organization and there was no possibility the Europeans as a whole would buy this type of organization. If we could get a national conservation program going on Georges Bank haddock, which we were then attempting, we would be in a better position. Then we might get the one or few European countries which later expanded their operations in this area, to participate in a more effective type of management commitment than was possible with the entire European group.

Herrington served as special assistant to the undersecretary for fisheries and wildlife, Department of State, from 1951 to 1966.

4. Telegram sent October 19, 1943 from Washington to the American embassy, London, Department of State MS File 811.0145/8-1944.

5. Letter from Ministry of Agriculture and Fisheries, London, to Department of Natural Resources, Newfoundland, Feb. 12, 1945 (FGB.2420A).

6. Naval War College, *International Law*, 1956, pp. 317-324; Whiteman, *Digest*, 4, 977-980.

7. D'Arcy O'Donnell, "Members Outline Problems Canadian Fishing Industry," *Daily News* (St. John, Newfoundland), September 4, 1946.

8. Canadian embassy, Washington, to secretary of state, June 5, 1947, Department of State MS File 811.0145/6-547.

9. Commonwealth Relations Office to Newfoundland and Canada, 3 September 1947.

10. Commercial Department, British embassy, Washington, to North American Department, London, September 22, 1947 (C.241/36).

11. Ibid.

12. U.S. TIAS 2089; 1 UST 477; 157 UNTS 157. Text may be found in Naval War College, *International Law*, 1956, pp. 324-345.

13. For an excellent overview of Latin American claims see Francisco Orrego Vicuña, *Los Fondos Marinos y Oceánicos* (Santiago: Editorial Andres Bello, 1976), pp. 65-96.

14. UN Legislative Series: *Laws and Regulations on the Regime of the*

High Seas, New York, 1951, ST/LEG/SER.B/1, p. 13; Naval War College, *International Law*, 1956, pp. 185-186; Whiteman, *Digest*, 4, 1219-1220.

15. With the adoption of a new constitution in 1960, this claim was dropped, but not until a number of fishing disputes had arisen with the United States over this and another Mexican claim.

16. Presidential Decree of August 29, 1935, *Diario Oficial*, XCI, No. 54 (August 31, 1935), 1055-1056. It is reprinted in Whiteman, *Digest*, 4, 1209-1210.

17. Much of the correspondence is reprinted in Whiteman, *Digest*, 4, 1210-1219, and U.S. Department of State, *Foreign Relations of the United States 1936*, v, 758-770. It is noteworthy that Texas also based its claim to a nine-mile band of the continental shelf on the same 1848 treaty and was successful in the U.S. courts (May 31, 1960, *U.S. v. Texas*, 363 U.S. 1), although the Supreme Court stipulated that its decision was for domestic purposes and did not relate to "the effectiveness of this boundary as against other nations."

18. Whiteman, *Digest*, 4, 1226.

19. *Foreign Relations 1946*, XI, 1056 and *Foreign Relations 1948*, IX, 645. As late as the 1920s, the two governments shared similar attitudes toward offshore jurisdiction and in 1926 had agreed on a 50-mile conservation zone. The U.S. subsequently repudiated this agreement. Whiteman, *Digest*, 4, 1226.

20. Carmen Baez, "Plataforma Geografica Continental," *El Nacional*, October 31, 1945.

21. Telegram from Department of State to American embassy, Mexico City, December 11, 1947, Dept. of State MS File 812.628/12-1147.

22. Draft Treaty with Respect to the Pacific Fisheries of Common Concern and Protocol, August 20, 1945, Dept. of State MS File FW 812.-628/4-1445.

23. Wilbert McLeod Chapman, "The United States Fish Industry and the 1958 and 1960 United Nations Conferences on the Law of the Sea," p. 37 in *The Law of the Sea*.

24. *Foreign Relations 1946*, XI, 1054-1058.

25. Ibid., p. 1056.

26. Ibid., p. 1061.

27. *Foreign Relations 1947*, VIII, 805 ff.

28. The conditions stipulated by the United States in the Truman Proclamation for the establishment of a fishery conservation zone and reiterated to the Mexicans were (1) if warranted by scientific investigations, and (2) if agreed to by nations which had previously also fished in the area in question. Of note is the fact that as of late 1946 State officials were still concerned to protect the U.S. option to unilaterally implement conservation zones off its own shores. *Foreign Relations 1946*, XI, 1065.

29. *Foreign Relations 1946*, XI, 1062-1067.

30. Whiteman, *Digest*, 4, 1223-1224.

31. Memorandum Sobre Dos Proyectos de Tratados de Pesca y Protocol Presentados por los Estados Unidos de America al Gobierno de Mexico, January 27, 1947, Dept. of State MS File 812.628/1-3147.

32. *Foreign Relations 1947*, VIII, 804-805.

33. U.S. TIAS 2094; 1 UST 513; 99 UNTS 3. Text of treaty may be found in Department of State Press Release 53, issued January 25, 1949.

34. Whiteman, *Digest*, 4, 1226-1227.

35. *Foreign Relations 1948*, IX, 263-264.

36. Whiteman, *Digest*, 4, 1230.

37. Amendment to the Constitution of Panama, Article 209, added by decree No. 9938, March 1, 1946, *Gaceta Oficial*, 4 March 1946. See UN Legislative Series *High Seas*, ST/LEG/SER.B/1, p. 15.

38. Decree No. 449, December 17, 1946.

39. Decree No. 1386 (Art. 2) Concerning Mineral Reserves, *Boletin Oficial*, 17 March 1944. Text in UN Legislative Series *High Seas*, ST/LEG/SER.B/1, p. 3.

40. Presidential Decree No. 14,708, Concerning National Sovereignty over the Epicontinental Sea and the Continental Shelf, October 11, 1946, *Boletin Oficial*, 5 Dec. 1946. Text in UN Legislative Series *High Seas*, ibid., p. 4.

41. Whiteman, *Digest*, 4, 793-794.

42. *Foreign Relations 1948*, IX, 298.

43. Memorandum of conversation, tuna fisheries and conservation measures, November 24, 1948, Dept. of State MS File 711.188/11-2448.

44. Aide-mémoire delivered by U.S. embassy to Foreign Office on June 18, 1947, Enclosure No. 1, Dispatch 69, from American embassy, San Jose, August 14, 1947, Dept. of State MS File 818.628A/8-1447.

45. Letter from Pacific Exploration Co. to Costa Rican chamber of commerce, San Jose, April 22, 1947, Dept. of State MS File 818.628A/8-1447.

46. Letter from chargé d'affaires to secretary of state, regarding Costa Rican fisheries and proposed legislation, August 14, 1947. Dept. of State MS File 818.628A/8-1447.

47. Aide-mémoire, Enclosure No. 1, Dispatch 69, dated August 14, 1947, from the American embassy, San Jose, Dept. of State MS File 818.628A/8-1447.

48. *Foreign Relations 1947*, VIII, 598-599.

49. Ibid., pp. 599-601.

50. Promulgated in the *Gaceta Oficial*, September 27, 1947.

51. Decree No. 5, October 18, 1947.

52. *Foreign Relations 1947*, VIII, 601-602.

53. Ibid., pp. 602-603.

54. Decree No. 116, *Gaceta Oficial*, July 28, 1948.

55. *Foreign Relations 1948*, IX, 263-264.

56. Cable No. 375, *Subject: Decree No. 116*, American embassy to secretary of state, July 28, 1948, Dept. of State MS File 819.0145/7-2848.

57. *Foreign Relations 1948*, IX, 265-268.

58. Memorandum of conversation, November 24, 1948, tuna fisheries and conservation measures, Dept. of State MS File 711-188/11-2448.

59. Decree Law No. 190, *Gaceta Oficial*, October 9, 1948.

60. Airgram 3089, American embassy, Costa Rica, dispatched October 13, 1948, Dept. of State MS File 818.0145/10-1348.

61. UN Legislative Series *High Seas*, ST/LEG/SER.B/1, p. 8.

62. U.S. TIAS 2044; 1 UST 230; 80 UNTS 3. On the evolution of IATTC to the mid-1960s, see J. E. Carroz, *Establishment, Structure, Functions and Actions of International Fisheries Bodies, II, Inter-American Tropical Tuna Commission (IATTC)*, Fisheries Technical Paper No. 58 FIb/T58 (Rome: FAO, 1965).

63. Panama adhered in 1953 (Panamanian ambassador to the secretary of state, note No. D-1107, September 4, 1953, Dept. of State MS File 611.0061/9-453; excerpt of telegram also in Whiteman, *Digest*, 4, 1033). Ecuador adhered in 1961 (American embassy, Quito, to Department of State, dispatch No. 436, February 14, 1961, Dept. of State MS File 371.8245/2-1461). Mexico adhered in 1964 (*Department of State Bulletin*, No. 1286, February 17, 1964, p. 269).

64. UN Legislative Series *High Seas*, ST/LEG/SER.B/1, p. 9.

65. Scholars not involved in the initial process of selecting a zone have subsequently sought to justify the 200-mile figure on a number of grounds. One argument is that 200 miles represents the width of the Humboldt Current off the coasts of Chile and Peru (Garcia Sayan, *Notas sobre la Soberania Maritime del Peru* [1955]). Related arguments based on one or another form of nature's determinism include (1) the relationship between the offshore fisheries and the guano birds, (2) the relationship between the land and the waters, and (3) the relationship of the narrow continental shelf to the vast expanse of ocean (lecture delivered by director of sovereignty and frontiers, Ministry of Foreign Affairs, at the CAEM Lima, April 9, 1970).

Others have sought in vain for legal precedents in the actions of other countries. One such precedent was a 200-mile patrol zone reportedly declared by President Roosevelt on September 5, 1939. The width of this zone was attributed to the prevailing technology, that is, the range in which radar operated (Andres A. Aramburu Menchaca, *Historia de las 200 Millas de Mar Territorial* [Lima: Universidad de Piura, 1973]). No evidence of a presidential proclamation of a 200-mile zone can be found, however, in governmental records of the period or subsequent compilations of U.S. claims to "defensive sea areas," "maritime control areas," and "customs enforcement areas" (U.S. Naval War College, *International Law, 1948-1949*, XLVI, 157-180 and *International Law, 1956*, pp. 601-607). The president's September 5, 1939 declaration of neutrality refers only to "areas under national jurisdiction" (Proclamation Concerning Neutrality of United States, *Federal Register*, 4, No. 171, Sept. 6, 1939, 3809-3812; Executive Order 8233, F.R. Doc. 39-3240, filed Sept. 5, 1939). Similarly, a subsequent elaboration of naval duties under this proclamation makes no reference to a

200-mile zone. (*Federal Register*, 4, No. 172, 3819-3823.) Naval duties, as elaborated by the president's secretary, were to include the establishment of a patrol force of at least 150 vessels to provide intelligence on the movements of belligerent submarines and warships. As the patrol force grew, the area covered would be extended gradually "until it has reached the waters adjacent to Puerto Rico, the Antilles and the Canal Zone." Ultimately the patrol system would operate up to 200 to 300 miles off the U.S. shores ("U.S. Coastal Patrol Swings into Action," *New York Times*, Sept. 7, 1939, p. 13). Roosevelt was explicit that the patrol was merely to gain information and did not determine U.S. territorial limits. He preferred to define America's territorial waters flexibly—as extending "as far as our interests need it to go out." (Press Conference 579, September 15, 1939, in *Complete Presidential Press Conferences of Franklin D. Roosevelt*, 14 [New York: De Capo Press, 1972], 166-174.) As for a connection between the size of a patrol zone and the state of military technology, it should be noted that the operational range of radar was less than 200 miles in 1939.

66. "Declaration of Panama," *Department of State Bulletin*, 1, No. 15 (Oct. 7, 1939), 331-333.

67. Letter to author from Jermán L. Fischer, March 15, 1976.

68. *Foreign Relations 1944*, II, 934 ff.

69. The first international agreement was negotiated under the auspices of the League of Nations in 1931 (Convention for the Regulation of Whaling, concluded September 24, 1931; USTS 880; 49 *Stat.* 3079; 155 LNTS 349; signed but not ratified by 26 states). The convention was limited to baleen (whale bone) whales and did not fix a total or species limit on harvesting. Then in 1937, an Agreement on the Regulation of Whaling (signed June 8, 1937 by nine governments; USTS 933; 52 *Stat.* 1460; 190 LNTS 79) introduced several new principles into the conservation of whales. It provided for inspectors, certain closed areas, an open season in waters south of 40° south latitude from December 8 to March 7, and a maximum of six months operation per year for any land station. A review conference was held the following year and adopted a protocol amending the 1937 agreement (Protocol Amending the Agreement of 1937, London, June 24, 1938, USTS 944; 53 *Stat.* 1794; 196 LNTS 131). A further conference was held before the war and adopted several additional recommendations (*Department of State Bulletin*, 1, No. 2 [July 8, 1939]). An excellent summary of prewar whaling and whaling agreements may be found in L. Larry Leonard, *International Regulation of Fisheries*, Monograph No. 7 (New York: Carnegie Endowment for International Peace, 1944), pp. 98-109.

70. *Foreign Relations 1944*, II, pp. 942-943.

71. Ibid., pp. 939 ff.

72. Supplementary Protocol Concerning Whaling, signed at London, October 5, 1945; British Treaty Series, No. 44 (1946), Cmd. 6941; Sen. Ex. J. 79 Cong., 1 Sess., November 23, 1945.

73. 146 British and Foreign State Papers (1946), p. 498; British Treaty Series No. 44 (1946), Cmd. 6941.

74. U.S. TIAS 1708; 62 *Stat.* 1577; 161 UNTS 361.

75. James E. Scarff, "The International Management of Whales, Dolphins and Porpoises: An Interdisciplinary Assessment (Part One)," *Ecology Law Quarterly*, 6, No. 2 (1977), 352.

76. *Foreign Relations 1947*, VI, 195 ff.

77. Ibid., p. 212 ff.

78. Whiteman, *Digest*, 4, 1056.

79. Story may be found in Tobías Barros, "Las Doscientos Millas," *Mercurio*, July 19, 1974; also in letter from Jermán Fischer to author, 15 March 1976.

80. Article by Juan Bardina, *La Semana Internacional*, Valparaiso, January 1940.

81. "Declaration of Panama," *Department of State Bulletin*, 1, No. 15 (October 7, 1939), 331-333. Among the nations represented at the Consultative Meeting of Foreign Ministers of the American Republics, Brazil explicitly declared that "the sea outside territorial waters, only three miles from our coast . . . not only is not ours, but in it we are at the mercy of any action contrary to the free and peaceful expansion of our sovereignty."

82. The U.S. government was responsible for determining the size of the security zone in the Declaration of Panama. The State Department's Office of the Geographer was first asked to draw zones using radii ranging from 300 to 1,000 miles. The 300-mile radius was determined to be adequate and a map embodying this width was sent to President Franklin Roosevelt. Roosevelt personally drew the straight lines linking the outermost points of the 300-mile circles. It was this map, only slightly altered by the Office of the Geographer, that became the officially delineated zone for the Declaration of Panama. For the accurate map and description of its origins, see *Foreign Relations 1939*, V, 35.

83. President Gonzalez evidences his enthusiasm for this policy in Gabriel Gonzalez Videla, *Memorias* (Santiago: Editorial Gabriela Mistral, 1975), pp. 835-837.

84. *Foreign Relations 1948*, IX, 731-732.

85. Bobbie B. Smetherman and Robert M. Smetherman, *Territorial Seas and Inter-American Relations*, p. 91; W. M. Chapman Memo to Harold F. Cary, "Disposition of the Marine Research Committee," January 24, 1965, Wilbert McLeod Chapman Collection, Manuscript Division, University of Washington, Seattle, Washington (hereafter cited as W. M. Chapman Collection).

86. Presidential Decree No. 781 of August 1, 1947. UN Legislative Series *High Seas*, ST/LEG/SER.B/1, p. 16; Whiteman, *Digest*, 4, 797-798.

87. For text of, and preparatory work on, the treaty, see *Foreign Relations 1947*, VIII, 59-60, 79-80 and Council on Foreign Relations, *Documents on American Foreign Relations 1947*, pp. 531-543.

88. Telegrams to Washington from U.S. embassies contain pleas for clarification of policy and instructions on how to proceed.

89. For a discussion of these forces see Bernard C. Cohen, *The Political Process and Foreign Policy*, chap. 12.

90. Subsequent to his government service, Mr. Chapman went to work for the American Tunaboat Association and Ralston Purina.

91. Approved August 8, 1956, 70 *Stat.* 1119; 16 U.S.C. 742a-742j; Whiteman, *Digest*, 4, 939-940.

92. U.S., President, *Dwight D. Eisenhower 1956, Public Papers of the Presidents of the United States* (Washington, D.C.: Office of the Federal Register, National Archives and Records Service, 1958), pp. 672-673; Whiteman, *Digest*, 4, 940.

93. Mr. Chapman explained U.S. fisheries policy at length in a speech before the California State Chamber of Commerce at San Francisco on December 2, 1948. The speech was circulated among U.S. embassies abroad, and was reprinted in the *Department of State Bulletin*, 26, No. 498 (January 16, 1949), 67-80.

94. Whiteman, *Digest*, 4, 793-799.

95. Smetherman and Smetherman, *Territorial Seas*, p. 91.

96. Letter to author from August Felando, American Tunaboat Association, February 22, 1977.

97. Peru seized a U.S. tuna vessel in 1947. (Thomas Wolff, "Peruvian-United States Relations Over Maritime Fishing: 1945-1969," Law of the Sea Institute, Occasional Paper No. 4, March 1970.)

98. Bobbie B. Smetherman and Robert M. Smetherman, "The CEP Claims, U.S. Tuna Fishing and Inter-American Relations," *Orbis*, No. 3 (Fall 1971), p. 955.

99. The Political Constitution of 1 November 1950 (Art. 5), UN Legislative Series *High Seas*, ST/LEG/SER.B/1, p. 15.

100. Congressional Decree of 6 November 1950, UN Legislative Series *High Seas*, ST/LEG/SER.B/1/Add 1, July 1952.

101. Presidential Decree No. 28,840, 8 November 1950, UN Legislative Series *High Seas*, ST/LEG/SER.B/1, p. 299.

102. Naval War College, *International Law*, 1956, p. 463.

103. Ibid., p. 460. Constitution of El Salvador (Art. 7), 149 *Diario Oficial*, No. 196, Sept. 8, 1950; Whiteman, *Digest*, 4, 801-802; UN Legislative Series *High Seas*, ST/LEG/SER.B/1, p. 300.

104. Whiteman, *Digest*, 4, 802; *Department of State Bulletin*, 29, January 1, 1954, 24.

105. Naval War College, *International Law*, 1956, pp. 464-466.

106. Congressional Decree No. 25 (approving Presidential Decree No. 96 of 28 January 1950), 17 January 1951, *La Gaceta*, 76, No. 14306 (January 22, 1951), 1; Naval War College, *International Law*, 1956, pp. 464-466.

107. There seems to have been some confusion in the drafting of the Ecuadorian law. While the law itself specifies a territorial sea at twelve Spanish leagues, subsequent Ecuadorian clarifications have referred to twelve

miles. Maritime Hunting and Fishing Law (Decree No. 003, February 22, 1951), Ano III, *Registro Oficial*, No. 756, March 6, 1951, pp. 6219-6220; Whiteman, *Digest*, 4, 799-800; UN Legislative Series *High Seas*, ST/LEG/ SER.B/1/Add 1, July 1952.

108. Thomas Wolff, "Something Fishy in Ecuador," *Latin American Digest*, 9, No. 3 (Spring 1975), 17.

109. American ambassador at Quito to Department of State, Dispatch 6, July 3, 1951, enclosing copy of note No. 355, June 7, 1951, Department of State MS File 722.022-7/351; Whiteman, *Digest*, 4, 800-801.

110. On the issue of baselines, England was disputing Norway's claim to straight baselines off her shores. The ICJ decision of December 18, 1951 (ICJ Reports, 1951, p. 116) supported Norway's claim.

111. Naval War College, *International Law*, 1956, pp. 401-502.

112. U.S. Congress, House, Committee on Merchant Marine and Fisheries, *Hearings to Protect Rights of United States Vessels on High Seas*, on HR 9584, 83rd Cong., 2nd Sess., July 2, 1954, p. 20.

113. Texts of agreements reproduced in *Revista Peruana de Derecho Internacional*, xiv, No. 45 (Jan.-June 1954), 104-113; translated into English in Naval War College, *International Law*, 1956, pp. 265-274.

114. The use of these terms rather than "freedom of the seas" implied a full territorial sea claim. The wording, however, is assumed by many to have been a mistake. Karin Hjertonsson, *The New Law of the Sea*, pp. 25-26; Francisco Orrego Vicuña, *Los Fondos Marinos y Oceánicos*, p. 93.

115. Executive Decree No. 275, February 7, 1955. *Registro Oficial*, 24 January 1956.

116. Legislative Resolution No. 12305, May 6, 1955. *El Peruano*, 12 May 1955.

117. Presidential Decree No. 0160, January 29, 1952, published in *Registro Oficial*, No. 1027, January 31, 1952.

118. Law No. 1166, July 16, 1952.

119. Whiteman, *Digest*, 4, 1092-1096.

120. Naval War College, *International Law*, 1956, p. 289; Whiteman, *Digest*, 4, 1198-1200.

121. "Judgment of Peruvian Port Officer," in Naval War College, *International Law*, 1956, pp. 289-294; Whiteman, *Digest*, 4, 1062-1070.

122. Thomas Wolff, "Peruvian-United States Relations," p. 9.

123. P.L. 680, August 27, 1954 in U.S., *Statutes at Large*, 89th Cong., LXXIX, 1965, p. 660.

124. S. A. Bayitch, *Interamerican Law of Fisheries*, pp. 39-40.

125. Naval War College, *International Law*, 1956, pp. 448-450. Countries such as France adopted the position that, although the claim was illegal, there was no need to protest it since the French government had not received official notification.

126. William Herrington, in a letter to the author of February 5, 1977, explains it thus: "To move the argument regarding the requirements for

sound conservation and sustainable yields, from the narrow dispute between the U.S. fishery experts and those of the CEP countries (mostly lawyers) was one of the principal reasons the U.S. pressed for a U.N. conference which would include leading fishery experts and international lawyers from all countries. We were also impressed with the need to develop world understanding of the importance of conservation considerations as fishing operations expanded and to develop agreement on the measures and research required."

127. *Revista Peruana de Derecho Internacional,* xiv, No. 46 (1954), 276-286. Naval War College, *International Law,* 1956, pp. 275-282.

128. Whiteman, *Digest,* 4, 1198-1199.

129. Ibid., p. 1102.

130. Ibid., pp. 1102-1103, pp. 1200-1201.

131. Whiteman, *Digest,* 4, 1103 and 1089-1101; Naval War College, *International Law,* 1956, pp. 214-237.

132. William Herrington explains this as follows: "Actually the CEP countries had agreed with the step-by-step conclusions regarding the measures required for conservation. When the Conference came to summarize these conclusions they perceived that the final conclusion to which this led was adverse to their position on extreme claims," and stalled accordingly. "They were the exceptions." Letter to the author, February 5, 1977.

133. For a detailed account of the deliberations, see Whiteman, *Digest,* 4, 1101-1110, and documents on pp. 1201-1207.

134. It is interesting that by 1955 the reference contained in the Truman Proclamation to countries that "traditionally fished" a stock had been replaced with a simple reference to countries that "fish" a stock. This may reflect the fact that the U.S. had temporarily succeeded in protecting its own coastal fisheries and that U.S. distant-water fleets were trying to move into new fishing grounds.

135. In August 1954, the U.S. Congress had passed the "Fishermen's Protective Act" (68 *Stat.* 883; 22 U.S.C. 1971-1976) which reimbursed fines levied on U.S. fishing boats seized in waters recognized as high seas by the United States.

136. "Regulations Governing the Issuance of Fishing Permits to Foreign Vessels in the Jurisdictional Waters of Peru," *El Peruano,* January 17, 1956; Smetherman and Smetherman, *Territorial Seas,* p. 25; Frederick Dutton, assistant secretary of state, "Statement on Tuna Fishing Problems," to Subcommittee on International Affairs, House Committee on Foreign Affairs, August 16, 1962, W. M. Chapman Collection; Letter from W. M. Chapman to Mr. Fred E. Taylor, Department of State, April 2, 1956, W. M. Chapman Collection.

137. Thomas Wolff, "Peruvian-United States Relations," p. 18.

138. Ibid.

139. Smetherman and Smetherman, "The CEP Claims," p. 954; David C. Loring, "The United States-Peruvian 'Fisheries Dispute,'" p. 408.

140. Smetherman and Smetherman, *Territorial Seas,* p. 25.

141. 2 UST 2394; TIAS 2361; 119 UNTS 3; Naval War College, *International Law, 1948-49*, pp. 1-25.

142. Bayitch, *Interamerican Law of Fisheries*, p. 48; Naval War College, *International Law, 1956*, p. 237; Whiteman, *Digest*, 1, 150-151; 4, 68-69.

143. U.S. Congress, *Hearing to Protect Rights of United States Vessels on High Seas*, pp. 39-44; Naval War College, *International Law, 1956*, pp. 238-239.

144. Bayitch, *Interamerican Law*, pp. 49-50.

145. Ibid., pp. 51-52; Naval War College, *International Law, 1956*, pp. 242-244; Whiteman, *Digest*, 4, 1096-1097.

146. Chapman, "The United States Fish Industry," p. 42.

147. Reiff, *Treaty Law*, p. 311.

148. Naval War College, *International Law, 1956*, pp. 245-246; Bayitch, *Interamerican Law*, pp. 52-55; Whiteman, *Digest*, 4, 69-70, 72.

149. Reiff, *Treaty Law*, pp. 312-313.

150. Naval War College, *International Law, 1956*, pp. 246-255; Whiteman, *Digest*, 4, 69-70, 72.

151. Among the U.S. presentations to the conference is one distinguishing the Truman Proclamations from the claims of other countries that had purported to use U.S. actions as precedent. Over eleven years after the promulgation of the Truman Proclamations, U.S. diplomats were still struggling with their aftereffects. Whiteman, *Digest*, 4, 959-961.

152. Naval War College, *International Law, 1956*, p. 263; Reiff, *Treaty Law*, p. 314.

153. Text of resolution and delegation statements may be found in Naval War College, *International Law, 1956*, pp. 256-265; Bayitch, *Interamerican Law*, pp. 55-62; Whiteman, *Digest*, 4, 1111-1113.

154. Ibid.

155. Stillman Wright, chief, Office of Foreign Activities, to commissioner of fish and wildlife service, August 19, 1957; Fish and Wildlife Service Files, Federal Records Center, Suitland, Maryland. 67A-1358, Box 80.

156. Members included China, Australia, the USSR, the Netherlands, Philippines, the United Kingdom, and the United States.

157. *Foreign Relations 1947*, VI, 160-477.

158. Ibid., p. 195.

159. Ibid., p. 179.

160. Ibid., p. 161

161. Ibid., p. 162. William Herrington, in a letter to the author of February 5, 1977, offers the following comments: "At the time (1946-   ) Japan was very short of food and SCAP was intent on encouraging Japanese efforts to increase food production. Australia, USSR and others opposed expansion of Japanese fishing operations on the grounds that Japanese fishermen operated with no regard to conservation principles and the conservation measures applied by others (whaling, etc.). Thus the primary objective behind SCAP's stress on conservation was to reduce the opposition to expanded Japanese fishing operations. The State Department had not cleared

any fisheries policy regarding Japan until the draft prepared in 1951, which included abstention from certain stocks, based on severe conservation requirements."

162. Whiteman, *Digest*, 4, 988-989.

163. Ibid., p. 990. The domestic political impact of this letter is described in Cohen, *The Political Process*, pp. 265-267.

164. U.S., TIAS 2490; 3 UST 3169, 3177; 136 UNTS 45.

165. US., TIAS 2786; 4 UST 380; 205 UNTS 65.

166. Whiteman, *Digest*, 4, 991.

167. Among the proposals considered at the time was one to restrict Japanese fishing within 150 miles from the coastline. Whiteman, *Digest*, 4, 992.

168. Ibid., p. 992.

169. Mr. Herrington's account of the origins of the abstention principle are set out in his letter to the author, February 5, 1977: "The U.S. fishing industry wanted a treaty which would keep Japanese fishing boats out of the Eastern Pacific indefinitely. The Japanese appeared prepared to accept temporary restriction on their operations off the Canadian and U.S. coasts but no more. When I returned from Japan in 1951, with my knowledge of Japanese fisheries and fishery interests and of the concern of the U.S. industry, I had an idea for a solution which I thought might provide a barely acceptable compromise. Essentially it provided that where a country or countries had carried out extensive research and fisheries conservation management for a stock of fish and could show with scientific evidence that they were taking the maximum sustainable yield from that resource, Japan would not fish on such stocks. The determination of full utilization would be subject to continuing proof or the "abstention" would be lost. Such a provision presumably would keep Japan at the least out of the salmon and halibut fisheries along the North American coast as long as the U.S. and Canada maintained sound conservation programs and were making maximum use of the resource. It would allow Japan to enter the fisheries for other species such as Alaskan pollock, codfish, etc. which were much more abundant than salmon and halibut. It would also stimulate the U.S. and Canada to continue to improve their research and management efforts.

"This approach presently secured the support of the Dept. of State, and then the rather reluctant support of the U.S. fishery industry and, following this, of Canada. In the course of prolonged negotiations between the U.S., Canada and Japan, it evolved in its present form of 'abstention.' "

170. Whiteman, *Digest*, 4, 996.

171. Ibid., pp. 1006-1009.

172. Mr. Herrington notes that "the line was included at the insistence of the Japanese delegation so that it would be agreed where their boats could fish without molestation by U.S. or Canadian enforcement officials and without charges of treaty violation." Letter to the author, February 5, 1977.

173. Herrington states: "It was a compromise location based on the best

information we had on salmon migration at the time. Achieving agreement on this location stalled negotiations for some time." Ibid.

174. Herrington comments: "The line almost completely protects all Canadian salmon stocks and all, or nearly all, U.S. stocks except those originating from Bristol Bay streams. Most of the fish from Bristol Bay runs are protected except in years of abnormal migration." Ibid.

175. An additional threat to Japanese fishing came in the form of legislation to prohibit the import of salmon into the United States from any country whose nationals fished salmon with nets on the high seas. (H.R. 10244, known as the "Pelly Bill" was introduced in the 85th Congress [1958] and reintroduced in the 86th Congress [1959].) Whiteman, *Digest*, 4, 1189-1193.

176. Herrington explains the policy as follows: "The fishing area restrictions on Japanese fishing operations were established to keep Japanese fishermen from going far afield and stimulating friction and incidents where they came into conflict and/or competed with fishermen from countries which had recently been their bitter enemies. This area was expanded as the Japanese fishing fleet increased in size and procedures were developed for policing SCAP regulations. This expansion was done in spite of constant pressure from other members of the F.E.C. to closely restrict Japanese fishing operations." Letter to the author, February 5, 1977.

177. Mr. Chapman points out that underlying the tuna industry's willingness to support Mr. Herrington's pursuit of the abstention principle was the recognition that it would never receive international acceptance in a UN forum because it too closely resembled the exclusionary policies of Latin America. Chapman, "The United States Fish Industry," pp. 39-49.

178. Ibid.

Chapter 4

THE CONTINENTAL SHELF DEBATE: 1945-1956

1. Executive Order No. 9633, September 28, 1945, 10 *Fed. Reg.* 12305.

2. Marjorie Whiteman, *Digest of International Law*, 4, 756.

3. *Annual Report of the Secretary of the Interior*, FY 1945 (Washington, D.C.: Gov't. Printing Office, 1945), p. ix.

4. It is interesting to note what was in contention between the states and the executive branch during this eight-year period—the prospect, not the certainty of valuable resources. The press release accompanying the Truman Proclamation described the continental shelf as "submerged land which is contiguous to the continent and which is covered by no more than 100 fathoms [600 feet] of water." (*Department of State Bulletin*, 13, No. 327 [September 30, 1945], 484-485.) Estimated at an underwater area of 750,000 square miles, the shelf was expected to contain "valuable oil deposits" and "valuable deposits of minerals other than oil." The Interior Department's annual report specified rutile, sulphur, ilemenite, chromite, monazite, and other heavy minerals. By Ickes's own admission, however, oil

had never been recovered beyond two miles off Texas, and then only in shallow water. Exploration, however, had taken place twenty-six miles off Louisiana's coast and the prospect of technological capabilities to operate in the areas was sufficient to whet acquisitive appetites. A legal history of the offshore dispute to 1953 may be found in Ernest R. Bartley, *The Tidelands Oil Controversy: A Legal and Historical Analysis.*

5. Harry S. Truman, *Memoirs,* II, 482.

6. It is ironic that despite the coincidence of the president's and Ickes's views regarding offshore oil, they were to have a falling out on exactly this issue. The precipitating incident was the president's nomination of Edwin Pauley to be under secretary of the navy in January 1946. As a California oil operator, Pauley had sought to secure the grant of the submerged lands to the states. At the hearings on Pauley's appointment, Ickes charged Pauley with having offered the Democratic campaign a considerable contribution in exchange for dropping the pending federal suit against the states to secure title to offshore lands. When Ickes then staged a press conference to announce his resignation from "an administration where I'm expected to commit perjury for the sake of the party," President Truman was so irate that he gave the secretary seventy-two hours to vacate his office. Gerald D. Nash, *United States Oil Policy 1890-1964* (Pittsburgh: University of Pittsburgh Press, 1968), pp. 180-185.

7. *United States v. California,* 332 U.S. 19 (1947). When this decision was handed down there were seventy-eight producing leases on offshore lands issued by California with a monthly production of one million barrels of oil. One estimate of the total amount of oil withdrawn to that date was 150 million barrels.

8. *Congressional Record,* February 18, 1948, pp. 1356-1359. The proposal in the Senate was S. 2165 and in the House of Representatives was H.R. 5528 and H.R. 5890 (80th Cong., 1st sess.). This act introduced a system of competitive bidding and increased the size of acreage limitations over those provided for in onshore leasing.

9. H.J. Res. 118, S.J. Res. 48 and H.J. Res. 225, 79th Cong., 1st sess.

10. Veto Message, H. Doc. 765, 79th Cong., 2nd sess.

11. S. 1988, H.R. 5992, and companion House bills, 80th Cong., 2nd sess.

12. S. 2165, H.R. 5528, H.R. 5890, 80th Cong., 2nd sess.; S. 923, 81st Cong., 1st sess.

13. Louisiana Act 55 of 1938.

14. Texas Act of May 23, 1947, L. Tex. 50th Leg., p. 451, Vernon's Tex. Civ. Stats., art. 5415a.

15. *United States v. Louisiana,* 339 U.S. 699, 705-706 (1950), and *United States v. Texas,* 339 U.S. 699, 719-720 (1950).

16. U.S. House of Representatives, Committee on the Judiciary, House Report No. 215, *Submerged Lands Act,* March 27, 1953, 83rd Cong., 1st sess.

17. Truman, *Memoirs*, II, 482.

18. Letter to Alben W. Barkley, president of the Senate, Manuscript Division, Library of Congress, 51363.

19. U.S. House of Representatives, *Submerged Lands Act*, p. 14.

20. H.R. 5991 contained language acceptable to the state representatives providing it was also accepted by the federal government. H.R. 5992, on the other hand, contained language on revenue sharing which the federal representatives had agreed to support if it were accepted by state representatives. With the breakdown in negotiations, however, federal officials withdrew support from H.R. 5992 and urged enactment of S. 923 and S. 2153, bills which were identical to the original management bills introduced at the request of Justice, Defense, and Interior in 1948. The House, in response, approved in committee the language of H.R. 5991 which, with amendments, was reintroduced as H.R. 4884 (81st Cong.). This confirmed and established the rights of the states to the offshore lands within their boundaries and provided for leasing by the secretary of the interior of those areas of the continental shelf lying outside of state boundaries.

21. S. 1700 (81st Cong., 1st sess.), for example, would create a federal waters land reserve, but dedicate a portion of the revenues therefrom to the public schools. Along the same line, Senator Joseph C. O'Mahoney sponsored S.J. Res. 195 (81st Cong., 2nd sess.), which would recognize federal jurisdiction over the entire continental shelf but give the states 37½ percent of revenues inside their sea boundaries.

22. S.J. Res. 20 was introduced by Senator O'Mahoney on January 11, 1951 (with a companion bill H.J. Res. 131 introduced by Emanuel Celler). It allowed the federal government to retain title to offshore lands but provided for continued offshore mineral leases under the jurisdiction of the states. Like its predecessor, the O'Mahoney-Anderson resolution granted the adjacent coastal states 37½ percent of the revenues from operations off their shores. On June 7, Senator Lister Hill (D-Ala.) introduced an amendment to S.J. Res. 20. It provided for royalties from offshore oil and gas to be used for defense needs during the remainder of the Korean War. Thereafter, 100 percent of the royalties from the outer continental shelf and 62½ percent from the inner shelf would be used for grants-in-aid to education throughout the country. In February, Senator Spessard I. Holland (D-Fla.) introduced S. 940 which, unlike S.J. Res. 20, would establish definite title to the submerged lands in the coastal states.

23. S. Doc. No. 139, 82nd Cong., 2nd sess., 98 *Congressional Record* 6251.

24. Truman, *Memoirs*, II, 483.

25. Message from the President of the United States, 82nd Cong., 2nd sess., Doc. 139; Hearings, Senate Committee on Interior and Insular Affairs, S.J. Res. 13, 83rd Cong., 1st sess., pp. 649-656.

26. Truman, *Memoirs*, II, 484.

27. Ibid., p. 485.

28. Ibid., p. 486.

29. Dwight D. Eisenhower, *Mandate for Change: 1953-1956*, pp. 203-204, 205-206.

30. James P. McGranery, Attorney General, "Memorandum Re Executive Order No. 10426 of January 16, 1953, entitled 'Setting Aside Submerged Lands of the Continental Shelf as a Naval Petroleum Reserve,'" U.S. Senate, Committee on Interior and Insular Affairs, *Hearings on Submerged Lands*, pp. 960-962.

31. Of note is the fact that the Interior Department initiated this last-ditch effort to retain ownership of the offshore lands in federal hands, and that the Navy was only brought into the picture at the last minute. Only three and a half years earlier, in 1949, the president had attempted such a move but was advised against it by the solicitor general of the Interior Department. The argument then used was that the continuing uncertainty as to the status of the area would make it difficult for the Navy to administer as a petroleum reserve. Given the subsequent reversal of Interior's position, one might surmise with the benefit of hindsight that in 1949, Interior's primary concern was to retain operating authority in its own hands. When, with the advent of a new administration, it seemed likely that the federal government would lose these resources altogether, Interior officials were willing to try to strengthen the federal claim by converting these lands to a naval petroleum reserve. U.S. Senate, *Hearings on Submerged Lands*, p. 172.

32. Eisenhower, *Mandate for Change*, p. 206.

33. U.S. Senate, *Hearings on Submerged Lands*, pp. 962-963.

34. Ibid., p. 1088. It is noteworthy that Assistant Secretary Morton's account of earlier reactions to U.S. claims overlooks the existence of the Truman Proclamation on fisheries. It was perhaps thought that a stronger case could be made against the continental shelf legislation if foreign reactions to the Truman Proclamations were attributed exclusively to that on the continental shelf. Alternatively, the State Department may have preferred to forget the 1945 fisheries proclamation altogether since it was clear by that point that it would never be implemented through legislation.

35. James E. Webb to J. Howard McGrath, November 13, 1951, in U.S. Senate, *Hearings on Submerged Lands*, p. 460.

36. Ibid., p. 462.

37. As noted elsewhere, of course, other nations who had already laid claim to their shelf areas had not restricted themselves solely to resources.

38. Testimony of Jack B. Tate, deputy legal advisor, Department of State, in U.S. Senate, *Hearings on Submerged Lands*, pp. 1051-1086, and U.S. Senate, Committee on Interior and Insular Affairs, *Hearings on Outer Continental Shelf*, pp. 572-607. Of interest is the fact that the American tuna industry adopted the same positions as the State Department on the need to moderate national claims to take account of possible foreign responses. U.S. Senate, *Hearings on Submerged Lands*, p. 667.

39. U.S. Senate, *Hearings on Submerged Lands*, p. 125.

40. Ibid., p. 642.

41. Ibid., p. 513.

42. Eisenhower, *Mandate for Change*, pp. 206-207.

43. 67 Stat. 29, U.S.C. secs. 1301-1315. A history of the background of the Submerged Lands Act may be found in vol. 1 of Robert B. Krueger, *Study of the Outer Continental Shelf Lands of the United States*. The Submerged Lands Act of May 22, 1953 was captioned H.R. 4198, but in fact it consisted of the Senate's S.J. Res. 13, which the Senate had substituted in its entirety for the House bill. (*Congressional Record*, May 5, 1953, p. 4488; May 13, 1953, pp. 4897-4898.)

44. *Congressional Record*, April 28, 1953, p. 4114.

45. Sec. 2 (c), 43 U.S.C. sec. 1301 (c).

46. The issue of state boundaries in the Gulf of Mexico returned to the Supreme Court as a result of congressional unwillingness to specify exactly which states should enjoy a three-league limit. In May of 1960, the Court granted a three-league limit to Texas and Florida and set a three-mile limit for the rest of the Gulf states. (May 31, 1960, *United States v. Louisiana et al.*, 363 U.S. 1, *United States v. Florida et al.*, 363 U.S. 121.)

47. George S. Swarth, "Offshore Submerged Lands," p. 133.

48. 67 *Stat.* 462, 43 U.S.C. secs. 1331-1343; P.L. 83-212. The background of this act and its subsequent administration may be found in vol. 1 of Krueger, *Outer Continental Shelf Lands*.

49. U.S. Senate, Committee on Interior and Insular Affairs, *Outer Continental Shelf Lands Act*, Report No. 411, 83rd Cong., 1st sess., p. 2.

50. Ibid., p. 4.

51. Contention over the continental shelf question did not subside with the passage of the 1953 legislation. Indeed, three types of litigation immediately ensued. The first consisted of suits brought by states who opposed the congressional grant of offshore lands to a few states and who felt moreover that it was discriminatory to give some states (i.e., Gulf states) more offshore land than others. *Alabama v. Texas: Rhode Island v. Louisiana*, 347 U.S. 272. In 1954, leave to file these complaints was denied by the Supreme Court. The second type of litigation concerned which of the Gulf states could establish a successful claim to the seabed out to three leagues. The Supreme Court announced its opinion in these cases on May 31, 1960. It supported the claims of Texas and Florida to continental shelf boundaries of three leagues but denied those of Louisiana, Mississippi, and Alabama. The Court stated that its decision was made "for domestic purposes" only and did not relate to "the effectiveness of this boundary as against other nations." (*United States v. Louisiana, Texas, Mississippi, Alabama*, 363 U.S. 1, *United States v. Florida et al.*, 363 U.S. 121.) The third form of contention deriving from the Submerged Lands Act related to the drawing of baselines from which the seaward boundaries were to be measured. (This is discussed in Aaron L. Shalowitz, *Shore and Sea Boundaries*, 1, U.S.

431

Department of Commerce [Washington, D.C.: Government Printing Office, 1962].)

For information on the subsequent administration of U.S. offshore leasing see Frank J. Barry, "The Administration of the Outer Continental Shelf Lands Act," *Natural Resources Lawyer*, 1, No. 3 (July 1968), 38-48; Robert B. Krueger, "Mineral Development on the Continental Shelf and Beyond," *Journal of the State Bar of California*, 42, No. 4 (July-August 1967), 515-533.

52. U.S. Senate, *Outer Continental Shelf Lands Act*, Report No. 411, p. 5.

53. Eisenhower, *Mandate for Change*, p. 207.

54. Chapter 3, pp. 67-80.

55. Declaration of Mexico of 29 October 1945; Presidential Decree of 25 February 1945.

56. Panama, Amendment to the Constitution (new Art. 209 added by Decree No. 9938, March 4, 1946).

57. Declaration of Argentina of 9 October 1946; text in *American Journal of International Law, Supplements*, 41, 11.

58. Britain's early interest in areas off its protectorates was evidenced in the treaty with Venezuela on the submarine areas of the Gulf of Paria; Trinidad and Tobago Submarine Areas of the Gulf of Paria (Annexation Order) 1942, Statutory Rules and Orders, 1, 919. Text is in Whiteman, *Digest*, 4, 789-792.

59. Bahamas (Alteration of Boundaries) Order in Council, Statutory Instruments, 1948, No. 2574.

60. Jamaica (Alteration of Boundaries) Order in Council, Statutory Instruments, 1948, No. 3574.

61. British Honduras (Alteration of Boundaries) Order in Council, Statutory Instruments, 1950, No. 1649.

62. Falkland Islands (Continental Shelf) Order in Council, Statutory Instruments, 1950, No. 2100.

63. In the 1954 General Assembly, for instance, the Legal Advisor's Office worked hard to achieve a separate resolution of the continental shelf issue while the Fisheries Office supported efforts to deal with all law of the sea issues in a single forum.

64. In Texas, Florida, and Louisiana, for instance, the interests of the shrimp industries were overlooked where they conflicted with state policies on offshore oil of the continental shelf. Wilbert McLeod Chapman, "The U.S. Fish Industry and the 1958 and 1960 United Nations Conferences on the Law of the Sea," p. 43.

65. Declaration of the Governor General, March 9, 1950; *Gazette of Pakistan*, "Extraordinary," 14 March 1950.

66. Nicaragua Political Constitution, November 1, 1950, Art. 5; Text appears in *Revista Española de Derecho Internacional*, 2, 64.

67. Decree No. 28, 840, Art. 1, 18 November 1950.

68. Honduras Legislative Decree No. 102, 7 March 1950; Legislative Decrees Nos. 103 and 105, March 7, 1950.

69. Legislative Decree No. 25, January 17, 1951.

70. Article 7 of the political constitution, 1950.

71. Francisco Orrego Vicuña, *Los Fondos Marinos y Oceánicos* (Santiago: Editorial Andres Bello, 1976), p. 79.

72. Ecuadorian Congressional Decree of February 21, 1951; Laws and Regulations on the Regime of the High Seas (UN Legislative Series 1951) ST/LEG/SER.B/1/Add 1, July 1952, p. 300. In 1952 Ecuador joined Chile and Peru in claiming a 200-mile zone.

73. Naval War College, *International Law: Situation and Documents*, pp. 238-239.

74. The territorial sea was one of the items considered by the League of Nations Hague Conference on the Progressive Codification of International Law in 1930. The conference was unable to reach agreement on the question of breadth.

75. General Assembly Resolution 174 (II) on November 21, 1947.

76. Dr. Manley O. Hudson, an American jurist and formerly a judge of the Permanent Court of International Justice served until 1953. He was succeeded by Douglas L. Edmonds. In 1956 the commission membership was increased to twenty-one by General Assembly Resolution 1103 (XI), December 18, 1956.

77. *Yearbook of the International Law Commission*, 1949 (UN Doc. A/CN.4/SR.1 to 38). The ILC "yearbooks" are actually summary records of their meetings.

78. The annual reports of the ILC were reprinted regularly in the *American Journal of International Law, Supplements*: Vol. 44 (1950), pp. 1, 105 (1st and 2nd sess.); Vol. 45 (1951), p. 103 (3rd sess.); Vol. 47 (1953), p. 1 (4th sess.); Vol. 48 (1954), p. 1 (5th sess.); Vol. 49 (1955), p. 1 (6th sess.), and *Official Documents*, Vol. 50 (1956), p. 190 (7th sess.); Vol. 51 (1957), p. 154 (8th sess.).

79. *Report of the International Law Commission Covering the Work of its Fifth Session*, 1 June-14 August 1953, UN General Assembly *Official Records*, Eighth Session, Supplement No. 9 (A/2456).

80. *Report of the International Law Commission Covering the Work of its Eighth Session*, 23 April-4 July, 1956, UN General Assembly *Official Records*, Eleventh Session, Supplement No. 9 (A/3159).

81. Two hundred meters is 109 fathoms or 654 feet.

82. U.S. Naval War College, *International Law*, 1959-60, 53, 19-30.

83. UN General Assembly, A/1858, pp. 17-19, p. 80.

84. The adoption of the 200-meter depth contour rather than that of 100 fathoms is due to the fact that a vast majority of states used meters as a depth unit for nautical charts.

85. *Report of the International Law Commission* (A/2456), chap. 3.

86. The United States government was seemingly indifferent as between

the two limits. Naval War College, *International Law*, 1959-60, p. 26; (A/CN.4/55/Add.2, June 21, 1952). For its part, the Interior Department expressed a strong preference for the potentially expansive depth of exploitation limit (Letter of secretary of the interior, Chapman, to secretary of state, Acheson, July 30, 1951. Department of the Interior files, Box 2208, pt. 29, National Archives, Washington, D.C.). The legal advisor of the State Department expressed his own preference for the fixed limit of 200 miles (Herman Phleger, "Recent Developments Affecting the Regime of the High Seas," *Department of State Bulletin*, 32, No. 832 [June 6, 1955], p. 938).

87. UN General Assembly, *Official Records*, 11th sess., plenary meeting 685th, February 21, 1957, Resolution 1105 (xi).

Chapter 5
THE FIRST AND SECOND UN CONFERENCES ON THE LAW
OF THE SEA: 1958 AND 1960

1. General Assembly Resolution 374 (iv), December 6, 1949.

2. D.H.N. Johnson points out that the contribution of governments to the work of the ILC was limited because only a few governments issued comments on the drafts submitted to them and some of these comments were fragmentary. "The Preparation of the 1958 Geneva Conference on the Law of the Sea," *International and Comparative Law Quarterly*, viii, Jan. 1959, 126.

3. "(a) A convention should cover either: (i) One or more stocks of marine animals capable of separate identification and regulation; or (ii) A defined area, taking into account scientific and technical factors, where, because of intermingling of stocks or for other reasons, research on and regulation of specific stocks as defined in (i) is impracticable." *Report of the International Technical Conference on the Conservation of the Living Resources of the Sea*, 18 April to 10 May 1955, Rome (UN 1955), A/CONF.10/6, July 1955, pp. 1-10.

4. See Chapter 4, (pp. 122-126) for discussion of ILC work on the continental shelf.

5. *Report of the International Technical Conference*, p. 2.

6. The commentary to this Article 53 noted the principle of abstention favored by the United States but declined to make any concrete proposal relating to it, claiming the lack of the necessary scientific and economic competence.

7. Another contentious issue was the requirement for compulsory dispute settlement in the ILC proposals.

8. See Edward S. Greenbaum, U.S. representative to the General Assembly, statement, December 14, 1956 in Marjorie Whiteman, *Digest of International Law*, 4, 1129-1131 and *Department of State Bulletin*, 36, No. 916 (January 14, 1957), 60-65.

9. See for instance the policy adopted by the Council of Jurists in Mexico City a few months earlier. "The distance of three miles as the limit of territorial waters is insufficient, and does not constitute a general rule of international law. . . . Each State is competent to establish its territorial waters within reasonable limits, taking into account geographical, and biological factors, as well as the economic needs of its population, and its security and defense." Resolution XIII, Final Act of the Third Meeting of the Inter-American Council of Jurists, Mexico City, Mexico, January 17-February 4, 1956 (Washington, D.C.: Pan American Union, 1956), CIJ-29, p. 36; Whiteman, *Digest*, 4, 72.

10. Resolution 1, Final Act, Inter-American Specialized Conference on "Conservation of Natural Resources: The Continental Shelf and Marine Waters," Ciudad Trujillo, March 15-28, 1956 (Washington, D.C.: Pan American Union, 1956), p. 14; Whiteman, *Digest*, 4, 72.

11. Commentary of the International Law Commission with respect to its final draft on the "Breadth of the Territorial Sea," United Nations, *Yearbook of the International Law Commission*, 1956, II, 265-266; Whiteman, *Digest*, 4, 74-75.

12. UN, A/CN.4/53, April 4, 1952, *Yearbook of the International Law Commission*, 1952, pp. 25, 28; Whiteman, *Digest*, 4, 76.

13. *Yearbook of the International Law Commission*, 1952, I, 155, 164.

14. *Report of the International Law Commission Covering the Work of Its Seventh Session*, 2 May-8 July, 1955, UN General Assembly, *Official Records*, 10th session, Supp. No. 9 (A/2934), p. 16; *Yearbook of the International Law Commission*, 1955, II, 35.

15. See comment by U.S. government with respect to this article. The United States mission to the United Nations to the secretary-general of the United Nations, *note verbale*, March 12, 1956, Doc. A/CN.4/99/Add.1; *Yearbook of the International Law Commission*, 1956, II, 91, 93-94; Whiteman, *Digest*, 4, 73-74.

16. *Report of the International Law Commission Covering the Work of Its Eighth Session*, 23 April-4 July, 1956, UN General Assembly, *Official Records*, 11th session, Supp. No. 9 (A/3159); *Yearbook of the International Law Commission*, 1956, II, 256; Whiteman, *Digest*, 4, 73.

17. Verbatim record of the debate is found in UN, A/CONG.13/19, Vols. 1 and 2; Summary record is in UN General Assembly, *Official Records*, 11th session, 6th committee, 485th to 505th meetings.

18. UN, A/C.6/L.385. The draft resolution was sponsored by Australia, Brazil, Ceylon, Cuba, Denmark, the Dominican Republic, France, Greece, Guatemala, the Netherlands, New Zealand, Panama, the Philippines, Portugal, Sweden, Thailand, the United Kingdom, the United States, and Uruguay. They were later joined by Pakistan, Norway, and Spain (Add. 1, 2, and 3).

19. UN, A/CONF.13/19, pp. 258-259 and 495. (UN documents cited throughout this chapter will hereafter be referred to by document number only.)

20. A/CONF.13/19, p. 177.

21. Ibid., pp. 258-259, 495.

22. UN General Assembly, *Official Records*, 11th sess., plenary meeting 658th, Feb. 21, 1957, Res. 1105 (XI).

23. The sixth committee recommended that the conference be held in Rome, but the fifth committee (administrative and budgetary) recommended Geneva instead in the interests of economy. The General Assembly left the choice of site to the secretary-general who chose Geneva and allotted nine weeks for the meeting. A/3520, p. 37.

24. A/CONF.13/5.

25. February 4, 1958.

26. Afghanistan, Austria, Bolivia, Czechoslovakia, Nepal, and Paraguay, A/C.6/L.393.

27. Memorandum Concerning the Question of Free Access to the Sea of Land-Locked Countries, A/CONF.13/29, January 14, 1958.

28. FAO, ICAO, ILO, ITU, UNESCO, WHO, WMO.

29. For an overview of the major conference groupings see Robert L. Friedheim, "The Politics of the Sea," chap. 4.

30. Arthur H. Dean, "Freedom of the Sea," *Foreign Affairs*, XXXVII (October 1958), 83-94; Arthur H. Dean, "The Geneva Conference on the Law of the Sea," pp. 607-628.

31. Friedheim, "The Politics of the Sea," p. 157.

32. A/CONF.13/40, 21st meeting, par. 15.

33. A/CONF.13/38, 10th plenary meeting, pars. 35-50.

34. Not only were the Eastern Europeans largely distant-water fishing nations, but the Soviet Union had also undertaken in the mid-1950s to develop its distant-water fishing capabilities. See Soviet proposal in A/CONF.13/C.3/L.30.

35. Whiteman, *Digest*, 4, 81.

36. Wilbert McLeod Chapman, "The United States Fish Industry and the 1958 and 1960 Conferences on the Law of the Sea," pp. 51-52.

37. Alvin Hamilton, "Report on Law of the Sea Conference," *External Affairs*, 10, No. 7 (July 1958), 195-202.

38. W. M. Chapman, proposed letter to Arthur Dean, LS 60-7, February 13, 1960 in Wilbert McLeod Chapman Collection (hereafter W. M. Chapman Collection).

39. A/CONF.13/18: On the Philippine position, see W. M. Chapman, Memo to the Resources Committee on the End of the Second U.N. Conference on the Law of the Sea, GC 60-7, April 28, 1960, W. M. Chapman Collection.

40. Dean, "The Geneva Conference," pp. 615-616.

41. Friedheim, "Politics of the Sea," pp. 162 ff.

42. W. M. Chapman, proposed letter to Arthur Dean, W. M. Chapman Collection.

43. Dean, "Freedom of the Sea," pp. 84 and 90.

44. "We were advised by those charged with the responsibility for our national security that the importance of preserving the three-mile limit was such that we were bound to make every effort to preserve it." Loftus Becker, "The Breadth of the Territorial Sea and Fisheries Jurisdiction," *Department of State Bulletin*, March 16, 1959, p. 372.

45. A/CONF.13/C.1/L.140: "After a careful, and I may say agonizing review of every possibility, the United States decided, if we could gain general acceptance for a 3-mile territorial sea, to concede to coastal states an additional 9-mile contiguous zone in which they would have exclusive fishing rights." Becker, ibid., p. 372.

46. A/CONF.13/C.1/L.159 or A/CONF.13/L.29: "This proposal likewise was put forward only after it had received consideration at the highest levels of our Government." Becker, ibid., p. 372.

47. A/CONF.13/38.

48. The fishing industry had been organized to deal with the law of the sea for several years. In August 1956, the industry and state advisers met to consider the ILC fisheries articles at the request of the State Department's Office for Fisheries and Wildlife (see memo from William C. Herrington to Industry Advisers, January 23, 1957 in W. M. Chapman Collection). The group met again in September 1958 and December 1959 to consider the desirability of and strategy for a second law of the sea conference. (Memos from William C. Herrington to industry and state fisheries advisers summarizing aforementioned meetings, W. M. Chapman Collection.)

49. A/CONF.13/38, first plenary meeting, pars. 14-31.

50. A/CONF.13/C.2/L.46.

51. A/CONF.13/40, 29th meeting.

52. A/CONF.13/C.2/L.30.

53. A/CONF.13/C.2/L.71/Rev. 1; A/CONF.13/40, 17th and 18th meetings.

54. Whiteman, *Digest*, 4, 465-477; Dwight D. Eisenhower, *Waging Peace*, 1959-61, pp. 183-193.

55. *Report of the International Law Commission*, UN General Assembly *Official Records*, 11th sess., Supp. No. 9 (A/3159).

56. Report of the First Committee, A/CONF.13/L.28/Rev. 1; UN Conference on the Law of the Sea, 2, plenary meetings (A/CONF.13/38), 115-116; Whiteman, *Digest*, 4, 92-94.

57. The original U.S. proposal provided for a three-mile territorial sea with a nine-mile exclusive fisheries zone beyond.

58. A/CONF.13/C.1/L.159/Rev. 2; UN Conference on the Law of the Sea, First Committee (A/CONF.13/39), pp. 253-254; Whiteman, *Digest*, 4, 97-98.

59. A/CONF.13/C.1/L.77/Rev. 3; UN Conference on the Law of the Sea, First Committee (A/CONF.13/39), p. 232; Whiteman, *Digest*, 4, 99.

60. A/CONF.13/L.34; UN Conference on the Law of the Sea, plenary meetings (A/CONF.13/38), p. 1, 28; Whiteman, *Digest*, 4, 102.

61. A/CONF.13/C.1/L.80; UN Conference on Law of the Sea, First Committee (A/CONF.13/30); Whiteman, *Digest*, 4, 103.

62. For an account of the voting, see Friedheim, "Politics of the Sea," pp. 39-43.

63. Judgment of 18 December, 1951; ICJ Reports, 1951, pp. 116-142; *British Year Book of International Law*, XXXI (1957), 371-429.

64. C.1/L.62 Corr.1: A/CONF.13/39, 43rd meeting, 51st meeting.

65. A/CONF.13/39, 52nd meeting.

66. A/CONF.13/C.1/L.62, L.63, L102, L.109.

67. A/CONF.13/C.1/L.103 and A/CONF.13/L.105.

68. Whiteman, *Digest*, 4, 228-229.

69. Art. 14, A/CONF.13/L.52. The United States made the proposal to eliminate the reference to acts, a move that it came to regret when it realized that coastal-state competence was thereby expanded beyond the actual conduct of ships to include destination, cargo, etc. Myres S. McDougal and William T. Burke, *The Public Order of the Oceans*, pp. 757-763.

70. Whiteman, *Digest*, 4, 465-471.

71. A/CONF.13/C.1/L.71.

72. Whiteman, *Digest*, 4, 464-465.

73. Art. 16, A/CONF.13/L.52.

74. A/CONF.13/39, 43rd meeting.

75. J.P.A. François, "Second International Conference on Law of the Sea," *United Nations Review*, IV, June 1960, 13.

76. A/CONF.13/L.53.

77. A/CONF.13/C.2/L.34.

78. A/CONF.13/C.2/L.7. Scientific research was explicitly cited in the International Law Commission's commentaries of 1955 and 1956.

79. McDougal and Burke, *Public Order of the Oceans*, pp. 757-763.

80. A/CONF.13/C.2/L.6.

81. A/CONF.13/C.2/L.32 and A/CONF.13/40, 22nd meeting, par. 18.

82. A/CONF.13/C.2/L.30 and A/CONF.13/40, 17th meeting, pars. 5-8, 35-37.

83. A/CONF.13/C.2/L.64.

84. A/CONF.13/C.2/L.71, Rev. 1.

85. A/CONF.13/40, 20th meeting, pars. 1-16.

86. A/CONF.13/C.2/L.15 and L.29.

87. A/CONF.13/C.2/L.68 and A/CONF.13/L.53, Art. 2.

88. A/CONF.12/C.2/L.107 and A/CONF.13/40, 31st meeting, par. 31.

89. A/CONF.13/C.2/L.121, Rev. 1.

90. A/CONF.13/C.2/40, 33rd meeting, par. 34.

91. A/CONF.13/C.2/L.121/Rev. 2 and A/CONF.13/C.2, 34th meeting, pars. 8-14.

92. A/CONF.13/C.2, 25th meeting, pars. 16-30.

93. The U.S. had played a role in the development of these principles. See Chapter 3.

94. A/CONF.13/C.2/L.76.

95. A/CONF.13/40, 27th meeting, par. 12.

96. *Report of the International Law Commission* (A/3159), Articles 49-59.

97. A/CONF.13/C.3/L.49 and A/CONF.13/C.3/L.21.

98. A/CONF.13/L.21, part III.

99. A/CONF.13/C.3/L.1.

100. The Soviet Union objected in principle to any form of compulsory dispute settlement.

101. A/CONF.13/C.3/L.67.

102. A/CONF.13/C.3/L.65 and A/CONF.13/30th meeting, par. 12.

103. A/CONF.13/C.3/L.55.

104. A/CONF.13/C.3/L.33, L.36, L.41, L.42.

105. A/CONF.13/C.3/L.65.

106. A/CONF.13/C.3/L.43.

107. A/CONF.13/C.3/L.71.

108. A/CONF.13/C.3/L.66 and A/CONF.13/C.3/L.66/Rev. 1.

109. A/CONF.13/41, 25th meeting, pars. 1-44; 27th meeting, pars. 1-57.

110. A/CONF.13/C.3/L.3; A/CONF.13/41, 21st meeting, par. 38.

111. For a description of these efforts see Chapman, "United States Fish Industry," pp. 50-53.

112. See Chapter 3, pp. 101-102.

113. Chapman, "United States Fish Industry," p. 52.

114. A/CONF.13/L.54.

115. Chapman, "United States Fish Industry," p. 50.

116. The United States, it should be noted, adopted a low profile in the discussions of Committee Four. Having initiated this legal concept through the Truman Proclamation of 1945, the U.S. had a clear interest in seeing it incorporated into international law. On the other hand, the United States could not afford a rupture with its European allies on other maritime issues.

117. UN General Assembly, *Official Records*, 11th sess., Supp. No. 9 (A/3159).

118. A/CONF.13/C.4/L.6.

119. A/CONF.13/C.4/L.26.

120. A/CONF.13/C.4/L.2.

121. A/CONF.13/C.4/L.43.

122. A/CONF.13/C.4/L.31.

123. A/CONF.13/38, 8th plenary meeting, pars. 45-61, 64.

124. Sweden, A/CONF.13/C.4/L.9; Greece, A/CONF.13/C.4/L.39; Germany, A/CONF.13/C.4/L.43.

125. Burma, A/CONF.13/C.4/L.3; Yugoslavia, A/CONF.13/C.4/L.13.

126. A/CONF.13/C.4/L.36; A/CONF.13/42, 24th meeting, par. 29 and 8th plenary session, par. 64.

127. A/CONF.13/C.4/L.27; A/CONF.13/42, 27th meeting, par. 47.

128. A/CONF.13/C.4/L.49.

129. A/CONF.13/C.4/L.56.

130. A/CONF.13/C.4/L.15.

131. A/CONF.13/C.4/L.28.

132. A/CONF.13/L.52.

133. A/CONF.13/L.53.

134. A/CONF.13/L.54.

135. A/CONF.13/L.55.

136. A/CONF.13/L.56.

137. A/CONF.13/L.57.

138. 71 in favor, 0 opposed, 6 abstentions.

139. Whiteman, *Digest*, 4, 83.

140. Republic of Panama Law No. 58, December 18, 1958, published in *Official Gazette*, December 24, 1958.

141. Whiteman, *Digest*, 4, 120 and 1157.

142. Ibid., p. 120.

143. Decree of November 17, 1958, published in the *Iraq Times*, November 19, 1958.

144. Law No. 21959, published in *Official Gazette*, March 31, 1959.

145. Iranian decree signed April 16, 1959. Whiteman, *Digest*, 4, 83.

146. For an elaboration of this assumption, see memos of William C. Herrington to industry advisers summarizing 1958 and 1959 meetings, W. M. Chapman Collection.

147. See, for instance, the Japanese response to Mexico's nine-mile territorial claim (Whiteman, *Digest*, 4, 114-115); U.S. note of November 20, 1958 to the Mexican government (Whiteman, *Digest*, 4, 115-118).

148. Ibid., 4, 118, 120.

149. *New York Times*, July 21, 1958, p. 12.

150. *New York Times*, September 5, 1958, p. 1; Dean, "The Geneva Conference," pp. 607-628.

151. Morris Davis, "British Public Relations: A Political Case Study," *Journal of Politics*, 24 (1962), 63. See also W. M. Chapman, Proposed Letter to Arthur Dean, LS 60-7, February 13, 1960, W. M. Chapman Collection.

152. Whiteman, *Digest*, 4, 121; memo from William Herrington to industry advisers, January 11, 1960, W. M. Chapman Collection.

153. Acting Secretary of State Dillon to American embassy, Rio de Janeiro, circular airgram, July 30, 1959. MS Department of State File 399.731/7-3059. See also Whiteman, *Digest*, 4, 120-121. The Canadians had proposed in 1958 a six-mile territorial sea with an additional six-mile exclusive fishing zone. The U.S. had proposed that in the outer six-mile fishing zone, historic fishing rights would apply—that is, nations that had fished in the area for at least five years would continue to have the right to do so. (Chapter 5, p. 141.) The U.S. proposal, it will be recalled, fell seven votes short of a two-thirds majority required in plenary.

154. Acting Secretary of State Dillon to American embassy, Rio de Janeiro, circular airgram, July 30, 1959. MS Department of State File 399.731/7-3059.

155. Memo of William C. Herrington to industry advisers summarizing meeting of December 1959, W. M. Chapman Collection.

156. Memorandum of meeting in Seattle, January 16, 1960, W. M. Chapman Collection.

157. Summary of U.S. Alternative Positions for 1960 Conference, February 12, 1960, MS Department of State File, 711.11-EI/2-1260.

158. The Peruvians had released the Chileans and Ecuadoreans from their 1952 agreement so they were free to vote as they wished. (W. M. Chapman Memo to Resources Committee on the End of the Second UN Conference on the Law of the Sea, GC 60-7, April 28, 1960, W. M. Chapman Collection.)

159. François, "Second International Conference," pp. 12-14.

160. A/CONF.19/C.1/L.1.

161. A/CONF.19/C.1/L.2.

162. A/CONF.19/C.1/L.3.

163. A/CONF.19/C.1/L.4.

164. Iran, Indonesia, Iraq, Philippines, Jordan, Lebanon, Saudi Arabia, the UAR, Libya, Tunisia, Morocco, Ghana, Guinea, Sudan, Ethiopia, and Yeman. A/CONF.19/C.1./L.6.

165. A/CONF.19/C.1/L.7.

166. A/CONF.19/C.1/L.10.

167. Tunisia and Mexico joined the earlier sixteen-nation group as co-sponsors.

168. A/CONF.19/C.1/L.2/Rev. 1.

169. A/CONF.19/C.1/L.11 and L.12.

170. A/CONF.19/8, 28th meeting, pars. 3, 5-6, 10; Whiteman, *Digest*, 4, 130.

171. Indonesia, Iraq, Lebanon, Mexico, Morocco, Saudi Arabia, Sudan, UAR, Venezuela, Yemen.

172. A/CONF.19/L.9.

173. A/CONF.19/L.12.

174. Chapman, "United States Fish Industry," p. 55. W. M. Chapman Memo to the Resources Committee on the End of the Second UN Conference on Law of the Sea.

175. Chapman, "United States Fish Industry," p. 55.

176. For a dramatic account of these closing weeks, see W. M. Chapman Memo to the Resources Committee on the End of the Second UN Conference on Law of the Sea.

177. A/CONF.19/L.8 (adopted. See Final Act A/CONF.19/L.15, Res. II).

178. A/CONF.19/L.3 (adopted. See Final Act A/CONF.19/L.15, Res. I).

179. Chapman, "United States Fish Industry," p. 55; W. M. Chapman Memo to Resources Committee on the End of the Second UN Conference on Law of the Sea.

180. For a critique of the convention, see James A. Crutchfield, "The

Convention on Fishing and Living Resources of the High Seas," *Natural Resources Lawyer*, 1, No. 2 (June 1968), 114-124.

181. President Eisenhower sent the Geneva Conventions to the Senate in September 1959. The U.S. officially ratified them in March 1961.

Chapter 6
OCEAN POLICY INTERREGNUM: THE 1960s

1. Convention on the Territorial Sea and Contiguous Zone, A/CONF.-13/L.52; Convention on the High Seas, A/CONF.13/L.53; Convention on Fishing and Conservation of the Living Resources of the High Seas, A/CONF.13/L.54; and Convention on the Continental Shelf, A/CONF.-13/L.55.

2. It will be recalled that the twelve-mile contiguous zone specified in the 1958 Convention was for fiscal, sanitation, and immigration purposes —not fishing.

3. Summary Minutes, Meeting of State Department's Fishing Industry Advisory Committee, Seattle, Washington, May 5, 1962, Wilbert McLeod Chapman Collection.

4. Ann L. Hollick, "Canadian-American Relations," p. 762.

5. Drawbacks of such a multilateral approach from the U.S. perspective were spelled out to U.S. officials by Wilbert McLeod Chapman, among others. He noted that the proponents of a twelve-mile territorial sea could undertake a similar multilateral effort and gain a significant number of adherents among the newly independent states. Memorandum to the Resources Committee on "Post Geneva Conference Activity on the Law of the Sea," May 16, 1960, W. M. Chapman Collection.

6. Canada, Laws, Statutes, etc. *Territorial Sea and Fishing Zones Act,* 1964, 13 Elizabeth 2, Ch. 22, 26th Parl., 2nd sess. (1964). The parliamentary debate accompanying this move may be found in 113 Senate Deb. 349 (Hansard's, Canada), April 30, 1964; 372 (May 4, 1964); 381-383, 385, 389 (May 5, 1964); 399, 403 (May 6, 1964).

7. Statistics are found in *Major Issues of the Law of the Sea* (Durham, N.H.: University of New Hampshire, 1976).

8. Austria, Belgium, Denmark, France, Federal Republic of Germany, Ireland, Italy, Luxembourg, the Netherlands, Portugal, Spain, Sweden, Switzerland, United Kingdom.

9. Final Act of the European Fisheries Conference, London, December 3, 1963 to March 2, 1964, with Fisheries Convention, Protocol of Provisional Application and Agreements as to Transitional Rights, Misc. No. 11 (1964) Cmnd. 2355; Marjorie Whiteman, *Digest of International Law*, 4, 1040.

10. P.L. 89-658, 80 U.S. Statutes at Large 908 (October 14, 1966). In 1964 the U.S. passed the "Bartlett Act" which made it unlawful for any non-U.S. vessel to fish within U.S. territorial waters (or within any waters in which the United States had the same rights with respect to its fisheries)

or to take any continental shelf fishery resource which appertained to the United States. P.L. 88-308, 78 U.S. Statutes at Large 194, 196 (May 20, 1964); see also Whiteman, *Digest*, 4, 787, 937.

11. Act of 13 December 1966 on the Exclusive Fishing Zone of the Nation. *Diario Oficial* of 20 January 1967.

12. Decree No. 11 of 5 April 1964 Delimiting the National Fishing Zone to 200 Nautical Miles, *La Gaceta*, No. 82 of 8 April 1965.

13. Amendment to Article 633 of the Civil Code by Decree No. 1542 of 10 November 1966, published in *Registro Oficial*, No. 158, 11 November 1966. See also UN Doc. ST/LEG/SER.B/15 at 78.

14. Law No. 17,094-M 24 of 29 December 1966. *Boletin Oficial*, 10 January 1967. See UN Doc. ST/LEG/SER.B/15 at 45.

15. Panama, Act No. 31 of 2 February 1967, amending and supplementing Act No. 58 of 18 December 1958.

16. Uruguay, Decree 604-969 of 3 December 1969. *Diario Oficial*, 9 December 1969.

17. Brazil, Decree-Law 1098 of 25 March 1970. *Diario Oficial* of the Federal Republic of Brazil, March 30, 1970.

18. Summary Minutes, Meeting of State Department's Fishing Industry Advisory Committee, Seattle, Washington, March 5, 1962, W. M. Chapman Collection.

19. Data of Seizures of U.S. Flag Tuna Clippers During Period January 1961-December 1973 was compiled by the American Tunaboat Association and reproduced in U.S. Senate, Committee on Commerce, *Interim Fisheries Zone Extension and Management Act of 1973*, pp. 574-598. April 18, 19, 26, May 3, 13, 14, and June 14, 1974.

20. U.S. Congress, House Merchant Marine and Fisheries Committee, Subcommittee on Fisheries and Wildlife Conservation, Hearings on H.R. 4153, 4346, 4350, 4451, 4452, 9015, 5148, 6785, 90th Cong., 1st sess., 1967, p. 58.

21. "An Act to Protect the Rights of Vessels of the United States on the High Seas and in Territorial Waters of Foreign Countries," P.L. 680, approved August 27, 1954, 68 U.S. Statutes at Large 883; 22 U.S.C.; Whiteman, *Digest*, 4, 1231.

22. P.L. 89-171, Approved September 6, 1965, U.S. Statutes at Large 79; Sec. 620, 653 (1965); J. Y. Smith, "Aid Cutoff Threatened in Fishing Rights Row," *Washington Post*, February 24, 1967, p. A5.

23. P.L. 90-482, 82 U.S. Statutes at Large 729. This act was amended again in 1972 to speed the process of reimbursing vessel owners from a Fishermen's Protective Fund. If a seizing government refused to pay U.S. claims against it, the funds would be transferred from the financial aid appropriated for the country and put in the Fishermen's Protective Fund. The president could intervene to prevent the transfer by certifying that it was not in the national interest. P.L. 92-569, 86, U.S. Statutes at Large 1182.

24. P.L. 90-224, 81 U.S. Statutes at Large 729 (December 26, 1967).

25. Section 3, P.L. 90-629, 82 U.S. Statutes at Large 1320, approved October 22, 1968. See also U.S. Congress, House, *Congressional Record*, 90th Cong., 2nd sess., September 10, 1968, p. 8455. This act was amended again in 1970 to tighten up the language on vessel seizures. It was provided that no sales, guarantees, or credits could be issued to a country for one year after it illegally seized a U.S. vessel. P.L. 91-672, 84 U.S. Statutes at Large 2053.

26. Benjamin Welles, "U.S. and Peru are Closer," *Excelsior*, June 15, 1969, p. 26A; Diego E. Gonzalez, "Habra Junta de E. U. con Chile, Peru, y Ecuador Sobre Aguas," *Excelsior*, July 5, 1969, p. 3A.

27. Fisheries agreements already in existence in the early 1960s were renegotiated and amended as necessary, but were generally maintained where they had proven useful. See for instance: International Pacific Halibut Commission (U.S. and Canada)—1925, revised 1953; International Pacific Salmon Fisheries Commission (U.S. and Canada)—1930, amended 1956; Northwest Atlantic Fisheries Convention (U.S., Canada and others)—1949; Japan and USSR—Convention Concerning Fisheries on the High Seas of the Northwest Pacific Ocean—1956, amended 1970; Japan and China—Intergovernmental Agreement Concerning Fishing Operations in the Yellow Sea and the East China Sea, 1955, 1963, 1965, 1970, 1975; China and North Korea—1959.

For a comparative study of the fisheries treaties in existence by 1962, see Food and Agriculture Organization, *Comparison and Abstracts of Selected Conventions Establishing Fisheries Commissions*, Legislative Research Branch, Rome, 1962. For more on fisheries arrangements in the North Pacific, see Hiroshi Kasahara and William T. Burke, *North Pacific Fisheries Management*, Resources for the Future Program of International Studies of Fishery Arrangements, Paper No. 2 (Washington, D.C., 1973).

28. Frederick Dutton, assistant secretary of state, Statement on Tuna to House Committee on Foreign Affairs, Subcommittee on Inter-American Affairs, August 16, 1962, W. M. Chapman Collection. W. M. Chapman reports on the complex Ecuadorian politics pertaining to the seizures in memoranda to the Resources Committee of the American Tunaboat Association. GC 60-10, May 16, 1960; Ecuador 60-6, July 11, 1960; Ecuador 60-10, September 25, 1960; Ecuador 61-1, February 15, 1961, W. M. Chapman Collection.

29. David C. Loring, "The United States-Peruvian 'Fisheries Dispute'"; Thomas Wolff, "Something Fishy in Ecuador," *Latin American Digest*, 9, No. 3 (Spring 1975), 27; U.S. Congress, House, Committee on Merchant Marine and Fisheries, Subcommittee on Fisheries and Wildlife Conservation, *Commercial Fisheries*, Hearings, 92nd Cong., 1st sess., 10 February, 11 March, 3 June, 8 July 1971, p. 6.

30. Of nine vessel seizures by Ecuador and Peru from June 1963 to February 1965, none resulted in fines. U.S. Congress, *Interim Fisheries Zone Extension and Management Act of 1973*, Hearings, pp. 577-578.

31. W. M. Chapman, Resources Committee Memo, Ecuador 60-15, November 7, 1960, W. M. Chapman Collection.

32. Leyde Aeronautica Civil del Peru (1965) 57 Legislacion Peruana, 139-155.

33. U.S. Congress, House, Committee on Merchant Marine and Fisheries, *Foreign Seizures of U.S. Fishing Vessels*, Hearings, 90th Cong., 1st sess., June 22, 1967, p. 59.

34. Karin Hjertonsson, *The New Law of the Sea*, p. 37.

35. U.S. Congress, House, Committee on Foreign Affairs, Subcommittee on Inter-American Affairs, *Fishing Rights and United States-Latin American Relations*, Hearings, pp. 75-78.

36. Bobbie B. Smetherman and Robert M. Smetherman, "The CEP Claims, U.S. Tuna Fishing and Inter-American Relations," *Orbis*, xv (Fall 1971), 964.

37. For an example of the draft fisheries agreement proposed by the U.S. for discussion with the CEP at Buenos Aires in September 1970, see U.S. Congress, House, Committee on Foreign Affairs, *Fishing Rights and United States-Latin American Relations*, pp. 4-6.

38. For instance, by mutual agreement, herring of Alaskan origin was removed from the abstention list on May 24, 1960, and opened to Japanese fishing. Whiteman, *Digest*, 4, 1010-1011. Also on May 8, 1963, the Japanese were permitted to fish for halibut in the Bering Sea and for herring off the west coast of Queen Charlotte Islands. 11 U.S.T. 1503; T.I.A.S. 4493; 13 U.S.T. 372; T.I.A.S. 4992; 14 U.S.T. 953; T.I.A.S. 5385.

39. Guenter Weissberg, *Recent Developments in the Law of the Sea and the Japanese-Korean Fishery Dispute*, p. 61. On the 1964 negotiations see Ralph W. Johnson, "The Japanese-United States Salmon Conflict," *Washington Law Review*, 43, No. 1 (October 1967), 1-43.

40. The "MacArthur Line" is detailed in *The Japan Yearbook, 1949-52* (Tokyo, 1952), pp. 435-448.

41. Choon-Ho Park, "Fisheries Issues in the Yellow Sea and the East China Sea," Occasional Paper #18, Law of the Sea Institute (Kingston, R.I.: University of Rhode Island, 1973).

42. Weissberg, *Recent Developments*, pp. 67-78.

43. Agreement Concerning Fisheries together with supplementary arrangements, June 22, 1965, in American Society of International Law, *International Legal Materials*, 4, 1128.

44. P.L. 88-308, 88th Cong., 2nd sess., 78 U.S. Statutes at Large 194 (May 21, 1964).

45. Weissberg, *Recent Developments*, p. 20.

46. T.I.A.S. No. 6155, 6601, 7527. Extended to 1966, 1968, and 1970.

47. David Widley, "International Practice Regarding Traditional Privileges of Foreign Fishermen in Zones of Extended Maritime Jurisdiction," *American Journal of International Law*, 63 (1969), 492.

48. T.I.A.S. No. 5752.

49. T.I.A.S. No. 6217, 6635, 7044, 7541.

50. Whiteman, *Digest*, 4, 1041. On this negotiation, see W. M. Chapman, Memorandum to Resources Committee of ATA, LS 60-18, November 11, 1960, W. M. Chapman Collection.

51. Whiteman, *Digest*, 4, 1041.

52. Convention for Regulating the Police of the North Sea Fisheries, signed at the Hague, May 6, 1882; Anglo-French Fishery Convention of 1839, Whiteman, *Digest*, 4, 1040.

53. Whiteman, *Digest*, 4, 1038-1041.

54. 13 Eliz. II, Ch. 72 (1964); Fishery Limits Act 1964 (Commencement) Order 1964, S.I. 1964, No. 1553 (C.20).

55. C. E. Lucas, "International Fishery Bodies of the North Atlantic," Occasional Paper No. 5, Law of the Sea Institute (Kingston, R.I.: University of Rhode Island, 1970).

56. The Soviet Union has the longest coastline, followed by Indonesia, Australia, the United States, Canada, Philippines, Mexico, Japan, Brazil, and China. Eight Latin American countries have coastlines exceedng 1,000 nautical miles; only three African countries have coastlines of that length.

57. The phrase "common heritage of mankind" contained in Maltese Ambassador Arvid Pardo's 1967 proposal to the UN was not long in becoming established in law of the sea vernacular, particularly as a rallying cry for developing nations.

58. On changing Canadian policy see Jacques-Yvan Morin, "The Quiet Revolution: Canadian Approaches to the Law of the Sea," in Ralph Zacklin, ed., *The Changing Law of the Sea* (Leiden: Sijthoff, 1974), pp. 17-31; R. M. Logan, *Canada, the United States and the Third Law of the Sea Conference*.

59. Canada, Laws, Statutes, etc. *Territorial Sea and Fishing Zones Act*, 1964, 13 Eliz. 2, Ch. 22.

60. P.L. 89-658, U.S. Statutes at Large 908 (October 14, 1966).

61. W. M. Chapman, Law of the Sea: Memorandum to Harold F. Cary, October 25, 1966, W. M. Chapman Collection.

62. Canada, Privy Council, "Order Representing Geographical Coordinates of Points from Which Baselines May Be Determined Pursuant to the Territorial Sea and Fishing Zones Act," 26 October 1967, *Canada Gazette*, part 2, 8 November 1967.

63. These went into effect in June 1969. *Canada Gazette*, 11 June 1969; Canada, Department of External Affairs, "Law of the Sea," Press Release No. 34, 4 June 1969.

64. U.S., Department of State, "Canadian Fisheries Closing Lines Legislation," Press Release No. 53, 12 March 1971.

65. Canada, Bill C-203, Act to Amend Territorial Sea and Fishing Zones Act, 1970, 18 and 19 Eliz. 2.

66. J. A. Beesley, "Rights and Responsibilities of Arctic Coastal States; The Canadian View," *Journal of Maritime Law and Commerce*, 3, October 1971, 7.

67. W. M. Chapman, Memo to the Resources Committee, Discussion with Col. Stewart Chant, Nov. 11, 1960, W. M. Chapman Collection.

68. Center for Strategic and International Studies, *Soviet Sea Power*, Georgetown University Special Report Series No. 10 (Washington, D.C.: Georgetown University, 1969).

69. Soviet trawlers had been ordered out of Argentine waters in 1966 (*New York Times*, October 2, 1966). Soviet fishing provoked Argentina to claim a 200-mile zone in December 1966.

70. Hjertonsson, *New Law of the Sea*, p. 42.

71. For an account of the evolution of these Soviet policies, see William E. Butler, "Some Recent Developments in Soviet Maritime Law," pp. 695-708.

72. The total value of fish taken in 1966 was around $9 billion, more than twice the value of ocean mineral resources recovered, including petroleum. Wilbert McLeod Chapman, "Toward a More Effective Use of Food from the Sea by the United States and Man," in U.S. Congress, House, Committee on Merchant Marine and Fisheries, *National Oceanographic Program—1969*, Hearings before the Subcommittee on Oceanography, Part 2, 91st Cong., 1st sess., August, September, and October 1969, p. 1120.

73. Thomas H. Lineaweaver III, "Our Catch-as-Catch-Can Fisheries," *The Reporter*, 37, September 7, 1967, 38; Chapman, "Toward a More Effective Use," p. 1117 ff.; United Nations, Food and Agriculture Organization, *Yearbook of Fishery Statistics*, Vols. 18 (1964) and 28 (1969).

74. For expressions of congressional concern regarding this state of affairs, see U.S. Congress, House, Committee on Merchant Marine and Fisheries, *Report on the Soviets and the Seas*, No. 1809, 89th Cong., 2nd sess., and U.S. Congress, Senate, Committee on Commerce, *The Post-War Expansion of Russia's Fishing Industry*, Report, January 23, 1964, 88th Cong., 2nd sess.

75. W. M. Chapman, "Discussions with McKernan, Terry, and McHugh, Concerning the Eastern Pacific Tuna Affairs," December 8, 1964, W. M. Chapman Collection.

76. Public Law 89-658, 80 U.S. Statutes at Large 908 (approved October 14, 1966).

77. One example of this was the bill introduced by Senator Bartlett of Alaska in 1964 to prevent foreign fishing within U.S. territorial waters and of U.S. continental shelf fishery resources (S. 1988, 88th Cong., 1st sess.). William Herrington, the special assistant for fisheries and wildlife, recognized the possible harmful effects on U.S. distant-water interests if the U.S. were to move to any broad claim of continental shelf fisheries (U.S. Congress, House, Committee on Merchant Marine and Fisheries, *Fishing in U.S. Territorial Waters*, 88th Cong., 2nd sess., pp. 69-70, 74-75). He argued that if the continental shelf provision had to be included in the legislation, it should be made clear that foreign fishing over the continental

shelf would not be restricted except in accordance with the Geneva Convention on the Continental Shelf. Senator Bartlett's effort to protect the king crab was simply one of an increasing number of instances where the policies favored by U.S. coastal interests jeopardized the concerns of U.S. distant-water fishermen.

78. See pages 87-88, 163-166.

79. W. M. Chapman to Harold F. Cary, "Joint Symposium by the Department of State, NAS and ICO Dissecting the Role of Marine Sciences in Foreign Affairs, 20 April 1965," May 8, 1965, W. M. Chapman Collection.

80. A typical combination of national and international goals to be served by marine science includes (1) military security, (2) ocean resources, (3) international cooperation, and (4) knowledge for its own sake. Dr. Edward Wenk, Jr., U.S. Congress, House, Committee on Science and Astronautics, *Ocean Science and National Security*, Report No. 2078, 86th Cong., 2nd sess., pp. 2-4.

81. Elisabeth Mann Borgese, "The Prospects for Peace in the Oceans," *Saturday Review*, September 26, 1970, pp. 16-17.

82. Stewart Riley, "The Legal Implications of the Sea Use Program," *Marine Technology Society Journal*, 4, January-February 1970, 31.

83. National Academy of Sciences-National Research Council, *Oceanography 1960 to 1970: Introduction and Summary of Recommendations*, Washington, D.C., 1959; Harold M. Schmerck, Jr., "Nation Is Warned to Retain Its Lead in Science Fields," *New York Times*, May 9, 1970, p. 1.

84. U.S., President's Science Advisory Committee, *Effective Use of the Sea*, Report of the Panel on Oceanography, Washington, D.C., June 1966, p. 1.

85. Savings were expected from improvements in shipping, weather forecasting, and sewage disposal. Increased production was expected in the development of ocean fisheries, seabed minerals, and marine recreation. National Academy of Sciences-National Research Council, *Economic Benefits from Oceanographic Research*, Report of the Committee on Oceanography, Publication 1228, Washington, D.C., 1964, pp. 1-2. For a critique of this approach see James A. Crutchfield, Robert W. Kates, and W. R. Derrick Sewell, "Benefit-Cost Analysis and the National Oceanographic Program," *Natural Resources Journal*, 7, July 1967, 361-375.

86. "Marine science interests of the United States, which are shared by scientists around the world, involve observation, description, and understanding of physical, chemical, and biological phenomena of the marine environment." U.S., President's Science Advisory Committee, *Effective Use of the Sea*, p. 1.

87. It is evident that worldwide activity is required if research is to accomplish scientific goals." William T. Burke, *Report on International Legal Problems of Scientific Research in the Oceans*, U.S., Department of Commerce, Clearinghouse for Federal Scientific and Technical Information, PB 177 724 (August 1967), p. 8.

88. Milner B. Schaefer, "The Changing Law of the Sea—Effects on Freedom of Scientific Investigation," in Lewis Alexander, ed., *Law of the Sea: Future of the Sea's Resources*, Law of the Sea Institute (Kingston, R.I.: University of Rhode Island, 1967), pp. 113 ff.

89. Burke, *International Legal Problems*, p. 12. On the need for access to coastal waters, see Warren S. Wooster and Michael D. Bradley, "Access Requirements of Oceanic Research: The Scientists' Perspective," in Warren Wooster, ed., *Freedom of Oceanic Research*, pp. 29-39.

90. Arvid Pardo in United Nations, General Assembly, 23rd Session, *Official Records* (A/C.1/PV.1589), 1968; Herman Franssen, "Developing Country Views of Sea Law and Marine Science," in Wooster, *Freedom of Oceanic Research*, pp. 137-178.

91. Judith A. Tegger Kildow, "Nature of the Present Restrictions on Oceanic Research" in Wooster, *Freedom of Oceanic Research*, pp. 5-28. Donald L. McKernan, special assistant for fisheries and wildlife, letter to John A. Knauss, provost for marine affairs, University of Rhode Island, April 10, 1970, W. M. Chapman Collection.

92. Robert Engler, *The Politics of Oil*, p. 35.

93. Cities Service, Gulf, Phillips, Shell Group, Sinclair, Socony Mobil, Standard of California, Standard (Indiana), Standard (New Jersey), and Texaco. Engler, *Politics of Oil*, p. 38.

94. This investment had been based on estimates of sizeable potential resources in place on the U.S. continental margin. To the depth of 200 meters the U.S. Geological Survey estimated there were between 660 and 780 billion barrels of oil and between 1,640 and 2,220 trillion cubic feet of natural gas. Between the 200-meter isobath and the edge of the U.S. continental margin, potential resources were expected to be about the same. U.S., Department of the Interior, *Petroleum and Sulfur on the U.S. Continental Shelf*, December 1969, p. 49.

95. "Our Yellow Submarine," *The Humble Way*, VIII (1969), 13. F. Ward Pain, "Oceanography—Investment Prospects and Pitfalls in a Growing Environment," *Wall Street Transcript*, June 19, 1967, p. 10356.

96. U.S., Department of the Interior, *Petroleum Production, Drilling and Leasing on the Outer Continental Shelf* (May 1966), p. 8.

97. Letter to secretary of the interior, March 2, 1962, Office of the Secretary, Submerged Lands File, Department of the Interior.

98. This was apparent from a survey of its board of directors in the 1960s. Engler, *Politics of Oil*, p. 60.

99. Ibid., p. 292.

100. Hollis M. Dole, assistant secretary for mineral resources, Interior Department, "Ocean Minerals and the Law," *Natural Resources Lawyer*, II, November 1969, 354.

101. Melvin Conant, "Industry's Needs—Political," in Lewis Alexander, ed., *Law of the Sea: International Rules and Organization for the Sea*, Law of the Sea Institute (Kingston, R.I.: University of Rhode Island, 1968), p. 325.

102. On the subject of the depletion allowance, oil import restrictions, and tax write-offs, see Ronnie Dugger, "Oil and Politics," *The Atlantic*, 224 (September 1969), 66 ff.

103. J. R. Dozier, "Offshore Oil and Gas Operations—Present and Future," Paper presented at the First Annual Conference of the Law of the Sea Institute, June-July 1966, Kingston, Rhode Island; Frank N. Ikard, "Offshore Petroleum Recovery—Status and Outlook," *Exploiting the Ocean, Supplement*, and T. W. Nelson and C. A. Burk, "Petroleum Resources of the Continental Margins of the United States," *Exploiting the Ocean*, Transactions of the 2nd Annual Marine Technology Science Conference and Exhibit, June 1966, Washington, D.C.

104. U.S., Department of the Interior, Geological Survey, "Geologic Boundary of the Continents," Statement of W. T. Pecora, February 21, 1968.

105. The total obligational authority for 1969 was $79.4 billion for the Defense Department and $23.3 billion for the Navy. Figures for the Defense Department include the Military Assistance Program.

106. E. D. Brown, *Arms Control in Hydrospace: Legal Aspects* (Washington, D.C.: Woodrow Wilson International Center for Scholars, 1971), pp. 11, 13, 33.

107. Seymour M. Hersch, "An Arms Race on the Seabed?" *War/Peace Report*, August-September 1968, p. 21; Sven Hirdman, "Weapons in the Deep Sea," *Environment* 13 (1971), 40-41.

108. Rear Adm. Wilfred A. Hearn, judge advocate general of the Navy, in U.S. Congress, House, Committee on Foreign Affairs, *The United Nations and the Issue of Deep Ocean Resources*, pp. 189 ff.; Captain L. E. Zeni, "Defense Needs in Accommodations Among Ocean Users," Alexander, ed., *Law of the Sea: International Rules and Organization*, p. 334; Commander Larry G. Parks, "The Law of—and Under—the Sea," *U.S. Naval Institute Proceedings*, February 1966, p. 57.

109. Captain John R. Brock, director, International Law Division, Office of the Judge Advocate General of the Navy, "Mineral Resources and the Future Development of the International Law of the Sea," *JAG Journal*, 22, September-October-November 1967, 43.

110. Parks, "The Law of—and Under—the Sea," p. 55; Lieutenant Commander Bruce A. Harlow, head, Law of the Sea Branch, International Law Division, Office of the Judge Advocate General of the Navy, "Contemporary Principles of the International Law of the Sea," *JAG Journal*, 22, September-October-November 1967, 29-30.

111. Harlow, "Contemporary Principles," p. 38.

112. Rear Admiral Wilfred A. Hearn, "Principles of International Legal Development," *JAG Journal*, 22, September-October-November 1967, 46.

113. Brock, "Mineral Resources and the Development of the Law of the Sea," p. 41.

114. Parks, "The Law of—and Under—the Sea," p. 58.

115. Rear Admiral Wilfred A. Hearn, "The Fourth Dimension of Sea-power—Ocean Technology and International Law: Introduction," *JAG Journal*, 22, September-October-November 1967, 25.

116. Robert A. Frosch, assistant secretary of the Navy, "Exploiting Marine Mineral Resources: Problems of National Security and Jurisdiction," *Vital Speeches of the Day*, 35, November 15, 1968, 70.

117. "It is militarily desirable to: (1) minimize any extension of terri-toral seas, (2) very closely limit sovereignty over the continental shelves, and (3) maintain freedom of the air space above the high seas." Robert A. Frosch, "Military Uses of the Oceans," Address at the Second Annual Mershon-Carnegie Conference on Law, Organization and Security in the Use of the Ocean, Columbus, Ohio, October 1967, p. 21.

118. This conflict is documented in Lawrence Juda, *Ocean Space Rights: Developing U.S. Policy* (New York: Praeger, 1975), pp. 66-68.

119. Treaty on the Prohibition of the Emplacement of Nuclear Weapons and other Weapons of Mass Destruction on the Seabed and the Ocean Floor and in the Subsoil Thereof, Opened for Signature February 11, 1971. Came into force May 18, 1972.

120. For a discussion of the Defense Department's concern with main-taining organizational capabilities, see Morton Halperin, "Why Bureaucrats Play Games," p. 70 ff.

121. Admiral Elmo R. Zumwalt quoted by Brooke Nihard, "Entering a Desperate Era of Seapower," *Armed Forces Journal*, March 15, 1971, p. 22.

122. Frosch, "Exploiting Marine Mineral Resources," p. 68; see also Robert A. Frosch, "Military Uses of the Ocean," Admiral Zumwalt, chief of naval operations, described the four functional categories of U.S. naval forces as strategic deterrence, projection of power overseas, sea control, and overseas presence. "Future Needs at the Expense of Present Capability," *Armed Forces Journal*, January 4, 1971, p. 15.

123. Paul C. Warnke, assistant secretary of defense, International Se-curity Affairs, in U.S. Congress, Senate, Committee on Foreign Relations, *Governing the Use of Ocean Space*, Hearings, 90th Cong., 1st sess., No-vember 29, 1967, p. 35.

124. U.S., National Council on Marine Resources and Engineering De-velopment, *Marine Science Affairs—A Year of Plans and Progress*, March 1968, p. 189.

125. *Law for the Sea's Mineral Resources*, Institute for the Study of Science in Human Affairs, Columbia University, New York, 1968, see pp. 70 ff.; also Department of Commerce, Clearinghouse for Federal Scientific and Technical Information, PB 177 725, 1967.

126. U.S., National Commission on Marine Science, Engineering and Resources, *Our Nation and the Sea*, pp. 144 ff.; U.S. National Commission on Marine Science, Engineering and Resources, International Panel, *Marine Resources and Legal-Political Arrangements for Their Development*, p. 15 ff.

127. G. Warren Nutter, assistant secretary of defense for international security affairs, U.S. Congress, Senate, Committee on Commerce, *Special Study on United Nations Suboceanic Lands Policy*, Hearings, p. 23.

128. Leigh Ratiner, in U.S. Congress, House, Committee on Armed Services, *Territorial Sea Boundaries*, Hearings, 91st Cong., 2nd sess., June 25, 1970, p. 9288.

129. Nutter, in U.S. Congress, Senate, Committee on Commerce, *United Nations Suboceanic Lands Policy*, p. 24.

130. U.S. Congress, House, Committee on Merchant Marine and Fisheries, *Oceanography in the U.S.*, Hearings before the Special Subcommittee on Oceanography, 86th Cong., 1st sess., p. 135.

131. National Academy of Sciences-National Research Council, *Oceanography 1960 to 1970*.

132. Original members were the Department of Defense, National Science Foundation, Atomic Energy Commission, Department of Commerce, Department of the Interior, with the Bureau of the Budget as observer. In 1960, the Department of Health, Education and Welfare and the Treasury Department joined while the National Academy of Sciences Committee on Oceanography became an observer. On the ICO mission, see W. M. Chapman to Harold F. Cary, Report of Meeting at Pentagon on May 6, May 9, 1965, W. M. Chapman Collection.

133. U.S. Congress, House, Committee on Merchant Marine and Fisheries, *Study of the Effectiveness of the Committee on Oceanography of the Federal Council for Science and Technology*, Hearings before the Subcommittee on Oceanography, 87th Cong., 2nd sess., 1962, pp. 2 ff., 118 ff.

134. The members of PIPICO included representatives from the State Department, the Office of Naval Research, the Office of the Assistant Secretary of the Navy, the Office of the Chief of Naval Operations, the Coast and Geodetic Survey and the Bureau of Commercial Fisheries of the Department of the Interior, the Atomic Energy Commission, the National Science Foundation, and the National Academy of Sciences.

135. U.S. Congress, House, Committee on Merchant Marine and Fisheries, *Study of the Effectiveness of the Committee on Oceanography*, pp. 9, 143. The IOC was a result of persistent efforts by the National Academy of Sciences, Committee on Oceanography to create a world oceanic organization within a UN specialized agency. The committee first made the proposal in 1958 and found itself facing U.S. government opposition to creating any new UN agencies. An additional difficulty arose over the location of such a body. The FAO would have been a possible site if it had had an interest in scientific research. UNESCO was the other alternative. W. M. Chapman to Harold F. Cary, General Assembly Resolution, November 22, 1966, W. M. Chapman Collection.

136. See letter of President John F. Kennedy to the president of the Senate on increasing the national effort in oceanography, March 29, 1961, in U.S., President, *Public Papers of the Presidents of the United States* (Wash-

ington, D.C.: Office of the Federal Register, National Archives and Records Service, 1961), Item 100, pp. 240-244.

137. Evidence of this concern was to be found in the report of the Panel on Oceanography of the president's Scientific Advisory Committee. Released in June 1966, the report on *Effective Use of the Sea* recommended national oceanic goals and programs and stressed the importance to national security of a strong naval program.

138. Marine Resources and Engineering Development Act of 1966, Statutes at Large, Vol. 80, Pt. 1, 1966, pp. 203-208.

139. The commission report, "Our Nation and the Sea," was released in January 1969. It called for establishment of an independent agency, the National Oceanic and Atmospheric Agency (NOAA), to unify the national program in marine affairs and for a National Committee on the Oceans and Atmosphere (NACOA) outside the government. The Marine Sciences Council was to remain active through 1970.

140. This committee subsequently became the permanent Committee on International Policy in the Marine Environment. U.S. Congress, House, Committee on Foreign Affairs, *The United Nations and the Issue of Deep Ocean Resources*, Hearings, p. 173.

141. Ibid., p. 183. See Chart A for the structure established by the Marine Resources and Engineering Development Act.

142. Ibid., p. 199.

143. W. M. Chapman to Harold F. Cary, Reorganization of the Work of the Office of the Special Assistant, May 9, 1965, W. M. Chapman Collection.

144. U.S. Congress, House, Committee on Merchant Marine and Fisheries, *National Oceanographic Program Legislation*, Hearings before the Subcommittee on Oceanography, 89th Cong., 1st sess., 1965, p. 102.

145. U.S. Congress, House, Committee on Merchant Marine and Fisheries, *National Marine Sciences Program*, Part I, Hearings before the Subcommittee on Oceanography, 90th Cong., 1st sess., 1967, p. 505.

146. W. M. Chapman to Harold F. Cary, General Assembly Resolutions, November 22, 1966, W. M. Chapman Collection.

Chapter 7
A NEW BEGINNING: THE U.S. ADOPTS AN OCEANS POLICY

1. United Nations, General Assembly, 22nd Session (A/6695), August 16, 1967.

2. United Nations, General Assembly, 22nd Session, September 21, 1967, *Summary Records* (A/BUR/SR.166), p. 3.

3. H.J. Res. 816-824, H.J. Res. 828-830, H.J. Res. 834-835, H.J. Res. 837, H.J. Res. 839-840, H.J. Res. 843-844, H.J. Res. 850, H.J. Res. 854-857, H.J. Res. 865, H.J. Res. 876, H.J. Res. 881, H.J. Res. 916, 90th Cong., 1st sess., 1967.

4. S.J. Res. 111, 90th Cong., 1st sess., 1967.

5. U.S. Congress, House, Committee on Foreign Affairs, *Interim Report on the United Nations and the Issue of Deep Ocean Resources*, together with Hearings by the Subcommittee on International Organizations and Movements, pp. 38-42, 70-71. For discussion of the Maltese proposal and reactions to it in the United States and the United Nations, see: Guenter Weissberg, "International Law Meets the Short-Term National Interest: The Maltese Proposal on the Sea-Bed and Ocean Floor—Its Fate in Two Cities"; Daniel S. Cheever, "The Role of International Organization in Ocean Development."

6. U.S. Congress, House, Committee on Foreign Affairs, *United Nations and Deep Ocean Resources*, pp. 52, 56.

7. H. Con. Res. 558, H. Con. Res. 576-577, H. Con. Res. 580, 90th Cong., 1st sess., 1967.

8. S. Res. 172, S. Res. 186, 90th Cong., 1st sess., 1967.

9. U.S. Congress, Senate, Committee on Foreign Relations, *Governing the Use of Ocean Space*, Hearing on S.J. Res. 111, S. Res. 172, S. Res. 186, 90th Cong., 1st sess., 1967, p. 26.

10. U.S. Congress, House, Committee on Foreign Affairs, *United Nations and Deep Ocean Resources*, pp. 141-142.

11. U.S. Congress, Senate, Committee on Foreign Relations, *Governing the Use of Ocean Space*, p. 27.

12. A direct statement of the official position at the time was made by a Department of the Interior official to Congress. "The Federal position," as his agency construed it, was "that the Malta proposal is not acceptable to us. It is premature. We do not have the information to make decisions with respect to the questions that are raised by the Malta proposal. We don't want to have to take any position with respect to some of these questions." This point of view had been carried to the interagency deliberations by Interior. Interior recognized, however, that "no nation . . . likes to have to go before the General Assembly of the United Nations in a strictly negative position, especially if the negative position for one reason or another would be unpopular. Therefore you look for positive suggestions as alternates." Statement of Dr. Stanley A. Cain, assistant secretary for fish and wildlife and parks, Department of the Interior, in U.S. Congress, House, Committee on Foreign Affairs, *United Nations and Deep Ocean Resources*, p. 176.

13. U.S., Department of State, *Department of State Bulletin*, 57, No. 1483 (November 27, 1967), 723-725 or U.S./UN Press Release 182 or United Nations, General Assembly, 22nd Session (A/C.1/PV 1524), November 8, 1967.

14. United Nations, General Assembly, 22nd Session (A/RES/2340), 18 December 1967.

15. U.S. Congress, Senate, Committee on Commerce, *Special Study on United Nations Suboceanic Lands Policy*, Hearings, p. 64.

16. U.S. Congress, Senate, Committee on Foreign Relations, *Activities*

of Nations in Ocean Space, Hearings before the Subcommittee on Ocean Space, p. 220.

17. United Nations, General Assembly, 23rd Session, A/AC.135/20 (1968).

18. Thomas J. Hamilton, "U.S. Prepares Proposal for Treaty to Bar Nuclear Weapons from Seabed," *New York Times*, March 24, 1969, p. 13. Thomas J. Hamilton, "U.S. Rejects Soviet Proposal for Seabed Treaty," *New York Times*, May 16, 1969, p. 2.

19. U.S. Congress, House, Committee on Merchant Marine and Fisheries, Subcommittee on Oceanography, *Oceanography in the 90th Congress*, by George A. Doumani, 91st Cong., 1st sess., 1969, p. 71.

20. Ibid., p. 71.

21. U.S., Department of State, *Department of State Bulletin*, 58, No. 1493 (February 5, 1968), 161.

22. White House Press Release, "To Renew a Nation," March 8, 1968.

23. U.S., National Council on Marine Resources and Engineering Development, Executive Office of the President, *International Decade of Ocean Exploration*, May 1968, p. 1.

24. U.S. Congress, Committee on Merchant Marine and Fisheries, *Oceanography Legislation*, Hearings before the Subcommittee on Oceanography, 90th Cong., 1968, pp. 211-215.

25. U.S. Congress, House, Committee on Foreign Affairs and Committee on Merchant Marine and Fisheries, *The U.N. Ad Hoc Committee on the Seabeds*, Hearings before the Subcommittee on International Organizations and Movements and the Subcommittee on Oceanography, 90th Cong., 2nd sess., 1968, pp. 15, 28.

26. Press Release of U.S. Mission, USUN—100 (68), 20 June 1968 or UN Press Release GA/3669, 20 June 1968, pp. 4-6.

27. Harold M. Schmerck, Jr., "Johnson Asks Joint Exploitation of Sea Resources," *New York Times*, July 14, 1966, p. 10.

28. United Nations, General Assembly, 23rd Session, June 7, 1968, *General Assembly Official Records* (A/AC/135/12), pp. 6-9. For other descriptions of efforts to agree on principles at the 23rd General Assembly see George Winthrop Haight, "United Nations Affairs—Ad Hoc Committee on Seabed and Ocean Floor," *International Lawyer*, 3 (October 1968), 23-27, and "Developments in the United Nations Relating to Sea-Bed and Ocean Floor," *Natural Resources Lawyer*, 2 (June 1969), 121-129; Oliver Stone, "The Marine Environment—Recent Legal Developments," *Natural Resources Lawyer*, 2 (January 1969), 36-40.

29. U.S. Congress, House, Committee on Foreign Affairs, *UN Ad Hoc Committee*, pp. 122-123.

30. United Nations, General Assembly, 23rd Session, *General Assembly Official Records* (A/2730), 1968, Paragraphs 88 (a) and (b), pp. 17-19.

31. U.S. Congress, House, Committee on Foreign Affairs, *UN Ad Hoc Committee*, p. 56.

32. U.S., Congress, House, Committee on Foreign Affairs, *The Oceans:*

A Challenging New Frontier, Report by the Subcommittee on International Organizations and Movements, H. Reprt. 1957, 90th Cong., 2nd sess., 1968, p. 3R.

33. A comprehensive discussion of the work of the UN Ad Hoc Seabed Committee and its legal and economic technical working group can be found in Judy Joye, "The United Nations and its Interest in the Sea-Bed and Ocean Floor," *The Decade Ahead, 1970-1980* (Washington, D.C.: Marine Technology Society, 1969).

34. The resolution had the rather cumbersome title "Examination of the question of the reservation exclusively for peaceful purposes of the seabed and the ocean floor, and the sub-soil thereof, underlying the high seas beyond the limits of present national jurisdiction, and the use of their resources in the interests of mankind," United Nations, General Assembly, 23rd Session, December 21, 1968, *General Assembly Official Records* (A/PV.1752), pp. 13-20.

35. U.S. Congress, Senate, Committee on Foreign Relations, *Activities of Nations in Ocean Space,* p. 215.

36. A discussion of the resolutions and of the accomplishments of the ad hoc committee may be found in K. Krishna Rao, "The Legal Regime of the Sea-Bed and Ocean Floor."

37. U.S. Congress, House, Committee on Foreign Affairs, *United Nations and Deep Ocean Resources,* pp. 164, 231.

38. U.S., Department of the Interior, *Petroleum and Sulfur on the U.S. Continental Shelf . . . A Summary of Activity in Exploration and Production of Oil, Gas and Sulfur, 1963-1968* (Washington, D.C.: Government Printing Office, 1969), p. 12.

39. Ibid., p. 17.

40. U.S. Congress, Senate, Committee on Commerce, *Special Study on United Nations Suboceanic Lands Policy,* p. 103.

41. "Our Yellow Submarine," *The Humble Way,* 8, No. 3 (1969), 15.

42. U.S., Department of the Interior, V. E. McKelvey et al., "Potential Mineral Resources of the United States Outer Continental Shelves," unpublished report of the Geological Survey to the Public Land Law Review Commission, March 1968. A year later the U.S.G.S. estimated potential reserves in place to a depth of 200 meters to be 660-780 billion barrels of oil and 1,640-2,200 trillion cubic feet of gas with reserves of the same magnitude in the area between the 200- and 2500-meter isobaths.

43. U.S. Congress, Senate, Committee on Commerce, *United Nations Suboceanic Lands Policy,* p. 103.

44. Murray Seeger, "The Oilmen and Politics," *The Washington Post,* January 17, 1971, p. B1.

45. National Petroleum Council, *Petroleum Resources Under the Ocean Floor* (Washington, D.C.: National Petroleum Council, March 1969), pp. 70-72.

46. Ibid.

47. U.S. Congress, House, Committee on Foreign Affairs, *United Nations and Deep Ocean Resources*, p. 164.

48. U.S. Congress, House, Committee on Foreign Affairs, *UN Ad Hoc Committee*, pp. 2-3.

49. U.S. Congress, Senate, Committee on Commerce, *United Nations Suboceanic Lands Policy*, p. 108.

50. Ibid., p. 110.

51. Ibid., pp. 107, 124.

52. U.S. Congress, House, Committee on Foreign Affairs, *United Nations and Deep Ocean Resources*, pp. 190-192.

53. U.S. Congress, Senate, Committee on Commerce, *United Nations Suboceanic Lands Policy*, p. 24.

54. U.S. Congress, Senate, Committee on Foreign Relations, *Activities of Nations in Ocean Space*, pp. 244-246.

55. U.S. Congress, Senate, Committee on Commerce, *United Nations Suboceanic Lands Policy*, p. 24.

56. Assistant Secretary of the Navy Robert A. Frosch argued in 1968 that "sovereignty over the continental shelves (whatever their seaward boundary) should be closely limited." "Exploiting Marine Mineral Resources," *Vital Speeches of the Day*, 35 (November 15, 1968), 71. A year earlier Mr. Frosch had pointed out "that the Navy has used the sea bottom for many purposes for many years." (U.S. Congress, House, Committee on Foreign Affairs, *United Nations and Deep Ocean Resources*, p. 192.) Mr. Frosch noted elsewhere that "certain policies which might favor our military and our defense systems in this respect are: The rules should not deny freedom of the seas for the deployment of strategic forces by all nations. The rules should not deny freedom of the seas for deployment of strategic detection and warning devices. Future development of international agreements should allow use of the ocean surface, the air and space above it, and the ocean bottom for warning devices." ("Military Uses of the Ocean," Paper presented at *Second Conference on Law, Organization and Security, in the Use of the Ocean*, Mershon Center for Education in National Security, Ohio State University, pp. 154-174.)

See also Captain L. E. Zeni, "Defense Needs in Accommodations Among Ocean Users," Lewis M. Alexander, ed., *Law of the Sea*, p. 35.

57. For a comprehensive discussion of ASW detection devices, see Stockholm International Peace Research Institute, *SIPRI Yearbook of World Armaments and Disarmament*, 1969/70 (Stockholm: Almquist and Wiksell, 1970), pp. 106-129, 148-152.

58. For discussion of the seabed disarmament debate, see *SIPRI Yearbook*, pp. 154-179.

59. U.S., Department of State, *Department of State Bulletin*, 60, No. 1556 (April 21, 1969), 343.

60. For text of U.S. proposal see U.S. Congress, Senate, Committee on Foreign Relations, *Activities of Nations in Ocean Space*, pp. 15-16. Also,

U.S., Department of State, *Department of State Bulletin*, 60, No. 1564 (June 16, 1969), pp. 520-524; Thomas J. Hamilton, "U.S. Prepares Proposal for Treaty to Ban Nuclear Weapons from Seabed," *New York Times*, March 24, 1969, p. 13.

61. For text of Soviet proposal to ENDC, see U.S. Congress, Senate, Committee on Foreign Relations, *Activities of Nations in Ocean Space*, pp. 16-17. See also Thomas J. Hamilton, "Russians Submit Pact to Bar Arms from Ocean Bed," *New York Times*, March 19, 1969, p. 1. Thomas J. Hamilton, "U.S. Rejects Call by Soviets to Ban Arms on Seabed," *New York Times*, March 26, 1969, p. 1. Thomas J. Hamilton, "U.S. Rejects Soviet Proposal for Seabed Treaty," *New York Times*, May 16, 1969, p. 2. Y. Listvinov, "Pentagon and the Seabed," *New Times*, No. 27, July 9, 1969, pp. 14-15.

62. Since many of the detection systems of the Navy Sound Surveillance System (SOSUS) program relied on shore-based generators, the military was accustomed to dealing with "friendly" nations in the installation of such facilities. With the development of self-contained battery-powered systems, the military no doubt hoped to get away from this requirement. *SIPRI Yearbook*, pp. 149-150.

63. Chalmers M. Roberts, "U.S. Joins Russia in Sea A-Ban," *Washington Post*, October 8, 1969, p. A1. Thomas F. Hamilton, "U.S.-Soviet Draft Bans Atom Arms on Ocean Floor," *New York Times*, October 8, 1969, p. 1.

64. "Ninth Annual Report of the United States Arms Control and Disarmament Agency," (1969); U.S., Department of State, *Department of State Bulletin*, 62, May 4, 1970; see pp. 592-594.

65. Henry Tanner, "U.N. Group Balks on Seabed Treaty," *New York Times*, December 13, 1969, p. 7. Thomas J. Hamilton, "Seabed Draft to Bar Atoms Revised," *New York Times*, April 21, 1970, p. 4. Kathleen Teltsch, "U.N. Adopts Pact on Seabed Arms," *New York Times*, November 18, 1970, p. 1.

66. U.S. Congress, Senate, Committee on Foreign Relations, *Seabed Arms Control Treaty*, 92nd Cong., 2nd sess., pp. 39-41.

67. David C. Brooks, "Deep Sea Manganese Nodules: From Scientific Phenomenon to World Resource," *Natural Resources Journal*, 8, July 1968, 406-407; Arnold J. Rothstein, "Deep Ocean Mining Today and Tomorrow," *Columbia Journal of World Business*, 6, Jan.-Feb. 1971, 43-50.

68. Joint Report sent to the American Bar Association House of Delegates by the Sections of Natural Resources Law, International and Comparative Law, and the Standing Committee on Peace and Law Through the United Nations.

69. American Bar Association, "Non-Living Resources of the Sea (A Critique)," *Natural Resources Lawyer*, 2, November 1969, 429.

70. John G. Laylin, attorney at law, in U.S. Congress, Senate, Committee on Interior and Insular Affairs, *Outer Continental Shelf*, p. 136. "Those who

have primarily in mind the extraction of oil are interested only in the area landward of the foot of the continental slope. They have been informed, it would appear, that there is little likelihood of oil pools below the bed of the deep sea. In consequence they are not concerned with the regime to be established for the deep sea bed. It does not matter to them that their demands may hurt the efforts of the United States to bring about a satisfactory regime for the deep sea.

"In contrast . . . [those] . . . who have in mind the interests of hard metal miners find themselves agreeing with many of the contentions of the Navy and the scientists. They do not object to a broad shelf, but they do object to sacrificing the chances of reaching agreement on a satisfactory deep sea regime by insisting willy nilly that the United States now take the position that the outer limit of the shelf is now at the foot of the continental slope."

71. A useful discussion of the role of the legal advisor within the Department of State may be found in Richard B. Bilder, "The Office of the Legal Adviser."

72. U.S. Congress, House, Committee on Armed Services, *Territorial Sea Boundaries*, Hearings before the Subcommittee on Seapower, 91st Cong., 2nd sess., June 25, 1970, p. 9299.

73. U.S. Congress, House, Committee on Merchant Marine and Fisheries, *National Marine Sciences Program*, Hearings, Part 1, 90th cong., 1st sess., 1967, pp. 166-167.

74. U.S. Congress, House, Committee on Foreign Affairs, *UN Ad Hoc Committee*, p. 204.

75. U.S. Congress, Senate, Committee on Commerce, *Federal Oceanic and Atmospheric Organization*, Hearings before the Subcommittee on Oceanography, Part 2, 91st Cong., 1st and 2nd sess., pp. 1121-1122.

76. The date of the Seabed NSSM given by John P. Leacocos was April 11, 1969 in "Kissinger Apparat," *Foreign Policy*, 5, Winter 1971-1972, 25.

77. For discussions of the Kissinger NSC system, see David Landau, "Henry Kissinger: Nixon's Metternich," *Washington Post*, July 11, 1971, p. B1; Chester A. Crocker, "The Nixon-Kissinger National Security Council System, 1969-1972," in *Commission on the Organization of the Government for the Conduct of Foreign Policy, June 1975*, 6 (Washington, D.C.: Government Printing Office, 1975), Appendix O, pp. 79-99.

78. It should be noted that the options system in this case diverged from the usual pattern. Typically, the NSSM was a probing questionnaire setting out the problem and requesting policy options. Agency replies were then reviewed and sifted through a network of interdepartmental groups before going to the president with Mr. Kissinger's covering memorandum. Passage through this committee structure could be a lengthy process. It is likely that the resort to the Under Secretaries Committee without extensive review by interdepartmental study groups was intended to avoid undue delay in reach-

ing a decision. It was also generally the case that matters believed to be of lesser importance passed to the Under Secretaries Committee rather than to the Senior Review Group.

79. While four of the five committees of the Marine Science Council were dissolved by the Nixon administration and replaced by a single Committee for Policy Review, CIPME remained unaffected, confirming if nothing else its claim to be a State Department committee.

80. U.S., National Council on Marine Resources and Engineering Development, *Marine Science Affairs—Selecting Priority Programs*, Annual Report (Washington, D.C.: Government Printing Office, 1970), p. 10.

81. U.S. Congress, Senate, Committee on Foreign Relations, *Activities in Ocean Space*, July 24, 25, 28, and 30, 1969.

82. U.S. Congress, Senate, Committee on Commerce, *United Nations Suboceanic Lands Policy*, p. 1.

83. U.S. Congress, Senate, *Congressional Record*, 91st Cong., 1st sess., August 4, 1969, S. 9045. On the role of these committees see Kenneth H. Kolb, "Congress and the Ocean Policy Process," *Ocean Development and International Law*, 3, No. 3 (1976), 268-269.

84. U.S. Congress, Senate, Committee on Commerce, *United Nations Suboceanic Lands Policy*, p. 18.

85. An excellent discussion of the State Department's diminished influence under the Nixon administration may be found in Terence Smith, "Foreign Policy: Decision Power Ebbing at the State Department," *New York Times*, January 18, 1971, p. 1.

86. U.S. Congress, Senate, Committee on Foreign Relations, *Activities of Nations in Ocean Space*, p. 232.

87. Ibid., p. 220.

88. U.S. Congress, Senate, Committee on Commerce, *United Nations Suboceanic Lands Policy*, pp. 4-7.

89. U.S., Department of State, *Department of State Bulletin*, 61, September 29, 1969, 288.

90. U.S. Congress, Senate, Committee on Commerce, *United Nations Suboceanic Lands Policy*, pp. 5-6.

91. Ibid., pp. 30, 112.

92. Ibid., p. 15.

93. The concept of the intermediate zone for seabed resources was first proposed by Louis Henkin in his study *Law for the Sea's Mineral Resources* prepared for the Marine Sciences Council (Department of Commerce, Clearinghouse for Federal Scientific and Technical Information, PB 177, 725, 1967). It was also adopted by the Commission on Marine Science, Engineering and Resources Development in its report, *Our Nation and the Sea*.

94. American Bar Association, "Non-Living Resources of the Sea," p. 435; Jerry Landauer, "Sharing the Wealth: Nixon is Urged to Yield Some

Ocean-Floor Oil to Help the World's Poor," *Wall Street Journal*, March 27, 1970, p. 1.

95. For evaluations of this resort to majority rule in the Twenty-fourth General Assembly, see: Louis Henkin, "Activities of the United Nations General Assembly," Lewis M. Alexander, ed., *The Law of the Sea: The United Nations and Ocean Management*, Proceedings of the Fifth Annual Conference of the Law of the Sea Institute (Kingston, R.I.: University of Rhode Island, 1970), pp. 2-22; and David P. Stang, "Recent United Nations Developments Concerning the Seabeds," *Marine Technology*, 1970, Sixth Annual Conference and Exposition of the Marine Technology Society, Washington, D.C., 1970, pp. 593-609.

96. Henry Tanner, "U.S. and Soviets Ask UN Backing for a Seabed Pact," *New York Times*, November 18, 1969, p. 17. Henry Tanner, "UN Group Balks on Seabed Treaty," *New York Times*, December 13, 1969, p. 7.

97. UN, General Assembly, 24th Session, December 15, 1969, *General Assembly Official Records* (A/Res. 2574).

98. U.S./UN Press Release 183 (69), December 2, 1969.

99. Henry Tanner, "U.N. Votes to Stop Civil Seabed Uses," *New York Times*, December 16, 1969, p. 8; "U.N. Votes to Halt Deep-Ocean Exploitation," *Ocean Industry*, 5, January 1970.

100. Letter from John Stevenson, in U.S. Congress, Senate, Committee on Interior and Insular Affairs, *Outer Continental Shelf*, pp. 210-211.

101. U.S. opposition to Resolutions 2574A and 2574B is explained in detail in U.S., Department of State, *Department of State Bulletin*, 62, January 26, 1970, 89-95, and in *Department of State Bulletin*, 62, February 9, 1970, 164-165.

102. Henry Tanner, "U.N. Votes to Stop Civil Seabed Uses."

103. U.S. Congress, Senate, Committee on Foreign Relations, *Activities of Nations in Ocean Space*, p. 246.

104. The Under Secretaries Committee meeting, agency positions, and the outcome are described in Edward Wenk, Jr., *The Politics of the Ocean*, pp. 274 ff.

105. In addition to Under Secretary Richardson, John Stevenson, the legal advisor, was present to represent the Department of State. General Earl Wheeler, chairman of the Joint Chiefs of Staff, and David Packard, the deputy secretary of defense, were present on behalf of their agency, while Russell Train represented the Department of the Interior in his capacity as under secretary. Also in attendance were Richard G. Kleindienst, the deputy attorney general, David Peacock, the under secretary of commerce, Robert E. Osgood of the National Security Council, James E. Beggs, the under secretary of transportation, and Charles Maechling, the deputy general counsel of the National Science Foundation. Other agencies represented that afternoon were the Treasury Department, the Bureau of the Budget, the Central

Intelligence Agency, the Office of Science and Technology, and the National Council for Marine Science, Engineering and Resources Development.

106. For a description of the role and stature of the Under Secretaries Committee in the National Security Council committee hierarchy, see: Hedrick Smith, "Foreign Policy: Kissinger at Hub," *New York Times*, January 19, 1971, p. 1, and James Reston, "The Kissinger Role," *New York Times*, March 3, 1971, p. 39.

107. Letter from Elliot L. Richardson to the author, March 22, 1977.

108. H. Gary Knight, "The Draft United Nations Convention on the International Seabed Area," p. 486.

109. On the agency positions that were considered by the president, see: Jerry Landauer, "Nixon is Urged to Yield Some Ocean-Floor Oil to Help the World's Poor," *Wall Street Journal*, March 27, 1970, p. 1; U.S. Congress, Senate, Committee on Interior and Insular Affairs, *Outer Continental Shelf*, Part 2, pp. 361 ff.; Samuel C. Orr, "Domestic Pressures Quicken U.S. Policy-Making on Seabed Jurisdiction," *CPR National Journal*, March 28, 1970, pp. 676 ff.

110. U.S. Congress, Senate, Committee on Interior and Insular Affairs, *Outer Continental Shelf*, Part 2, p. 399.

111. On the operations of these two power centers in the White House, see Robert B. Semple, Jr., "Nixon's Style as Boss Combines Desire for Order and Solitude," *New York Times*, January 12, 1970, p. 1.

112. For the background to the Brazilian decision, see Michael A. Morris, "The Domestic Context of Brazilian Maritime Policy."

113. "Secret Crisis," *Wall Street Journal*, March 20, 1970, p. 1.

114. For an excellent discussion of the U.S. reaction to this legislation, see Robert H. Neuman, "Oil on Troubled Waters: The International Control of Marine Pollution," *Journal of Maritime Law and Commerce*, 2, January 1971, 1.

115. For a discussion of the impact on decision-making of the need to seek outside support, see R. Harrison Wagner, *United States Policy Toward Latin America: A Study in Domestic and International Politics* (Stanford: Stanford University Press, 1970), pp. 74-78.

116. Examples include: Landauer, "Nixon Urged to Yield Ocean-Floor Oil"; Orr, "Domestic Pressures Quicken U.S. Policy-Making"; and "Oceans of Oil," *National Observer*, April 6, 1970.

117. See for instance, Alton Lennon, chairman of the Subcommittee on Oceanography, Committee on Merchant Marine and Fisheries, House, letter to the president, April 7, 1970; U.S. Congress, Senate, Senator Pell speaking on the Seaward Limits of National Jurisdiction over the Continental Shelf, 91st Cong., 2nd sess., April 16, 1970, *Congressional Record*, S. 5933-5936.

118. U.S. Congress, Senate, Committee on Interior and Insular Affairs, *Outer Continental Shelf*, Part 2, p. 363.

119. U.S. Congress, Senate, Senator Metcalf speaking on the Seaward

Limit of Our Legal Continental Shelf, 91st Cong., 2nd sess., April 13, 1970, *Congressional Record*, S. 5590.

120. U.S. Congress, Senate, Committee on Interior and Insular Affairs, *Outer Continental Shelf*, Part 2, p. 423.

121. Ibid., p. 427.

122. "United States Policy for the Seabed," *Weekly Compilation of Presidential Documents*, 6 (1970), 677. Also in U.S., Department of State, *Department of State Bulletin*, 62, June 15, 1970, 737-738. For the press response to the Nixon proposal, see: Victor Cohn, "Nixon Urges World Treaty for Sharing Seabed Riches," *Washington Post*, May 24, 1970, p. A1; Richard D. Lyons, "Nixon Proposes a Treaty to Exploit Seabed for All," *New York Times*, May 24, 1970, p. 28; "New Frontier Under the Sea," *Washington Post*, May 27, 1970, p. 18; "Man's Ocean Heritage," *New York Times*, May 27, 1970, p. 46.

123. U.S. Congress, Senate, Committee on Interior and Insular Affairs, *Outer Continental Shelf*, Part 2, p. 434.

124. Ibid., p. 454.

125. Ibid., p. 435.

126. Committee members included Bernard H. Oxman, Louis B. Sohn, and Stuart McIntyre of the State Department, Vincent McKelvey of the Interior, and Leigh S. Ratiner of the Defense Department (three international lawyers, one political scientist, and one geologist).

127. Samuel C. Orr, "Administration Insists Oil Industry Benefits from Proposed Seabed Treaty," *CPR National Journal*, June 6, 1970, pp. 1184-1185.

128. Invited to participate were representatives of the National Petroleum Council, American Petroleum Institute, Jersey Standard, Kennecott Copper, Union Carbide, and Deep Sea Ventures. See "A Draft Treaty for the Nixon Deep Seabed Regime," *Ocean Science News*, 12, July 17, 1970, 1.

129. "The U.S. Should Not Present a Seabed Treaty at Geneva," *Ocean Science News*, 12, July 24, 1970, 1.

130. For congressional reactions to the proposal, see: U.S., Congress, House, Congressman Bush Speaking on Treaty to Renounce All National Claims on Seabed Resources, 91st Cong., 2nd sess., June 30, 1970, *Congressional Record*, H. 6272-6273; U.S., Congress, Senate, Senator Hollings speaking on "Draft U.S. Seabeds Treaty Discussions Should Begin," 91st Cong., 2nd sess., July 24, 1970, *Congressional Record*, S. 12065-12067; U.S., Congress, Senate, Senator Tower Speaking on Seabed Treaty, 91st Cong., 2nd sess., July 31, 1970, *Congressional Record*, S. 12523.

131. U.S. Congress, Senate, Committee on Interior and Insular Affairs, *Outer Continental Shelf*, Part 2, p. 463.

132. U.S. Congress, Senate, Committee on Interior and Insular Affairs, *Outer Continental Shelf*, p. 25. The letter was signed by Senator Henry M. Jackson, Chairman of the Interior and Insular Affairs Committee, Senator

Gordon Allott, the committee's ranking minority member, Senator Lee Metcalf, chairman of the committee's Special Subcommittee on the Outer Continental Shelf, and Senator Henry L. Bellmon, ranking minority member of the subcommittee.

133. Samuel C. Orr, "Soviet, Latin Opposition Blocks Agreement on Seabeds Treaty," CPR *National Journal*, September 12, 1970, pp. 197 ff.; "The U.S. Should Not Present a Seabed Treaty at Geneva."

134. U.S. Congress, Senate, Committee on Interior and Insular Affairs, *Outer Continental Shelf*, p. 25.

135. For the final provisions of the draft working paper, see Ann L. Hollick, "United States Ocean Policy: 1948-1971," pp. 25 ff.

136. U.S., President, Report to the Congress, *U.S. Foreign Policy for the 1970s*, February 18, 1970; see also U.S., Department of State, *Department of State Bulletin*, 62, March 9, 1970.

137. Speech to the Philadelphia Bar Association and the Philadelphia World Affairs Council, February 18, 1970; Press Release 49, *Department of State Bulletin*, 62, March 16, 1970, 341. For comments see: "U.S. Shifts Position on Territorial Seas," *Washington Post*, February 19, 1970, p. A16; "12-Mile Territorial Seas," *Washington Post*, February 21, 1970, p. A14; Sam Pope Brewer, "U.S. Will Support 12-Mile Sea Limit," *New York Times*, February 22, 1970; "Redefining the Law of the Sea," *New York Times*, March 16, 1970, p. 40.

138. A question naturally arises as to what sort of concession is constituted by an agreement to recognize a twelve-mile territorial sea when, in practice, the United States already observes (or does not violate) the territorial seas of nations that already claim twelve miles. The answer is not entirely clear.

139. Press Release 64, *Department of State Bulletin*, 62, No. 1603 (March 16, 1970), 343.

140. U.S., Department of Defense, "United States Policy with Respect to Territorial Seas," Department of Defense Press Release, February 25, 1970.

141. There has been disagreement on this number: 116 is the more-or-less official U.S. government figure. A chart prepared by the geographer of the State Department for the 1958 UN Conference (entitled "World Straits Affected by a Twelve-Mile Territorial Sea") lists 121. The State Department Pamphlet *Sovereignty of the Sea* (Geographic Bulletin No. 3, Revised October 1969) includes 94 candidates between seven and twenty-four miles.

142. The right of innocent passage through territorial waters is exercised subject to compliance with the regulations of the coastal state. In practice it may be considerably restricted. Submarines are required to navigate on the surface of territorial waters; the right of warships to passage without express consent is widely disputed; and no provision is made for innocent passage of aircraft, possibly precluding civilian as well as military rights to fly over territorial seas. See Articles 14 and 23 of the Geneva Convention

on the Territorial Sea and the Contiguous Zone, adopted by the United Nations Conference on the Law of the Sea, April 29, 1958 (A/CONF. 12/L.52).

143. On the history of Soviet claims to coastal waters, and discrepancies in legal classification of water expanses along Soviet coasts, see William E. Butler, *The Soviet Union and the Law of the Sea*, pp. 19 ff.

144. Leigh S. Ratiner, "United States Oceans Policy, pp. 248-249.

145. U.S. Congress, House, Committee on Armed Services, *Territorial Sea Boundaries*, p. 9291.

146. The declaration of Basic Principles on the Law of the Sea made at the Montevideo meeting is translated in UN Doc. A/AC.138/34, April 1971. For an excellent discussion of the motivating forces at this and subsequent Latin American conferences, see Karin Hjertonsson, *The New Law of the Sea*, pp. 44-45; 68-73.

147. UN General Assembly Resolution 2749 (xxv), December 17, 1970.

148. The U.S. view was that the meaning of the principle of "common heritage" would be established through negotiation on an international regime. Until then, mining constituted a reasonable use of the high seas under international law. Testimony of John Norton Moore before Senate Subcommittee on Minerals, Materials and Fuels, 92nd Cong., 2nd sess., Washington, D.C., September 1974.

149. UN General Assembly Resolution 2750A (xxv), December 17, 1970; UN General Assembly Resolution 2750B (xxv), December 17, 1970; UN General Assembly Resolution 2750C (xxv), December 17, 1970.

Chapter 8
PREPARATIONS FOR A THIRD UN CONFERENCE: 1971-1973

1. The committee also met in New York on October 14, 15, and 22 to complete adoption of its report. The 1971 sessions are described in David P. Stang, "The Donnybrook Fair of the Oceans."

2. The tripartite structure of the negotiations reflected political rather than substantive considerations. Obviously, the work could have been divided between the issue of the deep seabed regime and problems associated with the extent of national jurisdiction. The establishment of three committees served the political goal of providing positions on the bureau for each of the major regional groups.

3. The work of the Seabed Committee in 1971 is fully reviewed in a Senate committee staff report. See U.S. Congress, Senate, Committee on Interior and Insular Affairs, *The Law of the Sea Crisis*, 92nd Cong., 1st sess., December 1971.

4. UN General Assembly Resolution 2881 (xxvi).

5. See Report of the Committee on the Peaceful Uses of the Sea-Bed and the Ocean Floor Beyond the Limits of National Jurisdiction, UN General Assembly Official Records, Supplement No. 21, A/8721 (xxvii). The

spring session of the Seabed Committee is described in U.S. Congress, Senate, Committee on Interior and Insular Affairs, *The Law of the Sea Crisis: A Staff Report*, Part 2, 92nd Cong., 2nd sess., May 1972. The U.S. delegation report on the spring session is in U.S. Congress, House, Committee on Foreign Affairs, Subcommittee on International Organizations and Movements, *Law of the Sea and Peaceful Uses of the Seabeds*, Hearings, 92nd Cong., 2nd sess., April 10 and 11, 1972, pp. 9-12. The delegation report on the summer session is in U.S. Congress, House, Committee on Merchant Marine and Fisheries, Subcommittee on Oceanography, *Oceanography Miscellaneous, Hearings*, 92nd Cong., 2nd sess., pp. 237-273.

6. UN General Assembly, Document No. A/AC.138/56. (Hereafter, UN documents will be cited by number only.)

7. A/AC.138/58.

8. A/AC.138/66.

9. A/AC.138/68-72.

10. See Appendix 2.

11. Organizations with which the subcommittee hoped to coordinate its efforts included the Food and Agriculture Organization of the UN (FAO), the UN Conference on the Human Environment, the Intergovernmental Maritime Consultative Organization (IMCO), and the Intergovernmental Oceanographic Commission of UNESCO.

12. UN General Assembly Resolution 3029A (XXVII).

13. See Report of the Committee on the Peaceful Uses of the Sea-Bed and the Ocean Floor Beyond the Limits of National Jurisdiction, UN General Assembly Official Records, Supplement No. 21, A/9021, Vols. 1-6 (XXVIII).

14. For discussion of the texts prepared by the Seabed Committee, see U.S. Congress, Senate, Committee on Interior and Insular Affairs, Subcommittee on Minerals, Materials and Fuels, *Status Report on Law of the Sea Conference*, and John R. Stevenson and Bernard H. Oxman, "The Preparations for the Law of the Sea Conference," *American Journal of International Law*, 68, No. 1 (January 1974).

15. Due to the unrest in Chile following the overthrow of the Allende government in late 1973, the site of the conference was moved to Caracas.

16. These and other negotiating groups are described in Edward Miles, "The Structure and Effects of the Decision Process in the Seabed Committee and the Third United Nations Conference on the Law of the Sea," pp. 161-166.

17. See Appendix 3.

18. The African regional group was particularly attentive to the problems of landlocked states since they comprised thirteen members of their forty-eight-nation group.

19. For a discussion of the territorialist, broad margin, and patrimonialist positions in the Latin American context, see Karin Hjertonsson, *The New*

Law of the Sea; Alvaro de Soto, "The Latin American View of the Law of the Sea," *India Quarterly,* 29, No. 2 (April-June 1973), 126-137.

20. See for example A/AC.138/SC.II/L.27, L.47 and L.54.

21. See A/AC.138/SC.II/L.25 n which Brazil interprets "innocent passage" in the territorial sea to allow free transit for navigation.

22. A/CONF.62/L.4.

23. Canada, secretary of state for external affairs, "Third United Nations Conference on the Law of the Sea," bound typescript.

24. The text of the meeting is in UN General Assembly Official Records, Supplement 21, A/8721 (xxvii) or A/AC.138/80.

25. Joint proposal A/AC.138/SC.II/L.21.

26. The conclusions of their report are in UN General Assembly Official Records, Supplement 21, A/8721, or A/AC.138/79.

27. A/CONF.62/C.2/L.82.

28. Ibid.

29. The Philippines made a special claim to historic waters based on an historic title or right. A/CONF.62/C.2/L.24.

30. A/CONF.62/C.2/L.49.

31. Ibid., and A/CONF.62/C.2/L.13.

32. A/CONF.62/C.2/L.69.

33. Miles, "The Structure and Effects of the Decision Process," p. 165.

34. A/CONF.62/C.2/L.38; V. Yaroslavtsev, "The World Ocean and International Law," *International Affairs,* No. 2, February 1975, pp. 61-71.

35. A/AC.138/SC.II/L.7 (1972); A/CONF.62/C.2/L.11.

36. A/CONF.62/C.2/L.3.

37. Japan (A/AC.138/SC.II/L.12 and A/CONF.62/C.2/L.46); Soviet Union (A/CONF.62/C.2/L.38); United States (A/CONF.62/C.2/L.47 and 80).

38. A/CONF.62/C.2/L.40.

39. A/AC.138/81.

40. A/AC.138/52.

41. A/CONF.62/C.2/L.39 (Afghanistan, Austria, Belgium, Bhutan, Bolivia, Botswana, Finland, Germany, Iraq, Laos, Lesotho, Luxembourg, Nepal, Netherlands, Paraguay, Singapore, Swaziland, Sweden, Switzerland, Uganda, Upper Volta, Zambia).

42. A/CONF.62/C.2/L.33.

43. A/CONF.62/C.2/L.19.

44. A/AC.138/49 sponsored by thirteen Latin American nations.

45. See A/AC.138/33 by Tanzania, A/CONF.62/C.3/L.13 by Colombia, and A/AC.138/49 by Brazil.

46. A/CONF.62/C.1/L.8 by Belgium, Denmark, France, Germany, Italy, Luxembourg, Netherlands, UK; A/CONF.62/C.1/L.6 by the United States; A/CONF.62/C.1/L.9 by Japan.

47. For a detailed discussion of U.S. government organization for law of the sea, see Otho E. Eskin, *Law of the Sea and the Management of*

Multilateral Diplomacy, Oceans Policy Study 1:5, Center for Oceans Law and Policy, University of Virginia, 1978.

48. See Appendix 4.

49. National Petroleum Council, *Petroleum Resources Under the Ocean Floor*, Supplemental Report, March 4, 1971.

50. See U.S. Congress, Senate, Committee on Interior and Insular Affairs, Subcommittee on Outer Continental Shelf, *Outer Continental Shelf*, Report, 91st Cong., 2nd sess., December 21, 1970.

51. American Mining Congress, *Statement with Respect to Working Paper of the Draft United Nations Convention on the International Seabed Area*, by T. S. Ary, Washington, D.C., January 27, 1971.

52. For a discussion of the important congressional contribution to the ocean policy process see House, Committee on Merchant Marine and Fisheries, Subcommittee on Oceanography, *Ocean Affairs in the 93rd Congress*, Report, 94th Cong., 1st sess., 1975, pp. 35-43. See also Kenneth H. Kolb, "Congress and the Ocean Policy Process," *Ocean Development and International Law*, 3, No. 3 (1976), 261-286.

53. U.S. officials signalled this shift in public meetings as early as June of 1971. *Ocean Science News*, 13, No. 26 (June 25, 1971).

54. Statement of John R. Stevenson, A/AC.138/SR.77-89 at p. 63 (August 10, 1972). See also, *United States Foreign Policy for the 1970s*, a report by President Nixon to the Congress, May 3, 1973, p. 217.

55. A/AC.138/SC.II/L.35 (1973) and statement of John R. Stevenson, A/AC.138/SC.II/SR.65 at 11 (1973).

56. National Petroleum Council, *Petroleum Resources*.

57. National Petroleum Council, *U.S. Energy Outlook*, Summary Report (Washington, D.C.: National Petroleum Council, December 1972), p. 79.

58. National Petroleum Council, *Law of the Sea: Particular Aspects Affecting the Petroleum Industry* and *Ocean Petroleum Resources: An Interim Report* (Washington, D.C.: National Petroleum Council, May 1973 and July 1974).

59. *San Diego Law Review*, 9, May 1972, 625.

60. U.S. Congress, Senate, Committee on Interior and Insular Affairs, Subcommittee on Minerals, Materials and Fuels, *Development of Hard Mineral Resources of the Deep Seabed, Hearings*, 92nd Cong., 2nd sess., June 2, 1972; House, Committee on Merchant Marine and Fisheries, Subcommittee on Oceanography, *Oceanography in the 92nd Congress: A Report*, 92nd Cong., 2nd sess., December 15, 1972, pp. 41-58.

61. On the pros and cons of this legislation, see John G. Laylin, "A Law to Govern Deep-sea Mining Until Superseded by International Agreement," and H. Gary Knight, "The Deep Seabed Hard Mineral Resources Act—A Negative View," pp. 433-460 in *San Diego Law Review*, 10, No. 3 (May 1973).

62. The legislation was drafted and approved by all AMC member companies with one exception.

63. U.S., *Congressional Record*, daily ed., January 23, 1974, pp. S255-S266.

64. Statement of Chilean representative, A/AC.138/SC.I/SR.49, March 1972.

65. The launching of the Hughes *Glomar Explorer*, ostensibly by Summa Corporation, in November 1972 alarmed the other companies. By September 21, 1973, the *Wall Street Journal* reported that Summa had invested about $100 million in ocean mining with Kennecott and Deep Sea Ventures (Tenneco) trailing at about $20 million each. (It was subsequently revealed that the *Glomar Explorer* was in fact a CIA enterprise, built to recover a Russian submarine from the Pacific ocean floor.)

66. Deborah Shapley, "Law of the Sea: Energy, Economy Spur Secret Review of US Stance," *Science*, 183, No. 4122 (January 25, 1974), 290-292; "Sea Breezes," *Save Our Seas Newsletter*, 1, No. 9 (November-December 1973).

67. See *Federal Register*, Notices, 38, No. 76 (April 20, 1973), 9839; and 38, No. 212 (November 5, 1973), 30457.

68. Shapley, "Law of the Sea," p. 291. Memorandum to Senator Metcalf from administrative assistant, July 1973.

69. U.S. Congress, House, Committee on Armed Services, *Territorial Sea Boundaries*, Hearings before the Subcommittee on Seapower, 91st Cong., 2nd sess., June 25, 1970, p. 9291.

70. U.S. Congress, Senate, Senator Hatfield on Fish Industry Representation at United Nations Conference, December 13, 1971, *Congressional Record*, daily ed., S21555; Senator Hatfield on the U.S. Fishing Industry, November 20, 1971, *Congressional Record* S19908; U.S. Congress, House, Congressman Pelly on a Program to Conserve World Fishery Resources, December 7, 1971, *Congressional Record*, daily ed., E.13076.

71. On the creation of NOAA, see Edward Wenk, Jr., *The Politics of the Ocean*, pp. 341-360 and George A. Doumani, *Ocean Wealth: Policy and Potential* (New York: Spartan Books, Hayden Book Company, 1973), pp. 82-84.

72. A/AC.138/SC.II/L.4. Also available in *International Legal Materials*, 10 (Washington, D.C.: American Society of International Law, 1971), 1018.

73. A/AC.138/52, March 23, 1971.

74. On these discussions, see Chapter 6.

75. U.S. Congress, House, Committee on Foreign Affairs, Subcommittee on Inter-American Affairs, *Fishing Rights and United States-Latin American Relations*, Hearings, pp. 84 ff.

76. OAS/SER.F/II, 14 Doc. 11/Rev. 1.

77. U.S. Congress, House, Committee on Foreign Affairs, *Fishing Rights and U.S.-Latin American Relations*, pp. 6-9.

78. Ibid., p. 10.

79. *International Legal Materials*, 12 (1973), 468.

80. P.L. 92-594, October 27, 1972; 86 Stat. 1313. Theodor Meron, "The Fishermen's Protective Act: A Case Study in Contemporary Legal Strategy of the United States," *American Journal of International Law*, 69, No. 2 (April 1975), 293 ff.

81. "Recent Developments in the Law of the Sea," *San Diego Law Review*, 11, May 1974, p. 699.

82. A/AC.138/SC.II/L.9.

83. John Neary, "Chaos at Sea III," *Saturday Review/World*, December 4, 1973, p. 20.

84. A/AC.138/SC.II/L.20; summarized in A/AC.138/SC.II/SR.60.

85. A/CONF.62/C.2/L.47.

86. A/AC.138/SC.II/L.4.

87. For more on these articles, see: H. Gary Knight, "The 1971 United States Proposals on the Breadth of the Territorial Sea and Passage through International Straits," *Oregon Law Review*, 51, Summer 1972, 759-787.

88. In 1971 a number of personnel changes had occurred in Defense. David Packard retired from the government and law of the sea responsibilities were transferred from the Legal Counsel's Office to the offices of the Joint Chiefs of Staff (JCS) and International Security Affairs (ISA). In addition, the secretary of defense, Melvin Laird, and the secretary of the navy, John Warner, began to take a direct interest in the law of the sea negotiations.

89. Bill C-202, April 8, 1970 (first reading), second session, 28th Parl., 18 and 19, Eliz. 2, 1C.17, 1969-1970.

90. J. A. Beesley, "Rights and Responsibilities of Arctic Coastal States: The Canadian View," *Journal of Maritime Law and Commerce*, 3, October 1971, 7.

91. Ann L. Hollick, "Canadian-American Relations: Law of the Sea."

92. A/AC.138/SC.III/L.40 and A/AC.138/SC.III/SR.41 at 2.

93. A/AC.138/SC.III/L.44.

94. U.S. Congress, House, Committee on Foreign Affairs, Subcommittee on National Security Policy and Scientific Developments, *Exploiting the Resources of the Seabed*, by George Doumani, July 1971, pp. 76-79.

95. UN General Assembly Resolution 3067 (xxviii).

96. For an excellent discussion of the UNCLOS rules of procedure in the UN context see, Louis B. Sohn, "Voting Procedures in United Nations Conferences for the Codification of International Law."

97. A detailed discussion of this debate may be found in Edward Miles, "An Interpretation of the Caracas Proceedings," in Francis Christy, Jr. et al., eds., *Law of the Sea: Caracas and Beyond* (Cambridge, Mass.: Ballinger, 1975), pp. 47-55.

98. Appendix, *Rules of Procedure*, A/CONF.62/30.

99. A record of these discussions is available in the official records of the conference: United Nations, *Third United Nations Conference on Law of the Sea*, 1st and 2nd sess., 1975, I, 16-59; Amendments offered by individual nations are summarized in Vol. III, pp. 67-80 (A/CONF.62/L.1).

Chapter 9
UNCLOS III: Variations on a Theme

1. United Nations, *Third United Nations Conference on the Law of the Sea*, Document No. A/CONF.62/28, June 20, 1974. (Conference documents hereafter cited by number and date, or number only. A/CONF.62 is the series designation for the conference proper, while A/AC.138 designates documents of the Seabed Committee prior to the convening of the conference.)

2. The first "Evensen Group" of juridical experts was established during the deliberations of the Seabed Committee to facilitate the work of Subcommittee II.

3. The definition of "geographically disadvantaged" offered by Haiti and Jamaica in 1974 was:

developing States which

(a) Are land-locked; or

(b) For geographical, biological or ecological reasons:

(i) Derive no substantial economic advantage from establishing an economic zone or patrimonial sea; or

(ii) Are adversely affected in their economics by the establishment of economic zones or patrimonial seas by other States; or

(iii) Have short coastlines and cannot extend uniformly their national jurisdiction.

A/CONF.62/C.2/L.35, August 1, 1974, and A/CONF.62/C.2/L.36, August 5, 1974. Other definitions (or refinements in definition) were still being submitted in 1976.

4. Detailed reports on the Caracas session of UNCLOS III include the following: Edward Miles, "An Interpretation of the Caracas Proceedings," in Francis T. Christy, Jr. et al., eds., *Law of the Sea: Caracas and Beyond* (Cambridge: Ballinger, 1975); U.S. Congress, Senate, Committee on Interior and Insular Affairs, *Status Report on Law of the Sea Conference*, Hearing, Pt. 2, 93rd Cong., 2nd sess., September 17, 1974; U.S. Congress, Senate, Committee on Commerce, National Ocean Policy Study, *The Third U.N. Law of the Sea Conference*, 94th Cong., 1st sess., 1975; U.S. Comptroller General, *Results of the Third Law of the Sea Conference, 1974 to 1976*.

5. Declaration of Kampala. A/CONF.62/63, May 2, 1974.

6. A/CONF.62/SR.21-42, June 28-July 15, 1974.

7. A/CONF.62/SR.22, June 28, 1974.

8. A/CONF.62/SR.29, July 9, 1974.

9. A/CONF.62/SR.38, July 11, 1974.

10. A/CONF.62/C.1/SR.1, July 10, 1974. Statement of Work Program in A/CONF.62/C.1/L.1, July 10, 1974.

11. See the alternative treaty articles designated as "Article 9" in A/CONF.62/C.1/L.3, August 5, 1974.

12. The U.S. proposed a $50,000 application fee to receive a site no greater than 30,000 square kilometers for fifty years. U.S. Draft Appendix to the Law of the Sea Treaty Concerning Mineral Resources Development in the International Seabed Area, A/CONF.62/C.1/L.6, August 13, 1974.

13. UN, Office of Public Information, Press Release SEA/100, July 31, 1974.

14. United States Proposal A/CONF.62/C.1/L.6, August 13, 1974; European Economic Community Proposal, A/CONF.62/C.1/L.8, August 16, 1974; Japan Proposal, A/CONF.62/C.1/L.9, August 19, 1974.

15. John R. Stevenson, Statement before Senate Committee on Interior and Insular Affairs, *Status Report*, Pt. 2, p. 858.

16. It took the Group of 77 a week to formulate a list of general guidelines (A/CONF.62/C.1/L.7) during which time the work of the committee ground to a halt.

17. Chile Working Paper, A/CONF.62/C.1/L.11, August 26, 1974.

18. A/AC.138/36, May 28, 1971 and supplement A/AC.138/73, May 12, 1972; A/CONF.62/25, May 22, 1974; U.S. Working Paper A/CONF.-62/C.1/L.5, August 8, 1974.

19. Another important example of the difficulty of structuring a negotiating situation occurred toward the end of the session. With the work program of the committee and the working group completed, efforts were directed at setting up a representative negotiating group to review the articles before the committee. The negotiating group would have fifty members selected on the basis of regional or interest groups, but would be formally open-ended. This effort was immediately attacked by those members of the Group of 77 who knew they would not be among the chosen fifty and who refused to delegate to other states the right to negotiate on their behalf. Although the negotiating group was finally established, its powers were severely restricted. The problem of creating groups with the authority to negotiate was to recur at every session of the conference.

20. Summary statement of work in Committee I, A/CONF.62/C.1/L.10, August 23, 1974.

21. A/CONF.62/C.1/L.3, August 5, 1974.

22. A/CONF.62/C.2/SR.1, July 3, 1974; Chairman's Statement of Program in A/CONF.62/L.2, July 3, 1974; and A/CONF.62/C.2/L.77, August 23, 1974.

23. A/CONF.62/C.2/SR.2, July 9, 1974 to end of session.

24. A/CONF.62/L.3-84, July 3-August 26, 1974.

25. Summary statement of work in Committee II, A/CONF.62/C.2/L.25, August 28, 1974.

26. The "territorialists," such as Peru, Brazil, Ecuador, Panama, and Uruguay, continued to advocate a 200-mile territorial sea and coastal African states periodically threatened to join them. See, for instance, the Ecuadorian position in A/CONF.62/C.2/L.10, July 16, 1974.

27. Statement of John Norton Moore before Committee II, July 22, 1974, Department of State Press Release No. 326.

28. See U.K. proposal, A/CONF.62/C.2/L.3, July 3, 1974; Soviet proposal, A/CONF.62/C.2/L.6, July 10, 1974, and A/CONF.62/C.2/L.11, July 17, 1974.

29. UN General Assembly, A/9021, Supplement No. 21, Vol. III, p. 4.

30. A/CONF.62/C.2/L.29, July 30, 1974; A/CONF.62/C.2/L.35, August 1, 1974; A/CONF.62/C.2/L.36, August 5, 1974; A/CONF.62/C.2/L.39, August 5, 1974; A/CONF.62/C.2/L.45, August 8, 1974; A/CONF.-62/C.2/L.48, August 8, 1974.

31. Brazil, A/AC.138/SC.II/L.25; Ecuador, A/CONF.62/C.2/L.10; Panama and Peru, A/AC.138/SC.II/L.27; A/AC.138/SC.II/L.47; A/AC.-138/SC.II/L.54.

32. See for instance, Guyana, A/CONF.62/C.2/L.5, July 9, 1974; Nicaragua, A/CONF.62/C.2/L.17, July 23, 1974; Nigeria, A/CONF.62/C.2/L.21/Rev. 1, August 5, 1974; El Salvador, A/CONF.62/C.2/L.60, August 14, 1974; African States, A/CONF.62/C.2/L.82, August 26, 1974.

33. A/CONF.62/C.2/L.38, August 5, 1974.

34. See A/CONF.62/C.2/L.39, August 5, 1974; A/CONF.62/C.2/L.36, August 5, 1974.

35. A/CONF.62/C.2/L.40/Add 1, August 5 and 28, 1974.

36. A/CONF.62/C.2/L.47, August 8, 1974.

37. Ireland, A/CONF.62/C.2/L.41, August 5, 1974; U.S., A/CONF.-62/C.2/L.47, August 5, 1974; Canada, A/CONF.62/C.2/L.81, August 23, 1974.

38. A/CONF.62/C.2/L.46, August 8, 1974. Japan was supported by Denmark, A/CONF.62/C.2/L.37, August 5, 1974.

39. A/CONF.62/C.2/L.47, August 8, 1974.

40. A/CONF.62/C.2/L.21, July 30, 1974; A/CONF.62/C.2/L.31/Rev. 1, August 16, 1974.

41. A/CONF.62/C.2/L.24, July 26, 1974; A/CONF.62/C.2/L.49, August 9, 1974; A/CONF.62/C.2/L.64, August 16, 1974; A/CONF.62/C.2/L.67, August 16, 1974; and A/CONF.62/C.2/L.70, August 20, 1974.

42. Turkey, A/CONF.62/C.2/L.9, July 15, 1974; A/CONF.62/C.2/L.23, July 26, 1974; A/CONF.62/C.2/L.34, August 1, 1974; A/CONF.-62/C.2/L.55, August 13, 1974; Greece, A/CONF.62/C.2/L.22, July 25, 1974; A/CONF.62/C.2/L.50, August 9, 1974.

43. A/CONF.62/C.2/L.85, August 28, 1974.

44. A/CONF.62/C.3/SR.1-2, July 4 and 11, 1974.

45. The work of Committee III is summarized in A/CONF.62/C.3/L.20, August 23, 1974.

46. The results of the informal working group are summarized in A/CONF.62/C.3/L.14-15, August 22, 1974.

47. See Kenya proposal, A/CONF.62/C.3/L.2, July 23, 1974.

48. Proposal of Federal Republic of Germany, A/CONF.62/C.3/L.7, August 1, 1974.

49. A/CONF.62/C.3/L.6, July 31, 1974.

50. Most of the proposals on scientific research are in informal conference room papers and are not a part of the UN documentation.

51. A/CONF.62/C.3/L.19, August 23, 1974.

52. A/CONF.62/C.3/L.13, August 22, 1974.

53. A/CONF.62/C.3/L.11-12, August 22, 1974.

54. A/CONF.62/C.3/SR.8, pp. 2-5; A/CONF.62/C.3/L.19, August 23, 1974.

55. A/CONF.62/L.7, August 27, 1974.

56. John R. Stevenson, "U.S. Urges Early Conclusion of Law of the Sea Treaty," Statement to UN General Assembly, December 17, 1974 in *Department of State Bulletin*, 72, No. 1858 (February 3, 1975), 153-154.

57. Detailed reviews of this session may be found in Edward Miles, "An Interpretation of the Geneva Proceedings," Pts. 1 and 2 in *Ocean Development and International Law*; U.S. Congress, Senate, Committee on Interior and Insular Affairs, *Status Report on Law of the Sea Conference*, Hearing, Pt. 3, 94th Cong., 1st sess., June 4, 1975; and John R. Stevenson and Bernard H. Oxman, "The Third United Nations Conference on the Law of the Sea.

58. See Appendix 5.

59. Debate in General Committee on April 7 is summarized in United Nations, *Conference on the Law of the Sea*, Official Records, 4, 31-36.

60. Debate in General Committee on April 15, ibid., pp. 36-41.

61. See Appendix 6.

62. As found in A/CONF.62/C.1/L.7, August 16, 1974.

63. "U.S. Delegation Report: UNCLOS III, Geneva March 17-May 9, 1975," pp. 1220, 1225-1226; U.S. Congress, Senate, Committee on Interior and Insular Affairs, *Status Report*, Pt. 3.

64. CP/cab.12/C.1, issued April 9, 1975.

65. For discussion of other changes see Miles, "An Interpretation of the Geneva Proceedings, Pt. 1," pp. 214-215.

66. Convention on the Seabed and the Ocean Floor and the Subsoil Thereof Beyond the Limits of National Jurisdiction, A/CONF.62/WP.8, Pt. 1, May 7, 1975.

67. A/CONF.62/L.8/Rev. 1, October 17, 1974.

68. Statement on the Work of the Second Committee, A/CONF.62/C.2/L.89/Rev. 1, July 15, 1975.

69. See Appendix 6.

70. Spain, Iran, Oman, Morocco, Yemen, and Egypt.

71. A/CONF.62/C.2/L.3, July 3, 1974; A/CONF.62/C.2/L.18, July 23, 1974.

72. Proposed by Uganda and Zambia, A/AC.138/SC.II/L.41, July 1973.

73. Draft Articles on the Prevention, Reduction and Control of Marine Pollution, A/CONF.62/C.3/L.24, Belgium, Bulgaria, Denmark, German Democratic Republic, Federal Republic of Germany, Greece, Netherlands, Poland, and United Kingdom, March 21, 1975.

74. To buy the backing of the less developed countries Canada had even supported a double standard at Caracas, A/CONF.C.3/L.6, July 31, 1974.

75. Articles 20-42 dealt with standard setting and enforcement.

76. A/CONF.62/C.3/L.13/Rev. 2, introduced by Iraq, April 21, 1975.

77. A/CONF.62/C.3/L.19, August 23, 1974.

78. A/CONF.62/C.3/L.28, April 24, 1975.

79. A/CONF.62/C.3/L.26, April 3, 1975.

80. A/CONF.62/C.3/L.29, introduced by Colombia, El Salvador, Mexico, and Nigeria, May 6, 1975.

81. A detailed discussion of the work of the group is available in A. O. Adede, "Settlement of Disputes Arising Under the Law of the Sea Convention."

82. Detailed reports on the 1976 sessions of UNCLOS III may be found in Edward Miles, "The Structure and Effects of the Decision Process in the Seabed Committee and the Third United Nations Conference on the Law of the Sea" (see especially pp. 214-234); Bernard H. Oxman, "The Third United Nations Conference on the Law of the Sea: The 1976 New York Sessions"; Subcommittee on International Relations of the Advisory Committee on the Law of the Sea, "Third United Nations Conference on the Law of the Sea: Report on the 1976 New York Sessions," *San Diego Law Review*, 14, No. 3 (April 1977), 736-750; U.S. Congress, Senate, Committee on Foreign Relations, Subcommittee on Oceans and International Environment, *Law of the Sea*, Hearing, 94th Cong., 2nd sess., May 20, 1976.

83. A/CONF.62/WP.8/Rev. 1, May 6, 1976. The president of the conference produced a single negotiating text on dispute settlement.

84. A/CONF.62/L.16, September 6, 1976.

85. Fishery Conservation and Management Act of 1976. Public Law 94-265, 16 USC 1801, 90 Stat. 331.

86. "The Law of the Sea: A Test of International Cooperation," Address before the Foreign Policy Association, U.S. Council of the International Chamber of Commerce, and UN Association of the U.S.A., New York, April 8, 1976, Department of State Press Release No. 162.

87. Secretary Kissinger's inattentiveness in previous years had become the object of scathing attacks. See, for example, John Norton Moore, "Neglect of the Oceans," Address to the World Affairs Council of Northern California and the Bar Association of San Francisco, August 18, 1976; "Organizing for a National Oceans Program," Address to Oceans '76 Conference, Washington, D.C., September 13, 1976; and "The Crisis in Oceans Policy: Time for a Change."

88. Introductory note by chairman to the RSNT, Pt. II. A/CONF.62/WP.8/Rev. 1/Pt. II, May 6, 1976.

89. Articles 57, 58, and 59, Pt. II of ISNT.

90. Hollis D. Hedberg, "Ocean Boundaries for the Law of the Sea."

91. Article 71, Pt. 2. For a review of the history of delimitation problems, see Myres S. McDougal and William T. Burke, *The Public Order of the Oceans*, chaps. 4 and 5.

92. Marine mammals and management of fishery resources were largely neglected.

93. A/CONF.62/WP.9/Rev. 1, Pt. IV, May 6, 1976.

94. A/CONF.62/WP.9/Rev. 2, Pt. IV, November 23, 1976.

95. The sixth session is reviewed in Bernard H. Oxman, "The Third United Nations Conference on the Law of the Sea: The 1977 New York Session"; U.S. Congress, Senate, Committee on Energy and Natural Resources, Subcommittee on Public Lands and Resources, *Status Report on Law of the Sea Conference*, Hearing, 95th Cong., 1st sess., July 26, 1977, U.S. Congress, House, Committee on International Relations, *Law of the Sea Conference: Status Report*, Hearing, July 25, 1977, 95th Cong., 1st sess.

96. United Nations, *Third United Nations Conference on the Law of the Sea*, A/CONF.62/WP.10, July 20, 1977.

97. Oxman, "The Third United Nations Conference: The 1977 New York Session."

98. The intersessional was called by Jens Evensen with the acquiescence of the Secretariat and the president of the conference. Chairman Engo was not there and Christopher Pinto attended only briefly.

99. See, for instance, Ambassador Richardson's statements on May 26, June 10, and June 13, 1977; typescript.

100. Statement by Ambassador Elliot L. Richardson, July 20, 1977, reprinted in Oxman, "The Third United Nations Conference: The 1977 New York Session."

101. See Chairman Aguilar's explanatory memorandum in the ICNT.

102. President's Message to Congress Regarding Oil Pollution of the Oceans, 13 Weekly Compilation of Presidential Documents 908-909 (March 21, 1977).

103. The seventh session is reviewed in Bernard H. Oxman, "The Third United Nations Conference on the Law of the Sea: The Seventh Session (1978)," *American Journal of International Law*, 73, No. 1, January 1979, pp. 1-41; U.S. Congress, House, Committee on International Relations, *Law of the Sea Conference, Status Report, Summer 1978*, Hearing, May 24, 1978, 95th Cong., 2nd sess.; U.S. Congress, House, Committee on Merchant Marine and Fisheries, Subcommittee on Oceanography, *Oceanography Miscellaneous*, Pt. 2, Hearings, 95th Cong., pp. 1-294.

104. United Nations, *Third United Nations Conference on the Law of the Sea*, Reports of the Committees and Negotiating Groups on Negotiations at the Seventh Session contained in a single document both for the purpose of record and for the convenience of delegations, May 19, 1978.

105. A decision to formalize the text would move the conference to a new stage in which the text would be subject to formal amendments that would have to be acted on in accordance with the decision-making process adopted in 1974.

106. The first part of the item was the formulation required by the group

of coastal states; the second part was the formulation required by the LL/GDS.

107. A/CONF.62/61, p. 3.

108. NG4/9/Rev. 2. Reports of the Committees and Negotiating Groups, pp. 71-78.

109. As reflected in amendments to the Federal Water Pollution Control Act, P.L. 95-576.

110. Reports of the Committees and Negotiating Groups, pp. 87-90.

111. Ibid., pp. 90-98.

112. The eighth session is reviewed in Bernard H. Oxman, "The United Nations Conference on the Law of the Sea: The Eighth Session (1979), *American Journal of International Law*, 74, January 1980, pp. 1-47; U.S. Congress, House, Committee on Foreign Affairs, *The Status of the Third United Nations Conference on the Law of the Sea*, Hearing, 96th Cong., 1st sess., May 16, 1979; U.S. Congress, House, Committee on Foreign Affairs, *Briefing on the Eighth Session of the Third United Nations Conference on the Law of the Sea*, 96th Cong., 1st sess., March 7, 1979.

113. See Report of the Chairman of Negotiating Group 6, NG6/19, August 22, 1979.

114. See Report of the Chairman of Negotiating Group 7, NG7/45, August 22, 1979.

115. Report by the Chairman of the Third Committee, A/CONF.62/L.41, August 23, 1979.

116. The ninth session is reviewed in Bernard H. Oxman, "The United Nations Conference on the Law of the Sea: The Ninth Session (1980), *American Journal of International Law*, 75, No. 1, January 1981.

117. A/CONF.62/WP.10/Rev. 3, August 27, 1980.

Chapter 10
UNITED STATES POLICY AND LESSONS FOR THE FUTURE

1. Edward Miles describes the Group of 5 in, "The Structure and Effects of the Decision Process in the Seabed Committee and the Third United Nations Conference on the Law of the Sea," p. 165.

2. U.S. Congress, Senate, Committee on Commerce and National Ocean Policy Study, *A Legislative History of the Fisheries Conservation and Management Act of 1976*, Committee Print, 94th Cong., 2nd sess., October 1976.

3. John Norton Moore, "Foreign Policy and Fidelity to Law: The Anatomy of a Treaty Violation"; John Norton Moore, "Neglect of the Oceans," address to World Affairs Council of Northern California, San Francisco Bar Association and the Comstock Club, August 16 and 18, 1976.

4. For additional discussion of State Department organization for law of the sea, see Otho E. Eskin, "Law of the Sea and the Management of Multi-

lateral Diplomacy," Oceans Policy Study 1:5 (Charlottesville, Va.: University of Virginia, Center for Oceans Law and Policy, 1978).

5. A/CONF.62/C.1/L.5, August 8, 1974 and A/CONF.62/C.1/L.6, August 13, 1974.

6. Henry A. Kissinger, "The Law of the Sea: A Test of International Cooperation," *Congressional Record*, April 8, 1976, pp. S5223-S5227; also April 12, 1976, pp. S5445-S5449; Henry A. Kissinger, U.S. Mission to the United Nations, Press Release USUN-99 (76), September 1, 1976.

7. On this policy see, W. Michael Reisman, "The Regime of Straits and National Security," and the reply of John Norton Moore, "The Regime of Straits and the Third United Nations Conference on the Law of the Sea: A Review of the Record."

8. A/AC.138/SC.III/L.40, July 13, 1973.

9. A/AC.138/SC.III/L.44, July 19, 1973.

10. A/CONF.62/C.2/L.47, August 8, 1974; A/CONF.62/C.2/L.79, August 23, 1974; A/CONF.62/C.2/L.80, August 23, 1974.

11. Kissinger, "The Law of the Sea," April 8, 1976.

12. As noted elsewhere, the committee chairman was already following the Soviet lead to a full consent regime.

13. This growth segment was stated as six percent per year. Thus the production control was either six percent of accumulated growth of six percent per year, or the actual growth of the nickel market, whichever was greater.

14. The interest in precedent was not an explicit matter of delegation policy but is reflected in Darman's and Smith's writings upon leaving the delegation. Richard G. Darman, "The Law of the Sea: Rethinking U.S. Interests"; Richard G. Darman, "Precedential Implications of a Deep Seabed Mining Regime," testimony before House Committee on Merchant Marine and Fisheries, Subcommittee on Oceanography, *Oceanography Miscellaneous*, Pt. 2, Hearings 95th Cong., pp. 131-136; John Thomas Smith, II, "The Seabed Negotiations and the Law of the Sea Conference—Ready for a Divorce?" *Virginia Journal of International Law*, 18, No. 1 (Fall 1977), 43-59.

15. Elliot L. Richardson, statement to press, March 16, 1978, p. 6.

16. Although Darman and Smith agreed on this strategy and on their assessment of the negotiating realities, their preferred prescriptions varied. For Darman's view, see his "Law of the Sea"; and "Precedential Implications of a Deep Seabed Mining Regime"; also Richard G. Darman, "Choices in the Law of the Sea Negotiations: An Analytical Framework and Personal Assessment," Oceans Policy Series 1;4 (Charlottesville, Va.: University of Virginia, Center for Oceans Law and Policy, April 1978). Smith preferred to detach the seabed negotiation from the rest of the conference. See his "Seabed Negotiations and the Law of the Sea Conference—Ready for a Divorce?" For their joint analysis of the ICNT see Darman and Smith, Report of the Committee on Law of the Sea, International Law Association, American Branch, New York, 1978.

17. Questions and Answers at Press Conference Given by Ambassador Richardson, March 16, 1978; typescript.

18. Ibid.

19. U.S. Congress, Senate, Committee on Foreign Relations, Subcommittee on Arms Control, Oceans and International Environment, *Law of the Sea*, Hearing, 95th Cong., 2nd sess., June 16, 1978.

20. U.S. Congress, House, Committee on Merchant Marine and Fisheries, Subcommittee on Oceanography, *Oceanography Miscellaneous*, Pt. 2, p. 64.

21. Elliot L. Richardson, testimony before Senate Committee on Commerce, Science and Transportation and the Subcommittee on Public Lands and Resources of the Committee on Energy and Natural Resources, *Mining of the Deep Seabed*, Hearing, 95th Cong., 1st sess., October 4, 1977, pp. 378-390; Testimony before House International Relations Committee, Subcommittee on International Organizations and Subcommittee on International Economic Policy, 95th Cong., 2nd sess., January 23, 1978.

22. The legal argument sustaining the administration's case for legislation pending completion of the negotiations was set out most eloquently by Ambassador Richardson before the plenary of the law of the sea conference on September 15, 1978. See also, statement by Elliot L. Richardson, March 16, 1978 Press Conference.

23. In the House, the Deep Seabed Hard Minerals Resources Act was reported in 1977 by the Merchant Marine and Fisheries Committee and the Interior and Insular Affairs Committee (*Deep Seabed Hard Minerals Act*, Report, together with dissenting, separate, and additional views, 95th Cong., 1st sess., August 9, 1977, H.R. 95-588, pt. 1). In 1978 the International Relations Committee reported the bill (House, Committee on International Relations, *Deep Seabed Hard Mineral Resources Act*, Report, together with supplemental views, 95th Cong., 2nd sess., February 16, 1978, H.R. 95-588, pt. 3). The bill was next referred to the Committee on Ways and Means to consider its taxation and revenue-sharing provisions (House, Committee on Ways and Means, *International Revenue Sharing Provisions in Deep Seabed Mining Legislation*, Hearing, 95th Cong., 2nd sess., April 13, 1978; House, Committee on Ways and Means, *Explanation of Ways and Means Committee Amendment to H.R. 3350 [Deep Seabed Hard Minerals Resources Act*, together with dissenting views, 95th Cong., 2nd sess., June 7, 1978]). On July 26, 1978, the bill passed the House with amendments.

The Senate Committees on Commerce, Science and Transportation, and Energy and Natural Resources jointly reported the mining bill in the summer of 1978 (Committees on Commerce, Science and Transportation, and Energy and Natural Resources, *Deep Seabed Mineral Resources Act*, Report together with additional views, 95th Cong., 2nd sess., August 18, 1978). The Senate Foreign Relations Committee reported the bill last (Committee on Foreign Relations, *Deep Seabed Mineral Resources Act*, Report, 95th Cong., 2nd sess., September 11, 1978, Report No. 95-1180).

24. See pp. 360-361 for the U.S. interpretation of the Kissinger compromises in 1977.

25. "Top Federal Aides Meet," *New York Times*, February 7, 1978, p. 14; Section 311 of Clean Water Act, Federal Water Pollution Control Act as amended 33 U.S.C. 466 et seq.

26. A catalog of the adverse impacts of the amendments may be found in J. Peter Bernhardt, "The 1977 Clean Water Act Amendments—Conflicts and Contradictions," *Marine Technology Society Journal*, 12, No. 5 (October-November 1978), 28-31.

27. The 1969 and 1971 amendments to the International Convention for the Prevention of Pollution of the Sea by Oil were implemented for the U.S. by the 93rd Congress (P.L. 93-119).

28. The *Argo Merchant* went aground on the Nantucket Shoals; the *Sansihena* exploded in Los Angeles Harbor; the *Oregon Peace* spilled bunker oil off New London, Connecticut; and the *Olympic Games* discharged crude oil into the Delaware River.

29. International Conference on Marine Pollution: International Convention for the Prevention of Pollution from Ships (done at London, November 2, 1973). For text see *International Legal Materials*, 12 (Washington, D.C.: American Society of International Law, November 1973), 1319-1444.

30. 33 Code of *Federal Regulations*, pt. 157.

31. IMCO held the International Conference on Tanker Safety and Pollution Prevention (TSPP) in London on February 6-17, 1978. The Conference considered U.S. proposals for modifications to MARPOL 1973 and to the International Convention for the Safety of Life at Sea (SOLAS 1974), as well as other proposals developed in preparatory meetings. The conference produced two protocols: the Protocol of 1978 Relating to the International Convention for the Prevention of Pollution from Ships (MARPOL Protocol) and the Protocol of 1978 Relating to the International Convention for the Safety of Life at Seas (SOLAS Protocol). Among the features of these protocols are provisions that new crude oil tankers 20,000 dwt and over have segregated ballast, that crude oil washing be used, as well as inert gas systems and backup radar and collision avoidance systems. For hearings on the results of this conference, see U.S. Congress, Senate, Committee on Commerce, Science and Transportation, *1978 IMCO Protocols*, Hearing, 95th Cong., 2nd sess., April 5, 1978.

32. U.S. Congress, Senate, Committee on Environment and Public Works, *Oil Pollution Liability and Compensation Act of 1978*, Report together with additional views, 95th Cong., 2nd sess., August 25, 1978.

33. See, for instance, the Fishery Conservation Zone Transition Act (P.L. 95-6) and its amendments (P.L. 95-8 and P.L. 95-314).

34. North Pacific Fisheries Act, amendments P.L. 95-326.

35. Unpublished letter to Secretary of State Cyrus R. Vance from Senators Jacob K. Javits and Frank Church, October 30, 1979.

36. *New York Times*, August 10, 1979.

37. For an explanation of the reasoning behind this policy, see Elliot L.

Richardson, "Power, Mobility and the Law of the Sea," *Foreign Affairs*, 58, No. 4 (Spring 1980), 902-919.

38. The accident at the Three-Mile Island nuclear plant in Pennsylvania on March 28, 1979, and the worldwide attention it received, served to mobilize existing opposition to nuclear power and to attract new converts to the antinuclear movement.

39. Thomas O'Toole, "Merchant Ships Sink at Rate of One a Day," *Washington Post*, August 7, 1972, p. A1.

BIBLIOGRAPHY

BOOKS

Bartley, Ernest R. *The Tidelands Oil Controversy: A Legal and Historical Analysis*. Austin: University of Texas Press, 1953.

Bayitch, S. A. *Interamerican Law of Fisheries*. New York: Oceana, 1957.

Bingham, Joseph Walter. *Report on the International Law of Pacific Coast Fisheries*. Palo Alto: Stanford University Press, 1938.

Butler, William E. *The Soviet Union and the Law of the Sea*. Baltimore: The Johns Hopkins Press, 1971.

Cohen, Bernard C. *The Political Process and Foreign Policy*. Princeton: Princeton University Press, 1957.

Crutchfield, James A., and Pontecorvo, Guilio. *The Pacific Salmon Fisheries*. Baltimore: The Johns Hopkins Press, 1969.

Eckert, Ross D. *The Enclosure of Ocean Resources*. Stanford: Stanford University Press, 1978.

Eisenhower, Dwight D. *Mandate for Change, 1953-1956*. Garden City: Doubleday and Company, 1963.

————. *Waging Peace, 1959-1961*. Garden City: Doubleday and Company, 1965.

Engler, Robert. *The Politics of Oil*. Chicago: University of Chicago Press, 1961.

Friedheim, Robert L. "The Politics of the Sea: A Study of Law Making by Conference." Ph.D. Dissertation, University of Washington, 1962.

Gamble, John King, Jr., ed. *Law of the Sea: Neglected Issues*. Proceedings of the Twelfth Annual Conference, Law of the Sea Institute. Honolulu: Law of the Sea Institute, University of Hawaii, 1978.

Gardner, Richard N. *In Pursuit of World Order: U.S. Foreign Policy and International Organizations*. New York: Praeger, 1964.

Graebner, Norman A. *Cold War Diplomacy, 1945-60*. Princeton: Van Nostrand, 1962.

Hjertonsson, Karin. *The New Law of the Sea: Influence of the Latin American States on Recent Developments in the Law of the Sea*. Leiden: A. W. Sijthoff, 1973.

Hollick, Ann L. "United States Ocean Policy: 1948-1971." Ph.D. Dissertation, Johns Hopkins University, 1971.

Hollick, Ann L. and Osgood, Robert E. *New Era of Ocean Politics*. Baltimore: The Johns Hopkins Press, 1974.

Ickes, Harold L. *The Secret Diary of Harold L. Ickes*. Vol. I: *The First Thousand Days, 1933-36*. New York: Simon and Schuster, 1954.

————. *The Secret Diary of Harold L. Ickes*. Vol. II: *The Inside Struggle, 1936-39*. New York: Simon and Schuster, 1952.

483

————. *The Secret Diary of Harold L. Ickes*, Vol. III: *The Lowering Clouds, 1939-41*. New York: Simon and Schuster, 1955.

Institute for the Study of Science in Human Affairs, *Law for the Sea's Mineral Resources*. New York: Columbia University, 1968.

Krueger, Robert B. *Study of the Outer Continental Shelf Lands of the United States*. 2 vols. Public Land Law Review Commission, 1968.

Logan, R. M. *Canada, the United States and the Third Law of the Sea Conference*. Washington, D.C.: National Planning Association, 1974.

McDougal, Myres S. and Burke, William T. *The Public Order of the Oceans*. New Haven: Yale University Press, 1962.

Major Issues of the Law of the Sea. Durham, N.H.: University of New Hampshire, 1976.

National Academy of Sciences—National Research Council. *Oceanography 1960-1970*. Washington, D.C.: National Academy of Sciences, 1959.

Orrego-Vicuna, Francisco. *Los Fondos Marinos y Oceanicos*. Santiago: Editorial Andres Bello, 1976.

Osgood, Robert E.; Hollick, Ann L.; Pearson, Charles S.; and Orr, James C. *Toward a National Ocean Policy, 1976 and Beyond*. Washington, D.C.: U.S. Government Printing Office for National Science Foundation, 1976.

Reiff, Henry. *The United States and the Treaty Law of the Sea*. Minneapolis: University of Minnesota Press, 1959.

Schlaffer, Harold Samuel. "The Eighty-Second and Eighty-Third Congresses and the Submerged Lands Controversy." M.A. Dissertation, American University, 1955.

Smetherman, Bobbie B. and Smetherman, Robert M. *Territorial Seas and Inter-American Relations*. New York: Praeger, 1974.

Spanier, John. *American Foreign Policy Since World War II*. New York: Praeger, 1965.

Szekely, Alberto. *Latin America and the Development of the Law of the Sea*. Vols. I and II. New York: Oceana, 1976.

Truman, Harry S. *Memoirs*. Vol. I: *Year of Decision*. Garden City: Doubleday, 1955.

————. *Memoirs*. Vol. II: *Years of Trial and Hope*. Garden City: Doubleday, 1966.

Weissberg, Guenter. *Recent Developments in the Law of the Sea and the Japanese-Korean Fishery Dispute*. The Hague: Martinus Nijoff, 1966.

Wenk, Edward, Jr. *The Politics of the Ocean*. Seattle: University of Washington Press, 1972.

Wooster, Warren, ed. *Freedom of Oceanic Research*. New York: Crane Russak, 1973.

ARTICLES

Adede, A. O. "Settlement of Disputes Arising Under the Law of the Sea Convention." *American Journal of International Law*, 69 (October 1975), 798-818.

Bilder, Richard B. "The Office of the Legal Advisor: The State Department Lawyer and Foreign Affairs." *American Journal of International Law*, 56 (July 1962), 633-684.

Butler, William E. "Some Recent Developments in Soviet Maritime Law." *International Lawyer*, 4 (July 1970), 695-708.

Chapman, Wilbert McLeod. "The United States Fish Industry and the 1958 and 1960 United Nations Conferences on the Law of the Sea." In *Law of the Sea: International Rules and Organization for the Sea*, Proceedings of the Third Annual Conference of the Law of the Sea Institute, edited by Lewis M. Alexander, pp. 35-63. Kingston: University of Rhode Island, 1969.

Cheever, Daniel S. "The Role of International Organization in Ocean Development." *International Organization*, 22 (Summer 1968), 629-648.

Darman, Richard G. "The Law of the Sea: Rethinking U.S. Interests." *Foreign Affairs*, 56 (January 1978), 373-395.

Dean, Arthur H. "The Geneva Conference on the Law of the Sea: What was Accomplished." *American Journal of International Law*, 52 (October 1958), 751-789.

Halperin, Morton. "Why Bureaucrats Play Games." *Foreign Policy*, No. 2 (Spring 1971), 70-90.

Hedberg, Hollis D. "Ocean Boundaries for the Law of the Sea." *Marine Technology Society Journal*, 10, No. 5 (June 1976), 6-11.

Hollick, Ann L. "Canadian-American Relations: Law of the Sea." *International Organization*, 28, No. 4 (Autumn 1974), 755-780.

Knauss, John A. "Factors Influencing a U.S. Position in a Future Law of the Sea Conference." Occasional Paper No. 10. Kingston, R.I.: Law of the Sea Institute, April 1971.

Knight, H. Gary. "The Draft United Nations Convention on the International Seabed Area: Background, Description and Some Preliminary Thoughts." *San Diego Law Review*, 8 (May 1971), 459-550.

Loring, David C. "The United States-Peruvian 'Fisheries Dispute,'" *Stanford Law Review*, 23, No. 3 (February 1971), 391-453.

Miles, Edward. "An Interpretation of the Geneva Proceedings." *Ocean Development and International Law*: Part 1 in Vol. 3, No. 3 (1976), 187-224; Part 2 in Vol. 3, No. 4 (1976), 303-340.

————. "The Structure and Effects of the Decision Process in the Seabed Committee and the Third United Nations Conference on the Law of the Sea." *International Organization*, 31, No. 2 (Spring 1977), 159-234.

Moore, John Norton. "The Crisis in Oceans Policy: Time for a Change." *Marine Technology Society Journal*, 10, No. 8 (October-November 1976), 3-10.

————. "Foreign Policy and Fidelity to Law: The Anatomy of a Treaty Violation." *American Journal of International Law*, 70, No. 4 (October 1976), 802-808.

————. "The Regime of Straits and the Third United Nations Conference on the Law of the Sea: A Review of the Record." *American Journal of International Law*, 74 (January 1980), 77-121.

Morris, Michael A. "The Domestic Context of Brazilian Maritime Policy." *Ocean Development and International Law*, 4, No. 2 (1977), 143-170.

Oxman, Bernard H. "The Third United Nations Conference on the Law of the Sea: The 1976 New York Sessions." *American Journal of International Law*, 71, No. 2 (April 1977), 247-269.

————. "The Third United Nations Conference on the Law of the Sea: The 1977 New York Session." *American Journal of International Law*, 72 (January 1978), 67-75.

Rao, K. Krishna. "The Legal Regime of the Sea-Bed and Ocean Floor." *Indian Journal of International Law*, 9 (January 1969), 1-18.

Ratiner, Leigh S. "United States Oceans Policy: An Analysis." *Journal of Maritime Law and Commerce*, 2 (January 1971), 225-266.

Reisman, W. Michael. "The Regime of Straits and National Security." *American Journal of International Law*, 74 (January 1980), 48-76.

Richardson, Elliot L. "Power, Mobility and the Law of the Sea." *Foreign Affairs*, 58, No. 4 (Spring 1980), 902-919.

Sohn, Louis B. "Voting Procedures in United Nations Conferences for the Codification of International Law." *American Journal of International Law*, 69, No. 2 (April 1975), 333-353.

Stang, David. "The Donnybrook Fair of the Oceans." *San Diego Law Review*, 9, No. 3 (May 1972), 569-607.

Stevenson, John R. and Oxman, Bernard H. "The Third United Nations Conference on the Law of the Sea: The 1975 Geneva Session." *American Journal of International Law*, 19, No. 4 (October 1975), 763-797.

Swarth, George S. "Offshore Submerged Lands: An Historical Synopsis." *Land and Natural Resources Division Journal*, U.S. Department of Justice, 6 (April 1968), 109-157.

Weissberg, Guenter. "International Law Meets the Short-Term National Interest: The Maltese Proposal on the Sea-Bed and Ocean Floor—Its Fate in Two Cities." *The International and Comparative Law Quarterly*, 18 (January 1969), 41-102.

GOVERNMENT PUBLICATIONS

U.S. Comptroller General. *Federal Agencies Administering Programs Related to Marine Science Activities and Oceanic Affairs*. Report to the Congress. February 25, 1975.

————. *The Law of the Sea Conference—Status of the Issues, 1978*. Report to the Congress, March 9, 1979.

————. *Results of the Third Law of the Sea Conference, 1974 to 1976*. Report to the Congress, June 3, 1977.

U.S. Congress. House. Committee on Foreign Affairs. *The United Nations and the Issue of Deep Ocean Resources*. Hearings before the Subcommittee on International Organizations and Movements. 90th Cong., 1st sess., 1967.

U.S. Congress. House. Committee on Foreign Affairs. Subcommittee on Inter-American Affairs. *Fishing Rights and United States-Latin American Relations*. Hearings. 92nd Cong., 2nd sess., 1972.

U.S. Congress. House. Committee on Merchant Marine and Fisheries. *Deep Seabed Mining*. Hearings before the Subcommittee on Oceanography. 94th Cong., 2nd sess., 1976.

U.S. Congress. Office of Technology Assessment. *Establishing a 200-Mile Fisheries Zone*. June 1977.

U.S. Congress. Senate. Committee on Commerce. *Interim Fisheries Zone Extension and Management Act of 1973*. 93rd Cong., 2nd sess., 1973.

———. *Special Study on United Nations Suboceanic Lands Policy*. Hearings. 91st Cong., 1st sess., 1969.

U.S. Congress. Senate. Committee on Foreign Relations. *Activities of Nations in Ocean Space*. Hearings before the Subcommittee on Ocean Space. 91st Cong., 1st sess., 1969.

U.S. Congress. Senate. Committee on Interior and Insular Affairs. *Hearings on Outer Continental Shelf*, 83rd Cong., 1st sess., 1953.

———. *Hearings on Submerged Lands*. 83rd Cong., 1st sess., 1953.

———. *Mineral Resources of the Deep Seabed*. Hearings before the Subcommittee on Minerals, Materials and Fuels. 93rd Cong., 1st sess., 1973; Part 2, 93rd Cong., 2nd sess., 1974.

———. *Ocean Manganese Nodules*. Committee Print prepared by the Congressional Research Service, June 1975; Second Edition, February 1976.

———. *Outer Continental Shelf*. Hearings before the Subcommittee on Outer Continental Shelf, Parts 1 and 2, 91st Cong., 1st and 2nd sess., 1969 and 1970.

———. *Status Report on Law of the Sea Conference*. Hearing before the Subcommittee on Minerals, Materials and Fuels. 93rd Cong., 1st sess., 1973.

U.S. Congress. Senate. House. House Judiciary Committee and Special Subcommittee of the Senate Judiciary Committee. *Title to Lands Beneath Tidal and Navigable Waters*. Joint Hearings. 79th Cong., 1st sess., 1945.

U.S. National Commission on Marine Science, Engineering and Resources Development. International Panel. *Marine Resources and Legal-Political Arrangements for Their Development*. Vol. 3. Washington, D.C.: Government Printing Office, 1969.

U.S. National Commission on Marine Science, Engineering and Resources Development. *Our Nation and the Sea*. Washington, D.C.: Government Printing Office, 1969.

487

DOCUMENT COLLECTIONS

Council on Foreign Relations. *Documents on American Foreign Relations.* New York: Harper, various years.

Knight, H. Gary. *The Law of the Sea: Cases, Documents, and Readings.* Washington, D.C.: Nautilus Press, 1975.

Lay, S. Houston, Churchill, Robin, and Nordquist, Myron, eds. *New Directions in the Law of the Sea.* Vols. I and II. Dobbs Ferry, N.Y.: Oceana, 1973.

Oda, Shigeru. *The International Law of the Ocean Development: Basic Documents.* Leiden: Sijthoff, 1972.

United Nations. *Conference on the Law of the Sea, 24 February-27 April 1958. Official Records.* Vols. I-VII (A/CONF.13/37-42).

United Nations. General Assembly. *Report of the Committee on the Peaceful Uses of the Sea-Bed and the Ocean Floor Beyond the Limits of National Jurisdiction.* Official Records: Twenty-Sixth Session, Supplement 21 (A/8421), 1971; Twenty-Seventh Session, Supplement 21 (A/8721), 1972; Twenty-Eighth Session, Supplement 21 (A/9021), 1973, Vols. I-IV.

United Nations. *Second United Nations Conference on the Law of the Sea, 17 March-26 April 1960. Official Records* (A/CONF.19/8).

———. *Third United Nations Conference on the Law of the Sea.* Official Records. Vols. I-VIII (A/CONF.62/ . . .).

———. *Yearbook of the International Law Commission, 1956.*

U.S. Department of State. *Foreign Relations of the United States.* Washington, D.C.: Government Printing Office, various years.

U.S. Department of State Manuscript Files 711, 811, 812, 818.

U.S. National Archives. Record Group 48.

U.S. Naval War College. *International Law: Situation and Documents.* Washington, D.C.: Government Printing Office, various years.

Whiteman, Marjorie. *Digest of International Law.* U.S. Department of State. Washington, D.C.: Government Printing Office, Vol. 4.

Wilbert McLeod Chapman Collection. Manuscript Division, University of Washington, Seattle, Washington.

Library of Congress Cataloging in Publication Data

Hollick, Ann L
   U.S. foreign policy and the law of the sea.

   Bibliography: p.
   Includes index.
   1. Maritime law—United States.   2. United States—
Foreign relations—1945-   .   3. Maritime law.   I. Title.
JX4422.U5H64   341.4'5   80-8554
ISBN 0-691-09387-3
ISBN 0-691-10114-0 (pbk.)

Ann L. Hollick is currently Director of the Policy Assessment Staff, Bureau of Oceans, Environmental, and Scientific Affairs, at the Department of State.